Windows® 2000 System Administrator's Black Book

Second Edition

Deborah Haralson
Stu Sjouwerman
Barry Shilmover
James Michael Stewart

President and CEO
Roland Elgey

Publisher
Al Valvano

Associate Publisher
Katherine R. Hartlove

Acquisitions Editor
Charlotte Carpentier

Developmental Editor
Jessica Choi

Product Marketing Manager
Tracy Rooney

Project Editor
Sharon McCarson

Technical Reviewer
Doug Bassett

Production Coordinator
Wendy Littley

Cover Designer
Laura Wellander

CD-ROM Developer
Michelle McConnell

Windows® 2000 System Administrator's Black Book, Second Edition

The Coriolis Group, LLC
14455 N. Hayden Road
Suite 220
Scottsdale, Arizona 85260

(480) 483-0192
FAX (480) 483-0193
www.coriolis.com

Library of Congress Cataloging-in-Publication Data
Windows 2000 system administrator's black book / by Deborah Haralson ... [et al.].–2nd ed.
    p. cm.
  Includes index.
  ISBN 1-58880-162-4
   1. Microsoft Windows (Computer file) 2. Operating systems (Computers) I. Haralson, Deborah.

QA76.76.O63 W5646715   2001
005.4'4769–dc21
    2001047660
    CIP

Printed in the United States of America
10 9 8 7 6 5 4 3 2 1

⊙

The Coriolis Group, LLC • 14455 North Hayden Road, Suite 220 • Scottsdale, Arizona 85260

A Note from Coriolis

Coriolis Technology Press was founded to create a very elite group of books: the ones you keep closest to your machine. In the real world, you have to choose the books you rely on every day *very* carefully, and we understand that.

To win a place for our books on that coveted shelf beside your PC, we guarantee several important qualities in every book we publish. These qualities are:

- *Technical accuracy*—It's no good if it doesn't work. Every Coriolis Technology Press book is reviewed by technical experts in the topic field, and is sent through several editing and proofreading passes in order to create the piece of work you now hold in your hands.

- *Innovative editorial design*—We've put years of research and refinement into the ways we present information in our books. Our books' editorial approach is uniquely designed to reflect the way people learn new technologies and search for solutions to technology problems.

- *Practical focus*—We put only pertinent information into our books and avoid any fluff. Every fact included between these two covers must serve the mission of the book as a whole.

- *Accessibility*—The information in a book is worthless unless you can find it quickly when you need it. We put a lot of effort into our indexes, and heavily cross-reference our chapters, to make it easy for you to move right to the information you need.

Here at The Coriolis Group we have been publishing and packaging books, technical journals, and training materials since 1989. We have put a lot of thought into our books; please write to us at **ctp@coriolis.com** and let us know what you think. We hope that you're happy with the book in your hands, and that in the future, when you reach for software development and networking information, you'll turn to one of our books first.

Coriolis Technology Press
The Coriolis Group
14455 N. Hayden Road, Suite 220
Scottsdale, Arizona
85260

Email: ctp@coriolis.com
Phone: (480) 483-0192
Toll free: (800) 410-0192

Look for these related books from The Coriolis Group:

Windows 2000 Systems Programming Black Book
By Al Williams

Windows XP Professional Little Black Book
By Brian Proffitt

Windows 2000 Security Little Black Book
By Ian McLean

Windows 2000 Mac Support Little Black Book
By Gene Steinberg and Pieter Paulson

Exchange 2000 Server Black Book
By Marcus Goncalves

Also Recently Published by Coriolis Technology Press:

Exchange 2000 .NET Server Black Book
By Evan Benjamin, Phillip Schein, and Cherry Beado

C# Black Book
By Matthew Telles

Windows XP Professional—The Ultimate User's Guide
By Joli Ballew

God bless America. This is for all Americans past, present, and future, whose love for land and liberty prompt them to stand beside this country and guide her by the light from above. Thank you for giving us liberty.

And also, this is for my precious husband, without whose love, support, guidance, and generosity this book wouldn't have happened.

❧

About the Author

Deborah Haralson (MCSE, MCP+I) has been a computer geek since elementary school, learning Basic programming on her father's CommodorVIC20. High school brought the technological bleeding edge, learning GWBASIC programming on an 8086 AT&T backplaned box with no hard disk drive. While going to school for engineering, she discovered that her true passion was for IT, and began working on Windows, DOS, and Macintosh network clients, quickly graduating to network servers and WAN technologies. With over ten years of experience in the IT field, she has worked for companies such as Honeywell, MicroAge, Moon Valley Software, and Mastering Computers. Along the way, she has become proficient in a wide array of hardware, software, and operating systems, along with both Windows and Novell networking technologies to bring them all together, with an occasional stint as a PBX & ACD admin, DBA, trainer, Webmaster, and application programmer. Deborah is currently an independent consultant with recent experience in IT management for large real-estate companies. Deborah has worked with Microsoft server products since the original NT 3.1 beta, and has (ahem) enjoyed the experiences ever since then.

While questing for the perfect ISP, Deborah can be reached at **deb.haralson @bigfoot.com**.

Stu Sjouwerman is president of Sunbelt Software, an international B2B Internet company specializing in providing system management tools and network utilities to manage eBusinesses running on Windows NT/2000. He is the editor of Sunbelt's *W2Knews* (the original *NTools E-news*) that goes to 600,000 subscribers, and also the primary system operator for the MCSE, NTSYSADMIN, Exchange, and MSSQL discussion lists.

Barry Shilmover operates a computer training and consulting company in Calgary, Alberta. He has authored and co-authored several books ranging in topics from Exchange 5.5 to Windows NT to Novell NetWare. He specializes in Windows NT/2000 installation and configuration, network design, and Exchange 5.5/2000 implementations. When not working (rarely), he spends time with his wife Shawna, his son Jory, and his golden retriever (Vicky). You can reach Barry via email at **books@shilmover.com**.

James Michael Stewart is a fulltime writer focusing on Windows NT and Internet topics. Most recently, he has worked on several titles in the Exam Cram and Exam Prep series. Michael has written articles for numerous print and online publications, including *C\Net, Computer Currents, InfoWorld, Windows NT Magazine,* and *Datamation.* He is also a regular speaker at Networld+Interop and TISC. Michael has been with LANWrights, Inc., a wholly owned subsidiary of LeapIT.com, developing Windows NT and Windows 2000 MCSE-level courseware and training materials for several years, including both print and online publication, as well as classroom presentation of training materials. He has been an MCSE since 1997. Michael graduated in 1992 from the University of Texas at Austin with a bachelor's degree in philosophy. Despite his degree, his computer knowledge is self-acquired, based on over 17 years of hands-on experience. He spends his spare time learning to do everything, one hobby at a time. You can reach Michael by email at **michael@lanw.com**, or via the Web at **www.lanw.com/jmsbio.htm**.

Acknowledgments

Thank you goes to so many people who worked on, supported, and helped me during the writing of this book. Our support staff: Paula Kmetz, Wendy Littley, and Tracy Rooney—thanks for your quality work and support during those deadlines. Thank you to Charlotte Carpentier for your patience and perseverence...especially when we were first getting started, and especially for your moral support during this adventure. Thank you, Doug Bassett, for lending your technical expertise and diplomatic skills toward ensuring that everything was technically correct, understandable, and pertinent. Thanks also to Chris Ward for helping in a crunch. Thank you to Sharon McCarson: I couldn't ask for a better friend and confidante who just happened to be my project editor. Thank you to Jeff, Johnathan, Raymond, Mom and Dad, Randy and Michelle, Alex and Faith: Without your love and support I would not be doing this. Thank you to all who serve our country in times of trouble. And humble gratitude and love to our Father in Heaven, for the ability to write, for the blessings and challenges of life in general, and for the knowledge of your love for all of us. Thank you.
—*Deb Haralson*

All three of us would like to thank the team at LANWrights, Inc., for helping us put together a great book. We'd also like to thank the folks at The Coriolis Group: Charlotte Carpentier, Paula Kmetz, Sharon McCarson, and Meg Turecek for their help in geting this book to publication. Finally, thanks to Michelle Stroup, Bart Reed, and Emmett Dulaney for their wonderful attention to detail in their editorial and technical reviews of this book.

A book like this is usually a team effort. In this case, I'd like to thank Barry and Ed for their tireless efforts in making this into a useful resource that is also fun to read.
—*Stuart Sjouwerman*

I would like to extend a special thanks to my wife, Shawna, and my son, Jory. While writing this book, I had moved away to the Seattle area to work on a project. As expected, it was extremely difficult for my 2-year-old son to understand why Daddy did not live with us anymore. All is back to normal now. Shawna, thanks for being there for me when I needed you. While writing this book, my grandfather passed away at the ripe young age of 91. This book is therefore dedicated to

him, Dr. S. Shilmover. We miss you. Special thanks also go to Dawn Rader (for keeping me on track) and Ed Tittel (for your constant help).
—*Barry Shilmover*

Thanks to my boss, Ed Tittel, for including me in this book. To my parents, Dave and Sue, thanks for your love and consistent support. To Mark, as best friends go, I couldn't have found better. To HERbert, I hope you adjust well to our new home and all the new roommates. And finally, as always, to Elvis—your strength, your will, and your passion are an inspiration to us all; I just wish we could all grow lamb chops.

—*James Michael Stewart*

Contents at a Glance

Table of Contents

Immediate Solutions

Introduction

Welcome to the *Windows 2000 System Administrator's Black Book*. This book is designed to give you all the information that you need to manage a Windows 2000 system successfully. Each chapter provides in-depth coverage of the terms and concepts involved in Windows 2000 systems management. Windows 2000 is by far the most advanced operating system released by Microsoft to date. It includes advanced management features that were sorely missing from Windows NT and previous versions of Windows operating systems.

This book provides in-depth detail of all the functions and features of installing, configuring, and maintaining Windows 2000. Each chapter provides hands-on solutions that give you the first-hand experience that you'll need to work with Windows 2000 configuration and management.

What This Book Contains

Chapter 1 discusses the architecture of Windows 2000. This chapter explores how the environment is designed and how each element functions and provides the abilities you know and love.

Chapter 2 examines the differences and similarities between Windows 2000 and Windows NT 4.

Chapter 3 looks at the Windows 2000 directory services system called Active Directory. I discuss the physical components and logical structure and how everything is laid out.

Chapter 4 covers different account types within Windows 2000 Active Directory, such as users and computers, and different ways that the accounts can be grouped together, managed, and administered.

Chapter 5 covers Group Policies within Active Directory. This includes how to create, use, administer, and troubleshoot them, as well as helpful tips on what they can do for any situation that you might encounter.

Chapter 6 details the steps necessary for migrating from Windows NT 4 to Windows 2000. This move can be beneficial, but there are some pitfalls to watch out for.

Chapter 7 covers restructuring Windows 2000 in the event that you want to change the existing structure or layout of an Active Directory forest. I also cover the restructuring method of Windows NT to Windows 2000 migration.

Chapter 8 discusses Windows 2000 installation, which is even more straightforward than ever, but you won't believe how many options or methods of installation are available.

Chapter 9 explores the capabilities of Windows 2000, such as faxing, resource management, file recovery, offline files, drive mount points, and more. This chapter discusses many of these features and how to configure them.

Chapter 10 discusses Windows 2000 file system support, including the file allocation table (FAT), FAT32, and Windows NT File System (NTFS) file systems. With the addition of encryption and new methods of inheritance, you'll need to refamiliarize yourself with the file systems.

Chapter 11 takes a look at the abilities of Windows 2000 to interact with other systems across an integrated small business network.

Chapter 12 discusses implementing Windows 2000 in an enterprise environment. Topics covered in chapters 11 and 12 range from clustering and Terminal Services to distributed file systems and Domain Name Service (DNS), Windows Internet Naming Service (WINS), and Dynamic Host Control Protocol (DHCP).

Chapter 13 discusses the boot process, which is an essential function of Windows 2000. You learn about each step in the boot process and how you can modify booting to meet your needs or even perform troubleshooting and recovery.

Chapter 14 covers Windows 2000's new breed of administration tools made possible by the Microsoft Management Console.

Chapter 15 discusses the Windows 2000 registry, which contains operating and parameter information for every aspect of the system. You learn about the registry and how to safely modify it.

Chapter 16 looks at scripting and automation, and how to use command-line tools for both administration and automation. You learn about the Windows Scripting Host and how to simplify your repetitive administrative tasks.

Chapter 17 discusses Windows 2000 tuning and performance. You can use System Monitor to watch for performance degradations, locate bottlenecks, and even perform capacity planning analysis.

Chapter 18 discusses remote access and routing, which have been fully integrated into the networking architecture of Windows 2000. You learn how to configure a system for any inbound, outbound, or internal connection from dial-up to Virtual Private Network (VPN).

Chapter 19 examines Windows 2000 security. With the addition of Kerberos, encryption, Group Policies, and more, maintaining a security environment with Windows 2000 is easier than ever.

Chapter 20 takes a look at the Windows 2000 print system, which has been enhanced with new features, including Internet printing.

Chapter 21 takes a look at some common troubleshooting techniques. When problems occur, use this handy collection of troubleshooting tips, tricks, and resolutions to restore your Windows 2000 system back to normal.

How to Use This Book

If you're a newcomer to Windows 2000, you should read the book from beginning to end because some topics build upon one another to provide complete coverage of Windows 2000 topics. If you are not familiar with some of the more basic tasks covered in earlier chapters, the more detailed, advanced management functions discussed in later chapters might not make much sense. This is particularly true in the areas of networking and Active Directory.

On the other hand, if you're a seasoned Windows veteran and need information on how to perform a certain action, thumb through the index or Table of Contents, and jump right in. The Immediate Solutions sections of each chapter give you step-by-step instructions on how to install, manage, configure, and troubleshoot all areas of Windows 2000.

Thanks, and enjoy the book!

Chapter 1

Windows 2000 Architecture and Overview

In Depth

During the past few years, the world has been transformed by the proliferation of computing devices—from networks to handheld assistants—and the explosion of the Internet. Microsoft has endeavored to stay at the forefront of this tidal wave by producing ever more advanced operating systems to take advantage of the new technologies and to provide users with the broadest range of resource access capabilities possible. Microsoft's latest operating system manifestation is Windows 2000, which boasts the strengths of Windows NT and Windows 98, combined with many new technologies and features. This new network operating system offers a solid platform for building communication and information delivery systems of all sizes.

Windows 2000 Product Family

Microsoft has once again defined the standard against which all other operating systems are judged and all third-party vendors must compete. The Windows 2000 product family has four current members: Windows 2000 Professional, Windows 2000 Server, Windows 2000 Advanced Server, and Windows 2000 Datacenter Server. Although all are based on a common core, each version has specific features and components designed to support its unique purpose. Windows 2000 offers solid solutions for standalone systems and global networks alike.

Although Windows 2000 is the latest operating system release from Microsoft, it is by no means the only or the last. Microsoft has definitive goals to provide full-featured operating systems for every computing device imaginable.

Windows 2000 Professional

Windows 2000 is Microsoft's answer to the perfect business desktop operating system. The reasoning behind this presumptuous statement is that Windows 2000 Professional provides all of the arguable user-friendliness of Windows 9x with the stability and security of Windows NT. Windows 2000 Professional is designed primarily to serve as a client on a Windows 2000 network. It can, however, serve as a client on other networks, including Windows NT, Novell NetWare, Unix, and Linux, or function as a standalone system for isolated professional or personal home use. Windows 2000 Professional replaces Windows NT 4 Workstation as the business network client of choice from Microsoft. Using features like Internet Connection Sharing (ICS), Windows 2000 is also ideal in several pseudoserver roles within a peer-to-peer networking environment.

This version of Windows 2000 is tuned to maximize performance for foreground applications and Internet resource access, while still being scalable to truly heavy-duty functions that you just won't find in other operating systems. It offers a platform rich in multimedia support (audio and video), full support for Internet standards, support for up to two central processing unit (CPU) chips, and several unique server-type functions, such as accepting inbound analog connections and ICS. All these features function reliably without sacrificing high performance, reliability, and security control.

Windows 2000 Server

Windows 2000 Server is optimally designed to function as a network server within a Windows 2000 domain. However, it can be configured as a member server within the same Windows 2000 domain or in other networked environments, such as Unix, Linux, or Novell NetWare.

Standard server functionality can include file and print sharing, Web services, remote access, and terminal services right out of the box. Networking services—such as Domain Name Service (DNS), Dynamic Host Control Protocol (DHCP), and Windows Internet Naming Service (WINS)—are also available at no extra charge. Windows 2000 Server was designed for a primarily Windows 2000 network; however, it is backward compatible with Windows NT and is interoperable with other networking clients, such as Unix and NetWare. One really nifty feature is that you can create a domain network where a Windows 2000 primary domain controller (PDC) and Windows NT servers, acting as backup domain controllers (BDCs), coexist. Windows 2000 Server can also be deployed in heterogeneous networks with NetWare and Unix systems.

As a domain controller, the first Windows 2000 server in a network establishes the domain and its directory services, provided by Active Directory. A *directory service* is a networking service that tracks and manages network resources to include security, access control, and other features. In addition to standard directory services, Active Directory also allows for centralized (and/or distributed) management of users, groups, security services, and network resources. Unlike Windows NT, all Windows 2000 domain controllers become peers in supporting and updating the domain and its directory services. What this means is that, in the event that the main domain controller fails, all other domain controllers remain available to handle resource and network security and authentication. The added bonus is that this is accomplished without additional administrative intervention.

Windows 2000 Server is tuned to maximize the performance of network services for a small to midsized company base. It offers a stable platform for hosting up to 256 inbound remote access connections and can handle up to four CPUs and four gigabytes (GB) of random access memory (RAM). Windows 2000 Server offers sufficient capabilities to support small- to medium-sized networks. However, it would be wise to consider using Windows 2000 Advanced Server or Datacenter Server for more heavy-duty and specialized network, Web, or client/server applications.

NOTE: *Any operating system that claims to support four-way symmetric multiprocessing (SMP) is really just saying that it supports four CPUs. With SMP, system and application processes can use any processor that is available to service requests.*

Windows 2000 Advanced Server

Windows 2000 Advanced Server is designed to function as a high-end network server in a Windows 2000 domain. It has all the same base features and capabilities as Windows 2000 Server, but it offers more power and scalability. Advanced Server includes support for eight-way multiprocessing (which means that it can handle up to eight CPUs), up to eight GB of RAM, network load balancing, and clustering. Although it can be deployed as a domain controller or a typical application server in a network, it is designed to offer enhanced performance for e-commerce and line-of-business applications.

Load balancing is an incredible technology advance that has actually been available in other operating and hardware systems for quite a while. That's one of the unique things about Microsoft. It manages to take technology that has existed in the mainframe, minicomputer, and Unix world and actually make it work in the personal computer (PC) arena. Load balancing is a process where, if a single server becomes inundated with processes and tasks, other servers are available to assist with the workload. Quite often, you will see similar technologies, such as round-robin DNS, in effect. However, true load balancing with Windows 2000 Advanced Server is a new feature to the PC NOS server world. You typically encounter load balancing and clustering in the same set of servers because they provide very similar services.

Clustering is a computing technology in which two or more computers are connected to share the workload on a common application. Clustering allows more computing power to be leveraged against a single computing task while offering *fault tolerance* (the ability to continue functioning if a cluster member goes offline).

Both load balancing and clustering are ideal for environments where mission-critical availability and response are essential. Good examples are Web servers, call center servers, or any system where 100 percent availability and accessibility is required for business. Load balancing, in particular, should be considered for systems where a large number of transactions are processed in a relatively short amount of time. For instance, your company's entire sales staff arrives at the office at 8:00 A.M. The first thing that they do is download the current product catalog pricing changes from the previous evening. Having 200 people access the same database at the same time can be a problem for a single server. Load balancing can assist with this by moving the additional traffic to another server.

Windows 2000 Datacenter Server

Windows 2000 Datacenter Server is designed to handle high-end memory and CPU-intensive applications, which are much more than file and print servers. It has all the same base features and capabilities as Windows 2000 Advanced Server (including network advanced load balancing and clustering), with added support for up to 32 CPUs and 64GB of addressable physical RAM. Microsoft developed Datacenter Server to provide unparalleled power to support applications, such as data warehousing, complex graphics rendering, realtime e-commerce transaction processing, and more. In order to take advantage of these types of features properly, it becomes necessary to customize the applications and solutions that go on a Datacenter Server machine. As a result, Datacenter Server is available only from original equipment manufacturers (OEMs), such as Compaq, Hewlett Packard, and Dell. These OEMs configure and tune the operating system and hardware (specifically built to take advantage of Datacenter Server) to optimal efficiency specific to the applications that will be installed on the system.

Windows 2000 Solutions

Microsoft does not just offer operating systems to handle your networking needs; it also offers networking and office applications that are specifically tuned to interoperate and work with the Windows 2000 Server product line.

Additional Windows 2000 Server Applications

Although this book focuses on the administrative skill sets for Windows 2000, you will most likely be working with other applications that run on Windows 2000. Because of this, we will briefly mention other Windows 2000 Server applications that may become useful as a complete solution to you or the company you work for. Take a look at these applications when you are considering solutions and technologies for your company. More information on these products is available on the Microsoft Web site at **http://www.microsoft.com**.

Quite a few of the applications can be specifically integrated into Windows 2000 Active Directory. This allows for additional security and a good reduction in administrative overhead. For example, adding a new user requires an hour's worth of administrative time in order to add user accounts and profiles on five different systems. Integrating these systems with Active Directory reduces that hour to 15 minutes because the administrator only needs to enter the user data once and then subsequently point the respective applications to the correct account within Active Directory. The following applications can also be integrated with Windows 2000 Server to create any number of different corporate solutions:

- Application Center offers advanced load balancing and Web application management, thus enabling a potential 99.999 percent uptime.

- Mobile Information 2001 Server enables remote access to email; email applets, such as contacts, calendars, and task lists; and basically any intranet application from any mobile device.

- Host Integration Server replaces and is upgradable from Microsoft SNA Server. Host Integration Server allows desktop access and management of minicomputer and mainframe sessions.

- System Management Server (SMS) allows administration and management of desktop hardware and software inventory. Software distribution, maintenance, and deployment also round out this administrative dream tool.

- Exchange Server is email. Exchange Server, along with an Outlook client, can be the heart and soul of your company. Together, they can provide email, contacts, tasks, calendars, centralized appointments, customized data entry forms and management, shared scheduling, delegated tasks, and rules-based email management.

- Structured Query Language (SQL) Server is the Microsoft database solution of choice. Although it can be tuned and optimized for heavy-duty access and response—such as what would be necessary for Datacenter Server—SQL Server is ideal for small to midsized database solutions. If you are not a database administrator (DBA) and you are considering SQL Server as a solution, keep in mind that, unlike Microsoft Access, SQL Server is just the backend database. A front-end interface is necessary in order to provide a complete solution. This usually involves development. However, the solution can be as simple as creating an Access interface and pointing the backend toward your database. Rumor has it that Exchange Server will soon have the capability of allowing its backend database to reside on SQL Server. If this is the case, your front-end interface could very well be Outlook configured with customized forms.

- BizTalk Server is a business process and management application server that enables your company to build, integrate, and manage applications and data with other companies and business partners. Similar to pieces of Lotus Notes, BizTalk can be configured to route and track business documents.

- Commerce Server is a Web server add-on that allows e-commerce forms and permits data transactions to occur.

- Site Server is an application that allows you to publish and find mass quantities of data easily in an intranet/Internet-based system.

- Internet Security and Acceleration (ISA) Server 2000 is designed to replace Proxy Server. ISA provides Internet proxy services by tracking all Internet usage and maintaining copies of recent and frequently used Web sites. Additional firewall, scheduled content download, and intrusion-detection features create a more rounded Internet security system.

- SharePoint Portal Server—code named Tahoe—is a document management and collaboration system. High points include lifecycle management, document check-in and check-out control, and version control. This is ideal if your company employs developers and programmers.

Application Bundles

The cost for these applications can become quite expensive, especially for the small to midsized company. Quite often, Microsoft will create bundles of applications specifically grouped for certain functionalities. Two bundles have been around for quite a while in their different versions, and others have been available for limited times under differing names and in target markets.

BackOffice Suite

The BackOffice Suite is the most common server bundle purchased by both large and small businesses alike. BackOffice includes Windows 2000, Exchange Server, SQL Server, ISA Server, Host Integration Server, and SMS. These applications should be adequate for any fairly large corporation. Licensing methods vary, but licenses are usually either sold in bundles or handled by online purchases and open licensing. Generally, you may get sticker shock from the price of the complete BackOffice Suite. If this is the case, consider the pricing (including licenses) for each component in the bundle. Even if you choose not to use one of the applications, the bundle price is still better than purchasing the programs separately.

Small Business Server

A few years ago, Microsoft realized that the entire BackOffice Suite was still too cost-prohibitive for the small to midsized company. The result was a new bundle called Small Business Server, or SBS for short. SBS contains Windows 2000 Server, Exchange Server, ISA Server, SQL Server, shared fax and modem services, Microsoft Health Monitor, and FrontPage 2000. By and large, these features are more tuned for the small business that does not have the money for professionally outsourced Web sites or expensive fax and modem pools. Again, the component prices are larger than the bundle prices, yet if your company is particularly budget-conscious, you can still see a great return on the SBS product in comparison with BackOffice just in the Exchange, ISA, and SQL Server functionalities because each of these is in high demand for small and midsized companies.

What's Right for Your Company?

Implementing Windows 2000 within an organization is rarely an isolated event, as other applications often need to be upgraded or installed as well. Quite often, we as administrators want to see the features of Windows 2000 implemented in order to both make our lives easier and be able to provide more services to our customers. It's these services—in the form of added applications and features—that may become the deciding factor in getting management to approve a Windows 2000 budget.

Getting Buyoff from Management

On your quest to become a Windows 2000 guru, you will be asked about what solutions and systems are best for the company. This is a good thing. It shows that your peers and management respect your opinion and that you have some input into the decision-making process. Quite often, after you request or tell management what would be best for the company, management is uncomfortable with the price of the systems. This is when you bring up how the investment will reduce downtime for mission-critical systems.

Of course, all companies will insist that their <insert system name here> is mission-critical and essential to the business, but it seems that, all too often, when you propose a technological safety net, the application is suddenly not important enough to keep it from failing. If applications were that important, companies would be flocking to purchase Advanced Server and Datacenter Server because of their increased reliability. In reality, the definition of the word "critical" is misunderstood. Personally, when you analyze the criticality of a system, you should be asking yourself these questions:

- If this application dies, will I get fired?
- If this application does not work, will the company close its doors?
- If this application does not work, is there no other way that the company can make money?

If the answer to any of these is yes, the system is truly mission-critical. This is why it becomes even more important to propose these technological safety nets and to get them approved.

The means of getting approval for these critical powerhouse purchases, such as anything in the Windows 2000 suite, is in one of two ways. First, you can compute something known as cost of downtime and convince management that the cost of downtime, combined with your current known downtime, outweighs the cost of the systems that you wish to purchase. Here's the basic formula: One hour of downtime equals x many people not working when they're paid $\$y$ per hour. Average sales, income, and calls for that hour can usually be calculated based upon daily revenue levels (call this r) divided by the number of hours in the work day (let's say eight for our example here). If the company is 24 by 7, your company probably has revenue numbers for each shift. Use the revenue from the applicable shift as r, and divide r by the duration of the shift itself. The final cost of downtime calculation is H$((pw)+(r/8))$ where (pw) is the number of personnel affected, multiplied by the average wages of each person. (pw) ultimately ends up being the cost of personnel goofing off while the network is down, and $(r/8)$ is the estimated hourly revenue. Both of these numbers add to the total cost of downtime for a single hour. Multiply this by the number of downtime hours (H) in, let's say a week or a month, and you have a pretty good number to use to support your request.

You could also compute the increased productivity levels as a result of a complete Windows 2000 solution. There is no easy way to calculate a true productivity increase. However, there are means of creating an estimate based completely upon a single function's difference. For example, you notice that Judy spends quite a bit of time surfing the Web, but you aren't sure how much. You could find out, however, if you had ISA Server. As a result, you could determine exactly where and how long Judy is surfing and could provide management with tangible data faster than any other means. The increased productivity is seen when management gets in the habit of detecting personnel issues like this early. A multipronged proposal can occur here when you pitch Windows 2000 Professional and SMS as additional means of increasing security and of reducing administrative overhead. Why? Windows 2000 Professional can be configured to use mandatory roaming profiles, which along with group policies can help restrict what users can do on their computers, thus reducing the likeliness of users both goofing off and blowing up their systems. SMS can be coupled with Windows 2000 Remote Installation Services (RIS) to quickly rebuild and deploy systems with the proper applications and profiles intact.

In many ways, both cost of downtime and productivity can be the same. After all, if you decrease downtime from 12 hours a week to 6 hours a week, and 20 phone reps are paid at $10 per hour, you've decreased the cost of downtime by at least $1,200, depending on revenue numbers. On the flip side, you've increased productivity by that much also. Computing productivity is usually the better tactic to take with management when you are dealing with application purchases rather than hardware or operating system purchases. This is because applications are usually more user-based and are more likely to improve productivity.

When you make your proposal with this information, you are more likely to be considered. All too often, IT professionals complain that management doesn't understand the effort that goes into supporting them in their everyday lives. Unfortunately, management complains that IT just doesn't see the big picture. The solution is to come up with as many solid facts and numbers as possible. Management will always pay attention to dollars, and solid arguments that equal increased revenue and profits will always be listened to.

Researching Your Proposal

Before you put together the battle plan for getting your recommended Microsoft solution, you can also do several other things. First of all, ask your manager. Make sure that you communicate everything that you'd like to do and get her buyoff and support before doing anything or going anywhere. Not only might your manager receive questions, but she is your first and most powerful ally toward improving the company. If your plans include things like profit, money, and time savings, you've come full circle toward getting your Windows 2000 solutions approved and implemented.

Next, you can talk to other departments. This is usually handled by a member of the IT management staff. If it is not, or if you need additional clarification, volunteer to do it yourself. The idea is to get a better idea of any recurring problems a particular group of people might have, which can mean anything from budget overruns to employees goofing off to standard IT "it doesn't work" issues. Chances are that, during your conversation, you will at least find one annoyance that can be easily solved, and, at most, a real gem of a problem with a resolution can be worked into the return on investment (ROI) plan for acquiring new equipment and software. The overall goal of talking to other departments is to gain allies and to let them help push and prod for the capital equipment. One time, I really wanted to purchase a phone switch for the company I worked for instead of having it live on an outgrown key system. The biggest leverage point was that we had lots of sales employees making phone calls, so I spoke with the marketing director and explained to him the benefits of a small call center setup for that phone system. The president of the company was soon asking me if the contract was ready to sign. The advantages of communicating with other departments are huge, and they will undoubtedly help in your day-to-day operations as well.

Finally, take a good look at the processes that the company has right now. This is very similar to talking to other departments, but quite often you will miss broad processes that span more than one department. For instance, take a look at how new employees are hired. When and how do you receive names and requirements to create accounts for and enter them into the IT computer systems? Who gives you this information, and how soon before the person walks in the door do you hear about it? This is the perfect example of an interdepartmental process. Human resources recruits and handles administrative hiring, department managers have the need for a new person, and other departments like IT and facilities are in charge of ensuring the new employees have a place to sit and the appropriate equipment to get their job done. Look at processes like these, figure out how they might be streamlined, and see if anything can be worked into your software and hardware request. Again, talk to other departments, but be careful that you listen to any objections or thoughts that they have.

The Windows 2000 Installation

How Windows 2000 is installed and deployed can play a big part in how the overall implementation plan develops. Specific information on installation processes is covered in Chapter 8. However, some installation factors are covered in Table 1.1 to allow you to get a good idea of what will be involved.

You may notice in Table 1.1 that certain information is missing. We assume that you are aware that all versions of Windows 2000 require a Video Graphics Array (VGA) or better monitor, a keyboard, and a mouse. Additional features, such as ICS, are not listed because they similarly exist for all versions of Windows 2000.

Installing Windows 2000 usually occurs using a local CD-ROM. Similar to the Windows NT installation, a 3.5-inch high-density floppy disk drive (along with three disks) is required only if the CD-ROM drive will not boot to the Windows 2000 installation CD.

If you are rolling out several Windows 2000 systems, if the CD-ROM drive is not available, or if you simply need to keep the CD safe, the installation may require some additional effort; however, some new Windows 2000 features make the work well worth it.

Unique Installation Methods

You can set up Windows 2000 using a standard network installation, along with answer files to allow for unattended installations. In this process, the installing computer boots to a floppy disk that enables network connectivity and attaches

Table 1.1   The base features and minimum system requirements for each type of Windows 2000.

Feature	Professional	Server	Advanced Server	Datacenter Server
Processor limit	2	4	8	32
Memory support	4GB	4GB	8GB	64GB
Clustering	No	No	2 maximum	4 maximum
Load balancing	No	No	32 maximum	32 maximum
HCL	Standard	Standard	Standard	Gold HCL
Processor	133MHz	133MHz	133MHz	Pentium III Xeon
RAM	64MB	128MB*	128MB*	256MB
HDD/free HDD	2GB/650MB	2GB/1GB	2GB/1GB	2GB/1GB

256MB recommended minimum

to a network share that has the Windows 2000 installation files. The boot disk needs to be created, the installation files need to be placed on the network with appropriate permissions, and the proper network drivers and connections need to be present in order for this to work. After this particular functionality is accomplished, the installation can be kicked off either by the floppy disk or by manual entry. You can create an automated answer file using Windows 2000 Server Resource Kit tools to make the installation completely automated. However, you should know that this is the point, during rollout, where the project may become truly time-consuming.

Requirements for installing from a network include:

- A compatible network interface card (NIC) and associated media cable
- Connection or access to a network share containing the setup files, that is, a shared folder or a shared CD-ROM or digital video disk (DVD) drive

You can also set up Windows 2000 using a new feature of Windows 2000 called RIS. In order to use RIS, you need a Windows 2000 Server running DNS, a DHCP server from which to receive a Transmission Control Protocol/Internet Protocol (TCP/IP) address, and a Pre-Boot eXecution Environment (PXE)-compliant boot disk or network card. In preparation, you need to take a preconfigured Windows 2000 system (along with applications) and run a utility that creates a system image with the licensing and system-specific software data stripped. Then, when you are ready to install the same image onto another system, you boot it to the network and choose the image that was created. This does require a small amount of user interface, but it may be worthwhile considering the time that it would take to install both Windows 2000 and additional applications.

NOTE: *Windows 2000 is the first Microsoft operating system since Windows 3.1 that is somewhat portable. What this means is that you can literally pull a hard drive from one PC and install it onto a completely different PC and the system will usually boot. You may have some tweaking to do, of course, but, then again, you always did. It's the plug-and-play piece of Windows 2000 that makes this possible. As a result, quite often you can use a single RIS image for multiple computers during installation. You may receive some errors specific to hardware devices, such as a particular Universal Serial Bus (USB) hub or disk controller, but Windows 2000 functions just fine with a huge savings in time and effort. This is great for large rollouts where the systems are not all guaranteed to be the same. One piece of advice, though, is to try to avoid radical RIS image differences, such as installing an RIS image created on a laptop onto a desktop or server machine. Because laptop equipment is usually proprietary, this can quite often cause problems.*

Requirements for installing using RIS include:

- A network-bootable, PXE-compliant network interface card
- Network access to a Windows 2000 domain controller, DNS Server, and DHCP server
- Administrative-equivalent permissions on the Windows 2000 server

One last method for Windows 2000 installation involves a tool that we've used in the industry for quite some time. Utilities such as Symantec's Ghost and PowerQuest's Drive Image Pro have been ideal for backup and restore, as well as disaster recovery tools. Most OEM hardware manufacturers also use imaging tools like this to install the software that is on the new computers we buy. The problem with Windows 2000 (and Windows NT to a lesser extent) is due to something known as a globally unique identifier (GUID). The GUID is a special number that is created by Windows 2000 based upon the hardware configuration of the machine on which it is installed. It sounds innocent enough until you accidentally blast the same image onto two machines on the same Windows 2000 network, and all sorts of confusion occurs. Windows 2000 offers us the same luxury of using image tools like Ghost and Drive Image Pro while stripping the install-specific data, such as the GUID, from the software before the imaging program takes the snapshot. The result is a somewhat genericized drive image that can be distributed to any other system that supports the same drive and partition configuration. Ideally, the target machine should be identical, but, again, because of Windows 2000's plug-and-play features, usually only the drive size needs to be the same, or larger. Most imaging applications will adjust the partitions if they are different. Similar to the RIS solution, the biggest advantage is that both Windows 2000 and the installed applications get distributed. The downside again is the potential for hardware glitches if the target system is drastically different from the source.

Hardware

Although Windows 2000 supports a much wider range of hardware devices than Windows NT, you should still verify that all devices present in a computer are fully compatible before performing the installation. You can ensure that your devices are compatible by checking each device against the Hardware Compatibility List (HCL) maintained by Microsoft. Datacenter Server reportedly deals with a more refined list of supported hardware, but, because Datacenter Server is only distributed through OEM channels, the HCL for it is by and large unavailable. The standard list is available on the Windows 2000 distribution CD and the Microsoft Web site.

The HCL version on the CD is only as useful as it is current. Because the information on the CD was finalized in January 2000, any hardware and drivers released after that are not included. Therefore, this version of the HCL should be used with caution, especially because it is more than six months out of date. The HCL is stored on the distribution CD in the \Support subdirectory and is contained in the file named hcl.txt.

The version of the HCL on the Microsoft Web site is constantly updated and is the best resource available. The online HCL is located at **http://www.microsoft.com/ hcl/default.asp**. This URL is subject to change; if this one is no longer valid, you can manually find it by starting from **www.microsoft.com/windows/**.

A compatible device is a device with a driver that is distributed on the Windows 2000 CD or that has a new or updated driver available for download from Microsoft or the device's manufacturer. Be sure you have all drivers for all devices on hand before starting the installation. You should also check manufacturers' Web sites and the Microsoft Windows 2000 Web site for special instructions on installing software with drivers not already present on the distribution CD.

Windows 2000 Architecture and Design

Windows 2000 is not a single monolithic program, but rather a collection of many small components designed to interact and interface with one another. This modular design has several benefits, which range from versatility of features to ease of upgrade, administration, and repair. This structure is evident in the division of user- and kernel-level processes and services.

The Windows 2000 operating system environment is separated into two distinct layers: user mode and kernel mode. All user applications like Microsoft Office and Exchange reside in user mode, and all system and hardware operations reside in kernel mode. Instructions are passed between the two modes through a few processes that act as messengers between the two. In other words, applications cannot talk directly to the hardware. They need to use Windows as a messenger to pass instructions and requests to the hardware for them. In the process of being messenger, Windows makes sure that the messages are all civil and appropriate. Once in a while, the messages are inappropriate, and the message is not delivered. When this happens, the application usually terminates. This particular functionality has been around since Windows NT, and it provides a great amount of system integrity because it keeps all applications playing fair. This is why Windows NT and 2000 are known to be more stable than many other operating systems. What's the downside? Many 16-bit disk operating system (DOS) and Windows applications were programmed to access the hardware directly and are still available today. Although this compatibility-by-design issue has been reduced significantly in the past several years, many video-intensive games still talk to the hardware directly in order to improve speed, but also to go beyond the capabilities of the Windows drivers installed on the system.

Although it is not necessary to know the specifics of user and kernel modes in order to be a Windows 2000 administrator, you need to understand some memory-related basics to assess your environments and to determine if Windows 2000 is the appropriate system to use. The basic structure of the user and kernel modes and their related components is shown in Figure 1.1. More information on Windows 2000 architecture is available in the Windows 2000 Server Resource Kit and also online at **http://www.microsoft.com**.

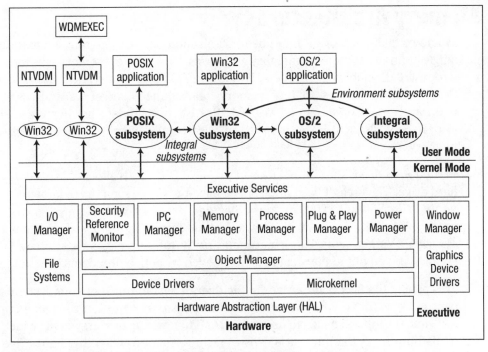

Figure 1.1   The system architecture of Windows 2000.

By using this same isolationist-type model, Windows 2000 can also support the following types of applications:

- Windows 32-bit applications (Win32)
- Windows 16-bit applications (Win16)
- DOS applications
- Operating System 2, second generation (OS/2) 1.x character-mode applications
- POSIX.1 applications

Not all these environments are actually useful. The OS/2 and POSIX subsystems only support text-only applications and are present only to meet the purchasing requirement minimums for government agencies. Third-party services must be installed to provide true OS/2 and POSIX support.

Also keep in mind that just because Windows 2000 supports all of these different types of applications doesn't mean that the applications will successfully run on Windows 2000. Any application that attempts to access the hardware directly will either hang or terminate.

Memory Architecture

Windows 2000 employs a flat, linear, 32-bit memory scheme that is basically a single contiguous block of memory addresses. This type of memory provides for a robust and reliable environment. Windows 2000 Professional and Windows 2000 Server can both address 4GB of memory, but Advanced Server can address 8GB, and Datacenter Server can address 64GB. Although modern hardware can support 4GB of physical RAM, the 4GB of addressable memory is actually virtual memory.

Virtual memory is the combination of physical RAM with allocated space from a hard drive. The area of hard drive space used by virtual memory is known as the *paging file*. Windows 2000 creates a paging file one and a half times as large as the amount of physical RAM present at the time of installation. The Virtual Memory Manager (VMM) manages virtual memory by moving pages (4 kilobyte [KB] chunks) in and out of physical RAM as needed by active processes.

This paging file is very important in the overall performance of your system and even more so for servers and mission-critical systems. Consider the real picture. Any time the system needs to use more RAM than what's on the system (which is, by definition, all the time), it swaps other information out to the hard drive to make room for the new information that needs to be in RAM. As a result, your hard drive might be in use quite a bit more than anticipated, particularly if you do not have enough RAM on the system. If, for example, this swap file is located on the same hard drive as the boot partition (which contains all of the Windows 2000 information) or the Active Directory database (which handles all resource authentication), you could run into performance issues where the entire system slows down because the hard drive simply becomes too busy dealing with both the swap file and other tasks essential to system survival. In situations like this, it might be wise to place the swap file on a different drive. You can use Performance Monitor to determine if more RAM or another hard drive is necessary. Find out how in Chapter 17.

Despite the fact that the VMM only seems to swap data to the swap file, the VMM keeps track of the address pages created and used by each process within their assigned address space and maps those pages to actual locations within the available virtual memory of the computer. This process is depicted in Figure 1.2.

One additional concept concerning Windows 2000 architecture that, as an administrator, you should be aware of is the hardware abstraction layer (HAL). The HAL is a hardware platform-specific component compiled at the time of installation based on the foundational hardware devices of the computer. The HAL must

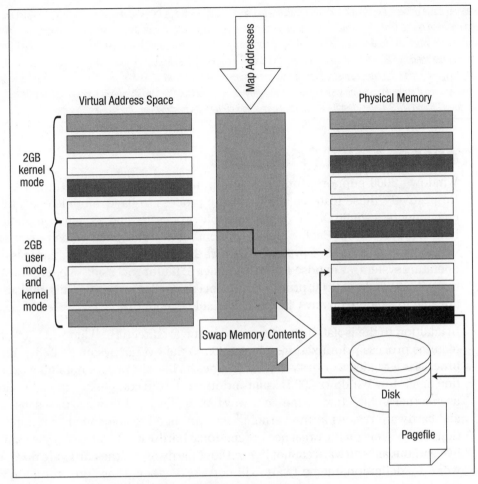

Figure 1.2   The Windows 2000 virtual memory architecture.

be rebuilt each time a significant change occurs to the system, such as adding a second CPU or upgrading the motherboard, so keep this in mind when transplanting Windows 2000 or upgrading the CPU.

NOTE: *You may be wondering how Windows 2000 can be transplanted from computer to computer, especially if the HAL must be recompiled (by performing an install process) when motherboards or CPUs change. Other than the plug-and-play factor, the reason that we are able to do these things is because many PC components on the motherboard stay the same from system to system. Specifically, it's a motherboard's chipset that manages the on-board disk; sound; and parallel, serial, Peripheral Component Interconnect (PCI) and Accelerated Graphics Port (AGP) drivers, along with a host of other mind-numbing functions. When Windows talks to the hardware, it specifically talks to these drivers. Because only a handful of popular chipset makers are on the market and because many of them use technical standards when* *creating these drivers, there's a good chance that a transplanted Windows 2000 hard disk drive will wake up just fine and not even notice that it's talking to new base-level hardware. On the off chance that Windows doesn't work properly, you'll know. When the blue screen of death (BSOD) appears, reboot. If it happens again, the solution is easy. Just run through the Windows 2000 installation process (the boot CD comes in handy here), choose to install in the current directory, and repair the current installation. If you don't know what the BSOD looks like, don't worry; you will know one when you see it sometime during your career as an administrator. Ancient BSODs have been spotted as early as Windows 95 and NT 3.1 and, despite all efforts, eradication of the little pests seems impossible.*

Processes and Priorities

Windows 2000 supports multithreading, multitasking, and multiprocessing. Respectively, these features allow a single process to have multiple executable components, a single CPU to juggle multiple processes, and a single computer to have multiple CPUs. Each of these computing advancements adds power and versatility to an operating system. Windows 2000 is a symmetric multiprocessing operating system, as opposed to an asymmetric multiprocessing one. This means that within Windows 2000, processes are not assigned to a specific CPU, but rather are able to execute on any CPU with available execution cycles.

In addition to the isolationism described in the architecture, Windows 2000 also features process prioritization, which adds to the overall system stability. Each process is assigned a priority that determines its importance for obtaining execution time. How Windows 2000 assigns priority is based completely upon the same user/kernel architecture. In the same way that applications reside in the user space and hardware resides in the kernel space, you need to remember that applications always rely on the presence of functional hardware. Just like people cannot live without air, software cannot live without hardware. If the hardware does not work, by definition, the software will not work either. Therefore, kernel mode (hardware) processes always have a higher execution priority than any user mode (application) process.

It is also possible to change the tone of the computer and how it automatically prioritizes tasks. By this, we mean that you can specifically tune the system to set a higher priority on system tasks, such as login and authentication or application tasks like Microsoft Office or Internet Information Server (IIS). This is done by changing the system's performance from the Control Panel.

NOTE: *As a user (or even as an administrator), you can also change the priority by which an application executes, but you will always be limited by the rule that hardware comes first. You are also limited to setting one of six priority levels at startup or during execution: Low, Below Normal, Normal, Above Normal, High, and Realtime (restricted to only administrators).*

The Windows 2000 Interface

The Windows 2000 interface is much like that of Windows 95 and 98, with several differences to accommodate the additional security and functional features seen in Windows NT, plus a few new features.

By default, you can double-click any icon to open the application that it is associated with. You can right-click that same icon to receive a pop-up menu that allows you to perform several functions upon that item, such as open, edit, and delete. You can also right-click the same icon, hold down the right mouse button, and drag that icon anywhere, including onto the Start menu or the quick-launch bar just to the right of the Start menu. To remove icons from these spaces, you do just the opposite. Right-click the item, and either click Delete from the pop-up menu or simply drag the item elsewhere. Similarly, you can get the path for an application by finding the application within Explorer, clicking the Start menu, selecting Run, and then dragging the application directly from Explorer onto the Run line. The entire path then appears there.

You can right-click anything else, too. If functionality is available, a pop-up menu appears. You need to pay attention because the pop-up menus change depending upon where you click. The following are different right-click functionalities that are available:

- Right-clicking the blank space on the desktop and selecting Properties gives you the same display settings that you would receive from Control Panel|Display.
- Right-clicking My Computer and selecting Properties gives you the same settings as you would receive from Control Panel|System.
- Right-clicking Network Neighborhood and selecting Properties gives you the same settings as you would receive from Control Panel|Network.
- Right-clicking the empty space on the taskbar and selecting Properties gives you the same settings as you would receive from Start|Settings|Taskbar And Start Menu.
- Right-clicking an item in the system tray (opposite from the Start menu button) usually presents you with options for that application.
- Right-clicking My Computer and selecting Manage gives you Computer Manager, which contains Event Viewer, Performance Monitor, Users And Groups, Disk Manager, and Services, along with a few new features, such as removable storage and logical drives.

The following additional specialized keystrokes are available:

- Ctrl+Alt+Delete brings up the Windows security dialog where you can lock the computer (similar to a Windows screensaver password, only more difficult to crack), log off, shut down, change your password, or access the Task Manager.

- Ctrl+Shift+Esc brings the Task Manager directly onto the screen.

- Alt+Tab switches from one active application to the next.

- Ctrl+Esc activates the Start menu.

- Ctrl+C copies highlighted text.

- Ctrl+V pastes highlighted text.

- Shift+right-clicking an icon brings up the same pop-up menu with an additional Run As function (in the event that the application requires administrative authority and the currently logged on user does not have administrator privileges).

- Any item in a menu bar within any application can be accessed by clicking the Alt key, holding it down, and hitting the underscored letter on the menu bar at the same time. For instance, Alt+F usually brings up the File menu.

As you can see, many of these features are new, and many others have been around for a while. The important thing to remember is that most applications developed under the Windows 95/98/2000 interface umbrella have similar behavior patterns, such as being able to right-click text to receive options and dragging tool and menu bars from the window. Additional brand-new interface features do exist, but in reality, these are few and far between, as well as unnoticeable. One exception to this is a function called Personalized Menus. This function is an intuitive algorithm that only shows you the Start menu items that you use most. You can still access all other items, but an extra step is involved. For those of you who have experience with the Windows 9x interface, this can be annoying because you expect certain things to appear and they usually don't. The solution is to turn this feature off within the Taskbar and Start Menu settings. Outside of these systemwide interface tips, specific functions—such as Active Directory User Management—are covered in subsequent chapters.

Immediate Solutions

Altering the Size of the Paging File

Windows 2000 automatically creates a paging file when installed. The default initial size is approximately one and a half times the amount of physical RAM, and the maximum size is set to two times the default initial size. Therefore, if you have 128 megabytes (MB) of RAM, the initial size will be 192MB, and the maximum size will be 384MB. Depending on the applications and services hosted by your computer and the tasks you perform, you may want to alter the size of the paging file. In addition, if you add more RAM to your system, you'll want to increase the paging file size. To alter the size of the paging file, perform the following steps:

1. Click the Start button and select Settings|Control Panel. The Control Panel window is displayed.

2. Locate and double-click the System applet icon in the Control Panel window. The System applet opens.

3. Click the Advanced tab (see Figure 1.3).

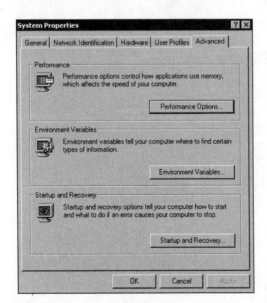

Figure 1.3   The Advanced tab of the System applet.

4. Click the Performance Options button. The Performance Options dialog box is displayed (see Figure 1.4).

5. Click the Change button in the Virtual Memory section of the Performance Options dialog box. The Virtual Memory dialog box is displayed (see Figure 1.5).

6. Select the drive that currently hosts the paging file. It's the one with the MB range defined under the Paging File Size column. Notice how the initial size and maximum size values appear in the text fields under the Paging File Size For Selected Drive section after you've selected the paging file host drive.

7. Change the initial size to reflect your needs. For example, suppose you added more RAM so your computer now has 256MB. In this case, you would change the initial size to 384 (256×1.5) and the maximum size to 768

Figure 1.4   The Performance Options dialog box.

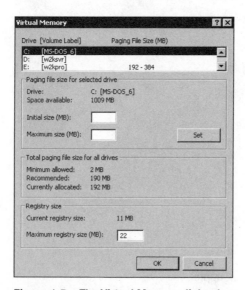

Figure 1.5   The Virtual Memory dialog box.

(384×2) and then click the Set button. Notice that new values are displayed in the Drive And Paging File Size table at the top of the dialog box.

8. Click OK to close the Virtual Memory dialog box.

9. Click OK to close the Performance Options dialog box.

10. Click OK to close the System applet dialog box.

11. Close the Control Panel by selecting File|Close.

A system reboot may be required; if so, you are prompted to reboot.

Moving the Paging File to a New Host Drive

If your boot partition (the partition hosting the main Windows 2000 system files) does not contain enough free space or if you want to speed system performance by placing the paging file on a different physical disk, you can move the paging file from its default location. To move the paging file to a new host drive, perform the following steps:

1. Click the Start button, and select Settings|Control Panel. The Control Panel window is displayed.

2. Locate and double-click the System applet icon in the Control Panel window. The System applet opens.

3. Click the Advanced tab (see Figure 1.6).

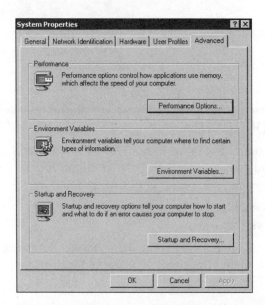

Figure 1.6   The Advanced tab of the System applet.

4. Click the Performance Options button. The Performance Options dialog box is displayed (refer to Figure 1.4).

5. Click the Change button under the Virtual Memory section of the Performance Options dialog box. The Virtual Memory dialog box is displayed (refer to Figure 1.5).

6. Note the initial and maximum size of the current paging file (for example, 192MB and 384MB).

7. Select the drive where you want to place the paging file in the Drive And Paging File Size table at the top of the Virtual Memory dialog box.

8. In the Initial Size field, type the initial size of the current paging file (for example, 192).

9. In the Maximum Size field, type the maximum size of the current paging file (for example, 384).

10. Click Set. Select the drive hosting the original default paging file.

11. Change the initial and maximum sizes of the paging file to 0, and click Set.

12. Click OK to close the Virtual Memory dialog box.

13. You should see a message stating that the computer must reboot for the changes to take effect. Click OK.

14. Click OK to close the Performance Options dialog box.

15. Click OK to close the System applet dialog box.

16. When prompted to reboot your computer, click Yes to reboot the system automatically.

17. When the system reboots, you may need to close the Control Panel by selecting File|Close.

Removing Windows Components

Windows 2000 may install components that you do not want installed on your system. By default, the removal tool does not display all the configurable components. To remove Windows components, perform the following steps:

1. Launch Windows Explorer by clicking the Start button and selecting Programs|Accessories|Windows Explorer.

2. Locate and select the boot partition in the left pane of Windows Explorer. The boot partition is where the main Windows 2000 system files reside. This is typically drive C: or D:.

3. Locate the %systemroot%\inf\sysoc.inf file; it is located within the main Windows 2000 directory (which may be named Windows, W2K, Winnt, or something similar). Double-click the file, which opens the file in Notepad.

4. Select Edit|Replace.

5. In the Find What: field, type ",hide," (be sure to include the commas).

6. In the Replace With: field, type "," (no space is required).

7. Click the Replace All button, and then click the Cancel button.

8. Select File|Save.

9. Select File|Exit to close Notepad.

10. Click the Start button, and select Settings|Control Panel. The Control Panel window is displayed.

11. Locate and double-click the Add/Remove Programs applet icon in the Control Panel window. The Add/Remove Programs applet opens.

12. Click the Add/Remove Windows Components button. The Windows Components portion of the Windows Components Wizard opens (see Figure 1.7).

13. Select the Accessories And Utilities component.

14. Click the Details button (see Figure 1.8).

15. Deselect the Accessibility Wizard checkbox.

16. Click OK.

17. Click Next.

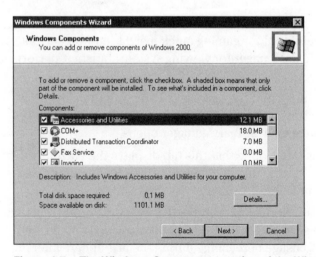

Figure 1.7   The Windows Components portion of the Windows Components Wizard.

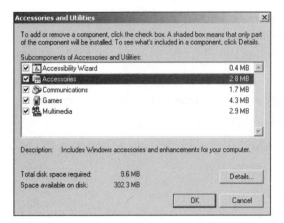

Figure 1.8   The Accessories And Utilities dialog box.

18. The Add/Remove service performs the necessary operations to add or remove the component. Eventually, a completed dialog box is displayed. Click Finish.

19. Click Close on the Add/Remove Programs dialog box.

20. Close the Control Panel and Windows Explorer by selecting File|Close on each window.

Using the Task Manager to View Application Status and Process Details

The Task Manager is a useful tool for gaining quick insight into the current state of the system. To use the Task Manager for viewing system statistics, perform the following steps:

1. Right-click over a blank area of the taskbar (be sure not to be over the Start button, the icon tray, or any application button). From the pop-up menu, select Task Manager. The Task Manager opens.

2. Click the Applications tab. Notice that this tab displays the currently active applications and their status (that is, Running or Not Responding). See Figure 1.9 for an example.

3. Click the Processes tab. Notice that this tab displays the currently active processes along with several details. The default displayed details are process ID (PID), CPU usage percentage during the last update interval, total CPU usage time, and current amount of virtual memory in use by the process (see Figure 1.10).

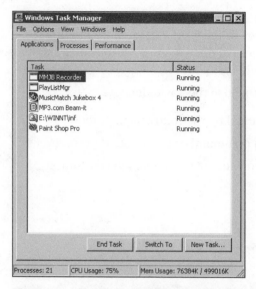

Figure 1.9   The Task Manager's Applications tab.

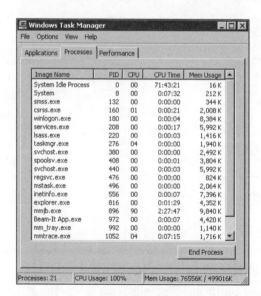

Figure 1.10   The Task Manager's Processes tab.

4. Click the Performance tab. Notice that this tab displays the current and brief historical operational levels of the CPU and memory in graphical format as well as provides numerical details about various memory aspects and system resources (see Figure 1.11).

5. Select File|Exit Task Manager to close the Task Manager.

The Task Manager can also be launched by the following methods:

- Executing **taskmgr** from the **run** command or a command prompt
- Pressing Ctrl+Alt+Delete and then clicking the Task Manager button
- Pressing Ctrl+Shift+Esc

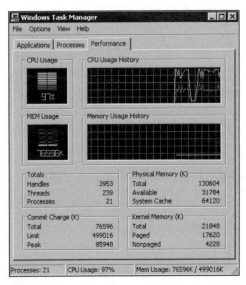

Figure 1.11   The Task Manager's Performance tab.

Launching an Application with a Non-Normal Priority

The default execution priority for user mode applications (that is, anything that a user can launch) is 13 (Normal). Using the **start** command from the command prompt, you can launch applications at other priority levels. To launch an application with a non-normal priority, perform the following steps:

1. Click the Start button, and select Programs|Applications|Command Prompt. The Command Prompt window is displayed.

2. At the command prompt, type "start /low notepad" and press Enter. The Notepad application launches. You can start any Windows or DOS

application in this screen, but you may need to navigate to the specific directory location of the application in order to execute it. More information on command-line functions is in Chapter 16.

3. Press Ctrl+Shift+Esc to launch the Task Manager.

4. Click the Processes tab.

5. Locate and select the notepad.exe process.

6. Right-click over the notepad.exe process and then select Set Priority from the pop-up menu. Notice the selected priority is currently Low.

7. Click the Notepad button on the taskbar.

8. Select File|Exit to close Notepad.

9. Click the Command Prompt button on the taskbar.

10. At the command prompt, type "start /high notepad" and press Enter. The Notepad application launches.

11. Click the Task Manager button on the taskbar.

12. Locate and select the notepad.exe process.

13. Right-click over the notepad.exe process and then select Set Priority from the pop-up menu. Notice the selected priority is currently High.

14. Click the Notepad button on the taskbar.

15. Select File|Exit to close Notepad.

16. Repeat Steps 9 through 15 for Below Normal, Above Normal, and Realtime.

NOTE: *Realtime priority can only be set by administrators.*

---

17. Click the Task Manager button on the taskbar.

18. Close the Task Manager by selecting File|Exit Task Manager.

19. Click the Command Prompt button on the taskbar.

20. Close the command prompt by typing "exit" and pressing Enter.

Changing the Priority of an Active Process

After an application is launched, you can still leverage some minor control of its execution priority. To change the priority of an active process, perform the following steps:

1. Click the Start button, and select Programs|Applications|Command Prompt. The Command Prompt window is displayed.

2. At the command prompt, type "start /low notepad" and press Enter. The Notepad application launches.

3. Press Ctrl+Shift+Esc to launch the Task Manager.

4. Click the Processes tab.

5. Locate and select the notepad.exe process. If you are running other apps and don't know which process to access, go to the Applications tab, right-click the application, and select Go To Process from the pop-up menu.

6. Right-click over the notepad.exe process, and select Set Priority from the pop-up menu. Notice the selected priority is currently Normal.

7. Click the High setting from the list of priorities in the pop-up menu.

8. A warning message may appear stating that changing the priority might cause system instability. Click Yes.

9. Right-click over the notepad.exe process and select Set Priority from the pop-up menu. Notice the selected priority is now High.

10. Click the Notepad button on the taskbar.

11. Select File|Exit to close Notepad.

12. Click the Task Manager button on the taskbar.

13. Close the Task Manager by selecting File|Exit Task Manager.

14. Click the Command Prompt button on the taskbar.

15. Close the command prompt by typing "exit" and pressing Enter.

Changing the System's Performance Optimization

Windows 2000 can be tuned to provide optimized performance for either applications (that is, foreground user mode processes) or background services (that is, applications and services accessed from the network or required to maintain the local system). Windows 2000 Professional is set to Applications by default, whereas all the Windows 2000 Server variants are set to Background Services. To optimize system performance, perform the following steps:

1. Click the Start button, and then select Settings|Control Panel. The Control Panel window is displayed.

2. Locate and double-click the System applet icon in the Control Panel window. The System applet opens.

3. Click the Advanced tab.

4. Click the Performance Options button. The Performance Options dialog box is displayed (refer to Figure 1.4).

5. Select the Applications radio button to optimize performance for applications, or select the Background Services radio button to optimize performance for background services.

6. Click OK to close the Performance Options dialog box.

7. Click OK to close the System applet.

8. Select File|Close to close the Control Panel.

Customizing the Activities of the Start Menu

The default enabled features of the Start menu might not be the best configuration for your method of interacting with Windows 2000. To customize the Start menu, perform the following steps:

1. Right-click over a blank area of the taskbar. Select Properties from the pop-up menu.

2. The Taskbar And Start Menu Properties dialog box appears with the General tab selected (see Figure 1.12).

3. If you want the taskbar to automatically disappear from the desktop when not in use, select the Auto Hide checkbox. If you want the taskbar to always appear, deselect the Auto Hide checkbox.

4. To compress the displayed size of the Start menu, select the Show Small Icons In Start Menu checkbox.

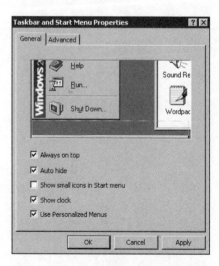

Figure 1.12   The General tab of the Taskbar And Start Menu Properties dialog box.

5. If you want the clock to appear on the taskbar, select the Show Clock checkbox.

6. Click the Advanced tab (see Figure 1.13).

7. To display the Administrative Tools menu on the Start menu, select the Display Administrative Tools checkbox, located in the Start Menu Settings area.

8. To show the Control Panel applets from the Start menu, select the Expand Control Panel checkbox.

9. To expand the Network And Dial-Up Connections objects from the Start menu, select the Expand Network And Dial-Up Connections checkbox.

10. To expand the Printers folder from the Start menu, select the Expand Printers checkbox.

11. Click OK to save these changes and close the Taskbar And Start Menu Properties dialog box.

12. Explore the Start menu and taskbar to see the changes you just made.

Adding a New Shortcut to the Start Menu Method 1

The Start menu is fully customizable. All you need to do is add, remove, or shuffle shortcuts to create the layout you desire. This solution explains how to add new shortcuts. To add a shortcut to the Start menu, perform the following steps:

1. Click the Start menu, and select Settings|Taskbar And Start Menu. The Taskbar And Start Menu Properties dialog box appears.

2. Click the Advanced tab.

3. Click the Add button. The Create Shortcut dialog box is displayed.

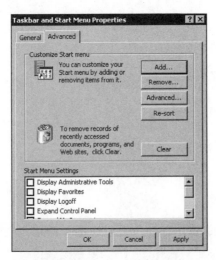

Figure 1.13   The Advanced tab of the Taskbar And Start Menu Properties dialog box.

4. Click the Browse button. The Browse For Folder dialog box appears; it displays all local drive letters.

5. Double-click the drive letter hosting your main Windows 2000 files. The dialog box now displays the top-level contents of this drive.

6. Double-click the main Windows 2000 directory name. The dialog box now displays the contents of the Windows 2000 directory.

7. Locate and select regedit.exe, and then click OK. The path and file name of the selected application is now displayed in the Type The Location Of The Item: field of the Create Shortcut dialog box.

8. Click Next. The hierarchy of the Start menu is displayed.

9. Locate and select the Administrative Tools folder, located under Programs.

10. Click Next.

11. Type a name for the shortcut, such as 16-bit Registry Editor. Click Finish.

12. Click OK to close the Taskbar And Start Menu Properties dialog box.

13. Click the Start menu and select Properties|Administrative Tools. (You must have the Display Administrative Tools setting enabled; see the solution "Customizing the Activities of the Start Menu.") Notice the new shortcut now appears.

Adding a New Shortcut to the Start Menu Method 2

To use the second method for adding a new shortcut to the Start menu, perform the following steps:

1. Click on the Start menu, and select Programs|Accessories.

2. Right-click Notepad.

3. Drag the mouse away from Accessories and over Programs, and release the mouse.

4. Click Copy Here to leave a copy of the Notepad icon in that location.

Adding a New Shortcut to the Start Menu Method 3

To add a new shortcut to the Start menu using Method 3, perform the following steps:

1. Use Explorer to locate an application and drag that application over the Start menu.

2. After the Start menu appears, drag the application over Programs, which causes the Programs submenu to open.

3. After you have found the suitable location for the application, release it, and select Create Shortcut Here from the pop-up menu.

Removing a Shortcut from the Start Menu Method 1

The Start menu is fully customizable. All you need to do is add, remove, or shuffle shortcuts to create the layout you desire. This solution explains how to remove existing shortcuts. To remove a shortcut form the Start menu, perform the following steps:

1. Click the Start menu and select Settings|Taskbar And Start Menu. The Taskbar And Start Menu Properties dialog box appears.

2. Click the Advanced tab.

3. Click the Remove button. The Remove Shortcuts/Folder dialog box is displayed.

4. This dialog box displays the current Start menu hierarchy. Locate and select the Address Book item in the Accessories subsection. (If you wish to keep the Address Book item, select some other item to delete. Otherwise, skip this solution.)

5. Click Remove.

6. Click Yes when prompted to confirm.

7. Click Close to close the Remove Shortcuts/Folder dialog box.

8. Click OK to close the Taskbar And Start Menu Properties dialog box.

9. Click the Start menu, and select Properties|Accessories. Notice the shortcut no longer appears.

Removing a Shortcut from the Start Menu Method 2

To remove a shortcut from the Start menu using Method 2, perform the following steps:

1. Click the Start Menu, and select Programs|Accessories.

2. Right-click on Notepad.

3. Select Delete from the pop-up menu.

4. A dialog box appears to confirm the removal. Click Yes.

This is an ideal process for removing items from the Startup folder.

Customizing the Structure of the Start Menu

The Start menu is fully customizable. All you need to do is add, remove, or shuffle shortcuts to create the layout you desire. This solution explains how to reorganize existing shortcuts. To customize the structure of the Start menu, perform the following steps:

1. Click the Start menu, and select Settings|Taskbar And Start Menu. The Taskbar And Start Menu Properties dialog box appears.

2. Click the Advanced tab.

3. Click the Advanced button. A Windows Explorer dialog box is opened with the Start Menu folder selected from the current user's profile (see Figure 1.14).

NOTE: *The Start menu is nothing more than a set of folders and subfolders stored in the Start Menu folder within a user's profile. The shortcuts in the subfolders of the Start Menu folder can be edited, added, removed, and rearranged, just like any typical file.*

---

4. The Start menu you see is a combination of the Start Menu folder from your user profile and the contents of the Start Menu folder from the All Users profile. Therefore, be sure to view and edit both these folders to fully customize your Start menu.

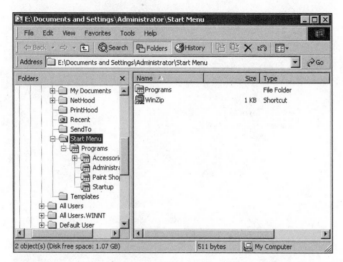

Figure 1.14   Editing the Advanced Start Menu properties.

Chapter 2

Comparing Windows 2000 to Windows NT

In Depth

The Windows 2000 product line is the result of starting from the foundation of Windows NT and adding features from Windows 98, along with new innovative technologies. The resulting network operating system (NOS) is a flexible and robust Internet-capable computing platform. Microsoft directed the development of Windows 2000 into a multipurpose platform instead of a single- or limited-use system. This adds strength, options, and versatility to an already impressive NOS.

Most of the differences between Windows NT and Windows 2000 can be found within system administration, directory services, security enhancements, and networking. This chapter looks at some of these improvements from Windows NT and makes comparisons between the new Windows 2000 operating system and its predecessors.

System Administration

Although Windows 2000 has many new features and improvements from Windows NT, it's the changes in system administration and overhead that probably have the greatest impact on how you manage and administer your network. If you're an old hat at Windows NT administration, you will definitely become frustrated while trying to figure out where the previous functions are now. As you read through this chapter, you'll notice that many user and group functions have been moved into Active Directory while several Windows NT Control Panel applets have been moved into network management.

Plug and Play

Through the long-awaited addition of plug and play to Windows NT, Windows 2000 now boasts the ease of configuration that only Windows 95 and Windows 98 previously enjoyed. Windows 2000 does not support quite the broad range of hardware as its desktop predecessors, but it is still significantly broader than that of Windows NT. The benefits of plug-and-play support include:

- Fewer reboots due to configuration changes
- Easier installation of new hardware through automatic detection and driver installation
- On-the-fly reconfiguration, connection, and removal of devices
- Power management capabilities

- Support for hot-swappable and hot-plug-enabled devices
- Better functionality on notebook and portable systems with removable devices and docking stations
- Support for infrared, Universal Serial Bus (USB), and Institute of Electrical and Electronic Engineers (IEEE) 1394 (firewire)

In case you're not already familiar with plug and play, it's a technology that enables an operating system (OS) to identify and alter hardware configurations with little or no user intervention. This grants a user the ability to add and remove devices dynamically without extensive knowledge of the computer's resource structure and state or of hardware manipulation.

If you are familiar with the phrase "plug and pray," don't forget it: plug-and-play problems can still occur. In the server world where every minute of downtime can be a lifetime to a stressed admin, don't forget that even the smallest hardware installations should be carefully planned and scheduled, lest you end up praying louder than usual.

From an administration perspective, the inclusion of plug and play with the Windows 2000 environment simplifies all hardware issues. However, because most of us are working on hardware that has been around for a while, it's important to know how plug and play works on a basic level and why it is so different.

All hardware on a computer needs certain resources in order to function properly. For example, personal computer (PC) hardware works in the same way that most people do when they work for a living. People need certain things in order to do their job, such as a computer, a chair, and a desk. Most PC hardware components need to process interrupt requests (IRQs), direct memory accesses (DMAs), and memory addresses in order to do their job. This isn't really a hardware book, so I won't go into the definitions for these things, but you should just know that these things are necessary in order for the hardware to work.

Not too long ago, everything in the PC market ran on an Industry Standard Architecture (ISA) bus. Hardware that was plugged into an ISA bus—such as modems, sound cards, and network cards—needed to be physically configured in order to set their IRQs, DMAs, and memory addresses. This was painful and annoying because if administrators didn't document a PC appropriately (and when do we really ever have time for that?), it was highly possible to configure two cards for the same settings. Quite often, when this happened, both cards would not work, and troubleshooting for the issue could get quite thorny because most cards don't get up and introduce themselves.

A few years back, a new bus type came along called Peripheral Component Interconnect (PCI). This was great because not only did PCI run faster, but you didn't have to touch the hardware after installing it in order to get the hardware up and running. The hardware got its information from its drivers, which basically made sure that an address didn't conflict with any other address. The advent of PCI technology was the single greatest factor for plug and play. Does this sound unlikely? Take a look at what happened next.

Motherboard manufacturers figured out that they could use the basic input/output system (BIOS) to actively search, find, and assign addresses to PCI hardware automatically when the system boots. Then, a plug-and-play operating system could come along, find out what the addresses are from the hardware itself, and everything would be just great. Then, if the operating system (like Windows 95, 98, and now 2000) needed to make changes to the hardware addresses, the operating system could reprogram the hardware in the same way that the old PCI drivers used to. What's more, the plug-and-play operating system could then create umbrella drivers for hardware that might change while running Windows, just like USB. These umbrella drivers would be on the lookout for new hardware to show up and would handle all of the intricacies of actually getting the hardware to work.

Historically, Windows NT entered the marketplace before Windows 95 and was definitely not designed to be a plug-and-play operating system. Although Windows NT did have some hardware detection features during installation—like CD-ROM and Small Computer System Interface (SCSI) support—basically Windows NT remained a hardware-static OS. In the early Windows NT days, administrators had to provide hardware drivers with their addresses. Although this was painful and confusing, it was still better than cracking the case and risking potential damage to the hardware itself. Later, as Windows NT evolved a bit, hardware drivers became better about automatically determining what addresses were available for the hardware to use. Unfortunately, when plug-and-play motherboards became available, this caused a problem because the BIOS would assign addresses to the hardware when the system booted, and the hardware drivers would then assign different addresses again when Windows NT loaded. The result was the potential of having more than one card programmed with the same addresses. Again, troubleshooting could be thorny and even more unpredictable. Windows NT often required that plug and play be disabled in BIOS settings in order to survive.

That's not necessary anymore. The only remaining consideration that you, as a Windows 2000 administrator, need to be aware of is that your Windows NT computer may still have ISA or PCI cards that are not plug and play compatible. (ISA, by definition, will not be). You will need to force the BIOS not to assign the addresses for this hardware to other plug-and-play devices on the system. The result is that the BIOS will allocate addresses to the other hardware without reallocating those addresses that have been reserved for older hardware.

Basically, adding and removing hardware is now mostly painless. New plug-and-play devices are detected, their drivers are installed automatically, and drivers for removed devices are not loaded into memory. If you need to alter the configuration of one device to accommodate another, just use the Device Manager (accessed on the Hardware tab of the System applet or through the Computer Management utility), plus (hooray!) not all configuration changes require a reboot.

Don't assume, however, that just because plug and play is here that hardware is just a breeze. Particularly with Windows 2000, you need to be especially aware of what is Windows 2000 compatible. First, check the Hardware Compatibility List (HCL) on the Microsoft Web site. Second, check the hardware manufacturer's Web site for Windows 2000 drivers. Hindsight is 20/20, and my hindsight advises you not to purchase anything that's not Windows 2000 compatible. If "Windows 2000 Compatible" is not on the label, it probably won't work.

If on the off chance you still manage to end up with hardware that doesn't have a Windows 2000 driver, feel free to try the Windows 95, 98, ME, or Windows NT drivers. Most of these alternative drivers will not work. However, you will have the greatest chance of success with Windows Me drivers.

For more information on Windows 2000 support for plug and play, see the *Windows 2000 Server Resource Kit*, ISBN: 1-57231-805-8.

Power Management

Plug and play incorporates two standards that are directly responsible for the USB support that we enjoy in Windows 98 and 2000. Although Advanced Power Management (APM) has been around for a while, Advanced Configuration and Power Interface (ACPI) promises to be a truly useful tool.

APM is a BIOS-based standard that allows computers to automatically shut down or suspend specific components after set latency times. This can be useful for laptop computers when battery life is at a premium. Temporarily suspending a hard drive and monitor (two of the most power-intensive components in any computer) after a brief period of nonusage can come in handy. Windows NT Workstation and Windows 2000 Professional are both able to take advantage of these features; however, for the most part, it's not recommended. This is because quite often, when a hard drive would go into suspension, other background applications and services would stop or terminate. When using a laptop, this could become particularly annoying when the dial-up networking connection terminated when the hard drive suspended itself after 10 minutes. Windows 2000 server does not support APM for reasons just like this.

ACPI is very similar in intent to APM because the goal is to save energy when computer components are not essentially needed. The biggest difference is that ACPI allows the operating system to control when and how hardware should become susceptible to energy conservation features. This allows the OS to put critical applications and services on life support before tampering with the hardware. The difference is just like a light switch. APM is strictly an on/off variety, but ACPI is like a dimmer switch where power can be adjusted and increased to handle only what is necessary to maintain critical lifeline components.

All Windows 2000 products support ACPI, but Windows 2000 Professional only supports APM in a single-processor configuration, and the Server product does not support APM at all. Keep in mind that for Windows 2000 Professional, both APM and ACPI can't be used at the same time because this would certainly cause conflicts.

USB Support

Finally, Microsoft has created a NOS that supports USB devices. Originally, USB was somewhat unstable. (Remember the infamous blue screen of death [BSOD] that Bill got while demonstrating its features.) However, USB has improved since Windows 98, and it is even more stable under Windows 2000.

Administratively, USB comes in handy in situations where occasional hardware usage comes up. For instance, a server is handling a mission-critical call center application, and the application has malfunctioned. The only way to fix it is to allow the manufacturers to dial into the computer and fix the problem. Of course, this would require a modem and an analog phone line, and, because this is a once-in-a-blue-moon situation, USB provides the perfect feature set to get a modem on the system quickly and easily and with portability, too.

USB can be described as a child of plug and play. It's the first truly versatile means of connecting devices to a computer. USB devices can be plugged and unplugged from a system at any time, and the computer not only detects the device automatically, but also installs drivers for it. In addition, more than one device can be put onto the same USB connection. This is not possible with serial or parallel connections without frequently running into conflicts. What this means is that a modem, keyboard, microphone, and hard drive can be plugged into the same port on the back of the system, just not all at the same time. Because of this simple feature, a device called a USB hub is available where all of these devices can be plugged in to function at the same time, and the hub itself is plugged into the port on the computer. In the server example above, all I need to do is find a USB modem, plug it in, install Windows 2000 drivers (if necessary), and go. The USB modem can then be unplugged and removed for usage elsewhere, saving money and shelf space.

USB also comes in handy for laptops. Personal Computer Memory Card Industry Association (PCMCIA) network and modem cards can be very expensive, especially considering that dongles and connectors are easily damaged, easy to lose, and expensive to replace. An ideal USB solution is to purchase a USB modem and network connection. The results are more reliable, cheaper, and easily replaceable on the road because replacement cables are available in any department store.

One word of warning in regard to USB, however. Just like video, serial, sound, and parallel devices, on-board USB connections are becoming popular with motherboard manufacturers. Be cautious, however, of the possibility that certain motherboard chipsets are not 100 percent ready for the USB revolution, despite the on-board connections. Most motherboards will function fine for most USB devices. However, be particularly alert for high input/output (I/O) devices, such as external drives and removable media. As with any hardware issue, it becomes difficult to trace the problem toward faulty software or drivers versus a device problem. Just because we are so accustomed to the base hardware working, it's sometimes difficult to recognize (let alone resolve) motherboard issues. USB problems of this type will never bring a server to its knees. However, it is well advised that, if you wish to add USB hard drives or external storage devices, you might look for any known issues on the motherboard manufacturer's Web site, or you may simply consider purchasing a $30 USB controller card and installing it instead.

NOTE: *Be very aware of the part USB can or should play in your server configuration. Remember that USB keyboards and mice exist, and because USB is plug and play, this can open a security risk by allowing someone to install hardware and change the configuration of your server.*

Storage

Windows NT data storage functionality was actually pretty feature-rich compared to other operating systems on the market. With Windows 2000, it has only been improved.

Fault Tolerance

Software redundant array of inexpensive disks (RAID) support continues to be a feature with Windows 2000. However, the following additional changes are required with the advent of dynamic disks:

- *RAID 0*—Disk striping is still around and is a popular choice for systems where data access speeds are crucial. RAID 0 technically does not provide any fault tolerance because data is split across multiple drives and a single drive failure cannot be recovered.

- *RAID 1*—Disk mirroring is a good solution for allowing quick recoverability for boot and system partitions and drives when a single hard drive goes bad. There are relatively few additional features here because the mirror still needs to be broken in order to remove and replace the damaged hardware.

- *RAID 5*—Disk striping with parity will remain the preferred method for providing fault tolerance, increasing disk I/O speeds (but not as much as RAID 0), and allowing for recoverability in the event that a hard drive fails. Administrative intervention is not immediately necessary in order to provide adequate services because the parity information will automatically rebuild the missing data until the system can be taken down and the affected hard drive replaced. After the hard drive is replaced, the parity information is again brought into play to populate the new drive with the missing informatfin previously found on its damaged counterpart.

Basic and Dynamic Disks

Dynamic disks were created to allow some features seen in NetWare and Unix to be available to the Microsoft market. Put simply, basic disks are the hard drive physical and logical partitions that we've used for years. Dynamic disks accommodate volumes instead of partitions. This is actually a blessing for the overworked administrator. Normally, when a hard drive becomes full, you either need to add a new hard drive, assign new drive letters and make it available on the network, or simply replace it with a larger capacity hard drive and transfer the data. Neither solution is ideal in server and networked environments just because of extended system downtime and end user training. Dynamic disk functionality allows you to add a new hard drive and instruct the system to integrate all or part of it into the current volume, also known as a partition. This is called disk spanning and can be useful for an organization that outgrows itself quite often. Keep in mind, however, that Windows 2000 RAID cannot be implemented for spanned volumes. Also be aware that Windows 2000 RAID requires dynamic disk functionality. RAID implementations in Windows NT will be upgraded intact into their respective basic disk configuration. However, changing and creating new RAID configurations is reserved for dynamic disk functionality. In situations where Windows NT RAID has been upgraded, it is best to upgrade all basic disks to dynamic disks and not worry about it anymore.

Distributed File System

Distributed File System (DFS), although technically not a storage solution, should be mentioned here because it works well with the concept of spanned volumes and can be used to overcome the fact that RAID cannot be implemented for spanned volumes.

DFS is a service that allows network access to multiple network disk resources that appear to be coming from the same location. In other words, data from the marketing department resides on the second partition of the C: drive on Server One and the third partition of the D: drive on Server Two. DFS can make all of this data appear as though it resides in the same place.

Therefore, using our disk space scenario described in the previous section, we have another potential solution: add another disk, assign a drive letter, and implement DFS in such a manner that all new data will be written to and read from the new disk, yet appear as though it is coming from the same place as it always has.

One word of caution, however. DFS can become a documentation nightmare if not cared for properly. A rapidly growing organization can generate a huge DFS tree where a single data request can hit many servers and potentially cause bandwidth and server performance issues. Keep DFS as simple as you possibly can, even if this means that you might need to move data from one drive to another.

Removable Storage

Windows 2000 now formally supports removable storage. Primarily built to support tape backup and management, removable storage can also support Zip, Jaz, and Orb disks. Although all this is great, Windows NT backup will not write directly to these devices without assigning a drive letter first, and compression is a foregone conclusion. On the plus side, removable storage will format, prepare, mount, and dismount storage devices, and it also allows you to create tape pools for usage with backup programs.

Computer Management

Even though administering and managing the system involves the biggest group of changes from Windows NT to Windows 2000, the means of actually administering and managing the system still remain much the same, especially if you are familiar with Windows 95 and 98. Again, many functions have moved to Active Directory, and, because that will be covered in the "Directory Services" section later in this chapter, we will focus on Windows NT Control Panel functions and other administrative tasks that don't fall under Active Directory.

Control Panel

By and large, Windows NT hardware configuration and installation was done through components of the Control Panel. This has changed. In addition to the standard add-and-remove hardware functionality, most hardware can be installed and configured using the Device Manager and also using the appropriate Control Panel applet.

A Devices applet now exists as part of Device Manager, and it can be accessed either through Control Panel|System|Hardware|Device Manager or by right-clicking My Computer and selecting Properties|Hardware|Device Manager. Specific devices can be enabled, disabled, and uninstalled from this applet. Device properties, including drivers and resource allocation, can also be updated from here. The changes to these applets include:

- *Phone And Modem applet*—The functionality of the Modem And Telephony applet has moved to this applet. The control of the dialing location, modem hardware, and configuration occurs here. One great additional feature is that Windows 2000 can run modem diagnostics in order to confirm functionality.

- *Sounds And Multimedia applet*—The Multimedia outlet now exists as this applet. From here, you can not only make system sound assignments, but you can also configure audio and multimedia hardware.

- *Tape Devices and SCSI Adapters applets*—These are now found with Device Manager.

- *Services applet*—This performs computer management and is available by right-clicking My Computer and selecting Manage from the drop-down menu.

- *Uninterruptible power supply (UPS) applet*—This is now found with Device Manager.

- *Network applet*—This is now the same as Network And Dial-Up Connections. This will be discussed in more detail in the section called "Networking Changes."

Administrative Tools

One of the biggest changes with Windows 2000 involves the almost exclusive use of the Microsoft Management Console (MMC) to administer the system and network. Technically, the MMC has been around since Windows NT 4.0 SP5, and is used in administering applications like Internet Information Server (IIS).

The MMC is in reality an interface shell wrapped around administrative applets that must be plugged into the MMC in order to function. By design, this is an advantage because this open architecture allows other applications to use the MMC as the administrative interface. As an administrator, the biggest advantage of the MMC is the ability to mix and match administrative utilities (called snap-ins) to create a customized MMC console that contains only the administrative tools that we need. Hooray! No more moving from program to program to accomplish everyday tasks.

Although it's not necessary to cover every administrative tool within Windows NT, some changes can and will be useful. Windows NT Workstation formerly contained Administrative Tools, which was located on Start|Programs. Many of these tools still exist; however, most of the "managing this computer"-type administration items have been moved to computer management, which is best found by right-clicking My Computer and selecting Manage from the pop-up menu.

Most of the Windows NT Server administrative tools are intact, but with several additions for different domain and local security policies, DFS, component services, Routing And Remote Access Server (RRAS), and Active Directory administrative snap-ins.

Synchronization and Replication

Synchronization and replication with Windows 2000 has changed drastically in comparison with Windows NT. Windows NT supported a replication schema called LMRepl. This was the process where a designated folder and/or document was created for export to another computer or computers. This automated file transfer was driven by a replication service. Windows 2000 replaced this methodology by simply replicating everything located in the Windows 2000 SYSVOL folder with all other servers in the domain. This functionality is called File Replication Service (FRS) and is covered in greater detail in Chapter 12.

Windows 2000 also supports functionality in a similar way as My Briefcase in Windows 95 and 98. Unlike the bugs and glitches with My Briefcase, the Microsoft solution—called Offline Files—is very stable and reliable. Configuration is simply accomplished by designating files and data located on the network that need to be made available in the event that the network itself becomes unavailable. This can come in handy if servers go down, thus reducing the cost of downtime, but we've primarily seen it implemented for laptop users. Synchronization occurs based upon a schedule that is set during configuration. When the network becomes unavailable, the end user simply refers to the local copies rather than attempting (and hanging) on the network. After the network resource becomes available again, synchronization occurs automatically.

Installation and Configuration

Windows NT installation is much the same as Windows 2000 with a few brilliant differences. Both operating systems can install using CD-ROM, floppy disk, and bootable CD-ROM, and also from the network. However, Windows 2000 supports the IntelliMirror feature of Remote Installation Services (RIS). RIS does require some configuration and also requires that the target system be able to boot to the network, but for major workstation rollouts, RIS is an awesome feature to be able to rely on, especially because installed applications can be rolled out as part of an RIS package. Unattended installations of Windows 2000 are possible; however, RIS and System Preparation Tool (Sysprep) were designed to eliminate that need.

Sysprep, an additional installation/configuration feature for Windows 2000, is very similar to RIS in that both the operating system and installed applications can be rolled out. The difference between the two is that, although RIS uses a Microsoft-generated image, Sysprep uses imaging software of your choice and simply strips the current installation of instance-specific information. Both applications install Windows 2000 with a minimum of user intervention. However, images created with Sysprep can be rolled out without the assistance and use of a Windows 2000 server. Both RIS and Sysprep are still a far cry, however, from installing Windows NT through an unattended installation and then using SYSDIFF to install applications.

Security Enhancements

Windows 2000 offers many new security enhancements at nearly every point that users access resources. The new security features include changes to user authentication, networking, remote access/virtual private network (VPN), file access, data storage, encryption, and Internet Information Server (IIS). Most of the improvements to the security system used by Windows 2000 focus on authentication (proving identities) and communications (protecting data transfer). Some of the noteworthy security improvements are:

• *Kerberos Authentication Protocol v5*—Kerberos is a means of allowing Windows 2000 clients to authenticate into a Windows 2000 domain without dumping the user name and password onto the network wire. If the data doesn't hit the wire, it cannot be hacked.

• *Encrypting File System (EFS)*—This uses public key infrastructure (PKI) to encrypt files and folders. An added feature is that data that is moved into an encrypted folder is automatically encrypted after it gets there.

• *Internet Protocol Security (IPSec)*—This is a method of secure Transmission Control Protocol/Internet Protocol (TCP/IP) communications. IPSec is used to encrypt communications between computers and devices regardless of the running application.

• *Smart card support*—This can allow access to a computer based solely upon a card or USB key attached to the system.

• *Transitive trusts*—This is a new feature of Active Directory that virtually eliminates multimaster and meshed trust enterprise problems. Windows NT trusts function in such a manner that if A trusts B and B trusts C, A does not trust C. Windows 2000 allows A to trust C through the use of transitive trusts, which, incidentally, are created between all domains in a forest. More information can be found in Chapter 3.

• *Group Policies*—These aren't like system policies for Windows NT. Windows 2000 Group Policies can be used to restrict and configure hardware, software, Windows settings, and component access, as well as to install applications in a mini-System Management Server (SMS)-type functionality.

From a day-to-day administration perspective, the new security features offer subtle improvements to the administrative workload and a tremendous increase in personal, local, and network security. The presence of encrypted transmissions and a guaranteed source and receiver requires less work in the long run for monitoring, testing, and improving communications. In most cases, after you define and configure a security feature within Windows 2000, you can almost just forget about it. The security system is always there, and it's always working, verifying identities and restricting access as needed.

With that said, you can't simply forget about security. However, after you configure the security of a resource, users are not confronted with the security barriers if a user account meets the requirements to access that resource. The only time security should really be noticed is when it's properly restricting access to a protected resource.

Security is covered in this book in Chapters 9, 10, and 20. For more information on the security improvements of Windows 2000, consult the *Windows 2000 Server Resource Kit*.

Directory Services

Directory services, put simply, are a service that maintains, monitors, and proctors resource access and control. Windows NT relied on Security Account Manager (SAM) to handle both user authentication and network resource access. The Windows 2000 equivalent is Active Directory.

In addition to standard directory services, Active Directory also contains elements that have never before been associated with directory services, which include the following:

- Active Directory uses a somewhat new administrative tool called the Microsoft Management Console (MMC). This allows Active Directory to be administered and viewed in a logical, Explorer-like hierarchy.

- MMCs exist for many different types of administrative tools. Custom MMCs can be created that contain child or sub-MMCs that are more unique to administrative needs.

- Unlike Windows NT domains that contain a primary domain controller (PDC) and multiple backup domain controllers (BDCs), pure Windows 2000 domains contain domain controllers that are all peers.

- Active Directory does not have the Windows NT SAM limitation on objects. Therefore, it is easier to configure, migrate, and maintain a flatter, more organized domain structure.

- Active Directory can accommodate not only multiple domains, but also multiple trees of domains. Without getting into complex terminology here, it is now possible to integrate two completely separate enterprises into a single structure without completely changing either organization.

- User and object replication between domains is handled by Active Directory, which is smart enough to be able not only to calculate the best means of accomplishing replication, but it can also do it in the least amount of time, taking up the least amount of bandwidth, and all with the greater success rate than Windows NT.

- Active Directory is backward compatible with Windows NT SAM, therefore allowing Windows NT BDCs to reside in the same domain as Windows 2000 domains.

- Windows 2000 client domain validation is more secure and stable than any other validation or authorization process previously offered by Microsoft.

- Trusts have changed, too. Both transitive and nontransitive trusts are supported within Windows 2000 Active Directory. Transitive trusts, being dynamic, allow users that have been authenticated in one domain to access data in another domain when all they share is a trust to a third domain.

- Groups have changed somewhat. Universal and Domain Local group types have been created, and full group nesting is supported.

- User functionality has also improved somewhat. A single user interface is used to enter account information, including name, address, password options, organizational notes, group memberships, VPN and Remote Access Service (RAS) permissions, application startup upon login, and Terminal Services options for that user.

- Group Policies are completely different compared to Windows NT policies. Group Policies can now be applied to either computers or logged-in users belonging to an organizational unit (OU). An OU is an Active Directory base component. Group Policies can install software; impose startup, shutdown, and logoff scripts (not just login scripts anymore); define services based on the logged-in user; redirect local folders to reside on the network; and, of course, change and restrict Windows configurations and settings.

Active Directory is arguably the heart and soul of a Windows 2000 network with all of the beauty and grace to allow for interoperability and additional and continued functionality with Windows NT, Unix, and NetWare.

Networking Changes

Improvements to networking include a simplified networking component-management scheme. The Networking And Dial-Up Connections interface brings all the networking capabilities and features of Windows 2000 into a single, easy-to-use interface. Now, all communication lines from modems to high-speed networks are managed through a single utility. Some of the changes to Windows 2000 network include:

- VPNs have been improved with the addition of IPSec and Layer Two Tunneling Protocol (L2TP), which is a more secure version of the Point-To-Point Tunneling Protocol (PPTP).

- The routing has been more thoroughly and natively integrated into both remote access and local networking. This allows Windows 2000 to serve as a remote access server, an Internet connection point for a network, a domain router, or even a gateway between networks. The routing services of Windows 2000, previously only available to Windows NT through the RRAS add-on, now include enterprise routing features, such as Network Address Translation (NAT), Open Shortest Path First (OSPF), and Routing Information Protocol (RIP2) for IP networks, as well as RIP and Service Advertising Protocol (SAP) for Internetwork Packet Exchange (IPX) networks.

- Windows 2000 also improves private Domain Name Service (DNS) through the introduction of dynamic Domain Name Service (DNS). This new networking utility simplifies the task of maintaining a DNS by automating the addition and removal of systems. See Chapter 12 for more information.

- DNS services improve with Active Directory integration, automatic aging and scavenging, flexible zone transfer options, and even active DNS diagnostics.

- DNS becomes a system requirement for a Windows 2000 domain.

- Windows 2000 Advanced Server includes clustering and network load balancing services. *Clustering* is a technology that enables two or more servers to be linked to share a common task. Windows 2000 can leverage several distinct computers against a single application, plus it provides failover capabilities if a member of the cluster goes offline. *Network load balancing* distributes TCP/IP traffic between multiple servers. Network load balancing and clustering display their true capabilities when employed against Internet services, such as high-traffic Web sites, by managing more traffic with excellent performance.

- Dynamic Host Control Protocol (DHCP) can update the DNS database with non-Windows 2000 client information.

- Native support for a large assortment of high-speed networking devices, including Asynchronous Transfer Mode (ATM) and Fibre Channel, make Windows 2000 the most advanced network operating system available.

- Limited Terminal Server comes with Windows 2000 Server. Although only two concurrent connections are allowed per server, this is a huge administrative advantage when it becomes necessary to administer the server itself.

- Delegated network administration is available on many levels, such as DNS, user and group administration, and Group Policy.

- Interdomain replication has been automated.

Additional information on networking is provided in Chapters 11 and 12. For more information on the networking improvements of Windows 2000, consult the *Windows 2000 Server Resource Kit*.

New Services

Windows 2000 has also introduced several new breeds of services to Windows 2000. These include the following:

- *Recovery Console*—A command-line control system used in system recovery in the event of a failure of a core system component or driver. Through the Recovery Console, simple commands can be used to restore the operating system to a functional state. See Chapter 22 for information on this issue.

- *Windows file protection*—An automated protection measure that prevents in-use system files, such as SYS, DDL, OCX, TTF, and EXE, from being overwritten by other programs or installation routines.

- *IntelliMirror*—A network desktop management system that allows administrators to retain control of systems not permanently connected to the network. Each time a portable computer logs back onto the network, the domain's Group Policies are reinforced, software is added or removed, and user data files are updated. See Chapters 5 and 8 for information on this issue.

- *Web-Based Enterprise Management (WBEM)*—The Distributed Management Force (DMTF) initiative, included in Windows 2000 through Windows Management Instrumentation (WMI), grants you the ability to remotely manage, configure, and control nearly every aspect of your systems and networks—from software to hardware.

- *RIS*—With RIS, clients can be easily installed across the network by booting from a PXE read-only memory (ROM) network interface card (NIC) or a boot floppy. The installation routine can be fully automated after the destination computer is turned on, or a full or partial user interaction-required installation can be customized. See Chapter 8 for information on this issue.

- *IIS 5*—The latest generation of Microsoft's IIS is included with Windows 2000. IIS offers a solid platform for building personal Web pages through true distributed, dynamic e-commerce Web sites. IIS integrates with the Windows 2000 system, seamlessly granting Web administrators access to networked resources, security, and management controls.

- *Internet connection sharing*—Built into Windows 2000's routing support is a basic proxy server. This tool can be used to grant Internet access to a small network without requiring additional hardware or applications, plus the network clients are automatically configured to use the shared connection. See Chapters 12 and 22 for information on this issue.

- *Terminal Services*—Windows 2000 includes native Terminal Services (previously available to Windows NT only as an add-on), which allows thin clients to be employed as network clients. Terminal Services grants remote access to applications and offers limitation controls for application access. See Chapter 20 for information on this issue.

Comparing Windows NT Workstation to Windows 2000 Professional

Windows 2000 Professional is the new desktop client equivalent to Windows NT Workstation. From a basic functional standpoint, these two versions are quite similar. Both provide complete integrated access to a Microsoft domain and all the resources contained there. They offer secured, multiuser environments that can be customized by the user to any extent allowed by the system administrator. However, Windows 2000 Professional is a more advanced operating system, offering more reliable application support, more hardware support, and more features throughout the OS.

The Windows 2000 platform includes many significant changes and improvements compared to Windows NT. The client version of Windows 2000 still does not include the network services of DNS, DHCP, and domain controller. However, this should be a fairly common-sense issue. Windows 2000 Professional is designed to act as a network client, not a network server. To get the tools and services to truly host, manage, and serve resources to a network, you need Windows 2000 Server (or greater).

Both Windows 2000 Professional and Windows NT Workstation take advantage of the Windows 95 desktop environment look and feel. This is primarily identified with the Start menu, taskbar, and desktop icons, along with common utilities, such as Windows Explorer, Control Panel, Printers, Recycle Bin, My Computer, and Network Neighborhood (called My Network Places in Windows 2000). The basic methods of navigating the environments are the same. However, Windows 2000 boasts many improvements to these now-familiar interface elements, such as more advanced search tools, a user-adaptive Start menu, more intuitively useful dialog boxes (such as Open and Save As), autocomplete dialog boxes, pervasive most-used-recently lists, and more.

With the support for more hardware and the addition of plug and play, Windows 2000 offers control of hardware and drivers through the Add/Remove Hardware applet and the Device Manager (through the System applet or the Computer Management tool). Windows 2000 Professional now boasts true support for notebook, portable, and mobile computers through plug and play, power management, versatile hardware profiles, and offline files and synchronization. The offline files feature provides Windows 2000 the capability to cache network resources locally so they can still be used when the computer is not connected to the network. This includes both local network resources and Internet resources. A synchronization tool is integrated with the offline files service that can automatically update the cached content when a network connection is established.

Creating new network connections or managing existing connections is now easier than ever. The Network And Dial-Up Connections interface combines control mechanisms previously located in different utilities in Windows NT. From this interface, you can manage any type of network link, from local NIC connections to RAS links to VPNs. In addition, a wizard is used to walk you through the creation of new links, thus eliminating the possibility for gross configuration errors.

Windows 2000 has added support for the file allocation table (FAT)32 file system, thus expanding Windows NT's support for only FAT and New Technology File System (NTFS). FAT32 uses smaller clusters than FAT (FAT16) and supports larger drives (up to 4 terabytes [TB]). NTFS has been improved with features such as EFS and content indexing. Other advances in the storage realm include fault-tolerant drive configuration support on the client. Windows 2000 now offers dynamic storage, which is an alternative method to partitioning. Dynamic storage is not restricted by partitioning rules (that is, only four primary partitions per drive) and allows for on-the-fly reconfiguration of storage devices without rebooting. Windows 2000 also includes a disk defragmenter and a disk cleanup tool. The former increases disk performance due to scattered file storage, and the later removes orphaned and temporary files to regain valuable storage space.

The list of new features in Windows 2000 is seemingly endless. Here are several more new features you may want to investigate further if they pique your interest:

- *Multiple monitors*—You can configure up to 10 monitors to display an expanded desktop.

- *Driver signing*—All drivers from Microsoft and approved vendors are signed. You can configure Windows 2000 to refuse to install any nonsigned drivers.

- *Improved graphics*—Support for DirectX 7.0 and OpenGL 1.2 provide a richer graphics-rendering environment for productivity and entertainment applications.

- *MMC*—This is a new standardized Web-capable management interface. Most of the Windows 2000 administration tasks are accessible through an MMC snap-in.

- *Boot options*—A useful set of optional boot methods can offer an easy out when specific problems occur. Boot options include booting without network support, booting with base Video Graphics Array (VGA) support, booting to a command prompt, and booting with the Last Known Good Configuration (LKGC).

- *Windows Scripting Host (WSH)*—Native scripting capabilities of Windows 2000 grant administrators a wider set of automation options. Most tasks can be accomplished through command-line utilities. Using WSH, an administrator can automate many redundant tasks.

For more information about Windows 2000 Professional and its new features, visit the Microsoft Web site or consult the *Windows 2000 Professional Resource Kit*.

Comparing Windows NT Server to Windows 2000 Server

Windows 2000 Server includes all the improvements found in Windows 2000 Professional as well as many networking server-specific enhancements. Making a comparison between Windows 2000 Server and Windows NT Server reveals just how advanced the latest NOS from Microsoft truly is.

Both Windows NT and Windows 2000 include solid network capabilities, such as TCP/IP networking—routing, DHCP, DNS, and Windows Internet Naming Service (WINS)—and remote access (encrypted authentication, callback security, and VPNs). However, Windows 2000 has several new benefits, including the following:

- IPSec
- L2TP
- Quality of Service (QoS) control
- Dynamic DNS
- Native ATM and gigabit Ethernet support
- Improved routing capabilities
- A broader range of native telephony services

In addition, the networking capabilities of Windows 2000 are integrated with Active Directory for better overall control and security.

Both Windows NT and Windows 2000 include solid storage services, such as a 64-bit file system (NTFS) and fault-tolerant drive configurations. However, Windows 2000 boasts hierarchical storage management, dynamic volume management, native disk defragmentation, an encrypted file system, and automated content indexing and searching.

Both Windows NT and Windows 2000 include a solid printing subsystem, which offers features such as priority printing, printer pooling, spooling management, network attached printers, and more. However, Windows 2000 adds Internet printing support, which not only grants access to the printer queues using a Web browser, but supports Hypertext Transfer Protocol (HTTP) printing as well.

Both Windows NT and Windows 2000 include centralized management of security and resource access based on a user's network logon and authentication. Windows 2000 has greatly improved on this through the introduction of Active Directory (see Chapters 3 through 6 for details). Active Directory offers noncomplex scalability. It's also based on Internet standards, is flexible and secure, includes built-in synchronization, and is supported by a wide range of products from various vendors. In addition to the system policies of Windows NT, Windows 2000 adds Group Policy control for the entire computing and network environment, thus granting true control of users.

Both Windows NT and Windows 2000 are designed around a virtual memory architecture. The base Server versions of both NOSs support up to 4GB of memory, whereas the Advanced Server and Datacenter Server versions of Windows 2000 can manage 8GB and 64GB of memory, respectively.

Both Windows NT and Windows 2000 are multitasking, multithreading, and multiprocessor operating systems, with the base Server version supporting up to four CPUs. The Advanced Server and Datacenter Server versions of Windows 2000 can support 8 and 32 CPUs, respectively, plus Windows 2000 includes native support for server clustering and network load balancing.

Both Windows NT and Windows 2000 support several application types: Win32, Win16, disk operating system (DOS), OS/2 character mode, and POSIX.1. Both employ Component Object Model (COM) and Win32 application programming interfaces (APIs) to provide a solid applications platform. However, Windows 2000 has improved on its application support through Distributed COM (DCOM) and native Microsoft Transaction Server (MTS), Active Server Pages (ASP), and Microsoft Message Queuing (MSMQ)—all four of which could be added to Windows NT through the Option Pack.

Table 2.1 provides further comparisons between Windows 2000 Server and Windows NT Server.

The content of this table was derived from the Microsoft document "Comparing Windows NT Server and Windows 2000 Server with NetWare 5.0," available from the **www.microsoft.com/windows/** Web site. For more information on any of the items listed in this table, consult this comparison document, the Windows 2000 documentation manuals, the Microsoft Web site, or the *Windows 2000 Server Resource Kit.*

Table 2.1   A comparison of features.

Feature	Windows NT Server 4	Windows 2000 Server
Same security model for catalog and native directory	No	Yes
Lightweight Directory Access Protocol (LDAP) support	No	Yes
DNS/directory namespace integration	No	Yes
Autodetection of devices after installation	No	Yes
Hardware configuration as part of OS	No	Yes
Plug-and-play support	No	Yes
Power management support	No	Yes
Reboot required for configuration changes	Yes	No
DHCP statistics and analysis reporting	No	Yes
Dynamic DNS	No	Yes
Server-to-server VPN support	No	Yes
Radius server	No	Yes
Connection sharing	No	Yes
ATM routing support	No	Yes
Dynamic bandwidth allocation (admission control service)	No	Yes
DHCP relay agent support	Yes	Yes
DNS proxy support	No	Yes
Internet Group Management Protocol (IGMP) support (multicast)	No	Yes
Network address translator	No	Yes
Internet printing	No	Yes
Print server clustering	No	Yes
Synchronization between client/server of user data	No	Yes
Desktop application management	No	Yes
Remote operating system installation	No	Yes
Extensible Markup Language (XML) integration	No	Yes
Customized Web error handling	No	Yes
Server script support	No	Yes
HTTP compression	No	Yes
File Transfer Protocol (FTP) restart	No	Yes

Immediate Solutions

Demonstrating Plug and Play under Windows 2000

The plug-and-play architecture is fully integrated into Windows 2000. It operates seamlessly and automatically. In fact, it's difficult to demonstrate without actually altering your system to force it to function. To view how plug and play works, perform the following steps:

NOTE: *This solution should only be performed if you're using a mouse or pointing device fully compatible with Windows 2000.*

---

1. Click the Start button, and select Settings|Control Panel. The Control Panel is displayed.

2. Double-click the System applet. The System applet opens.

3. Click the Hardware tab.

4. Click Device Manager. The Device Manager dialog box is displayed.

5. Expand the Mice And Other Pointing Devices section by clicking the plus sign.

6. Select the listed mouse. In Figure 2.1, this is a Microsoft Serial Mouse.

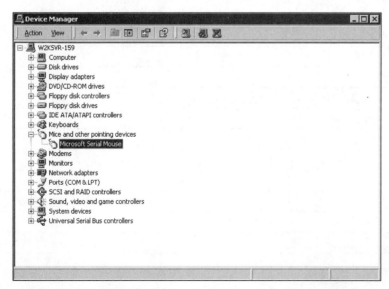

Figure 2.1   The Device Manager with the installed mouse selected.

7. Select Action|Uninstall.

8. On the Confirm Device Removal dialog box, click OK.

9. You will receive a message indicating that the system needs to be shut down. Click on the Yes button.

10. Upon rebooting your computer, press Ctrl+Alt+Del when prompted by the logon splash screen.

11. Provide your account credentials, and then press Enter.

12. As your desktop loads, you may see a New Hardware dialog box. The system automatically determines the type of device and reenables the driver already stored on the hard drive. Your mouse functionality is restored.

Installing a Plug-and-Play Device

To install a plug-and-play device, perform the following steps:

NOTE: *This solution requires an external plug-and-play device, such as a camera or scanner with USB or infrared capabilities. It also requires that the Windows 2000 computer have the corresponding USB or infrared hardware to support external peripherals.*

1. Boot into Windows 2000.

2. Attach your external peripheral. In this example, it is an Epson digital camera.

3. Watch as Windows 2000 automatically detects the new device and attempts to install the correct drivers.

4. If drivers are not already stored locally, Windows 2000 prompts you for drivers. Follow those prompts to provide the drivers for your device.

5. After the system installs the newly discovered hardware, you can view its configuration through either the Device Manager or the Control Panel applet dedicated to its specific type of hardware.

6. If you installed a digital camera or scanner, you can view information about the device through the Scanners And Cameras applet.

7. Click the Start button, and select Settings|Control Panel. The Control Panel is displayed.

8. Double-click the Scanners And Cameras applet. The Scanners And Cameras applet opens.

9. Your installed device should be displayed, as shown in Figure 2.2.

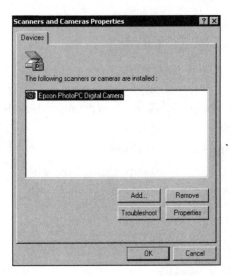

Figure 2.2   The Scanners And Cameras applet.

10. Click OK to close the applet.

11. Select File|Close to close the Control Panel.

Changing Display Properties without Rebooting

Windows 2000 no longer requires a system reset on nearly 40 system configuration changes that required reboots under Windows NT. For example, changing the Display properties no longer requires a reboot. To change the Display properties, perform the following steps:

1. Right-click an empty area of the desktop. Select Properties from the pop-up menu that appears.

2. Click Settings. The Display Properties dialog box opens (see Figure 2.3).

3. In the Colors section, take note of the current setting. Change the setting using the pull-down list. For example, change from 256 Colors to High Color (16-bit), or vice versa.

4. In the Screen Area section, take note of the current setting. Change the setting using the slider control. For example, change from 640 × 480 to 800 × 600, or vice versa.

5. Click OK.

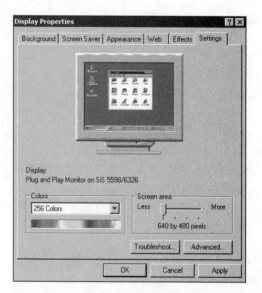

Figure 2.3 The Display Properties dialog box with the Settings tab selected.

6. A Display Properties warning dialog box appears to warn you that the current changes will be applied, and, if the settings fail, the previous settings will be automatically restored in 15 seconds. Click OK.

7. After the screen resolves with the new settings, click Yes. Notice that you did not have to reboot to change the display settings.

8. Restore the previous settings using Steps 1 through 7.

Configuring Power Management

Conserving energy is good for the environment and your wallet. If you leave your computers on 24 hours a day, you may want to consider employing the power management capabilities of Windows 2000 to reduce their power drain when they're idle. To configure power management, perform the following steps:

1. Click the Start button, and select Settings|Control Panel. The Control Panel is displayed.

2. Double-click the Power Options applet. The Power Options Properties dialog box opens (see Figure 2.4).

3. Select After 10 Minutes from the Turn Off Monitor pull-down list.

4. Select After 10 Minutes from the Turn Off Hard Disks pull-down list.

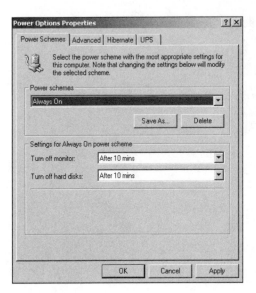

Figure 2.4   The Power Options Properties dialog box.

5. Click OK.

6. Wait 11 minutes, watch your monitor turn off, and listen to your hard drives power down.

7. Press any key on the keyboard or move the mouse to reawaken your system.

Changing a Hard Drive to Dynamic Disk

Changing a hard disk drive to dynamic disk changes all partitions on a disk into volumes and allows for the spanning feature to occur. When upgrading to dynamic disk, keep in mind that any other operating systems located on these drives become inoperable after the upgrade. To change a hard drive to dynamic disk, perform the following steps:

1. Right-click My Computer and select Management from the pop-up menu. The Computer Management window appears.

2. Three items appear under the Local Computer: System Tools, Storage, and Services And Applications. Expand the Storage item, and click the Disk Manager folder. Disk Manager initializes in the right-hand side of the window.

3. Right-click the gray square that lists the disk's name, size, status, and that it's a basic disk (see Figure 2.5).

4. Select Upgrade To Dynamic Disk from the pop-up menu.

5. A prompt appears listing all disks that can be upgraded to dynamic disk. The disk that was originally selected will be checked. Click Upgrade.

6. Another prompt appears reminding you that other operating systems will become invalid after the upgrade occurs. Click Yes.

7. Another prompt appears indicating that you will not be able to downgrade back into a basic disk configuration and asks if you want to continue. Click Continue.

8. The system reboots after the process is complete, and plug and play will detect the changes and configure your system appropriately. Another reboot is required after this final configuration.

9. Right-click My Computer, and select Manage from the pop-up menu. The Computer Management window appears.

10. The storage item should already be expanded. Click the Disk Manager folder.

11. Notice that the gray square indicated in Figure 2.5 now shows that the drive is a dynamic disk.

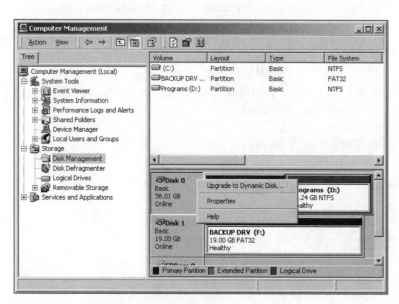

Figure 2.5   Selecting a disk to upgrade.

Seeing the Options for IPSec

The inclusion of IPSec in Windows 2000 offers a more secure communications protocol than standard TCP/IP. To view the options for IPSec, perform the following steps:

1. Click the Start menu, and select Settings|Network And Dial-Up Connections. The Network And Dial-Up Connections dialog box opens.

2. Select the Local Area Connection option.

3. Select File|Properties. The Local Area Connections Properties dialog box opens.

4. Select Internet Protocol (TCP/IP).

5. Click Properties. The Internet Protocol (TCP/IP) Properties dialog box opens.

6. Click Advanced. The Advanced TCP/IP Settings dialog box opens.

7. Click the Options tab.

8. Select IP Security.

9. Click Properties. The IP Security dialog box opens.

10. Select the Use This IP Security Policy radio button (see Figure 2.6).

11. Read the text in the Selected IP Security Policy Description area.

12. Change the selection in the pull-down list from Client (Respond Only) to Secure Server (Require Security).

13. Read the text in the Selected IP Security Policy Description area.

14. Change the selection in the pull-down list from Secure Server (Require Security) to Server (Request Security).

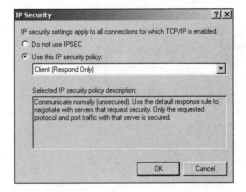

Figure 2.6   The IP Security dialog box.

15. Read the text in the Selected IP Security Policy Description area.

16. Click Cancel to close the IP Security dialog box without saving any changes.

17. Click Cancel to close the Advanced TCP/IP Settings dialog box.

18. Click Cancel to close the Internet Protocol (TCP/IP) Properties dialog box.

19. Click Cancel to close the Local Area Connection Properties dialog box.

20. On the Network And Dial-Up Connections dialog box, select File|Close.

Applying an IPSec Policy to Computers in a Windows 2000 Domain

The beauty of IPSec is that it can be applied to single computers or to groups of systems within an Active Directory OU. To apply an IPSec policy, perform the following steps:

1. Click the Start button, and select Program Files|Administrative Tools|Active Directory Users And Computers.

2. Right-click an OU within the domain, and select Properties from the pop-up menu.

3. Click the Group Policy tab, and click New.

4. A New policy appears. Rename it to IPSEC POLICY, and press Enter.

5. Click Edit. The Group Policy window appears.

6. Click the plus sign next to the Windows Settings folder under Computer Settings to expand the list. Do the same under Security Settings.

7. Highlight the IP Security Policy at the bottom of the expanded list, and right-click the Client (Respond Only) policy in the right-hand side of the window.

8. Select Assign from the pop-up menu.

9. Notice that the policy appears as Assigned in the Group Policy window.

10. Close the Group Policy window. Click OK, and close the Active Directory Users And Computers window.

Viewing the Local Security Policy

The local security policy is the local version of the group security policy, which can apply to an entire domain. It's used to define various aspects of Windows 2000 security. To view a local security policy, perform the following steps:

1. Click the Start menu, select Programs|Administrative Tools, and then click Local Security Policy. The Local Security Policy dialog box opens.

2. Take your time to review the contents of the local security policy. Expand the Account Polices and Local Policies nodes, and then select each subnode in turn (see Figure 2.7).

3. As you select a subnode, the policies of that subnode are displayed in the right-hand side of the window. Read through each listed policy.

4. For more details on any specific policy, highlight the policy, and then select Action|Security. Do not make any changes to the dialog boxes you open and be sure to close them, using the Cancel button to discard any accidental changes.

5. After you've finished exploring, close the window by clicking the close button (the X button) on the title bar.

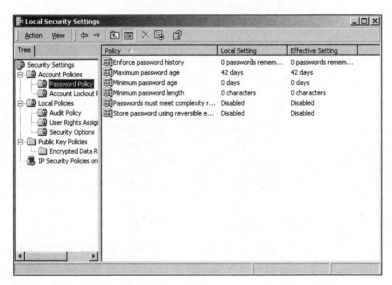

Figure 2.7   The local security policy.

Encrypting a File or Folder

The improved security of Windows 2000 includes EFS. This new capability allows you to encrypt data to prevent prying eyes from discovering its contents. To encrypt a file or folder, perform the following steps:

NOTE: *This solution requires that an encryption recovery agent be defined.*

1. Click the Start menu, and select Programs|Accessories|Windows Explorer.
2. Use Windows Explorer to locate a file or folder to encrypt; select it in the right-hand side of the window.
3. Select File|Properties. The Properties dialog box opens.
4. Click Advanced. The Advanced Attributes dialog box opens (see Figure 2.8).
5. Select the Encrypt Contents To Secure Data checkbox.

NOTE: *You cannot use both encryption and compression on a file or folder. They are mutually exclusive.*

6. Click OK to close the Advanced Attributes dialog box.
7. Click OK to close the Properties dialog box.
8. If you selected a folder, you'll see a dialog box asking you to confirm your selection to encrypt and whether to encrypt only the selected folder or the folder and all its contents. Select the Apply Changes To This Folder, Subfolders, And Files option, and then click OK.

    If you selected a file, you'll see a dialog box asking you to confirm your selection to encrypt and whether to encrypt only the selected file or the file and its parent folder. Select the Encrypt The File Only option, and then click OK.

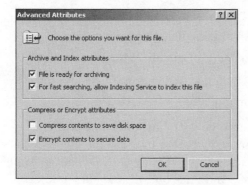

Figure 2.8   The Advanced Attributes dialog box.

9. A warning may appear that states that no valid encryption recovery policy has been configured for this system. If so, click Cancel. This indicates that you do not have an encryption recovery policy properly defined, and encryption cannot occur.

10. You'll briefly see a progress dialog box as the system encrypts the selected files.

11. Select File|Close to close Windows Explorer.

Related solution:	Found on page:
Working with Encryption	762

Decrypting a File or Folder

If you have encrypted a file or folder and need to grant access to other users, you should remove the encryption. To decrypt a file or folder, perform the following steps:

NOTE: *This solution requires that an encryption recovery agent be defined. It also requires that a file or folder be encrypted.*

1. Click the Start menu, and select Programs|Accessories|Windows Explorer.

2. Use Windows Explorer to locate and select the file or folder that's already encrypted; select it in the right-hand side of the window.

TIP: *The encryption state of a file is not indicated in the default or main Windows Explorer window. If you want to see if a file is encrypted, you must look at the Advanced properties of the object.*

3. Select File|Properties. The Properties dialog box opens.

4. Click Advanced. The Advanced Attributes dialog box opens.

5. Deselect the Encrypt Contents To Secure Data checkbox.

6. Click OK to close the Advanced Attributes dialog box.

7. Click OK to close the Properties dialog box.

8. If you're decrypting a file, it is decrypted with further prompts. If you're decrypting a folder, you'll be prompted whether to apply the changes to this folder only or to its contents as well (see Figure 2.9). Select the Apply Change To This Folder, Subfolders, And Files option, and click OK.

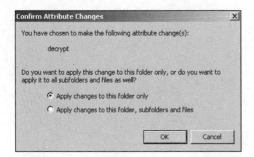

Figure 2.9   The Confirm Attribute Changes dialog box.

9. You'll briefly see a progress dialog box as the system decrypts the selected files.

10. Select File|Close to close Windows Explorer.

Related solution:	Found on page:
Working with Encryption	762

Enabling Internet Connection Sharing

If you have a small network and only one computer has a modem or if you only have a single Internet service provider (ISP) account, you can share that link to the Internet with your network. To enable Internet connection sharing, perform the following steps:

NOTE: *This solution requires that you have a connection object (modem or other dialing device) predefined for connecting to the Internet.*

1. Click the Start menu, and select Settings|Network And Dial-Up Connections. The Network And Dial-Up Connection dialog box opens.

2. Select the connection object used to connect to the Internet.

3. Select File|Properties. The Properties dialog box for the connection object opens.

4. Click the Sharing tab.

5. Select the Enable Internet Connection Sharing For This Connection checkbox (see Figure 2.10).

6. Click OK.

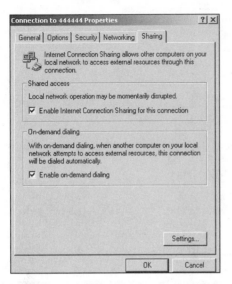

Figure 2.10   The Sharing tab of a connection object's Properties dialog box.

7. A message appears stating that your network adapter is being reconfigured to a new NAT-compatible address. Also, all clients on the network that need Internet access should be reconfigured to obtain their IP configurations automatically. Click Yes.

Your Internet connection is now shared, but you must perform two further steps before real access is possible:

1. Reconfigure all clients to obtain their IP configurations automatically. There is a workaround for this that is covered in Chapter 11.

2. Define the applications (that is, their protocols and ports) that will be proxied by the shared connection.

Using Advanced Search Tools

Do you need to locate a file and can't remember where you put it, but you remember a bit about its contents? If so, the search tools of Windows 2000 can help. To use the Windows 2000 advanced search tools, perform the following steps:

1. Click the Start menu, and select Find|Search For Files And Folders. The Search Results dialog box appears.

2. In the Containing field, type your keywords (for example, "1993–1999").

3. Verify that the Look In pull-down list has Local Hard Drives selected.

4. Click Search Now.

5. After a few moments, you should see the hosts file listed in the results (see Figure 2.11). This file happens to contain the string "1993–1999".

6. Select File|Close to close the Search Results window.

Figure 2.11   The Search Results window after a successful search operation.

Chapter 3

Active Directory Physical and Logical Structure

In Depth

Before you can install and implement Active Directory, you must understand the purpose of a directory service. You should also understand the role that Active Directory plays in the overall scheme of a Windows 2000 network. This chapter examines the key features that play a role in Active Directory design, which will help you properly implement Active Directory in your Windows 2000 network.

A directory service is a network service that is used to store and control all resources on a network, making them available and accessible to all users and applications on the network. These resources include user accounts, group accounts, email addresses, computers, and peripheral devices, such as scanners and printers. Ideally, the directory service would be extensible, meaning that an administrator or an application could modify the objects and the object properties stored in the directory service.

Active Directory Features

Many people assume that Active Directory is Microsoft's first operating system directory service (not including the directory service that was included in Microsoft Exchange Server), but Windows NT does use a directory service called the Security Account Manager (SAM). This directory service, however, uses what is known as a *flat file* system. This makes the directory service difficult or impossible to modify or to extend for third-party applications and services that want to add features and peripherals to the Windows NT network. In a flat file system, all information is stored in the directory in a specific order. For example, a flat file directory service might store the following information about a user:

- User name
- Full name
- Description
- Password

NOTE: *This example is simplified and does not coincide with the Windows NT directory service. It is only used to illustrate the limitations of a flat file directory service.*

Similarly, a flat file directory service may store the following information about user groups:

- Group name
- Description
- Member 1
- Member 2
- Member 3

To understand how the data is stored, imagine that you're about to go shopping. You'll be visiting four different stores in four different locations (Stores A, B, C, and D). On a piece of paper, you write your shopping list with only one item on a line, as follows:

- Store A: Item 1
- Store A: Item 2
- Store A: Item 3
- Store B: Item 1
- Store B: Item 2
- Store C: Item 1
- Store C: Item 2
- Store D: Item 1

Now, assume that you must buy these items in the order that they're listed. You cannot write between the lines, place more than one item on a line, or erase any items. What would happen if you forgot to add Item 3 from Store B? You would have to do one of two things: rewrite the list, or add the item after the last line of the list. Now, imagine that this list has 5,000 items on it from 2,000 stores. As you can see, this way of making a list becomes extremely difficult to modify and maintain.

Windows NT's directory system operates in a manner similar to this, which limits how many objects (users, groups, and computers) that the Windows NT directory model can store and maintain, which is up to approximately 40,000 user, group, and computer acounts. The results of this limitation in the Windows NT world are pretty drastic. This limitation is called the Security Account Manager (SAM) database limitation, and the results in the Windows NT world are pretty drastic. Any time a company exceeded this limitation, the workaround was to create a new domain and to set up trusts between the domains. You now know why Windows NT required many domains with trust relationships for organizations with a large number of users, groups, and computers.

Active Directory, on the other hand, is an object-oriented directory service, which is essentially a database where everything is an object. Several years ago, a new methodology called *object-oriented programming* came along in the programming world. Although the programmers may lay claim to what became the object-oriented revolution, realistically it's just plain ol' common sense. The basic idea is that instead of making a linear shopping list, as we did in the previous example, each item on the list becomes its own object that knows what it is and what it does. After all, a shopping list isn't just a list. It's a representation of items that you need to do things in your house, from food to cook with to bulbs that light the home. Any item can be shuffled, modified, and moved providing that the base attributes of what it is and what it does remain intact. For example, let's say that Item 3 from Store D is a lightbulb. It is glass, wire, a special connector, and it requires an input of a certain voltage of electricity to do its job: lighting a room. We can move the lightbulb anywhere where the connector fits, paint it, and cover it. However, if we puncture the glass, break the wire, remove the metal, or input too much voltage, it ceases to become a lightbulb object and becomes a junk object. This is how Active Directory works, too. Everything is an object, and all objects have attributes that basically paint a picture of what the object is and what it does.

Now let's take this a step further. What if you needed to have information on 100 different lightbulbs that were all the same except for the serial number? The Windows NT SAM database would store all 100 different lightbulbs. The Active Directory database does it a bit differently. It stores a single list of those attributes (glass, wire, connector, and voltage) and simply references that list along with each serial number 100 different times. Tables 3.1 and 3.2 illustrate how Windows NT and Active Directory would store information on these lightbulbs.

Table 3.1   An example of how Windows NT might list lightbulbs.

Serial Number	Glass	Wire	Connector	Voltage
Bulb 1	1 oz	3 in	T40	40
Bulb 2	1 oz	3 in	T40	40
Bulb 3	1 oz	3 in	T40	40

Table 3.2   An example of how Active Directory might list lightbulbs.

Serial Number	Attributes
Bulb1	List1*
Bulb2	List1
Bulb3	List1

*List1 = 1 oz glass, 3 in wire, T40 connector, 40 voltage.

Table 3.2 shows how Active Directory stores a list of the attributes in a single place and then references that list rather than storing the entire list 100 times. This saves a lot of space.

Active Directory is also a *distributed directory*, which means that all the information within Active Directory can be placed across multiple computers in multiple locations. Not only does this allow for fault tolerance, but it also enables faster access to the directory information. In a Windows NT environment, if the primary domain controller (PDC) is in company headquarters in New York and your office is in California, all changes to the directory (adding or removing users and groups, or changing a user password) must be done on the PDC in New York and then replicated back to the backup domain controller (BDC) in your location. This doesn't mean that administrative control is based in New York because administrative tools can be installed in California. The hidden gotcha is that the changes that you would be making are actually going across the wire to New York. If you just made a change—from California—to a password on a user account, you'd still have to wait for replication to occur in order for those changes to be visible in California. This can tie up wide area network (WAN) bandwidth and can cause some problems if the WAN connection is anything less than fast and reliable. Again, the Windows NT solution was to create another domain so that reliable administration could occur.

With Active Directory, all the domain controllers (DCs) maintain a read/write version of the directory where changes can be made on any DC and replication occurs to any other DC. This is called *multimaster replication*. It eliminates the need for the DCs to replicate all the information from a centralized source. In the previous example, under Windows 2000, you'd not only be making changes on the local DC, but the changes would be active immediately where it's most important. Those changes will be copied to New York when the next replication cycle hits.

Another great feature in Windows 2000 that has been a long time in the making is the ability to convert member servers in the network into DCs without reinstalling the operating system. With Windows NT, after you selected the server's role (DC or member server), you had to reinstall the operating system to change that role. As you'll see in "Immediate Solutions," the utility that allows you to accomplish this is dcpromo.

TIP: *You can also demote a DC to a member server using dcpromo.*

Keep in mind that the Windows NT SAM directory service just handled user accounts, groups, and machine accounts. Active Directory takes care of so much more that it is undoubtedly the single most important object in a Windows 2000 network, and it is certainly the most complex. The following features are included in Active Directory:

- Active Directory supports Kerberos V5 security, which not only increases security in general, but also opens up interoperability to other networks that use Kerberos as their security and authentication method.

- Logon scripts and roaming profiles have been integrated into Active Directory.

- Active Directory supports Lightweight Directory Access Protocol (LDAP) V3, Messaging Application Programming Interface (MAPI), and Remote Procedure Call (MAPI-RPC). It also supports X.500, which accomplishes several things. X.500 allows us to communicate and share information with other LDAP and X.500 systems, such as NetWare, and it also allows third-party applications to be created that will integrate with Active Directory. For example, at some point you've probably been stuck with adding a single user into several different systems in order to get them up and running. Imagine network applications like email, fax, and databases all referencing Active Directory for user information so that you only have to enter information once.

- Active Directory includes Active Directory Services Interfaces (ADSI), which allow scripted administration.

- Active Directory includes folder redirection, which is a feature commonly used to redirect the contents of certain local folders to the network so that the folders can be available for backup. Folder redirection is most often used to redirect the My Documents folder, which is the default file saving location for almost every Windows application.

- Active Directory Group Policies in Windows 2000 aren't like Windows NT Group Policies at all. Group Policies can be used to install applications and to customize and restrict Windows and security on a user and/or computer level. This can all be done on different levels on the system affecting different levels and groups of people and computers.

- Active Directory now handles domain structure and replication, thus making it easier to administer users and permissions by reducing the redundant workload.

- Active Directory requires Domain Name System (DNS), which now has a dynamic update feature that drastically reduces overhead by receiving host information from the Dynamic Host Control Protocol (DHCP) database. There are many reasons for this, but basically DNS is needed to locate various services on the network by name. Naming conventions are handled in the next section, but it's important to know that DNS is required to resolve names to addresses. Don't be alarmed. Many additional features have been added to assist with overall DNS administration and interoperability. For more information, see Chapters 11 and 12.

- Active Directory handles replication. It figures out the best way to replicate data between controllers and how to do it at the best time of day with the least amount of bandwidth.

- Simple Network Time Protocol (SNTP) keeps your servers in sync with time servers available on the Web, but also allows network clients to reliably synchronize with your local servers.

- Simple Mail Transfer Protocol (SMTP) handles message transfer for certain customizable aspects of administration and replication.

- Active Directory uses X.509 V3 certificate authentication.

All of these things combine to form a truly powerful and unique directory service that seems to be able to handle anything and everything necessary on a network. During the course of this book, we will investigate not only the scope of Windows 2000, but also how Active Directory weaves and bobs through nearly every aspect of the system.

Naming Conventions

Every object in Active Directory has a name assigned to it. Every object in Active Directory also belongs to at least one container. Unfortunately (or fortunately, depending on your point of view), you can have duplicated names within the same organization (as long as they're in different containers and have different logon names). For Active Directory to be able to distinguish one name from another, it uses several different methods. These include the following:

- Distinguished name (DN)
- Relative distinguished name (RDN)
- User principal names (UPN)
- Globally unique identifier (GUID)

DN

Every object in Active Directory has a DN, which is an LDAP standard that allows information exchange between LDAP-compliant systems because the object naming method is the same. The DN is actually a string of information containing the full address of the object. Each DN must be unique in Active Directory. Here's an example. Joe Smith is a supervisor in the Accounting domain of the WidgetsRUs corporation. The Active Directory DN would be written as follows:

```
Joe Smith.supervisors.accounting.widgetsrus.com  <<OR>>
/com/widgetsrus/accounting/supervisors/Joe Smith
```

The previous example depends upon who and what is creating the address and whether the address is a user, computer, or other object.

When thinking about a DN, just consider that everything in it is nested or located inside something else. When considering Joe Smith's address, look at it like this. Joe Smith is a member of the Supervisors group, which belongs to the Accounting domain, which is a child domain of widgetsrus.com.

Each item in a DN address corresponds to up to one of three attributes:

- Domain component (DC)
- Organizational unit (OU)
- Canonical name (CN)

If we were to label these attributes for each item in Joe Smith's address, we would see this:

```
DC=com/DC=widgetsrus/DC=accounting/OU=supervisors/CN=Joe Smith
```

NOTE: *If you were to compare Active Directory DNs to some of the other directory services out there, such as Novell Directory Service (NDS) or LDAP, you would notice that they have a /C option (/C = Country). Microsoft's Active Directory does not support the Country DN field.*

RDN

An RDN is simply a part of the DN that helps define the relationship between that part and the rest of the DN. Writing a DN is somewhat like introducing yourself along with your family tree. A well-known example would be the Biblical Ephraim. Ephraim's DN would be Abraham/Isaac/Jacob/Ephraim. Ephraim's RDN would simply be "Ephraim" with the understanding that he was the son of Jacob. Back in the computer world, if you were trying to access the C:\Program Files\Application\App.exe application, you can use the full path (C:\Program Files\Application\App.exe) from anywhere in the command prompt, and the application would be executed. This is the same as the DN. If you're in the C:\Program Files\Application directory (that is, you issued a **CD C:\Program Files\ Application** command), you can simply type "App.exe", and the application will execute. The operating system will look for App.exe in the current context (C:\Program Files\Application) and run the application if it is found. This shortened name is the RDN.

UPNs

Each user account in Active Directory has a UPN assigned to it. This UPN can be referred to as a friendly name for the user account object. The UPN is a combination of the alias of the user account and the DNS name of the domain. In the previous example, Joe Smith's UPN might be **joes@widgetsrus.com**. The primary reason for this is simple. When Joe logs in to the system, he does not need to enter the full DN in order to log in. What he needs is an alias login that points to his specific DN so that the system can get to his account. (Don't forget that the DN is an address.) The UPN is created as this type of alias. Also, if Joe Smith's account is moved from the Supervisors OU to the Managers OU, his DN would change from /com/widgetsrus/accounting/supervisors/Joe Smith to /com/widgetsrus/accounting/managers/Joe Smith, but his UPN wouldn't change at all. It looks the same to Joe and is simply updated to point to the new DN.

GUID

Most Windows NT administrators are aware of what security identifiers (SIDs) are. Each object in the Windows NT directory is assigned a unique ID. This is how the operating system recognizes the object. With Active Directory, a SID is still used, but a GUID is also assigned. The GUID is a 128-bit value that not only makes the object unique in the enterprise, but it also makes the object unique in the world. This is a great feature because it's flexible enough that you will never have naming issues—no matter what domain you need to trust or what corporation joins your Active Directory forest or tree—and it does this with all of the grace and poise of a secure system, too.

Active Directory Files

Active Directory can be backed up via normal backups, but a true Windows 2000-compliant backup program will back up the system state, which is essentially the AD. The Active Directory file structure itself is built to handle full and complete restoration even when time has elapsed since the backup occurred (no more than 60 days). By default, the Active Directory database installs itself in the %system%\ntds folder along with several log and support files, which include:

- NTDS.DIT is the Active Directory database itself.

- EDB.LOG is a log file containing all of the transactions that have occurred since the last backup. It is less than 10 megabytes (MB) in size.

- EDB001.log, EDB002.log, and so forth are all log files similar to EDB.LOG and are created when EDB.LOG is full.

- EDB.CHK is an authoritative list of all transactions contained in the EDB files.

WARNING! The feature known as circular logging can be turned on. Circular logging changes the EDB.LOG into a first in, first out (FIFO) bucket and essentially makes the data that the file contains up-to-date. This is not recommended, however. Why? Because if a restore becomes necessary, the system will restore NTDS.DIT from tape, look at the EDB.CHK file to get a list of all the transactions that occurred since the last backup, and pull in the EDB log files to restore all the changes that occurred since the NTDS.DIT was last backed up. If circular logging is turned on and the Active Directory database hasn't been backed up in a while, transactions that have been kicked out of that FIFO bucket are gone forever, and the restore will be incomplete. In addition, remember that some changes are based upon other changes that rely on other changes, so you run a serious risk of a not-so-immediate-meltdown when attempting an incomplete restore.

- RESn.LOG are a series of reserved log files that are created in a manner similar to how the EDB.NNN files are created, but RESn.LOG files are created specifically when EDB.LOG creation fails. Immediately after backing up NTDS.DIT, EDB.LOG is deleted, and a blank 10MB file is created. If that creation fails due to lack of disk space, a warning event is placed in the event log, and these smaller RESn.LOGs (where n is a number that's incremented for every file) are created for every transaction or change that occurs to the database. As you can imagine, creating so many files can be time-consuming, but it is certainly better than running the risk of completely losing those transactions in the event that a restore becomes necessary. A restore will become necessary if disk space isn't cleared very soon, especially if these files are located on the same partition as the system files. Obviously, the sum of all of these RES files must be less than 10MB.

TIP: *Because of all these advanced features, backing up the Active Directory database isn't simply backing up the contents of the NTDS folder; it's backing up what's known as the system state, which handles several other sensitive things also. This is why it's so very important to make sure that your backup/restore program supports Windows 2000 and will specifically back up the system state.*

- The *.pat files may also exist in the NTDS folder. These files are created when a transaction is split between log files. The *.pat files are used to patch broken transactions back together when a restore occurs.

During Active Directory installation (covered in Chapter 8), you are asked where you want the Active Directory database to be installed. In a system with multiple partitions or drives, this can be a very important decision because Active Directory will probably be the busiest service on your DC, and a large database belonging to a corporation can slow itself and other important processes down when it's on the same drive as the system and boot files. The Active Directory database files can get quite large, too. When you are considering the size required for Active Directory, you can calculate the approximate space that it will occupy based upon the number of objects it will contain. Basically, security principals (users, groups, and computers) should take about 3,600 bytes each. Other items, such as shared files and such, take approximately 1,100 bytes each. After that calculation is done—double it. Triple it, if you can, because these are approximate numbers, because you're always bound to forget or to be unaware of something or another, and also just to ensure that there is room for growth. In any case, miscalculation can be rectified with only a little bit of administrative woe (as opposed to the great pain and anguish you'd see with underestimating the SAM on Windows NT), thanks to two new features of Windows 2000. First—in the event that Active Directory gets bigger than the space available on a particular DC—remember that all DCs are peers on the network. You can promote a member server, create a new DC, or simply use an existing DC as your fallback. After that is done, you can demote the congested DC and reinstall Active Directory, placing the database in a more suitable location. In case you need help determining what suitable is, use the AD Sizer tool available on the Microsoft Web site. AD Sizer simply asks you several questions and estimates how large the AD would be in response to your answers.

Active Directory Tools and Utilities

Before we move on to Active Directory objects, it's important to get an overview of how you will spend your time administering Active Directory. Because Active Directory is compatible with so many different industry standards, like X.500 and LDAP, other third-party applications are available that allow you to see and change parts of Active Directory. It's important to keep in mind, however, that the Active Directory distributed architecture is exactly that—distributed—and it is very easy to get lost when wandering around using non-Microsoft non-graphical user interface (GUI) tools. In this section, we will discuss the Microsoft Management Console (MMC), Active Directory snap-ins, and a few command-line utilities that can be used to view and change specific parts of Active Directory.

The Windows 2000 MMC

The MMC has been around since Windows NT 4 SP5 and was initially introduced with applications like Internet Information Server (IIS) 5. The MMC is similar to your car stereo, which is a hole in your dashboard that you plug stereo equipment into so that you can get different kinds of music. Instead of being the primary source of music in your car, the MMC is the primary source for administrative functions within Windows 2000.

The MMC was designed to be immensely flexible and completely open in ways your stereo can't handle. For instance, you can plug more than one piece of equipment into the MMC. These pieces of equipment are called snap-ins, and the finished stereo or product is called a console. Any MMC console can have one or more snap-ins, and this is where the beauty comes in. You can create a custom console that handles only certain administrative tasks. Personally, I use a custom console that contains the snap-ins that I use every day (Active Directory Users

And Computers and Terminal Services Manager), and I put it as an icon on my desktop. A custom console containing snap-ins that are customized only for the computers and systems that they need to administer can be created specifically for remote administrators. If I have an administrative counterpart in Portland that only needs to administer a specific group of users located in Portland, I can create an MMC console that handles only those users. This comes in handy in a large or decentralized environment where you don't necessarily want remote administrators tampering with trusts or sites. Using the MMC creatively can also make administration something less of a headache by taking difficult or annoying pieces of administration and isolating them from other parts. The perfect example would be isolating Group Policies into their own console because they're somewhat difficult to track down within Active Directory Users And Computers and are even more difficult to troubleshoot. These custom consoles can be saved and distributed in much the same manner as any other application, and they will run on Windows 9x, Windows NT 4, and Windows 2000 systems as standalone items in the same way that an application will run.

When creating a custom console, consider the audience that will use it. If it is slated for distribution, it may be wise to consider saving the console with added security so that it cannot be changed by administrators or users who receive it. By default, all consoles are saved with full access security called Author Mode. Additional security can be added using the console options as shown in Figure 3.1.

What's more, certain snap-ins can be restricted or customized by allowing only certain components to appear on the snap-in after it's saved. These components

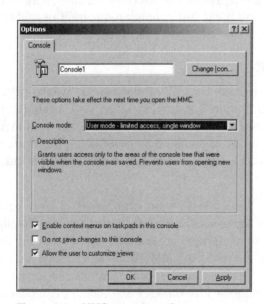

Figure 3.1   MMC console options.

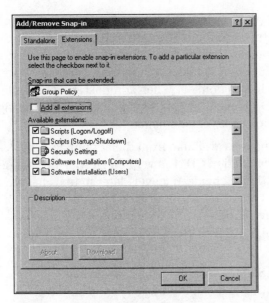

Figure 3.2   Snap-in extensions for customizing available items within the Group Policy snap-in.

are called extensions. In Figure 3.2, you'll see that several pieces of a Group Policy can be disabled. The result is that we can remove the more dangerous items from these types of interfaces and allow experience-challenged personnel to administer pieces of the network, such as only logon scripts or software installation.

We speak of the Windows 2000 MMC here because it is the primary means of administering Active Directory. You do need to be aware that MMC consoles and snap-ins exist for other Windows 2000 administrative tasks, like Windows Internet Naming Service (WINS), DHCP, and DNS. For a full list of what snap-ins are available for your system, click the Start menu, select Run, and type "MMC". Next, select Console|Add/Remove Snap-Ins. A list of available snap-ins will appear. You'll be surprised at how many different snap-ins are available by default. You should install the adminpak.msi located in the Windows 2000 installation CD.

In addition, Microsoft has created the MMC to be an open standard. What this means is that third-party applications can be administered using the MMC providing that they use the appropriate application programming interfaces (APIs) during development.

Active Directory MMC Snap-ins

Active Directory MMC snap-ins consist of the following:

- The Active Directory Domains And Trusts snap-in is used to administer domains within the forest. You need to be at least a domain administrator to run this console and preferably an Enterprise administrator so that you can view other domains within the tree and forest. Using the Active Directory Domains And Trusts snap-in, you can view and edit the trusts for domains listed and can use the manage function to kick off the Active Directory Users And Computers snap-in for a selected domain. When administering multiple domains, the Active Directory Domains And Trusts snap-in is a good starting place to be able to pick and choose between domains.

- The Active Directory Schema snap-in (available from the adminpak.msi located on the Windows 2000 installation CD) is a very dangerous place to go. As described in the section entitled "Schema Manager" later in this chapter, the schema contains an index of all of the attributes and properties that Active Directory objects can have. Modifying these attributes can be very dangerous and potentially lethal to Active Directory and therefore to your entire Windows 2000 network.

- The Active Directory Sites And Services snap-in is used to manage interdomain replication by creating and maintaining sites and subnets.

- The Active Directory Users And Computers snap-in is where you will spend most of your Windows 2000 administrative time. As the name indicates, the Users And Computers snap-in is used to administer users, computers, Group Policies, folder redirection, and a host of other features that are covered in Chapter 4.

- The Active Directory Migration Tool (available for download from the Microsoft Web site) is used to migrate Windows NT objects into Windows 2000 or simply to migrate objects from one Windows 2000 domain to another during a restructure process. More information on the Migration Tool is covered in Chapters 6 and 7.

Active Directory Command-Line Utilities

All of the following utilities are covered in more detail in Chapter 16:

- DCDIAG.EXE is a command-line utility that should be run from a command prompt. It performs tests on all DCs in a forest.

- DCPROMO.EXE isn't actually a utility. It's the program that installs and removes Active Directory. Because Active Directory is vitally linked to a DC, DCs can be demoted, and member servers can be promoted to DCs. DCPROMO is covered in more detail in Chapter 8.

- DSASTAT.EXE can be used to monitor replication status and should be run from a command prompt. DSASTAT.EXE is an LDAP utility and should work on other LDAP directories, such as NetWare and Lotus Notes.

- NETDOM.EXE should be run from the command prompt to query and move devices from Windows NT to Windows 2000 or between Windows 2000 systems.
- NTDSUTIL.EXE should be run from the command prompt to query and change several base-level functions, LDAP policies, domain management, and changing role masters within Active Directory.

Active Directory Objects

Active Directory is very different from the directory service used with Windows NT. Before you can truly administer Active Directory, you need to understand the structure of Active Directory. The Active Directory structure, also known as *logical structure*, consists of the following five components:

- Objects
- OUs
- Domains
- Trees
- Forests

With Active Directory, network administrators have the ability to access resources independent of their physical locations. It is the logical structure that makes this possible. The following sections examine the five logical structure components.

Objects

The directory is made up of network resources, such as computers, printers, users, groups, and contacts, which are all called objects. Each object has attributes associated with it. These can include the following:

- Name
- Description
- Alias
- Department
- Memory
- Model
- Employee number

As you can see, the amount of information that can be included with an object in Active Directory is vast compared to the Windows NT directory. Microsoft has also designed the Active Directory so that organizations and applications can extend Active Directory to add proprietary information, such as date of birth, credit card number, anniversary date, and so on.

OUs

An OU can be defined as a container that's used to organize objects into logical administration groups. OUs can contain objects, such as users, groups, printers, computers, file shares, and other OUs, and are exclusive to a single domain. Figure 3.3 illustrates the logical hierarchy of Active Directory.

OUs exist as administrative structures for your convenience and functionality. How you name and organize them can have a serious impact on how you administer your network. This is because OUs are the anchors by which Group Policies are implemented. Group Policy is covered in a separate chapter (see Chapter 5), so without giving too much away, it's safe to say that Group Policies are objects that restrict and grant specific computer and user configurations, as well as application installation and configuration. With this much power involved in Group Policy, you need to consider how you might want to group your users and computers in a way that will take advantage of Group Policy assignments.

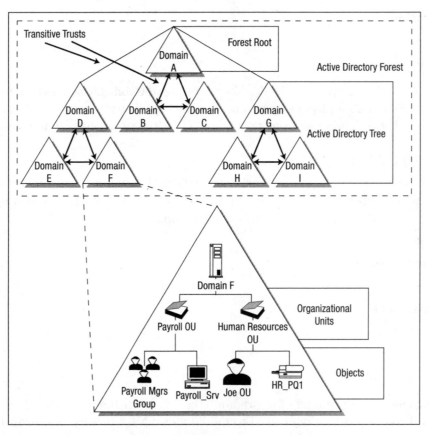

Figure 3.3   Logical hierarchy of Active Directory.

Considering that both Group Policies and users will be initially implemented and grouped into OUs, the OU structure should be well planned in order to maintain a structure that is stable enough not to require babysitting, yet flexible enough to allow for growth. There are three types of OUs that can be created: administrative, geographical, and departmental.

Administrative OUs

Administrative OUs are grouped according to administrators that own the resources located within these OUs. Let's say a given domain has been split into three different buildings, all connected together using a fiber backbone. In order to provide adequate information technology (IT) support for the users, administrative support IT personnel are assigned to each location. Administrative OUs would be created for each location so that the respective administrator only has the capability to administer his or her resources. Administrative OUs are also ideal for companies that have either an overworked IT staff or companies that traditionally hire entry-level IT administration personnel. Some of the more mundane administrative tasks can be safely assigned to other company personnel without having to worry that they might trip on something and take the network down. Administrative OUs are the preferred method of OU organization according to Microsoft. However, they don't work well for small organizations or companies with a centralized IT staff and equipment because the user/administrator ratio isn't enough to justify delegating administrative tasks for any reason outside of sheer process improvement.

Geographical OUs

Geographically-based OUs are grouped based upon physical location in a building, campus, city, state, or country or worldwide. Geographical OUs are ideal because they are the least likely to change depending upon which way the political winds blow within the corporation. The previous example of administrative OUs applies here also because each building would have its own OU. In both situations, it's important to keep in mind that OUs do not span domains, and locations that are far apart enough to warrant their own domains should not be considered for Geographical OUs unless a domain restructure is in the cards where multiple domains are slated to be integrated into the same domain.

Departmental OUs

Department-based OUs are perhaps the most common and usually the first logical organizational methodology that an administrator will implement. The reasoning makes sense. Departments usually have applications and rules that they want implemented across the entire department, so grouping users and computers together by department works ideally for smaller companies. Problems usually occur when growth happens, and the structure or function of the departments changes. Let's say you create OUs within your organization for Management, Administration, IT, and Sales. It works well for a while until the Sales department decides to start hiring people who work from home. As a result, the Group Policy restrictions based upon the Sales department shouldn't apply for everyone in the Sales department, but almost everyone. The solution is to create an OU within sales for each group of people and to move or modify the Group Policy from Sales to the appropriate child OU. Doesn't sound like much of a chore, does it? Well, what do we do when the Sales department decides to split a few people into a new department called Marketing? All three sets of groups require access to the same files on the network, but the computer and user restrictions are different depending upon their job function. I'm sure you get the idea here. When looking at a healthy midsized organization, department-based OUs can become an administrative nightmare rather than a relief.

Project-Based OUs

Project-based OUs have their place, but are not highly recommended. A project-based OU should be created for security purposes or when temporary tasks need to be performed. A risk is run, however, not only when the project ends, but also when users or computers need to grow during a project, requiring changes to the OU security and Group Policy. For example, a project OU has been created for temporary personnel that has fairly strict security that does not allow access to many computer and systems functions. What happens when a temp needs to use one of these restricted functions as part of the job? Ideally, project-based OUs are more suited to multiuser computers that are specifically available for a specific function.

You might be wondering why user groups still exist if OUs can hold groups of people and be named in the same type of structure and manner as a user group is. There are at least a dozen smaller answers, but the big answer is pure granularity and the ability to have more control of what happens to what objects contained within an OU. A single user can be assigned to multiple groups. However, that same user can only be a member of a single OU, and OUs cannot be assigned access privileges to network resources. Like user groups, OUs can be embedded within each other, thus allowing additional granularity and flexibility to be applied to the overall system. Administrators can quite often choose to implement a security feature or restrictive function at many different levels. OUs will only be seen in the Active Directory Users And Computers snap-in console. These items and more will be covered in Chapter 4.

Domains

The definition of a domain in Windows 2000 is similar to that of a domain in Windows NT. A *domain* is basically a logical security boundary that contains and manages all server-related network functions. A domain is sustained by one or more DCs, which are responsible for all of the physical tasks required to support and maintain the domain and all of the resources that belong to it.

DCs

The DC authenticates users and computers into the network and also provides access control services to allow those users to access requested network resources. Additionally, the DC—which houses a copy of Active Directory—also performs directory synchronization, inter- and intradomain replication, and other installed services, such as DNS, WINS, and DHCP. If you factor in additional applications, such as email or a relational database, a DC can become quite busy.

Additional DCs can be brought into a domain for several reasons:

- *To share the authentication and access control workload*—Quite often a smaller company will implement a DC and put additional applications on the server in order to better justify the cost of the equipment. Although this is reasonable and very common, Microsoft always tells you that a DC should be just that: a DC and not an application server. The reasoning behind this is solid, yet just not practical for these smaller companies. As a company grows, the domain-related loads on a server become more and more, and both domain functions and other installed applications may run slowly. One of two solutions is available: add another DC to the network or offload the application onto another server.

- *To provide fault tolerance in the event that a DC dies*—Remember, though, when a DC dies, the server-specific services that reside on it go down with it. Although having another DC is great for handling domain-specific tasks, keep in mind that other important services like DNS, DHCP, and WINS may still require attention.

- *To provide faster authentication and access control services to network users*—In many ways, this ties in with the first reason for adding a DC. The difference is that sharing the workload allows more resources on a DC to be available for other tasks, such as applications and services. Providing faster authentication by adding a DC solves problems where mass quantities of users overload a server's ability to respond quickly and efficiently. This is particularly common in larger companies where all of the employees log on in the same time period and subsequently overload the DC. What you see is a server grinding to a halt; what they see is the fact that it takes five minutes to get onto their computer.

Contrary to these reasons, it is not a good idea to make every server into a DC because this increases the directory synchronization and replication that must occur between each DC. Although it's necessary for each DC to be up-to-date in order to do its job properly, keep in mind that synchronization and replication eat network bandwidth, and when more DCs are on a network, less bandwidth is available for normal user-based network functions.

Domain Modes

Windows 2000 sports enough new features and improvements over Windows NT to make any Windows NT administrator seriously consider migrating to Windows 2000 until he or she remembers that upgrading and migrating is always a hassle, always painful, and not always worth it. The single brilliant star that changes people's minds is the fact that Windows 2000 is backward compatible and supports a slow migration that allows administrators to rest, prevent problems, and deal with fully upgrading a network with as little user disruption as possible. During the time when both Windows NT and Windows 2000 DCs will be on the network, the domain is considered to be in mixed mode. It's necessary to have one Windows 2000 DC emulate a Windows NT PDC in order to make everything work happily together. This emulation process happens automatically. However, after all of the DCs are upgraded, it's no longer necessary for the Windows 2000 DC to emulate Windows NT. At that time, the process needs to be turned off, and Active Directory needs to be modified slightly so that it doesn't need to cater specifically to a Windows NT structure. After this is done using the Active Directory Users And Computers snap-in or the Active Directory Domains And Trusts snap-in, the domain is then considered to be in native mode.

It is not always necessary to convert to native mode after a network is fully migrated, but converting to native mode is recommended for four reasons:

- Universal groups are a new type of group that spans domain and tree boundaries. A global group's membership is restricted to the domain that it belongs to. This might be difficult to understand, but in Windows NT, accessing data across domain boundaries required that users be a member of a global group within their domain, that global group had to be added to a local group on the guest domain, and that local group had to be granted access to the data in question. In Windows 2000, the same user can be a member of a universal group that gets assigned directly to the resource on the target domain, thus saving several disjointed (and tough to troubleshoot) administrative steps.

- Embedded groups are something of a new feature also. Windows NT would not allow local groups to belong to global groups; local groups could contain users and groups; and global groups could only contain users. Windows 2000 allows any group to belong to any other group, allowing for greater flexibility in resource access control.

- sIDHistory is a new feature available only with Windows 2000 that specifically involves migration and restructure. Here's the concept. Let's say that you work for a company that has been bought out by another company. You need to migrate (restructure) your Windows 2000 domain into the other company's domain. Think about how you'd move a given user account without dismantling the entire domain every night. You'd make sure both domains had the appropriate trusts in place, move the account to the new domain, and reestablish access to all resources located on the old domain. (The system doesn't look at the username to grant permission to a resource; it looks at the SID.) For a single user belonging to multiple groups assigned to many divergent resources, this can be nearly impossible without disrupting the user's ability to do his or her job. Instead of slogging through this, Windows 2000 features sIDHistory, which basically keeps track of all the old SIDs so that they can be referenced back to the old domain. The process for migrating a user from one domain to another then becomes a factor of the utility you use to migrate them and how well it updates group memberships as they are also moved. More information on sIDHistory and restructuring a domain is covered in Chapter 6 on restructuring Windows 2000 Active Directory.

- Active Directory runs faster when it is specifically tuned for an all-Windows 2000 network (meaning DCs).

Trees

A *tree* is simply a collection or group of one or more Windows 2000 domains. All domains within a tree share schema, trusts, and the global catalog (GC). The root domain (as shown in Figure 3.3) maintains the configuration and schema for the entire tree specifically on the Schema Role Master (discussed in the section called "Active Directory Servers").

Remember that a domain is a logical object. It can mirror or overlay the physical structure of the network, but it's not necessary. For the most part, multiple domains can be logically structured based upon administrative responsibilities, geography, or department. You might notice that logical domain structures can be put together similar to OUs. Remember the advantages and disadvantages of each when considering an overall solution for a company.

Administrative Domains

Administrative domains can be created for situations where distributed administration is required based upon security needs. With many different organizations today, each department has its own IT budget and therefore owns its part of the network. Although there might be an IT group that oversees the entire network, the department maintains control of daily tasks on its part of the network (creating users, for example). By creating a domain for each department and assigning a delegate from each department to control that domain, a network administrator can allow for the organization to maintain the overall domain while the department controls its portion of the network, setting policies as they fit that department's criteria. This same function can also be performed by delegating administrative authority for a department or administrative OU without creating a separate domain. This is the beauty of Active Directory. You can get the same results in several ways, and which one you choose is completely dependent upon the environment and what side effects or features you want to go with it. So when would you choose to create a domain? Certain security functions can only be implemented at the domain level, and this may be the reason why you'd choose a separate domain for a given department instead of delegating administrative authority. For example, the information stored on the payroll system is more critical and sensitive than that stored on the marketing system. The payroll department may choose to set the password length to 8 characters and have the password changed every 14 days, whereas the marketing department is not worried about password length or its expiration policy. Creating separate domains to handle this need would be the deciding factor between OU delegation versus delegated domain administration.

Geographic Domains

A domain can be structured based upon the geographic or physical layout of the network. Replication between servers in a single domain can take up precious bandwidth and can take time. Windows 2000 has several replication enhancements and features to help solve this problem, but it may still be necessary to create a separate domain for remote offices and locations where connectivity is less than ideal.

Departmental Domains

A domain can also be structured based upon departments, similar to administrative purposes. The difference here is usually related to resources and servers specific to a given department. Security may be a factor here, too. Basically, a department or division may have unique servers that require specialized administration.

Also, keep the following in mind when you are designing a domain structure for an enterprise with multiple locations. The Windows NT SAM database size limitation no longer applies to Windows 2000 Active Directory, but in many ways, it might as well. To put it simply, situations in Windows NT where you created a domain due to the size limitations may be the same situations in Windows 2000 where you ought to create a domain due to the sheer bulk of the Active Directory database. This is discussed in the section titled "Sites and Replication." However, keep in mind that, despite all of the Active Directory replication features, the larger and more spread out the domain is means the more that replication must occur. This can be just as prohibitive and costly as creating a new domain was under Windows NT.

Forests

Using the same logic, a *forest* is a collection of one or more trees. Forests share a Global Catalog, configuration, and schema and also use Kerberos and transitive trusts to allow resources to be shared. The single largest reason for Microsoft creating a forest-type object is to handle data exchange between separate companies, like for joint ventures, cooperative projects, and corporate mergers.

Each tree in a forest maintains its own separate DNS namespace and, for all intents and purposes, remains its own separate entity. This can be an advantage when dealing with a corporate merger because allowing immediate restructuring as a separate tree satisfies the need to share data, thus giving administrators more time to craft a more thorough restructuring plan.

Sites and Replication

In the same way that domains are logical security boundaries, sites are logical replication boundaries. A site is usually defined as all of the computers and network resources within a single well-connected network. This, of course, brings into question what a well-connected network is. Basically, any network where you aren't worrying about bandwidth use should be considered well connected.

Think of sites as you would a city. In a decent-sized city, there are several ways to get from Point A to Point B (on a good day). Now, if we were to add another site or city across a river and build a single bridge between the two, you could say that there is only one way to get from Point A to Point B. Everything within in these cities is well connected. The bridge between the two cities is not well connected because there's only one way to get between Point A and Point B, and we also have to worry about traffic and how many lanes are on the bridge.

Because of the way internetworking works, a site is a collection of one or more Transmission Control Protocol/Internet Protocol (TCP/IP) subnets. This is because the *physical* connection between cities usually has a router on each end, which (among other things) acts as a demarcation between one IP subnet and another. Subnets are sometimes created to reduce network traffic or to increase network security, so a site can also consist of more than one subnet. A subnet cannot belong to more than one site. Domains, forests, and trees have almost nothing to do with how a site is put together except in situations where it's been decided that the domain boundaries should match physical or geographical boundaries. Site placement, however, does have a direct impact on users. This is due to the additional placement of the GC server (see the section titled "Active Directory Servers"). All clients reference the GC when logging in. If the GC is placed on the other side of a site link that is not well connected, additional traffic will occur when users attempt to log in. This translates to the five-minute-logon complaint. It is highly recommended that a GC server be installed in every site created.

After a site is created and configured with its respective subnet information, Windows 2000 handles all other parts of replication. This is done using the Knowledge Consistency Checker (KCC). The KCC creates and maintains links between sites by analyzing cost and scheduling preferences input by you. It also designates replication partners for every DC on the network. The KCC's goal is to create site links and replication partners in such a way that full intrasite replication can occur within three hops from the original source. In English, this means that within each domain, every single DC is no more than three steps from every other DC. Administrators love this feature because all of the complex calculations and procedures for calculating appropriate replication paths are done automatically. The KCC also manages how and when replication occurs based upon set defaults. Advanced administrators can override these defaults and manually create or modify site links within the Active Directory Sites And Services snap-in. If a manually created site fails, the KCC automatically steps in and attempts to reestablish the site link. The Active Directory Sites And Services snap-in can also be used to force replication, which is a recommended maintenance process any time that major network changes occur.

Intrasite Replication

Intrasite replication is simply replication that occurs between DCs within a site. When a change occurs on a DC, all replication partners are notified within five minutes. Changes in security, such as password or permissions, trigger immediate notification. The replication partner DCs in turn pull the changed information from the source DC and begin their own replication process by notifying their replication partners of the changes. Replication partners are created in the KCC in a way that ensures that any given change will not circle back to a DC that already has the change.

The improvements in the intrasite replication process are numerous. Allowing each DC to one side of a replication transaction allowed for greater reliability to be implemented, too. Having changes wait for five minutes is also a great idea because it allows some time to pass where further changes could queue up waiting for the replication cycle. Again, this helps in traffic by restricting replication communications to specific periods of time.

Each change that is slated for replication is given a unique update sequence ID number that indicates the order of implementation both in how changes are sent across the wire and also how they should be integrated back into Active Directory. If a replication session fails, the sequence number is referenced, and replication is resumed with the last update successfully sent in the previous transaction.

Intersite Replication

Intersite replication is opposite from what occurs with intrasite replication. It's easy to get confused, so just remember that an interstate highway spans multiple states, and intersite replication spans multiple sites.

The intersite replication process begins every three hours instead of every five minutes, and the data is compressed. This is to reduce bandwidth use. Again, the KCC sets and maintains the intervals of when and how long replication should occur, so it may be wise to override the KCC and define intersite replication to only occur at times of low bandwidth use. The downside to this depends upon how fast updates need to be made available to the system or to the user population.

Intersite replication usually replicates changes to the schema, configuration data, and domain data. Changes to the GC fall into the configuration data category and are usually the most important piece of an intersite replication transaction. This is because the GC contains a subset of all Active Directory data that is limited to all objects and only those attributes and objects most commonly needed.

Trust Relationships

Much like in Windows NT, a trust relationship is an understanding between domains. You can also think of it as a link between two domains. This link enables one domain to trust (this domain is known as the *trusting domain*) that authenticated users from the other domain can access specific resources located on the first domain (the *trusted domain*) without duplicating user accounts or requiring that a separate authentication process occur.

One of the major differences between Windows NT and Windows 2000 trust relationships is that Windows 2000 supports the Kerberos V5 protocol. Kerberos V5 is an industry standard for encrypted authentication across different operating systems.

Windows 2000 trusts can be confusing, but at least they aren't nearly as confusing as Windows NT trusts. This is because every trust contains specific attributes that describe the direction of the trust, whether it's transitive or not, and if it's explicit.

Trust Direction

As with Windows NT, trusts can be one-way or two-way. A one-way trust is a relationship in which one of the domains trusts the users from another domain to access its resources. As the old Windows NT adage goes, the source domain is the trusting domain; the host domain is the trusted domain. The arrow goes to the trusted domain because it has lots of users named "Ted" trying to access the "tings" on the other side. Bad puns, but it's a good way to remember how a one-way trust works. Figure 3.4 shows how a one-way trust works. Two-way trusts are basically two one-way trusts where both domains are trusting and trusted.

Trusts can be configured by using the Active Directory Domains And Trusts MMC console and checking the properties of any domain on the list. A one-way trust as shown is simply when a domain is listed in one of the two windows shown in Figure 3.5, but not the other. A two-way trust is shown in both windows. When creating a one-way trust, be careful of the wording. You'll notice that the phrase "Domains Trusted By This Domain" can tie your thinking in a knot. Just consider it to translate into "This domain trusts these domains," or, if it works better for you, "These domains need access to my data."

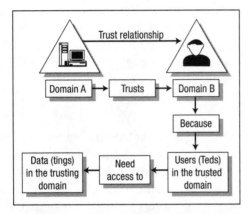

Figure 3.4 A one-way trust between two domains.

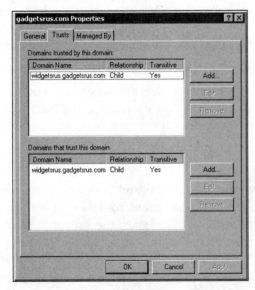

Figure 3.5 Trust configuration in Windows 2000.

Transitive and Nontransitive Trusts

Transitive trusts are new to Windows 2000 and effectively put an end to what was known as mesh trust topology in the Windows NT world. To properly understand why this is, we need to investigate how nontransitive trusts work.

Nontransitive trusts are trusts between two domains. As shown in Figure 3.6a, if Domain A trusts Domain B and Domain B trusts Domain C, Domain A does not trust Domain C even though they are linked together by Domain B. Nontransitive trusts are not associative in one of the few times where A=B and B=C, but A does not equal C. The only way to get communication between all three domains—and Domains A and C in particular—is to create another trust between the two domains as shown in Figure 3.6b. As you add more domains to the picture (Figure 3.6c), the trust relationships become exponentially more complex. This is called a mesh topology or a complete trust model.

Transitive trusts are associative in nature, which means that, when A=B and B=C, then A=C also. As shown in Figure 3.6d, domains that use transitive trusts require far fewer trusts than domains that use nontransitive trusts. This is done by the "any friend of yours is a friend of mine" principal. Let's say that a user belonging to Domain D needs to access data located in the B domain. Rather than maintaining a complex mesh of trusts, the Windows 2000 domain, tree, and forest hierarchy is followed in such a manner that the request for information would be sent

3. Active Directory Physical and Logical Structure

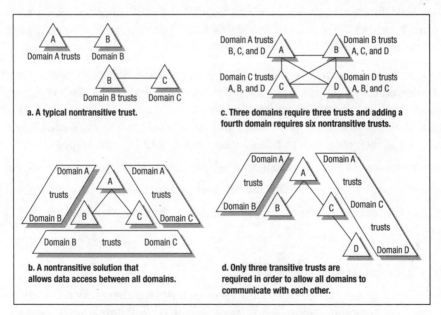

a. A typical nontransitive trust.

c. Three domains require three trusts and adding a fourth domain requires six nontransitive trusts.

b. A nontransitive solution that allows data access between all domains.

d. Only three transitive trusts are required in order to allow all domains to communicate with each other.

Figure 3.6   The differences between transitive and nontransitive trusts.

through successive parent domains and appropriately downstream to the target domain. In this situation, the request would go from Domain D to C to A and then down to B with each domain not only trusting another, but also trusting all of the trusts held by its trusted domain.

Transitive trusts have one potential drawback, and that is the latency that may occur in a large enterprise with multiple trees within a forest. The time it takes for Domain I in Figure 3.3 to access data located in Domain F may be inappropriate for the users and applications involved. This could be an argument for maintaining a nontransitive trust model. However, you will probably find that the overhead required to keep track of nontransitive trusts far outweighs the likelihood that trust latencies will become a problem.

Explicit and Dynamic Trusts

Explicit trusts are trusts that are manually created by an administrator on the system. Manual (explicit) trusts can be created to link divergent domains directly in order to remove latency issues in large domains as described in the previous section. These specialized trusts are called shortcut trusts. Explicit trusts may also be created to connect with Windows NT 4 domains, other trees within a forest, and Kerberos V5 realms.

Dynamic trusts are created automatically by Windows 2000. As part of the package, dynamic trusts are transitive and are also two-way. Windows NT trusts are also created automatically when a Windows NT domain is upgraded. Trusts that run from Windows NT domains to Windows 2000 domains are also upgraded as transitive, dynamic, and two-way trusts.

It's a good idea to get into the habit of referring to trust direction, transitive status, and explicit vs. dynamic creation when talking about trusts. This is generally to lessen confusion between yourself and your colleagues on how a trust is configured. The real world, however, does not always refer to trusts in this manner, so here are some guidelines to follow when reading or hearing about trusts:

- If the word "transitive" is not mentioned, assume that the trust is transitive.

- If the trust direction is not mentioned, assume that the trust is two-way.

- If the word "explicit" is not mentioned, assume that the trust was created by Windows 2000.

Active Directory Servers

Microsoft has gone to a lot of trouble to design Active Directory to be damage resistant by enhancing backup features and by also providing multiple database copies through additional DCs on the network. Despite all of this apparent redundancy, certain functions must still reside only on a single server or on a select few servers within any given domain, tree, or forest.

GC Server

Active Directory stores certain pieces of information, such as DCs, user logins, and commonly used information in a repository (or database) called the GC. Not all object attributes are stored in the GC (which would make replication in a large enterprise impractical). Instead, only the most commonly searched attributes for each object are stored, for example, the first and last names of the user, the logon name, and the universal group relationships.

The GC's primary purpose is to enable cross-domain functions to occur with little or no bandwidth. For example, let's say that you need to access information located in the WIDGETS domain, but you belong to the GADGETS domain within the same forest. Normally, with Windows NT, you request the information across the wire, wait until you're authenticated into the WIDGETS domain, wait again while file permissions are checked, and then look at the information. With Windows 2000, you request the information across the wire, a GC server handles your authentication and checks your universal group membership, and it then hands you over to the WIDGETS DC to handle the rest. The process is quicker and takes less bandwidth.

What time we save by querying the GC is usually spent elsewhere in the form of populating the GC itself. This could be very bandwidth expensive if it weren't for the fact that the GC is relatively small. It only contains objects in the tree and forest, and even then only a small set of attributes for each object. An attribute, as discussed earlier, can be anything that qualifies as a descriptor fitting into a what-it-is category or a what-it-does category. The attributes that are carried by the GC can be defined as frequently used. It might be more understandable, however, to compare the GC, objects, and attributes to traveling. If I'm traveling to New York City from Arizona, the GC will basically tell me to go northeast for a very long time. When I get to New York state, I'm in the domain that contains New York City, and because the domain is the authority on all things New York, I don't need to talk to the GC anymore. Basically, the closer I get to my target, the more I need to know, and until then, the GC has just enough information to get me there.

Because the GC is so important, one is installed on every Windows 2000 domain when the first DC is brought online, thus also making the Windows 2000 DC into a GC server. Even for single domain trees, a GC is created and integrated in such a manner that domain logon cannot occur without the GC being available. For all of the redundancy and safety measures incorporated into Active Directory, users cannot log in unless the GC server is alive and kicking. Microsoft (correctly) saw this as a problem and allowed multiple GC servers to exist within a forest, tree, or domain.

When designating an additional DC as a GC server, also consider what the GC server is there for: Its purpose is to handle interdomain tasks. It's probably a good idea to place at least one GC server at each site in the enterprise, or—if your site planning and placement is less than ideal—at each subnet. This will reduce the WAN link bandwidth significantly because clients won't be hitting the wire looking for a GC server when they have one within their own subnet or site. Ironically, the downside of placing GC servers like this is bandwidth. Why? Because every GC server generates replication traffic that is handled by Active Directory. By definition, every DC on the network will have replication traffic, but adding GC servers everywhere just adds to the load. Probably, the best idea for GC placement is to consider that any remote location worthy of a separate domain controller might be a good candidate for a GC server also.

GC servers can be changed and added using the Active Directory Sites And Services snap-in. The attributes that are carried by the GC can be changed using the Schema Manager MMC snap-in.

Flexible Single Master Operations, a.k.a. Role Masters

Flexible single master operations (FSMOs) are specific server functions that need to live and breathe on a single server. Reasoning for a given FSMO's existence can range from multiple update hassles to security to simply needing only a single authority. When a system that carries a role master fails, the consequences are far from dire. However, it is necessary to get these functions back online as soon as possible. FSMO roles are automatically assigned when the operating system (OS) is installed. However, the role masters can be transferred, or, in the case of a system failure, seized from one server to another.

Domain Naming Master

The domain naming master is the authority on domains within a forest. It maintains, tracks, and handles the security and functions involved when a new domain is created. When the domain naming master fails, domains cannot be added or removed. The domain naming master and the schema master should both reside on the same server. The domain naming master server can be changed using the Active Directory Domains And Trusts snap-in.

Infrastructure Master

Within every domain, the infrastructure master's sole existence is not based upon a single function's requirement, but rather upon speed. The infrastructure master owns the user group replication process in order to update group membership changes more quickly. Its existence is based solely upon Windows NT customer requests. If the infrastructure master is down, changes to group membership will not propagate to all DCs within a domain. Depending upon how demanding your users are, this could be one of the most critical FSMOs you will need to deal with. The infrastructure master server can be changed using the Active Directory Users And Computers snap-in.

PDC Emulator

Just as it sounds, every domain's PDC emulator is designed to be backward compatible with existing Windows NT BDCs on the network. Its purpose is, for all intents and purposes, to appear like a Windows NT PDC to Windows NT BDCs. The ideal Windows 2000 network contains Windows 2000 servers and no Windows NT DCs, so a PDC emulator is only supposed to be a temporary measure until the entire network is upgraded to Windows 2000. Migration will be discussed later in Chapter 7, but, in the meantime, you need to know that the PDC emulator also serves the purpose of being the SNTP server on the domain. SNTP is a protocol that allows a server or computer to receive time stamps from SNTP servers on the Web. Microsoft's adaptation of SNTP is called Windows Time Service (WTS) and can be updated using the **NET TIME** command on a command prompt window. The PDC emulator can be moved from server to server using the Active Directory Users And Computers MMC snap-in.

Relative ID Master

The Relative ID (RID) master tracks RID numbers for each domain. It may seem much ado about nothing, but all objects in a domain have a SID that is assigned by the DC that creates the object. An object's SID is a combination of the SID of the domain and a sequential number called the RID. In order to make sure that no duplicate RID numbers are assigned to any objects, a single RID master is necessary. However, the RID master behavior is different from all other FSMOs in that the privilege is passed from server to server. This is because DCs do not request a RID every time a new object is created; this would be time consuming. Instead, DCs allocate a bunch of RIDs for their usage, and when they run out of RIDs, DCs request more. The catch is that instead of making the request to receive more RIDs from the RID master, they actually become the RID master themselves until someone else needs more RIDs. If the RID master subsequently fails, objects can continue to be created within the domains until the domain runs out of their allocated RIDs. At that time, new objects won't be able to be created for that domain until another DC becomes the RID master. Just as with any other FSMO failure, it then becomes necessary to seize the RID master role using the Active Directory Users And Computers MMC snap-in.

Schema Master

The schema master contains the only editable copy of the Active Directory schema within a forest. The schema, put simply, is an index of all of the possible attributes for all of the possible objects within Active Directory. The schema master should reside on the same system as the domain naming master, and, like the domain naming master, failure simply means that the schema cannot be modified.

The schema is a very interesting and dangerous animal to tamper with, but it can be done using the Schema Manager MMC (SCHMMGMT.MSC) snap-in that can be installed from Adminpak.msi located on the Windows 2000 installation CD. When would the schema be modified? According to Microsoft, only advanced administrative functions and programming situations would need to touch the schema. I can't really see any advanced administrative functions that would need to touch the schema unless they would be really tied in with programming, so here's an example. Let's say a company is creating a human resources application that taps into the Active Directory database for its information. After all, Active Directory stores a lot of human resources-type user information, and a few extra fields (attributes) could be added to allow for additional data and functionality. In order to do this, two events would need to occur. First, the additional attributes would have to be created in the schema. This essentially initializes these attributes and makes them available for use within the Active Directory database. Second, the Active Directory database would have to actually use these new attributes using either a modified interface within the Active Directory Users And Computers MMC snap-in (highly unlikely) or a new interface created by the human resources company that uses the Active Directory database for its backend. This is exactly how Exchange Server 2000 and several other Microsoft applications make themselves Active Directory-integrated. As administrators, we can finally hope that this is the solution to us having to enter separate user accounts for the network, fax, phone, email, and database applications. The biggest drawback so far is that many software companies are reluctant to actually tamper with Active Directory for fear that Microsoft won't support Active Directory at all if it's been modified. The workaround to date has been to pull information from Active Directory and to store it in a separate database, thus making many applications only one-way or semi-Active Directory integrated. Take these factors into account when considering the purchase of a non-Microsoft Active Directory-integrated application.

Immediate Solutions

Creating a Custom MMC Console

As an administrator, you want to create your own set of tools to facilitate your common management tasks. Therefore, you should create your own MMC console. Here are the steps to follow:

1. Click the Start menu, and select Run. The Run dialog box appears.

2. Type "mmc", and then click OK. An empty MMC window appears.

3. Select Console|Add/Remove Snap-In. The Add/Remove Snap-In dialog box appears.

4. Click Add. The Add Standalone Snap-In dialog box appears.

5. Locate and select Device Manager (see Figure 3.7). Click Add.

6. Select the local computer, and click Finish.

7. Locate and select System Information. Click Add.

8. Select the local computer, and click Finish.

9. Click Close. You return to the Add/Remove Snap-In dialog box.

10. Click OK. You return to the MMC window.

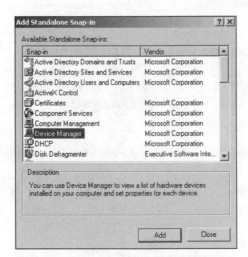

Figure 3.7   The Add Standalone Snap-In dialog box with Device Manager selected.

11. Select Console|Options. The Options dialog box appears.

12. Select User Mode - Limited Access, Single Window from the Console pull-down list.

13. Click OK.

14. Select Console|Save As.

15. Provide a file name, such as "devices". The default storage location should be within the Administrative Tools folder of the currently logged on user's Start menu. Click Save.

16. Select Console|Exit to close the MMC window.

17. Click the Start menu, select Programs|Administrative Tools|Devices.msc. Your newly created MMC console is launched.

18. Select Console|Exit to close the MMC window.

Configuring WTS to Use an SNTP Server

One benefit of having a PDC emulator is that it also handles WTS, which can be configured to synchronize the system clock with an SNTP server located on the Web. In turn, Windows 2000 DCs all synchronize to the DC containing the PDC emulator for their time. Final synchronization occurs when the clients log on to the network and synchronize their time with the DC. To configure WTS to use an SNTP server, perform the following steps:

1. Click on the Start menu, and select Run.

2. Type "CMD", and click OK.

3. Type the following, and press Enter: **net time /setsntp:192.5.41.209**.

NOTE: *There are several SNTP servers available on the Web. The server listed in Step 3 is the address for a server maintained by the United States Naval Observatory (USNO). Other USNO servers can be found at **http://www.usno.navy.mil**.*

---

4. Type the following to confirm that the SNTP server has been set: **net time /querysntp**.

5. The same IP address or fully qualified domain name (such as ntp2.usno.navy.mil) should appear as the set SNTP server.

6. Type "Exit", and press Enter.

Installing the Active Directory Schema Utility

The Active Directory schema utility is part of the Windows 2000 Administration Tools, which are available on the Windows 2000 Server CD-ROM. To install the Active Directory Schema utility, perform the following steps:

1. Insert the Windows 2000 Server CD-ROM into the CD-ROM drive.

2. Click the Start menu, and select Run.

3. In the Run dialog box, type "*<windows2000CD>*\i386\adminpak.msi" (where <windows2000CD> is your CD-ROM drive), and click OK. This starts Windows 2000 Administration Tools.

4. After the installer completes the installation, click the Start menu and select Run. In the Run dialog box, type "mmc", and click OK.

5. Select Console|Add/Remove Snap-In.

6. Click Add.

7. Choose the Active Directory Schema option, and click Add.

8. Click Close.

9. Click OK.

10. The Active Directory Schema utility is now installed. Save the MMC configuration for the next time you need this application.

Identifying the Schema Master

To identify the schema master, perform the following steps:

1. Click the Start menu, and select Programs|Administrative Tools|Active Directory Schema.

2. Right-click Active Directory Schema, and select Operations Master from the pop-up menu.

3. The name that appears in the Current Operations Master field is the schema master.

Modifying the Schema Master Role

To modify the schema master role, perform the following steps:

1. Click the Start menu, and select Programs|Administrative Tools|Active Directory Schema.

2. Right-click Active Directory Schema, and select Change Domain Controller.

3. Select the Any DC option to let Active Directory choose a new schema operations master.

4. Right-click Active Directory Schema, and choose Operations Manager.

5. Click Change, and choose the new schema master.

Determining a Server's Role Masters Using NTDSUTIL.EXE

NTDSUTIL.EXE is a command-line application that needs to be executed from a command prompt. NTDSUTIL can provide a single list showing which role masters are hosted on a selected DC without having to go through several applications to do so. To determine a server's role masters using NTDSUTIL, perform the following steps:

1. Make sure that you are logged on as a domain administrator for this function. When transferring forest role masters, an Enterprise Admin group membership is required.

2. Click the Start menu, and select Run. Type "CMD", and click OK.

3. Type "NTDSUTIL", and press Enter. An NTDSUTIL: prompt appears.

4. Type "?" at the prompt, and press Enter.

5. All of the NTDSUTIL options will appear. Type "ROLES" at the prompt in order to initiate FSMO maintenance, and press Enter.

6. The FSMO Maintenance prompt appears. Type "?" to display a list of options.

7. Type "CONNECTIONS" at the prompt in order to initiate server connections management.

8. The prompt changes to Server Connections:. Type "?" to display a list of options.

9. Type the following at the Server Connections prompt: "connect to domain <*domainname*>". The <domainname> should be the domain that contains the server that will be queried for its role masters.

10. Type the following at the Server Connections prompt: "connect to server *<servername>*". The <servername> should be the server that will hold the role masters.

11. Type "QUIT" at the Server Connections prompt. The prompt changes back to FSMO maintenance. Type "?" to see a list of the available options.

12. Type "SELECT OPERATION TARGET" from the FSMO maintenance prompt, and press Enter.

13. The prompt will change to Select Operation Target. Type "?" to see a list of the available options, and press Enter.

14. Type "LIST ROLES" for connected server at the Select Operation Target prompt, and press Enter.

15. A list of role masters for the connected server appears.

16. Type "QUIT", and press Enter. Do this three times to quit NTDSUTIL.EXE.

Transferring Role Masters Using NTDSUTIL.EXE

NTDSUTIL.EXE is a command-line application that needs to be executed from a command prompt. Transferring a role master occurs when a role master needs to change from one system to another. To transfer a role master, perform the following steps:

1. Make sure that you are logged on as a domain administrator for this function. When transferring forest role masters, an Enterprise Admin group membership is required.

2. Click the Start menu, and select Run. Type "CMD", and click OK.

3. Type "NTDSUTIL", and press Enter. An NTDSUTIL: prompt appears.

4. Type "?" at the prompt, and press Enter.

5. All of the NTDSUTIL options appear. Type "ROLES" at the prompt in order to initiate FSMO maintenance.

6. The prompt changes to FSMO maintenance:. Type "?" to display a list of options.

7. Type "CONNECTIONS" at the prompt in order to initiate server connections management.

8. The prompt changes to Server Connections:. Type "?" to display a list of options.

9. Type the following at the Server Connections prompt: "connect to domain *<domainname>*". The <domainname> should be the domain that contains the server that will be receiving the role master function. Press Enter.

10. Type the following at the Server Connections prompt: "connect to server *<servername>*". The <servername> should be the server that will receive the role master function.

11. Type "QUIT" at the Server Connections prompt. The prompt changes back to FSMO maintenance. Type "?" to see a list of the available options.

12. To transfer a role, type "TRANSFER", followed by any one of the following: "DOMAIN NAMING MASTER", "INFRASTRUCTURE MASTER", "PDC", "RID MASTER", or "SCHEMA MASTER". Press Enter.

13. A dialog box appears to confirm the role transfer. Click Yes.

14. The updated roles for the current server are listed on the window.

15. Type "QUIT", and press Enter. Do this twice to exit the NTDSUTIL app.

Seizing Role Masters Using NTDSUTIL.EXE

NTDSUTIL.EXE is a command-line application that needs to be executed from a command prompt. Seizing a role master occurs when a current role master has failed and is unavailable to properly transfer the responsibility. To seize a role master, perform the following steps:

1. Make sure that you are logged on as a domain administrator for this function. When seizing forest role masters, an Enterprise Admin group membership is required.

2. Click the Start menu, and select Run. Type "CMD", and click OK.

3. Type "NTDSUTIL", and press Enter.

4. An NTDSUTIL: prompt appears. Type "?" at the prompt, and press Enter.

5. All of the NTDSUTIL options appear. Type "ROLES" at the prompt in order to initiate FSMO maintenance.

6. The prompt changes to FSMO Maintenance:. Type "?" to display a list of options.

7. Type "CONNECTIONS" at the prompt in order to initiate server connections management.

8. The prompt changes to Server Connections:. Type "?" to display a list of options.

9. Type the following in at the Server Connections prompt: "connect to domain *<domainname>*". The <domainname> should be the domain that contains the server that will be receiving the role master function. Press Enter.

10. Type the following in at the Server Connections prompt: "connect to server *<servername>*". The <servername> should be the server that will receive the role master function.

11. Type "QUIT" at the Server Connections prompt. The prompt changes back to FSMO maintenance. Type "?" to see a list of the available options.

12. To seize a role, type "SEIZE" following by any one of the following: "DOMAIN NAMING MASTER", "INFRASTRUCTURE MASTER", "PDC", "RID MASTER", or "SCHEMA MASTER". Press Enter.

13. A window appears to confirm the role seizure. Click Yes.

14. The updated roles for the current server are listed on the screen.

15. Type "QUIT", and press Enter. Do this twice to exit the NTDSUTIL app.

Changing the Domain Naming Master Role

Changing the domain naming master role is not really recommended because of the insignificant load it has upon the network. If you do choose to change the role, remember that the domain naming master should reside on the same system as the Schema Master. To change the domain naming master role, perform the following steps:

1. Click the Start menu, and select Programs|Administrative Tools|Active Directory Domains And Trusts.

2. Right-click the Domains And Trusts icon at the top of the left-hand pane, and select Connect To Domain Controller from the pop-up menu.

3. Select the domain controller that will receive the transferred role, and click OK.

4. Right-click the Domains And Trusts icon at the top of the left-hand pane, and select Operations Master from the pop-up menu.

5. The current domain naming operations master is listed on the top. Click Change to change the role master to the computer listed on the bottom.

6. A dialog box appears requesting confirmation of the change. Click Yes.

Changing the PDC Emulator Master Role

To change the PDC emulator master role, perform the following steps:

1. Click the Start menu, and select Programs|Administrative Tools|Active Directory Users And Computers.

2. Right-click the Active Directory Users And Computers icon at the top, and select Connect To Domain Controller from the pop-up menu.

3. The Connect To Domain Controller dialog box appears. Select the DC that will be receiving the PDC emulator role, and click OK.

4. Right-click the Active Directory Users And Computers icon at the top, and select Operations Masters from the pop-up menu.

5. Click the PDC tab at the top of the window.

6. The current PDC emulator is listed on the top. Click Change to change the role master to the computer listed on the bottom.

7. A dialog box appears requesting confirmation of the change. Click Yes.

Changing the Infrastructure Master Role

To change the infrastructure master role, perform the following steps:

1. Click the Start menu, and select Programs|Administrative Tools|Active Directory Users And Computers.

2. Right-click the Active Directory Users And Computers icon at the top, and select Connect To Domain Controller from the pop-up menu.

3. The Connect To Domain Controller dialog box appears. Select the DC that will be receiving the infrastructure master role, and click OK.

4. Right-click the Active Directory Users And Computers icon at the top, and select Operations Masters from the pop-up menu.

5. Click the Infrastructure tab.

6. The current infrastructure master is listed on the top. Click Change to change the role master to the computer listed on the bottom.

7. A dialog box appears requesting confirmation of the change. Click Yes.

Changing the RID Master Role

Changing the RID master role may have some short-term value in offloading the function to a different system, but don't forget that the RID master role changes every time another DC requires a bank of RID numbers. To change the RID master role, perform the following steps:

1. Click the Start menu, and select Programs|Administrative Tools|Active Directory Users And Computers.

2. Right-click the Active Directory Users And Computers icon at the top, and select Connect To Domain Controller from the pop-up menu.

3. The Connect To Domain Controller dialog box appears. Select the DC that will be receiving the RID master role, and click OK.

4. Right-click the Active Directory Users And Computers icon at the top, and select Operations Masters from the pop-up menu.

5. The current RID master is listed on the top. Click Change to change the role master to the computer listed on the bottom.

6. A dialog box appears requesting confirmation of the change. Click Yes.

Enabling a Global Catalog

To enable a global catalog, perform the following steps:

1. Click the Start menu, and select Programs|Administrative Tools|Active Directory Sites And Services.

2. Navigate to the domain controller that's not currently hosting a global catalog.

3. Right-click NTDS Settings, and select Properties from the pop-up menu.

4. Ensure that the Global Catalog option is selected.

5. Click OK.

Disabling a Global Catalog

To disable a global catalog, perform the following steps:

1. Click the Start menu, and select Programs|Administrative Tools|Active Directory Sites And Services.

2. Navigate to the domain controller that's currently hosting a global catalog.

3. Right-click NTDS Settings, and select Properties from the pop-up menu.

4. Ensure that the Global Catalog option is unselected.

5. Click OK.

Working with Sites

A number of tasks are involved in managing sites in Active Directory. The following solutions address this important issue.

Creating a Site

To create a site, perform the following steps:

1. Click the Start menu, and select Programs|Administrative Tools|Active Directory Sites And Services.

2. Right-click the Sites container, and select the New Site option from the pop-up menu. (Alternatively, you can select New|Site.)

3. In the New Object - Site window, enter the name for the site.

4. Select the link that will be used to communicate with this site.

5. Click OK.

Deleting a Site

To delete a site, perform the following steps:

1. Click the Start menu, and select Programs|Administrative Tools|Active Directory Sites And Services.

2. Navigate to the site you would like to delete.

3. Right-click the desired site, and select Delete from the pop-up menu.

4. Click Yes to confirm the deletion.

Renaming a Site

To rename a site, perform the following steps:

1. Click the Start menu, and select Programs|Administrative Tools|Active Directory Sites And Services.

2. Navigate to the site you would like to rename.

3. Right-click the desired site, and select Rename from the pop-up menu.

4. Enter the new name for the site.

5. Press Enter.

Creating a Subnet

To create a subnet, perform the following steps:

1. Click the Start menu, and select Programs|Administrative Tools|Active Directory Sites And Services.

2. Navigate to the Subnets container.

3. Right-click the Subnets container, and select New Subnet from the pop-up menu.

4. In the Address field, shown in Figure 3.8, enter the address for the subnet.

5. In the Mask field, enter the subnet mask to be used with this subnet.

6. Select a site to associate with this new subnet.

7. Click OK.

Deleting a Subnet

To delete a subnet, perform the following steps:

1. Click the Start menu, and select Programs|Administrative Tools|Active Directory Sites And Services.

2. Navigate to the Subnets container.

3. Right-click the subnet you would like to delete, and choose Delete from the pop-up menu.

4. Click Yes to confirm the deletion.

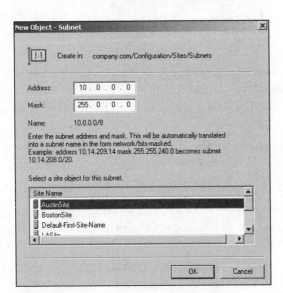

Figure 3.8   Creating a new subnet object.

Associating a Subnet with a Site

To associate a subnet with a site, perform the following steps:

1. Click the Start menu, and select Programs|Administrative Tools|Active Directory Sites And Services.

2. Navigate to the Subnets container.

3. Right-click the subnet you would like to associate with a site, and choose Properties from the pop-up menu.

4. Choose the site you would like associated with this subnet from the Site drop-down list, and click OK.

Creating a Site Link

Site links are created automatically by the KCC, but they can also be created manually for specific situations, such as when multiple sites need to communicate with another site using a single link. To create a site link, perform the following steps:

1. Click the Start menu, and select Programs|Administrative Tools|Active Directory Sites And Services.

2. Navigate to the Inter-Site Transports container, and double-click it.

3. Right-click the IP container, and select New Site Link from the pop-up menu.

4. Select a site from the left-hand column, and click Add. Do this at least twice so that two sites are in the link.

5. Click OK to create the site link.

Editing a Site Link

By default, site links are given equal preferential treatment with all other sites, and replication times are set at every three hours. The schedule of time that a site can replicate defaults to 24 hours a day, 7 days a week. To edit a site link, perform the following steps:

1. Click the Start menu, and select Programs|Administrative Tools|Active Directory Sites And Services.

2. Navigate to the Inter-Site Transports container, and double-click it.

3. Double-click the IP container, and double-click the listed site link in the right-hand window. Notice that, at the bottom of the properties window, entries exist for cost, replication frequency, and schedule.

4. Change the cost number if you have a preference that this site link be used rather than other site links. You can also designate the cost as the reliability factor of the network connection between the sites listed with 1 being the best speed and reliability, and higher numbers being worse.

5. Change the Replicate Every field when you wish to replicate more or less often.

6. Click Schedule to change the scheduled times when replication occurs. Quite often, due to bandwidth limitations, the schedule is modified to include only Monday through Friday evening hours. Try to create the replication schedule either before or after tape backup times in order to eliminate the possibility of corrupted backups.

7. The replication schedule is set by highlighting a block of times specific to a given day and then clicking on the appropriate radio button to indicate whether replication for that block is available or not available.

Creating a Server Object

To create a server object, perform the following steps:

1. Click the Start menu, and select Programs|Administrative Tools|Active Directory Sites And Services.

2. Navigate to the site where you would like the new domain controller server to be created (see Figure 3.9).

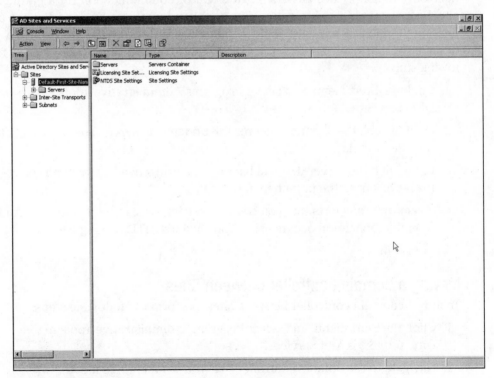

Figure 3.9   The Active Directory Sites And Services utility.

3. Right-click Servers, and select New|Server from the pop-up menu.

4. Enter a new name for the server object.

5. Click OK to create the server object.

Removing a Server Object from a Site

To remove a server object from a site, perform the following steps:

1. Click the Start menu, and select Programs|Administrative Tools|Active Directory Sites And Services.

2. Navigate to the server that you would like to remove.

3. Right-click the server, and select Delete from the pop-up menu.

4. Click Yes to confirm the deletion.

Creating a Bridgehead Server

A bridgehead server can be designated as a single tunnel by which intersite replication traffic can travel. Normally, replication traffic occurs between any DC that is available to do the job. In the event that mass replication is occurring, it may be necessary to simply designate a single point of communication for a particular site. Keep in mind that eliminating this extra bandwidth can be good, but you are limiting yourself to a single point of failure within the replication schema by designating a bridgehead server. To create a bridgehead server, perform the following steps:

1. Click the Start menu, and select Programs|Administrative Tools|Active Directory Sites And Services.

2. Double-click the site that requires the bridgehead server, and double click the Servers folder.

3. Right-click the server that will become the bridgehead server, and select Properties from the pop-up menu.

4. Select the transports that you wish to restrict to this server, and click Add. Intersite replication occurs using both IP and SMTP. See Figure 3.10.

5. Click OK.

Moving a Domain Controller between Sites

To move a domain controller between sites, perform the following steps:

1. Click the Start menu, and select Programs|Administrative Tools|Active Directory Sites And Services.

2. Navigate to the domain controller that you would like to move.

3. Right-click the domain controller object, and select Move from the pop-up menu. The Move Server window appears, as shown in Figure 3.11.

4. All available sites appear in the Move Server window. Select the destination site, and click OK.

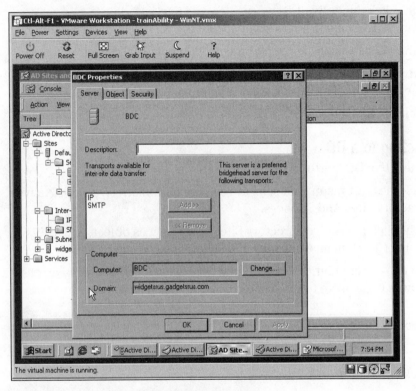

Figure 3.10   Designating a bridgehead server.

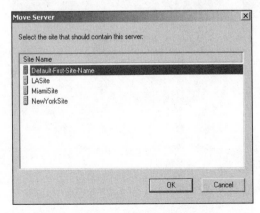

Figure 3.11   The Move Server window.

Connecting to a Forest

To connect to a forest, perform the following steps:

1. Click the Start menu, and select Programs|Administrative Tools|Active Directory Sites And Services.

2. Right-click the Active Directory Sites And Services object, and select Connect To Forest from the pop-up menu.

3. In the Root Domain field, enter the root domain of the desired forest.

4. If you would like this setting saved for this session, enable the Save This Domain Setting For The Current Console option.

5. Click OK.

Connecting to a DC

To connect to a DC, perform the following steps:

1. Click the Start menu, and select Programs|Administrative Tools|Active Directory Sites And Services.

2. Right-click the Active Directory Sites And Services object, and select Connect To Domain Controller from the pop-up menu.

3. You can either enter the name of the domain manually, or you can click Browse to navigate to the desired domain.

NOTE: *The available DCs for the selected domains are listed in the Available Controllers In section of the window (see Figure 3.12).*

---

4. Click OK to connect to the selected DC.

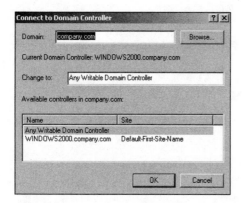

Figure 3.12   The Connect To Domain Controller window.

Starting Replication Manually

To start replication manually, perform the following steps:

1. Click the Start menu, and select Programs|Administrative Tools|Active Directory Sites And Services.

2. Double-click the site that you want to use to replicate.

3. Double-click the Servers folder, and double-click the server that you want to use to replicate.

4. In the left pane under the server is an entry labeled NTDS Site Settings. Click it.

5. Connections for this server are listed in the right window. Right-click the connection, and select Replicate Now from the pop-up menu.

6. A dialog box appears as shown in Figure 3.13 when replication is complete.

7. Click OK.

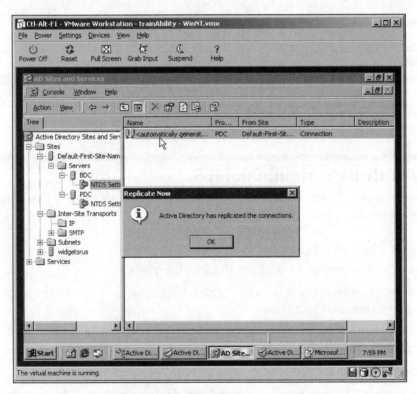

Figure 3.13   Forced replication completion.

Changing a Replication Partner

To change a replication partner, perform the following steps:

1. Click the Start menu, and select Programs|Administrative Tools|Active Directory Sites And Services.

2. Double-click the site that contains the servers involved.

3. Double-click the Servers folder, and double-click the server whose replication partners need to change.

4. Double-click the NTDS settings under the server.

5. Right-click the connection listed to the right, and select Properties. Replication partners are defined within connection settings.

6. Within the Replicate From section at the bottom of the Properties window is a server listing with a Change button to the right. Click Change.

7. A Find Domain Controllers dialog box appears listing all of the DCs within Active Directory. Select a DC, and click OK.

8. Click OK.

NOTE: *if you are modifying a system-generated connection, an additional dialog box appears. The message says that the KCC will tune and modify the changes you just made unless you tell it not to by marking the connection as being not automatically created. Click Yes.*

Working with Trust Relationships

A number of tasks are involved in managing trust relationships in Active Directory. The following solutions address this issue.

Creating a Trust Relationship

To create a trust relationship, perform the following steps:

1. Click the Start menu, and select Programs|Administrative Tools|Active Directory Domains And Trusts.

2. Right-click the domain you would like to administer, and select Properties from the pop-up menu.

3. Click the Trusts tab.

4. If you would like this domain to trust another domain, click Add under the Domains Trusted By This Domain section.

5. If you would like other domains to trust this domain, click Add under the Domains That Trust This Domain section.

6. Enter the domain name to be included in the trust.

TIP: *If you're creating a trust relationship with a Windows NT 4 domain, all you need to enter is the domain name. If, however, you're connecting with a Windows 2000 domain, you'll need to enter the fully qualified domain name.*

7. Type and confirm a password for the trust relationship.

8. Complete the trust by configuring the trust relationship on the DC in the partner domain.

Deleting a Trust Relationship

To delete a trust relationship, perform the following steps:

1. Click the Start menu, and select Programs|Administrative Tools|Active Directory Domains And Trusts.

2. Right-click the domain you would like to administer, and select Properties from the pop-up menu.

3. Click the Trusts tab.

4. Select the trust relationship you would like to delete, and click Remove.

5. Click Yes to confirm the deletion of the trust relationship.

6. Repeat this process on the other side of the trust relationship.

TIP: *Default two-way transitive trusts cannot be deleted.*

Modifying a Trust Relationship

To modify a trust relationship, perform the following steps:

1. Click the Start menu, and select Programs|Administrative Tools|Active Directory Domains And Trusts.

2. Right-click the domain you would like to administer, and select Properties from the pop-up menu.

3. Click the Trusts tab.

4. Select the trust relationship that you would like to edit, and click Edit.

5. Make any necessary changes to the trust.

6. Click OK.

7. Repeat this process on the other side of the trust relationship.

Verifying a Trust Relationship

To verify a trust relationship, perform the following steps:

1. Click the Start menu, and select Programs|Administrative Tools|Active Directory Domains And Trusts.

2. Right-click the domain you would like to administer, and select Properties from the pop-up menu.

3. Click the Trusts tab.

4. Select the trust relationship that you would like to verify, and click Edit.

5. Click Verify/Reset.

6. Click OK.

Changing a Domain Mode

To change a domain mode, perform the following steps:

1. Click the Start menu, and select Programs|Administrative Tools|Active Directory Domains And Trusts.

2. Right-click the domain you would like to administer, and select Properties from the pop-up menu. The domain's Properties window appears (see Figure 3.14).

3. Click Change Mode.

4. Click Yes to confirm the mode change.

WARNING! By changing the domain mode, you're changing the mode from mixed mode to native mode. This means that no Windows NT 4.0 DCs exist in the domain. This action is not reversible.

5. Click OK.

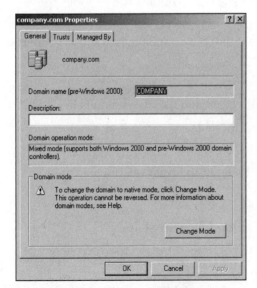

Figure 3.14   Changing the domain mode.

Chapter 4
Users, Groups, and Computers

In Depth

The fact of the matter is that, as an administrator, you'll spend about 50 to 80 percent of your administrative tasks on users and groups. The rest of your administrative time will be spent handling sharable resources, server administration and maintenance, and the occasional emergency.

Local Users and Groups

Windows 2000 Professional and Server systems residing outside of a Windows 2000 domain can be connected by what's known as a peer-to-peer network. What this means is simply that each computer has the capability of acting both as a server and as a workstation or client. This kind of network has several advantages. As with most companies, the reasons for choosing a peer-to-peer network model instead of a domain model are usually financially based. There is not a centralized authority, such as Active Directory, that tracks and maintains user and resource information. Without a centralized authority, there is no need for a centralized server, thus lessening the requirements for an information technology (IT) administrator to maintain a centralized network or domain. In order to maintain appropriate security access, each peer on the network must maintain its own security database containing information about shared resources (files and printers), users, and groups. This is called *decentralized administration*. The downside is that this decentralized administration requires that each computer user be trained on the appropriate administrative tasks for his or her computer system. Essentially, the money saved by not hiring an IT administrator is paid to distribute those same tasks to everyone. In very small environments, this additional training and administration requires little overhead and usually poses no problems. When the company grows, or when additional security requires specific and customized access privileges, this overhead can become a burden to the respective computer users. This is the point when a centralized or domain-based network should be considered. Of course, it is possible just to hire an administrator to handle the additional loads. However, at that point, this administrator would be spending more time administering individual workstations than she would be spending to administer a single server.

Local users and groups are created primarily to allow and restrict resource access over the network to a peer server system. On the other hand, this is by no means the only reason for local users and groups. Users and groups are also used to grant and restrict local access to resources for logged-on users.

TIP: *Be very aware that, especially when your users are technical or are prone to experimentation, peer-to-peer networking (otherwise known as file sharing) can occur in domains. If your company is concerned with security, file sharing might be a problem that should be fixed using group policies.*

Local user and group administration occurs within the Computer Management Microsoft Management Console (MMC) or while using Control Panel|Users And Passwords. It's a good idea to become familiar with both means of administering users and groups. During the course of desktop or server administration, restrictions may be in place that prevent easy access to either the Control Panel|Users And Passwords applet or the Computer Management MMC.

Computer Management and Local User Manager

The Computer Management MMC console can easily be accessed by right-clicking My Computer on the desktop and selecting Manage. You can also get there by clicking the Start menu, selecting Run, and typing "compmgmt.msc". The Computer Management console is the perfect example of an MMC console because every item you see is a separate MMC snap-in that can be run on its own. Because our purpose here is users and groups, we will focus on the Local User Manager snap-in. A quicker method to access users and groups would be to click the Start menu, select Run, and type "lusrmgr.msc". You'll also notice in Figure 4.1 that fewer administrative options are available from the Control Panel applet than are available within the Local User Manager snap-in. The other snap-ins located within Computer Management will be covered in detail in Chapters 9, 10, and 17, which

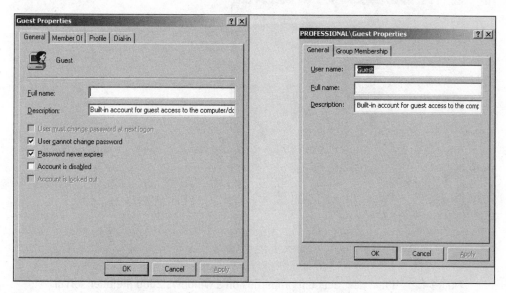

Figure 4.1 Guest user properties within Local User Manager on the left, and Guest user properties within Control Panel|Users And Passwords on the right.

4. Users, Groups, and Computers

cover configuration, disk and removable media management, and system optimization, respectively.

When dealing with local users and groups, remember that these users and groups apply both to people who log on locally to the computer and to people who would access resources on this computer over the network. This is less of a concern in a domain environment where local server access is usually restricted.

NOTE: *You may be asking yourself why you should move to a domain network when you could essentially designate a Windows 2000 Professional or member server as a centralized server that makes all network resources available for access. After all, centralizing administration solves many problems without the cost and hassle of administering a domain. The answer can be complex, so let's look at it as a study in probability. At the point in time where your company gets large enough to want a centralized administrative authority, your company is very likely also to want the additional security, scripts, and other application features available only with an Active Directory domain.*

One additional feature of the Computer Management console is that you can manage and administer other computer systems by connecting to another computer from the Action menu. More information on remote administration is in Chapter 14.

Additional user and group features are available depending upon whether the system is Windows 2000 Professional or Windows 2000 Server. Notice the differences between the available properties in Figures 4.1 and 4.2.

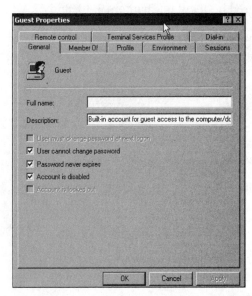

Figure 4.2   Guest user account properties on a Windows 2000 member server.

Local User Accounts

User accounts can easily be created by clicking the Action menu and selecting New User from the drop-down menu. A New User dialog box appears, and all you really need to know is a user login name. Of course, additional benefits can be seen when you provide the user's full name and description. You do not need to create a password, but it is beneficial.

Be aware that, in a peer-to-peer or workgroup network, user account names and passwords need to be the same for all systems that a user would need to access. This is all part of that distributed administration networking model. This isn't really a problem as long as you leave out all the fancy account options, such as requiring password changes. If anything, you might consider indicating that the passwords will never expire and that users cannot change their passwords. If this poses security risks within the environment, it's highly recommended that you implement a Windows 2000 domain. Trust me. You will spend far less time administering a domain than you will changing user passwords on a bunch of computers every time the users feel like changing passwords.

When you attempt to access a networked resource, your computer will automatically pass through your currently logged-in username and password to the system that you're trying to access. If the username and password do not match, you will be unable to access the data on the target machine without going through the additional step of providing a different username and password. A good rule of thumb in a peer-to-peer network is to keep usernames and passwords as simple and as unchanging as possible.

The basic creation of a user is simply coming up with a login name. Password and account disabling options are available at this point. However, you will need to check the properties of the newly created account in order to perform more advanced administrative functions. Right-clicking the account from within Computer Manager allows you to change the password and also to check properties. User account properties permit you to add the user to groups, define a profile location, assign a logon script, and define a home directory either locally or on the network. Dial-up options can be changed here as well; however, these are exclusive to Windows 2000 Server and will be discussed in Chapter 19. Logon scripts and home directories will rarely be used for local user accounts or in peer-to-peer networks simply because a centralized login point doesn't exist. Scripts certainly can be used for local logons, and home directories can also be used to point a locally logged-on user to a set of folders on the network automatically. Because these features are most common and most beneficial in domain environments, we will discuss these advanced user properties in the section called "Domain Users and Groups" later in this chapter.

NOTE: *When you're working in Local Users And Groups, keep in mind that the interface you see is somewhat generic and will contain domain-exclusive options.*

User Profiles

It has always been somewhat easy to confuse profiles with policies in the Microsoft networking world. It is less of an issue within Windows 2000 because Group Policies have become a powerhouse of administrative features, and user profiles have become a truly portable means of maintaining flexibility in a networked environment. Once we investigate Group Policies in Chapter 5, you'll never get the two mixed up again—because you'll either love or hate Group Policies, but you will never forget them.

User profiles contain information about the current desktop environment, application settings, and logon-specific data. They also exist on every Windows 2000 system for every person that logs into that system. Basically, the idea is that anything that is specific to you as a user is included in the user profile. Profile information can be stored both on the local hard disk and on the network. After a system is configured to store the profile on the network, the profile becomes a roaming profile. A roaming profile enables a user to log in to multiple machines with the same desktop settings, Start menu, My Documents, and other user-specific and customizable information. The roaming profile does this by essentially copying the profile from the network to the computer every time a user logs on. When the user logs off, the opposite occurs, and the profile is copied back up to the network. After the first profile is copied to the network for a user, only changes are copied back and forth, which improves network speeds and bandwidth. Keep in mind that, while all of this copying occurs, the user is patiently waiting for the computer to finish logging him or her into the system. An additional security feature is available for roaming profiles that essentially allows them to become read-only and unchangeable by the user. These are called mandatory roaming profiles. A standard roaming profile is good because it gives users the ability to log in to any system on the network and to begin working with all of their personal tools. The additional advantage of mandatory roaming profiles is that users cannot accidentally blow away their settings and render themselves unable to work.

NOTE: *Mandatory roaming profiles will also prevent users from making changes to their My Documents Folder. The only way to implement mandatory roaming profiles while still enabling users to save to My Documents is by implementing a group policy to redirect My Documents to a network folder. This, of course, requires that a Windows 2000 domain be in place.*

Roaming profiles are designed to work so that users can log in anywhere and still maintain the same settings. This only works when basic applications are installed on the system, and then only when those applications save their application data in the user's profile. In the real world, roaming profiles work kind of like those not-so-newfangled universal remote controls that you can get for your VCR and TV. The remote control has buttons for changing channels, volume, play, fast forward, stop, and rewind. If you press the play button on the remote, the VCR will play, but if you take that same remote to a different system that does not have a VCR and press the play button, nothing will happen. Windows 2000 roaming profiles work much the same way. When you move from one system to another, the desktop settings and icons will have the same buttons just like the universal remote control in our example did. However, if the installed applications and underlying equipment are not the same, some buttons won't work. Having a Microsoft Word icon doesn't do much good when Microsoft Word isn't installed on the system you are logged in to. Realistically, roaming user profiles are great for call centers or environments where every system is configured with the same software. As an administrator, you need to be hyperaware of the situation when you roll out roaming profiles. Configuring roaming profiles in nonhomogenous environments can cause users to complain that programs or settings do not work when they move from system to system. In the long run, these broken pieces can cause more harm than good, and the problems can outweigh the benefits of roaming profiles.

Also be aware that not all applications store user-specific data in the user profile, and this can cause problems even in environments where all the computers are the same (otherwise known as homogenous environments). The result would be that a user can move from one computer to another and run the applications, but another person's specific information shows up within the application. As time goes by, more and more applications will be created that store this type of information in the user profile. This is a good thing, but even Microsoft seems to be having problems putting together a truly seamless system. I've encountered issues with Microsoft Office 2000—and Outlook 2000 specifically—where most user-specific information is stored in application data. However, other information, such as customized forms and form assignments, were stored within the program directory. Symptoms of these types of issues are similar to those above, only more difficult to find, because it can take time for a user to notice that smaller details are different.

Profile data is located on the local drive in the Documents And Settings folder, which is located on the same drive as the WinNT directory. Every time a new person logs in to the computer, a folder is created with his account name under this Documents And Settings folder. If you look in the Documents And Settings folder, you'll notice a Default User folder and an All Users folder. When a user's profile folder is created, the contents of Default User are automatically copied into that directory. Ultimately, what users see is a combination of their personal profile and the All Users profile. Conflicts between the two will occur, in which case the user's profile is applied last, and thus takes precedence. Configuring roaming profiles in a peer-to-peer, workgroup, or nondomain environment is frankly a nightmare. Again, that distributed administration model comes into play because each user account on each computer would require that the profile be configured to reside on the same networked computer. In a domain, this is no problem because domain controllers and servers are designed to handle that kind of responsibility. Designating a Windows 2000 Professional system in a peer-to-peer environment to handle everyone's user profiles, however, could cause some performance issues for the person who uses the computer on a daily basis. Again, you can designate a Professional or Server machine to act as a server in a nondomain environment, but the efforts involved in administration would still be more than what would be required to maintain a Windows 2000 domain.

Built-In User and Group Accounts

The system by default will create an administrator and guest user when the system is installed. For standalone Windows 2000 servers, additional users may be added for installed services, such as Internet Information Server (IIS), Terminal Services, and Windows Media Services. The administrator account and password are created during the Windows 2000 installation. The guest user is created with the account name of Guest and a password that is null. Additional user accounts can be created by the administrator or someone with administrative authority. All default local and domain user, group, and computer accounts will have a description indicating that they are built into the system. The following list outlines built-in local groups:

- *Administrators*—This group is the ultimate authority over the Windows 2000 system. Other personnel with either authority to access information on this system fully or to administer the system should be added to this group.

- *Backup Operators*—There are no default members of this group because quite often it is not necessary or mission-critical to back up data on a workstation system. Backup operators can log in locally, read/write all data on the system, and shut down the computer. You may consider the backup operators an alternative to the Power Users group for personnel who simply need access to all resources on the system, but do not require administrative authority for user accounts and installed applications.

- *Guests*—By default, the only user belonging to the Guests group is the guest account. Guest users cannot create a user or group, but they can view all users and groups on the system. Similarly, guests cannot create or change items in Device Manager, performance logs, or services and applications, but the guests can see all of these items, which means that they can discern the exact configuration of the system. In high-security areas, this may be a problem. The good news is that the guest cannot even access Disk Management, Add/Remove Hardware, or the Date/Time applet within the Control Panel. Many restrictions are in place that enable the guest user to view, but not to change, system configuration settings, so be aware of potential security issues. Additionally, remember that the guest user is by default a member of the Everyone group. By default, the Everyone group is allowed full control access to every file and folder on the computer system. Again, be aware that guests who log on locally cannot only view the configuration of the system, but also have access to the entire contents of the hard drive. At the very least, you may consider removing everyone from full control capability for each drive on the system.

- *Power Users*—Nobody is assigned to the Power Users group automatically. Power Users have the ability to create and modify user accounts and also to install applications. Power users cannot see other user files and folders. Power users can make system changes, such as modifying the registry or performing disk management functions.

- *Replicator*—This is an underlying group whose sole purpose is to support file replication in a domain environment. Real people should never be members of the Replicator group because members of this group exist for the sole purpose of performing automated replication functions.

- *Users*—The Users group is the default user group for all user accounts in the system. Don't confuse this with the Everyone group because members of the Users group can be moved to other groups. The Users group is simply a handy storage place for users to be, especially in a small environment where complex user group assignments are not necessary.

TIP: *By default, all of these groups will exist on any Windows 2000 system—domain member, controller, or professional workstation. Be aware that in a domain environment, the Domain Users group is automatically added to the Users group. The Domain Administrators group is also added to the Administrators group. This can be a good thing and a bad thing. If you do not want domain users to be able to log on to a given machine, remove the Domain Users group from the Local Users group. On the other hand, if your Enterprise administrator suddenly is unable to administer a system on the domain, more than likely the Domain Administrators group has been removed from the Local Administrators group, or the Enterprise Administrators group has been removed from the Domain Administrators group.*

Restrictions are in place on what built-in accounts and groups can be modified or deleted. These are safety measures to make it less likely for you to accidentally lock yourself out of the domain. A prime example is that the administrator account cannot be deleted or even disabled. It can, however, be renamed. Renaming the administrator account is usually recommended in order to increase security.

This is a great new feature that is seldom used simply because, historically, we've never been able to rename the master or authority account for any network operating system (NOS), except for Unix. Face it—any hacker will automatically seek the administrative or root authority account because that account is always the quickest road to absolute dominion over a network's resources. In the Windows NT world, this is Administrator; NetWare has Supervisor; and Unix has Root. Changing the administrator account name just made it more difficult for hackers to penetrate the network, but only if the account name is changed by an administrator first.

TIP: *It is also a good idea to create a new account called Administrator as a carrot for hackers. Assign it specific Deny access and then audit its every move.*

System Groups

Windows 2000 creates another set of groups that are somewhat more complex and tricky to deal with. These are called system groups, and basically, you have no control of who is actively a member of these groups. These groups do, however, come in handy sometimes because they can be assigned resource access in just the same way that other groups are. When you assign resource access (covered in detail in Chapter 9), you'll notice that these system groups can be assigned access to files and folders as shown in Figure 4.3, but you will never be

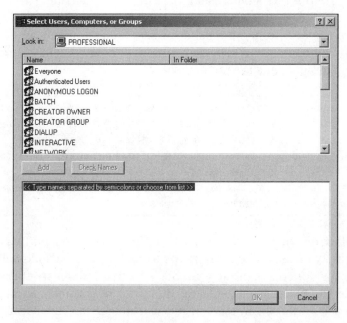

Figure 4.3   Several system groups can be assigned permissions to resources on a Windows 2000 system.

able to modify group membership. Try to remember that membership in these groups can be transient in nature because the members are usually added and removed based upon the way that the system is accessed and specifically, what is done.

The groups shown in the following list are not a complete list of those created in Windows 2000, but they are groups that can be used during your daily administrative job.

- *Everyone*—This group contains everyone who has a user account currently on the network. Be very careful how you assign resource access to the Everyone group simply because Everyone also includes Guest, which you might want to restrict somewhat due to the transient nature of the account. Also be aware that as soon as you share a folder or resource, the Everyone group is given full control over the resource by default. Unless you just don't care about who can access that information and what they can destroy, changing this permission should be the first thing you do after sharing a resource.

- *Authenticated Users*—Authenticated users are very similar to the Everyone group in that members include anyone who has a user account. The difference here is subtle. In a nondomain environment, users who attempt to log in to the system without an account are automatically allowed into the system as long as the guest account is enabled. The hitch is that they are given the same rights and privileges as members of the Guest group. This could be a problem if you've assigned the Everyone group access to sensitive information on the network. The Authenticated Users group can be used instead of the Everyone group because it will only contain members who truly have a legitimate nonguest user account on the system.

- *Batch*—Members of the Batch group basically have the ability to execute scripts and batch files. This can be an advantage in situations where all other script and command-line functionality and access has been restricted.

- *Network*—This group contains members who have a current network connection to some resource on the computer system. This group can be used to assign network-only access to resources. This would be ideal, for instance, on a server where you do not want local users to access the printer simply because such mundane tasks are best handled across the network rather than committing server resources to the task.

- *Interactive*—The members of this group are simply those who are currently logged onto the computer locally. This again would be ideal for allowing resource access to occur only with locally logged-on people. A great example would be to grant only Interactive members access to the WinNT directory on the hard drive, and to deny Network System group members access to this same folder. This, in effect, will allow only locally logged-on users to access the Windows system files.

- *Anonymous Logon*—While describing the Authenticated Users group, we covered a situation where a user can log in to the system without actually having a user account. Users who are automatically granted guest privileges in this manner are added to the Anonymous Logon group because they have not been formally authenticated into the system. A perfect application for using the Anonymous Logon group would be to create a customized logon script that notifies the user that they are a guest on the system and displays a nondisclosure screen where clicking on the OK button signifies acceptance.

- *Dialup*—Members of the Dialup group are similar to the Network group because they have active dial-up connections to the system.

- *Terminal Server User*—Members of the Terminal Server User group are just like the Dialup and Network group members except that they have an active connection to the terminal server. Again, remember that even though this and the Dialup groups are created on every Windows 2000 system, only Windows 2000 servers are capable of dial-up and terminal server services.

Domain Users, Groups, and Computers

Within a Windows 2000 domain, you will spend most of your time within the MMC Active Directory Users And Computers console working with organizational units (OUs), users, groups, computers, and a new-and-improved group policy editor. Windows group and system policies have been unified into a single interface along with a plethora of new features and capabilities. These Group Policy features are enough to warrant a separate chapter—Chapter 5—and certainly even enough for a completely separate book.

A Closer Look at the Active Directory Users And Computers Console

First, you can access the Active Directory Users And Computers console by either clicking the Start menu and selecting Programs|Administrative Tools|Active Directory Users And Computers or clicking the Start menu, selecting Run, and typing "DSA.MSC".

Any Windows 2000 domain administrator will gladly tell you that they spend a lot of their administrative time with this MMC console. Before we move directly into domain user, group, and computer administration, we should spend a few moments looking at the Active Directory Users And Computers console so that we can get a better idea of how it's laid out, how it works, and how you can plan and implement your Windows 2000 domain.

TIP: *Also, for you admins whose territory requires some walking between rooms, floors, or offices, remember that Windows 2000 has a new feature called Run As. It only works on Windows 2000 systems, but it is a definite timesaver. Let's say that you trip across a situation where a user needs to be added to a group in order to access certain resources and you are some distance from your system or any other computer that has the appropriate admin tools installed. With a little planning, you can make sure that DSA.MSC is loaded on every system on the network. When you need to, you can access the Active Directory Users And Computers console in one of two ways: log out the current user and log back in as administrator, or better yet, click the Start Menu, select Run, and type "CMD" (or just get yourself to a command prompt). Then, type the following:*

```
Runas /user:<domainname>\<adminname> dsa.msc
```

The <domainname> is the domain that contains the user account that needs to be modified, and the <adminname> is the administrator or admin equivalent login name that has permissions to modify this particular name or OU. The system will prompt for a password and will then run the program.

In Chapter 3, we discussed different ways and reasons for naming domains and OUs. Those same organizational ideas can be implemented into user groups as well. In fact, many of the ways you can manage and coordinate OUs will be mirrored by the organizational structure of groups. This is because OUs have Group Policy capabilities, and user groups don't. In the end, if a user group requires a separate Group Policy application, the best way to handle the situation would be to create a new OU and put the group inside that OU. OUs and Group Policies are discussed in detail in Chapter 5, but in the meantime, we need to look at how the Active Directory Users And Computers console works in order to better understand how we can lay out our network.

Nearly everything within the Active Directory Users And Computers console is one of the following six types of objects that can be added, modified, and administered:

- *Contact* objects contain information similar to what you would see in the contacts database within Microsoft Outlook or within the old address CARDFILE application used with Windows 3.1 and Windows 95. All of the information you'll see here can be found within user account properties also. The difference is that a contact cannot log in to the domain. Contacts exist within Active Directory for multiple purposes, all of them currently untapped. Microsoft has aggressive plans to unveil new interoperability and business-planning applications that will take advantages of non-systems-related information, such as contacts.

- *Computer* objects are all computers that are domain members. The computer machine account name is shown on the window.

- *Group* objects can reside within containers or within OUs, and they can contain users, groups, contacts, and computers. The reason contacts may be included is for organizational purposes only. The reason that computers are included here is because Group Policies (which are anchored at the OU level) can apply to either computers or users, or both.

- *Organizational unit* objects cannot reside within standard containers. They can, however, live as a child object of the domain controller, and also within other OUs. OUs can contain users, groups, contacts, printers, shares, computers, and other OUs.

- *Printer* objects are representations of shared printers on the network. After a printer has been shared to the network, it can also be published as a share within Active Directory. This allows Active Directory searches to find it. In a small network, you won't notice much difference, but in a large network, this is a wonderful administrative timesaver. To illustrate how Active Directory published printers can be of benefit, imagine you administer a network where a single printer was originally installed on one server, but was recently moved to a different server. While installing the networked printer on the users' machines, it is much easier to perform an Active Directory search to quickly find the printer, rather than manually browse the network or type in the server and printer name.

- *User* objects are exactly what they seem. They contain all of the information you would see in the contact object, plus information necessary to administer a domain account. Users can log on to the domain over the network. User objects can reside in any container within the Active Directory Users And Computers console, but they are most often placed within OUs for structure and administrative purposes.

- *Shared folder* objects are very similar to printer objects in that they present a published alias available for Active Directory searches. Shared printer objects seem to be more widely used than shared folders because shared folders are usually associated with mapped drives, which can be defined in the user profile and also in login scripts.

In looking at the Active Directory Users And Computers console, you'll notice that there is a single domain and several items with folder icons next to them. These are built-in containers that are created automatically when Active Directory is installed. Table 4.1 lists these containers and their default contents.

If you view the advanced settings, two more containers appear: LostAndFound and System. The LostAndFound container is a repository for orphaned or lost objects within the Active Directory Users And Computers Tree. Objects find themselves in the LostAndFound container most often during replication when replication has failed in some way or another. A conceivable situation would be where

Table 4.1   Built-in containers within the Active Directory Users And Computers console.

Container Name	Description
Builtin	The Builtin container contains all of the built-in local groups in the domain. You would see this same list of groups within Computer Management. User members of these groups will not be able to administer domain resources. The Builtin container can only contain computers, groups, and users.
Computers	The Computers container contains all of the computers belonging to the domain except the server itself. The Computers container can contain computers, contacts, users, groups, printers, and shared folders.
ForeignSecurityPrincipals	The ForeignSecurityPrincipals container is a repository for security identifiers (SIDs) associated with other domains. The ForeignSecurityPrincipals container can contain computers, contacts, users, groups, printers, and shared folders.
Users	The Users container is the default repository for all built-in domain user and group accounts. The Users container can contain computers, contacts, users, groups, printers, and shared folders.

the Global Catalog (GC) needs to delete an object, and the only problem is that, according to the remote GC, the object doesn't exist because the instructions to create it didn't make it across the wire during replication. All items in LostAndFound will be one of the following types of objects:

- Computer, contact, group, printer, user, shared folder (standard items)
- Licensing site settings
- Microsoft Message Queuing (MSMQ) or routing link
- Connection
- Site Settings, Site, Site Link, Site Link Bridge, or Sites container
- Organizational unit
- Server or Servers container
- Subnet

As you can see, many different types of objects, which apply to areas other than simply Users And Computers, can show up in LostAndFound. The System container, on the other hand, is a veritable cornucopia of information about various functions on the system, but nothing that really comes to bear while you administer, maintain, or monitor the network. You cannot modify any of the current settings, but you can add computers, contacts, groups, printers, users, and shared folders to it. Most of the contents are heavy-duty; however, you may want to take a look at the Internet Protocol (IP) Security Policies container in order to get a better idea of what's possible with Internet Protocol Security (IPSec) (more info on that is in Chapter 20). You can't perform any specific administrative frills from the System container, but you may consider viewing the advanced settings just for the LostAndFound container. Any items that show up in LostAndFound are good indicators that something is broken and needs to be looked at.

You'll also notice that one item is missing from this list: domain controllers. The Domain Controllers container is the only built-in OU in the system. It contains all of the domain controllers for the current domain. OUs are still containers, but they are different from standard containers in that the icon shown has a half-open book on top of the folder icon. When in doubt, you can check the properties of any container. If a Group Policy tab appears, you are dealing with an OU.

It is also possible to filter the objects and containers that you see in the Active Directory Users And Computers console by setting a filter from the Action menu. You can only view one or more of the following:

• Users

• Groups

• Contacts

• Computers

• Printers

• Shared folders

• Services

Another option is that you can create a custom filter based upon certain criteria from any one of previous items.

One more pretty nifty tidbit about the Active Directory Users And Computers console will definitely come in handy in larger environments. You can delegate administration of particular OUs. The specifics are covered in "Immediate Solutions" in this chapter, but the basics are that you can essentially create an OU, place a departmental or other logical group of users and computers within that OU, and delegate its administration to anyone in the domain. This is a huge plus when dealing with high user turnover or never-happy department heads who think that they just can't get any service or reasonable turnaround from the IT department. Delegating user and group administration in such a manner is great because it definitely requires less training for the new administrator and still keeps them out of a lot of trouble spots. Group Policy is definitely the most dangerous place for a delegatory administrator, so make sure that both you and the new admin are up to speed on Chapter 5.

Domain Users

Anything that can be created within the Active Directory Users And Computers console can be done by either right-clicking the parent object that will host the new object and then selecting New from the pop-up menu, or by selecting the parent object and then selecting Action from the menu bar.

NOTE: *Domain controllers do not support local users. This is primarily for security reasons, but it does come in handy in that you no longer have to coordinate server administration between two separate sets of users and groups.*

The system by default will create an administrator account and guest user when Active Directory is installed. Additional user accounts may be added for installed services, such as IIS, Terminal Services, and Windows Media Services. These accounts are not intended for you or anyone else to log in to the system. They are intended as service-related accounts that enable more complex functions to take place while still enabling some amount of administrative control.

User Properties

Similar to a local user account, all you really need is a login name in order to create a user account. Certain domain security policies, such as minimum password, may prevent you from creating accounts with certain properties, such as no passwords. Again, policies of this nature are discussed in Chapter 5. In the meantime, I will discuss specific user account properties and attributes that are slightly more than meets the eye. With the exception of passwords, all of the following properties can be viewed by double-clicking a user name from within the Active Directory Users And Computers console and then navigating through the tabs at the top of the window.

- *Display Name*—This is a handy feature for domain user accounts where the display name that shows both in active connections and also in the Active Directory Users And Computers console is something other than the specific account name. This is great when it's better to recognize people by something other than their full name or account name. Nicknames, aliases, or titles can be good substitutes and are a great way to differentiate between user accounts that are similar in name or nature.

- *Logon Name*—The logon name must be unique to Active Directory. What this means is that you can have more than one Joseph Smith in the directory, but we can only have one jsmith. Also, the login names can be a maximum of 20 characters, where any letter, number, and symbol can apply except for the following: / \ [ ] : ; | = + * ? < >.

- *Change Password*—This is the only feature not available from the Properties window of the user. As an administrator, you can change the password for someone else's account by right-clicking the account name from within the Active Directory Users And Computers console and then selecting Reset Password from the pop-up menu. Logon names are not case sensitive, but passwords are. Therefore, you may want to be aware of this when resetting passwords. Passwords can be a maximum of 128 characters, and they have the same restrictions as listed for logon name.

- *UPN Domain*—This shows the domain alias for the UPN. It defaults to the currently administered domain. You can change it to another domain, but this will not change the domain to which the user logs on.

- *Logon Hours*—This is a button that allows you to define the specific hours when users are allowed to log on. This is primarily a security feature in order to prevent users from logging on at inappropriate times. Logon hours can be modified by highlighting the hours and days affected and then selecting the appropriate Allow/Disallow Access radio button.

- *Logon To*—This security feature lets you restrict the computers that users can log on to. In the "User Profiles" section, we discussed roaming profiles and how it can be a problem when a user logs in to a system that doesn't have all of the applications installed, but the icons come through in the profile. You can reduce the likelihood of this becoming a problem by allowing roamable users to log on only to specific machines that have all applicable software installed. On the flip side, you can restrict users to log on to only their own computers to prevent unauthorized access to hardware and software. One word of warning is needed, however. This feature can be enabled, but it will not work properly unless NetBIOS Enhanced User Interface (NetBEUI) is installed on every applicable computer on the network. Unfortunately, the interface does not allow for network browsing and requires that you enter the computer name and add it to a list so that you won't know if it works until you try it.

- *Account Is Locked Out*—This feature kicks in when a user attempts to log in to the system and fails after x number of attempts. The number of failed attempts is configured as a Group Policy applying to the domain. When the account is locked out, the user is unable to log in for a specified time that is also configured in the same Group Policy. This feature is simply a checkbox within the account properties. If the user requires immediate access, the account can be reenabled by having the administrator or someone with an administrative equivalent clearing this checkbox.

- *User Must Change Password At Next Logon/User Cannot Change Password*—These are actually two features that cannot be used at the same time. The only thing you need to be aware of is that users cannot change the password at the next logon if they cannot change the password at all. Microsoft helps you here in Local User Manager by graying out one option when the other is chosen.

- *Password Never Expires*—Again, this is another feature that is tied into the Group Policy associated with domain security. The domain security policy can be configured to require that the password be changed at a preconfigured span of time. Of course, it's a good idea to implement this feature on any network, along with other security features that we'll discuss in the next chapter. The only time that you should use this particular feature is when you have designated an automatic account that handles system, service, or scheduled functions, such as any virus, tape backup, or anything residing on the scheduler applet. The system will warn users when their password is about to expire, and, when it has expired, they simply will not be able to log in without making a password change. Automated processes, such as backup or scheduler, aren't programmed to react to such prompts, and they will fail simply because they cannot access the required resources. Monitoring automated tasks isn't always a top priority, and such failures can occur for days or weeks before detection. It is better to set the password on these accounts to never expire so that nobody gets fired when no tape backup is available.

- *Store Password Using Reversible Encryption*—This feature offers compatibility with Shiva devices, such as a LAN Rover or dial-up server. These devices use Shiva Password Authentication Protocol (SPAP) to authenticate users into their system prior to passing the credentials on to Active Directory for authentication. SPAP is a better authentication method than plain text, but it is not as solid as Challenge Handshake Authentication Protocol (CHAP). Normally, devices such as Shiva boxes will synchronize passwords with Active Directory when you change passwords. Be aware, however (and this has been a feature for many years), that, if you change your network password during an active Shiva session, the password change will not synchronize automatically.

- *Smart Card Is Required For Interactive Logon*—Smart cards are a newfangled twist on an older technology. Once upon a time, higher-end personal computer (PC) and server applications had a key that attached to the parallel port on the back of the computer. The application basically queried the parallel port for the correct pinout and started the program. Some applications even customized the parallel pinout to indicate certain features and licensing privileges. This ensured that the software wasn't being bootlegged. Windows 2000 supports a similar technology called smart cards where specific smart card hardware is installed on the computer. A card—or key—must be inserted into the card reader, and a personal identification number (PIN) must be entered in order for logon to occur. Other systems can be configured where the card is never removed from the system, and the users are instead given a device that randomly generates an appropriate PIN number for them. Smart card technology is really great for high-security environments, such as banks and insurance agencies. The card keys themselves can be somewhat annoying to administer, but this technology is popping up in some very large, and very prominent, corporations in America. More information on smart cards is available in Chapter 20. In the meantime, this option must be checked in order to enable the smart card driver to intercept the logon process.

- *Account Is/Is Not Trusted For Delegation*—This is another Windows 2000 specialized Kerberos feature specifically created to allow or disallow Component Object Model (COM) objects to receive user authentication information through an intermediary computer. In other words, if it's OK to have an application residing on a different computer that impersonates your usernames and passwords, this feature is great. This would be necessary basically when a specialized application server is configured to call another application that requires authentication to function. If this occurs within your environment, more than likely you will already know it because the application or developers should be aware of the requirements. If this is not the case, it's a good idea to flag all accounts as not being trusted for delegation.

- *Use DES Encryption Types For This Account*—Data Encryption Standard (DES) encryption is supported within Windows 2000 under the IPSec umbrella with either one or two 56-bit encryption keys. Flagging an account to use DES encryption is required to properly implement IPSec.

- *Do Not Require Kerberos Preauthentication*—This Kerberos feature really requires some knowledge of the Kerberos world, which is covered in Chapter 20. Basically, the only time that this feature needs to be checked is when the system is using a non-Microsoft Kerberos implementation.

- *Manager/Direct Reports*—This contains information about the organizational structure and specifically how this account fits into it. Managers can be chosen from other accounts and contacts within Active Directory. Reports are then automatically placed into the appropriate managers' accounts.

- *Published Certificates*—Again, certificates are covered in detail in Chapter 20. Suffice it to say that certificates are a means of temporarily establishing trusts between two objects and bypassing authentication during the process.

Usually, a certificate authority system issues a certificate to a host computer where the certificate basically says that another system is safe. You might have additional experience with certificates in the Windows 2000 world when installing device drivers. If a certificate does not exist that indicates that the driver has been tested and is compliant with Microsoft standards, a warning appears indicating that Windows 2000 cannot determine if the driver is from a trustworthy source. Another scenario would exist where an application vendor has earned and purchased a certificate from a certificate authority in order to vouch for the stability of the product. Certificates can exist between users, computers, and programs.

- *Group Memberships*—These can be administered from within the user account properties or from within the properties of the group itself.

- *Primary Group*—This has more than likely been grayed out on your system. Primary groups only come into play when POSIX support or Windows 2000 Services For Macintosh have been installed on the server. A user's primary group must be defined as a global or universal group that has its sources in the same domain as the user account. When files and folders are created by POSIX apps or Macintosh clients, the owners are shown as the Primary group in order to allow access and administration by other operating systems and applications.

- *Remote Access Permissions (Dialin or VPN)*—Remote Access Service (RAS) and Virtual Private Network (VPN) are covered more thoroughly in Chapter 19. A domain user must be allowed access here in order to access the network either using dial-up networking or using a VPN. By default, several options will be grayed out until RAS is installed.

- *Callback Options*—These are set by default to No Callback. Callback is a security feature where a user calls in only long enough to identify him or herself and then hangs up. The system then calls the user's computer system back to confirm and establish the connection. The callback phone number can either be defined here or set by the user on the fly, but only when RRAS (Routing And Remote Access Service) is installed.

- *Assign Static IP Address*—This is only available when RAS is installed. When dial-up users are connected, it is possible to configure the system to provide them with a static IP address so that they may be able to use specific applications or functions that have been configured for a specific address.

- *Apply Static Routes*—This is primarily used for one-way demand-dial situations. Static routes are used to ensure that outbound traffic goes in only predefined directions. More information on static routing is covered in Chapter 11.

- *Security*—This covers users and groups that have various abilities to modify the account in question. Permissions themselves are covered in Chapter 9.

- *Starting Program*—Back in the old days, if you wanted an application to start or run automatically, you either had to fiddle with each computer on the network, or you had to add its execution to the login script. This new feature allows us to start an application automatically on an account by account basis.

- *Connect Client Drives, Printers And Default To Main Client Printer At Logon*—Basically, all of these are options to connect drives and printers during logon. The one exception, however, is the first one–connecting client drives–which is an interoperability hook to Citrix clients.

- *Terminal Services Timeout And Reconnection, Remote Control, And Profile*—Terminal Services is covered in detail in Chapter 12. In the meantime, you can leave most of these settings alone regardless of whether you're running Terminal Server on the network or not. The only setting change that I'd recommend is to change the End A Disconnected Session to something other than Never. Sometimes terminal server sessions disconnect for any number of unknown reasons, such as the client machine rebooting or network traffic killing the connection. When this happens, the terminal server still has a session that's alive and waiting for instructions, but there is absolutely no way to reconnect to that session. The terminal server (which can be any Windows 2000 server nowadays) then ends up supporting a full session—desktop, user profile, and settings included—indefinitely. Just one of these disconnected sessions can slow down the server and cause Terminal Services to become discombobulated in time. More than one disconnected session will bring the server to its knees for no visible reason. Rather than force yourself to check for orphaned sessions every few days, just change this feature to read anything other than Never.

Take a moment to look at Table 4.2. You'll notice that, as far as features are concerned, domain user properties definitely win out. Although Windows 2000 Professional and Server appear to be similar, the additional abilities and features that are inherent with Windows 2000 Server still make it a much more robust and flexible networked system than Windows 2000 Professional. This is not to say that Windows 2000 Professional networking performs anything less than excellently. A more appropriate term would be to say that Windows 2000 Professional is not designed to be a network server.

Table 4.2 Account properties comparison between contacts, domain user accounts, and local accounts for Windows 2000 Professional and Windows 2000 Server.

	Contacts	Windows 2000 Domain Users	Windows 2000 Professional	Server
First Name	X	X		
Initials		X		
Last Name	X	X		
Full Name		X	X	
Display Name	X	X		
Description	X	X	X	X
Office	X	X		
Multiple Phone Numbers	X	X		
Email	X	X		
Multiple Web Pages	X	X		
Street Address	X	X		
PO Box	X	X		
City	X	X		
State	X	X		
Zip	X	X		
Country	X	X		
User Logon Name		X		
UPN Domain			X	
Logon Hours		X		
Logon To		X		
Account Is Locked Out		X	X	X
User Must Change Password At Next Logon		X	X	X
User Cannot Change Password		X	X	X
Password Never Expires		X	X	X
Store Password Using Reversible Encryption			X	
Account Is Disabled		X	X	X
Smart Card Is Required For Interactive Logon		X		
Account Is Trusted For Delegation		X		

(continued)

Table 4.2   Account properties comparison between contacts, domain user accounts, and local accounts for Windows 2000 Professional and Windows 2000 Server (continued).

	Contacts	Domain Users	Windows 2000 Professional	Windows 2000 Server
Account Is Sensitive And Cannot Be Delegated		X		
Use DES Encryption Types For This Account			X	
Does Not Require Kerberos Preauthentication		X		
Account Expiration		X		
User Profile Path		X	X	X
Logon Script		X	X	X
Home Folder Local Path Or Drive Connection		X	X	X
Multiple Home #s	X	X		
Multiple Pagers	X	X		
Multiple Mobile #s	X	X		
Multiple Fax #s	X	X		
Multiple IP Phones	X	X		
Notes	X	X		
Title	X	X		
Department	X	X		
Company	X	X		
Manager	X	X		
Direct Reports	X	X		
Published Certificates		X		
Group Memberships	X	X	X	X
Primary Group		X		
Remote Access Dialin And VPN Permissions			X	X
Callback Options		X		
Assign Static IP Address		X		
Apply Static Routes		X		
Security	X	X		
Starting Program		X		X

(continued)

Table 4.2 **Account properties comparison between contacts, domain user accounts, and local accounts for Windows 2000 Professional and Windows 2000 Server** *(continued).*

	Contacts	Domain Users	Windows 2000 Professional	Windows 2000 Server
Connect Client Drives At Logon		X		X
Connect Client Printers At Logon		X		X
Default To Main Client Printer		X		X
Terminal Services Timeout And Reconnection		X		X
Terminal Services Remote Control		X		X
Terminal Services User Profile		X		X

User Profiles

User profiles can be local only or roaming, plus user profiles can be customizable or mandatory. A local-only user profile only exists on a single computer. A roaming user profile is available no matter where on the network the user logs on. A customizable user profile records the changes to the environment each time that the user logs off; this allows the last saved state of the environment to be returned to her at the next logon. A mandatory user profile does not save changes made during a logon session; this means the original mandatory environment will be returned to the user at the next logon. A mandatory profile can be shared by multiple users because no customization is possible.

User profiles from Windows 2000 and Windows NT are compatible with each other, but user profiles from Windows 98 or Windows 95 are not. Therefore, users can move from Windows 2000 clients to Windows NT clients and back while (for the most part) maintaining the same environment throughout. However, after a user moves to a Windows 98 or Windows 95 system, he will not be presented with the normal profile, but rather with the default local profile for that system. Both Windows 98 and Windows 95 and Windows 2000 and Windows NT user profiles can exist on the same network, and both types support roaming and mandatory configuration. However, to keep confusion to a minimum, users should stick with one system type or the other.

The first time that a user logs in to a computer, the system looks for a roaming profile on a network share for that user. The path to the storage location of a user's roaming profile is defined in his domain user account's properties. If no roaming user profile is found, a local user profile is created by duplicating the local default user profile. When a local user profile is created on a Windows 2000 system (whether from a copy of the local default user profile or from a copy of

4. Users, Groups, and Computers

the roaming user profile from its network storage location), it is placed in a subfolder of the \Documents and Settings directory, which has the same name as the user account. If a roaming user profile path is defined for a user, but no profile is stored there, when the system checks, the newly created user profile is copied to the network share location. The next time that the user logs on anywhere, his roaming user profile will be found and loaded. If a roaming user profile path is not defined for the user, the newly created user profile will remain a local profile, which will only be available on the one system where it is created. To transform a local user profile into a roaming user profile, just add a user profile path to the user account's properties. The next time that the user logs on and then logs off, the user's profile will become a roaming user profile stored on the provided network share path.

NOTE: *By default, all user profiles can be customized by the user. This means that all changes made to the environment during a logon session will be saved when the user logs out. This is true both for local and roaming user profiles.*

The only user account that does not have or cannot have its own unique user profile is the Guest account. Each time that the Guest account is used to log on, the default user profile is given to that user. No changes made by the guest user are saved, and no user profile directory is created.

Each time that a user logs on to a system, his roaming user profile will be cached locally. This means the next time the user logs onto the same system, only the changed items will be transferred across the network. This also allows users to log on even if the domain controller cannot be contacted to authenticate them. However, if the user profile is a mandatory profile and the domain controller cannot be contacted, the user will not be allowed to log on.

Roaming user profiles are created or defined simply by providing a Universal Naming Convention (UNC) path statement for the storage location for the profile. This is done on the Profile tab, shown in Figure 4.4, of a user account's Properties dialog box, accessed through the Active Directory Users And Computers console. A UNC path statement takes the form of \\<*servername*>\<*sharename*>\ <*directoryname*>, where *directoryname* is often the user account name.

NOTE: *The directory name can be a folder tree path as well, such as \users\profiles\admins\department1\jsmith.*

If you examine the contents of a user profile's storage folder, you'll see the following subfolders:

- *Application Data*—Contains application-specific data, such as configuration files, custom dictionaries, and file caches for Internet Explorer or Outlook Express

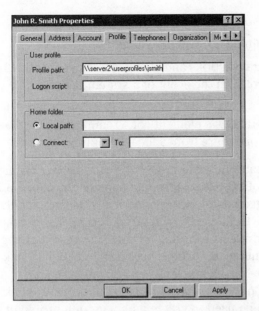

Figure 4.4 The Profile tab of a user account's Properties dialog box, accessed through the Active Directory Users And Computers console.

- *Cookies*—Contains the cookies accepted by the user
- *Desktop*—Contains the icons, files, shortcuts, and folders found on the desktop
- *Favorites*—Contains the list of bookmarked uniform resource locators (URLs) from Internet Explorer
- *Local Settings*—Contains user-specific application data, history data, and temporary files
- *My Documents*—Contains a user's saved files
- *NetHood*—Contains network mappings and items in Network Places
- *PrintHood*—Contains printer mappings and items in the Printer folder
- *Recent*—Contains links to the most recently used resources (documents and folders)
- *SendTo*—Contains items found under the Send To option of the right-click pop-up menu
- *Start Menu*—Contains the user-specific portions of the Start menu
- *Templates*—Contains a user's templates

The user profile's storage folder also contains the following items:

- *Ntuser.dat*—A registry file containing user-specific data

- *Ntuser.dat.log*—A file that logs transactions and changes to a user profile for the purpose of re-creating the profile in the event of a system failure or element corruption

- *Ntuser.ini*—A configuration file that lists elements of a roaming profile that are not to be uploaded to a network share from a local computer

The system applet's User Profiles tab, shown in Figure 4.5, offers a few management functions. This tab lists all profiles stored or cached locally. Therefore, only the profiles for users who have logged on to the system locally will appear here. This interface can be used to delete local copies of local user profiles or roaming user profiles from the local hard drive. It can also be used to prevent changes made on the local machine to a roaming user profile from being uploaded back to its network share storage location. This is known as converting a roaming user profile to a local user profile. The Copy To button is used to duplicate an existing profile to a new location. This can be used to create a backup of a profile or to jump-start a new user's profile with something other than the default user profile.

Any profile can be converted to a mandatory profile simply by renaming the registry file from ntuser.dat to ntuser.man. This name change must be made in the main storage location of the profile (that is, the network share instead of a local cache in the case of a roaming user profile). After a profile is set to mandatory, no

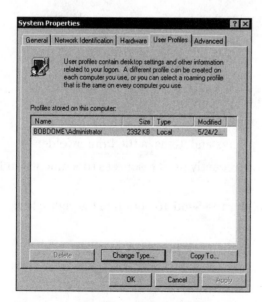

Figure 4.5   The User Profiles tab of the system applet.

changes made by the user during a logon session will be saved. To return a profile to a customizable state, just change the name of the registry file back to ntuser.dat.

Logon Scripts

Logon scripts can be created using Notepad or any editor capable of saving a text file. By default, logon scripts should be located in the %systemroot%\SYSVOL\ sysvol\<domainname>\scripts directory. (%systemroot% is an environment variable that represents the drive and path that contains the \WinNT directory.) This is because everything located in the SYSVOL directory tree is replicated to every other domain controller within the domain. This is how we can be assured that all login scripts and domain policies remain the same from one domain controller to another. You can set logon scripts to reside elsewhere by changing the location within the user account properties under the Profile tab. Scripts can be batch files (*.bat), command files (*.cmd), or Visual Basic scripts (*.vbs). If you don't know much about Visual Basic, Jscript, batch commands, or scripting in general, don't worry; more information is available in Chapter 16.

Batch files usually are used to map drives for the users. We can add logic and display information on the monitor, but the best thing to remember is that keeping it simple keeps it easy to troubleshoot.

Variables can be added to batch files in order to customize or add logic to the script. Variables come in two flavors: environmental and user-defined. Environmental variables are defined and maintained automatically by the system. The following is a list of environmental variables specifically used for logon scripts:

- *%userprofile%*—The local path to the user's profile.

- *%allusersprofile%*—The path to the profile located in the All Users folder.

- *%computername%*—The NetBIOS name of the current computer. If NetBIOS is not installed, the name will appear as the name in computer properties.

- *%homedrive%*—The drive letter that points to the home directory as defined in the account properties.

- *%homepath%*—The UNC of the home directory.

- *%logonserver%*—The NetBIOS name of the authenticating server.

- *%os%*—The operating system.

- *%userdomain%*—The domain that the user is logged on to.

- *%username%*—The username.

Several dozen other standard disk operating system (DOS) variables can be used within login scripts. Again, these will be discussed more thoroughly in Chapter 16. In the meantime, you can see all of the possible current variables by opening

4. Users, Groups, and Computers

a command prompt and typing "set" followed by a the Enter key. Variables in general can be viewed, modified, and defined using the **set** command. To view an existing variable, open a command prompt (Start Menu|Run|cmd), and type the word "set", followed by the variable name without the percent signs. Percent signs are used only within batch or command files in order to alert the system that you are referencing a variable as opposed to a normal word. Modifying a variable is the same process of **set** followed by the variable name and "=" followed by the new variable definition. The following code snippet is an example of what you can do with a logon script.

```
@echo off
ifmember "accounting"
        if not errorlevel 1 goto everyone
        net use p: \\payroll\shared
        goto everyone
:everyone
        net use j: \\fnps\apps
        set logdir=\\%logonserver%\profiles
    echo Hello there %username%, the time is %time% on %date%>>%logdir%
      \%username%.dat
        echo Hello there %username%, the time is %time% on %date%
    attrib %logdir%\%username%.dat +h
```

Line 2 demonstrates the use of the ifmember application that is available in the Windows 2000 Server Resource Kit. The ifmember app checks to see if the user is a member of a user group and performs the logic that follows. Login scripts can also be created using a program called KiXtart, which is a much more advanced, Basic-like scripting language. KiXtart is also in the Windows 2000 Server Resource Kit. I've indented lines 3 to 5 in order to make it easier to understand and read. If the current user is not a member of the accounting group, the script will go to the **everyone** subroutine, which starts on line 6. If the user is a member of the accounting group, a drive mapping is created for the shared directory on the payroll server, and the script will then execute the **everyone** subroutine, which starts on line 6. The purpose of the **everyone** subroutine is basically to perform those tasks that belong to everyone on the domain. We start by mapping a drive to the apps share on the fnps server. Then, we define a variable called **logdir** as what appears to be a literal path to the profiles share on the server that the user logged on to. The first **echo** statement uses several different features available in batch files. The **echo** command simply repeats everything following the word, replacing literal variable listings with their real world equivalents. The **%time%** and **%date%** variables are standard environmental variables that have been available since DOS 4. The **>>%logdir%\%username%.dat** piece of this line simply redirects that echo output from the window to a file named after the user that is located in the profiles directory of the logon server. The **>>** will specifically create the file if it is not there, and it will add this information to the file if it is there. The purpose of this statement is to produce a log file for every user that tells me when she has logged onto the system. The final **echo** statement echoes the information on the window. The last line in the file, the **attrib** statement, changes the log file to be hidden.

This code was designed to be a working example. Perhaps a better definition for the **%logdir%** variable would be to define a more centralized server because the current **%logonserver%** variable may change when a user logs in to the domain through different domain controllers. The purpose of the little security log was simply to provide an easy and quick way of checking when a user is logging into the system. Security logs can be created to track this information, but they can be confusing and misleading to read. Again, finding a more centralized storage place for this file would be more ideal in order to provide a single place for lookups.

Windows 2000 logon scripts such as this will function for all Windows 2000 clients that log in to the domain. Windows NT and Windows 2000 both recognize the **ifmember** command. However, if you want Windows 9x clients to handle group membership logic within the login script, you'll probably need to use KiXtart.

One final note on login scripts is that you can define login and logout scripts within a Group Policy. This is an ideal way to get a better picture of user logon hours, but there's a hitch. These types of script definitions only work for Windows 2000 clients. If you have clients running Windows 9x and Windows NT, not only will you not be able to define a logoff script, but the logon scripts will have to be defined within the account properties and will need to have a .bat or .cmd extension on the file.

Home Folders

Home folders are more commonly known as home drives. Home folders are very simple to create, and they quite often eliminate the pressing need for login scripts. When defining the home folder within the user account properties, you may use any of the variables listed previously to make it easier and less annoying. As a matter of fact, I particularly encourage you to use the **%username%** variable in order to avoid annoyances and mistakes while entering account names.

Looking at all of the features available for account properties, it's a good idea to create a template user account for your more complex or often used user accounts. What you do is create a user as you normally would and call it "template", or some other name indicative of the role it plays. Make sure that it has all of the group memberships and accesses that you would want anybody in this particular group to have, and then disable it. When you need to add a user, simply right-click the template account, click Copy on the pop-up menu, and fill in the username blanks. Be sure to go back and enable the account, and then check that the home directory is changed appropriately and that the profiles are configured for the new user and not the template. If your company has a high turnover rate in certain departments, you might also consider simply disabling accounts rather than deleting them. Similar to copying a template, all you need to do is rename the account, enable it, make sure that the home folder and profiles are reconfigured, and you're set to go.

When an account is created, a SID is created for that account. All security privileges—such as file, folder, and resource permissions—are hooked into the SID attached to the account and not to the username or login name for the account. This is how we can essentially rename and recycle accounts without disrupting resource access.

Domain User Groups

Domain user groups are drastically different from local user groups in that they are *routable,* or essentially available outside of the boundaries of the server, domain controller, or domain. Basically, if a user requires access to multiple computers, membership to a domain user group is necessary in order to avoid creating user accounts on each computer. Similarly, if a user requires access to computers in multiple domains, membership to a domain user group is also necessary in order to avoid creating user accounts within each domain.

Group Types

Domain groups come in two types: security groups or distribution groups. Basically, security groups deal with permissions, access, authentication, and other stuff that makes up the nuts and bolts of the system. Almost every group that you deal with in Windows 2000 will be a security group.

Distribution groups, compared to security groups, are fluff. Windows 2000 distribution groups are just like Exchange or other email groups—just a bunch of people who are related enough to warrant a grouping for distribution or reference purposes. This is not to say that distribution groups aren't important; they just aren't where you're going to be spending the bulk of your administrative time. Distribution groups are useless until and unless they are referenced by applications specifically designed to interact with Active Directory. To date, these applications are few and far between. As usual, Microsoft continues to blaze the trail with current and forthcoming applications like Exchange 2000 and servers in the .NET suite of applications.

Group Scope

Every domain group must apply to a certain range or scope. A group's scope can be defined as domain local, global, or universal.

Domain local groups can contain members from any domain, but can access resources only in the domain that the group was created in. In a mixed mode domain, users, computers, and global groups can all be members of a domain local group. In a native mode domain, users, groups, global and universal groups from any domain, and other domain local groups can be members of a given domain local group.

Global groups can contain members only from the domain that the group was created in, but can access resources in any domain. In a mixed mode domain, user and computer accounts from the same domain can be members, but global groups that live in a native mode domain support users, computers, and global groups from the same domain.

Universal Security groups can contain members from any domain, can access resources in any domain, and are available only with native mode domains.

It's easy to get confused about which type of group can belong to which other types of groups. Hopefully, Figure 4.6 can help sort things out a bit. It's very tempting to just create universal groups and use nothing else. Although this might not be an issue in a smaller environment, it can be devastating in an enterprise

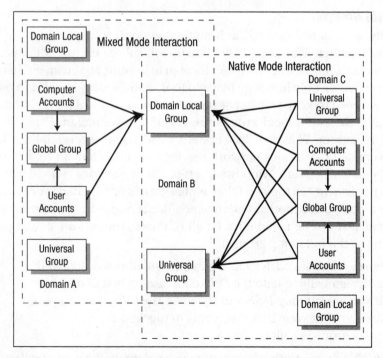

Figure 4.6   Mixed mode and native mode group interactions between domains A and B and domains B and C.

4. Users, Groups, and Computers

because universal group memberships are replicated to every GC server in the Active Directory tree. If your entire group memberships are universal groups, then a huge chunk of your Active Directory is also being replicated, which can cause bandwidth and timing issues. A better rule of thumb for both domain and local groups is that, in order to grant resource access, large things are usually stuffed into smaller things. What this means is that universal groups stuff into global groups or domain local groups. Global groups are stuffed into domain local groups in order to access data between domains.

Figure 4.6 shows that:

- Mixed mode domain user and computer accounts go into global groups

- Mixed mode domain global groups go into domain local groups

- Native mode computer and user accounts can go into global groups, domain local groups, or universal groups

- Native mode global groups can go into domain local groups or universal groups

- Native mode universal groups can go into domain local groups or other universal groups

Default Domain Groups

Several domain groups are created automatically when Active Directory is installed. Remember that Windows 2000 domain controllers do not administer local users through the Local User Manager located in Computer Manager. This is a good thing because we only have one place to look, and then again, this is a bad thing because we need to keep track of several different flavors of administrator groups. Basically, the same local groups are created in a domain as are in a standalone or workgroup Windows 2000 system. In addition, several domain local groups are created for various network services, such as Domain Name Service (DNS) admins, RAS servers, Windows Internet Naming Service (WINS) users, and certificate publishers. On top of all that, global groups are created for domain admins, domain computers, domain controllers, domain guests, domain users, Enterprise admins, and schema admins. Of all of these groups, you should pay special attention to the following groups:

- *DnsUpdateProxy*—Dynamic DNS has a feature that allows designated computers to dynamically update the DNS database on behalf of other computers. If you are running DNS and Dynamic Host Control Protocol (DHCP), make sure that your DHCP server is in this list. The DnsUpdateProxy group is a global group.

- *DHCP and WINS Users*—Both of these groups, by default, have no members. It is not necessary to add members to these groups unless you specifically need to deny or grant a small group of users access to use the DHCP and WINS servers. A possible application would be in a call center where agents do not require access to the Internet, but supervisors and managers do. In that case, adding the supervisors and managers groups to the DHCP and WINS Users groups is an ideal way of granting access without tampering with individual computers.

- *DNSAdmins and DHCP Administrators*—Both of these groups are empty by default. Domain and enterprise administrators will have, by default, the ability to administer DNS and DHCP. These groups should be used to delegate administrative authority for DNS and DHCP.

- *Domain Admins and Enterprise Admins*—Domain Admins defaults to the administrator. Enterprise Admins will also default to the administrator, but only in the forest root domain. An administrative-equivalent user account should at least be a member of the Domain Admins group.

Domain Computers

Administering computer accounts within a domain is relatively easy compared to user accounts. What you are essentially doing is allowing computers to join the domain. Don't forget that computers can provide resource access on the domain without having someone logged in at the time. In order to provide appropriate security, these computers must be members of the domain all by themselves, with or without a user logon. This is what domain computer administration is all about.

By default, all domain controllers are added to the domain and inserted into the Domain Controllers OU from the Active Directory Users And Computers console. All computers that are added to the domain are placed in the Computers folder. We recommend that the domain controllers remain where they are unless you need to delegate administration for the domain controller along with a specific OU.

Computers can join the domain in one of two ways. The first way is to log on to the computer as an administrator and, from within computer properties, join the domain. You need to be a local administrator equivalent on the computer in order to get to the Properties window for the computer, and the system will prompt you for the domain administrative account and password before the computer officially joins the domain. When the computer enters the domain, a computer account is automatically created within the Computers container in the Active Directory Users And Computers console. In order to keep things straight, it's probably a good idea to keep the computer in the same OU or container that has the user account for the primary user of that system. This is basically to give you a head start on troubleshooting Group Policy issues if and when they come along. If you are so lucky as to have a fairly stable homogenous network where the computer policies will all be the same, by all means, create an appropriate OU for all of your computers to live in, and proceed down the Group Policy trail.

The second way is, from the Active Directory Users And Computers console, add the computer account to the appropriate container or OU. When you are done, it will still be necessary to join the computer to the domain formally by changing the domain within Computer Properties.

For smaller networks, I prefer the first method because it gets everything done for me in one step. If you administer a large network, the second method is better because you can change the option for who can join the computer to the domain into another group, such as the built-in Local Administrators group. The local administrator can join the domain without requiring a full domain administrative logon.

Computer Account Options and Properties

The first option you have while creating a computer account is deciding whether or not to allow non-Windows 2000 systems to join the domain. Although it's great to be able to maintain a list of all computers on the network, there is no other reason for maintaining non-Windows 2000 systems within the Active Directory because Active Directory simply won't administer and maintain non-Windows 2000 or non-Windows NT network resources. The reason behind this is primarily security-based, which is certainly understandable if you consider the relative weakness of Windows 95 and 98 and the potential security breaches of having a security-feeble Windows 95 system be a member of a Windows 2000 domain.

After a computer account is created, we still have many customizable features available. There is a great set of features here. Unfortunately, most of the IT world focuses on users and groups, and a thorough balance of attention isn't paid to computer account properties. One of the first features to choose from is service delegation. This allows the local system services to request assistance from other server services. This is a subset feature similar to clustering and load balancing, so you will not see this on the system by default. Application-based load balancing and clustering applications do exist. However, the documentation will most likely instruct you to turn on this feature in order to allow the application's services to forward the proper requests to other servers. Also, don't forget that groups can contain computer accounts as well as user accounts and other groups, so you also have the option to add the computer account to a group. For inventory purposes, you may wish to record the location of the computer. You can modify the Active Directory schema to include other pieces of information in order to possibly implement an inventory system. These types of schema modifications are usually associated with development projects and are certainly not for the fainthearted. More information on schema modification is available in the *Windows 2000 Active Directory Black Book*. In addition to location, you can also change the security permissions that grant and deny access and the ability to administer this computer account.

Immediate Solutions

Defining a Network Share-Hosted Home Folder

To encourage users to store data in folder hierarchies that are protected by IntelliMirror, use a home folder designation to orient the user in the proper location each time a new file save is attempted by performing the following steps:

1. Open the Active Directory Users And Computers console.
2. Select the Users section.
3. Locate and select a user account for which to define a home folder.
4. Double-click the account to open the Properties dialog box for the selected user.
5. Click the Profile tab.
6. Select the Connect radio button under the Home Folder heading.
7. Select an unused drive letter in the pull-down list.
8. Type in the UNC name of the folder in a network share to be used as this user's home folder.
9. Click OK to save.
10. Repeat this procedure for all users. Be sure to define a unique folder for each user.
11. Close the Active Directory Users And Computers console.

Creating a Roaming User Profile

To create a roaming user profile, perform the following steps:

1. On a network server, create a share with sufficient drive space.
2. Open the Active Directory Users And Computers console.
3. Select the Users section.
4. Locate and select a user account for which to define a roaming profile.
5. Open the Properties dialog box for the selected user.

6. Click the Profile tab.

7. In the Profile Path field, type in the UNC of the network share location where the user profile should be stored. This should be in the form of *\\servername\sharename\%username%*. The system automatically fills in the username.

8. Click OK to save these changes.

9. Close the Active Directory Users And Computers console.

10. From a client system, log in with the user account, and then log out. Until the user account logs on and then logs off of the network, the roaming profile is not actually created.

Designating a Mandatory Roaming User Profile

To change a roaming profile into a mandatory roaming profile, perform the following steps:

1. Open the Active Directory Users And Computers console.

2. Select the Users section.

3. Locate and double-click a user account that requires a mandatory roaming profile.

4. Click the Profile tab, and make a note of the location of the profile.

5. Using Windows Explorer, browse to the location shown on the Profile tab.

6. Right-click the ntuser.dat file. It is hidden, so you may need to view hidden files by selecting Tools|Folder Options|View|Advanced Settings|Show Hidden Files and Folders.

7. Select Rename from the pop-up menu, and rename the file to ntuser.man.

Designating a Logon Script

To designate a logon script for use in a user account, perform the following steps:

1. Open the Active Directory Users And Computers console.

2. Select the Users section.

3. Locate and double-click a user account that requires a logon script.

4. Click the Profile tab, and type the name of the script in the Logon Script field.

5. If the script is located anywhere other than the %SystemRoot%\SYSVOL\sysvol\<domainname>\scripts folder, you need to enter the full UNC name that leads to the script, for example, \\<*servername*>\<*sharename*>\<*folder*>\<*scriptname*>.

Creating a User in Active Directory

To create a user in Active Directory, follow these steps:

1. Click the Start menu, and select Programs|Administrative Tools|Active Directory Users And Computers.

2. Select the container in which you would like the user to be created. Right-click the container, and select New|User.

TIP: *The Active Directory Users And Computers MMC snap-in provides several different ways to perform a task. For example, you can create a new user in the following ways: right-clicking the container and choosing New|User, clicking Action and choosing New|User, and clicking New User.*

---

3. Enter the desired information (such as first name, middle initial, last name, and user logon name), and click Next. The Create New User Wizard will autofill the Full Name field based on the information entered in the First Name, Initial, and Last Name fields. By default, it will also assume that the non-Windows 2000 name is the same as the Windows 2000 username. If you have multiple domains in your organization, select the desired domain from the drop-down menu.

NOTE: *To create a new user, you must complete the User Logon Name and at least one of the following: First Name, Middle Initial, or Last Name. If you do not have at least these selected, Next will be disabled.*

---

4. Enter the user's password and confirm it. Choose any other options for this account (User Must Change Password At Next Logon, User Cannot Change Password, Password Never Expires, or Account Is Disabled). Click Next.

NOTE: *By default, the Domain Security Policy allows you to create a password of zero length (that is, no password).*

---

5. Click Finish to create the user.

Creating a User in Active Directory Using the Command Line without Assigning a Password

To create an account using the command line without assigning a password, perform the following steps:

1. Click Start, and select Programs|Accessories|Command Prompt.

2. At the command prompt, type the following:

```
Net user Username /add
```

3. Press Enter. The account is now created without a password.

WARNING! This operation will fail if your password length policy is set to anything other than zero length.

Creating a User in Active Directory Using the Command Line and Assigning a Password

To create an account using the command line and to assign it a password, follow these steps:

1. Click Start, and select Programs|Accessories|Command Prompt.

2. At the command prompt, type the following:

```
Net user Username password /add
```

3. Press Enter. The account is now created with the desired password.

TIP: *Instead of typing in the password at the command line, you can substitute the desired password with the asterisk (*) symbol. This causes Windows 2000 to ask you to enter the password (which is hidden at this point) and then to confirm it.*

Working with Users

A number of tasks are involved in managing users in Active Directory. The following solutions address this important issue.

NOTE: *As with any other Windows 2000 application, keep in mind that quite often you can accomplish similar steps and functions by right-clicking on an object or double-clicking on it.*

Editing a User in Active Directory

To edit users in Active Directory, perform the following steps:

1. Click Start, and select Programs|Administrative Tools|Active Directory Users And Computers.

2. Navigate to the container in which the user you would like to modify resides. Click the user object to select it.

3. Click Action, and select Properties from the drop-down menu.

4. The User Properties window will appear. Make your desired changes, and click OK to finish.

TIP: *You can also access the Properties page of any object by simply double-clicking the object.*

Deleting a User in Active Directory

1. Click Start, and select Programs|Administrative Tools|Active Directory Users And Computers.

2. Navigate to the container in which the user you would like to delete resides. Click the user object to select it.

3. Click Action, and select Delete from the drop-down menu.

4. A dialog box will appear asking you to confirm the deletion of this user. Click OK to delete the user.

Deleting a User in Active Directory Using the Command Prompt

To delete an account using the command line, follow these steps:

1. Click Start, and select Programs|Accessories|Command Prompt.

2. At the command prompt, type the following:

```
Net user Username /delete
```

WARNING! *Make sure you're deleting the correct account. When using the command line, you are not asked to confirm the deletion.*

3. Press Enter. The account is now deleted.

Renaming a User in Active Directory

1. Click Start, and select Programs|Administrative Tools|Active Directory Users And Computers.

2. Navigate to the container in which the user you would like to rename resides. Click the user object to select it.

3. Click Action, and select Rename from the drop-down menu.

4. Type the new name for the user, and press Enter.

5. The Rename User window will appear. Enter any necessary information (including full name, first and last name, display name, login name and domain, and the pre-Windows 2000 name), and click OK.

Disabling a User in Active Directory

Three methods are used for disabling user accounts in Active Directory. One is not necessarily better than another, but you should be aware of the various ways of performing user management.

Here is the first method:

1. Click Start, and select Programs|Administrative Tools|Active Directory Users And Computers.

2. Navigate to the container in which the user you would like to disable resides. Click the user object to select it.

3. Click Action, and select Disable Account from the drop-down menu.

TIP: *Alternately, you can select the Disable Account option from the All Tasks Action submenu.*

---

4. A dialog box notifying you that the account has been disabled will appear. Click OK. Notice that the user icon now has a red X on it.

Here is the second method:

1. Click Start, and select Programs|Administrative Tools|Active Directory Users And Computers.

2. Navigate to the container in which the user you would like to disable resides. Click the user object to select it.

3. Right-click the selected user, and select Disable Account from the pop-up menu.

   4. A dialog box notifying you that the account has been disabled will appear. Click OK. Notice that the user icon now has a red X on it.

Here is the third method:

   1. Click Start, and select Programs|Administrative Tools|Active Directory Users And Computers.

   2. Navigate to the container in which the user you would like to disable resides. Double-click the user object to open its properties page.

   3. Click the Account tab.

   4. Under Account Options, select the Account Is Disabled option. Click OK.

   5. A dialog box notifying you that the account has been disabled will appear. Click OK. Notice that the user icon now has a red X on it.

Enabling a Disabled Account

To enable a disabled user account in Active Directory, perform the following steps:

   1. Click Start, and select Programs|Administrative Tools|Active Directory Users And Computers.

   2. Navigate to the container in which the user you would like to enable resides. Click the user object to select it.

   3. Click Action, and select Enable Account from the drop-down menu.

TIP: *Alternately, you can choose the Enable Account from the All Tasks Action submenu.*

---

   4. A dialog box notifying you that the account has been enabled will appear. Click OK. Notice that the red X disappears.

Finding a User in Active Directory in a Domain

To find an Active Directory user in a domain, perform the following steps:

   1. Click Start, and select Programs|Administrative Tools|Active Directory Users And Computers.

   2. To search the entire domain, right-click the domain node, and select Find from the pop-up menu.

   3. In the Name field, type the name of the user you want to find.

   4. Click Find Now.

Finding a User in Active Directory in an OU

To find an Active Directory user in an OU, perform the following steps:

   1. Click Start, and select Programs|Administrative Tools|Active Directory Users And Computers.

2. To search an OU, right-click the OU node, and select Find from the pop-up menu.

3. In the Name field, type the name of the user you want to find.

4. Click Find Now.

Copying a User in Active Directory

To copy user accounts in Active Directory, perform the following steps:

1. Click Start, and select Programs|Administrative Tools|Active Directory Users And Computers.

2. Navigate to the container in which the user you would like to copy resides. Click the user object to select it.

3. Click Action, and select Copy from the drop-down menu.

TIP: *Alternately, you can choose the Copy from the All Tasks Action submenu.*

---

4. The Copy Object - User window appears. Enter the required information, and click Next.

5. Enter the password (if any), and confirm it. Select any other desired options, and click Next.

6. Click Finish to complete the user account copy.

Changing the User Rights

To change local user rights, perform the following steps:

1. Click Start, and select Programs|Administrative Tools|Local Security Policy. A window like the one shown in Figure 4.7 will appear.

2. Expand the Security Settings item.

3. Expand Local Policies.

4. Select the User Rights Assignment item.

5. Choose the desired policy (for example, Access This Computer From The Network), right-click it, and select Security from the pop-up menu.

6. Click Add.

7. Choose a group or user to be added to this policy.

8. Click Add.

9. Repeat these steps for any additional users or groups.

10. When finished, click OK.

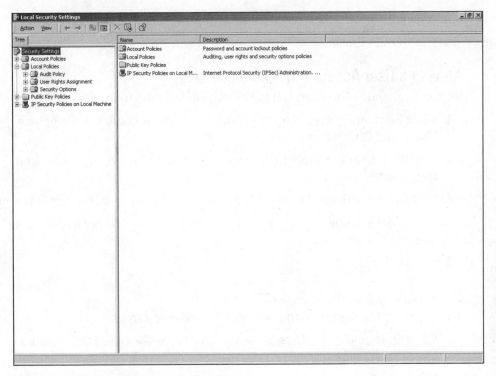

Figure 4.7   The Local Security Policy utility.

TIP: *Because you're dealing with both local and domain security settings, an effective policy exists. The effective policy displays the security attribute value that's currently enforced.*

Changing the Domain Rights

To change domain rights, follow these steps:

1. Click Start, and select Programs|Administrative Tools|Domain Security Settings.

2. Expand the Security Settings item.

3. Expand Local Policies.

4. Select the User Rights Assignment item.

5. Choose the desired policy (for example, Increase Quotas), right-click it, and select Security from the pop-up menu.

6. Enable the Define These Policy Settings option.

7. Click Add.

8. Add users and/or groups.

9. Repeat these steps for any additional desired users or groups.

10. Click OK to finish.

Moving a User Account in Active Directory

To move an Active Directory user account, perform the following steps:

1. Click Start, and select Programs|Administrative Tools|Active Directory Users And Computers.

2. Select the Users container (or any other container in which the desired user resides).

3. Right-click the desired user account, and select Move from the pop-up menu.

4. In the Move dialog box, click the folder to which you would like the user account moved.

5. Click OK.

Reactivating a Locked Account

To reactivate a locked account, perform the following steps:

1. Click Start, and select Programs|Administrative Tools|Active Directory Users And Computers.

2. Select the Users container (or any other container in which the desired user resides).

3. Right-click the desired user account, and select Properties from the pop-up menu.

4. Clear the Account Disabled checkbox.

5. Click OK.

Changing Passwords

To change a password, perform the following steps:

1. Click Start, and select Programs|Administrative Tools|Active Directory Users And Computers.

2. Select the Users container (or any other container in which the desired user resides).

3. Right-click the desired user account, and select Reset Password from the pop-up menu.

4. Enter the desired password, and confirm it.

5. If the user is to change the password the next time that he or she logs in, select the User Must Change Password At Next Logon checkbox.

6. Click the OK button.

Changing a User's Primary Group

To change a user's primary group, perform the following steps:

1. Click Start, and select Programs|Administrative Tools|Active Directory Users And Computers.

2. Select the Users container (or any other container in which the desired user resides).

3. Right-click the desired user account, and select Properties from the pop-up menu.

4. Click the Members tab.

5. Select the group that you would like to act as the user's primary group, and click the Set Primary Group button.

6. Click OK.

Working with Contacts

A number of tasks are involved in managing contacts in Active Directory. The following solutions address this important issue.

Creating a New Contact in Active Directory

To create a new Active Directory contact, perform the following steps:

1. Click Start, and select Programs|Administrative Tools|Active Directory Users And Computers.

2. Right-click the container where you would like the contact to be created, and select New|Contact.

3. Enter the contact information, and click OK.

Modifying a Contact in Active Directory

To modify an Active Directory contact, perform the following steps:

1. Click Start, and select Programs|Administrative Tools|Active Directory Users And Computers.

2. Choose the contact that you would like to modify.

3. Right-click it, and select Properties from the pop-up menu.

4. Modify any desired properties, and click OK.

Deleting a Contact in Active Directory

To delete an Active Directory contact, perform the following steps:

1. Click Start, and select Programs|Administrative Tools|Active Directory Users And Computers.

2. Right-click the contact you would like to delete, and select Delete from the pop-up menu.

3. Click Yes to delete the contact.

Finding a Contact in Active Directory

To search for a contact in an entire domain, follow these steps:

1. Click Start, and select Programs|Administrative Tools|Active Directory Users And Computers.

2. Right-click the desired domain node, and select Find from the pop-up menu. The Find utility will appear.

3. Ensure that Users, Contacts, And Groups is selected in the Find field.

4. Enter the name you would like to search for in the Name field.

5. Click Find Now to begin the search. All matching entries will be displayed in the lower part of the Find window.

TIP: *By clicking the Advanced tab, you can create extremely powerful search criteria. For example, you can search for all users who do not have a manager assigned to them.*

Adding a Computer in Active Directory

To add an Active Directory computer, perform the following steps:

1. Click Start, and select Programs|Administrative Tools|Active Directory Users And Computers.

2. Navigate to the Computers container (or any other container where you would like to add the computer), and select it.

3. Right-click the container, and select New|Computer from the pop-up menu.

4. Enter the computer name in the Computer Name field. Notice that the system will automatically create a pre-Windows 2000 name for your new computer.

5. By default, members of the Domain Admins group is allowed to join this new computer to the domain. If you would like to modify this, you can click Change, and select a new group or groups.

6. If this new system is a non-Windows 2000 computer, enable the Allow Pre-Windows 2000 Computer To Use This Account option.

7. Click OK to create the account.

Working with Computer Accounts

A number of tasks are involved in managing user accounts in Active Directory. The following solutions address this important issue.

Modifying a Computer's Properties

To modify a computer's properties, perform the following steps:

1. Click Start, and select Programs|Administrative Tools|Active Directory Users And Computers.

2. Navigate to the Computers container (or any other container where the computer you would like to modify resides).

3. Right-click the computer, and select Properties from the pop-up menu. The Properties window will appear, as shown in Figure 4.8.

4. Modify any desired properties, and click OK to finish.

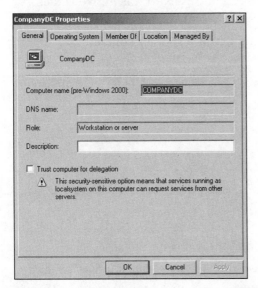

Figure 4.8   The computer's Properties window.

Adding a Computer Account to a Group

To add a computer account to a group, perform the following steps:

1. Click Start, and select Programs|Administrative Tools|Active Directory Users And Computers.

2. Navigate to the Computers container (or any other container where the computer you would like to modify resides).

3. Right-click the computer, and select Properties from the pop-up menu.

4. On the Member Of tab, click Add.

5. Select the desired group or groups, and click Add.

TIP: *If you need to add more than one group, you can select them by pressing and holding Ctrl while clicking the groups. You can also select several groups that follow one another in the group list by clicking the first group in the list and then pressing Shift and clicking the last group in the list.*

---

6. Click OK to return the Properties window.

7. Click OK to finish.

Disabling a Computer Account

To disable a computer account, perform the following steps:

1. Click Start, and select Programs|Administrative Tools|Active Directory Users And Computers.

2. Navigate to the Computers container (or any other container where the computer you would like to disable resides).

3. Right-click the computer, and select Disable Account from the pop-up menu.

4. Click Yes.

5. Click OK to disable the account.

NOTE: *Notice that a red X appears on the computer icon of the disabled account.*

Enabling a Computer Account

To enable a computer account, perform the following steps:

1. Click Start, and select Programs|Administrative Tools|Active Directory Users And Computers.

2. Navigate to the Computers container (or any other container where the computer you would like to enable resides).

3. Right-click the computer, and select Enable Account from the pop-up menu.

4. Click OK to enable the account.

Finding a Computer Account in Active Directory

To find a computer account in Active Directory, perform the following steps:

1. Click Start, and select Programs|Administrative Tools|Active Directory Users And Computers.

2. Right-click the domain where you would like to search for the computer, and select Find from the pop-up menu.

3. In the Find list box, select Computer.

4. In the Name field, enter the name of the computer you would like to search for.

TIP: *You can customize your search to the role of the computer. By choosing the Domain Controller role, only domain controllers will be displayed. Similarly, by choosing the Workstations and Servers role, only workstations and servers will be displayed.*

5. Click Find Now.

To search a specific container, perform the following steps:

1. Click Start, and select Programs|Administrative Tools|Active Directory Users And Computers.

2. Right-click the container where you would like to search for the computer, and select Find from the pop-up menu.

3. In the Find list box, select Computer.

4. In the Name field, enter the name of the computer that you would like to search for.

5. Click Find Now.

Resetting a Computer Account

To reset a computer account, perform the following steps:

1. Click Start, and select Programs|Administrative Tools|Active Directory Users And Computers.

2. Navigate to the Computers container (or any other container where the computer you would like to reset resides).

3. Right-click the computer, and select Reset Account from the pop-up menu.

4. Click Yes.

5. Click OK to reset the account.

WARNING! After you reset the computer account, the computer will have to rejoin the domain. This is very handy when an old computer is removed from the domain and a new system with the same name is taking its place. Because the SID of the computer is different, the domain controllers will think that the account already exists and will not allow the new computer to connect.

Moving a Computer Account

To move a computer account, perform the following steps:

1. Click Start, and select Programs|Administrative Tools|Active Directory Users And Computers.

2. Navigate to the Computers container (or any other container where the computer you would like to move resides).

3. Right-click the computer, and select Move from the pop-up menu.

4. Navigate to the destination container where you would like the computer moved to.

5. Click OK to move the computer.

Managing a Computer Account

To manage a computer account, perform the following steps:

1. Click Start, and select Programs|Administrative Tools|Active Directory Users And Computers.

2. Navigate to the Computers container (or any other container where the computer you would like to manage resides).

3. Right-click the computer to be modified, and select Manage from the pop-up menu.

4. The Computer Management utility will appear (see Figure 4.9).

5. You can now manage any component for which you have permissions assigned on the remote computer, including system tools, services and applications, and storage.

Deleting a Computer Account

To delete a computer account, perform the following steps:

1. Click Start, and select Programs|Administrative Tools|Active Directory Users And Computers.

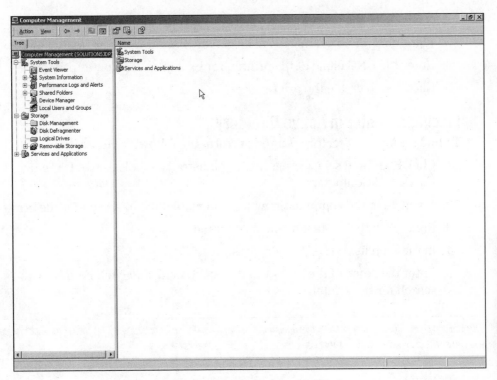

Figure 4.9   The Computer Management utility.

2. Navigate to the Computers container (or any other container where the computer you would like to delete resides).

3. Right-click the computer to be deleted, and select Delete from the pop-up menu.

4. Click Yes to delete the computer account.

Working with Printers in Active Directory

A number of tasks are involved in managing printers in Active Directory. The following solutions address this important issue.

Creating a New Printer in Active Directory

To create a new Active Directory printer, perform the following steps:

1. Click Start, and select Programs|Administrative Tools|Active Directory Users And Computers.

2. Navigate to the container in which you would like the printer created.

3. Right-click the container, and select New|Printer from the pop-up menu.

4. Enter the UNC name of the printer, for example, \\computer\printer.

5. Click OK to create the printer.

Finding a Printer in Active Directory

To find an Active Directory printer, perform the following steps:

1. Click Start, and select Programs|Administrative Tools|Active Directory Users And Computers.

2. Navigate to the container in which you would like to search for the printer.

3. Right-click the container, and select Find.

4. In the Find list box, select Printers.

5. Enter the name of the printer in the Name field, and click Find Now to search for the printer.

TIP: *You can search for a printer not only by name, but also by its capabilities. For example, if you click the Features tab, you can select to search for printers that can print double sided or that can staple.*

Deleting a Printer in Active Directory

To delete a printer in Active Directory, perform the following steps:

1. Click Start, and select Programs|Administrative Tools|Active Directory Users And Computers.

2. Navigate to the container in which you would like the printer deleted.

3. Right-click the desired printer, and select Delete.

4. Click Yes to delete the printer.

Working with Shared Folders in Active Directory

A number of tasks are involved in managing shared folders in Active Directory. The following solutions address this important issue.

Publishing a Shared Folder in Active Directory

To create a new shared folder in Active Directory, perform the following steps:

1. Click Start, and select Programs|Administrative Tools|Active Directory Users And Computers.

2. Navigate to the container in which you would like the Shared Folder object created.

3. Right-click the desired folder, and select New|Shared Folder.

4. Enter the name and the UNC path to the shared folder.

5. Click OK.

Modifying a Shared Folder in Active Directory

To modify a shared folder in Active Directory, perform the following steps:

1. Click Start, and select Programs|Administrative Tools|Active Directory Users And Computers.

2. Navigate to the container in which the shared folder you would like to modify resides.

3. Right-click the shared folder, and select Properties from the pop-up menu.

4. Make any desired changes, and click OK when done.

Finding a Shared Folder in Active Directory

To find a shared folder in Active Directory, perform the following steps:

1. Click Start, and select Programs|Administrative Tools|Active Directory Users And Computers.

2. Right-click the domain or container in which you would like to search for the shared folder, and select Find from the pop-up menu.

3. Select Shared Folder from the Find list box.

4. Enter the name of the shared folder in the Name field.

5. Click Find Now to begin the search.

Deleting a Shared Folder in Active Directory

To delete a shared folder in Active Directory, perform the following steps:

1. Click Start, and select Programs|Administrative Tools|Active Directory Users And Computers.

2. Navigate to the container that contains the shared folder you would like to delete.

3. Right-click the desired shared folder, and select Delete from the pop-up menu.

4. Click Yes to delete the shared folder.

Working with Groups

A number of tasks are involved in managing groups in Active Directory. The following solutions address this important issue.

Creating a Group in Active Directory

To create a user group in Active Directory, perform the following steps:

1. Click Start, and select Programs|Administrative Tools|Active Directory Users And Computers.

2. Navigate to the container in which you would like the group created.

3. Right-click the container, and select New|Group from the pop-up menu.

4. Enter a name for the group.

5. Click OK to create the group.

Removing a Group in Active Directory

To remove a group in Active Directory, perform the following steps:

1. Click Start, and select Programs|Administrative Tools|Active Directory Users And Computers.

2. Navigate to the container that contains the group you would like to delete.

3. Right-click the group, and select Delete from the pop-up menu.

4. Click Yes to delete the group.

Adding Members to a Group

To add members to a user group, perform the following steps:

1. Click Start, and select Programs|Administrative Tools|Active Directory Users And Computers.

2. Navigate to the container that contains the group you would like to modify the membership for.

3. Right-click the desired group, and select Properties from the pop-up menu.

4. Click the Members tab.

5. Click Add.

6. Choose the user(s) or group(s) that you would like to become members of this group.

7. Click OK.

8. Click OK to create the group membership.

Finding a Group in Active Directory

To find a group in Active Directory, perform the following steps:

1. Click Start, and select Programs|Administrative Tools|Active Directory Users And Computers.

2. Right-click the domain or container in which you would like to search for the group.

3. In the Name field, enter the name of the group you would like to search for.

4. Click Find Now.

Finding a Group's User Membership in Active Directory

To find the members of a group, perform the following steps:

1. Click Start, and select Programs|Administrative Tools|Active Directory Users And Computers.

2. Navigate to the container in which the group resides.

3. Right-click the desired group, and select Properties from the pop-up menu.

4. Click the Members tab. The group's members are listed in this window.

5. Click OK to close the membership window.

Removing Members from a Group

To remove members from a group, perform the following steps:

1. Click Start, and select Programs|Administrative Tools|Active Directory Users And Computers.

2. Navigate to the container in which the desired group exists.

3. Right-click the group, and select Properties from the pop-up menu.

4. Click the Member tab.

5. Select the user(s) or group(s) you would like to remove, and click Remove.

6. Click Yes to remove the selections.

7. Click OK to close the group membership window.

Renaming a Group in Active Directory

To rename a group in Active Directory, perform the following steps:

1. Click Start, and select Programs|Administrative Tools|Active Directory Users And Computers.

2. Right-click the group you would like to rename, and select Rename from the pop-up menu.

3. Enter a new name for the group, and press Enter.

4. Users, Groups, and Computers

Changing a Group's Scope

To change a group's scope, perform the following steps:

1. Click Start, and select Programs|Administrative Tools|Active Directory Users And Computers.

2. Navigate to the container in which the desired group resides.

3. Right-click the group, and select Properties from the pop-up menu.

4. In the Group Scope section, change the scope to the desired group scope.

5. Click OK to commit the changes.

NOTE: *A domain local group cannot be converted to a global group. Similarly, a global group cannot be converted to a domain local group.*

Change Group Type in Active Directory

To change a group type in Active Directory, perform the following steps:

1. Click Start, and select Programs|Administrative Tools|Active Directory Users And Computers.

2. Navigate to the container in which the desired group resides.

3. Right-click the group, and select Properties from the pop-up menu.

4. In the Group Type section, change the group type to the desired type.

5. Click OK.

Editing a User Group in Active Directory

To edit a user group in Active Directory, perform the following steps:

1. Click Start, and select Programs|Administrative Tools|Active Directory Users And Computers.

2. Navigate to the container that contains the group you would like to edit.

3. Right-click the group, and select Properties from the pop-up menu.

4. Edit any desired properties for the group, and click OK to commit the changes.

Using the **runas** Command to Launch the Active Directory Users And Computers Console

When you need to access the Active Directory Users And Computers console with another person logged into the system, perform the following steps:

1. Click Start, and select Run.

2. Type "cmd", and press Enter. A command prompt window will appear.

3. Type "runas /user:", followed by the domain name, "\", admin username "dsa.msc", and press Enter.

4. The Active Directory Users And Computers console should appear.

NOTE: *The application dsa.msc can be replaced with any application that is accessible by the current machine. It may be necessary to type in the full path to the program.*

Working with OUs

A number of tasks are involved in managing OUs in Active Directory. The following solutions address this important issue.

Adding an OU to Active Directory

To add an OU to Active Directory, perform the following steps:

1. Click Start, and select Programs|Administrative Tools|Active Directory Users And Computers.

2. Right-click the container in which you would like to create the OU, and select New|Organizational Unit from the pop-up menu.

3. Enter the name of the new OU.

4. Click OK to create the OU.

Deleting an OU in Active Directory

To delete an OU in Active Directory, perform the following steps:

1. Click Start, and select Programs|Administrative Tools|Active Directory Users And Computers.

2. Navigate to the container in which the OU resides.

3. Right-click the OU, and select Delete from the pop-up menu.

4. Click Yes to delete the OU.

Finding an OU in Active Directory

To find an OU in Active Directory, perform the following steps:

1. Click Start, and select Programs|Administrative Tools|Active Directory Users And Computers.

2. Navigate to the domain or container in which you would like to search for the OU.

3. Right-click domain or container, and select Find from the pop-up menu.

4. Select Organizational Unit from the Find list box.

5. Enter the name of the OU that you would like to search for.

6. Click Find Now.

Modifying an OU's Properties in Active Directory

To modify an OU's properties in Active Directory, perform the following steps:

1. Click Start, and select Programs|Administrative Tools|Active Directory Users And Computers.

2. Navigate to the desired container in which the OU resides.

3. Right-click the OU, and select Properties from the pop-up menu.

4. Modify any desired properties, and click OK to finish.

Renaming an OU in Active Directory

To rename an OU in Active Directory, perform the following steps:

1. Click Start, and select Programs|Administrative Tools|Active Directory Users And Computers.

2. Navigate to the OU that you would like to rename.

3. Right-click the OU, and select Rename from the pop-up menu.

4. Enter the new name for the OU, and press Enter.

Moving an OU in Active Directory

To move an OU in Active Directory, perform the following steps:

1. Click Start, and select Programs|Administrative Tools|Active Directory Users And Computers.

2. Navigate to the container in which the OU resides.

3. Right-click the OU, and select Move from the pop-up menu.

4. Navigate to the destination container, and click OK.

Assigning Delegate Control to an OU in Active Directory

To assign delegate control to an OU in Active Directory, perform the following steps:

1. Click Start, and select Programs|Administrative Tools|Active Directory Users And Computers.

2. Right-click the OU, and select Delegate Control from the pop-up menu. The Delegation of Control Wizard will appear, as shown in Figure 4.10.

3. Click Next.

4. Click Add.

5. Select the desired users and/or groups, and click Add.

6. Click OK.

7. Click Next.

8. Select the tasks for which you would like to grant these users and/or groups permissions.

9. Click Next.

10. Click Finish.

Figure 4.10   The Delegation of Control Wizard.

Chapter 5

Group Policy

In Depth

Group Policy comprises approximately one half of a new Windows 2000 feature called IntelliMirror. IntelliMirror is a collection of Windows 2000 services and applications that offer administrators control of desktops, user data, software installation, and more. IntelliMirror is not actually a standalone service or a feature of Windows 2000; instead, it consists of the capabilities created through the interaction and integration of native Windows 2000 components. To understand Group Policies and how they interact with the overall system, we need to get an idea of what IntelliMirror is and how its components interact with Windows 2000 Professional and Windows 2000 Server.

Group Policy Overview

Group Policy functionality covers a stunning array of features and functions through the use of several applications and tools gathered together by Microsoft under a single feature set known as IntelliMirror. IntelliMirror is a suite of applications and tools that is used primarily for network client management and configuration. IntelliMirror, administratively synonymous with Group Policy, has three core features or capabilities:

- Management of user data

- Installation and maintenance of software

- Management of user settings and desktop environments

These capabilities can be used independently or combined into a total management solution. With all the Group Policy features in use, in combination with Remote Installation Services (RIS) and roaming profiles, it is possible to replace, rebuild, and restore a user's system. This grants administrators control of users' desktops and grants users the ability to focus on work tasks instead of system maintenance and data management.

The user data management centers around maintaining the integrity and accessibility of data that's essential to users' work tasks. The User Data Management portion of Group Policy grants users reliable access to data no matter where they are located on the network and even when they're offline.

Installing and maintaining software ensures that users will always have the software necessary for accomplishing their work tasks. This portion of Group Policy can automatically install software on clients as needed by the users. Furthermore, Group Policy can update, repair, and remove software as well.

Managing user settings and the desktop environment centers on maintaining a consistent user environment no matter where a user logs in. This includes retaining a user's customized desktop as well as enforcing environment restrictions. Group Policy ensures that the user's desktop settings are always present so that the user can focus on work tasks instead of an unfamiliar layout and desktop scheme. These user settings are most often accomplished through temporary changes to the system registry, which governs items such as the Control Panel and Explorer.

To get an idea of the true scope of Group Policy, you should be aware that Group Policy can be used for the following tasks:

• Modifying the registry

• Redirecting folders

• Administering logon and logoff scripts

• Handling security issues

• Installing software

• Maintaining disk quotas

• Managing data encryption capabilities

• Customizing Internet Explorer

• Controlling how group policies are applied

Portions of Group Policy can be employed on a standalone system in the form of a local computer policy without Active Directory or as a Domain Group Policy. After a Group Policy has been applied to a system, those changes remain in effect even when the system is not connected to the network.

Group Policy eases the requirement and frequency of administrative intervention and simplifies a user's computing experience by performing all the necessary functions to maintain a consistent and functional computing environment for all network users, whether online or offline. Group Policy also offers another level of disaster protection and data recovery from a client system perspective. Every custom user-critical element on a client system present at the moment of the most recent graceful network disconnection is available for restoration, reinstallation, or reapplication at the next logon, all without administrative intervention.

In addition to the disaster protection it offers, Group Policy is also a control mechanism. Through the use of Group Policy on Windows 2000 Active Directory objects, which include domains, sites, and custom-defined OUs, an administrator can retain control of the environment on all clients, even when they are discon-nected from the network. This control ranges from implementing mandatory user profiles; to installing required software and removing unapproved software; to distributing patches, upgrades, and service packs (or *service releases*); to grant-ing or restricting access to native tools, Control Panel applets, the registry, and more.

Total Cost of Ownership

One of the most significant benefits of Group Policy is its ability to reduce the cost in actual dollars and man-hours needed to sustain a growing network. Group Policy can be used to reduce the cost of client management for small and large networks alike. Obviously, the more desktops that are automatically managed, the larger the time and monetary savings. These cost of ownership benefits are afforded you through Group Policy due to the following components:

- *Windows Installer*—This element of Group Policy is affectionately known as a *smart technology*. Windows Installer eliminates the need for an administra-tor to install software manually on every desktop. An installation package is added to the Group Policy, and it is instantly available to every client on the network. In addition to reducing installation costs, it also reduces ongoing support, upgrade, and removal costs.

- *Data redirection*—This element is a combination of folder redirection and offline files, which makes user and network data available at all times from any client on or off the network. By centrally managing data and storing data on network servers, data redirection decreases the cost of data management and reduces the risk of data loss, primarily through the fact that data stored in a single location is easier to back up and will most likely be stored on a fault-tolerant drive system.

- *RIS*—This component, when combined with Group Policy, reduces the cost of deploying new clients or restoring damaged clients.

Enhancement through Systems Management Server

Group Policy and RIS can be further enhanced through the addition of Systems Management Server (SMS). The primary benefit of adding SMS to Windows 2000's Group Policy is the added support for non-Windows 2000 systems. This is espe-cially helpful in environments that are not or will not fully migrate to Windows 2000 Professional on the desktop. SMS provides client management support for all Microsoft operating systems from Windows 3.x through Windows 2000. Table 5.1 shows a comparison of SMS and Group Policy and what their combined fea-tures can offer.

Table 5.1   The features of SMS and Group Policy.

Feature	SMS	Group Policy	Combined
Distribution	Yes	Yes	Yes
Targeting	Collection	Active Directory	Collection or group
Platform	All platforms	Windows 2000 only	All platforms
Installation	SMS or Windows Installer	Windows Installer	SMS or Windows Installer
Additional management support	Yes	No	Yes

SMS offers several management facilities:

- *Hardware and software inventory*—Through Windows Management Instrumentation (WMI) and various software scanners, SMS is able to maintain a detailed inventory of the hardware and software present on individual systems and ultimately the entire network. This data is stored in a Structured Query Language (SQL) Server-based system that can be used for budgeting, growth projection, and trending. The inventory is maintained automatically by SMS so that a current, accurate, and complete inventory is available with a click of the mouse. Additionally, the inventory gathered from systems can be processed by the compliance comparative database tool to determine which systems require hardware upgrades to support operating system upgrades or software deployments properly.

- *Software distribution and installation*—Software can be distributed on a computer, user, or group basis. Rules-based deployment techniques can be employed to target application deployment on an even more detailed or controlled basis. SMS includes immediate deployment as well as rollback capabilities. This allows administrators to control the application environment of users, including situations where a user moves from one department to another, where a user's job description is drastically changed, or when a project requires a specific application.

- *Software metering*—Managing how much an application package is used is often important, especially when license restrictions limit the number of simultaneous users. SMS offers complete software usage tracking by user, group, client, time, and license. Reports can be generated to outline the usage scenarios based on real activity. These reports can be used for growth planning and budgeting for new hardware and software acquisitions. In addition to tracking and logging, SMS can control software use by issuing alerts and warnings, as well as by preventing applications from launching when specific triggers are tripped.

- *Diagnostics and troubleshooting*—Overseeing an entire network can be quite a time-consuming task. SMS offers automated oversight through numerous advanced diagnostic tools, ranging from network traffic monitors to performance monitors. SMS is able to track activity and can even offer troubleshooting and improvement advice for all Microsoft operating systems and most Microsoft software products, including the Microsoft BackOffice and Office suites.

TIP: *Microsoft provides two Group Policy troubleshooting tools in the Windows 2000 Resource Kit: GPRESULT and GPOTOOL. GPRESULT will document, in varying degrees, what Group Policies have been applied to a given domain computer or user. GPOTOOL will actively check the health and fitness of Group Policies within the domain.*

Software Distribution

Whether you need to distribute a new software application, a recent patch, or an upgrade, or if you need to add older software to a new system, Group Policy offers centralized management of client software. Through the use of Windows Installer and Group Policy, new applications can be installed on a user's system as needed, and existing applications can be upgraded.

Mobile System Management

Managing the software and user data on a notebook is difficult. However, when you add in security controls, access restrictions, software patches and upgrades, and access to network resources when offline, the task becomes a nightmare. Fortunately, Group Policy was designed to eliminate this specific horror. Notebook systems are fully controllable through Group Policy, and all user data and network data can be made available to roaming users even when they're not connected to the network. Group Policy automatically manages version conflicts, alterations of folder hierarchies, and damaged or deleted files.

Group Policy Navigation

Before delving into the specifics on what Group Policy can do, we need to investigate the mechanics of how you will manage, maintain, create, link, and administer Group Policy. As with most other Windows 2000 administrative tools, Group Policy is administered through a Microsoft Management Console (MMC) snap-in. Unlike most MMCs, however, Group Policy is generally accessed, viewed, and modified from its respective associations within the Active Directory Users And Computers snap-in. To gain a better understanding of how a Group Policy can be accessed, as well as the other functions you need to learn, let's begin by talking about how a Group Policy is created.

Local computer policies are created from within the Group Policy editor console, GPEDIT.MSC. What you see with this console is very similar to what you will see while administering domain Group Policy. The biggest difference is that many of the built-in policy elements are missing. This is due to the many network-related Group Policy features that are available exclusively within a domain environment.

Active Directory Group Policy Objects (GPOs) are created and linked to a site, domain, or OU container. Put simply, a Group Policy cannot be created without first having an association to one of these parent-type objects. As such, you need to first consider not just what you want to accomplish with a given Group Policy, but also with whom you want to associate that accomplishment. Consider it like this: It does no good to enforce a screen saver or restrict Control Panel access if you have no people or computers to impose these restrictions upon. After a GPO is created, it is stored as an object and can be associated to other OUs through a process known as linking. Subsequent filtering based upon groups that belong to an OU can occur within the GPO properties. After a GPO has been created, it is usually modified using the Active Directory Users And Computers snap-in. In situations where you have delegated Group Policy administration, you may want to create a specialized MMC console containing only specific Group Policies. This is done by adding a Group Policy standalone snap-in from within a blank MMC window, but it will still require your knowledge of which Active Directory objects act as parents to the Group Policy.

Group Policy is one of the most difficult, complex, and powerful tools within the entire Windows 2000 platform. The complexity and power can be attributed to the features and broad range of positive impacts that Group Policy can have upon a network. Unfortunately, the difficult part comes into play as a result of three specific features of Group Policy:

- *Embedded*—Group Policy is by nature always embedded within an Active Directory OU or group object. There is no quick and dirty way of looking at an OU or group and determining if a Group Policy is associated with it. What you must do is check into the properties for the OU or group and then look at the Group Policy tab.

- *Shared*—Group Policies can be recycled. My personal opinion would be that a Group Policy should be created as a completely generic object within a program where I could assign it to OUs and groups simply by dragging the policy object over the OU or group. This is not the case. Group Policies are stored either in the sysvol volume or as an association to a domain, site, OU, or group within Active Directory. A Group Policy can also be shared as independent-looking objects and associated with other OUs and groups.

5. Group Policy

Looking at the Group Policy picture with both embedded and shared properties makes it impossible to quickly determine not just where Group Policies are, but which OUs and groups might be using the same Group Policy.

- *Inherited*—You would assume that by assigning a Group Policy at the domain level, all OUs and sub-OUs within that domain would also automatically have the same policies applied without having to relink each object manually to the Group Policy. This concept is known as inheritance, which means that all of the Group Policies assigned to a parent object (OU) are passed down and inherited by all child objects. By itself, inheritance isn't a big deal. When attempting to troubleshoot problems, inheritance is not unlike some unknown disease where you see all of the symptoms, but not the problem, and you cannot directly see what may be causing the problem. A child object's properties will not tell you that a parent object's Group Policy is being applied. In addition, a Group Policy may be functioning just fine for a parent object, but may have completely unexpected results for a child object. If that child object were to have other Group Policies assigned to it, you might begin to understand how confusing it can be for an administrator to sort through the directly assigned Group Policies and the invisibly inherited Group Policies.

Any one of these features might present a small challenge to the average administrator, but if you consider the overall picture, you might begin to understand how very important it is to document your Group Policy functions, assignments, and properties before things get out of control. If Group Policy is not documented, you are unable to troubleshoot or control how your Group Policies are working. You can block inheritance upon child objects in order to prevent Group Policies of the parent objects from flowing downhill and being applied to the child objects. I really recommend against this, however, because it simply adds more complexity to an already potentially confusing picture.

TIP: *Keep in mind that a Group Policy can be assigned to OUs, which can be embedded within other OUs. This process of embedding is also known as nesting. Remember that policies are applied to systems or users when they log in to the domain. If a computer or user is a member of an OU that is nested several times over (that is to say, the OU has multiple generations of parent objects), it will take longer for the logon process to complete because the domain controller will process each Group Policy associated with each parent OU prior to moving on to the child OU. If multiple generations are involved, this could take some time. If at all possible, it is best to maintain a relatively flat OU hierarchy in order to reduce these types of delays.*

Other methods can be used to make it easier to track and troubleshoot Group Policies, but most of those are associated with practical layout rather than documenting the Group Policies.

When a user logs in to a computer that resides within a domain, Group Policies are applied to that computer and user in the following order:

1. Local computer
2. Site
3. Domain
4. OU
5. Domain computer
6. Domain user

If an OU policy states that a user cannot shut down the computer, yet the user policy allows that functionality, the user policy will prevail because it completely overwrites that particular feature with its own policy. Policy inheritance is simply a matter of he who is last, wins.

The easiest method of accessing domain GPOs is through the Active Directory Users And Computers snap-in. Whether editing an existing Group Policy or creating a new one, you must access the properties of either the domain, site, or OU. After you are in the properties, you need to check the Group Policy tab. Within this tab, you will see that all object-related Group Policy attributes can be divided into three groups: how Group Policy applies from the outside, how each Group Policy is treated, and the properties and functions of each Group Policy. A small window lists all of the Group Policies applied to the object. Within the Group Policy tab, these other options are available:

- The Options button allows you to select whether the highlighted Group Policy can be overridden by another Group Policy. This is particularly valuable in a situation where a user policy is more permissive than the computer policy, and the computer policy is what ideally should prevail. In this situation, the domain computer policies that should not be overridden should be checked to see if this option has been activated. Also under Options, we can disable the Group Policy altogether. This disables the Group Policy so that it is not only not being used on this particular object, but it cannot be assigned to another object either.

- The Properties button allows you to disable the computer or user portions of a particular Group Policy. This will help speed up the logon process when policies are applied because the computer will ignore an entire section rather than check for policy components. This is also where you can determine what other links exist for this particular policy.

Note that, for both of these buttons, the point of view has changed from being the properties of the Active Directory object to being the properties and options for each Group Policy. In order to take full advantage of the features allowed with the Options and Properties buttons, it's a good idea to get in the habit of creating Group Policies that do only one thing, or essentially have one goal. It is possible to have a single policy that contains several restrictions. However, for the sake of both troubleshooting and properties such as override and inheritance, it's a good idea to keep each group policy limited to a single task such as password or software installation or display settings.

The New and Add buttons can be confusing because the interface will not gray one of the buttons out when the focus is on an existing policy. Adding a policy is the process of linking a preexisting policy into the current object. The New button will allow you to create a brand-new policy and will simply create a blank policy in the window for you to rename. After you have named the new policy, you will still need to click the Edit button in order to configure it.

You can also highlight a particular policy and click the Delete, Up, or Down buttons in this window. The Delete button will delete the policy after a suitable warning, and the up and down arrow buttons will move the policies up or down within the window. The system will implement object policies in order from bottom to top. Just remember that each policy will override the one below it. All this is done while still following standard policy inheritance rules. Again, the last policy to be applied is the one that has the final word on a given item or attribute.

The last option in this window is Block Policy Inheritance. With all of these features, it is sometimes difficult to remember whether the feature we look at is coming from the object's point of view or a Group Policy's point of view. In this case, the policy inheritance applies for the entire object. This feature will keep a parent Group Policy from applying to a particular child object. It will not prevent other child objects from inheriting the parent Group Policy, unless the child object is a grandchild of the original parent and a child of an inheritance-blocked parent.

Group Policies that Control How Group Policies Are Processed

No, you are not misunderstanding the statement. Yes, a Group Policy can define and guide how Group Policies are applied to users and computers. This section will explain how these policies might be important in certain situations. You'll also notice that several areas cover Group Policy Group Policies, just as several areas cover similar functions within Group Policy itself. Appendix A contains a Group Policy dictionary that may be able to assist you in your efforts in understanding what Group Policies can be applied to accomplish what overall tasks.

All of the sections below represent Group Policy locations that contain Group Policies that control how other group policies are processed.

Computer Configuration|Administrative Templates| System|Group Policy

All of the policies in this section are found under Computer Configuration| Administrative Templates|System|Group Policy. As you read through computer configuration policies, please remember that the policy applies to the computer itself and has an impact upon all users that log on to that computer. The only time that computer policies will not have this user impact is when a user policy overrides the computer policy. Computer configuration policies include:

- *Disable Background Refresh Of Group Policy*—After a policy is applied to a user and/or computer, the system checks for policy changes every 60-120 minutes and applies any changes that aren't software deployment or folder redirection related to the computer. You might not want this to happen if you have concerns about bandwidth, do not want policy changes to kick in during the middle of the day, or have any number of other control-related administrative issues. Disable Background Refresh Of Group Policy turns this particular feature off so that the system does not check for policy updates.

- *Group Policy Refresh Interval For Computers*—In most situations, you won't even notice when the system looks for policy changes. In some situations, however, you might want to change the frequency that the system does look for these changes. This refresh interval is measured in minutes. If you want to increase this frequency, lower the number of minutes. If you want the system to check for changes less often, increase the number of minutes.

- *Group Policy Refresh Interval For Domain Controllers*—Domain controllers, although they are still computers on the network, fall into their own set of rules that may be different than other computers'. Your goal as an administrator should be to obtain and maintain as stable an environment as possible, which may mean setting a different Group Policy refresh interval for domain controllers.

- *User Group Policy Loopback Processing Mode*—Recall that the Group Policy order of inheritance starts with the local computer policy and ends with the domain user policy. In some situations, such as with high usage library or kiosk computers, you might not want a user's policy to override the computer policy on a system. Turning on this policy will prevent this from happening by basically reapplying the computer policy after the user policy has been implemented.

- *Group Policy Slow Link Detection*—There are also situations where you might not want software installation or Group Policy processing to occur. One prime example is for remote users. Preventing certain Group Policy processing starts by turning on slow link detection to allow the system to be aware of when slow links exist. You can further pick and choose Group Policy elements that will and will not be processed across a slow link by choosing their specific elements within the policy itself.

- *Registry, Internet Explorer Maintenance, Software Installation, Folder Redirection,* and *Scripts Policy Processing*—Each of these is its own separate Group Policy option. After the option is enabled, the particular policy type will not be run across slow link connections unless specified here. One additional feature is also available, which is to process all Group Policies even when Group Policy objects have not changed. This is just an option that allows you to apply a policy redundantly even when the policy has not been changed within Active Directory. Generally, you would think that this is a waste of time. However, sometimes there are ways around policies at the computer or user level, and you may want to reapply a Group Policy at every interval in order to maintain the level of integrity that you originally planned for.

User Configuration|Administrative Templates|Microsoft Management Console|Group Policy

When dealing with Group Policies, always remember the differences between user and computer configurations. User configuration specifically looks at restrictions that you might want to impose on a user or group of users, or any group of users (not necessarily a "User Group") that a Group Policy can apply to. Remember that you can delegate administrative authority on an OU level, which means that by default, you can also delegate Group Policy creation and modification on that level. Each of the items in this section simply provides an additional means for you to restrict items and sections that can be administered (or tampered with, depending upon your point of view) by your delegated administrator. Within this section, you can deny access to the following:

- Group Policy snap-in
- Group Policy tab for Active Directory tools
- Administrative templates (computers)
- Administrative templates (users)
- Folder redirection
- Internet Explorer maintenance
- RIS

- Scripts (logon/logoff)
- Scripts (startup/shutdown)
- Security settings
- Software installation (computers)
- Software installation (users)

The purpose of Group Policy is to make your administrative job easier. The last thing that you need to do is to clean up a Group Policy nightmare (especially because they're so difficult to troubleshoot) that was created when a delegated administrator naively changed an access feature.

User Configuration\|Administrative Templates\|System\| Group Policy

In general, you will find duplicate or very similar policies between identical branches of user and computer configuration. Again, this is because very real differences exist between having a policy apply to a computer and having the same policy apply just to a user. This is a huge improvement over Windows NT policies because most truly dangerous policies don't exist at the computer level anymore. With Windows NT, it was possible to remove any possibility of accessing Control Panel from a computer. With Windows 2000, that is not a possibility, and, instead, Control Panel restrictions are specific to user logon, thus making Group Policy much safer than it used to be. This additional safety factor comes into play not just because the policies are user-specific, but also because they are not permanently written to the registry. The following policies are all found within the User Configuration\|Administrative Templates\|System\|Group Policy section of the Group Policy Window:

- *Group Policy Refresh Interval For Users*—This is very similar to the same option described for computers; Group Policy refresh intervals can occur for users, too. Be careful with this, though. It is not necessarily required for you to set intervals for both users and computers. When a policy is refreshed, it is refreshed for both user and computer configuration components within the policy. In other words, policy refreshment occurs for the entire policy.

- *Group Policy Slow Link Detection*—This property is identical to the one under Computer Configuration. Again, remember that the difference lies strictly in how you prefer to deal with things. My personal recommendation is that slow link detection should only be necessary for laptops that are not necessarily anchored to the office. It doesn't matter who is logged in to the system; the system determines whether a link is slow or not. In this case, I'd recommend using slow link detection under the Computer Configuration option.

- *Group Policy Domain Controller Selection*—Standard operating procedure indicates that, after a user is authenticated in the domain, it receives Group Policies from the same domain controller that performed the authentication. For large corporate environments, however, you may have a specific domain controller that is better equipped to handle massive amounts of policy traffic. In cases like this, you can designate a specific domain controller as a Group Policy server of sorts. Keep in mind that the opposite can also be done with this feature. You can distribute Group Policy processing across multiple domain controllers based upon different OUs.

Management of User Data

Data management can be controlled on an OU basis through Group Policies or on an individual basis through manual configuration. Group Policy can maintain a copy of network resources on clients so that, when they are offline, the data is still available to the user. In fact, the data is still accessed in the same manner from the user's perspective; it is as if he or she were still connected to the network. This feature is primarily enabled through offline files.

Offline Files

Offline files (discussed in detail in Chapter 11) are used to provide continuous access to network data even when the network is down. Offline files can be configured on a user-by-user basis or through a Group Policy in the Administrative Templates|Network|Offline Files section of either the Computer Configuration or User Configuration (see Figure 5.1) node on the Group Policy window. After a file is managed by offline files, the file can be restored when corrupted or deleted. Also, when multiple versions of the same file come into existence, you are prompted whether to keep both versions or to overwrite one with the other. The offline files option offers administrators a networkwide intelligent document management and version control solution that operates with connected and transient clients.

Folder Redirection

Data management is also accomplished through intelligent positioning and mapping of user home and data directories (such as the My Documents folder). In most cases, the home directory and all user data directories should be stored on a network share, and these folders should be made available offline (using offline files manually or through Group Policy). Additionally, you can use Group Policy to map common local folders to network share-stored versions of these folders as necessary. This is known as *folder redirection*. After folder redirection is configured, users' data and folder hierarchies are available no matter where they log in, and they're also available on portable systems disconnected from the network. Folder redirection (Figure 5.2) is defined in the User Configuration|Windows Settings|Folder Redirection area of the Group Policy window.

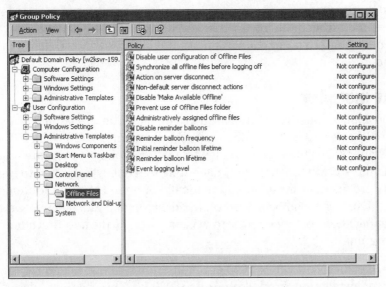

Figure 5.1 The Group Policy|Offline Folders section of the Group Policy window.

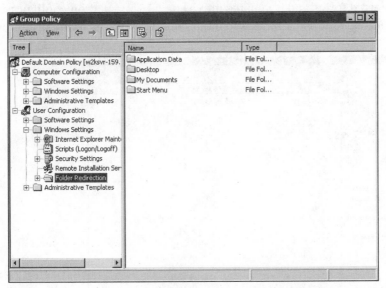

Figure 5.2 The Group Policy|Folder Redirection section of the Group Policy window.

5. Group Policy

201

Installing and Maintaining Software

Software management is a key tool on many networks. It can be used to ensure that software is always available to users, that the latest version of the software is installed, and that no unapproved software is present. These control mechanisms are often essential for maintaining a virus- and corruption-free network and for fostering a computing environment sufficient for all necessary work tasks to be accomplished.

Microsoft Installer

Many desktop applications are created in such a manner that the setup.exe application essentially refers to an *.msi file for all subsequent installation tasks. These Microsoft Installer (MSI) files can be added to a Group Policy (see Figure 5.3) in order to facilitate software installation. Each time this policy is applied to a system, the software is either installed automatically or added to the Add/Remove Programs list. Icons can also be placed on the desktop and Start menu, and the appropriate application components are then installed when the user first attempts to use the program.

Applications like Microsoft Office 2000 are built around MSI files and rely upon them heavily for installation. In addition, Office 2000 Premium has administrative tools to further integrate with Windows 2000. These tools allow an administrator to add customized forms and templates into a specific installation configuration. Other applications that use MSI files make it quite easy for us to integrate them

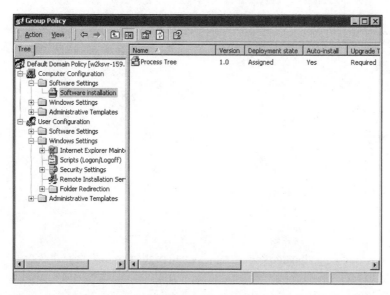

Figure 5.3   The Group Policy|Software Installation section of the Group Policy window.

into a Group Policy. If Group Policy and automated software distribution are important, you may want to visit the software or program manufacturer's Web site or check with technical support to determine if MSI files are used. If they are not, fear not; Microsoft has other alternatives built in to Windows 2000 that still allow us to take advantage of Group Policy software distribution. These alternatives are WinINSTALL and ZAP.

TIP: *Group Policy-assigned installation packages will install automatically for any computer or person belonging to the object that the Group Policy is assigned to. This also includes remote users. In order to prevent application updates from occurring when users are on the road, you can create a domain Group Policy that disables Group Policy from being applied across slow links.*

WinINSTALL

WinINSTALL is an application produced by Veritas software. Put simply, it creates MSI files for you. You can download a smaller version of the WinINSTALL application from the Veritas Web site, and it is also located on the Windows 2000 Server and Advanced Server installation CDs. A full version is available that has more features to allow postpackage editing and modification. Although not as ideal as having a built-in MSI file for an application, WinINSTALL will work quite well under the right circumstances.

WinINSTALL works very much like a snapshot image program. You create an MSI file simply by starting WinINSTALL on a computer that meets the following two criteria:

- Does not have the application in question installed on it
- Is most like the computers that will be using the installer package to install the application

WinINSTALL scans the hard disk drive, prompts you to install the target application on the computer, and then sits back and waits for you to finish. Quite often, an application will require that the system be restarted. Never fear; WinINSTALL will recognize where you were when you restart the program after a reboot. When you let it know that the installation is complete, scan your hard drive again, and produce an MSI file ready for distribution.

As you can imagine, WinINSTALL is very similar to the old SYSDIFF/SNAP days of Windows NT. This time, however, it's easier to create the image file and easier to distribute it (using Group Policy), and the overall distribution methods are far more sophisticated and automated.

Some applications just don't work well with WinINSTALL. You have to consider that sometimes application developers won't package the program with an MSI file simply because they couldn't get it to work. This will happen usually when several multistep registry changes or user interactions need to occur post-setup in order to complete installation. It can also happen when an application legally references hardware that is unique to the system where the MSI file was created. In order to get the best chances of success, avoid creating MSI files on a laptop when the target computer is a desktop and vice versa. Try to create the MSI files on one of the target computers. Also, try to run the application once before you tell WinINSTALL that the installation is complete. This should clean up any lingering registration or registry tweaks that the new application might perform. Also, be aware that service-related applications are thorny just in their nature. If you're using RIS (discussed in detail in Chapter 8) to install the operating system, you might consider installing the antivirus application prior to imaging the computer.

NOTE: *If you administer a diverse environment where you'll need to deploy a WinINSTALL MSI file on systems that are not identical, you may consider creating the WinINSTALL on a completely clean system. WinINSTALL will only track files that are installed or updated on the system. Many applications use shared files and simply check that a shared file exists during the installation process. Creating an MSI on a clean computer will ensure that both shared and application files are caught by WinINSTALL.*

ZAP Files

ZAP files are a last resort for Group Policy application installation. Once upon a time, with Windows 9x and Windows NT, a registry hack essentially turned on a Network tab within the Control Panel|Add/Remove Programs applet and pointed the contents of that tab toward an .ini file that could reside on the local hard disk or on the network. Basically, you configured the .ini file to list network installable application names and their corresponding setup files. The application then showed up in Add/Remove Programs under the new Network tab. If a program needed to be installed, all you needed to do was go to that spot, click the application, and click the Add button. This was a great and wonderful feature for us administrators who didn't have SMS and who really couldn't afford to risk walking around with expensive CDs just to install desktop applications. The same functionality now applies for Windows 2000 without the registry hack, but the .ini file has been replaced by a ZAP file for each application.

You may be thinking that, if ZAP files are only text files with a few commands, it might be easier just to use ZAP files rather than try to create an MSI file on your own. There are several good reasons why you might want to stick with MSI files:

- MSI files with Group Policy can automatically install an application or can be configured to await installation using the Add/Remove Programs applet. ZAP solutions can only be implemented within Add/Remove Programs.

- MSI-installed Group Policy applications can repair themselves when components are deleted, missing, or corrupted beyond recognition. ZAP-installed applications are not proactive about their own health.

- MSI files install using elevated permissions that are in nature higher than your average user and similar to the Administrator account. ZAP-installed programs are installed using the currently logged-on users' permissions.

- MSI files can roll back from a failed installation. What this means is that, if an install fails, MSI is smart enough to remove all traces of the application and installation attempt—both registry and other—from the system. ZAP installations are just like any other installation. If the install fails, you might be getting odd error messages

- MSI files will install applications with little or no user intervention. ZAP installations require just as much user involvement as manually running the application.

Again, ZAP files are plain text files that can be created, edited, and viewed in Notepad or any other word processing editor. Unlike the Windows 9x or the Windows NT solution, a ZAP file is created for each application that needs to be viewed within Add/Remove Programs. The format of a ZAP file is as follows:

```
[Application]
FriendlyName=MaxMain Database Application
SetupCommand=\\server1\installs\install.exe
[Ext]
MAX=
```

The first line of the ZAP file must contain the **[Application]** header. The **FriendlyName** is what the application is labeled as within Control Panel's Add/Remove Programs. The **SetupCommand** is a pointer to the setup or install application that will install the program for you. This can be a local application or a network share. You might not want to assign a drive letter to the directory containing your application installs, so for security purposes, it's a good idea to just enter a Universal Naming Convention (UNC) for the setup command. Other entries, such as Display Version, Publisher, and uniform resource locator (URL) are fluff, but can be added to the ZAP in situations where you would like to provide that extra level of professionalism. An additional entry actually provides some value. The **[ext]** section lists all file extensions that should be associated with this application. Most installer applications will do this on their own, but some homegrown applications might need this extra boost.

You can name the file any name that you want, as long as you maintain the ZAP file extension. After you are done, you still need to assign the ZAP file as a new software package within a Group Policy. You will also need to place both the ZAP file and the data located in the **SetupCommand** location on the network with Read permissions for everyone who will be affected by the Group Policy.

Published vs. Assigned

There are two ways of distributing applications using Group Policy: published and assigned. Published group policy applications show up as installable applications from within Control Panel|Add/Remove Programs. Assigned user group policy applications will automatically install icons and file extensions (and repair/update) on the system when a user logs in. As soon as the user attempts to use one of the icons or file associations, the application installs in its entirety. Assigned computer group policy applications will just install the application entirely as soon as the computer group policy is executed. In most situations, you will probably want to publish applications because they are fully automated. This is to take full advantage of the features, such as automatic installation and repair. This type of installation of Group Policy is known as being *assigned*. An assigned installation policy will automatically install the application as soon as the computer joins the network and/or as soon as the user tries to run the application or a file with an associated extension. The difference lies in whether a computer software or user software policy is being applied.

As I described in the previous section on ZAP files, software can be deployed in a selective manner by publishing the Group Policy package from within Control Panel|Add/Remove Programs. This is known as *published software*. Keep in mind that both MSI and ZAP files can be published. The only difference between the two in this case is that all of the MSI smart features are no longer proactive, but are restricted to the user manually clicking the Install button from within Add/Remove Programs. Optional or bonus software that users can selectively install as desired can also be included. The software portion of Group Policy can also be used to remove previously distributed software. This capability will restore damaged or corrupted software files so that a reliable and functional system is always available for the users.

Final Words for Group Policy Software Installations

After a Group Policy software package has been created, you can still check the properties for the package and change some additional features:

- *Deployment options*—These can determine the scope of user involvement in the installation as well as other deployment options. Deployment options range from triggering installation by double-clicking a file association to uninstalling the application when a user or computer is moved out of the territory that the Group Policy covers.

- *Upgrades*—These are similar to modifications. Rather than create an entirely new MSI file, which is sometimes impossible, a package can be created specifically to perform an upgrade. This Upgrades property indicates whether an upgrade should be applied to the current package or whether the current package is an upgrade.

- *Categories*—You can categorize the software package associated with a Group Policy. This allows packages to be displayed with other packages of the same type. This can come in handy when building groups of packages that are specific to departments or job types.

- *Modifications*—Many applications that use MSI files also have the capability of adding custom features. Rather than re-create the entire package, these customizations are applied as adjuncts or add-ons to the main package. These adjuncts are called transform files and end with an *.mst extension.

- *Security options*—These list personnel that have authority to change the assigned GPO package.

Software can be installed either at the computer or the user level of a Group Policy. There are differences between the two levels and how they ultimately interact with different logged-in user profiles. Applications that deal with hardware or the computer itself should be installed at the computer level of the GPO. Service applications, such as antivirus and backup applications, should also be installed at the computer level because they are independent of any specific user logon. Applications that are user specific should be placed at the user level of the software package's GPO. You might be tempted to install default corporate applications (programs that everyone in the company needs) at the computer level, but I recommend against this because the application icons and user-based registry changes will not show up for logged-on users. In essence, the application will need to be installed again.

Placing an MSI package at the user level also requires some additional awareness. When a user logs in to the computer, the policy is applied, and the application is installed appropriately for the first time. When another user logs in to the same machine, the entire process is repeated. In situations where a given computer is truly a multiuser system or when dealing with a high turnover rate, a 10-minute install process can be tedious even when user intervention is not involved. Instead, this is another situation where RIS comes in handy. In addition to creating the same software package GPO, install the operating system using RIS and include the installed application in the RIS image. The application will install itself for every logged-in user, but it only copies user-specific items, rather than overwriting the entire application. It will change a 10-minute wait to a 30-second pause.

One more thing that you need to be aware of with regards to Group Policy software packages: User profiles can make or break the entire project. Let's say that one of your users—Mike—is a member of the accounting OU. Mike has Microsoft Office installed on his computer. Nobody else in the accounting group has it installed, yet they all need it. To save yourself some time, you deploy Microsoft Office as an installer package within a Group Policy assigned to the accounting OU. Group Policies are initially applied upon system startup and domain logon. After that, they are updated every 90 minutes (give or take a random offset that Microsoft put in there just to keep us guessing). Software deployment and folder redirection do not follow this rule, as these policies are only executed upon system login. The first thing of which you need to be aware is that if you enable the Group Policy in the middle of the day, users might become alarmed when a computer automatically begins doing things on its own as it's installing Office when they log in right after lunch. The second thing to be aware of deals specifically with the user Mike. Because he's a member of the same OU, the program will reinstall itself for him along with all of his coworkers. This is bad because not only will it cause an unnecessary delay, but any application customizations that he's made will be erased, which could possibly take Mike offline longer than it would have taken to install Office manually at each computer. I use Microsoft Office as an example here specifically because of Microsoft Outlook (which is included in the Office suite of applications). Not only will you need to reconfigure mail services and profiles, but local custom forms and templates within Outlook will be completely gone. My best advice to you would be to test the packages thoroughly by deploying them to a pilot OU with a few user assignments under it.

Managing User Settings and the Desktop Environment

User profiles are nothing new to Windows networking administrators. However, under Windows 2000, roaming user profiles, when used in conjunction with Group Policies, offer users greater flexibility and administrators more control. User profiles and all related environmental settings, files, and controls can be protected from corruption or loss in the same manner as user data. Keep in mind that a roaming user profile is defined on the Profile tab of a user's Properties dialog box (see Figure 5.4).

The proper management of environmental data through Group Policy ensures that the user's personal desktop is always accessible, that administrative control is maintained, and that the least amount of data must be transferred to the client system each time the user logs on.

With all of the different options available throughout Group Policy, let's take a look in detail at some of the more important Group Policy features available and

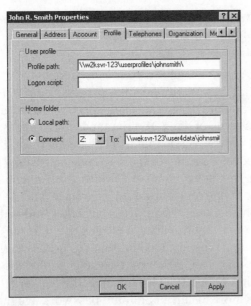

Figure 5.4 The Profile tab of a user's Properties dialog box.

what they can do for you. Because of the complex nature of Group Policies, we have added a Group Policy dictionary in Appendix A. As you become more and more familiar with Group Policy, you'll probably find yourself becoming frustrated with the fact that similar types of policies that all seem the same are located in different places. Particularly, I speak of the similarities between the policy folders under computer and user configurations. Appendix A should help you get your bearings by grouping similar functions together.

Computer Configuration|Windows Settings|Security Settings|Account Policies

By definition, everything under Security Settings for Group Policy will be covered in Chapter 20. However, some specifics are important enough to be mentioned here, especially in relation to the direct impact upon the users. Specifically, we are talking about password policies and account lockout policies. Due to the security nature of these types of policies, they can only be implemented at the domain level. If you attempt to assign a password policy to an OU, the system will simply ignore that portion of the policy. Security Settings account policies include:

• *Enforce Password History*—This is a policy similar to NetWare where the system remembers a set number of prior passwords. Most people have dealt with the annoyances that occur when they are forced to change passwords every so often, and many people will attempt to leapfrog between two passwords. In a higher security environment, this is not a good idea. In order to prevent this from happening, turn this policy on.

- *Maximum/Minimum Password Age*—This allows you to set a password expiration to occur every so often. The standard account properties have a similar feature. However, that particular trigger causes the account to expire on a specific date rather than on a cycle of days. Minimum password age is similar, with the specific intent of preventing people from changing their passwords too quickly. You may consider many of these security measures to be overkill. However, I assure you that many companies—the government included—are very concerned about hackers, corporate espionage, and international intrigue. Instead, consider a situation where a hacker finds out the password to an important account that has access to sensitive information. Let's also say that this account is the only account that has access to this sensitive information. During that time, the hacker may be able to view the sensitive information, but with other Group Policies in place, the hacker may not be able to download it. What's more, using a minimum password age that is very close to the maximum password age will prevent the hacker from changing the password inappropriately, which would make it difficult for you to get to your data.

- *Minimum Password Length*—This is another security feature that requires that a defined number of characters exist for any password.

- *Passwords Complexity Requirements*—This is probably the most powerful tool you have in this particular batch of policies. Between minimum password length and this policy, you can build a pretty good password policy that can make it very difficult for hackers to crack a password. Using this policy, you can require that passwords not include the username and that they contain numbers or symbols.

- *Account Lockout Duration*—For users, this is usually an annoyance that pops up when a good case of butterfingers occurs. When someone repeatedly attempts to log in to the network and fails, it might not be a good idea to let them keep trying until they get it right. Most of the time, we know that this happens when users mistype their passwords when setting them or when they forgot the password altogether. For security purposes, however, you might want to consider setting the account lockout policies so that the users cannot get into the account at all, even when the password is correct. The account lockout duration is a timer of how long that account is not allowed to log in to the network.

- *Account Lockout Threshold*—This allows you to define how many failed attempts it takes before the account is locked out of the system. Traditionally, this is set to three.

- *Reset Account Lockout Counter After*—This resets the counter that is tracking the failed logon attempts. If a user gets a case of noodlefingers twice, but then logs in successfully, it's not appropriate to lock the account out three days later when the user slips again.

User Configuration\Windows Settings\Folder Redirection

As promised, this is where you can configure specific local folders and directories to be redirected to a location on the network. The redirection process is seamless to the users. They can browse to the redirected folders using Explorer, My Computers or even the command line, and, in reality, the folder is located on the network. Folders that are automatically predefined as capable of folder redirection include the following:

- Application Data
- Desktop
- My Documents
- My Pictures (within My Documents)
- Start Menu

Enabling folder redirection occurs by accessing the properties for one of the listed folders. From there, you can choose to redirect the folder to the same location for everyone that the policy affects, or you can redirect the folder to different locations depending upon the user groups. The same location feature can be used to designate these folders as sourcing from the same location for everyone on this policy, but you can also use system variables, such as **%username%**, to designate a folder that is unique to a given user. The end result of redirecting the My Documents folder to \\server1\users\%username% for the user jvann would be a My Documents folder located in \\server1\users\jvann.

After setting the redirection option, you also have the opportunity to define if the folder is used exclusively by the user in question, if the local contents are moved to the network location, and what to do with the data if and when the policy is eliminated or the target redirection location is changed. When moving the local contents to the network location, I highly recommend that you leave this setting at the default. The folder redirection policy will indeed copy the contents of the local folder to the network, and the user will continually reference that location. However, synchronization between the true network and local folders is not created or maintained. What this means is that, when the network becomes available, the user will look for the folder in the usual places and notice that it is grossly outdated. You do not want to deal with this when a network is down.

User Configuration\Administrative Templates\ Windows Explorer

For some unknown reason, Microsoft has become fond of the term "Explorer" for any number of its products, including a mouse, an Internet browser, a file management tool, and an operating system shell. In this particular section, we discuss policies that can be applied to the file management tool. This includes both Windows Explorer and also other tools that perform similar functions, such as My Network Places, My Computer, and anything that happens in association with the **Explore** or **Browse** commands. This is where we begin to see the restrictions that average users would normally see:

- *Remove File Menu From Windows Explorer*—There are several instances where you might not want the File menu to appear within Windows Explorer. Remember that the **Delete** and **Cut** commands are located on the File menu, so removing this menu might come in handy, especially in situations where you really do not trust a user or group of users not to delete the WINNT or another important folder. Windows NT policies had the ability to do similar functions, but there always seemed to be ways to work around many restrictions. There are many fewer ways to do this with Windows 2000 policies because, rather than restricting the instance of an event, you are restricting the event itself. When this or any other restriction is in place, all but the most obscure workarounds are restricted as well. The bottom line is that removing the File menu removes all of the File menu entries and all other instances of those entries. This means that you cannot right-click on a file and rename, delete, or cut it because those options are all part of the File menu.

- *Remove Map Network Drive And Disconnect Network Drive*—This option will remove these options from the Tool menu within Explorer.

- *Remove Search Button From Windows Explorer*—This option will remove the Search button and search options from within Windows Explorer. This might come in handy when you want to prevent users from accessing or scanning network resources.

- *Hide These Specified Drives In My Computer*—This option allows you to hide specific drive icons from Explorer. These drives will still be accessible by their drive letters, but they will not be browsable.

- *Prevent Access To Drives From My Computer*—This option is used to restrict access to local disk drives, such as the A: drive or the CD-ROM drive. This is used frequently to reduce the risk of virus infection and also to reduce the possibility of a user walking off with sensitive data.

- *Hide Hardware Tab*—From within My Computer or Explorer, you have the capability of changing the drivers and settings associated with any local drive on the system. This is done by accessing the properties of the disk and selecting the Hardware tab from the Properties window.

- *No Computers Near Me In My Network Places* and *No Entire Network In My Network Places*—These two options can be used in conjunction to eliminate the curiosity factor from My Network Places.

- *Do Not Request Alternate Credentials*—Certain system functions will require user privileges that are greater than the currently logged-on user's credentials. Some of these same functions like to reiteratively ask for the credentials even when the currently logged-on user is an administrator. Turning on this particular policy will prevent the system from requesting an alternate username and password. Again, this is one more security measure to keep administrative access under control. Before thinking that this is one more overboard security issue, just remember that usually the only times that alternate credentials are requested are those dealing with domain-level security. This option is definitely worthy of some attention.

- *Request Credentials For Network Installations*—Remember this particular option. By default, Group Policy software installations for ZAP files run with the same authority as the logged-on user. With MSI files within Group Policy, you don't have this problem because these files are automatically run with elevated permissions that are capable of modifying the registry and other key elements of the system. When you turn this policy on, the system will prompt for user authentication when ZAP files are triggered for installation.

User Configuration|Administrative Templates|Start Menu And Taskbar

The Start Menu And Taskbar restrictions are particularly important for security reasons. In addition, the Start Menu can be configured as a redirected network folder. Start Menu And Taskbar restrictions include:

- *Remove User's Folders From The Start Menu*—This particular policy comes in handy when multiple users are referencing the same Start menu using folder redirection. In situations like this, it is not appropriate to store links to user-specific folders within the Start menu.

- *Remove Common Program Groups From Start Menu*—With this additional security feature, common program groups, such as Accessories And Startup, can be removed in order to reduce the possibility of a user inadvertently damaging the functionality of the operating system.

- *Remove My Documents Menu From Start Menu*—Similar to Remove User's Folders From The Start Menu, this policy removes references to My Documents from the Start menu for the same reasons.

- *Remove Network And Dialup Connections From Start Menu*—This particular policy removes the Network And Dialup Connections object from the Settings option within the Start menu. In general, if you apply Group Policy, it's probably a good idea to turn this on for the preventative value unless you want users to have the easy opportunity to kill their own network settings. The Network And Dialup Connections option contains all network hardware, software, and protocol configuration information. Standard access to Network And Dialup Connections is available by viewing properties from My Network Neighborhood Places.

- *Remove Favorites/Search/Help/Run Menu From Start Menu*—Each of these options is a separate policy that removes these items from the Start menu.

- *Add/Disable Logoff To The Start Menu*—These are two separate policies. Adding the Logoff To The Start Menu performs two tasks. It helps Windows 98 personnel in logging off the system, and, perhaps more importantly, it provides one less conduit for users to tamper with system resources (Task Manager) during the normal course of work.

- *Disable And Remove The Shut Down Command*—It's not uncommon to want to disable the **Shut Down** command in computers that are either high-usage, multiuser, or kiosk systems.

- *Disable Changes To Taskbar And Start Menu Settings*—This is another great feature for multiuser shared Start menu environments.

- *Disable Personalized Menus*—The personalized menu feature is new in Windows 2000 and only shows you the most recently used programs. Just about everyone I know disables this because it drives them nuts. This policy will disable personalized menus automatically.

- *Add Run In Separate Memory Space Checkbox To Run Dialog Box*—This particular policy is a good feature to have around for people who frequently test or compile applications, especially developers, who sometimes program things that get out of hand. This policy can prevent an entire system meltdown.

User Configuration|Administrative Templates|Desktop

These desktop policies include the following:

- *Hide All Icons On Desktop*—This literally hides both system-generated and user icons on the desktop. The icons still exist, but they are hidden. This is good because an installer application will usually burp when an attempt to place an icon on the desktop fails, and it's also great for kiosk systems.

- *Remove My Documents Icon From Desktop/Start Menu*—These two separate policies combined essentially remove the My Documents icon from general view. My Documents is still available by browsing Explorer. Unlike hiding an icon, the My Documents icon is completely removed from the desktop for the affected users.

- *Hide My Network Places/Internet Explorer Icon On Desktop*—This removes these two icons from the desktop with the intention of providing less temptation for personnel to wander away from their designated tasks. If the environment is this strict, however, you may consider simply hiding all icons on the desktop.

- *Prohibit User From Changing My Documents Path*—The My Documents icon on the desktop is a shortcut to the My Documents folder located in the user profile. If folder redirection is implemented for My Documents (which is the most frequent use of folder redirection because My Documents is the default save point for many applications), you probably don't want a user tampering with that particular setup. The user can still change the path, and it will be reimplemented when the policy is refreshed. However, it's a good idea to use this particular policy in conjunction with folder redirection in order to prevent files from being misplaced during that span of time.

- *Don't Save Settings On Exit*—The last time that we really used this was when it was a visible option within Windows 3.1. Since then, Windows 95, Windows 98, Windows Me, and Windows NT all save desktop settings (icon placement, system fonts, backdrops, and so forth) by default. This policy can be implemented in situations where the desktop is either shared or tightly controlled in order to prevent user changes from becoming permanent.

User Configuration|Administrative Templates| Control Panel

Control Panel policies include the following:

- *Add/Remove Programs*—Several separate policies reside under the Add/ Remove Programs option for Control Panel. These policies are as follows: Disable Add/Remove Programs; Hide Change Or Remove Programs Page; Hide Add New Programs Page; Hide Add/Remove Windows Components Page; Hide The Add A Program From CD-ROM Or Floppy Disk option; Hide The Add Programs From Microsoft option; Hide The Add Programs From Your Network option; Go Directly To Components Wizard; Disable Support Information; and Specify Default Category For Add New Programs. These policies can be turned on to allow a user to add specific types of programs, add only programs located on the network, view only specific items within Add/Remove Programs, or disable user access altogether.

- *Display*—The most important policies within the Display section of Group Policies are probably Screen Saver Executable Name and Password Protect

The Screen Saver. You can configure these two policies in conjunction with requiring a specific screen saver to appear that requires the logon or administrative password to be entered in order to disable it. This is great for accounting, human resources, or any other personnel who frequently work with sensitive information.

• *Disable Control Panel*—Disabling Control Panel is a quick and easy policy that allows administrators to breathe a sigh of relief almost instantly. The sheer fact that users are unable to access most hardware and system settings is a huge plus. One word of caution, however. Before rolling out a policy such as this, first make sure that all desktop, display, wallpaper, and screen saver settings are properly configured, and then test it with a small group of users. I once applied this particular policy and was very happy with it until I had a user who was visually impaired and required a different screen resolution from everyone else. In the end, it might be better to disable portions of Control Panel and filter the group policy specifically for that person to enable access to display properties.

• *Hide/Show Specified Control Panel Applets*—Hiding and showing specific Control Panel applets is a significant improvement over the features of Windows NT policies. If you implement Group Policies at all, I'd recommend that, at a minimum, you hide the Add/Remove Hardware applet. At the same time, keep in mind that hardware management is both centralized and decentralized. Hardware device drivers can be installed by using the My Computer/ Properties/Hardware/Device Manager tab, by using Control Panel's Add/ Remove Hardware, or even from peripheral Control Panel applets, such as Mouse, Network And Dial-Up Connections, Keyboard, and Display. Nearly every item in Control Panel can become mission-critical if misconfigured in many, if not all, situations. If security is truly a concern, think through your Control Panel policies thoroughly, and test them to ensure that all issues are ironed out prior to a full deployment.

User Configuration|Administrative Templates|System| Logon/Logoff

Logon/logoff policies found here include the following:

• *Disable Task Manager*—Contrary to first impressions, Task Manager has much more system-critical power than you would assume. Most of this power is tied up in its very easy accessibility and frequent usage, both in conjunction with troubleshooting and simple curiosity. Task Manager can be dangerous because applications and tasks can be run and stopped from here. A background application or task that is ultimately essential to the function of a server or computer can be stopped manually by a user. This action can potentially cause great harm not just in availability, but it also runs corruption risks by abruptly halting the application. Disabling Task Manager is certainly a reasonable policy to implement.

- *Disable Lock Computer*—This policy, on the other hand, is not used frequently because, in the absence of a password-protected screen saver, locking the computer is the fastest and easiest way of securing sensitive data and allowing a user to walk away. However, there are situations where having a user tie up a computer, its resources, and its data by locking the computer can be dangerous, especially in environments where not everyone is either friendly or aware.

- *Disable Change Password/Logoff*—The Disable Change Password policy is redundant because the same feature can be enabled from within user properties in the Active Directory Users And Computers snap-in. You may want to implement this policy in order to save a few key clicks while creating users. However, if you create a template account with this feature included, it's much easier to place the feature there rather than within a Group Policy. In general, a decent rule to follow is that anything that is handled in Group Policy that can be handled elsewhere should be handled elsewhere. The primary reason for this is because Group Policy configuration and documentation quite often take longer than making the change elsewhere. In addition, troubleshooting Group Policies can be hard.

- *Run Logon Scripts Synchronously*—This policy is used to run logon scripts at the same time that Group Policies and profiles are being applied to the system. Normally, logon scripts are run after all group policies are applied, which makes the users wait that much longer before they can use the computer. Running logon scripts at the same time can shave a few seconds off of login time, especially with complex logon scripts, large user profiles, or extensive Group Policies.

- *Run Logon/Logoff Scripts Visible*—Remember this feature when troubleshooting both Group Policies and logon scripts. When troubleshooting Group Policies, be sure to disable the Run Logon Scripts Synchronously policy so that you can properly target where a computer may be hanging up—before or after the logon script. Additionally, just having this policy on allows us to see logon scripts and all of the system responses, which can be essential when troubleshooting logon scripts.

User Configuration|Administrative Templates|System

Of all of the frequently used Group Policies, only a few are left to cover in this chapter that are not covered more appropriately elsewhere. These system Group Policies allow you to disable the command prompt (including typing "CMD" in the Run field), to disable registry editing tools, to run only allowed Windows applications, and not to run specified Windows applications. The first two policies, disabling the command prompt and disabling registry editing tools, can be quite valuable. However, because much of today's computer population is afraid of the "big black window," disabling the command prompt isn't as urgent as it used to be. Disabling registry editors, however, can be a very good thing because anyone who shouldn't be in regedit or regedt32 and who knows how to run either of these programs could very well cause some serious harm. Basically, if they can get there, it can't be a good thing. Running or disallowing specific Windows applications can come in handy as the final touch to locking down a computer and restricting it to a single and limited purpose. Adding this policy to an already comprehensive policy of hiding Control Panel components and desktop icons can be quite effective. Before you do this, however, just make sure that all settings and configurations are installed, configured, and stable; in addition, test the policy to make sure that everyone—both users who are affected by the policy and users who are not (such as administrators)—can access the applications and system tools that they need to.

Immediate Solutions

Creating a GPO

To create a GPO, perform the following steps:

1. Click the Start menu, and select Programs|Administrative Tools|Active Directory Users And Computers.

2. Right-click the domain object or an OU, and select Properties from the pop-up menu.

3. Click the Group Policy tab at the top of the Properties window.

4. Click New.

5. An unnamed policy appears in the Link window. Enter a descriptive name.

6. Click Edit to configure the Group Policy further.

Linking an Existing Group Policy to a Different OU

To link an existing Group Policy to a different OU, perform the following steps:

1. Click the Start menu, and select Programs|Administrative Tools|Active Directory Users And Computers.

2. Right-click an OU, and select Properties from the pop-up menu.

3. Click the Group Policy tab at the top of the Properties window.

4. Click Add.

5. A window will appear showing all of the objects within Active Directory. Browse to and double-click the object that contains the Group Policy that will be applied here.

6. Double-click the Group Policy that will be applied here.

7. Click Close.

8. Close the Active Directory Users And Computers snap-in.

Configuring a Group Policy for No Override

Setting the No Override feature on a policy flags the system that items within this policy will not be overridden by subsequent or child. This does not mean that a policy that is applied to a child OU will not be applied. It does mean, however, that any duplicate policy elements within a child or subsequently applied OU will not be overlaid onto the policy that is flagged as no override. To configure a Group Policy for No Override, perform the following steps:

1. Click the Start Menu, and select Programs|Administrative Tools|Active Directory Users And Computers.

2. Right-click an OU, and select Properties from the pop-up menu.

3. Click the Group Policy tab at the top of the Properties window.

4. Highlight the Group Policy that will take on the No Override property.

5. Click Options. A dialog box will appear as shown in Figure 5.5.

6. Click the No Override checkbox.

7. A window appears to confirm that you want to mark the Group Policy as No Override. Click Yes.

8. Click OK, and then click Close.

9. Close the Active Directory Users And Computers snap-in.

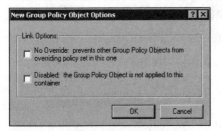

Figure 5.5   Group Policy Properties.

Disabling a Group Policy

Disabling a Group Policy turns it off for the OU or domain that the Group Policy is currently linked to. This also turns off its effectiveness for any child objects under the current OU or domain, but if this same Group Policy has been linked to another object within Active Directory, the Group Policy will continue to be effective in that location. To disable a Group Policy, perform the following steps:

1. Click the Start menu, and select Programs|Administrative Tools|Active Directory Users And Computers.

2. Right-click an OU, and select Properties from the pop-up menu.

3. Click the Group Policy tab at the top of the Properties window.

4. Highlight the Group Policy that will be disabled.

5. Click Options. A dialog box will appear as shown in Figure 5.5.

6. Click the Disabled checkbox.

7. A window appears to confirm that you want to disable the Group Policy. Click Yes.

8. Click OK, and then click Close.

9. Close the Active Directory Users And Computers snap-in.

Deleting a Group Policy

To delete a Group Policy, perform the following steps:

1. Click the Start menu, and select Programs|Administrative Tools|Active Directory Users And Computers.

2. Right-click an OU, and select Properties from the pop-up menu.

3. Click the Group Policy tab at the top of the Properties window.

4. Highlight the Group Policy that will be deleted.

5. Click Delete.

6. A Delete dialog box will appear.

NOTE: *From here, you have the option to delete the entire Group Policy or just the instance where it was linked to this object. If you delete the link, the Group Policy will still exist and be available for use. For lack of any better reason, I prefer to always delete the link. This ensures that the Group Policy is still available in the event that it has been linked to other objects. When it isn't linked to any other objects, I prefer to rename it and keep it around just as a reference. Group Policy can be quite confusing, so it's always been a good idea for me to keep examples of what did and did not work. This avoids the time-consuming troubleshooting involved with a failure that I forgot I had.*

---

7. Click OK, and then click Close.

8. Close the Active Directory Users And Computers snap-in.

Configuring a Group Policy to Hide My Network Places on the Desktop

To configure a Group Policy to hide My Network Places on the desktop, perform the following steps:

1. Click the Start Menu, and select Programs|Administrative Tools|Active Directory Users And Computers snap-in.

2. Right-click an OU, and select properties from the pop-up menu.

3. Click the Group Policy tab at the top of the Properties window.

4. Click on a preexisting policy (or create a new one) specific to this task, and click Edit.

5. The Group Policy window appears. Expand the User Configuration entry.

6. Entries appear for Software Settings, Windows Settings, and Administrative Templates. Expand the Administrative Templates section and then the Desktop section.

7. Several options appear as shown in Figure 5.6. Double-click the policy labeled Hide My Network Places Icon On Desktop.

8. The properties for this policy will appear. Click the Enabled checkbox, and click OK.

9. Close the Group Policy Window, click Close, and close the Active Directory Users And Computers snap-in.

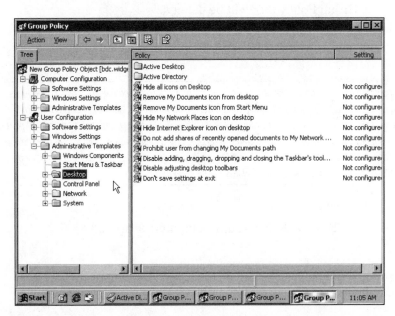

Figure 5.6   User Configuration|Administrative Templates|Desktop Policies.

Creating a Custom Group Policy MMC Console

Although not the most popular method of accessing Group Policies, you can create a custom Group Policy console that contains only the policies that you or an
administrator need to work on. Be alert, though, for situations where a Group
Policy might be linked to multiple Active Directory objects. To create a custom
Group Policy MMC console, perform the following steps:

1. Click the Start menu, and select Run.

2. Type "MMC", and click OK. An empty MMC console appears.

3. Right-click the console root folder, and select Add/Remove Snap-in.

4. Click Add, and a standalone snap-in window appears listing all possible
   snap-ins that can be added to this MMC console. Scroll down, select the
   Group Policy entry, and click Add.

5. Click Browse. A new window appears. Click the All tab at the top of the
   window.

6. Ensure that the appropriate domain is shown in the Look In field at the top
   of the window.

7. Double-click any of the listed Group Policies.

8. Click Close, and the Console window should appear with the new snap-in
   included.

9. Save the console by selecting Console|Save As.

10. Close the console, and make a note of the new console.

Configuring Folder Redirection

To use folder redirection to ensure that a user's data will follow him or her around
the network and will be available (even when he or she is offline) through a network share, perform the following steps:

1. Open the Active Directory Users And Computers snap-in. To manage the
   Group Policy for a site instead of a domain or OU, launch the Active
   Directory Sites And Services snap-in.

2. Locate and select the domain or OU for which to configure folder redirection.

3. Open the Properties dialog box for the container.

4. Click the Group Policy tab.

5. Group Policy

5. Select a listed Group Policy for this container.

6. Click Edit.

NOTE: *If you want to add a new Group Policy instead of editing an existing Group Policy, click New.*

---

7. Expand the User Configuration section.

8. Expand the Windows Settings section under User Configuration.

9. Expand the Folder Redirection section.

10. Select the Application Data item in the right pane.

11. Open the Properties dialog box for this item.

12. On the Target tab, select whether to redirect all users' folders to the same location or specify different locations for users and groups.

13. If One Location For All (Basic) is selected, provide the UNC for the network share location for this folder.

14. If unique locations will be defined for users and groups, add each unique user and group along with the UNC for the network share location for this folder.

15. Click the Settings tab.

16. Select whether to grant exclusive access rights to the Application Data folder to each user.

17. Select whether to move the contents of the local location of the folder to its newly defined location.

18. Select whether to leave the contents of the folder in the new location or to return the contents to the local original location in the event that this policy is removed.

19. Close the Application Data Properties dialog box by clicking OK.

20. Repeat Steps 11 through 19 for the Desktop, My Documents, and Start Menu items.

21. Close the Group Policy editor.

22. Click OK in the container's Properties dialog box.

23. Close the Active Directory Users And Computers snap-in.

Adding a Software Package to Group Policy

To add a software installation package to Group Policy, perform the following steps:

NOTE: *A Windows Installer software distribution package (MSI file) must be available.*

1. Open the Active Directory Users And Computers snap-in. To manage the Group Policy for a site instead of a domain or OU, launch the Active Directory Sites And Services snap-in.

2. Locate and select the domain or OU for which to configure software distribution.

3. Open the Properties dialog box for the container.

4. Click the Group Policy tab.

5. Select a listed Group Policy for this container.

6. Click Edit.

NOTE: *If you want to add a new Group Policy instead of editing an existing Group Policy, click New.*

7. Expand the Computer Configuration section.

8. Expand the Software Settings section under Computer Configuration.

9. Select the Software Installation section.

10. Select Action|New|Package.

11. Use the Open dialog box to locate and select the MSI file (the software distribution package). Be sure to select the file through a network path (that is, use My Network Places) instead of a local path.

12. Click Open.

NOTE: *If you select a local path, a warning dialog box will be displayed asking whether to go ahead and use the local path that is known. Most network users will be unable to access the installation files or to abort the configuration procedure. If this message appears, click No to abort and start over; then, be sure to select the MSI file using a network path.*

13. Select what method of deployment to configure this software for. The options are Published, Assigned, and Advanced Published or Assigned. Keep in mind that a published package will only be installed when a user manually initiates the installation from the Add/Remove Programs applet and that an assigned package will be installed automatically when a user selects the application's preexisting Start menu shortcut icon.

5. Group Policy

NOTE: *You need to know that group policy application assignments are different for computer group policies and user group policies. Computer group policy applications can only be assigned, while user group policy applications can be either published, assigned, or Advanced Published or Assigned.*

---

14. Click OK.

15. If you selected Published or Assigned, the new installation package will appear in the list of packages in the right pane of the Group Policy MMC snap-in display. At this point, the basic configuration of the software package is complete. To fine-tune or customize the settings, select the listed package, select Action|Properties, and then continue from Step 17.

16. If you selected Advanced Published or Assigned, the Properties dialog box for the installation package will open.

17. The General tab shows the displayed name of the process that can be customized along with details about the package itself, including version, publisher, language, platform, and support contact information.

18. Review this data; alter the displayed name if desired.

19. Click the Deployment tab.

20. This tab can be used to configure several options:

    - *Deployment Type*—Used to set the installation package deployment type to Published or Assigned.

    - *Deployment Options*—Used to enable or disable various deployment options, including Auto-Install This Application By File Extension Activation, Uninstall This Application When It Falls Out Of The Scope Of Management, and Do Not Display This Package In The Add/Remove Programs Control Panel.

    - *Installation User Interface Options*—Used to specify whether only basic minimal displays are shown to the user or complete messages, screens, and installation data are shown to the user.

21. Click the Upgrades tab.

22. Use this tab to specify whether this installation package is an upgrade to another installation package. When making this specification, you can also select whether to uninstall the existing package before installing the upgrade or to use this package to upgrade the existing installation.

23. Click the Categories tab.

24. Use this tab to place the installation package under a category displayed through the Add/Remove Programs applet.

25. Click the Modifications tab.

26. This tab is used to define modification scripts or to install routines that should be used against this package after it is installed. These modification elements are MST (Microsoft Transform) files. Multiple MST files can be applied in a specified order.

27. Click the Security tab.

28. This tab is used to define which users have access to this installation package. Users who will be installing this package need Read access only.

29. Click OK to return to the container's Properties dialog box.

30. Click OK to return to the Group Policy MMC snap-in window.

31. Close the MMC window.

Creating a ZAP File

The first step in creating a ZAP-based software installation is to copy the software package's install CD to a network location that is accessible by all of the users that will be affected by this Group Policy. The following example is specific for installing a fictitious application called Whizbang.

1. Click the Start menu, select Run, enter Notepad, and click OK.

2. Type the following:

```
[Application]
FriendlyName=Whizbang
SetupCommand=\\server1\installs\whizbang\setup.exe
[Ext]
wb=
```

NOTE: *The FriendlyName should be changed to whatever you want to appear within Add/Remove Programs. The SetupCommand should be replaced with the absolute path—either UNC or drive letter—to the software's installer application. File extensions that you want to be associated with this application should each go on a separate line under [Ext].*

3. Select File|Save As. Browse to a location on the network that is appropriate to store all ZAP files and is also accessible by all users that will be affected by this policy.

4. Name the file anything you want, followed by ".ZAP", for example, WHIZBANG.ZAP. Press Tab, and in the Save as Type field, select All Files.

Linking a ZAP File to a Software Package within Group Policy

To link a ZAP file to a software package within Group Policy, perform the following steps:

1. Open the Active Directory Users And Computers snap-in. To manage the Group Policy for a site instead of a domain or OU, launch the Active Directory Sites And Services snap-in.

2. Locate and select the domain or OU to configure software distribution.

3. Open the Properties dialog box for the container.

4. Click the Group Policy tab.

5. Select a listed Group Policy for this container.

6. Click Edit.

NOTE: If you want to add a new Group Policy instead of editing an existing Group Policy, click New.

---

7. Expand the Computer Configuration section.

8. Expand the Software Settings section under Computer Configuration.

9. Select the Software Installation section.

10. Select Action|New|Package.

11. In the Open dialog box, change the file type to ZAW Software Package (ZAP Files). Locate and select the ZAP file. Be sure to select the file through a network path (that is, use My Network Places) instead of a local path.

12. Click Open, and then click OK.

13. Click Close, and close the Active Directory Users And Computers snap-in.

Applying a Policy to a Specific User or Computer Group

Group Policies by default are assigned to domain, site, or OU objects within Active Directory. You can, however, restrict how a Group Policy is applied within an OU based upon user or computer group membership. Even though a policy can be filtered on a per-user basis, we recommend against it just because of the additional administrative overhead necessary to document and keep track of such granularity. If a single user or group in a different OU needs the same policy, you should link the same policy to the parent OU and restrict access to all other users and groups for that policy. To apply a policy to a specific user or computer group, perform the following steps:

1. Click the Start menu, and select Programs|Administrative Tools|Active Directory Users And Computers.

2. Right-click an OU, and select Properties from the pop-up menu.

3. Click the Group Policy tab at the top of the Properties window.

4. Click a configured policy (or create a new one and configure it), and click Properties.

5. Click Security. You will notice that, by default, all security groups belonging to the affected OU are listed with at least the Apply Group Policy property shown as allowed.

6. Click a security group that you do not want to be affected by this policy, and select Deny in the lower window.

7. Click OK.

8. Click Close, and close the Active Directory Users And Computers snap-in.

Instantly Applying Policy Changes at the Desktop

By default, domain computers will refresh the Group Policies that aren't software deployment or folder redirection on their own every 60 to 120 minutes. In the event that you are testing Group Policy changes or need to implement a fix quickly, perform the following steps:

1. Click the Start menu, and select Run.

2. Type "CMD", and click OK.

3. Type in the following to refresh computer configuration policies:

```
secedit /refreshpolicy machine_policy /enforce
```

4. Type in the following to refresh user configuration policies.

```
secedit /refreshpolicy user_policy /enforce
```

5. Type "EXIT", and press Enter.

5. Group Policy

Chapter 6

Migrating from Windows NT to Windows 2000

In Depth

The process of migrating from a Windows NT environment (workgroup or domain) to a Windows 2000 environment can be a huge and daunting task, especially if you aren't thoroughly familiar with the details and tasks involved. Microsoft seems to have finally figured out that if it really wants you to use its network operating system (NOS), it might be a good idea to actually help you migrate there from your current environment. It's difficult to migrate to Windows 2000 when you currently live on Unix or NetWare. Tools and utilities are available to assist in transitions of these types. However, for the most part, we need to focus strictly on migrating the Windows products. In the past, Microsoft has been kind enough to provide tools and third-party utilities to get you from NetWare or Unix to Windows, but it was sadly lacking in getting you from earlier versions of Windows to current versions of Windows. That's all changed. Not only does Windows 2000 offer upgrade paths that I've never seen before, along with heterogeneous support for older versions, but Windows 2000 has a flexibility in directory services that I've never seen before either. What this means is that you can perform an upgrade or migration piecemeal, which provides time to adjust and troubleshoot and to create your own upgrade schedule based upon your environment, rather than upon what the NOS required to function. The icing on the cake is that Windows 2000's Active Directory is flexible enough to allow you to reorganize the structure without losing information.

Remember that Windows 2000 and Windows NT are vastly different operating systems. Also be aware that as far as a Windows NT 4 system can tell, it is the newest server operating system from Microsoft. It was not created to communicate with Windows 2000. Thankfully, however, the developers at Microsoft kept in mind that there are numerous Windows NT installations in the world. Therefore, Windows 2000 can look and feel like Windows NT to a Windows NT system.

When a Windows 2000 domain controller is installed or upgraded into a domain that consists of one or more Windows NT domain controllers, it runs in what is known as *mixed mode*. With mixed mode, the Windows 2000 domain controllers must be an upgrade of, and will emulate, the Windows NT primary domain controller (PDC) of the domain and will use this role to communicate with Windows NT systems and users.

Migration Types

In order to back up its claims that migrating to Windows 2000 from Windows NT is fully supported, Microsoft first needed to look at the different situations where you might be upgrading and to build migration plans around those situations. In the end, it found that there were three different migration plans, each modularly based around different environments and requirements that you might have while upgrading and migrating to Windows 2000. As you read through these three different types of migration strategies, keep in mind that everything is modular and domain based. This is only realistic because you cannot expect to migrate or upgrade an entire multidomain enterprise all at once. This is by design. The idea is to migrate domains one by one so that you can troubleshoot potential problems and also reduce downtime before moving on to the next phase in migration.

Domain Upgrade

A domain upgrade is exactly what it sounds like. The idea is to upgrade the Windows NT PDC to Windows 2000 and to establish it as the forest root domain controller that anchors the forest root. Then, as time allows, backup domain controllers (BDCs) are upgraded appropriate to criticality and functionality. After all domain controllers are upgraded and everything is settled, the domain is officially upgraded.

You want to perform a domain upgrade process when system downtime (necessary for the actual upgrade process) can be scheduled and when the environment does not require 100 percent uptime. The upgrade process is also ideal because it is not necessary to enter new user or computer accounts, groups, profiles, or policies. Nearly all native domain information is automatically migrated during the upgrade process.

Domain Restructure

A domain restructure is the exact opposite of an upgrade. Basically, all Windows NT accounts and resources are moved into a separate and pre-existing Windows 2000 structure. Reasons for not performing an upgrade fall into one or more of these four categories:

- The existing server hardware may not be compatible with Windows 2000.
- System downtime may not be available.
- You may want to test Windows 2000 thoroughly in an isolated environment in such a manner that you can duplicate all mission-critical systems.
- Your current domain infrastructure is so unstable or undesirable that it's important to consolidate domains as soon as possible.

The possibility of not having existing server hardware that is compatible with Windows 2000 pretty much indicates that a restructure involves new hardware. The unique thing about it is that you install Windows 2000 Server or Advanced Server on a clean server system and test it until you're ready to begin migration. Migration itself occurs when you either copy or move resources from the source domain into the new Windows 2000 forest. Moving or copying small groups of resources will accomplish the same piecemeal result that you see with a domain upgrade, but with almost no system downtime. Low downtime is possible because all applications and services that reside on the Windows NT domain controllers have already been installed and tested in the laboratory environment before they get converted into production.

TIP: *I'm sure that you are thinking about the ramifications on other servers—Structured Query Language (SQL), Internet Information Server (IIS), Exchange, and other application servers. For the most part, Microsoft has always recommended that application servers reside separate from domain controllers. If this is the case in your environment, the restructure process is the same for your member servers as it is for your desktops. Change the domain that the system logs in to. If you are blessed with having both applications and domain controller functions residing on the same machine, this might be a good time to recommend splitting the functionality into a new system. After all, you're already purchasing or recycling server hardware; it might be a great opportunity to refine the environment further.*

For the previous bullets 1, 2, and 3, I would definitely recommend that you perform a restructure. Bullet 4, however, might not be enough justification for an outright restructure. My personal preference in situations such as this is to upgrade the domain and then restructure other domains accordingly.

Upgrade then Restructure

Quite often, performing an upgrade followed by a restructure is the ideal solution for your environment. This applies particularly in multidomain enterprises. More than likely, the overriding reason that you've gotten management to buy off on Windows 2000 is due to the features available with Active Directory. Unless you have an overwhelming need to reduce system downtime as much as possible, the quickest way to get from point A (Windows NT) to point B (Windows 2000) is to perform an upgrade process. One possible reason for restructuring lies with an inherent flaw within Windows NT: Security Account Manager (SAM) database size limitation. The SAM database has a limit on how many objects it can store. Many corporations, in order to work around this particular problem, created multiple domains and linked them together with trusts. Sometimes these domains were just extensions of the original domain, but for the most part, these additional domains were structured to hold either accounts or resources in order to reduce the overhead necessary to administer these workaround domains. These specialized domains are called *resource domains* (domains that hold servers, printers, and data) and *account domains* (that hold user accounts, computer accounts, groups, policies, and so forth). In situations where multiple domains lie under one roof or location and also where domains were created to allow departmental administration, you may be thinking that restructuring these domains into a single domain might be the way to go.

For those domains that were created to overcome the Windows NT SAM limitation, there really is no reason not to consolidate them. Administratively created domains are somewhat more annoying to consolidate due to potential office politics, but, with the newer advances of Group Policy and the delegation of administration, it should be easier for you to provide departmental personnel with the ability to control and administer user accounts and resources more appropriately, without giving them the ability to inadvertently shoot themselves in the proverbial foot.

Despite the fact that you can see a need to restructure, especially with the additional features of Active Directory, there still may be no overriding justification for performing a restructure-only migration. There is certainly no justification if you don't have the hardware available to create a laboratory environment to emulate production and if the domains structurally and organizationally work and function just the way they are. In this situation, you can upgrade the domain(s) as they are, let the proverbial dust settle for a while, and then tackle the political and organizational task of collapsing the newly upgraded Windows 2000 domains into the structure that you feel is most efficient for your environment. You may be wondering at what point you should consider leaving separate domains intact. Ideally, this should be when intradomain traffic and replication becomes a bandwidth issue. Specifically, when a domain resides in a remote location that requires wide area network (WAN) links to communicate with other domains. See, the ideal Active Directory structure should be where all domain members and resources exist on the same local area network (LAN) or metropolitan area network (MAN) so that these resources can take advantage of the speed and availability that Active Directory provides for that domain. Remote locations that are connected by slower WAN links or slow connections should be separated from the central domain in order to take advantage of the replication features that are designed to handle remote locations.

NOTE: *Remember that, with Windows 2000, you can restructure your domain on the fly. You are no longer presented with the problem of domain controllers being locked into their domains. You can now dynamically move them between domains. I discuss this in detail in Chapter 7.*

Analyzing the Current Environment

Before you jump right in and upgrade your network to Windows 2000, you should check out all the ramifications this might have. What follows is a recommendation of the steps that you should follow when migrating your existing Windows NT network to a Windows 2000 network. Obviously, the more complex your network means the more complex the migration plan will be.

The migration plan can be divided into several sections:

1. Discover and assess your current network. This includes the existing domain model and trusts, accounts, data, and applications.

2. Model and design your Active Directory infrastructure.

3. Optionally, you can cleanse your data. Fix any corruptions, streamline processes, and basically get everything in order and ready to perform the migration.

4. Perform the migration.

In most organizations, servers are added as budgets are approved, needs change, and projects arise. If you administer a medium-to-large network, chances are that you occasionally find new servers with new resources. Because the Microsoft suite of server software is so easy to install, anyone can do so (installing it *properly* is another story, though). To most end users, Windows is Windows is Windows. To most users, Windows 95 is the same as Windows 98, which is the same as Windows NT, which is the same as Windows 2000. Maybe this is a marketing fault of Microsoft, but it is not uncommon to hear "Another version of Windows? No way I am installing Windows 2000 on my home system!" Remember, Windows 2000 is designed for the office environment. Nonetheless, if users require Windows to be installed on their system and they cannot find you, the users just might grab the first Windows CD-ROM they find and install it.

One of the most important tasks that you must perform is to discover your existing domain structure. Again, if you administer a small network, that structure is usually simple—just one domain. Many organizations, however, will have many domains with trust relationships between them. The Windows 2000 networking model (with Active Directory) is usually a single forest with a single domain (although larger organizations might have several domains). The following subsections cover what you should consider before you migrate your network to Windows 2000.

Existing Domain Model

The most common domain structure is a single domain for a small to midsized company. Upgrades and restructures for these types of environments are remarkably shorter and simpler than a multiple domain environment. Domain structures in the Windows NT 4 world with one or more account domains with one or more resource domains, on the other hand, can be more complex and, overall, a longer project. For your own peace of mind, after you design your Active Directory model, try to just focus on one domain at a time, as if it was the only domain that you needed to migrate. For your own sanity, take this advice: Never ever migrate more than one domain at the same time unless you absolutely have to. When you look at the existing domain model, you need to do several things:

- Look at all of the existing domain controllers. Just because one or two domain controllers aren't up to par for Windows 2000 doesn't necessarily mean that you must perform a restructure-type migration.

- Look at all of the servers within the domain. You might have member servers that are better able to handle the Windows 2000 loads than your existing domain controllers. Now, usually member servers exist as application servers, which shouldn't mix with domain controllers, so you might consider trading roles between a less-than-ideal domain controller and a member server. This makes the member server into a domain controller and installs the applications on the domain controller. If you plan to upgrade the member servers to Windows 2000 eventually (which is a separate process from a domain migration), all you need to do is upgrade the member server/BDC and not install Active Directory when you're done with the migration. Remember that any Windows NT domain controller that is upgraded will automatically run DCPROMO to install Active Directory. If you do not wish for the PDC or BDC to be a Windows 2000 DC then you'll need to cancel out of the program.

- If you live in a multidomain environment, do some research. Find out (if you don't already know) exactly what the boundaries are for each domain and why it has been created. If it was created for departmental administration, start laying the political groundwork now. Start telling the decision makers about the great new features and benefits that come with a consolidated domain.

Existing Trust Relationships

Two different trust relationship types exist in a Windows NT 4 network: one-way and two-way trusts. Going back to the most common domain model, the account domains trust each other using two-way trusts whereas the resource domains trust the account domains. This makes sense to you if you have implemented domains and trust relationships before. If not, think of it this way. If two domains exist (account domain A and resource domain B), domain B will trust domain A (in other words, domain B will trust the *accounts* from domain A to use its *resources*).

NOTE: A two-way trust is actually two one-way trusts flowing in the opposite direction.

Trust relationships are important. Recall from Chapter 3 that Windows 2000 trust relationships are transitive, which means that trusts are (for the most part) automatically created and maintained by the system. If, for some odd reason, you are responsible for an enterprise that contains an isolated domain, you will probably want to upgrade or migrate it into its own forest.

Also be aware that, within any restructuring scenario, you will need to create trusts manually between the Windows NT and Windows 2000 domains. To the contrary, when you upgrade the PDC in a Windows NT domain to Windows 2000, trusts will be upgraded automatically as explicit trusts. This is the only time where Windows 2000 will automatically create a trust for you that is not dynamically transitive.

Domain Controllers

Knowing how many domain controllers you have as well as their geographical and logical locations will help tremendously in the migration. Be extremely careful when upgrading a domain that does not have BDCs. As a matter of fact, if you don't have a BDC, make one, even if only temporarily. More details on why are in the section called "Keys to a Successful Upgrade."

Accounts

Recalling again that Windows 2000 uses transitive trust relationships, you'll want to compose a list of all the user accounts and groups that exist in your domains. This is particularly valuable when performing a restructure of any kind. In larger environments, it may not be necessary to document every single user, but rather to document groups. One of the restructuring tools, Active Directory Migration Tool (ADMT) will migrate all user accounts associated with a selected group, so you won't need to worry so much about making sure that every single account is copied or moved. No matter how you plan on performing a restructure, be sure that you get a list of user groups that exist within the Windows NT domain and a list of the resources to which they have been given permissions. If you have time, also document the users belonging to those groups. Remember that user accounts can belong to multiple groups, so you might also want to keep an eye on which groups contain duplicate users so that you can take the appropriate precautions as in the ADMT section.

One last thing regarding accounts that you should consider when you're doing a domain restructure, keep user and group account changes to a minimum. If you can lock down and restrict changes altogether, that's better. The reason is this: Let's say that you migrate a user group from the source Windows NT domain into the target Windows 2000 domain. Two weeks later, you need to migrate another user group. Now, let's suppose that one user was a member of both groups. He was initially migrated to the new domain when the first group was cloned. You have the option to overwrite the account information (when you use ADMT) when the second group is migrated. If neither Windows 2000 nor Windows NT account properties or privileges have changed since the first go-round, you can recopy the account during the second user group migration and not worry. If changes have been made, you'll need to migrate the Windows NT account under a different account name and then work to piece together the differences between the remigrated NT account and the existing Windows 2000 account. Otherwise, any changes on the Windows 2000 side will be lost when you overwrite the account with the original Windows NT account.

Data

Data is at the root of everything in a network. In the midst of user logins, scripts, and passwords, data sharing and security are the sole reasons for a network's existence. In a domain restructure, data will certainly end up on the back burner while attempting to migrate users, groups, profiles, and everything that makes one domain unique from another.

Normally, we don't even consider data an issue during a domain upgrade, except for environments where Windows NT intradomain synchronization and replication has been configured. Now, it's easy to get confused between synchronization and replication within the Windows NT and Windows 2000 environments because Microsoft seems to have changed the definitions on the sly between one and the other. Windows NT synchronization is what occurs when a PDC shares SAM information to BDCs within a domain. Windows NT replication (also known as the LMRepl service) is what occurs when you have configured a specific folder to be shared from one replication server to another. Within Windows 2000, the term "synchronization" doesn't really seem to exist anymore, and, if it does, it's used interchangeably with the term replication. I could probably start a trend by coining Windows 2000 synchronization as being the process where Active Directory data is interchanged between domain controllers within a single domain. Windows 2000 replication is the process where Active Directory information is exchanged with other domains within the Active Directory tree and forest.

Windows NT replication is not supported within Windows 2000. This is because it has been replaced by an automated process where all data located within the

SYSVOL share is replicated to all other domain controllers in the domain. Although this may seem annoying at first, it's really a blessing because you can finally be assured that your login scripts are being disseminated appropriately. At the time of this writing, no other process for establishing replication is available. I will discuss the intricacies of dealing with replication in a mixed mode domain in the section called "Keys to a Successful Upgrade."

Maintaining Accessibility during Migration

Compared to a domain restructure, domain upgrades are easy as long as you're upgrading from a stable and working environment. Doing a domain restructure is not unlike moving an infantry unit from point A to point B. One of the biggest concerns of any Army general is to make sure that the supply lines carrying food, equipment, and fuel are available not just to the soldiers at the front of the march, but to the entire platoon in transit. For the individual soldier, it doesn't matter where you are. If you don't get food, you can't go on. If you (and your fellows) can't go on, the war is lost because of food. In a domain restructure, the soldiers are your user accounts, and network access is the supply line. It's of the utmost importance in your company's battle for survival that migrating users—no matter where they are—have access to the network.

sIDHistory

During an upgrade, all user data, permissions, group assignments, and other details are upgraded when the PDC is upgraded, so we don't have to worry about that information. During a restructure, we will need to take some care to ensure that users can still access the data after they—or the data—have been copied, cloned, or moved from one domain to another. On the surface, this seems like not such a big deal, but think about it. What happens if a user is moved (or even copied) from the Windows NT domain to the Windows 2000 domain? By definition, the user account will get a new security identifier (SID). Because resource access is granted and denied based upon an account's SID, the user won't be able to access the data still located in the Windows NT domain because the Windows NT domain is looking for the SID that was attached to the original account.

Windows 2000 has a feature called sIDHistory that is designed to eliminate this particular issue. Certain restructure tools have the feature (either automatic or user defined) to keep a copy of the source domain user account's SID embedded with the new SID when the account is migrated. Ultimately, what happens is that a migrated user account will attempt to access the source Windows NT domain using both SIDs, and, providing the old SID had the appropriate permissions, data access is granted. It is possible to create duplicate account names and passwords between the two domains, but, if you're going to do that, you might as well just manually enter in all of the information because, even with trusts in place, you'll still need to reassign user access to the resources. Far better to clone user accounts and groups and take advantage of sIDHistory than to spend hours (if not days) reentering user accounts and access privileges.

Application Access

Another lurking issue that you'll need to look into deals with application servers. Applications like Windows NT Domain Name Service (DNS), Windows Internet Naming Service (WINS), and IIS will be automatically upgraded, but other applications such as Exchange and SQL will not. The first thing you'll need to do is determine if any of your networking applications are incompatible with Windows 2000, either as Windows 2000 domain members or on a Windows 2000 domain controller (or member server, if you plan on eventually upgrading Windows NT member servers to Windows 2000).

You'll also need to prepare for any application that hooks application user accounts into the Windows NT SAM's domain user accounts. Real-life situations where an application directly references SAM user accounts are generally few and far between, but you still need to be aware of them. If you do happen to be running one of these applications, you need to check with the manufacturer to see if it has any utilities to reestablish those hooks after the application is migrated or moved from one domain to another. One exception to this is Microsoft Exchange.

Without going into Exchange 101, Exchange is configured in your environment in two basic ways. The first is to run it completely separate from the Windows NT domain. When users open Outlook or another email client, the system will prompt them for a username and password, which is stored on the Exchange server. This is how companies use Exchange in non-Microsoft networking environments. The second way Exchange has been set up is to link user mailboxes directly to user accounts within Windows NT. This has the same effect that trusts have between domains. Exchange trusts that the domain authentication process is accurate and allows the domain user to access whatever mailbox has been linked to the SAM user account. During an upgrade, these links should be maintained because all account names and SIDs have not changed. The same is not true for a domain restructure, however. When an account (or group of accounts, for that matter) is migrated from one domain to another, it will still be able to access its Exchange mailboxes in the Windows NT source domain as long as the Exchange server remains there because sIDHistory takes care of that pass-through authentication. When the Exchange server is moved (be it member server or domain controller) into the new domain, those account links are broken because the mailboxes were linked to the user account's SID. Although sIDHistory will take care of making sure that the Windows NT domain will still recognize you, Exchange does not have such a rear-guard function. Instead, you need to relink all of the Exchange email accounts to the new Active Directory accounts in order to allow the same pass-through authentication to occur as it did before the migration. Don't worry. ADMT has a tool to do this for you.

Keys to a Successful Upgrade

Although Microsoft would like you to believe that the upgrade process is easy and glitch-free, there are a few things that you should do in order to ensure that upgrading is as easy as it seems.

DNS Health and Happiness

Before we go much further, you need to be aware (if you aren't already) that DNS resolves domain names to Transmission Control Protocol/Internet Protocol (TCP/IP) addresses that, in turn, allow computers to find each other on the Web, and most likely, within your network also.

Windows 2000 Active Directory requires DNS. If you're migrating from Windows NT DNS, this is no problem because Active Directory will upgrade DNS for you. If you aren't running DNS, this isn't an issue either because DCPROMO (the Active Directory Installer application) will install DNS for you.

If you are running Microsoft DNS, it's a good idea to go into DNS prior to the upgrade and safely eliminate any unnecessary or dead entries in order to prevent any glitches from occurring during the upgrade. Upgrade failures don't happen on healthy systems, but, when an upgrade does fail, there's a 99 percent chance that there's something wrong with DNS. Before you get to the failure part, make sure that DNS is working okay. Clean it up, make sure it works, and test it just before starting the upgrade. If you're uncomfortable wandering around DNS, check out Chapters 11 and 12, where I discuss functionality and concepts in detail.

If you are running in a non-Microsoft DNS environment, you have some research to do and some decisions to make. First of all, Active Directory doesn't require Microsoft DNS; it just requires support for dynamic DNS (DDNS) and pointer (PTR) records. Unix-based DNS people might recognize this as Berkley Internet Naming System (BIND) 8.1.2 or higher. Technically, Win2k will support BIND 4.9.7, however Microsoft seems to be a bit wobbly on what supported features go with what version of BIND. Check the Microsoft website for the latest 'recommendations' in the DNS arena. No matter what version you may be running, this is the research part. If the current DNS either supports DDNS and PTR records or is BIND 4.9.7 or higher, you're okay. Write down the IP address and server name of the DNS server.

If the existing DNS does not support DDNS and PTR records or isn't BIND 8.1.2 or higher, three options are available that will allow Active Directory to exist on the network:

- Talk to the existing DNS staff (if that's not you) and see if a DNS upgrade to BIND 8.1.2 is possible. If that's not possible, see if an upgrade to 4.9.7 is. If management is behind the move to Windows 2000 and Active Directory, they might also support a DNS upgrade to support it. Keep this in mind as you speak with people. DNS traditionally lives in the realm of Unix, and Unix administrators aren't always friendly toward Windows folk. There are several reasons for this, but primarily it's due to the fact that Windows (pick a version—any version) still doesn't hold a candle to Unix in the realm of stability and flexibility. Yes, both Windows NT and Windows 2000 were originally based on Unix, but the user interface that Microsoft added that we all know and love came at the price of a lot of the stability and flexibility that you see in the Unix world.

- Create a separate Windows 2000 DNS domain, and configure it to forward to the corporate Internet service provider (ISP). This is not an ideal situation because you will be forced to administer a real-live DNS system. I discuss DNS in detail in Chapters 11 and 12, but, for now, you need to be aware that, if you already have a Unix DNS in place, there's at least one person whose job is to take care of it. This is not without justification. One of the features of Windows 2000 DNS, BIND 8.1.2, and DDNS is the fact that certain network clients can automatically register themselves in the DNS database. Before this, all network clients had to be entered manually into the DNS database in order for proper name resolution to occur. This still must occur for several different types of servers. A lot of administrative overhead is associated with Unix DNS in a large corporation. Think twice before attempting to duplicate work by setting up and maintaining your own DNS.

- You can also request a delegated subdomain in the existing DNS structure that belongs exclusively to your Windows 2000 network. What this does is allow you to install Windows 2000 DNS in its own zone and domain and still use the existing DNS by configuring forwarding to the Unix DNS system. All domain members will receive their DNS information from Windows 2000 DNS, and, if Windows 2000 DNS is stumped, it'll pass the request on to the Unix DNS server.

The first suggestion is the ideal solution for environments that require non-Microsoft DNS. If that's not possible, the third suggestion is your next best choice. If you are unable to obtain a delegated subdomain, you may again consider pulling management out of your pocket, not just for getting Windows 2000 installed and functional, but also to avoid the extra resources that would be needed for a second solution.

Dynamic Host Control Protocol Clients

Prior to upgrading the first PDC, you'll need to ensure that the network has no activity. The easiest way to do this is to reboot the domain controller before upgrading it. For non-Windows 2000 clients, this will knock any currently logged on users off of the domain, but it will not prevent them from logging in after the server is up again. Ideally, you should notify all management and users that the network will be unavailable during the scheduled upgrade time.

In addition to this, you'll also need to set Dynamic Host Control Protocol (DHCP) client addresses to expire on the day of the upgrade. Normally, you'll have a set time where DHCP addresses automatically expire, such as seven days. In order to ensure that everyone's address expires on the same day, you'll need to decrement this automatic expiration by one day, each day, starting X number of days before the upgrade. X is the automatic expiration configured within DHCP. If, for example, DHCP is set to expire and renew IP leases every seven days, seven days before the upgrade you'll need to change the expiration to six days. On the following day, change it to five days, and so on. This will ensure that every client IP configuration lease is released on the day of the upgrade without requiring more renewals than necessary.

BDC Backout

If your Windows NT domain doesn't have a BDC, get one, make one, or promote one. Whatever you need to do, do it because it's absolutely essential that you have a BDC available. Why? You'll need it if the upgrade fails. What you'll do is synchronize the entire Windows NT domain and then physically unplug the designated BDC from the network. Don't get me wrong. Performing an upgrade migration is the least complicated of all scenarios to work with. This doesn't mean that there aren't potential issues, especially if your Windows NT DNS isn't in good working order before you upgrade it. In the event that an upgrade failure occurs, you'll need to take the failed domain controller off the network, plug in the BDC, promote it to a PDC, synchronize the domain again, and then go back to the drawing board and figure out what went wrong.

Synchronization and Replication

As we mentioned earlier, Windows NT replication is something that needs to be addressed if you're using replication in your current environment and are planning on maintaining a mixed mode domain with both Windows NT and Windows 2000 domain controllers for any length of time. If you're not using Windows NT replication, don't worry. Move on. If you are using Windows NT replication, read on.

Windows NT replication works by designating an import and export directory within Windows NT and then enabling replication. Frankly, it never worked very well for large amounts of data, and it always seemed to have real synchronization issues. I think it was originally designed to be just a mechanism to replicate login scripts and custom data. Windows 2000 solved these problems by defining the SYSVOL volume as being synchronized between all domain controllers within a domain. Literally, any file or folder placed in the SYSVOL volume will find itself copied to all other domain controllers within the domain—no configuration, no interference, and no administration. Although this is a great feature, Windows 2000 does not directly support Windows NT replication (LMRepl). This isn't a problem in native mode domains. It only becomes an issue in mixed mode domains where LMRepl has been configured. As soon as you upgrade the PDC to Windows 2000, you may need to deal with this particular issue because users will still be successfully authenticating against your Windows NT BDCs, but your Windows 2000 is still viewed as a Windows NT box and will also be authenticating users. In order to maintain any login scripts (or any other replicated data you've got going) that are still being replicated on the Windows NT side of the domain, you'll need to fabricate a bridge between the Windows 2000 domain controller and what amounts to the lead Windows NT dog in the LMRepl scheme. Windows NT replication can also have an impact on which servers are upgraded when. LMRepl can be configured on any Windows NT server, and, if it is occurring on member servers exclusively, you don't have anything to worry about until you begin upgrading member servers separately from the domain upgrade process.

When you configure LMRepl in a Windows NT environment, it can get out of hand rather quickly because replication paths aren't necessarily linear. Let's say that you have three different servers in your Windows NT environment:

- Server 1 can replicate data to server 2, which then replicates it to server 3. This is ideally the type of linear replication topology that you'll need to maintain your sanity in a mixed mode domain.

- Server 1 can replicate data to server 2 and server 3. This is also known as a star replication topology.

- Server 1 can replicate data to servers 2 and 3. Server 2 then replicates the same data to servers 3 and 1. Server 3 replicates the same data to servers 2 and 1. The original intention when creating this type of replication is to ensure that data will be replicated redundantly in order to avoid failure. The immediate downside of this is that there is a high risk of losing data anyway. Changed data is replicated one direction, and unchanged data is replicated back before the changed data can reach all branches of the replication tree. Windows 2000 helps avoid this by inherently only synchronizing changed information instead of the entire directory, as LMRepl did.

If you're planning a domain upgrade, it's highly recommended that you restructure your Windows NT replication scheme to match the first or second scenario in the previous bullets in order to ensure that data is replicated appropriately. It will become clearer in a moment why this is necessary.

The example in Figure 6.1 shows a basic network with five Windows NT servers (member servers or domain controllers) all performing replication among themselves. The plan is to upgrade each server according to its number on the network, starting with NT Server 1 and finishing with NT Server 5. When planning replication, start with the server that will be performing replication between the Windows NT network and the Windows 2000 network. This is called the *replication bridge*. This Windows NT export server should be among the last to be migrated to Windows 2000. Otherwise, you would have to reconfigure the replication bridge every time the Windows NT server was upgraded. Let's say that, in Phase 1

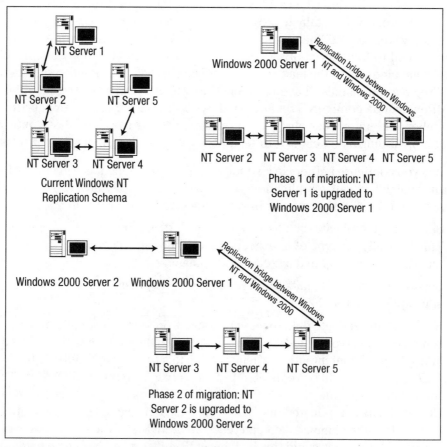

Figure 6.1   Replication during a Windows NT to 2000 migration.

of the migration, NT Server 2 was designated as the replication bridge. Phase 2 might become a problem because, after NT server 2 is upgraded according to plan, the replication bridge would need to be reconfigured for a different server. In our example, it is far better to designate NT Server 5 as the replication bridge. In the case of Figure 6.1, keep in mind that after NT Server 2 is upgraded, NT Server 3 will need to be reconfigured to no longer replicate with NT Server 2 because the replication to that server will then automatically be handled as a member of the Windows 2000 network. As you can see by the overall idea, it's very important that you discover, document, and restructure Windows NT replication as necessary within your network.

This process of discovering and changing Windows NT replication is relatively simple, but it can be time-consuming if you have a complex replication scheme in place. To discover your Windows NT replication scheme, open Server Manager from the server's administrative tools, and click the Replication button. If replication has been configured, it will show entries for import and export. The default import directory is for receiving, and the export directory is for outbound data. This can be changed so that both import and export directories are the same. You'll see this type of situation for the previous scenarios 1 or 3. If you choose to make any changes, you'll need to stop and restart the replication service (from within Control Panel|Services) in order to fully implement those changes.

After the PDC has been upgraded, you'll need to set up this replication bridge. Technically, this is a postmigration task, but we'll discuss the process here in order to help ease information overload.

After the first PDC has been upgraded, you'll need to configure a replication bridge to synchronize login scripts and other data between the Windows 2000 domain controller and the rest of the soon-to-be-upgraded Windows NT domain. You should already have replication structured linearly as shown in Figure 6.1. Just like building a bridge between two cities, we have a Windows NT city and a Windows 2000 city. First, we need to anchor the sides of the bridge by designating a Windows NT replication server and a Windows 2000 domain controller. Then, we make sure that the roads on the Windows NT side of the bridge are open to designated locations (servers) within the Windows NT city. Next, we open traffic going to the Windows NT city and then open traffic going to the Windows 2000 city. It is not necessary to make sure that the roads on the Windows 2000 side are open to designated locations because the Windows 2000 city is a much more advanced city that automatically conveys traffic where it needs to go. The steps are as follows:

1. Anchor each side of the bridge to a designated Windows NT replication server and a Windows 2000 domain controller. In order to avoid rebuilding the bridge after every server upgrade, the Windows NT replication server should be one of the last to be upgraded.

6. Migrating from Windows NT to Windows 2000

2. Make sure that the roads on the Windows NT side are open. Using your documentation of known import and export servers on the network, reconfigure all Windows NT import servers to expect data from the appropriate designated upstream or central replication server. You configure these roads going from the Windows NT side of the bridge by checking the properties of each import server within Server Manager and clicking the Replication button. Remove any entries from the Import window, and then add the appropriate entries back into the Import window so that they point to the Windows NT replication server.

3. Allow traffic to go to the Windows NT city. Create a batch file on the Windows 2000 domain controller that will be the Windows 2000 replication server. The batch file will copy the contents of the SYSVOL share into the import directory of the Windows NT replication server. A similar batch file called l_bridge.cmd can be found in the Windows 2000 Resource Kit. The batch file should look like this:

```
XCOPY \\WIN2K\SYSVOL \\NTREPL\EXPORT /S /D
```

Where **WIN2K** represents the Windows 2000 replication server, and **NTREPL** represents the centralized Windows NT replication server. The switch **/S** will copy subdirectories, and **/D** will copy updated files. Within the batch file, another similar line should be implemented that brings any Windows NT data into the Windows 2000 system. If you want to simplify life a bit, leave that line out, and be sure to restrict any changes from occurring anywhere other than within the Windows 2000 environment. The export directory must be shared with appropriate permissions so that the Windows 2000 replication server can access and write to that directory. Configure the Windows 2000 task scheduler to run this batch file as often as necessary.

4. Open traffic to go to the Windows 2000 city. Configure the Windows NT replication server to ship all the data located in the export directory out to the other Windows NT import servers on the network. Again, do this using Server Properties within Server Manager. Steps 1 and 4 will handle the Windows NT side of the replication bridge.

5. The Windows 2000 replication of the SYSVOL volume will occur automatically, thus handling the Windows 2000 side of the bridge.

Take One Last Look at the Hardware

Even though your current server hardware might be compatible with Windows 2000, that doesn't necessarily mean that it'll provide adequate services or thrive after it is upgraded to Windows 2000. In many ways, Windows 2000 is more intense than Windows NT, especially with all of the added features, so it's a good idea to get a hunch about how your servers will behave after they're upgraded. You can use a couple of tools to get a better idea of if a server is truly ready for prime time, such as the following:

With the CHECKUPGRADEONLY switch you can manually kick off the Windows 2000 install using the WINNT32.EXE application located on the CD drive. As always, numerous switches can be used. One of these is the /CHECKUPGRADEONLY switch. This switch will check the current OS and hardware for compatibility. This comes in handy if you don't want to, or can't, determine whether all of the components are up to snuff.

Keep Your Eye on the Ball

Think of any and every issue you've been called on with regards to the network. Consider whether this may become an issue again after the upgrade. This is simple advice, but difficult to keep track of in the real world when you're dealing with so many details involved with a migration. Try to anticipate any and every problem that you might see after the upgrade. Determine which ones are valid, and try to prevent them from becoming issues. At worst, you'll be anticipating complications and can appropriately notify management and your users of the impacts and solutions.

Upgrade Process

It's easy to get lost in the details associated with any migration strategy. In order to assist you with an upgrade migration, let's talk about upgrading within a single domain and then talk about upgrading in an entire enterprise.

Domain Upgrade

When it's time to upgrade, the first system that needs to be upgraded is the Windows NT PDC. The "Immediate Solutions" section shows that this is a relatively easy task because the Windows 2000 setup program does all the work.

The first real step in the upgrade is to ensure that the BDCs have the most up-to-date domain information. If you are upgrading a domain that does not have at least one BDC, you should install one (even if just for the upgrade). Having a BDC taken offline just prior to the upgrade ensures that all the user, group, and security information is backed up in case the PDC upgrade fails for any reason. Another reason for having a BDC on the network during the upgrade is to allow users to continue to log in to the network. If a BDC does not exist, non-Win2k users will not be able to log in to the network while the system is being upgraded.

The Windows 2000 setup program is smart. It recognizes that the server you are upgrading is a PDC and will automatically launch the Active Directory Installation Wizard (DCPromo.exe) after the core Windows 2000 operating system is installed. The options available during the Active Directory installation can become confusing. You will need to be prepared to provide locations for the SYSVOL share, Active Directory database, and logging files. If you have multiple drives, it's recommended that these things be separated from the boot drive in order to boost efficiency. If this isn't a possibility, just leave the defaults in place and move on.

As previously mentioned, when the Active Directory setup process is completed, the Windows 2000 domain will run in mixed mode. This means that it is fully backward compatible. It does this by masquerading as a Windows NT domain controller using a flat store system, which is commonly referred to as a PDC emulator. A Windows 2000 domain controller appears as follows on the network:

- Other Windows 2000 computers on the network will see the Windows 2000 domain controller as a Windows 2000 system.

- Windows NT systems will see the domain controller as a Windows NT PDC.

- All new accounts in Active Directory will still appear to be part of SAM to Windows NT systems.

- Windows NT and Windows 9x systems will still use the PDC as a logon server. The difference is that the upgraded PDC now runs the PDC emulator service, and NT and 9x clients won't know the difference.

- If the Windows 2000 domain controller becomes unavailable, an existing Windows NT BDC may be promoted to the role of a PDC.

After the PDC has been upgraded, you can continue with the migration by upgrading each of the BDCs to Windows 2000. Your network will continue to run in mixed mode until you manually set the mode to native. Although native mode provides access to new Windows 2000 features, many organizations decide to run in mixed mode for a while.

One reason for this is the inability to upgrade BDCs. Windows 2000 has higher hardware requirements than Windows NT. For this reason, you may find that some systems that run very efficiently as Windows NT BDCs will cause a bottleneck on your network if upgraded to Windows 2000. Also, if you require the ability to fall back to a Windows NT network, mixed mode is your solution. Mixed mode essentially gives you a way out of your upgrade. Another reason for not upgrading all your Windows NT servers to Windows 2000 is software compatibility. Windows 2000 is not 100 percent backward compatible. Given the scores of different applications that currently exist in the Windows NT world, you are likely to find one (or more) that will not function under Windows 2000 (presently). If such applications exist in your organization, you'll need to maintain some Windows NT systems to support them, thus running in mixed mode until such applications can be modified or upgraded.

At this point, all your domain controllers should be running Windows 2000. If the installation went smoothly, none of your users even noticed that anything changed (other than some servers not being available for short periods of time). One thing that you should be aware of is that to get the full power of Windows 2000 (both feature based and performance based), you should upgrade all your servers and your clients to Windows 2000 as well.

After all your domain controllers are upgraded, you're ready to switch to native mode. You might consider migrating all of your member servers, too, but it is not a necessary part of the domain migration process.

Before I move on, let's recap the basic process of performing a domain upgrade:

1. Synchronize the domain.
2. Take the designated fallback BDC offline.
3. Upgrade the PDC.
4. Configure the replication bridge between Windows NT and Windows 2000.
5. Upgrade BDCs as appropriate.
6. Upgrade the Windows NT replication server last.
7. Upgrade mission-critical application servers that are also domain controllers last.
8. After all BDCs have been upgraded, switch the domain to native mode.

Upgrading the Enterprise

We've already discussed upgrading a domain itself, but what do you do when you need to upgrade more than one domain, and which domain should be upgraded first? In many ways, you'll need to consider this before you do the domain upgrade. Basically, you'll need to choose a domain that will become the forest root for Active Directory. Usually, this would be a master domain, but it can be an account or resource domain. Microsoft recommends that you upgrade an account domain first because you'll see more benefits from Active Directory within a user environment than you will from a resource environment. No matter what, keep in mind that the first domain that ends up being migrated ends up being the Windows 2000 forest root, which holds some specific FSMO roles that you may want to have nearby for administrative purposes. Also, factor mission criticality and downtime in your decision-making process. My recommendation is to start by upgrading the core domain as the forest root. By this, I mean the domain that either holds the most resources, is closest to the central hub of the corporation, or is closest to you. When upgrading an enterprise, you're more than likely going to need to travel to remote locations, and it's probably not a good idea to use a remote location for your first upgrade experience, primarily because it's difficult to troubleshoot post-upgrade issues remotely. After the forest root has been upgraded, move on to child domains in order of preference. If your child domains can be categorized as account or resource domains, always upgrade the account domain first.

Now that you have a good idea (from Chapter 3) what Active Directory trees and forests are, you should really have no problems. However, you may want to follow these few guidelines:

- When upgrading a PDC in an isolated domain, choose to create a new domain tree and then create a new forest. When the system prompts, be prepared with a fully qualified domain name (FQDN) for DNS. Even if DNS doesn't exist, don't worry. The system will prompt to install it for you.

- When upgrading the first PDC in a master domain, create a new domain tree and then create a new forest. Be prepared to enter a FQDN for DNS.

- When upgrading the first PDC in a secondary master domain (an NT domain that is a master domain in an enterprise that has multiple master domains and is not slated to be the first master domain to be upgraded), choose to create a new domain tree and to join an existing forest. You will need to provide administrative credentials for the forest root domain.

- When upgrading the first PDC in any resource, account, or child domains, you'll need to create a child domain in an existing domain tree. Be prepared with administrative credentials for the parent Windows 2000 domain.

- When upgrading a BDC in any domain that has already upgraded the PDC, you'll choose to create a replica of an existing domain, and you will have to provide administrative credentials to the domain.

Keys to a Successful Restructure

In the event that you will need to perform a restructure process in order to get from Windows NT to Windows 2000, there are several tools available for use that will make this potentially daunting task easier. The number one key you'll need for any restructure is planning. Once you get a good idea of what tools are available, you'll need to make sure that you've planned every stage of the restructure process in order to ensure success.

ADMT

ADMT is usually used for domain restructures where it's necessary to consolidate or collapse Windows 2000 domains, but it is used to perform migrations such as a Windows NT-to-2000 restructure. It is the crown jewel of the Microsoft suite of flexible Active Directory products.

ADMT is discussed in thorough detail in Chapter 7. For the purposes of restructuring from Windows NT, you'll need to establish trusts between the source and target domains and make sure that you have administrative authority for both domains. Technically, you can run ADMT in either domain, but it's recommended that you run it within the Windows 2000 domain for stability purposes.

ADMT is actually a collection of wizards that perform each piece of a restructure procedure. You'll need to choose whether you want to clone accounts or to move them. In situations like this (also known as an interforest restructure), you always want to clone accounts so that you'll have the capability of having users log in to the old Windows NT domain in the event that something went wrong during the restructure process. You'll also need to decide whether or not to migrate users by accounts or groups of accounts. You have the ability to select groups of individual users or Windows NT user groups. It's recommended that you migrate Windows NT user groups because you kill two proverbial birds with one stone. User group migrations have the option also to migrate user accounts that are members of the affected groups. Migrating users on their own offers no tagalong group migration. Because most well-constructed domain resources are assigned using groups, it's probably a good idea to migrate groups rather than single users.

Microsoft realizes that any migration can take days, if not weeks, to accomplish successfully. This is why ADMT has been split into separate wizards that allow you to perform specific tasks in a modular or incremental fashion. Table 6.1 shows which of these wizards are used to perform which restructuring processes. One additional factor that I touched on earlier occurs when redundantly restructuring users. Because ADMT will migrate users when their groups are migrated, and because it often happens that users belong to multiple groups, it's a probability that at least a few users will be migrated more than once. ADMT has a switch that will target duplicate accounts and give you the option not to migrate them or to migrate them and change the names of the accounts so that you can fix them. I mention this particular point here because of its importance. Ideally, you should lock down all user account changes on both domains while the restructure is in process. However, because this might not be possible (especially when the

6. Migrating from Windows NT to Windows 2000

Table 6.1   Which wizards to use to migrate what objects.

Restructure or Migration Process	Wizard
Establish trusts	Trust Migration Wizard
Global groups	Group Migration Wizard
Domain local groups	Group Migration Wizard
User accounts	User Migration Wizard
Roaming profiles	User Migration Wizard
Target Service accounts	Service Account Migration Wizard
Workstations and servers	Computer Migration Wizard
Local profile updates	Security Translation Wizard

restructure takes a long time), you might see changes occurring within the Windows NT domain that aren't mirrored in the Windows 2000 domain, or vice versa. It will save you countless hours of time if you thoroughly document any changes in either domain so that you can determine which accounts can be remigrated and overwritten or remigrated and renamed so that you can subsequently fix the differences between the two accounts.

ClonePrincipal

ClonePrincipal is a tool that is used exclusively for restructuring and is covered in detail in Chapter 7. It is used to clone users and groups between domains, and its primary feature is supposedly being able to do so without interfering with the production environment. ClonePrincipal is more difficult to use and has fewer features than ADMT. If you're restructuring a Windows NT domain into Windows 2000, there's a good chance that you're more familiar with the workings of Windows NT than Windows 2000. If this is the case, don't use ClonePrincipal. This is not to say that it is a bad tool. It's great for certain situations, but if you want to be sure that all your i's are dotted and t's are crossed during this migration, use ADMT.

Restructure Process

Unlike upgrades, where you'll see the greatest return on efforts invested by first upgrading account domains, Microsoft recommends that any resource domains be migrated prior to account domains during a restructure process. Because all the players are already within Windows 2000, migrating users first has no advantage. As such, the restructure process is a bit different from an upgrade and includes the following steps:

1. Move workstations and member servers from the source domain to the target domain.

2. Migrate service accounts.

3. Update user rights and group memberships at this point while migrating resource domains because several network resources have been relocated while the bulk of users accessing those resources have not. Between sIDHistory and updating user rights and group memberships, you should be able to stabilize the situation.

4. Move domain local groups, users, and profiles.

5. Decommission the domain.

Postmigration Tasks

There's nothing worse than completing all or part of a domain migration successfully and not knowing whether it worked. Waiting for Murphy's Law to kick in can be excruciating, especially when everything works fine up until the point where users start calling in with problems. You can do several things to help prevent an unknown shoe from dropping from out of nowhere.

Check Connectivity

Log in to the domain, and make sure that you can get in. Log in not just as yourself or as an administrator, but also as a general user. Check to ensure that connectivity to the company intranet, network applications, and Web work also.

Checking DNS

Check to make sure that DNS is working. The quickest way is to make sure that you can get to the Internet. You can also use the Packet Internet Groper (**PING**) command to check DNS by pinging a server's FQDN. Start by pinging a known Internet server, such as **www.yahoo.com** or **www.microsoft.com**. Also ping your Windows 2000 server(s), such as dc1.gadgetsrus.com. Don't just ping the name of the server because Network Basic Input/Output System (NetBIOS) name resolution is handled by WINS. You must ping the *<servername>.<domainname>* where the *<servername>* is the server in question, and the *<domainname>* is the domain that it resides in.

Another method for checking DNS functionality is to run diagnostics on the DNS server itself. To do this, perform the following steps:

1. Get into DNS Manager by clicking Start and selecting Administrative Tools.

2. Then, right-click the DNS server name, select Properties, and then click the Monitoring tab.

3. Select the A Simple Query Against This DNS Server option, and click Test Now. The results will appear in the window. If anything other than PASS shows up, you may have a problem. Start troubleshooting by looking in the event log.

Checking Active Directory

Check Active Directory by going into the Active Directory Users And Computers console, creating a new account, and then using it to log in. If you have time, actually go through the entire process of creating a new user—everything inside and outside of Windows 2000, including network applications—and make sure that you can log in as that user and access all applications and data that that user should be able to.

You can also use the NETDIAG and NETDOM utilities to check for Active Directory object health and happiness. Both of these tools are in the \support\tools folder on the Windows 2000 installation CD. NETDIAG is a quick and dirty way of getting a well-rounded idea of what the Active Directory network looks like.

NETDOM is used to query (and sometimes change) specific Active Directory objects. Both can be used in troubleshooting.

Checking Trusts

You can check trusts in three ways:

- Select Administrative Tools|Active Directory Domains And Trusts, right-click the domain and select Properties, and click the Trusts tab.
- Run the ADMT Trust Migration Wizard in Test mode.
- Log in as a user, and attempt to access information in a different domain.

Checking Replication and Synchronization

Configure the replication bridge as I discussed earlier. Test it by making a change on the Windows 2000 side within the SYSVOL share and then manually kick off the replication using scheduled tasks. Check to see if the changes appear on at least the lead Windows NT replication server.

Converting to Native Mode

Okay, you have now upgraded all your domain controllers to Windows 2000 and are happy with the installation. The network has been running smoothly with the new operating system. Many administrators would like to flip the switch now and convert to native mode. Honestly, Windows 2000 has so many new cool features to make your life easier that you'll want to use them as soon as is humanly possible. Take heed, though. After the switch from mixed mode to native mode is made, you cannot go back without reinstalling your entire network.

Let the network run under the new operating system for as long as possible. Some applications (such as month-end applications) might not be used every day, and you won't find out that they failed under Windows 2000 until it is too late.

The best approach to take on your upgrade is to treat it like Microsoft treated Windows 2000. Instead of releasing the application on the original promised date, Microsoft decided to hold the operating system back until all major bugs could be fixed. When Windows 2000 finally shipped, it delivered a very stable product. This was done with testing. Windows 2000 was tested more than any other application in the history of the computer world. Treat your network in the same way—test, test, test.

When you are finally ready to convert your network to a native Windows 2000 network, you need to be prepared. Murphy's Law exists in the computer world as well. You can be assured that as soon as you switch the mode of your network, some application will appear that cannot run under Windows 2000. Just be prepared.

Immediate Solutions

Promoting a Windows NT BDC to PDC

To promote a Windows NT BDC to a PDC, perform the following steps:

1. Click Start, and select Programs|Administrative Tools.

2. Select Server Manager.

3. When the PDC is not available (such as after a failed upgrade), a message will appear stating that the PDC isn't available. Click OK.

4. Select Computer|Promote To Primary Domain Controller.

5. The Server Manager dialog box appears. Click Yes.

6. Another Server Manager dialog box appears. Click OK.

7. After the promotion is complete, Server Manager appears, indicating that the BDC computer is now the PDC.

Demoting a Windows NT PDC

In the event that a failed upgrade or restructure occurs, it will be necessary to promote a fallback BDC to a PDC in order to handle the necessary authentication functionality on the network. After the original PDC has been restored from tape, it will be necessary to demote the promoted PDC back into BDC status. To do this, perform the following steps:

1. Click Start, and select Programs|Administrative Tools|Server Manager.

2. Select Computer|Demote To Backup Domain Controller.

3. Click Yes.

4. Close the window.

Synchronizing a Windows NT Domain

The following steps outline the process of synchronizing a Windows NT domain:

1. Click Start, and select Programs|Administrative Tools|Server Manager.

2. Select the PDC.

3. Select Computer|Synchronize Entire Domain.

4. Click Yes to synchronize the domain.

5. Click OK.

Synchronizing a Single Windows NT BDC

To synchronize a single Windows NT BDC, perform the following steps:

1. Click Start, and select Programs|Administrative Tools|Server Manager.

2. Select the BDC that you would like to synchronize.

3. Select Computer|Synchronize With Primary Domain Controller.

4. Click Yes to begin synchronization.

Performing a Windows NT 4 DNS Cleanup

If you're planning on upgrading your NT DNS, you'll need to clean up the DNS database to make sure that duplicate or incorrect entries are removed. DNS may not function appropriately after the upgrade if it contains these types of errors. To clean up the DNS database, perform the following steps:

1. Click Start, and select Programs|Administrative tools.

2. Click DNS Manager.

3. Click the plus sign next to the entry for the DNS server.

4. Click the appropriate lookup zone, and make a note of any records that are unnecessarily duplicated or where the same name points to two different IP addresses. Make sure that these are not mistakes.

5. Click the appropriate entries for deletion, and press Delete.

6. A confirmation dialog box appears. Click Yes.

Upgrading

The following solutions discuss the various ways to upgrade your system.

Upgrading a Standalone Server without Converting the File System

Perform the following steps to upgrade a standalone server without converting the file system:

1. Insert the Windows 2000 Server CD-ROM. The autorun feature should start the CD automatically. If it does not, double-click My Computer, and then double-click the CD-ROM drive's icon.

2. A window appears stating that the CD-ROM contains a newer version of the operating system. Click Yes to begin the upgrade.

NOTE: *Alternatively, you can click the Install Windows 2000 option on the Microsoft Windows 2000 CD, or you can run the command-line executable by clicking Start, selecting Run, and typing either D:\WINNT.EXE or D:\WINNT32.EXE. You may need to replace d:\ with the drive letter of the current CD drive. You would also do the same by clicking on the browse button, browsing to the CD drive, and double-clicking on WINNT.EXE or WINNT32.EXE.*

---

3. Select the Upgrade To Windows 2000 (Recommended) option, and click Next.

4. After you have read the license agreement, select the I Accept This Agreement radio button, and click Next.

5. Enter the 25-digit product key as it appears on your Windows 2000 packaging, and click Next.

NOTE: *If the product key is entered incorrectly, you will be informed that it is invalid and will be required to enter it again.*

---

6. In the Upgrading To The Windows 2000 NTFS File System dialog box, choose not to convert the drive (you can do this at a later date) by selecting the No, Do Not Upgrade My Drive option and clicking Next.

7. Setup will now copy all the necessary setup files.

8. Click Finish. (You can also wait; the system will automatically reboot after 30 seconds.)

9. When the system reboots, choose the Microsoft Windows 2000 Server setup option from the boot menu, and press Enter. (You can also wait; the option will be automatically selected after about five seconds.)

10. Setup will then examine your disks and copy all necessary files.

11. When setup completes the copy, your system will reboot again.

12. Select the Microsoft Windows 2000 Server option from the boot menu, and press Enter. (Again, you can wait; the option will be automatically selected after about 30 seconds.)

13. Windows 2000 will start and detect and install devices.

14. Network settings will be set up and configured.

15. Components will be installed.

16. When the setup is done, click Restart Now.

17. Select the Microsoft Windows 2000 Server option from the boot menu, and press Enter.

18. When the system starts up, you'll be able to log in to the newly converted Windows 2000 system.

Upgrading a Standalone Server and Converting the File System

To upgrade a standalone server and to convert the file system, perform the following steps:

1. Insert the Windows 2000 Server CD-ROM. The autorun feature should start the CD automatically. If it does not, double-click My Computer, and then double-click the CD-ROM drive's icon.

2. A window appears stating that the CD-ROM contains a newer version of the operating system. Click Yes to begin the upgrade.

NOTE: Alternately, you can click the Install Windows 2000 option on the Microsoft Windows 2000 CD.

3. Choose the Upgrade To Windows 2000 (Recommended) option, and click Next.

4. After you have read the license agreement, select the I Accept This Agreement radio button, and click Next.

5. Enter the 25-digit product key as it appears on your Windows 2000 packaging, and click Next.

NOTE: If the product key is entered incorrectly, you will be informed that it is invalid and will be required to enter it again.

6. In the Upgrading To The Windows 2000 NTFS File System dialog box, choose not to convert the drive (you can do this at a later date) by selecting the No, Do Not Upgrade My Drive option and by clicking Next.

7. Setup will now copy all the necessary setup files.

8. Click Finish. (You can also wait; the system will automatically reboot after 30 seconds.)

6. Migrating from Windows NT to Windows 2000

9. When the system reboots, choose the Microsoft Windows 2000 Server setup option from the boot menu, and press Enter. (You can also wait; the option will be automatically selected after about five seconds.)

10. Setup will now examine your disks and copy all necessary files.

11. When the setup program completes the copy, your system will reboot again.

12. Select the Microsoft Windows 2000 Server option from the boot menu, and press Enter. (Again, you can wait; the option will be automatically selected after about 30 seconds.)

13. The setup program will now convert your drive to NTFS. When the conversion is done, the system will reboot.

14. Select the Microsoft Windows 2000 Server option from the boot menu, and press Enter.

15. Windows 2000 will start and detect and install devices.

16. Network settings will be set up and configured.

17. Components will be installed.

18. When the setup is done, click Restart Now.

19. Select the Microsoft Windows 2000 Server option from the boot menu, and press Enter.

20. When the system starts up, you'll be able to log in to the newly converted Windows 2000 system.

Upgrading a Primary Domain Controller Server Without Converting the File System

Perform the following steps to upgrade a domain controller without converting the file system:

NOTE: *At least one partition will have to be converted to NTFS for Active Directory to be installed.*

---

1. Insert the Windows 2000 Server CD-ROM. The autorun feature should start the CD automatically. If it does not, double-click My Computer, and then double-click the CD-ROM drive's icon.

2. A window appears stating that the CD-ROM contains a newer version of the operating system. Click Yes to begin the upgrade.

NOTE: *Alternately, you can click the Install Windows 2000 option on the Microsoft Windows 2000 CD.*

---

6. Migrating from Windows NT to Windows 2000

3. Choose the Upgrade To Windows 2000 (Recommended) option, and click Next.

4. After you have read the license agreement, select the I Accept This Agreement radio button, and click Next.

5. Enter the 25-digit product key as it appears on your Windows 2000 packaging, and click Next.

NOTE: *If the product key is entered incorrectly, you will be informed that it is invalid and will be required to enter it again.*

---

6. In the Upgrading To The Windows 2000 NTFS File System dialog box, choose not to convert the drive (you can do this at a later date) by selecting the No, Do Not Upgrade My Drive option and by clicking Next.

7. Setup will now copy all the necessary setup files.

8. Click Finish. (You can also wait; the system will automatically reboot after 30 seconds.)

9. When the system reboots, choose the Microsoft Windows 2000 Server setup option from the boot menu, and press Enter. (You can also wait; the option will be automatically selected after about five seconds.)

10. Setup will examine your disks and copy all necessary files.

11. When the setup program completes the copy, your system will reboot again.

12. Select the Microsoft Windows 2000 Server option from the boot menu, and press Enter. (Again, you can wait; the option will be automatically selected after about 30 seconds.)

13. Windows 2000 will start and detect and install devices.

14. Network settings will be set up and configured.

15. Components will be installed.

16. When the setup is done, click Restart Now.

17. Select the Microsoft Windows 2000 Server option from the boot menu, and press Enter.

18. When the system starts up, the setup program will automatically launch the Active Directory Installation Wizard (DCPromo.exe).

19. When the Active Directory Installation Wizard appears, click Next.

20. In the Domain Controller Type window, choose the Domain Controller For A New Domain option, and click Next.

21. In the Create Tree Or Child Domain window (see Figure 6.2), choose the Create A New Domain Tree option, and click Next.

22. If the forest root domain has been created already, you'll need to choose to join an existing forest as shown in figure 6.3 If this is a new forest, you'll need to choose to Create A New Forest and click the Next button.

23. Enter the full DNS name of the new domain, and click Next. The wizard will verify whether this domain name is duplicated on the network. If it is, click OK, and choose a new domain name.

24. Enter the NetBIOS name that is to be assigned to this domain. This name will be used when systems that are not Active Directory enabled need to communicate with this domain. The wizard will automatically create a

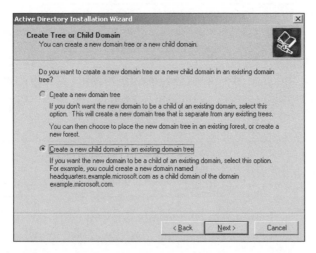

Figure 6.2   The Create Tree Or Child Domain window.

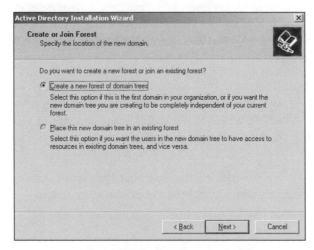

Figure 6.3   The Create Or Join Forest window.

NetBIOS domain name for you. You can choose to keep this name or to create a new one. If the NetBIOS domain name exists, the wizard will add a number to the end of the name. For example, if the NetBIOS domain name, DOMAIN, exists, the wizard will suggest the name DOMAIN0. When you have selected your NetBIOS domain name, click Next.

25. The wizard will ask you for the location where it should create the database and log directories. By default, these are stored in the %systemroot%\NTDS directory. You can, however, choose a different location. After you have selected the location for these directories, click Next.

NOTE: *The database directory is used to store the Active Directory information for the new domain, and the log directory is used temporarily to store changes that are made to the Active Directory database before the changes are committed. For best performance, you should place the database and log directories on separate physical hard disks.*

---

26. Choose the location for the shared system volume. By default, this is stored in the %systemroot%\Sysvol directory. After you have selected the location for this directory, click Next.

NOTE: *The shared system volume directory is used to store scripts and Group Policies. Every domain controller in Active Directory maintains such a directory that must reside on an NTFS volume. All file replication services use this volume to replicate the scripts and Group Policy information to all domain controllers.*

---

27. If the Active Directory Installation Wizard does not detect a DNS server, you'll be notified and must then decide whether you would like the wizard to install and configure DNS.

WARNING! For Active Directory to be installed on your system, at least one drive or partition must be formatted with Windows 2000 NTFS (NTFS 5). If no such partition exists, you will be presented with an error message and will not be able to continue the Active Directory installation until you create such a partition.

28. Next, the Windows NT 4.0 RAS Servers window will appear. This window allows you to choose whether Windows 2000 Active Directory will use permissions that are compatible with non-Windows 2000 systems or with native Windows 2000 permissions. Choose your desired option, and click Next.

29. In the Directory Services Restore Mode Administrator Password window, choose a password to be used when you need to restore your Active Directory information. Click Next.

TIP: *For security reasons, do not use your administrator password as the Directory Services Restore Mode administrator password.*

---

6. Migrating from Windows NT to Windows 2000

30. A summary window will appear informing you of all the options that you selected. Click Next to start the Active Directory installation.

31. A progress indicator will appear. When the installation is complete, the Complete Active Directory Installation Wizard window will appear. Click Finish.

32. A dialog box will appear notifying you that the system must be rebooted for the changes to take effect. Click Restart Now to complete the installation.

Upgrading a Domain Controller Server and Converting the File System

To upgrade a domain controller and convert the file system, perform the following steps:

1. Insert the Windows 2000 Server CD-ROM. The autorun feature should start the CD automatically. If it does not, double-click My Computer, and then double-click the CD-ROM drive's icon.

2. A window will appear stating that the CD-ROM contains a newer version of the operating system. Click Yes to begin the upgrade.

NOTE: *Alternately, you can click the Install Windows 2000 option on the Microsoft Windows 2000 CD.*

---

3. Choose the Upgrade To Windows 2000 (Recommended) option, and click Next.

4. After you have read the license agreement, select the I Accept This Agreement radio button, and click Next.

5. Enter the 25-digit product key as it appears on your Windows 2000 packaging, and click Next.

NOTE: *If the product key is entered incorrectly, you will be informed that it is invalid and will be required to enter it again.*

---

6. In the Upgrading To The Windows 2000 NTFS File System dialog box, choose not to convert the drive (you can do this at a later date) by selecting the No, Do Not Upgrade My Drive and by clicking Next.

7. Setup will now copy all the necessary setup files.

8. Click Finish. (You can also wait; the system will automatically reboot after 30 seconds.)

9. When the system reboots, choose the Microsoft Windows 2000 Server setup option from the boot menu, and press Enter. (You can also wait; the option will be automatically selected after about five seconds.)

10. Setup will now examine your disks and copy all necessary files.

11. When the setup program completes the copy, your system will reboot again.

12. Select the Microsoft Windows 2000 Server option from the boot menu, and press Enter. (Again, you can wait; the option will be automatically selected after about 30 seconds.)

13. The setup program will now convert your drive to NTFS. When the conversion is done, the system will reboot.

14. Select the Microsoft Windows 2000 Server option from the boot menu, and press Enter.

15. Windows 2000 will start and detect and install devices.

16. Network settings will be set up and configured.

17. Components will be installed.

18. When the setup is done, click Restart Now.

19. Select the Microsoft Windows 2000 Server option from the boot menu, and press Enter.

20. When the system starts up, the setup program will automatically launch the Active Directory Installation Wizard (DCPROMO.exe).

21. When the Active Directory Installation Wizard appears, click Next.

22. In the Domain Controller Type window, choose the Domain Controller For A New Domain option, and click Next.

23. In the Create Tree Or Child Domain window, choose the Create A New Domain Tree option, and click Next (refer to Figure 6.2).

24. If the forest root domain has been created already, you'll need to choose to join an existing forest as shown in Figure 6.3. If this is a new forest, you'll need to choose to Create A New Forest and click the Next button.

25. Enter the full DNS name of the new domain, and click Next. The wizard will now verify whether this domain name is duplicated on the network. If it is, click OK, and choose a new domain name.

26. Enter the NetBIOS name that is to be assigned to this domain. This name will be used when systems that are not Active Directory enabled need to communicate with this domain. The wizard will automatically create a NetBIOS domain name for you. You can choose to keep this name, or you can create a new one. If the NetBIOS domain name exists, the wizard will add a number to the end of the name. For example, if the NetBIOS domain name, DOMAIN, exists, the wizard will suggest the name DOMAIN0. When you have selected your NetBIOS domain name, click Next.

27. The wizard will ask for the location where it should create the database and log directories. By default, these are stored in the %systemroot%\NTDS directory. You can, however, choose a different location. After you have selected the location for these directories, click Next.

NOTE: *The database directory is used to store the Active Directory information for the new domain, and the log directory is used temporarily to store changes that are made to the Active Directory database before the changes are committed. For best performance, you should place the database and log directories on separate physical hard disks.*

28. Choose the location for the shared system volume. By default, this is stored in the %systemroot%\Sysvol directory. After you have selected the location for this directory, click Next.

NOTE: *The shared system volume directory is used to store scripts and Group Policies. Every domain controller in Active Directory maintains such a directory that must reside on an NTFS volume. All file replication services use this volume to replicate the scripts and Group Policy information to all domain controllers.*

29. If the Active Directory Installation Wizard does not detect a DNS server, you'll be notified and must then decide whether you would like the wizard to install and configure DNS (see Figure 6.4).

WARNING! For Active Directory to be installed on your system, at least one drive or partition must be formatted with Windows 2000 NTFS (NTFS v5.0). If no such partition exists, you will be presented with an error message and will not be able to continue the Active Directory installation until you create such a partition.

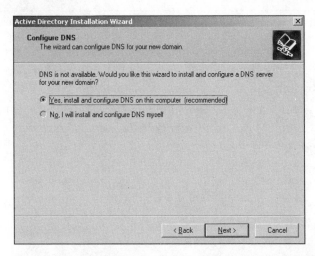

Figure 6.4   The Active Directory Installation Wizard: Configure DNS.

6. Migrating from Windows NT to Windows 2000

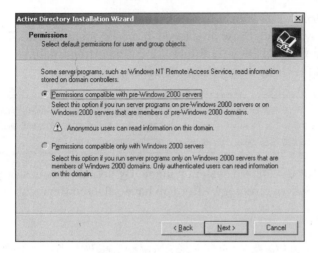

Figure 6.5   The Active Directory Installation Wizard: Permissions window.

30. The Windows NT 4.0 RAS Servers window will appear (see Figure 6.5). This window allows you to choose whether Windows 2000 Active Directory will use permissions that are compatible with non-Windows 2000 systems or with native Windows 2000 permissions. Choose your desired option, and click Next.

31. In the Directory Services Restore Mode Administrator Password window, choose a password to be used when you need to restore your Active Directory information. Click Next.

TIP: For security reasons, do not use your administrator password as the Directory Services Restore Mode administrator password.

---

32. A summary window will appear informing you of all the options that you selected. Click Next to start the Active Directory installation.

33. A progress indicator will appear, as shown in Figure 6.6. When the installation is complete, the Complete Active Directory Installation Wizard window appears. Click Finish.

34. A dialog box will appear notifying you that the system must be rebooted for the changes to take effect. Click Restart Now to complete the installation.

Figure 6.6   The Configuring Active Directory installation progress indicator.

Switching to Native Mode

To switch your system to native mode, perform the following steps:

1. Click Start, and select Programs|Administrative Tools|Active Directory Domains And Trusts.

2. Select the domain that you would like to administer.

3. Right-click, and select Properties from the drop-down menu.

4. On the General tab, click Change Mode.

5. Click Yes to change the mode from mixed mode to native mode.

WARNING! Remember that after this is done, it cannot be undone. A Windows 2000 domain controller running in mixed mode will look like a Windows NT domain controller to Windows NT machines.

Using ADMT to Migrate Users

1. Click Start, and select Programs|Administrative Tools.

2. Select Active Directory Migration Tool.

3. Right-click the Active Directory Migration Tool folder, and select User Migration Wizard from the drop-down menu.

4. Click Next, and click the Migrate Now? radio button.

5. Click Next.

6. Click Next, and click Add.

7. Double-click the accounts that you wish to migrate, and click OK.

8. Click Next.

9. Click Browse, and double-click the target OU where the users will be placed.

10. Click Next.

11. Click the Migrate User SIDS To Target Domain checkbox, and then click Next.

12. Click the Migrate Associated User Groups checkbox.

13. Click the Update Previously Migrated Objects checkbox.

14. Click Next twice, and then click Finish.

15. The migration status will appear. After the migration is complete, click Close.

Using NETDIAG To Analyze and Provide Hard-Copy Information about the Network

The NETDIAG utility is located in the \support\tools folder of the Windows 2000 installation disk. It provides various types of information about the health and happiness of clients, servers, and domain controllers on the network. To use the NETDIAG utility, perform the following steps:

1. Click Start, and then select Run.

2. Type "cmd", and click OK.

3. Click OK.

4. Type "netdiag > diag.txt".

5. Press Enter.

6. Steps 4 and 5 ran the NETDIAG utility and put the output into the file named diag.txt. Type "type diag.txt|more" to view the file.

Using NETDOM to Get Information about Network Objects

You can use NETDOM to query domain objects within the domain. Although NETDOM is a complex tool, it can also be used to change several domain attributes, such as trusts. To use the NETDOM utility, perform the following steps:

1. Click Start, and select Run.

2. Type "cmd", and click OK.

3. Type "netdom query /domain:*<domainname>* workstation" where *<domainname>* is the domain that you're working in.

4. Press Enter.

5. Successfully migrated workstations appear. Type "netdom query /domain *<domainname>* OU" where *<domainname>* is the domain that you're working in.

6. Press Enter.

7. Current OUs show on the window. Type "netdom query /domain *<domainname>* FSMO" where *<domainname>* is the domain that you're working in.

8. Press Enter.

9. Valid FSMO role servers will be listed on the window.

10. Type "netdom query /domain *<domainname>* trust". Replace domainname with the applicable domain name.

11. Press Enter.

12. Valid trusts will appear, also listing the trust types and status.

Testing Upgraded DNS for Functionality

1. Click Start, and select Programs|Administrative Tools.

2. Click DNS.

3. Select Action|Connect To Computer.

4. The Select Target Computer dialog box appears. Click OK.

5. Right-click the PDC icon, and select Properties from the drop-down list.

6. Click the Monitoring tab.

7. Click the A Simple Query Against This DNS Server checkbox.

8. Click Test Now.

9. The query test results of PASS should appear.

Chapter 7

Restructuring Windows 2000 Active Directory

In Depth

In Chapter 6, we discussed migrating to Windows 2000 from Windows NT using an upgrade process. It is possible to migrate to Windows 2000 by restructuring an existing Windows NT domain or multiple domains into another existing Windows 2000 domain, tree, or forest. In this chapter, we will discuss restructuring as it applies to migrating to Windows 2000. We will also discuss restructuring your existing Windows 2000 Active Directory structure in order to accommodate several different situations within your company.

The biggest concern when considering any restructuring or migration task is Active Directory. Because Active Directory only resides on domain controllers, we only need to concern ourselves with domain controllers. Sure, it's possible to restructure or migrate member servers, but that process is really an upgrade and not a restructure because we're not dealing with Active Directory. For the purposes of this chapter, we will be discussing migrations and restructures as they apply only to domain controllers.

Reasons for Restructuring Active Directory

Before we get much further, we need to discuss the reasons and the situations where you might want to restructure an Active Directory setup. By and large, Active Directory is flexible enough to handle many different situations and environments. However, it is possible that an Active Directory structure or layout might need to be changed. Unlike Windows NT domain structures, Microsoft has graced us with the ability to reorganize and change the structure of Active Directory with relatively little or no pain. Of course, as with any major change on the network, thorough planning is required, along with a complete understanding of the processes and limitations of restructuring Active Directory.

Scenario 1: Bought Another Company

Let's say that you are an administrator for a large company that just purchased another company. For all intents and purposes, you might find yourself as an administrator for either company and responsible for coordinating and/or cooperating in the process of merging and integrating both companies' Internet Protocol (IP) infrastructures or data center needs. Realistically, this other company might be running Unix, NetWare, Lotus Notes, Windows NT, or any number of other networking platforms. These interoperability issues will be handled in detail in Chapter 12. In this chapter, we will discuss how to migrate another company's Windows NT or Windows 2000 network into a preexisting Active Directory forest.

Scenario 2: Just Finished Upgrading from Windows NT

When considering migration from Windows NT to Windows 2000, one of the things that you might consider as an administrator is the possibility of immediately upgrading from Windows NT to Windows 2000 in order to take advantage of the added features of Active Directory and then restructuring the domains later. For companies that only run one Windows NT or Windows 2000 domain, an upgrade might be the only thing required to truly migrate and take advantage of Windows 2000. Corporations, on the other hand, can be a completely different situation, especially when dealing with multiple domains and complex trust relationships. After performing an upgrade to Windows 2000 for each domain, it might be a good idea to restructure each of these domains into a single Active Directory forest, tree, or even domain. Reasons for performing a postupgrade restructure include the following:

- Microsoft has built in several networking-related improvements to Windows 2000 in the form of replication efficiencies that might allow a multidomain corporation to restructure into a single domain, or at the least into the same Active Directory tree. Windows 2000 automatically builds and maintains both trust relationships and replication links in such a manner that domains that were originally created due to networking bandwidth issues could very well be restructured in a more compact manner.

- Additionally, Windows 2000 uses Active Directory instead of the Windows NT Security Account Manager (SAM) database. When designing Active Directory, Microsoft ensured that Active Directory did not have the same size limitations that the SAM database did. Once upon a time, when NT was first installed, configured, and set up, quite often it was necessary to create separate Windows NT domains to overcome the size limitations of the SAM database. Because those limitations no longer exist within Windows 2000, it would be foolish not to restructure these unnecessary domains into a single domain for the purpose of reducing administrative overhead.

- Sometimes, Windows NT domains were created for the purpose of allowing administrative control to remote personnel. With Group Policy being integrated into Active Directory and with the additional ability to delegate administrative control with varying levels of granularity, the need for many of these subdomains no longer exists. Again, it's a good idea to restructure these administrative domains into single domains and to delegate appropriate administration. This will not only eliminate a huge amount of administrative overhead, but it will also reduce many of the security-type risks that occur when administrative personnel inadvertently alter system-critical components.

Scenario 3: Business Reorganization

As with Scenario 1, a business reorganization can occur that might require changing the Active Directory setup, which could be one of the most complex restructuring situations that you could encounter. This is because many subdomains today have been created around organizational, departmental, or business unit boundaries. When these boundaries change, you might begin to question the wisdom of creating departmentally based domains. The subsequent restructuring of business rules, computers, and personnel can become confusing as bits of some domains are treated with other domains, while other bits remain intact. Unfortunately, as an administrator, you have little or no say on whether or not a business reorganization occurs and whether it will impact the flow of data for the corporation, let alone the magnitude of that impact. This is where you can only hope that you have the appropriate management (or that you are the appropriate management) that can make upper management aware of the impacts that such a reorganization has upon information technology (IT) and the company at large.

Scenario 4: Migrating from Windows NT

In a few situations, especially for large or mission-critical companies (such as 911 or emergency services), it is necessary to minimize datacenter or server downtime as much as possible. This is particularly true for any company that provides 24x7 services, which can be anything from 911 companies to call centers to Web e-commerce services. These situations require that a migration take place by creating an entirely new Windows 2000 domain/forest/tree and by literally moving resources bit by bit from the Windows NT structure to the Windows 2000 structure. An additional reason for performing this type of migration is simply because an upgrade cannot occur. If the Windows NT hardware is not capable of being upgraded, a restructure is your only option. This type of migration or restructure is essential to minimize downtime for the following reasons:

- The Windows 2000 network is new and clean. This can prevent glitches from occurring from the onset just because legacy hardware and software problems will be overcome before the system is ever brought into production.

- The Windows 2000 network can be thoroughly tested before throwing it into a production role and migrating any users, computers, or data from Windows NT.

- Administrative personnel can be trained on, and can experiment with, the Windows 2000 network in a lab-type or mockup environment. This is a particularly juicy nugget because you do not often get the opportunity to play with something that is exactly like your production environment.

- Mission-critical applications and application servers can be thoroughly tested without potentially interrupting the production environment.

Restructuring Types

As you can imagine from the previous scenarios, you can perform an Active Directory restructure in many ways. On the surface, it might not seem like a big deal, but speaking from experience, things change when you're in the middle of a restructure. Therefore, it's important to step through each restructure process in the appropriate order so as to not lose data or resource connectivity on the network. Now that we've taken a look at different reasons for performing a restructure, let's look at different types of restructure situations and how they can be performed.

As you read through this chapter, please take this one word of warning: Remember your Active Directory structure. Forests, trees, and domains are all logical components that make up part of Active Directory. Of the three, the smallest single object is a domain. Without a domain, you can't have a tree or forest. When we speak of these restructures, remember that everything happens one step at a time. Even though every domain is a part of a larger tree and forest, just remember that the real action occurs between domains.

Interforest Restructure

An interforest restructure is the technical term for restructuring two separate Active Directory forests into the same forest. Figure 7.1 represents a facsimile of what two separate Active Directory forests look like. Scenarios 1 and 4 in "Reasons for Restructuring Active Directory" fit into an interforest restructure scheme because both situations deal with merging two separate systems into one. This also applies for Windows NT migrations because an NT domain could be loosely considered a separate forest.

Based upon Figure 7.1, any of the following scenarios would be termed an interforest restructure:

- Migrating Domain 50 into Domain G, along with all of its subdomains, with the subdomain structure intact

- Migrating Domain 97 into Domain Y, along with all of its subdomains, and collapsing all domains into Domain Y

- Migrating Windows NT Domain 1 into the upper forest as a separate tree in the same forest, along with all of its subdomains

- Migrating Windows NT Domain 1 into Domain Y and collapsing all of its subdomains into Domain Y

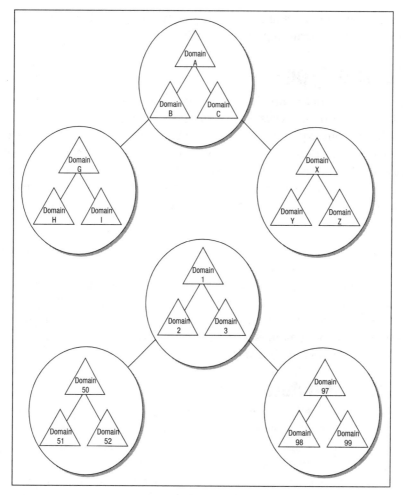

Figure 7.1   Two separate Active Directory forests.

Considerations for an Interforest Restructure

Several specifics need to be looked at prior to performing an interforest restructure. Although the process might seem tedious, those of us who've been around a while are just grateful that a process exists that might actually work (unlike some other "smooth" migrations that we've been through).

Accounts/Groups

Maintaining accounts and groups during an interforest restructure is usually the number one concern for any system administrator. Face it. The function of maintaining a server is to enable users to access network resources. When these resources are secured with access being tied into user and computer accounts and groups, these items become nearly as important as maintaining the data itself. After all, you can have all the information in the world, and it won't do you a bit of good if you can't get to it. Initially, our hope is to avoid reentering all user accounts and user groups. Rest assured, the tools exist that can either clone or move user and computer accounts and groups.

By and large, you will want to clone all of your accounts and groups between the two separate domains in question. This is just for the added safety of a fallback in the event that something goes wrong during the restructure and you need users to function from the original source domain.

Don't let these tools lull you into a false sense of security, because account management is a big deal. Why? Because after you re-create a user or group, you need to also reestablish all of the access permissions that have been created for that user or group. Again, this is more complex than it appears when the resources that need to be accessed might reside in a completely different environment.

Resource Access and Security

When we move or clone objects from one domain to another, a new security identifier (SID) is created and attached to that object. These objects (called security principals) can be users, groups, or computers. SIDs are what both Windows NT and Windows 2000 use to grant or deny users and computers access to network resources based upon the security permissions that are granted to the resources.

Imagine a situation where you're migrating user accounts from Windows NT to Windows 2000. You haven't moved the resources or data yet, and it's impossible to get it done all in one night. You still need to ensure that those accounts will be able to access data in the Windows NT domain from within the Windows 2000 domain until the time where you can move the other items in the domain. You could consider copying or cloning the user accounts from Windows NT to Windows 2000 and then configuring trusts to ensure that data access can occur back and forth, but you would still have a problem in the morning when the users came in and tried to access their data. After these accounts are moved, created, or cloned to a separate domain, they obtain a new SID. Even though a user name is the same, and all of the information is the same, Windows NT looks at the SID, not at the name, to determine if a user can be granted access to a particular resource. Therefore, when the user is in the new domain or forest and is attempting to gain access to a file that is residing in the older Windows NT domain, the old Windows NT domain will not recognize the user without some additional work on your part.

Luckily, Microsoft has added a function called sIDHistory. sIDHistory is a feature where any object that has a SID also maintains a history of older SIDs when the object is moved or cloned. In this case, sIDHistory maintains the older Windows

NT SID within the moved or cloned account and subsequently passes the older SID to the Windows NT domain so that access can occur as it would have if the account hadn't moved.

You need to be aware of one thing when cloning objects from one forest to another. Two identical active accounts residing in separate domains present a potential administrative annoyance if and when a change is made to one account and not the other. Because this type of dual personality is temporary and restricted to the period when the restructure takes place, Microsoft doesn't consider this worth creating a replication process to fix it. Just be aware that changes can occur on one side and not the other, and try as best you can to minimize changes as much as possible, and duplicate necessary changes as appropriate.

Profiles

Even local user profiles are stored and linked to users' accounts by their SIDs. When users whose accounts have been restructured attempt to log in to the domain, they will successfully log in, but they will receive the generic All Users profile that is stored locally on the system. Unfortunately, in this case, we cannot rely upon sIDHistory to save the day. Instead, we have the option of either copying the old profiles into new locations within the destination forest, or we can share the profiles between both domains.

Copying the profiles from the source domain or forest to the destination domain or forest is probably wiser in the long term because copying the profiles is a permanent solution. Sharing the profiles between the two domains, however, can be advantageous in a situation where you might need to fall back to the nonmigrated setup, or when the user might need to log in to either domain. Sharing the profile has one potential glitch, which is what to do with the profile when you need to decommission or remove the original domain. In that situation, the profile path within the user's account properties will need to be redirected to a permanent location within the destination domain. This can be done manually or by using scripts, which are covered in Chapter 16.

Equipment

Equipment becomes an issue, particularly when restructuring from Windows NT to Windows 2000, because you will need to set up and configure an entirely new set of Windows 2000 domain controllers that will eventually roll into place as your production environment. Again, remember that when we speak of a migration or restructure here, we are talking about domain controllers and not necessarily all servers.

Merging separate forests is less of an up-front concern because the equipment in both environments already exists. After all is said and done, however, the former equipment may still be valuable as a member server or upgraded and redeployed as a domain controller within the new environment.

Applications

Microsoft has spent a great deal of time telling us that domain controllers and network applications don't mix well on the same machine. Quite often, however, you don't have a choice, especially in smaller companies where finances are slim and you're trying your hardest to get the most bang for the few bucks that you have.

In the event that you will need to deal with an application server that is also a domain controller during a migration or restructure, the key is to test, test, test. Exchange 5.5 has been known to have fits when installed on a domain controller that houses the Global Catalog (GC). Of course, this was fixed with Exchange 2000 and may also be resolved in a Windows 2000 Service Pack, but the point is still valid. Applications might not work well in the Windows 2000 environment. You should not only make sure that your applications are compatible with Windows 2000, but you should also prove it by testing as much as you possibly can. This shouldn't be a problem for those of you restructuring from Windows NT because you'll have the ability to test the applications in your soon-to-be-production environment. As always, it's a good idea to check with the application manufacturer's Website to see if any known compatibility or migration issues exist.

If you are merging separate Windows 2000 forests, your application servers are more likely to be separate from domain controllers, so we might be discussing a dead issue. Just on the off chance that this is not a dead issue, it's a good idea to check with the software manufacturer to see if they have any special processes for migrating or moving applications from one server to another without tipping the apple cart. You might also consider decommissioning your application server/domain controller and moving it into the newer domain as a member server. However, be aware that Active Directory integrated applications might have problems living in a new Active Directory environment so again, you'll need to check with the application manufacturer.

Trusts

In order to clone or migrate resources from one domain or forest to another, you will need to establish trusts between the two domains in question. As we discussed in Chapter 3, a trust acts as a bridge between two domains and allows users and groups in one or both domains to access resources in the other domain. Additional security is required in order to complete the interdomain data access dance, but, for the most part, that's all we need to know here.

Most trusts between domains and trees are automatically generated by Active Directory. In the case of an interforest restructure, however, you will need to establish explicit trusts manually between the two domains involved. If you are planning on splitting and merging an existing Windows 2000 (or Windows NT for that matter) enterprise into a separate Windows 2000 forest, you will carefully need to plan and create the necessary trusts to provide a bridge between any given source domain and all respective destination domains.

Name Resolution Services

You might also consider how you perform name resolution services. As we discussed in Chapter 6, Active Directory requires Domain Name Service (DNS), but, due to newer DNS features such as Dynamic DNS, it's no longer necessary to maintain Windows Internet Naming Service (WINS) for Network Basic Input/Output System (NetBIOS) name resolution. The WINS debate is presented more in Chapter 12, but in the meantime you might consider eliminating WINS when restructuring unless you have application services that rely specifically upon WINS resolution.

Replication

Another hidden gotcha that can crop up with interforest restructures deals with replication. This is only true for multidomain forests where the restructure process has been split into stages spanning some time. For the most part, Windows 2000 replication will be handled automatically by Active Directory, and you don't need to worry about it. But because a separate forest denotes a separate Active Directory database, replication won't occur between the two. If you intend to maintain any replication between the two, you'll need to do it manually until the restructure is complete.

Domain Status

The target domain in an interforest restructure must be in native mode. Native mode domains contain domain controllers that are exclusively Windows 2000. Windows 2000 domains that were created from scratch are, by default, in native mode. Domains that have been upgraded require an administrator to manually change the domain to native mode after all NT domain controllers have been upgraded or decommissioned.

How, When, and Where

If you're restructuring from Windows NT to Windows 2000, one thing you need to be immediately aware of—especially if you are responsible for multiple domains—is that you don't have to do it all in one night. As a matter of fact, it's a good idea to allow some time between domain migrations simply because you and your staff will then have some time to deal with any lingering issues before proceeding to the next domain. Before you begin the interforest restructure process, look through the following steps and be sure to allocate an appropriate amount of downtime for the entire process to occur:

1. Create the target Windows 2000 domain. When migrating from Windows NT, this domain must be separate from the Windows NT domain. If you are restructuring two Windows 2000 domains, they both must reside in separate forests.

2. Establish appropriate explicit trusts between the domains. You will be unable to detect, let alone migrate, data between the two domains without an applicable trust.

3. Before you go any further, ensure that you are a member of the Enterprise Admins group in the target domain. Even if you choose not to use the Active Directory Migration Tool (ADMT), install it anyway. It will make some registry changes for you that are necessary to handle the migration process. You will need to run the restructure tools within the target domain, and specifically on the primary domain controller (PDC) emulator. Last, but not least, back up your data and Active Directory, and test to make sure that you will be able to restore from the backup.

TIP: *If you are migrating multiple domains within an enterprise or forest, it's a good idea to migrate account domains before resource domains. Both account and resource domains were usually created within Windows NT to overcome the SAM database size limitation. Again, if these extra domains are not needed anymore, you can basically collapse the structure into a single domain where each domain is its own organizational unit (OU). The reason for restructuring account domains first is to take advantage immediately of Active Directory features.*

---

4. Migrate applicable global groups and user accounts. Windows 2000 migration is fairly thorough, and you need to keep a good eye on what happens with each step of the migration. This is because when you migrate groups, the migration tools will also migrate the applicable users. If you choose to move groups instead of clone them, this can be a problem if users are migrated that you haven't planned to migrate. Again, I recommend that you clone everything that can be cloned, just to avoid problems like this. Even when you clone, keep a good eye on everything. If, at a later date, you clone a group that has users that have already been cloned, overwrite the cloned user information. The final key to success is to ensure that the environments in both domains are stable and that no user or group changes occur in the target domain that could be overwritten when the cloned user is cloned again.

5. Move or clone user computers and member servers (not domain controllers).

6. Copy or share profiles.

7. Clone or move service accounts. Service accounts are specific user-type accounts that are usually created by applications in order to handle certain automated tasks. Tape backup programs usually require either a service account or authorization to access data on behalf of an account with appropriate privileges. In order to ensure a successful restructure, service accounts will need to be migrated to the target domain.

7. Restructuring Windows 2000 Active Directory

8. As discussed in Step 4, it might be necessary for you to recopy accounts multiple times during a restructure. Because it is easy to let minute changes from one domain to another get away from you (especially in a team environment where not everything is documented), you have the ability to update user rights in order to bridge the gap. This is particularly useful for situations where a user has been copied to the new domain, but where some groups that the user belongs to haven't been copied.

9. Redeploy domain controllers, and formally decommission the source domain. After all users, groups, objects, resources, and data have been moved from the source domain to the target domain, the original domain is not really doing anything, which seems kind of unimportant in the end. At the point where you feel comfortable with removing the last vestiges of the old domain, you can either migrate domain controllers as domain controllers within the target domain, or you can simply decommission both domain and domain controllers at the same time. Redeploying domain controllers is a simple process of running dcpromo on the domain controller, then choosing to remove Active Directory, and then rerunning dcpromo and joining the new domain.

Intraforest Restructure

An intraforest restructure involves moving accounts, computers, and resources from one domain to another within the same Active Directory forest as shown in Figure 7.2. This applies for scenarios 2 and 3 mentioned earlier in this chapter. This process is usually called collapsing a tree because at least one domain is eliminated while its resources and members are usually moved into a single different domain. You are more likely to encounter an intraforest restructure situation than you are interforest restructures. In my experience, I have found that many Active Directory structures are built around a business model or organizational structure. Because companies reorganize sometimes (sometimes often, depending upon where you are), an intraforest restructure can occur just to keep up with the office politics.

After you have upgraded from Windows NT, you can also use an intraforest restructure to perform in two steps what an interforest restructure would have done in one. The idea is to first upgrade all domains into the same forest safely and then to collapse several domains into a single domain through an intraforest restructure process. My personal migration preference is to perform an upgrade followed by a restructure because you are allowing time to pass between each major event rather than having both occur at the same time. Traditional troubleshooting tactics support this position because troubleshooting one problem that sprouts from one major change is easier to do than troubleshooting a problem that sprouts from two major changes that occur at the same time. The same potential complications occur with this "upgrade then restructure" approach, which

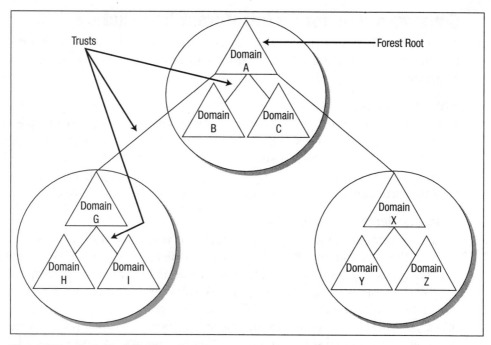

Figure 7.2 An Active Directory forest.

you will see with both the upgrade and restructure scenarios. In addition, what you gain in comfort level by splitting the entire project into phases is what you lose in fallback capability. You can still maintain the same fallback capabilities discussed with upgrading to Windows 2000, but you will be unable to clone security principals when doing an intraforest restructure, thus losing the fallback capability from the restructure piece of the project. Instead, you will be able to move security principals from one domain to another, but you will not be able to fall back to the original source domain in the event of a failure during migration.

One additional scenario that you might encounter technically qualifies as a restructure because you use the same tools, but it is not a full restructure process and does not require nearly as much planning. This is a situation where a single user or small group of users needs to move from one domain to another within the same company or forest.

Based upon Figure 7.2, all of the following situations apply as an intraforest restructure or migration:

- Migrating Domain X into Domain C and collapsing all of Domain X's subdomains into Domain C
- Migrating and collapsing Domain I into Domain G
- Migrating Domain H into Domain B

Considerations for an Intraforest Restructure

Although many of the same considerations apply for both intra- and interforest restructures, it is still important to note the differences and to modify any plans as necessary.

Accounts/Groups

Remember that an intraforest restructure involves moving security principles and not cloning them. The GC cannot handle having more than one object in the same forest that has the same SID or sIDHistory entry, so we really have no choice but to move objects. As with any major project, make sure you perform a good data backup, particularly of Active Directory, prior to making any moves.

Resource Access and Security

Security concerns are actually less of an issue with an intraforest restructure because the user cannot log in to two separate places. You do need to be aware that, after a user account is migrated from one domain to another, corresponding computer accounts should be moved at the same time. The reason for this is to eliminate footwork on your part. When users migrate from one domain to another, you will need to configure their systems (both Windows 2000 and earlier versions) to log in to a separate domain. When Windows NT and Windows 2000 computers migrate from one domain to another, you will need to configure the system to join and to be a member of the new domain. These are two separate processes that could wisely be placed into one.

Profiles

Local user profiles should be moved from the old domain to the new domain. When migrating accounts, you should have the new profiles already in place, and hopefully in a location similar to the previous one, in order to reduce the amount of busy work you'll need to do in order to rehook the profiles.

Equipment

Because this is an intraforest restructure, more than likely you will be looking at redeploying the domain controllers into the new domain at the same time that you're migrating resources. Redeploying a domain controller is easy. All you do is run dcpromo, remove Active Directory, and then run dcpromo again and join the new domain.

NOTE: *Usually when collapsing domains, the old users will rely on the logon scripts belonging to the new domain. In the midst of your planning, don't forget to add changes to the target domain's login scripts to accommodate the new users if necessary. This is one restructure task that you can perform before the restructure occurs because it doesn't require that the users be there for it to be implemented. You can either make changes that apply to all users in the domain or add a few variables to the scripts to restrict functions to the newer user OUs and groups.*

Applications

Moving application member servers on their own is just like moving any other non-domain controller system from one domain to another, which is not strictly part of a restructure process. You are, however, more likely to encounter an intraforest restructure that has an application server also acting the domain controller part. Again, this is especially true for smaller companies. If you are performing an intraforest restructure with an application server on board, just make sure that you back up your data thoroughly and secure the server before logically moving or redeploying the domain controller.

If you have the means to do so, now is an ideal time to justify an additional server and to split the domain controller functions from the application server. This is particularly justifiable when moving to a larger domain or any place that has more accounts and resources because your poor dual personality server will spend more time authenticating users and running profiles and login scripts than it has before. If the application server functionality is important (and it almost always is), the additional domain controller-related responsibilities might negatively impact the performance of the application server.

Trusts

By definition, an intraforest restructure consists of two domains within the same forest, so it stands to reason that trusts will already exist between the two domains. In the event that the two domains in question are distant cousins such as domains E and F in Figure 7.3, you may consider creating an explicit trust (also called a shortcut trust) directly between the two in order to save time and bandwidth.

Name Resolution Services

Because we're dealing exclusively with a preexisting Windows 2000 environment, DNS already exists and is probably at a sufficient caliber to handle the current load, no matter what domain configuration exists.

Replication

Replication within Active Directory occurs automatically, so again, you really will not need to do any replication tasks outside of checking to ensure that replication is complete. After the source domain is decommissioned, Windows 2000 will modify the replication links automatically. If your Active Directory forest spans multiple sites, you might consider modifying site boundaries appropriate to the changes involved.

Domain Status

The target domain must be a Windows 2000 native mode domain. There are technical reasons for this, primarily dealing with overhead and the capability of Active Directory to keep track of events. The true reasons for insisting on a native

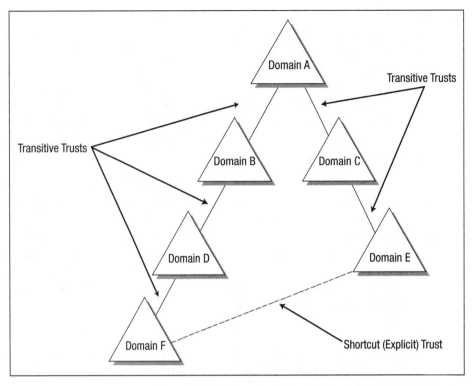

Figure 7.3   Transitive trusts in an Active Directory tree, with an explicit shortcut trust established between two domains.

mode domain for the target are more on the practical side. Realistically, when you restructure any domain, tree, or forest, the idea is to stabilize the situation into a more workable format that is beneficial to the company, and hopefully you, too. Restructuring a domain into a mixed mode domain would just be adding more complications into what is already probably an incomplete or failed restructure or upgrade to begin with.

Theoretically, it should be possible to make any Windows 2000 domain into a native domain by upgrading or migrating all of the domain controllers. The only exception could be a situation where an application server is doubling as a Windows NT domain controller. Again, if this is the case, it is highly recommended that you split these two functionalities. Also, don't forget the possibility that the application in question might not yet be compatible with Windows 2000, thus requiring a split. This will not just allow you to be able to perform Active Directory restructures, but will also allow you to take advantage of other benefits and functions that are available only with Windows 2000.

How, When, and Where

Generally, when performing an intraforest migration, Microsoft recommends that any resource domains be migrated prior to account domains. Because all the players are already within Windows 2000, there is no advantage in migrating users first. To perform an intraforest migration, perform the following steps:

1. Move workstations and member servers from the source domain to the target domain.

2. Migrate service accounts.

3. Update user rights and group memberships at this point while migrating resource domains because several network resources have been relocated while the bulk of users accessing those resources have not. Between sIDHistory and updating user rights and group memberships, you should be able to stabilize the situation.

4. Move domain local groups, users, and profiles.

5. Decommission the domain.

Restructuring Tools

Restructuring is not expected to be part of your daily, weekly, or even monthly task list as an administrator. By and large, it is possible to move single users from one domain to another, but usually this is accomplished by creating a new user in the target domain. If you are performing restructures that are larger in caliber than this on a regular basis, you might put some thought into redesigning your overall Active Directory structure to be more stable in the changing winds.

In the following section, I will describe the tools that can be used for restructuring Active Directory. Other tools are available from third-party sources, but, for the most part, the tools that I describe should be able to handle most, if not all, situations you'll come across. They're all available either from the Microsoft Web site or on the Windows 2000 Server installation CD.

ADMT

ADMT is probably the most frequently used restructuring and migration tool because it works through a graphical user interface and because it can handle most, if not all, of your migration tasks. ADMT can be used for both intra- and interforest restructures and should be run on the target domain for interforest restructures, and on either the source or target domain for intraforest migrations.

When you run ADMT, you need to make sure that you have at least administrative permissions on both domains. In an intraforest restructure, you'll need to be a member of enterprise admins in order to make all of the underlying Active Directory changes that are necessary.

ADMT works in a step-by-step manner by allowing you to run wizards for every piece of the overall restructuring project. This is a great feature when all you might need to do is move a couple of users. Additionally, ADMT has one huge feature that makes administrators grateful that someone in Microsoft actually understands what it's like to do their job. ADMT will dispatch a software agent to affected source domain workstations and computers and perform necessary configuration changes, such as moving domains and so forth. This single feature can save us hours of walking around and manually reconfiguring systems on our own. The following are a couple of gotchas that come with ADMT, but, for the most part, they're worth the trouble:

• The ADMT agent will only work for Windows NT 3.51 SP5, Windows NT 4 with SP4, Windows 2000 systems, or any system that's validly listed as a member of the domain.

• Each client system must be running both NetBIOS and the NetBIOS server service because the agents are dispatched across the network looking for the computer name. It has to be done this way because the other computer name is always associated with the domain, which is most likely going to change after the agent arrives at the destination.

• The ADMT user needs to have appropriate permissions on the target computers. Normally, if you're logged into the system running ADMT as a member of the domain administrators group, you should be all right because the domain admins global group is usually a member of the local administrators group on Windows NT or Windows 2000 machines. You might want to check on this if you encounter failures during dispatch. Again, if you're running an intraforest restructure, being a member of enterprise admins will solve most potential problems. When running an interforest restructure, you'll need to be careful. Usually, creating an account of the same name and password in each domain that is a member of the domain admins group should do the trick.

• Windows NT 3.51 did not by default configure an ADMIN$ share. You'll need to do this for any Windows 3.51 boxes because the agent uses the %systemroot% folder to apply several important changes. Make sure that the ADMIN$ share points to the %systemroot% folder.

ADMT is available on the Microsoft Website for download. After you install it, you'll notice a new entry in the Start Menu|Program Files|Administrative Tools for ADMT. After you start the program, each wizard is started from the Action menu as shown in Figure 7.4. Refer to Table 7.1 to determine the proper ADMT wizard when performing the various pieces of the restructure process.

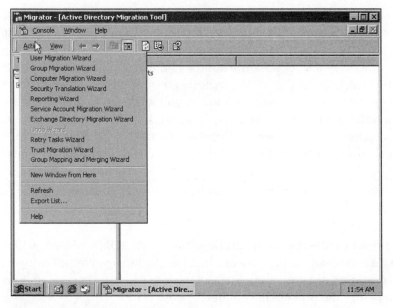

Figure 7.4   ADMT wizards.

Table 7.1   ADMT wizard functions.

Restructure Process	Wizard
Establish trusts	Trust Migration Wizard
Global groups	Group Migration Wizard
Domain local groups	Group Migration Wizard
User accounts	User Migration Wizard
Roaming profiles	User Migration Wizard
Service accounts	Service Account Migration Wizard
Workstations and servers	Computer Migration Wizard
Local profile updates	Security Translation Wizard

User Migration Wizard and Group Migration Wizard

Both the User and Group Migration Wizards look and feel the same. The difference between the two is really only logical. If you are doing a large restructure process, you've probably planned a phased approach where users will be migrated in groups. If this is the case, the Group Migration Wizard is the tool for you. On the other hand, if you are migrating individual or diverse groups of users, you would use the User Migration Wizard. The Migration Wizard will begin by prompting you to do a dry run of the process or to run the process live. It's always a good idea to do a dry run on the process before running it live just to get an idea of what options are available and what failures might occur. It is better to trouble-shoot problems like these before migration day rather than waste a lot of system downtime. ADMT will follow by detecting any and all domains that you are connected to. You will need to choose the source and target domains that you'll be working with. Nearly all of the ADMT wizards go through these two processes. After choosing the source and target domains, you will need to choose the users that will be migrated. You will be prompted to enter the distinguished name of the OU where the user will go. Rather than confuse yourself here, it's a good idea to just click the Browse button and select the applicable OU in the target domain.

TIP: ADMT will not add OUs on the fly for you, so you will need to ensure that the proper OU structure exists in the target domain before you begin.

In order to prevent authentication conflicts, nearly all ADMT wizards will also prompt you for a username and password that has administrative authority in the source domain. After authentication is checked, you will have several options to choose from before the process is complete.

- *Translate Roaming Profiles—* I already discussed the behavior of local profiles. However, you do not need to be concerned if everyone on the network is running roaming network profiles. If you choose this option, the system will copy roaming profiles from the source to the target domain and will also associate them properly to each user's account properties.

- *Update User Rights—*This is an option that updates the new user accounts in the target domain to be the same as they were in the source domain.

- *Migrate Associated User Groups—*This is an option that you need to keep track of. Normally, if you're performing any large or staged migration, you wouldn't be using the User Migration Wizard, but the Group Migration Wizard because you can migrate all the users belonging to specific groups that would fit into each stage you have planned. When you choose to migrate associated user groups or users, be sure to keep a good record of what those associations really are. This prevents you from inadvertently overwriting changed data if and when you remigrate users and groups when migrating subsequent stages in the overall plan.

- *Update Previously Migrated Objects—*This is an option that is available only when the previous option is selected. This option updates migrated groups even if or when the groups already exist in the target domain.

- *Do Not Rename Accounts, Rename With Prefix/Suffix—*You have the ability to rename migrated accounts. Generally, you wouldn't do this because users expect to be able to log in the next day using the same account name. Situations where you wish to create duplicate migrated accounts, or where you might want to work on the accounts before they are live, might warrant a prefix or suffix. Other methods of grouping migrated accounts can happen by simply placing them in a separate OU.

- *Naming Conflicts*—In the event that two accounts are named the same, the system will perform according to the options shown. By default, ADMT will not migrate duplicate accounts. However, you do have the option to replace or overwrite a duplicate account and group, with the additional capability of removing the old user rights or group members so that original associations won't exist with the newer user or group. If you choose to migrate duplicate accounts, one of the easier methods is to rename duplicate accounts and go back after the migration process is complete. Then, referencing the logs, compare the duplicate accounts, choose one, update it, rename it if necessary, and eliminate the other.

Computer Migration Wizard

The Computer Migration Wizard acts much the same as the User and Group Migration Wizards in that you have options to choose whether this is a live or practice migration, what computers are being migrated, and by what administrative authority they're being moved. Unique to computer objects, you have the ability to translate—or reapply Access Control Lists (ACLs)—files and folders, local groups, printers, the registry, shares, user profiles, and user rights. When ADMT reapplies the ACLs, it retunes these items for the new domain so that all resources local to that machine can now be addressed in relation to the new domain. What's more, ADMT will give you the option to replace, add, or remove references to source domain objects. For example, if a printer is referenced in the computer's profile that exists in the source domain, you may want to update that computer reference, add an identical reference for the new domain, or simply remove it altogether. We recommend that you stick with the default Add option because it does not require you to update the computers when the source object is moved from the original domain to the new one. If the object is slated to be eliminated or replaced, you can remove it or replace it if the object has already been migrated.

Again, you will have the option to rename migrated and conflicting computers in the same way you did with users and groups. The last option prior to migration is to set when the computers will reboot after the agent completes its job. It's particularly important here to do a dry run of the process because the system will attempt to contact the target computers and will notify you of any failures. This will give you a leg up on which systems might not be turned on or hooked to the network or any other problems. Rather than walk around checking for systems that are on, connected, and so forth, run a practice migration instead. In the end, it might just be faster to run the migration despite the failures and to fix and update the failed computers manually.

Security Translation Wizard

The Security Translation Wizard is specific to Windows NT-to-Windows 2000 interforest migrations. When performing a Windows NT-to-Windows 2000 restructure, you are unable to update the ACLs immediately when computers are moved as you can with the Computer Migration Wizard. As a result, the computers need to be migrated, and the Security Translation Wizard then needs to be run to update the appropriate resource information on each system.

Reporting Wizard

The Reporting Wizard is a wizard that creates reports that are similar in nature to database reports. What you do here is choose source and target domains and run the report. It subsequently shows up in the reports section of the main ADMT window. ADMT will track all activities performed using the tool, so you will not need to turn on logging in order to retrieve restructuring information that has already occurred.

From within the Reporting Wizard interface, you can choose one or more of the following: migrated user accounts, migrated computer accounts, expired accounts, account references, and account name conflicts. For the most part, the generated accounts do not show the dates that the objects were migrated, so you'll still need to keep track of what has been done when. In addition, despite the fact that the report icon is a picture of a printer, there appears to be no method of actually printing the reports, so you'll need to manually open the generated reports from their location in order to print them. ADMT will query you for report locations when you generate the report.

Service Account Migration Wizard

The Service Account Migration Wizard is used to target service accounts residing on chosen computers. All agent-related wizards will step through the process where the agents are dispatched to the applicable computers to make the appropriate changes. Again, logs are created to show which computers were accessed and which were not. Although the agents are outstanding, you have the option to turn on and monitor the activities.

Exchange Directory Migration Wizard

For those of you who are familiar with Exchange 5.5, you know that you need to associate a mailbox with a Windows NT login in order to link the security access to the Windows NT domain. This is a great feature that ensures that we don't have to enter a password to the domain login and again to access email. The Exchange Directory Migration Wizard will reassign those same mailbox associations to the proper Windows 2000 accounts.

Undo Wizard

The Undo Wizard is grayed out prior to any ADMT tasks being done. After your first migration task, however, the Undo Wizard becomes available. Note that the Undo Wizard will not function when the source domain is a mixed domain, so the Undo Wizard will also not work for Windows NT migrations. Also keep in mind that the undo part can only apply to the last migration action performed. The Undo Wizard will show you what action it can undo, but it will not show you what objects it is performing the action upon. If the affected domains are in the same forest, you will be prompted for proof of administrative authority in order to write the data back to the source domain.

Retry Tasks Wizard

The Retry Tasks Wizard is a great tool to use in failed tasks, especially those where agents have failed for some reason or another. ADMT keeps a list of failed tasks and allows you to select multiple tasks to be included in the retry process.

Trust Migration Wizard

Before you can migrate any objects from the source domain to the target domain, you must either manually (in the case of an interforest migration) establish the trusts between the two domains or check that the trusts are appropriately configured (in intraforest migrations). This handles the trusts necessary to perform the migration, but doesn't take care of those others that the source domain has that the target domain might not have. You can use the Trust Migration Wizard to establish either of these trusts. The Trust Migration Wizard will list all trusts for both source and target domains and will also let you know which trusts do not exist for both.

Group Mapping And Merging Wizard

The Group Mapping And Merging Wizard is used primarily for Windows NT migrations, but can be used for local groups when you need to convert components from a peer-to-peer network into Active Directory components. The Group Mapping And Merging Wizard requires that both domains be in separate forests.

ClonePrincipal

ClonePrincipal is restricted to interforest restructures. It is used to clone users and groups between domains, and its primary feature is supposedly being able to do so without interfering with the production environment. Theoretically, running only the User and Group Migration Wizards in ADMT should be able to produce the same results with an extra measure of safety. There's one gotcha involved with ClonePrincipal. It's not really an application. ClonePrincipal is actually a bunch of Visual Basic scripts that are included with the administration tool package. The administration tool package is in the \support directory of the Windows

2000 installation CD. We will discuss scripting in detail in Chapter 16. In the meantime, following are each of the Visual Basic scripts and the variables that they use. You can run each of these scripts from the command prompt using the syntax in the following sections.

Variables

The variables for the Visual Basic scripts are as follows:

```
Srcdc= the NetBIOS computer name of the source domain controller.
Srcdom=source domain name
Srcsam=SAM name of the object that is being moved from source to target
   domains
Dstdc=NetBIOS name of the destination domain controller. The script usually
   must run on this machine.
Dstdom=destination domain name (must be in FQDN formats i.e.widgetsrus.com)
Dstsam=SAM name of the object when it gets to the destination domain. This
   is your opportunity to rename the object.
Dstdn=distinguished name of the object at its destination. I.e. LDAP://
GADGETSRUS /OU=Supervisors,DC=gadgetsrus,DC=com
Dstou=destination OU for the copied data If the destination OU does not
   exist, the script will create it for you.
```

Clonegg.vbs

Clonegg copies global groups from a source domain to a destination domain. The syntax is as follows:

```
cscript clonegg.vbs /srcdc: <dcname> /srcdom: <domain> /dstdc: <dcname> /
dstdom:<domain> /dstou: <ouname>
```

Cloneggu.vbs

Cloneggu copies both global groups and users from a source domain. Cloneggu will not copy built-in accounts, such as administrator or guest. The syntax is as follows:

```
cscript cloneggu.vbs /srcdc: <dcname> /srcdom:<domain> /dstdc: dcname>
  /dstdom: <domain> /dstou: <ouname>
```

Clonelg.vbs

Clonelg copies local domain groups from the source to the target domain. The syntax is as follows:

```
Cscript clonelg.vbs /srcdc: <dcname> /srcdom:<domain> /dstdc:<dcname> /
dstdom:<domain> /dstou: <ouname>
```

Clonepr.vbs

Clonepr is used to copy security principals (user, computer, or group accounts) from the source to the target domain. Unlike clonegg, cloneggu, and clonelg, clonepr also automatically places the SID information from the source domain into the sIDHistory information in the target domain. The syntax is as follows:

```
Cscript clonepr.vbs /srcdc: <dcname> /srcdom: <domain> /srcsam: <name>
  /dstdc: <dcname> /dstdom: <domain> /dstsam: <name> /dstdn:
  <distinguished name>
```

Sidhist.vbs

Because clonegg, cloneggu, and clonelg do not copy the sIDHistory information, you will need to use sidhist to get the sIDHistory information from the source to the target domain. I can't imagine a situation where you won't need sIDHistory, but if indeed it is not necessary for you to maintain resource access, you don't need to run sidhist. Otherwise, it should be run after clonegg, cloneggu, and clonelg. The syntax is as follows:

```
Cscript sidhist.vbs /srcdc: <dcname> /srcdom: <domain> /srcsam: <name>
  /dstdc: <dcname> /dstdom: <domain> /dstsam: <name>
```

MoveTree

MoveTree is a command-line utility that moves Active Directory trees or branches of trees (domains) from one place to another. MoveTree is restricted to intraforest restructures and is usually used when collapsing or moving multiple domains. MoveTree takes advantage of sIDHistory, but only with native target domains. MoveTree is also located in the \support folder of the Windows 2000 installation CD and is installed locally when the administration pack is also installed.

Syntax

The syntax of MoveTree is as follows:

```
MoveTree [/start | /continue | /check /startnocheck] /s <SrcDSA> /d
  <DstDSA>
    /sdn <SrcDN> /ddn <DstDN> /u <Domain\Username> /p <Password> /verbose
```

Switches

One of the following switches must begin every instance of MoveTree:

• **/start**

• **/continue**

- **/check**

- **/startnocheck**

The switch **/check** will check the viability of the command and the integrity of the Active Directory subtree to be moved before anything gets moved. The switch **/start** automatically performs a check prior to actually moving items, and **/startnocheck** will immediately move objects. To restart a failed MoveTree operation, use **/continue**.

The switch **/verbose** will show all actions and activities on the screen.

Required Variables
The required variables include the following:

```
srcdsa=source domain controller's FQDN. i.e. widgdcl.widgetsrus.com
dstdsa=destination domain controller's FQDN. i.e. gadgdcl.gadgetsrus.com
srcdn=The 'lead' object in the source domain that will be moved. Must be in
  distinguished naming formats. I.e. /OU=Supervisors,DC=WIDGETSRUS,DC=com
dstdn=The full distinguished name of the same 'lead' or root object when it
  is grafted into the destination tree. i.e. /OU=Managers, /OU=Supervisors,
DC=GADGETSRUS, DC=com
```

Optional Variables
Although both of the variables in this section are optional, if they are not included in the command line, the system will prompt for the appropriate information.

The variable **domain\username=** is the domain and username that will have the authority to perform the actions (domain administrator equivalent for both domains or member of enterprise admins group).

For security purposes, if using the variable **password=**, it might be wise to eliminate the password from any batch files or scripts that you put MoveTree into.

Example
The following is an example of MoveTree:

```
Movetree /check /s widgdcl.widgetsrus.com /d gadgdcl.gadgetsrus.com /sdn /
OU=Supervisors,DC=WIDGETSRUS,DC=com /ddn
OU=supervisors,OU=managers,DC=GADGETSRUS,DC=dom /u gadgetsrus\dadmin /p
password
```

Immediate Solutions

Using ADMT to Migrate Groups

Group migration is part of an interforest migration and can also occur between two Windows 2000 domains. ADMT must be run on the target Windows 2000 domain. To use ADMT to migrate groups, perform the following steps:

1. After clicking Start, select Programs|Administrative Tools|Active Directory Migration Tools.
2. Right-click the Active Directory Migration Tool folder.
3. Select Group Migration Wizard from the drop-down menu, and click Next.
4. Click the Migrate Now radio button, and click Next.
5. Click the down arrow next to the Source domain line.
6. Select the appropriate domain.
7. Click the down arrow next to the Target domain line.
8. Select the appropriate domain, and click the Next button.
9. Click Add to select groups.
10. Double-click any groups that are slated for migration, and click OK.
11. Click Next.
12. Click Browse next to the Target OU line, and select the folder where the group should reside within the target domain.
13. Click OK.
14. Click Next.
15. Click the Update User Rights checkbox.
16. Click the Copy Group Members checkbox.
17. Click the Migrate Group SIDS To Target Domain checkbox, and then click Next.
18. Click on the Rename Conflicting Accounts By Adding The Following radio button.
19. Type an appropriate prefix or suffix, and click Next.
20. Carefully review the actions listed, and click Next.
21. Carefully review the actions listed. Note any failures, and click Finish.

Creating Trusts between a Windows 2000 and a Windows NT Domain

During an interforest migration from Windows NT to Windows 2000, it is necessary to create trusts between the target and destination domains. To do this, perform the following steps:

1. After clicking Start on the Windows NT machine, select Programs|Administrative Tools|User Manager For Domains.

2. Select Policies|Trust Relationships.

3. Click Add next to the Trusted Domains window.

4. Type the domain name.

5. Press Tab, and type the administrative username and password.

6. Click OK.

7. Because this trust has not been configured on the other side, click OK.

8. Click Add next to the Trusting Domain window.

9. Type the domain name in the Trusting Domain window.

10. Press Tab.

11. Type the administrative username and press Tab.

12. Type the administrative password again, and click OK.

13. Click Close.

14. Go to the Windows 2000 system, click Start, and select Programs|Administrative Tools|Active Directory Domains And Trusts.

15. Highlight and right-click the domain that requires the trust.

16. Click the Trusts tab.

17. Click Add next to the top window.

18. Type the Windows NT domain name as the trusted domain, and press Tab.

19. Type the administrative username and password, and press Tab.

20. Type the administrative password again.

21. Click OK.

22. Because this trust has been established on both domains, a confirmation dialog box appears. Click OK.

23. Click the Trusting Domain entry, and click Add next to the bottom window.

24. Type the Windows NT domain as the trusting domain, and press Tab.

25. Type the administrative password, press Tab, and then type the password and press Tab one more time.

26. Click OK.

27. In order to verify the trust, click OK again.

28. Type an administrator's username, press Tab, and type the password.

29. Click OK.

30. After the trust has been verified, click OK.

31. Click OK, and close the window.

Group Mapping And Merging Wizard

The Group Mapping And Merging Wizard will flag source and target groups and OUs for migration. To use the Group Mapping And Merging Wizard to flag these objects, perform these steps:

1. After clicking Start, select Programs|Administrative Tools|Active Directory Migration Tool.

2. Right-click the Active Directory Migration Tool folder.

3. Click Group Mapping And Merging Wizard, and click Next.

4. Click the Migrate Now radio button, and click Next.

5. Click Next again, and click Add.

6. Double-click any groups that need to be flagged, and click OK.

7. Click Next, and then click Browse.

8. Select a target location, and click Next.

9. Click Next.

10. Click Finish.

11. After the process has completed successfully, click Close.

Decommissioning a Windows 2000 Domain Controller

To decommission a Windows 2000 domain controller, perform the following steps:

1. Click Start.

2. Click Run.

3. Type "DCPROMO".

4. Click OK.

5. Click Next.

6. Click OK.

7. Click the This Server Is The Last Domain Controller In The Domain checkbox. Keep in mind that by server, Microsoft means Windows 2000 Server.

8. Click Next.

9. Type "administrator" in the User Name field.

10. Press Tab.

11. Type "administrator" in the Password field.

12. Click Next.

13. Click Next.

14. Click Next.

15. Wait while Active Directory is removed from the system.

16. Click Finish.

17. The system will prompt to restart the system. Click Restart Now.

Redeploying a Windows 2000 Server to a New Domain

This is also a method for changing a Windows 2000 server into a domain controller. To redeploy a decommissioned Windows 2000 server, perform the following steps:

1. Click on Start, and select Run.

2. Type "DCPROMO".

3. Click OK, and then click Next on the next four windows.

4. Type the domain that is being redeployed, and click Next.

5. The domain NetBIOS name is automatically filled in for you. Click Next.

6. The database and log locations are automatically filled in for you. Change them if necessary. If not, click Next.

7. The Sysvol location is automatically filled in for you. Change it if necessary. If not, click Next.

8. The system attempts to contact a DNS server in the entered domain. If or when it fails, it notifies you of the failure. Click OK.

9. Click Next.

10. Because this is the beginning of an intraforest restructure, click the Permissions Compatible Only With Windows 2000 Servers radio button.

11. Click Next.

12. Enter a Directory Services Restore Mode administrator password, and press Tab.

13. Type the password again, and click Next.

14. Click Next to begin the file copy and Active Directory configuration process.

15. Wait until the Active Directory configuration is complete.

16. When the installation is complete, click Finish.

Using ADMT to Migrate Users

During a pilot migration for an interforest migration, pilot groups of people may be designated, but individual users may also be designated for a pilot group. In the same manner that the Group Migration Wizard migrates associated users, the User Migration Wizard migrates associated groups. To use the User Migration Wizard to migrate associated groups, perform the following steps:

1. After clicking Start, select Programs|Administrative Tools|Active Directory Migration Tool.

2. Right-click the Active Directory Migration Tool folder.

3. Select User Migration Wizard from the drop-down menu.

4. Click Next.

5. Click the Migrate Now? radio button.

6. Click Next.

7. Because the Group Migration Wizard was run before, the domain entries are already filled in. Click Next.

8. Click Add.

9. Double-click the appropriate accounts, and then click on the down arrow on the scroll bar.

10. Double-click the appropriate accounts.

11. Click OK.

12. Click Next.

13. Because this was run through during the test, it was determined that the target OU was Users. Click Next.

14. Click Next.

15. Click the Migrate User SIDS To Target Domain checkbox, and then click Next.

16. Click the Migrate Associated User Groups checkbox.

17. Click the Update Previously Migrated Objects checkbox.

18. Click Next.

19. Click Next.

20. Click Finish.

21. The migration status will appear in this window. After it is complete, click Close.

Using ADMT to Migrate Computers

After user and group accounts have been migrated, workstations and other systems need to be migrated. To do this, perform the following steps:

1. After clicking Start, select Programs|Administrative Tools|Active Directory Migration Tool.

2. Right-click the Active Directory Migration Tool folder, and click the Computer Migration Wizard.

3. Click Next, and click the Migrate Now? radio button.

4. Click Next.

5. The source and target domains are probably already filled in. Change them if necessary, and click Next.

6. Click Add to select systems from the source domain.

7. Double-click computers to add them to the list, and click OK.

8. Click Next, and click Browse.

9. Click the folder or OU where the computers will be migrated into the target domain, and click OK.

10. Click Next.

11. Ensure that all entries are checked if necessary, and click Next.

12. Click the Add radio button, and click Next.

13. Enter an administrator's username, press Tab, enter the appropriate password, and click Next.

14. Click Next two more times.

15. Click Finish.

16. When the computers are migrated successfully, click Close.

17. The system will dispatch agents to change the system settings for the computers involved in this migration. This will eliminate the need for you to walk the floor to change the domain for every system that was migrated.

18. Click Close.

Using the Security Translation Wizard

Prior to migration, you'll need to identify service accounts in order to determine which ones need to be migrated using the Users And Groups wizard. Migrating system default service accounts can cause problems.

1. After clicking Start, select Programs|Administrative Tools|Active Directory Migration Tool.

2. Right-click the Active Directory Migration Tool folder, and select the Security Translation Wizard.

3. Click Next, and click the Migrate Now? radio button.

4. Click Next, and click Next again.

5. Click Add, and double-click computers that need this function performed. When you are done, click OK.

6. Click Next three times.

7. Type an administrator account for the username, press Tab, and type the appropriate password.

8. Click Next.

9. Click Finish.

10. The system will dispatch agents to perform the adjustments on the systems indicated. Wait a few moments.

11. After successful changes, click Close.

Chapter 8

Windows 2000 Installation

(continued)

In Depth

Before delving into the Windows 2000 installation process, you'll need to understand the Windows 2000 setup programs. Although they're still named winnt.exe and winnt32.exe, they have greatly changed from those that you used for Windows NT. This section will deal with some of the new changes. You'll also look at the system requirements that need to be met before Windows 2000 can be installed successfully.

Two different setup programs ship with Windows 2000. The first, winnt.exe, is used when installing or upgrading Windows 2000 when 32-bit operating systems do not exist. That is to say that the system is booting from either a disk operating system (DOS) floppy or a Windows 9x boot floppy. The second setup program, winnt32.exe, can be used when installing Windows 2000 on a system that already has a 32-bit operating system installed (Windows 9x, Windows NT, or Windows 2000). If your system has the ability to boot to the Windows 2000 installation CD, the boot program will automatically run the install program. This is particularly ideal for situations where no format on the hard disk will hold Windows 2000. I will discuss CD-ROM installation in the section called "Manual Installation."

NOTE: *Both of these setup programs reside in the i386 directory of the Windows 2000 CD-ROM.*

Each of these setup programs has its own unique set of command-line parameters that you can enter to get the program to accomplish different tasks. These command-line parameters are discussed in the following sections.

The winnt.exe Command-Line Parameters

As mentioned in the previous section, winnt.exe is the 16-bit version of the Windows 2000 setup program and can only be used to launch the setup program from a system booted with a DOS or Windows 9x boot disk.

The winnt.exe setup program is launched as follows:

```
winnt [/s[:sourcepath]] [/t[:tempdrive] [/u[:answer file]]
[/udf:id[,udf_file]] [/r:folder] [/r[x]:folder] [/e:command]
[/a] [/I:INF_file]
```

Typing "winnt /?" at the command prompt (from the i386 directory on the Windows 2000 installation CD) lists and describes all the command-line parameters available. All of the switches and options in the winnt.exe program are used to install Windows 2000 in different ways. These switches are discussed further throughout this chapter.

The Winnt32.exe Command-Line Parameters

Winnt32.exe is the 32-bit version of the Windows 2000 setup program. It allows for much greater performance by multithreading the setup process. As you'll notice, more preinstallation options are available.

The winnt32.exe setup program is launched as follows:

```
winnt32 [/s:sourcepath] [/tempdrive:drive_letter]
[/unattend[number]:[answer_file]] [/copydir:folder] [/copysource:folder]
[cmd:command] [/debug[level]:[filename]] [/udf:id[,UDF_file]
[/syspart:drive_letter] [/checkupgradeonly] [cmdcons] [/m:folder_name]
[/makelocalsource] [/noreboot]
```

Typing "winnt32 /?" at the command prompt (from the i386 directory) lists and describes all the command-line parameters available. Again, the options available with the winnt32.exe setup program are used for different types of installation.

System Requirements

Although Windows 2000 is a much more robust and scalable operating system than Windows NT, it does require more hardware resources. For this reason, Table 8.1 lists the recommended minimum requirements for installing Windows 2000 on your system.

NOTE: *Remember, these are minimum requirements. In the computer world, more is generally better.*

Windows 2000 is a fairly new operating system and may not support all existing hardware devices installed on your system. A couple of methods can be used to find out whether your system devices are supported. First, you can run the winnt32.exe application with the **/checkupgradeonly** command-line parameter. Results for this program are placed in a file called upgrade.txt for Windows 95 and Windows 98 systems or in winn32.log for Windows NT systems. Second, you can check the Hardware Compatibility List (HCL). A copy of an HCL exists in the Support directory on the Windows 2000 CD-ROM, but you should check the online version. The online version is updated regularly as new devices get certified to work with Windows 2000. You can find the online HCL at **www.microsoft.com/hcl/default.asp**.

Table 8.1   Minimum requirements for installing Windows 2000.

Item	Professional	Server	Advanced Server	Datacenter Server
Processor limit	2	4	8	32
Memory support	4GB	4GB	8GB	64GB
Clustering	No	No	2 maximum	4 maximum
Load balancing	No	No	32 maximum	32 maximum
Hardware Compatibility List (HCL)	Standard	Standard	Standard	Gold HCL
Processor	133MHz	133MHz	133MHz	Pentium III Xeon
RAM	64MB	128MB	128MB	256MB
Hard disk drive (HDD)/free HDD	2GB/650MB	2GB/1GB	2GB/1GB	2GB/1GB

Manual Installation

The following sections examine installing Windows 2000 manually.

Using Boot Floppies

Much like with Windows NT, you can install Windows 2000 using a set of boot floppy disks. Unlike Windows NT, however, these boot floppies do not ship with the product. Instead, two different applications exist. The first, makeboot.exe, is used to create the boot floppies from a DOS prompt or from Windows 9x. The second, makebt32.exe, is similarly used to create the boot floppies from Windows NT or Windows 2000.

To create these floppies, you'll need to run the makeboot.exe or makebt32.exe program from the Windows 2000 installation CD. Four floppy disks are required. After the boot disks are created, they can be used to start the Windows 2000 setup program. In essence, the floppy disks install enough of the Windows 2000 kernel to get the rest of the operating system installed. This includes support for some of the server-based devices and file system drivers.

From a CD-ROM

The Windows 2000 CD-ROM uses the El-Torito standard to boot. What this means to you is that, if your system can support this method of booting CD-ROMs, you can bypass the creation of the boot floppies. If your system can support Windows 2000, it should also support the El-Torito standard. This method is faster than using the floppy disks, but is not as fast as the hard drive method. This is also the most reasonable and painless method of manual installation when the target hard disk drive is blank or unformatted.

Although your system may support booting to a CD-ROM, you may need to change the basic input/output system (BIOS) boot order settings in order to take advantage of this. The BIOS contains a list of which devices should be queried for boot records when the system boots. Historically, the boot order was the floppy drive and then the hard disk drive. More recently, BIOS applications will allow more devices than just two to be queried, but, in any case, you will need to change one of the first boot devices to read the CD-ROM drive.

From a Hard Drive

The process of installing Windows 2000 from a hard drive is a simple one. All that needs to be done is to copy the distribution files (located in the i386 directory on the installation CD) to the hard drive and launch either the winnt.exe or winnt32.exe setup program. The setup after that is identical to the other methods.

From a Network Share

Similar to installing from a hard drive, installing Windows 2000 from a network share is also an easy process. All that needs to be done is to copy the distribution files to the server share point, map the client to that share, and launch either the winnt.exe or winnt32.exe setup program. The setup after that is identical to the other methods.

One glitch is involved with this type of installation, which is identical to the network-based installation from Windows NT. Partway through the installation process, the system reboots before network connectivity has been configured within Windows 2000. This causes problems because the system will still require the network share to copy and reference files. The solution to this is to create a unique boot disk that establishes access to a network share. Although these are sometimes difficult to create, you can do so by obtaining the Windows 3.1 or DOS drivers for the network card in question and by incorporating them into a boot disk. You may also check some imaging companies' Web sites, such as Symantec's Ghost or Powerquest's Drive Image Pro. Many images are too large to store on CD-ROM or other removable media, so they are often stored on the network. These imaging programs require that the system boot to floppy in order to get a clean image created or copied. The result is that many of the companies create network boot floppies to assist in the use of their products. These same boot floppies can help you perform a network installation of Windows 2000. The type of server that the installation files are located on should give you an idea of what commands you'll need to include on the disk. If the server that contains the setup files is a NetWare box, you'll need to use the **MAP** command to access the data. If the server is Microsoft-based, you can use the **NET USE** command to access the install files after the drivers have been loaded and initialized.

> **TIP:** *Several vendors have attempted to provide images for boot floppies that gain network access in order to assist in supporting their product. Check with vendors that do disk imaging, such as PowerQuest and Symantec. They may have a boot floppy image that has drivers for your network interface card (NIC). With a few modifications, you may be able to get up and running faster than if you built the disk yourself.*

Automated Installation

Sometimes you'll want to deploy or install Windows 2000 on several computer systems with little or no human intervention in order to get more done in less time. This type of fully or semiautomated installation can occur in several different ways, which I'll discuss in the following sections.

Using Automated Installation Tools

Several utilities are available from the Windows 2000 CD-ROM and the *Windows 2000 Server Resource Kit* (ISBN 1-57231-805-8) to automate the installation of Windows 2000. One of these is the Setup Manager Wizard, found in the "Deployment" section of the *Windows 2000 Server Resource Kit*.

This utility allows you to answer all the questions that the Windows 2000 setup program may request and store them in a text file. This text file is then used with the **/unattend** command-line parameter to answer these questions automatically.

Another feature is its ability to create a Uniqueness Database File (UDF). This file, when used in conjunction with the answer file, allows you to install multiple machines using the answer file, but to modify machine-specific information, such as the computer name, Transmission Control Protocol/Internet Protocol (TCP/IP) address, and so on. The UDF file is also used with the **/UDF** command-line parameter of the winnt.exe and winnt32.exe install programs.

Finally, you can create specialized directories in the distribution folder (for example, e:\i386) that will automatically install extra drivers or applications. These directories are outlined in Table 8.2.

Table 8.2   Folder options under the Distribution folder.

Directory	Purpose
\OEM	Contains all extra files to be copied to the system during the setup process
\$$	Is the same as %windir% (C:\winnt)
\$$\Help	Installs extra help files into the *%windir%*\help folder during setup
\$$\System32	Installs extra files into the *%windir%*\system32 folder during setup
\$1	Is the same as the root drive on the hard drive that Windows 2000 is installed on (for example, C:)

(continued)

Table 8.2   Folder options under the Distribution folder *(continued)*.

Directory	Purpose
\\$1*pnpdrivers*	Stores new and updated drivers for plug-and-play devices
\\$1\SysPrep	Contains the files used in the SysPrep process
\textmode	Stores extra drivers for mass storage devices and Hardware Abstraction Layers (HALs) to be used during the initial text-based phase of the setup program
drive_letter	Stores files that are copied to the root of the drive specified
*drive_letter**folder*	Stores files that are copied to the folder specified

Using Remote Installation Services

Another new feature of Windows 2000 is the Remote Installation Services (RIS). This service allows an administrator to create customized images that can then be used to install Windows 2000 Professional automatically on a workstation by inserting a boot disk and answering a few simple questions (such as username, password, and computer name). RIS does the rest.

RIS uses a technology known as a *Pre-boot Execution Environment* (PXE). PXE-compliant network cards are functional (with the appropriate BIOS support) before the operating system (OS) loads, thus allowing network communications before the NIC drivers are loaded. When the system boots using PXE, it first requests a TCP/IP address from a Dynamic Host Configuration Protocol (DHCP) server. Upon receiving this IP address, it contacts the server running the RIS service (which authenticates its right to be installed in Active Directory), and the image is installed to the client.

Using Ghosting or Cloning Tools

Many organizations are faced with installing Windows 2000 on a very large number of systems. Most of these organizations use products such as Norton's Ghost to duplicate their systems. What these applications do is duplicate the hard drive from one machine to another. It works well when the system hardware is identical from one system to the next. Although this is pretty rare in the real world, there is a place for this type of technology.

One of the problems with Windows 2000 is that each system has a unique ID. No two systems may have the same ID on the network and still function properly. To solve this problem, Microsoft released a product called SysPrep on the *Windows 2000 Server Resource Kit*. This utility, when executed after the system has been set up, removes some of these unique ID settings, and allows you to take the image of the system. After this image is restored on a different hard drive and that system is rebooted, the Windows 2000 setup completes these steps to present you with a Windows 2000 system that's unique on the network.

Although the basic descriptions between Sysprep and RIS may seem the same, they are very different tools and were created to handle certain situations. Basically, if you need to deploy to systems that are not all identical, you need to use RIS because it can handle many differences from computer to computer. The only exception to this is when you're deploying to different species of computers, such as laptops or servers. This is because many system-level device drivers are unique to that particular type of computer, such as Universal Serial Bus (USB) drivers. There are essentially two reasons to use Sysprep instead of RIS. First, if you want to be able to edit pieces of an image after it has been created, RIS will create the image for you and deploy it. However, if any changes occur, a new image will need to be built, and this can take up to several hours for complex or top-heavy systems. Sysprep basically allows editing because certain imaging applications allow you to browse components within an image and change those components. Although this can be a risky event when dealing with installed applications and such, I can definitely testify to the few times where I'd wished that I was using Sysprep instead of RIS for just this reason. The other reason that you may want to use Sysprep is actually a reason that you may not want to use it. The basic requirements for RIS include at least one server on the network that's running DHCP, RIS services, and a PXE-boot NIC on the client machine(s). With exception of the PXE-boot NIC, all of these components are free with Windows 2000 server and are easily installed and configured if not already on your server. Sysprep is unique in that it does not require a server (except perhaps to store the images), but it does require licenses for the imaging application. When you consider systems running on an enterprise, this can get to be expensive.

Active Directory Installation

After upgrading a Windows NT domain controller, the system will reboot and automatically start the dcpromo application. Dcpromo can also be started by either typing DCPROMO on the Run line from the start menu, or by selecting the Active Directory link from the Windows 2000 Configure Your Server wizard that appears once the system is rebooted. Dcpromo is the Active Directory Installation Wizard. If the server is destined to be a member server, you can automatically cancel out of the wizard. If the server is slated to become a domain controller within the domain, you'll need to continue with this wizard. As discussed in Chapters 6 and 7, Active Directory installation is central to several upgrade and restructuring processes. Although dcpromo is covered in more detail in those chapters, it is important for you to know a few facts before proceeding with the Active Directory installation.

You are presented with several options during the dcpromo installation process. You will need to know the following so that you can answer these options appropriately:

- Is this the first domain controller in the enterprise?

- Is this the first domain controller in a master domain?

- Is this the first domain controller in a child, resource, or account domain?

- Where do you want to store the log files? In the Active Directory database? In the SYSVOL volume?

- Is there a Windows 2000 Domain Name Service (DNS) server available? If not, is there a DNS server that supports SRV records?

If you are installing the first domain controller in the enterprise, you will need to choose the options to Create A New Domain Tree and then Create A New Forest. If you are installing the first domain controller in a master domain, but a domain controller is already in the enterprise, you'll need to create a new domain tree and join an existing forest. If you are installing the first domain controller in a child, resource, or account domain, you'll need to choose the option to create a child domain in an existing domain tree. If this is not the first domain controller for any of the choices in this paragraph, you will need to choose to Create A Replica Of An Existing Domain.

The fourth bullet in the previous list deals almost exclusively with performance. The log files, Active Directory database, and SYSVOL volume can all be the source for much disk usage and traffic. In many situations, you'll leave the options for these file's locations at the default. If you have separate hard disks and controllers, you may consider placing these files on a drive that is separate from the boot partition in order to distribute the physical and controller loads.

Active Directory requires DNS. Although Microsoft would prefer that we use a Windows 2000 DNS server, that may not be possible in larger enterprises. Any time that you install Active Directory, you should have thought through DNS and how it should be or is currently placed on your network. For example, you should consider the following:

- If you have already installed Windows 2000 DNS in your Active Directory forest, you'll need to know the server name and IP address (for good measure) while you're installing Active Directory on this server.

- If your company relies on a Unix flavor of DNS, you may want to check to see if it supports BIND 4.9.7. BIND 4.9.7 is the minimum supported by Windows 2000, but if you want to use features like dynamic DNS, you'll need BIND 8.1.2 or above. If your company has BIND 4.9.7 or above, you'll simply need to notify the Unix DNS administrators that Windows 2000 Active Directory will be using their DNS setup. You should be prepared with the DNS server's name and IP address during the dcpromo process.

- If the Unix DNS does not support BIND 4.9.7, the best advice is to speak with your current DNS administrators. If they cannot upgrade the DNS to be compliant, you can get them to allow a dedicated DNS subdomain for you to use. You'll need to allow dcpromo to install Windows 2000 DNS for you, and you'll use the new subdomain name as your zone and the Unix DNS parent domain as your forward lookup server. Also be aware that although BIND 4.9.7 is the minimum, you'll need version 8.1.2 for dynamic DNS support.

- If DNS does not exist at all in your company, dcpromo will install it for you. It will ask for the fully qualified domain name (FQDN) for the DNS server. Because one does not exist, move on appropriately, and dcpromo will prompt you to install DNS.

Immediate Solutions

Creating the Windows 2000 Installation Boot Disks

The following sections explore the various methods of creating boot disks.

From DOS

To create boot disks from DOS, perform the following steps:

1. Boot the system using a boot disk that installs all the necessary CD-ROM drivers.

NOTE: *If you need a boot disk, you can use the Windows 98 boot disk.*

2. Change to the drive assigned to the CD-ROM (for example, D:).
3. Type "cd bootdisk", and press Enter.
4. Type "makeboot", and press Enter.
5. When prompted, insert a blank, formatted floppy disk, and press Enter.
6. After the first floppy is created, repeat the process for the next three disks.

From Windows 9x

To create boot disks from Windows 95 or Windows 98, perform the following steps:

1. Click Start, and select Programs|Accessories|Windows Explorer.
2. Change to the drive assigned to the CD-ROM (for example, D:).
3. Open the Bootdisk folder, and double-click makeboot.exe.
4. Enter the drive letter for the floppy drive (A:).
5. When prompted, insert a blank, formatted floppy disk, and press Enter.
6. After the first floppy is created, repeat the process for the next three disks.

From Windows NT or Windows 2000

To create boot disks from Windows NT or Windows 2000, perform the following steps:

1. Click Start, and select Programs|Accessories|Windows Explorer.
2. Change to the drive assigned to the CD-ROM (for example, D:).

3. Open the Bootdisk folder, and double-click makebt32.exe.

4. Enter the drive letter for the floppy drive (A:).

5. When prompted, insert a blank, formatted floppy disk, and press Enter.

6. After the first floppy is created, repeat the process for the next three disks.

Installing Windows 2000 Using Boot Disks

To install Windows 2000 using boot disks, perform the following steps:

1. Insert Windows 2000 Boot Disk 1 into the floppy drive and the Windows 2000 CD-ROM into the CD-ROM drive. Then, turn on your system.

2. When prompted, replace Disk 1 with Disk 2.

3. Repeat for the rest of the disks when prompted.

4. When the Welcome To Windows 2000 window appears, press Enter.

5. Read the licensing agreement. You can use the Page Up and Page Down keys to scroll through it. Press F8 to continue.

6. The setup program then displays the disks and partitions available on your system. Choose the desired partition (partitions or unpartitioned space).

7. If you want to delete a partition, press D. If you want to create a partition, press C.

NOTE: *If you choose to create a new partition, Windows 2000 setup will prompt you to select whether to create a Windows NT File System (NTFS) partition or a file allocation table (FAT) partition. If you select the FAT partition option and the partition is less than 2GB, FAT16 will be used. If, however, the partition is greater than 2GB, FAT32 will be used automatically.*

---

8. When you've created your partition, select it, and press Enter.

9. The Windows 2000 setup program will confirm your partition selection; press Enter when you're ready. If the partition is formatted in a non-NTFS 5 file system, the setup program will ask you whether you want to convert it.

10. Your hard drives are now checked for errors, and all necessary Windows 2000 files are copied to the Windows 2000 folder (\Winnt by default).

11. When the file copy is complete, the Windows 2000 setup program will ask you to remove the CD-ROM and any floppies. Press Enter to reboot the system.

12. Windows setup will restart. You'll know that this has occurred when the splash screen appears.

13. The setup program will now detect and configure the hardware devices installed on your system. If, for some reason, the setup program cannot detect or install a driver for a particular device, it will prompt you to direct it to the correct drivers.

14. Specify the regional settings for your particular system. You can change your locale and your keyboard settings. After you've selected these criteria, click Next.

15. Enter the name of the person to whom this computer is registered, and then enter the company name. After you've entered this information, click Next.

TIP: *Instead of entering the name of each user, you may want to use a generic name, such as the company name. This will prevent any confusion over the computer name in case a different person inherits the system.*

---

16. Enter the 25-digit product key as it appears on the back of your Windows 2000 CD-ROM jewel case, and click Next.

17. Choose the licensing mode that will be used on this system. By default, a Per Server mode is selected. If you keep the Per Server selection, enter the number of Client Access Licenses (CALs) you purchased. Click Next when done.

TIP: *You can complete a one-time conversion from Per Server licensing to Per Seat. This can be done during setup or at a later date.*

---

18. Enter the name that will be assigned to this computer on the network in the Computer Name field. In this window, you can also choose the password that will be assigned to the administrator account on this system. This password can be left blank. Click Next.

19. You can now select the components that you would like to install on your system. Remember that you can add or remove these components at a later date. After you've completed your selection, click Next.

20. If setup detects a modem, it displays the Dialing Location window. Select the country, area code, and external line codes, and click Next.

21. Make sure the date, time, and time zone information is correct, and click Next.

22. If you chose to install the Windows Terminal Services in the Windows 2000 Components window, choose the mode of operation: Remote Administration Mode (the default) or Application Server Mode. After you've done so, click Next.

23. The Windows 2000 setup program will now ask you whether you would like to install the network settings using Typical settings or Custom settings. The Typical settings include Client For Microsoft Networks, File And Printer Sharing For Microsoft Networks, and the TCP/IP protocol configured to use either DHCP or Automatic Private IP Addressing (APIPA). Click Next.

24. If you selected to configure your own network options, enter the desired components, and click Next. Again, you can modify the network configuration at a later date.

25. You're now prompted to join either a workgroup or a domain. If you would like to join a workgroup, enter the name of the workgroup in the Workgroup field. To join a domain, select the Yes option, and enter the name of the domain in the Workgroup Or Computer Domain field. Click Next.

TIP: If you want to install a new domain, select the No option, and clear the Workgroup Or Computer Domain field.

---

26. If you chose to join a domain, the setup program will prompt you for the username and password of a user with sufficient rights to add your system to the domain. It will then contact the domain controller for the domain and add your computer account. Click Next to attempt to join the domain.

27. The selected components are now installed and configured. Windows 2000 is configured. When this phase is complete, the setup program deletes any temporary files and prompts you to remove the CD-ROM before it reboots.

28. Windows 2000 is now installed. You can log in to it as you would any other Windows 2000 system on your network.

Installing Windows 2000 from a DOS Prompt Using a CD-ROM

To install Windows 2000 from a DOS prompt using a CD-ROM, perform the following steps:

1. Boot into DOS with a boot disk that contains the correct CD-ROM drivers for your drive.

2. At the command prompt, type "*D:*" (where *D* is the drive letter assigned to your CD-ROM drive). Press Enter.

3. Type "cd i386", and press Enter.

8. Windows 2000 Installation

4. Type "winnt", and press Enter.

5. Windows 2000 setup will prompt you to enter the location of the Windows 2000 setup files. The default will be *drive_letter*:\i386.

NOTE: *You can exit the Windows 2000 setup program at any point during the text-based phase by pressing F3.*

---

6. The Windows 2000 setup program will now copy two sets of files. The first set includes the files necessary for the actual setup program. These files are the same as those found on the Windows 2000 boot floppies. The second set includes the actual Windows 2000 installation files.

7. When copying is completed, the setup program will prompt you to remove the floppy disk and CD-ROM from the drives, and press Enter to reboot.

8. When the system boots, the Windows 2000 setup program will continue.

9. When the Welcome To Windows 2000 window appears, press Enter.

10. Read the licensing agreement. You can use the Page Up and Page Down keys to scroll through it. Press F8 to continue.

11. The setup program will now display the disks and partitions available on your system. Choose the desired partition (partitions or unpartitioned space).

12. If you want to delete a partition, press D. If you want to create a partition, press C.

NOTE: *If you choose to create a new partition, Windows 2000 setup will prompt you to select whether to create an NTFS partition or a FAT partition. If you select the FAT partition option and the partition is less than 2GB, FAT16 will be used. If, however, the partition is greater than 2GB, FAT32 will be used.*

---

13. When you've created your partition, select it, and press Enter.

14. The Windows 2000 setup program will confirm your partition selection; press Enter when you're ready. If the partition is formatted in a non-NTFS 5 file system, the setup program will ask you whether you want to convert it.

15. Your hard drives are now checked for errors, and all necessary Windows 2000 files are copied to the Windows 2000 folder (\Winnt by default).

16. When the file copy is complete, the Windows 2000 setup program will ask you to remove the CD-ROM and any floppies. Press Enter to reboot the system.

17. Windows setup will restart. You'll know that this has occurred when the splash screen appears.

18. The setup program will now detect and configure the hardware devices installed on your system. If, for some reason, the setup program cannot detect or install a driver for a particular device, it will prompt you to direct it to the correct drivers.

19. Specify the regional settings for your particular system. You can change your locale and your keyboard settings. After you've selected these criteria, click Next.

20. Enter the name of the person to whom this computer is registered, followed by the company this system belongs to. After you've entered this information, click Next.

21. Enter the 25-digit product key as it appears on the back of your Windows 2000 CD-ROM jewel case, and click Next.

22. Choose the licensing mode that will be used on this system. By default, a Per Server mode is selected. If you keep the Per Server selection, enter the number of CALs that you purchased. Click Next when done.

23. Enter the name that will be assigned to this computer on the network in the Computer Name field. In this window, you can also choose the password that will be assigned to the administrator account on this system. This password can be left blank. Click Next when done.

24. You can now select the components that you would like to install on your system. Remember that you can add or remove these components at a later date. After you've completed your selection, click Next.

25. If setup detects a modem, it will now display the Dialing Location window. Select the country, area code, and external line codes, and click Next.

26. Make sure that the date, time, and time zone information is correct, and click Next.

27. If you chose to install the Windows Terminal Services in the Windows 2000 Components window, choose the mode of operation: Remote Administration Mode (the default) or Application Server Mode. After you have done so, click Next.

28. The Windows 2000 setup program will now ask you whether you would like to install the network settings using Typical settings or Custom settings. The Typical settings include Client For Microsoft Networks, File And Printer Sharing For Microsoft Networks, and the TCP/IP protocol configured to use either DHCP or APIPA. Click Next.

29. If you selected to configure your own network options, enter the desired components, and click Next. Again, you can modify the network configuration at a later date.

30. You're now prompted to join either a workgroup or a domain. If you would like to join a workgroup, enter the name of the workgroup in the Workgroup field. To join a domain, select the Yes option, and enter the name of the domain in the Workgroup Or Computer Domain field. Click Next.

31. If you chose to join a domain, the setup program will prompt you for the username and password of a user with sufficient rights to add your system to the domain. It will then contact the domain controller for the domain and add your computer account. Click Next to attempt to join the domain.

32. The selected components are now installed and configured. Windows 2000 is configured. When this phase is complete, the setup program deletes any temporary files and prompts you to remove the CD-ROM before it reboots.

33. Windows 2000 is now installed. You can log in to it as you would any other Windows 2000 system on your network.

Installing Windows 2000 from Windows 3.x Using a CD-ROM

To install Windows 2000 from Windows 3.x using a CD-ROM, perform the following steps:

1. Boot into Windows 3.x.

2. From File Manager, select the CD-ROM drive.

3. Navigate to the i386 directory.

4. Double-click winnt.exe.

5. The setup program will copy the necessary files to the hard drive and prompt you to reboot the system.

6. Insert the Windows 2000 Boot Disk 1 into the floppy drive and the Windows 2000 CD-ROM into the CD-ROM drive. Then, turn on your system.

7. When prompted, replace Disk 1 with Disk 2.

8. Repeat for the rest of the disks when prompted.

9. When the Welcome To Windows 2000 window appears, press Enter.

10. Read the licensing agreement. You can use the Page Up and Page Down keys to scroll through it. Press F8 to continue.

11. The setup program will now display the disks and partitions available on your system. Choose the desired partition (partitions or unpartitioned space).

12. If you want to delete a partition, press the D key. If you want to create a partition, press C.

NOTE: *If you choose to create a new partition, Windows 2000 setup will prompt you to select whether to create an NTFS partition or a FAT partition. If you select the FAT partition option and the partition is less than 2GB, FAT16 will be used. If, however, the partition is greater than 2GB, FAT32 will be used.*

---

13. When you've created your partition, select it, and press Enter.

14. The Windows 2000 setup program will confirm your partition selection; press Enter when you're ready. If the partition is formatted in a non-NTFS 5 file system, the setup program will ask you if you want to convert it.

15. Your hard drives are now checked for errors, and all necessary Windows 2000 files are copied to the Windows 2000 folder (\Winnt by default).

16. When the file copy is complete, the Windows 2000 setup program will ask you to remove the CD-ROM and any floppies. Press Enter to reboot the system.

17. Windows setup will restart. You'll know that this has occurred when the splash screen appears.

18. The setup program will now detect and configure the hardware devices installed on your system. If, for some reason, the setup program cannot detect or install a driver for a particular device, it will prompt you to direct it to the correct drivers.

19. Specify the regional settings for your particular system. You can change your locale and your keyboard settings. After you've selected these criteria, click Next.

20. Enter the name of the person to whom this computer is registered, followed by the company this system belongs to. After you've entered this information, click Next.

21. Enter the 25-digit product key as it appears on the back of your Windows 2000 CD-ROM jewel case, and click Next.

22. Choose the licensing mode that will be used on this system. By default, a Per Server mode is selected. If you keep the Per Server selection, enter the number of CALs that you purchased. Click Next when done.

23. Enter the name that will be assigned to this computer on the network in the Computer Name field. In this window, you can also choose the password that will be assigned to the administrator account on this system. This password can be left blank. Click Next when done.

8. Windows 2000 Installation

24. You can now select the components that you would like to install on your system. Remember that you can add or remove these components at a later date. After you have completed your selection, click Next.

25. If setup detects a modem, it will now display the Dialing Location window. Select the country, area code, and external line codes, and click Next.

26. Make sure that the date, time, and time zone information is correct, and click Next.

27. If you chose to install the Windows Terminal Services in the Windows 2000 Components window, choose the mode of operation: Remote Administration Mode (the default) or Application Server Mode. After you've done so, click Next.

28. The Windows 2000 setup program will now ask you whether you would like to install the network settings using Typical settings or Custom settings. The typical settings include Client For Microsoft Networks, File And Printer Sharing For Microsoft Networks, and the TCP/IP protocol configured to use either DHCP or APIPA. Click Next.

29. If you selected to configure your own network options, enter the desired components, and click Next. Again, you can modify the network configuration at a later date.

30. You're now prompted to join either a workgroup or a domain. If you would like to join a workgroup, enter the name of the workgroup in the Workgroup field. To join a domain, select the Yes option, and enter the name of the domain in the Workgroup Or Computer Domain field. Click Next.

31. If you chose to join a domain, the setup program will prompt you for the username and password of a user with sufficient rights to add your system to the domain. It will then contact the domain controller for the domain and add your computer account. Click Next to attempt to join the domain.

32. The selected components are now installed and configured. Windows 2000 is configured. When this phase is complete, the setup program deletes any temporary files and prompts you to remove the CD-ROM before it reboots.

33. Windows 2000 is now installed. You can log in to it as you would any other Windows 2000 system on your network.

Installing Windows 2000 from Windows 9x, Windows NT, or Windows 2000 Using a CD-ROM

To install Windows 2000 from Windows 95, Windows 98, Windows NT, or Windows 2000 using a CD-ROM, perform the following steps:

1. Insert the Windows 2000 CD-ROM. If autorun is enabled, the Windows 2000 Setup Wizard will automatically launch. If not, launch the Windows 2000 Setup Wizard by running the winnt32.exe file in the \i386 directory on the CD-ROM.

2. You can choose to upgrade your existing operating system to Windows 2000 or to install a new copy. Make your selection, and click Next.

3. Read the license agreement, select the I Agree radio button, and click Next.

4. Enter the 25-digit product key as it appears on the back of the CD-ROM jewel case. Click Next.

5. You can modify your Windows 2000 installations to support multiple languages and accessibility on this window. If you click the Advanced Options button, you'll be presented with some advanced Windows 2000 installation options. Click Next.

6. The Windows 2000 Setup Wizard will copy the necessary files to the hard drive and reboot your system.

7. The setup program will now display the disks and partitions available on your system. Choose the desired partition (partitions or unpartitioned space).

8. If you want to delete a partition, press D. If you want to create a partition, press C.

NOTE: *If you choose to create a new partition, Windows 2000 setup will prompt you to select whether to create an NTFS partition or a FAT partition. If you select the FAT partition option and the partition is less than 2GB, FAT16 will be used. If, however, the partition is greater than 2GB, FAT32 will be used.*

---

9. When you've created your partition, select it, and press Enter.

10. The Windows 2000 setup program will confirm your partition selection; press Enter when you're ready. If the partition is formatted in a non-NTFS 5 file system, the setup program will ask you if you want to convert it.

11. Your hard drives are now checked for errors, and all necessary Windows 2000 files are copied to the Windows 2000 folder (\Winnt by default).

12. When the file copy is complete, the Windows 2000 setup program will ask you to remove the CD-ROM and any floppies. Press Enter to reboot the system.

13. Windows setup will restart. You'll know that this has occurred when the splash screen appears.

14. The setup program will now detect and configure the hardware devices that are installed on your system. If, for some reason, the setup program cannot detect or install a driver for a particular device, it will prompt you to direct it to the correct drivers.

15. Specify the regional settings for your particular system. You can change your locale and your keyboard settings. After you've selected these criteria, click Next.

16. Enter the name of the person to whom this computer is registered, followed by the company this system belongs to. After you've entered this information, click Next.

17. Choose the licensing mode that will be used on this system. By default, a Per Server mode is selected. If you keep the Per Server selection, enter the number of CALs you purchased. Click Next when done.

18. Enter the name that will be assigned to this computer on the network in the Computer Name field. In this window, you can also choose the password that will be assigned to the administrator account on this system. This password can be left blank. Click Next when done.

19. You can now select the components that you would like to install on your system. Remember that you can add or remove these components at a later date. After you've completed your selection, click Next.

20. If setup detects a modem, it will now display the Dialing Location window. Select the country, area code, and external line codes, and click Next.

21. Make sure that the date, time, and time zone information is correct, and click Next.

22. If you chose to install the Windows Terminal Services in the Windows 2000 Components window, choose the mode of operation: Remote Administration Mode (the default) or Application Server Mode. After you have done so, click Next.

23. The Windows 2000 setup program will now ask you whether you would like to install the network settings using Typical settings or Custom settings. The Typical settings include Client For Microsoft Networks, File And Printer Sharing For Microsoft Networks, and the TCP/IP protocol configured to use either DHCP or APIPA. Click Next.

24. If you selected to configure your own network options, enter the desired components, and click Next. Again, you can modify the network configuration at a later date.

25. You're now prompted to join either a workgroup or a domain. If you would like to join a workgroup, enter the name of the workgroup in the Workgroup field. To join a domain, select the Yes option, and enter the name of the domain in the Workgroup Or Computer Domain field. Click Next.

26. If you chose to join a domain, the setup program will prompt you for the username and password of a user with sufficient rights to add your system to the domain. It will then contact the domain controller for the domain and add your computer account. Click Next to attempt to join the domain.

27. The selected components are now installed and configured. Windows 2000 is configured. When this phase is complete, the setup program deletes any temporary files and prompts you to remove the CD-ROM before it reboots.

28. Windows 2000 is now installed. You can log in to it as you would any other Windows 2000 system on your network.

Installing Windows 2000 from a Bootable CD-ROM

To install Windows 2000 from a bootable CD-ROM, perform the following steps:

1. Set your system's BIOS to boot off the CD-ROM drive prior to attempting to boot from the floppy drive and hard drive.

2. Insert the Windows 2000 CD-ROM into the CD-ROM drive, and turn on your system.

3. When the Welcome To Windows 2000 window appears, press Enter.

4. Read the licensing agreement. You can use the Page Up and Page Down keys to scroll through it. Press F8 to continue.

5. The setup program will now display the disks and partitions available on your system. Choose the desired partition (partitions or unpartitioned space).

6. If you want to delete a partition, press D. If you want to create a partition, press C.

NOTE: *If you choose to create a new partition, Windows 2000 setup will prompt you to select whether to create an NTFS partition or a FAT partition. If you select the FAT partition option and the partition is less than 2GB, FAT16 will be used. If, however, the partition is greater than 2GB, FAT32 will be used.*

7. When you've created your partition, select it, and press Enter.

8. Windows 2000 Installation

8. The Windows 2000 setup program will confirm your partition selection; press Enter when you're ready. If the partition is formatted in a non-NTFS 5 file system, setup will ask if you want to convert it.

9. Your hard drives are now checked for errors, and all necessary Windows 2000 files are copied to the Windows 2000 folder (\Winnt by default).

10. When the file copy is complete, the Windows 2000 setup program will ask you to remove the CD-ROM and any floppies. Press Enter to reboot the system.

11. Windows setup will restart. You'll know that this has occurred when the splash screen appears.

12. The setup program will now detect and configure the hardware devices installed on your system. If, for some reason, the setup program cannot detect or install a driver for a particular device, it will prompt you to direct it to the correct drivers.

13. Specify the regional settings for your particular system. You can change your locale and your keyboard settings. After you've selected these criteria, click Next.

14. Enter the name of the person to whom this computer is registered, followed by the company this system belongs to. After you've entered this information, click Next.

15. Choose the licensing mode that will be used on this system. By default, a Per Server mode is selected. If you keep the Per Server selection, enter the number of CALs you purchased. Click Next when done.

16. Enter the name that will be assigned to this computer on the network in the Computer Name field. In this window, you can also choose the password that will be assigned to the administrator account on this system. This password can be left blank. Click Next when done.

17. You can now select the components that you would like to install on your system. Remember that you can add or remove these components at a later date. After you've completed your selection, click Next.

18. If setup detects a modem, it will now display the Dialing Location window. Select the country, area code, and external line codes, and click Next.

19. Make sure that the date, time, and time zone information is correct, and click Next.

20. If you chose to install the Windows Terminal Services in the Windows 2000 Components window, choose the mode of operation: Remote Administration Mode (the default) or Application Server Mode. After you have done so, click Next.

21. The Windows 2000 setup program will now ask you whether you would like to install the network settings using Typical Settings or Custom settings. The typical settings include Client For Microsoft Networks, File And Printer Sharing For Microsoft Networks, and the TCP/IP protocol configured to use either DHCP or APIPA. Click Next.

22. If you selected to configure your own network options, enter the desired components, and click Next. Again, you can modify the network configuration at a later date.

23. You're now prompted to join either a workgroup or a domain. If you would like to join a workgroup, enter the name of the workgroup in the Workgroup field. To join a domain, select the Yes option, and enter the name of the domain in the Workgroup Or Computer Domain field. Click Next.

24. If you chose to join a domain, the setup program will prompt you for the username and password of a user with sufficient rights to add your system to the domain. It will then contact the domain controller for the domain and add your computer account. Click Next to attempt to join the domain.

25. The selected components are now installed and configured. Windows 2000 is configured. When this phase is completed, the setup program deletes any temporary files and prompts you to remove the CD-ROM before it reboots.

26. Windows 2000 is now installed. You can log in to it as you would any other Windows 2000 system on your network.

Installing Windows 2000 from a Hard Drive

To install Windows 2000 from a hard drive, perform the following steps:

1. Insert the Windows 2000 CD-ROM. If autorun in enabled, the Windows 2000 Setup Wizard will automatically launch. If not, launch the Windows 2000 Setup Wizard by running the winnt32.exe file in the \i386 directory on the CD-ROM.

2. You can choose to upgrade your existing operating system to Windows 2000 or install a new copy. Make your selection, and click Next.

3. Read the license agreement, select the I Agree radio button, and click Next.

4. Enter the 25-digit product key as it appears on the back of the CD-ROM jewel case, as shown in Figure 8.1. Click Next.

5. You can modify your Windows 2000 installation to support multiple languages and accessibility on the window shown in Figure 8.2. If you click

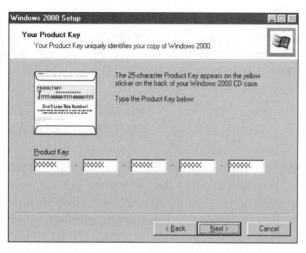

Figure 8.1   Entering the product key.

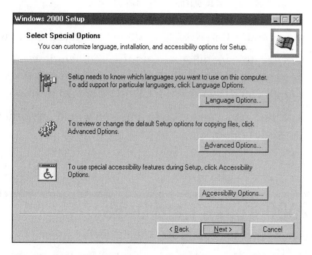

Figure 8.2   The Select Special Options window.

the Advanced Options button, you'll be presented with some advanced Windows 2000 installation options (see Figure 8.3). Click Next.

6. The Windows 2000 Setup Wizard will copy the necessary files to the hard drive and reboot your system.

7. The setup program will now display the disks and partitions available on your system. Choose the desired partition (partitions or unpartitioned space).

8. If you want to delete a partition, press D. If you want to create a partition, press C.

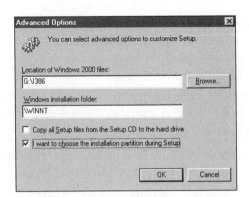

Figure 8.3   The Advanced Options window.

NOTE: *If you choose to create a new partition, Windows 2000 setup will prompt you to select whether to create an NTFS partition or a FAT partition. If you select the FAT partition option and the partition is less than 2GB, FAT16 will be used. If, however, the partition is greater than 2GB, FAT32 will be used.*

---

9. When you've created your partition, select it, and press Enter.

10. The Windows 2000 setup program will confirm your partition selection; press Enter when you're ready. If the partition is formatted in a non-NTFS 5 file system, the setup program will ask you if you want to convert it.

11. Your hard drives are now checked for errors, and all necessary Windows 2000 files are copied to the Windows 2000 folder (\Winnt by default).

12. When the file copy is complete, the Windows 2000 setup program will ask you to remove the CD-ROM and any floppies. Press Enter to reboot the system.

13. Windows setup will restart. You'll know that this has occurred when the splash screen appears.

14. The setup program will now detect and configure the hardware devices installed on your system. If, for some reason, the setup program cannot detect or install a driver for a particular device, it will prompt you to direct it to the correct drivers.

15. Specify the regional settings for your particular system. You can change your locale and your keyboard settings. After you've selected these criteria, click Next.

16. Enter the name of the person to whom this computer is registered, followed by the company this system belongs to. After you've entered this information, click Next.

17. Choose the licensing mode that will be used on this system. By default, a Per Server Mode is selected. If you keep the Per Server selection, enter the number of CALs you purchased. Click Next when done.

18. Enter the name that will be assigned to this computer on the network in the Computer Name field. In this window, you can also choose the password that will be assigned to the administrator account on this system. This password can be left blank. Click Next when done.

19. You can now select the components that you would like to install on your system. Remember that you can add or remove these components at a later date. After you've completed your selection, click Next.

20. If setup detects a modem, it will now display the Dialing Location window. Select the country, area code, and external line codes, and click Next.

21. Make sure that the date, time, and time zone information is correct, and click Next.

22. If you chose to install the Windows Terminal Services in the Windows 2000 Components window, choose the mode of operation: Remote Administration Mode (the default) or Application Server Mode. After you've done so, click Next.

23. The Windows 2000 setup program will now ask you whether you would like to install the network settings using Typical settings or Custom settings. The typical settings include Client For Microsoft Networks, File And Printer Sharing For Microsoft Networks, and the TCP/IP protocol configured to use either DHCP or APIPA. Click Next.

24. If you selected to configure your own network options, enter the desired components, and click Next. Again, you can modify the network configuration at a later date.

25. You're now prompted to join either a workgroup or a domain. If you would like to join a workgroup, enter the name of the workgroup in the Workgroup field. To join a domain, select the Yes option, and enter the name of the domain in the Workgroup Or Computer Domain field. Click Next.

26. If you chose to join a domain, the setup program will prompt you for the username and password of a user with sufficient rights to add your system to the domain. It will then contact the domain controller for the domain and add your computer account. Click Next to attempt to join the domain.

27. The selected components are now installed and configured. Windows 2000 is configured. When this phase is complete, the setup program deletes any temporary files and prompts you to remove the CD-ROM before it reboots.

28. Windows 2000 is now installed. You can log in to it as you would any other Windows 2000 system on your network.

Creating a Distribution Folder on the Local Machine

To create a local distribution folder, perform the following steps:

1. Using your favorite method, create a directory on the system, and give it a name that will easily identify it (for example, c:\win2000setup).

2. Copy the contents of the i386 directory on the Windows 2000 CD-ROM into this directory.

3. Create subfolders for any additional drivers or programs that will be installed. The entire contents of this folder will be temporarily copied to the hard drive of the system being installed.

4. Create any special folders that will be used by setup. These can include \$OEM$\textmode, \$OEM$\$$, \$Oem$\$1, and \$OEM$*drive_letter*.

Sharing the Distribution Folder

To share a distribution folder, perform the following steps:

1. Right-click the folder to be shared, and choose the Sharing option from the pop-up menu.

2. Select the Share radio button.

3. Enter a name for the shared folder.

4. Click Permissions, and assign the desired permissions to this folder.

5. Click OK.

TIP: *You'll most likely want to remove the Everyone: Full Control permission and assign the Read permission to the administration group that will complete the Windows 2000 installations.*

Creating a Distribution Folder on a Remote Machine

To create a distribution folder on a remote machine, perform the following steps:

1. Connect to the shared folder on the remote system (make sure you have Write permissions to this share).

2. Copy the contents of the i386 directory on the Windows 2000 CD-ROM to this directory.

8. Windows 2000 Installation

3. Create subfolders for any additional drivers or programs that will be installed. The entire contents of this folder will be temporarily copied to the hard drive of the system being installed.

4. Create any special folders that will be used by setup. These can include \$OEM$\textmode, \$OEM$\$$, \$Oem$\$1, and \$OEM$\\drive_letter.

Installing from a Network Share

To install Windows 2000 from a network share, perform the following steps:

1. Connect to the network share, and run the winnt32.exe file.

2. You can choose to upgrade your existing operating system to Windows 2000 or install a new copy. Make your selection, and click Next.

3. Read the license agreement, select the I Agree radio button, and click Next.

4. Enter the 25-digit product key as it appears on the back of the CD-ROM jewel case. Click Next.

5. You can modify your Windows 2000 installation to support multiple languages and accessibility on this window. If you click the Advanced Options button, you'll be presented with some advanced Windows 2000 installation options. Click Next.

6. The Windows 2000 Setup Wizard will copy the necessary files to the hard drive and reboot your system.

7. The setup program will now display the disks and partitions available on your system. Choose the desired partition (partitions or unpartitioned space).

8. If you want to delete a partition, press D. If you want to create a partition, press C.

NOTE: If you choose to create a new partition, Windows 2000 setup will prompt you to select whether to create an NTFS partition or a FAT partition. If you select the FAT partition option and the partition is less than 2GB, FAT16 will be used. If, however, the partition is greater than 2GB, FAT32 will be used.

---

9. When you've created your partition, select it, and press Enter.

10. The Windows 2000 setup program will confirm your partition selection; press Enter when you're ready. If the partition is formatted in a non-NTFS 5 file system, the setup program will ask you if you want to convert it.

11. Your hard drives are now checked for errors, and all necessary Windows 2000 files are copied to the Windows 2000 folder (\Winnt by default).

12. When the file copy is complete, the Windows 2000 setup program will ask you to remove the CD-ROM and any floppies. Press Enter to reboot the system.

13. Windows setup will restart. You'll know that this has occurred when the splash screen appears.

14. The setup program will now detect and configure the hardware devices that are installed on your system. If, for some reason, the setup program cannot detect or install a driver for a particular device, it will prompt you to direct it to the correct drivers.

15. Specify the regional settings for your particular system. You can change your locale and your keyboard settings. After you've selected these criteria, click Next.

16. Enter the name of the person to whom this computer is registered, followed by the company this system belongs to. After you've entered this information, click Next.

17. Choose the licensing mode that will be used on this system. By default, a Per Server mode is selected. If you keep the Per Server selection, enter the number of CALs you purchased. Click Next when done.

18. Enter the name that will be assigned to this computer on the network in the Computer Name field. In this window, you can also choose the password that will be assigned to the administrator account on this system. This password can be left blank. Click Next when done.

19. You can now select the components that you would like to install on your system. Remember that you can add or remove these components at a later date. After you've completed your selection, click Next.

20. If setup detects a modem, it will now display the Dialing Location window. Select the country, area code, and external line codes, and click Next.

21. Make sure that the date, time, and time zone information is correct, and click Next.

22. If you chose to install the Windows Terminal Services in the Windows 2000 Components window, choose the mode of operation: Remote Administration Mode (the default) or Application Server Mode. After you've done so, click Next.

23. The Windows 2000 setup program will now ask you whether you would like to install the network settings using Typical settings or Custom settings. The Typical settings include Client For Microsoft Networks, File And Printer Sharing For Microsoft Networks, and the TCP/IP protocol configured to use either DHCP or APIPA. Click Next.

24. If you selected to configure your own network options, enter the desired components, and click Next. Again, you can modify the network configuration at a later date.

25. You're now prompted to join either a workgroup or a domain. If you would like to join a workgroup, enter the name of the workgroup in the Workgroup field. To join a domain, select the Yes option, and enter the name of the domain in the Workgroup or Computer Domain field. Click Next.

26. If you chose to join a domain, the setup program will prompt you for the username and password of a user with sufficient rights to add your system to the domain. It will then contact the domain controller for the domain and add your computer account. Click Next to attempt to join the domain.

27. The selected components are now installed and configured. Windows 2000 is configured. When this phase is complete, the setup program deletes any temporary files and prompts you to remove the CD-ROM before it reboots.

28. Windows 2000 is now installed. You can log in to it as you would any other Windows 2000 system on your network.

Installing from Multiple Network Shares

To install Windows 2000 from multiple network shares, perform the following steps:

1. Map a network drive to the first network share. Click Start, and select Run. Enter "shared_drive:\i386\winnt32.exe /s:shared_drive:\i386 / s:\\server2\share2 /s:\\server3\share3", and so on. Click OK.

2. You can choose to upgrade your existing operating system to Windows 2000 or to install a new copy. Make your selection, and click Next.

3. Read the license agreement, select the I Agree radio button, and click Next.

4. Enter the 25-digit product key as it appears on the back of the CD-ROM jewel case. Click Next.

5. You can modify your Windows 2000 installation to support multiple languages and accessibility on this window. If you click the Advanced Options button, you'll be presented with some advanced Windows 2000 installation options. Click Next.

6. The Windows 2000 Setup Wizard will copy the necessary files to the hard drive and reboot your system.

7. The setup program will now display the disks and partitions available on your system. Choose the desired partition (partitions or unpartitioned space).

8. If you want to delete a partition, press D. If you want to create a partition, press C.

NOTE: *If you choose to create a new partition, Windows 2000 setup will prompt you to select whether to create an NTFS partition or a FAT partition. If you select the FAT partition option and the partition is less than 2GB, FAT16 will be used. If, however, the partition is greater than 2GB, FAT32 will be used.*

---

9. When you've created your partition, select it, and press Enter.

10. The Windows 2000 setup program will confirm your partition selection; press Enter when you're ready. If the partition is formatted in a non-NTFS 5 file system, the setup program will ask you if you want to convert it.

11. Your hard drives are now checked for errors, and all necessary Windows 2000 files are copied to the Windows 2000 folder (\Winnt by default).

12. When the file copy is complete, the Windows 2000 setup program will ask you to remove the CD-ROM and any floppies. Press Enter to reboot the system.

13. Windows setup will restart. You'll know that this has occurred when the splash screen appears.

14. The setup program will now detect and configure the hardware devices installed on your system. If, for some reason, the setup program cannot detect or install a driver for a particular device, it will prompt you to direct it to the correct drivers.

15. Specify the regional settings for your particular system. You can change your locale and your keyboard settings. After you've selected these criteria, click Next.

16. Enter the name of the person to whom this computer is registered, followed by the company that this system belongs to. After you've entered this information, click Next.

17. Choose the licensing mode that will be used on this system. By default, a Per Server mode is selected. If you keep the Per Server selection, enter the number of CALs that you purchased. Click Next when done.

18. Enter the name that will be assigned to this computer on the network in the Computer Name field. In this window, you can also choose the password that will be assigned to the administrator account on this system. This password can be left blank. Click Next when done.

19. You can now select the components that you would like to install on your system. Remember that you can add or remove these components at a later date. After you've completed your selection, click Next.

20. If setup detects a modem, it will now display the Dialing Location window. Select the country, area code, and external line codes, and click Next.

21. Make sure the date, time, and time zone information is correct, and click Next.

22. If you chose to install the Windows Terminal Services in the Windows 2000 Components window, choose the mode of operation: Remote Administration Mode (the default) or Application Server Mode. After you've done so, click Next.

23. The Windows 2000 setup program will now ask you whether you would like to install the network settings using Typical settings or Custom settings. The Typical settings include Client For Microsoft Networks, File And Printer Sharing For Microsoft Networks, and the TCP/IP protocol configured to use either DHCP or APIPA. Click Next.

24. If you selected to configure your own network options, enter the desired components, and click Next. Again, you can modify the network configuration at a later date.

25. You're now prompted to join either a workgroup or a domain. If you would like to join a workgroup, enter the name of the workgroup in the Workgroup field. To join a domain, select the Yes option, and enter the name of the domain in the Workgroup or Computer Domain field. Click Next.

26. If you chose to join a domain, the setup program will prompt you for the username and password of a user with sufficient rights to add your system to the domain. It will then contact the domain controller for the domain and add your computer account. Click Next to attempt to join the domain.

27. The selected components are now installed and configured. Windows 2000 is configured. When this phase is complete, the setup program deletes any temporary files and prompts you to remove the CD-ROM before it reboots.

28. Windows 2000 is now installed. You can log in to it as you would any other Windows 2000 system on your network.

Installing the Setup Manager Wizard

To install the Windows 2000 Setup Manager Wizard, perform the following steps:

1. Insert the *Windows 2000 Server Resource Kit* CD-ROM.

2. Double-click setup.exe from the CD-ROM drive.

3. Click Next to start the installation process.

4. Read through the licensing agreement, select the I Agree option, and click Next.

5. Enter your name and your organization's name, and click Next.

6. Choose the Custom option, and click Next.

7. Click Next to accept the selections.

8. Click Next to begin the file copy.

9. Click Finish to complete the setup.

TIP: *The Setup Manager (as well as the other installation utilities) resides in the Deployment section of the Windows 2000 Server Resource Kit.*

Creating an Answer File

To create an answer file, perform the following steps:

1. Click Start, and select Run. Enter "Setupmgr", and click OK. The Setup Manager Wizard will appear.

2. Click Next to begin the Setup Manager.

3. Choose the option to create a new answer file, and click Next.

4. Choose the type of installation that you would like to perform. Click Next.

5. Choose the platform that you would like to install, either Windows 2000 Professional or Windows 2000 Server. Click Next.

6. Choose the level of interaction that you would like the setup process to take. Click Next.

7. Enter the name and organization that you would like to use for the computer, and click Next.

8. If you chose to install Windows 2000 Server, select the licensing mode for the server (either Per Server or Per Seat). Click Next when done.

8. Windows 2000 Installation

9. At this point, you can choose to enter a single computer name or multiple names. If you choose to enter multiple names, a UDF file that partners up with the answer file will also be created. Click Next after you've added all the different computers.

10. Specify the method for supplying the administrator's password. When done, click Next.

WARNING! Remember that the answer file is a simple text file. If someone were to gain access to the file, the administrator's password could be discovered. For this reason, if you decide to enter the password into the answer file, make sure that you change the password file after the installation.

11. Choose the display settings for the new system, as shown in Figure 8.4. Three options are available to you: number of colors, screen resolution, and screen refresh rate. Make your desired selections, and click Next.

12. Specify your network settings, and click Next.

13. Select whether you would like the computer to belong to a workgroup or a domain. If you select a workgroup, enter the name of the workgroup in the Workgroup field. With a domain selection, you can have setup create a computer account in the domain. You supply a username and password with the correct security credentials to create the account or to create the account ahead of time. When done, click Next.

14. Select the time zone for the system, and click Next.

15. At this point, you get to decide whether additional settings are required. If you decide that no additional settings are required, click Next, and continue with Step 23. Otherwise, click Next.

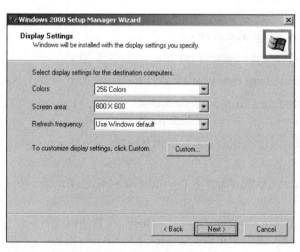

Figure 8.4   Configuring the installation display settings.

16. You can configure what telephony configuration will be set if the Setup Wizard detects any modems. Click Next to continue.

17. Specify the regional settings for the installation systems, and click Next.

18. Select any additional required languages for the system. Click Next.

TIP: *To select more than one language, you can press Ctrl+click to select items individually or press Shift+click to select a list of items.*

---

19. You're now given the option to configure the Internet browser installed on the system and additional Windows 2000 shell settings. Click Next when done.

20. By default, Windows 2000 will be installed in the \winnt folder. You can choose an alternate location in this window. Click Next when done.

21. Any local or network printers can be installed for the new system by configuring them in this window. Click Next to continue.

22. If you would like a specific application or command to be executed after the installation is complete, enter it here. Click Next to continue.

23. The Windows 2000 Setup Manager gives you the opportunity to have it automatically create a distribution folder for the Windows 2000 files (for example, the i386 folder). If you choose the No option and click Next, you can continue with Step 24. However, if you choose the Yes option and click Next, you'll be given the opportunity to configure the settings for the distribution folder (see Figure 8.5).

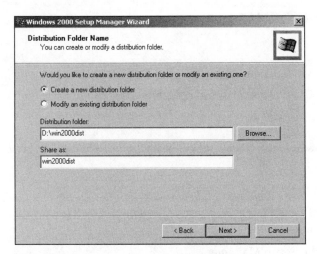

Figure 8.5   The setup distribution folder.

24. Enter the name of the answer file. This name will also be used for the UDF file as well as the batch file (BAT). Click Next to continue.

25. Click Finish to create the files and to exit the Setup Manager Wizard.

Installing Windows 2000 Using an Answer File

There are two methods to use an answer file. These methods are discussed in the following sections.

Using a Batch File

To use an answer file through a batch file, perform the following steps:

1. Copy the files created by the Setup Manager Wizard (assuming that you named these files unattended.bat, unattended.udf, and unattended.txt) to the distribution folder.

2. Navigate to the distribution folder, and double-click the batch file (unattend.bat).

Using the Command Line

To use an answer file from the command line, perform the following steps:

1. Copy the files created by the Setup Manager Wizard (assuming that you named these files unattended.udf and unattended.txt) to the distribution folder.

2. Open a command prompt, and navigate to the distribution folder.

3. Type the following:

```
distribution_folder:\i386\winnt32
/s:distribution_folder:\i386 /unattend:.\unattended.txt
```

Creating a UDF

To create a UDF, perform the following steps:

1. Click Start, and select Run. Enter "Setupmgr", and click OK. The Setup Manager Wizard will appear.

2. Click Next to begin the Setup Manager.

3. Choose the Create A New Answer File option, and click Next.

4. Choose the type of installation that you would like to perform. Click Next.

5. Choose the platform that you would like to install, either Windows 2000 Professional or Windows 2000 Server. Click Next.

6. Choose the level of interaction that you would like the setup process to take, and click Next.

7. Enter the name and organization that you would like to use for the computer, and click Next.

8. If you chose to install Windows 2000 Server, select the licensing mode for the server (either Per Server or Per Seat). Click Next when done.

9. At this point, you can choose to enter a single computer name or multiple names. If you choose to enter multiple names, a UDF file that partners up with the answer file will also be created. Click Next after you've added all the different computers.

10. Specify the method for supplying the administrator's password. When done, click Next.

11. Choose the display settings for the new system. Three options are available to you: number of colors, screen resolution, and screen refresh rate. Make your desired selections, and click Next.

12. Specify your network settings, and click Next.

13. Select whether you would like the computer to belong to a workgroup or a domain. If you select a workgroup, enter the name of the workgroup in the Workgroup field. With a domain selection, you can have setup create a computer account in the domain. You supply a username and password with the correct security credentials to create the account or to create the account ahead of time. When done, click Next.

14. Select the time zone for the system, and click Next.

15. At this point, you get to decide whether additional settings are required. If you decide that no additional settings are required, click Next, and continue with Step 23. Otherwise, click Next.

16. You can configure what telephony configuration will be set if the Setup Wizard detects any modems. Click Next to continue.

17. Specify the regional settings for the installation system, and click Next.

18. Select any additional required languages for the system. Click Next.

19. You're now given the option to configure the Internet browser installed on the system and additional Windows 2000 shell settings. Click Next when done.

20. By default, Windows 2000 will be installed in the /winnt folder. You can choose an alternate location in this window. Click Next when done.

21. Any local or network printers can be installed for the new system by configuring them in this window. Click Next to continue.

22. If you would like a specific application or command to be executed after the installation is complete, enter it here. Click Next to continue.

23. The Windows 2000 Setup Manager gives you the opportunity to have it automatically create a distribution folder for the Windows 2000 files (for example, the i386 folder). If you choose the No option and click Next, you can continue with Step 24. However, if you choose the Yes option and click Next, you'll be given the opportunity to configure the settings for the distribution folder.

24. Enter the name of the answer file. This name will also be used for the UDF file as well as the batch file (BAT). Click Next to continue.

25. Click Finish to create the files and to exit the Setup Manager Wizard.

Installing Windows 2000 Using a UDF

To install Windows 2000 using a UDF, perform the following steps:

1. Copy the files created by the Setup Manager Wizard (assuming that you named the files unattended.udf and unattended.txt) to the distribution folder.

2. Open a command prompt, and navigate to the distribution folder.

3. Type "*distribution_folder*:\i386\winnt32 /s:*distribution_folder*:\i386 / unattend:.\unattended.txt /udf:*id*:unattended.udf".

Installing Windows 2000 Using the /Sypart Switch

To install Windows 2000 using the **/syspart** switch, perform the following steps:

1. Attach the extra hard drive.

2. Connect to the distribution folder.

3. Click Start, select Run, and type the following:

```
winnt32 /unattend:unattended.txt /s:distribution_folder
/syspart:second_drive /tempdrive:second_drive
```

4. Shut down the reference computer, and remove the hard drive.

5. Install the hard drive in the new system.

6. Turn the new system on.

Running the SysPrep Application Manually

To run SysPrep manually, perform the following steps:

1. Click Start, and select Run. Type "cmd", and click OK.

2. At the command prompt, create a folder to be used by SysPrep at the root (for example, c:\sysprep). Type the following to create a folder called sysprep:

```
mkdir sysprep
```

3. Copy the sysprep.exe and setupcl.exe files from the *Windows 2000 Server Resource Kit* into this folder.

WARNING! *If you're using the sysprep.inf file, you'll have to copy it to the SysPrep folder as well.*

4. Change to the SysPrep folder.

5. Execute SysPrep with one of the optional parameters.

Running the SysPrep Application Automatically after Setup

To run SysPrep automatically, perform the following steps:

1. Create a folder named \$OEM$\$1\Sysprep, and copy the SysPrep files to it.

2. In the [GuiRunOnce] section of the answer file, enter the following command as the last line:

```
%systemdrive%\sysprep\sysprep.exe - quiet
```

3. Run the unattended setup as you normally would.

Installing RIS

To install Windows 2000 RIS, perform the following steps:

1. Click Start, and select Settings|Control Panel.

2. Double-click the Add/Remove Programs applet.

3. Click the Add/Remove Windows Components button on the left pane, and click the Components button to launch the Windows Components Wizard.

4. Scroll down and select the Remote Installation Services option. Click Next. The Remote Installation Services will be installed.

5. Click Finish, and reboot the server if necessary.

6. In the Add/Remove Programs applet, click the Add/Remove Windows Components button in the left pane, select Configure Remote Installation Services, and click the Configure button.

7. Click Next.

8. Enter the folder path where you want the root of the RIS operating system to reside. Click Next.

WARNING! The location of the RIS operating system's root must reside on an NTFS 5 partition and cannot be located on the same partition as the system partition.

9. If you want RIS to start immediately, select the Respond To Client Computers Requesting Service checkbox, and click Next (see Figure 8.6).

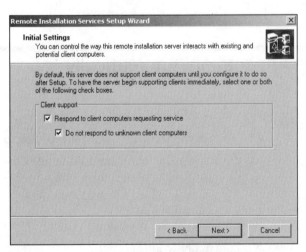

Figure 8.6 Configuring the initial settings for RIS.

10. Enter the path to the Windows 2000 Professional installation files, and click Next.

11. Enter a name for the folder that will be created to store the operating system image, and click Next.

12. Enter an explanatory name and a description for this operating system image, and click Next.

13. Click Finish to complete the setup. RIS will now create an image of the Windows 2000 Professional operating system and give you a status, as shown in Figure 8.7.

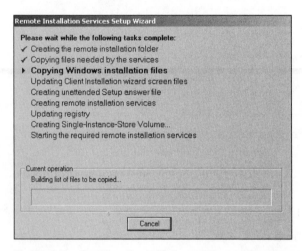

Figure 8.7   Creating the initial operating system image in RIS.

Enabling Remote Installation Preparation

To enable remote installation, perform the following steps:

1. Click Start, and select Programs|Administrative Tools|Active Directory Users And Computers.

2. Navigate to the server where you would like to enable RIS, right-click it, and choose Properties from the pop-up menu.

3. Click the Remote Install tab.

4. Select the Respond To Client Computers Requesting Service checkbox, and click OK.

Disabling Remote Installation Preparation

To disable remote installation, perform the following steps:

1. Click Start, and select Programs|Administrative Tools|Active Directory Users And Computers.

2. Navigate to the server where you would like to disable RIS, right-click it, and choose Properties from the pop-up menu.

3. Click the Remote Install tab.

4. Clear the Respond To Client Computers Requesting Service checkbox, and click OK.

Viewing Clients

To view RIS clients, perform the following steps:

1. Click Start, and select Programs|Administrative Tools|Active Directory Users And Computers.

2. Navigate to the server running RIS, right-click it, and choose Properties from the pop-up menu.

3. Click the Remote Install tab.

4. Click the Show Clients button.

Verifying Server Operation

To verify server operation, perform the following steps:

1. Click Start, and select Programs|Administrative Tools|Active Directory Users And Computers.

2. Navigate to the server running RIS, right-click it, and choose Properties from the pop-up menu.

3. Click the Remote Install tab.

4. Click the Verify Server button. The Check Server Wizard will appear (see Figure 8.8).

5. Click Next to start the server verification.

6. Click Finish when you're done reading the test result summary generated in Step 5.

Figure 8.8   The Check Server Wizard.

Creating a New OS Image

To create a new OS image, perform the following steps:

1. Click Start, and select Programs|Administrative Tools|Active Directory Users And Computers.

2. Navigate to the server running RIS, right-click it, and choose Properties from the pop-up menu.

3. Click the Remote Install tab.

4. Click the Advanced Settings button.

5. Click the Add button. The Add Wizard will launch.

6. Choose whether a new answer file is being used for an existing image by selecting the A New Answer File To An Existing Image option, or create a new image from the Windows 2000 Professional installation files by selecting the Add A New Installation Image option. Click Next.

TIP: *If you choose to use a new answer file with an existing image, you'll save a lot of disk space. Using this method, RIS will only copy the differences between the operating systems rather than the entire installation directory on the Windows 2000 Professional CD.*

7. Follow the wizard to create the new image.

8. Windows 2000 Installation

Modifying an Existing OS Image

To modify an OS image, perform the following steps:

1. Click Start, and select Programs|Administrative Tools|Active Directory Users And Computers.

2. Navigate to the server running RIS, right-click it, and choose Properties from the pop-up menu.

3. Click the Remote Install tab.

4. Click the Advanced Settings button.

5. Select the image that you would like to modify, and click the Properties button.

6. Notice that you may only change the friendly name and the description for this image. Click OK when done.

Deleting an OS Image

To delete an OS image, perform the following steps:

1. Click Start, and select Programs|Administrative Tools|Active Directory Users And Computers.

2. Navigate to the server running RIS, right-click it, and choose Properties from the pop-up menu.

3. Click the Remote Install tab.

4. Click the Advanced Settings button.

5. Select the image that you would like to delete, and click Remove.

6. Click the Yes button to confirm the image deletion.

Using Remote Installation Preparation (riprep.exe)

To use riprep.exe, perform the following steps:

1. Install Windows 2000 Professional on a reference system using RIS.

2. Install any desired applications.

3. Configure the system as required.

4. Shut down all services and applications.

5. Run the riprep.exe application from the RemoteInstall\Admin\i386 share on the RIS system. The Remote Installation Preparation Wizard will launch.

6. Click Next.

7. Enter the name of the RIS server that you would like to host the newly created image, and click Next.

8. Enter the folder name where the image will be stored, and click Next.

9. Enter a friendly name and description for the image, and click Next.

10. Review the settings, and click Next.

11. The image will be created. When you click Next, it will be copied to the RIS server.

Preparing a Client for Remote Installation

To prepare a client for remote installation, perform the following steps:

1. Click Start, and select Programs|Administrative Tools|Active Directory Users And Computers.

2. Navigate to the container where you would like the new computer created. Right-click the container, and select New|Computer from the pop-up menu.

3. In the New Object - Computer window, enter the name of the computer, and click Next.

4. Select the This Is A Managed Computer checkbox, enter the ID for the computer, and click Next.

5. Choose whether you would like the client to use the closest and/or fastest RIS server or a specific RIS server. Click Next when done.

6. Click Finish when done.

Creating a Remote Boot Disk

To create a remote boot disk, perform the following steps:

1. Insert a blank, formatted 1.44MB floppy disk, connect to the RIS server's \RemoteInstall\Admin\i386 share, and run the rbfg.exe file.

2. Select the floppy drive that you would like to use, and click Create Disk.

8. Windows 2000 Installation

Completing a Remote OS Installation

To complete a remote OS installation, perform the following steps:

1. Insert the remote boot disk, and turn on the system.

2. Press F12 to boot from the network.

3. Press Enter to begin the Client Installation Wizard.

4. Enter a username, a password, and the DNS name for the domain, and press Enter.

WARNING! If you did not prepare a client for installation as described in the "Preparing a Client for Remote Installation" section, make sure the username has sufficient privileges to create a computer account in the domain.

5. Choose either the Setup, Custom Setup, Restart A Previous Setup Attempt, or Maintenance And Troubleshooting Tools option, and press Enter.

6. Select the image that you would like to use, and press Enter.

7. Press Enter to begin the installation.

Installing Active Directory Using Dcpromo

To install Active Directory using dcpromo, perform the following steps:

1. Click Start, and select Run.

2. Type "DCPROMO".

3. Click OK. Be sure to choose the proper type of installation before clicking on the next button for each of the next four windows. Refer to the checklist in the Active Directory section for more information on which type to do.

4. Type the domain name that is being installed or added to, and click Next.

5. The domain network basic input/output system (NetBIOS) name is automatically filled in for you. Click Next.

6. The database and log locations are automatically filled in for you. Change them if necessary. If not, click Next.

7. The Sysvol location is automatically filled in for you. Change it if necessary. If not, click Next.

8. The system attempts to contact a DNS server in the entered domain. If or when it fails, the system notifies you of the failure. Click OK.

9. Click Next.

10. If Windows NT domain controllers are in the domain, click the Permissions Compatible Only With Windows 2000 Servers radio button.

11. Click Next.

12. Enter a Directory Services Restore Mode administrator password, and press Tab.

13. Type the password again, and click Next.

14. Click Next to begin the file copy and the Active Directory configuration process.

15. Wait until the Active Directory configuration is complete.

16. When installation is complete, click Finish.

Chapter 9

Windows 2000 Configuration

In Depth

Windows 2000 offers a wide range of capabilities and features. This chapter takes a brief look at access permissions on files and folders, faxing, the Recycle Bin, offline files, compression, encryption, mount points, disk cleanup, ScanDisk, Disk Defragmenter, and drive quotas.

Accessing Resources

There are two different ways to access resources on a given server or computer. The first is by being logged on to the local computer, and the second is across the network. Windows 2000 security is created in such a manner that resources can be flagged for access only to locally logged on users, only to users across the network, or both.

Accessing Local Resources

Local resource access security can be configured or viewed by checking an object's properties and looking at the Security tab as shown in Figure 9.1. What you see on this tab is also known as *Windows NT File System (NTFS) permissions*.

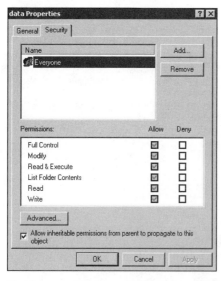

Figure 9.1   The Security tab from a folder's Properties dialog box.

These NTFS permissions allow you to apply access control and security locally for logged-on users. This is particularly useful in situations where you have multiple users using the same Windows 2000 Professional computer. Don't forget that much of this functionality can be taken advantage of by placing users in the proper user group, such as Power Users. Incidentally, NTFS permissions also apply for network resource access. If there are certain folders within a Windows 2000 Professional system that you want some users to access and others to be restricted from, NTFS permissions using the Security tab is the way to go.

As the name implies, NTFS permissions can only be used on systems that are formatted with NTFS. The reason for this is simple, yet requires some explanation on the differences between file formats.

The reason NTFS permissions work for local resource access is because each file on the disk has permission flags that, along with the Access Control List (ACL) for that file, will tell the system if it's okay for a logged-on user to access the data. In order to place the necessary flags on these files, Microsoft had to create a new disk format that allowed space for those extra flags to exist. Regular old Windows, Windows 9x, and disk operating system (DOS) disk formats (FAT and FAT32 for Windows 98) don't support these extra flags, which is one reason these operating systems aren't very secure. This is why an NTFS format is required to support NTFS permissions.

As shown in Figure 9.1, the basic NTFS permissions include Full Control, Modify, Read & Execute, List Folder Contents, Read, and Write. The following list defines each of these permissions, but notice the differences between applying these NTFS permissions to a file versus a folder or mounted volume:

- *Full Control (files)*—Allows users to perform any possible action on a file and to access any offered functions for the file.
- *Full Control (folders or mounted volumes)*—Allows users to perform any possible action on the folder or mounted volume and its contents.
- *List Folder Contents (folders or mounted volumes)*—Allows users to see the names of the contents of the folder or mounted volume.
- *Modify (files)*—Allows users to alter files through deletion, to change attributes, and to overwrite, as well as to launch applications and to view the files' contents.
- *Modify (folders or mounted volumes)*—Allows users to alter folders and mounted volumes through deletion and changing attributes. This permission also allows users to create new subfolders and files within the container and to view the contents of the objects within the container.
- *Read (files, folders, or mounted volumes)*—Allows users to open the file, folder, or mounted volume.

- *Read & Execute (files)*—Allows users to open files and to launch executables.

- *Read & Execute (folders or mounted volumes)*—Allows users to open folders and mounted volumes and grants Read access to the contents of these containers.

- *Write (files)*—Allows users to alter existing files by overwriting or changing attributes.

- *Write (folders or mounted volumes)*—Allows users to create new files and folders within the container.

NetWare has a feature where permissions assigned to a directory also apply to all directories or folders nested within the parent directory. By default, Windows 2000 will do this also, but the option can be removed by unchecking the Allow Inheritable Permissions From Parent To Propagate To This Object option at the bottom of the Security tab. You will know when parent permissions are inheriting to an object that you are looking at when you see the permissions grayed out. You can override these permissions in one of three ways: change the parent object, select current permissions that are opposite of the parent permissions, or clear the Allow Inheritable Permissions From Parent To Propagate To This Object checkbox.

By clicking the Advanced button, you open a dialog box that's used to manage detailed permissions, auditing, and ownership (see Figure 9.2). These detailed permissions are the literal components that go into the previous list of permissions. The detailed permissions, shown in Figure 9.3, that can be individually allowed or denied by user and group are the following:

- Traverse Folder/Execute File
- List Folder/Read Data
- Read Attributes
- Read Extended Attributes
- Create Files/Write Data
- Create Folders/Append Data
- Write Attributes
- Write Extended Attributes
- Delete Subfolders And Files
- Delete
- Read Permissions
- Change Permissions
- Take Ownership

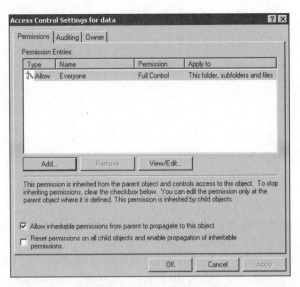

Figure 9.2   The Access Control Settings For Data dialog box.

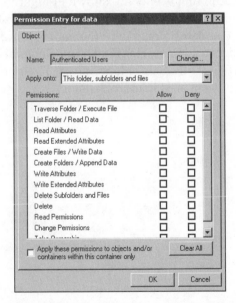

Figure 9.3   The Permission Entry For Data dialog box for setting detailed permissions.

Two inheritance controls also appear on the Permissions tab:

- Allow Inheritable Permissions From Parent To Propagate To This Object
- Reset Permissions On All Child Objects And Enable Propagation Of Inheritable Permissions

When a new permission entry is defined, you can determine where the new settings will apply using a pull-down list that offers the following selections:

- This Folder Only
- This Folder, Subfolder, And Files
- This Folder And Subfolders
- This Folder And Files
- Subfolders And Files Only
- Subfolders Only
- Files Only

You also have the ability to configure the system to be on the lookout for certain events to happen in association with the selected object and to report those events in the Event Viewer. This functionality is known as auditing. The Auditing tab is used to select which events generate entries in the Event Viewer. You can instruct the system to log certain events alone, or events that are initiated or associated with specific users or groups of users. Auditing events are shown in Figure 9.4. Notice that the user or user groups to be audited for the listed events can be changed at the top. Furthermore, you can determine where the audit setting is defined by selecting This Folder, Subfolders And Files, This Folder And Subfolders, This Folder And Files, Subfolders And Files Only, Subfolders Only, or Files Only. Because auditing is a security feature, it is covered in more detail in Chapter 20.

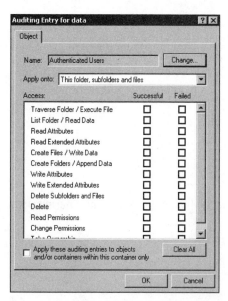

Figure 9.4   The Auditing Entry For Data dialog box.

The Owner tab, shown in Figure 9.5, is used to view the current ownership of the object and to take ownership. It is only possible to take ownership if you have the Take Ownership permission for this object or the universal user right.

When working with the permissions on a share, keep in mind that there are only three types of permissions: Full Control, Change, and Read. Each of these can be set to Allow or Deny for each individual user and group. You should also keep in mind that a resource can be shared multiple times under different share names. Each distinct share can have its own unique permission settings.

Accessing Network Resources

Objects accessed across a network are controlled through their network share. Unlike NTFS permissions that exist constantly and that apply to local users, network shares are specifically designed to allow users access to resources across the network. This doesn't mean that NTFS permissions don't apply for network resource access. The share itself has security controls that define which users and groups can use the share to access resources on other systems. These security controls are known as share permissions.

NOTE: *For information on printer shares and printer permissions, see Chapter 21.*

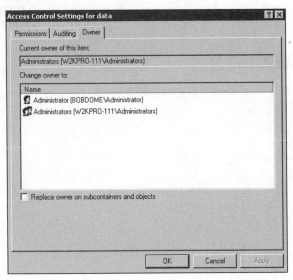

Figure 9.5   The Owner tab of the Access Control Settings For Data dialog box.

Creating a Share

A share is created by selecting the properties of an object, clicking on the Share tab, and sharing the object. You can also right-click the object from within Windows Explorer and click the Sharing option from the pop-up menu. Figure 9.6 shows a newly created share. This process is the same for creating shares in both Windows 2000 Professional and Windows 2000 Server. Although it may seem to be an easy and simple process, it can become quite complex. After a share is created, the local group Everyone (which includes Guest by default) is granted Full Control of the resources located in the object that has been shared.

Share Permissions

With the user group Everyone having Full Control of a share's resources, you'll probably want to change the permissions so that network access is a little bit more restricted.

Share permissions can be modified by clicking the Permissions button shown in Figure 9.6. Figure 9.7 shows the share permissions available. Just like NTFS (a.k.a. Security tab) permissions, you can add users and groups to the top window by clicking the Add button. You can then modify the selected user or group's permissions by selecting the permission in the bottom window. You'll notice that the applicable permissions will change when a different user or group is highlighted.

You'll notice that there are significantly fewer permission options for share permissions than for NTFS permissions. This allows a uniform functionality in

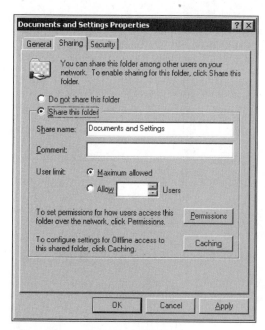

Figure 9.6   Creating a share.

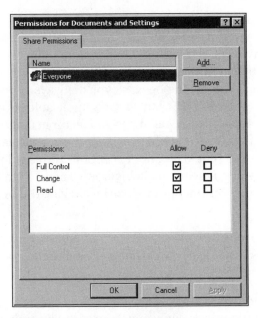

Figure 9.7   Share permissions.

network resource access even when the server's hard drive is not formatted for NTFS. Incidentally, this is similar to that you'd see when configuring shares in Windows 9x. If you want to allow the same permissions and security that you see with NTFS permissions and with the same access control you'd see across the network, you'll need to mix NTFS and share permissions.

Using Both Share and NTFS Permissions

When a network user attempts to access a folder that has both share and NTFS permissions applied, they first go through the share permissions that are applied. If they qualify to access the folder or file, they are then treated the same as if they were at the server itself, and NTFS permissions are applied against the user's credentials. This type of double-barreled security approach is ideal for environments where higher security is the norm. In order to configure optimum permissions for network clients, you'll need to combine both share and NTFS permissions. Many people don't know the true reasoning behind both permissions types. Default NTFS permissions vary from folder to folder on any given Windows 2000 Professional or Server system. As mentioned in the "Share Permissions" section, the default share permission, after a share is created, is Full Control for the Everyone group. If you want to mix the two types of permissions on a single resource, all you need to do is share the object and change the share permissions to be as restrictive as possible (outside of the No Access permission). You then go to the Security tab, add network users and groups (domain users and groups, too) as appropriate, and place the appropriate security permissions.

The rule of thumb when mixing share and NTFS permissions in the Windows NT world was that the most restrictive of the two wins. For example, if you place Read permissions on the share and assigned the NTFS Modify permission on the same folder, the end result would be only the ability to read the contents of the folder. As an administrator, this can be annoying because you'd always have to check not only both share and NTFS permissions, but also any applicable parent permissions when troubleshooting access problems. When you factor in multiple group memberships and restrictions, troubleshooting can become a nightmare. Windows 2000 permissions are no different. The only exception to this rule is anything that is explicitly denied. By this, I mean that in Figures 9.3 and 9.7, you'll notice that you have the ability to deny certain permissions by clicking the Deny checkbox.

By far, the best thing you can do is look at your current sets of permissions for both NTFS and shares. You can easily and quickly determine the current shares on a server by accessing the server using Windows Explorer.

By default, all hard drives on a Windows 2000 Professional or Server system are configured with a hidden administrative share. Only members of the administrative group can access this share. If you open Windows Explorer and enter "\\<servername>" and press Enter (where <servername> is the Windows 2000 Professional or Server in question), you'll receive a list of network advertised shares. The administrative share is hidden and will not be displayed. In order to access all data on a given hard drive using one of these administrative shares, you'll need to open Windows Explorer and enter "\\<servername>\<driveletter>" (where <servername> is the Windows 2000 Professional or Server system and <driveletter> is the drive letter on that server that you need to browse through, for example, \\exchange\C$).

Faxing

Windows 2000 includes fax support. This means that you can send and receive faxes without additional software if your computer has a supported fax or modem installed. In most cases, Windows 2000 will automatically detect your modem, or, when you install your modem, its fax capabilities will be recognized. This causes Windows 2000 to create a fax printer in the Printers folder. In fact, faxing is a similar process to printing. By default, only the ability to send out faxes is enabled.

Faxing is controlled through four interfaces: the Fax applet in the Control Panel, the Fax Service Management tool, the My Faxes folder, and the fax printer queue. The Fax applet is used to define user information (such as that contained on

Figure 9.8   The Fax Service Management tool.

cover pages), define and create cover pages, and configure received fax notifica-
tions. The Fax Service Management tool, shown in Figure 9.8, is used to configure fax devices and to log fax activities. Fax device configuration settings include
defining the station identifiers, such as transmitting station identifier (TSID) and
called subscriber identifier (CSID); the number of rings before answering; and
whether to send received faxes to a printer, folder, or local email box. The My
Faxes folder is a container where copies of all faxes handled by Windows 2000
are stored. The fax printer queue is used in the same manner as any other printer
queue to view, manage, and terminate active fax jobs.

To send a fax, just select the fax object from the list of printers from any application. You'll be prompted for the recipient's name and fax number, whether to use
dialing rules, whether to use a cover sheet, and whether to schedule the transmission for a later time. Recipient information can be pulled from an address book,
such as Outlook Express. Also, multiple recipients can be defined for a single fax
document. The only significant difference between Windows 2000 fax and normal printers is that a native fax device cannot be shared with the network.

File Deletion and Recovery

Windows 2000 offers file deletion protection through the Recycle Bin. This tool is
a temporary holding area for objects recently deleted from the desktop, Windows
Explorer, or My Computer. The Recycle Bin retains all deleted objects until it is
manually purged or a newly deleted object's size forces the oldest deleted object
to be removed. The Recycle Bin is configured to retain only a specific amount of
deleted data as a percentage of total disk space. The Properties dialog box, shown
in Figure 9.9, for the Recycle Bin is used to configure the following options:

- Whether a single setting is to be used for all drives or each drive is to be
  configured independently. A single setting is used by default.

- Whether files are to be removed from the system immediately or are to be
  retained in the Recycle Bin when deleted. This is enabled by default.

- What percentage of drive space should be used by the Recycle Bin. This is set to 10 percent by default.

- Whether to display a delete confirmation dialog box whenever a file is manually deleted. This is enabled by default.

- If each drive is configured independently, a tab for each volume is available to configure the Recycle Bin on each drive.

Opening the Recycle Bin reveals the currently retained deleted objects. Any listed object can be restored to its original location. To do so, select it, and then select File|Restore. If a file does not appear in the Recycle Bin, it cannot be recovered using native Windows 2000 tools.

Using Offline Files

Offline files are a mechanism within Windows 2000 that can cache network files and folders on a system. This allows those files and folders to be accessed when the system is not connected to the local area network (LAN), or when that particular system is offline. In addition, when the portable system is reconnected, updated files can be automatically saved back to the LAN, and new files on the LAN are added to the system's hard drive. Offline files are accessed in the same manner as they would be when connected to the LAN (that is, through Explorer).

To mark files to be stored in offline files, use My Network Places to locate the files and/or folders. Select File|Make Available Offline. This command will appear by default on Windows 2000 Professional systems, but it is not present by

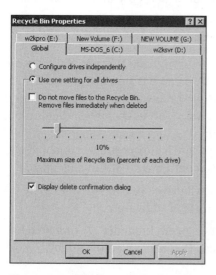

Figure 9.9   The Recycle Bin's Properties dialog box.

default on Windows 2000 Server systems. Offline files can be enabled or disabled on the Offline Folders tab of the Folder Options dialog box. All such marked files and folders will have a logo of two arrows in a circle added to their icons.

When offline files are used for the first time, a wizard appears to configure the system. Even after initial configuration, you can access the settings on the Offline Folders tab of the Folder Options dialog box (which is opened by selecting Tools|Folder Options or by using the Folder Options applet in the Control Panel). The configuration settings include:

- Enable/Disable Offline Files
- Synchronize Offline Files Before Logging Off
- Enable Reminders About Working Offline
- Add An Offline Files Shortcut To The Desktop
- Set The Amount Of Space Consumable By Offline Files
- Delete Cached Files
- View Cached Files
- Advanced Settings

Offline files and folders are pretty straightforward to use and implement. But keep in mind that the synchronization process takes time, and if you configure synchronization to take place before system shutdown or logoff, it may cause delays when users are trying to exit the office. There may not be enough space to copy the entire contents to the local hard drive, and the system will not notify you until your hard disk is already full.

Briefcase

Offline files and folders work for networked information, and you can configure them to be updated every time that the system starts and a user logs in. This makes the briefcase function obsolete in all but a very few situations. The briefcase application originally started with Windows 98. The purpose of the briefcase was to enable a user to tag network files for synchronization to the local machine so that those files could be used while offline and resynchronized when the user was back on the network.

The biggest problem with the briefcase function was that it was unable to automate the synchronization process. The result was that forgetful users would end up with two separate and unmergeable versions of a file: one on the network and another on the local drive. Other problems exist with the briefcase. One is that all files exist within the briefcase, and no effort is made to have synchronized files appear as they would in their natural networked environment. Another potential issue is that the improved Windows 2000 briefcase will determine if both documents have changed. If they have, it will not synchronize. Instead, you'll have to be on the lookout and catch these synchronization hiccups before something goes wrong and you end up losing data.

Personally, I prefer to use offline files because of the automation features and the fact that I just don't have to worry about whether my files have been updated. Unfortunately, I cannot use offline files and folders for local resources, such as removable media or external hard drives. Normally, this isn't a problem, but, if you're a technogeek like me, using both offline folders and the briefcase can come in handy as different backup components in a well-rounded, yet poor-man's, fault tolerant system. Here's how.

I have an external Universal Serial Bus (USB) hard disk drive. Originally, the drive was to be a backup device because it was cheaper than a tape drive and tapes, plus I had the added feature of being able to plug it in almost anywhere and use it. After a few system crashes, I learned that it was far more valuable as a primary location for all of my work and email folders. Everything that is mission-critical and that changes every day is stored on that drive. I still need the ability to have a backup of the data, so I perform backups in several different ways.

I use the briefcase and manually synchronize the most active parts of my external drive to my laptop (which is my primary working machine). This allows me to disconnect myself from my docking station and work anywhere in the office.

I share the entire external drive on the LAN. I have a laboratory computer that I routinely use to run tests and to play with new programs and technotoys. The laboratory computer has a huge disk drive and is connected to the external drive through the LAN. This mapped drive has also been defined as an offline folder. It will synchronize every time I log in and log out of the computer and also every night at midnight. This is essentially my backup copy of all my critical data.

This combined application of using an external drive along with the briefcase and offline files allows me several extra perks along with backing up data. There are many benefits just in having a laptop. The biggest extra benefit that I get is the ability to access any of these mission-critical files anywhere on the network while still having the portability that is at the core of both the offline and briefcase applications. Although this may not seem like such a big deal, it truly is because I can always rely on zero downtime if one of my networked machines goes down— or even if the external drive goes down. After configuring Microsoft Outlook with separate profiles, I am able to access my email, task, and contact data when I am on the network, off the network, connected to the Internet, or disconnected, and I can do all of this from any computer on the network, thanks to these different Outlook profiles.

Moving and Copying Objects

The processes of copying and moving files and folders can alter the settings on these moved objects in ways that you may not expect. In most cases, understanding how copying and moving actually works can help you avoid losing important security and functionality settings. Whenever a new file is created, it inherits the settings of its parent container. This means that a new file created within a directory, a new folder created within an existing folder, or a new file or directory created within the root of a drive will inherit the security settings of the parent container (that is, the directory, folder, or drive root).

In all cases, a copy process involves the creation of a new object at the destination location. However, a move process differs depending on whether the source and destinations are within the same or different partitions or volumes. When a move occurs within the same partition or volume, the only change to the file system is an alteration in the directory database pointing to the location of the object. Thus, the original object remains unmoved and just the pointer to its location is changed. In this instance, the object retains all its original settings. However, when a move occurs from one partition or volume to another, the process is now a two-step procedure. First, a new copy of the original object is created at the destination location. Then, the original object is deleted. Because this process creates a new object, the new object inherits the settings of its new container.

If you want to move objects from one partition or volume to another without losing the original settings, you must use the **XCOPY** command with the **/O** parameter to copy file ownership and ACL information. You can also use the **/X** command to copy auditing settings in addition to file ownership and ACL information. This **XCOPY** command can be used from a command prompt. For complete use information, issue the **XCOPY /?** command.

The preceding information about copy and move applies mainly when the source and destination locations are formatted with the same file system. When you're copying or moving objects from a partition or volume formatted with one file system to another formatted with a different file system, additional scenarios must be understood. When you're copying from an NTFS volume to a FAT or FAT32 volume, all security settings will be lost. When you're copying from a FAT or FAT32 volume to an NTFS volume, the objects will inherit the settings of the destination container.

Drive Letters and Mount Points

As with all other Microsoft operating systems, Windows 2000 can use the drive letters C through Z to reference various file resources, including network shares, local hard drives, and removable media drives. However, Windows 2000 now adds the ability of using mount points to remove the previous ceiling of 24 accessible volumes.

NOTE: *Drive configurations that are comprised of two or more volumes or partitions are only assigned a single drive letter.*

A *mount point* is a way to make a separate volume or drive appear as a subdirectory on an existing NTFS volume. A single drive or volume can be accessed on its own, or mounted to another NTFS volume. This is particularly useful if you do not want to administer Distributed File System (DFS) It can also come in handy for local users who do not need to deal with the added complexities of additional drives or volumes. The process is simple to configure within Disk Manager, and is invisible to the user and any applications (see Figure 9.10). A mount point can only be created on an NTFS volume, but the mounted volumes can be formatted with FAT, FAT32, or NTFS.

Disk Cleanup

During normal working conditions, many useless and forgotten files are created and deposited on the hard drive(s). In some cases, this can consume a significant portion of the drive(s). The Disk Cleanup tool can be used to regain access to hard drive space by deleting temporary, orphaned, or downloaded files; emptying the Recycle Bin; compressing little-used files; and condensing index catalog files (see Figure 9.11).

The Disk Cleanup tool can also be used to remove Windows components or installed programs to free space. The tool's More Options tab grants you easy access to the Windows Components Wizard and the Add/Remove Programs applet.

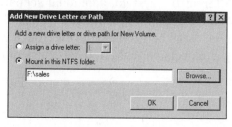

Figure 9.10   The Add New Drive Letter Or Path dialog box.

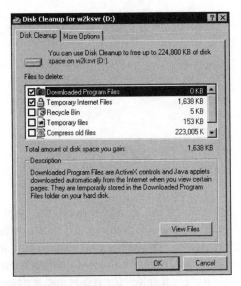

Figure 9.11   The Disk Cleanup tool.

Check Disk

Check Disk is a native tool used to discover and correct problems on hard drives. This tool was previously known as *ScanDisk*. Both physical and logical errors can be detected by Check Disk. When an error cannot be corrected, the area of the drive is marked as *bad*, and all other reads and writes to the hard drive will automatically avoid the bad sectors. Any data that is stored in a damaged location or that has become orphaned from its directory listing is copied into text files stored in the root of the drive with incrementing file names, such as FILE0001, FILE0002, and so on.

Check Disk can be launched from the Tools tab of a drive's Properties dialog box by clicking the Check Now button in the error-checking section. It cannot be launched from a command line as its ScanDisk predecessor could. Windows 2000 can also automatically launch Check Disk if it detects problems or if a nongraceful shutdown occurs. In some cases, Windows 2000 will need to schedule Check Disk to launch upon boot up before the graphical user interface (GUI) is loaded. Whenever Check Disk runs, you always have the option of aborting the activity of the tool. The GUI interface of Check Disk is very simple (see Figure 9.12). It offers two checkboxes: one to automatically fix errors and one to scan for and attempt recovery of bad sectors. The Start button initiates the scan; the Cancel button terminates the scan.

Only the version of Check Disk included with Windows 2000 should be used on volumes formatted by Windows 2000. Do not use ScanDisk from Windows NT, Windows 98, Windows 95, or DOS on Windows 2000-formatted volumes.

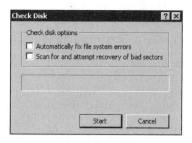

Figure 9.12   The Check Disk tool.

Defragmentation

As objects on a hard drive are written, deleted, changed, and moved, the organization of those objects becomes complex. Files may be broken into sections and stored in nonadjacent sectors of the drive. As free space becomes scattered and insufficient continuous free space is available, the fragmentation of files increases. The more fragmented a drive is means the longer it takes for reads and writes to occur. What's more, a highly fragmented drive can lose data through missing directory markers.

Defragmenting a drive reorganizes the files so that they are all stored in a contiguous manner. This improves drive performance. Windows 2000 includes a native defragmentation tool that can be used on any volume on a local drive formatted with FAT, FAT32, or NTFS. The Disk Defragmenter tool, shown in Figure 9.13, is

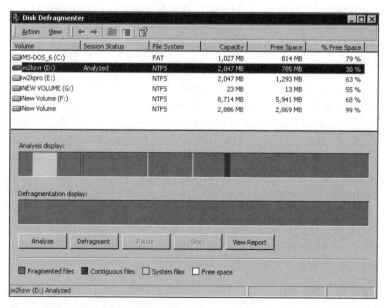

Figure 9.13   The Disk Defragmenter tool.

launched from the Tools tab of a drive's Properties dialog box. You can also get there by clicking on Start|Programs|Accessories|System Tools|Disk Defragmenter.

Just select one of the volumes listed, and click the Defragment button. The progress of the defragmentation is displayed alongside the original analysis of the volume. The process can be paused or stopped at any time. After the process is complete, you can view a report about the actions performed.

The Disk Defragmenter cannot be scheduled or launched from a batch file. You must obtain a third-party defragmentation tool to obtain scheduling capabilities.

Drive Quotas

Drive quotas grant you the ability to control the amount of disk space that a user can consume on both local systems and network shares. This feature is most often used in conjunction with roaming user profiles and network share-based home folders (and redirected folders). Quotas can be defined on a broad basis so that the same settings apply to all users or so that settings can be defined for individual users.

Quotas are defined on the Quota tab, shown in Figure 9.14, of a drive's Properties dialog box. Quotas are not enabled by default. You have the ability to set both a usage limit and a warning limit. When users exceed their limit, they are unable to log out until they reduce their space consumption.

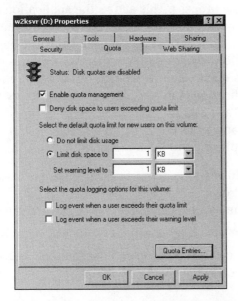

Figure 9.14   The Quota tab of a drive's Properties dialog box.

Task Manager

To gain a quick look at the state of the system, Task Manager is priceless. This tool allows you to see the standing of applications, the state of processes, and the status of system resources. You'll find yourself employing this utility often, especially when you suspect a problem is occurring. The Task Manager can be launched in several ways:

- Pressing Ctrl+Shift+Esc

- Pressing Ctrl+Alt+Delete and then clicking the Task Manager button on the WinLogon Security dialog box

- Right-clicking over an empty area of the taskbar and then selecting Task Manager from the pop-up menu

The Task Manager has three tabs: Applications, Processes, and Performance. Each of these tabs presents different information and offers content-specific controls or tasks.

The Applications tab, shown in Figure 9.15, displays a list of all currently active applications. This is the same list of applications that's present on the taskbar. Each application's status is included alongside its task name. The status will be Running or Not Responding. A program that has a status of Not Responding may be hung, have performed an illegal operation, or may simply be performing intensive calculations. You should wait 5 to 10 minutes after you notice an application is not responding before terminating the process. This allows the application to return to normal functionality on its own. If you deem an application stagnate and want to terminate it, select its name from the task list, and click the End Task button. After you confirm the termination when prompted, the application is removed from memory and the process queue, and its system resources are returned to the available pool. The Applications tab also offers you the ability to launch new programs using the New Task button. This opens a dialog box that functions exactly like the Run command from the Start menu. The Switch To button is used to bring the selected application to the foreground.

The Processes tab, shown in Figure 9.16, displays a list of all processes currently active on the system. By default, the Processes tab also displays the process ID (PID), central processing unit (CPU), cumulated execution time (CPU Time), and total consumed virtual memory (Mem Usage).

By selecting View|Select Columns, you can add or remove these four columns of data along with 18 others through the following checkboxes:

- Memory Usage Delta
- Peak Memory Usage

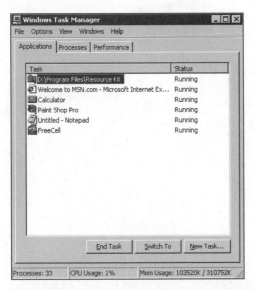

Figure 9.15   The Task Manager's Applications tab.

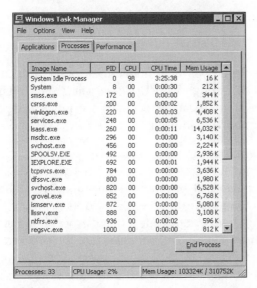

Figure 9.16   The Task Manager's Processes tab.

- Page Faults
- USER Objects
- Input/Output (I/O) Reads
- I/O Read Bytes
- Page Faults Delta
- Virtual Memory Size
- Paged Pool
- Non-Paged Pool
- Base Priority
- Handle Count
- Thread Count
- Graphics device interface (GDI) Objects
- I/O Writes
- I/O Write Bytes
- I/O Other
- I/O Other Bytes

By default, the data displayed on the Processes tab is updated every second. This interval can be increased or decreased through View|Update Speed. The Update Speed submenu offers the settings of High (twice per second), Normal (once per second), Low (once every four seconds), and Paused.

The Processes tab provides an excellent overview of the state of all processes operating on the system. Every process from both User mode and Kernel mode is listed here. You'll also notice a process that doesn't belong to either mode; it's called *System Idle Process*. This is a do-nothing task that the CPU works on when no other process is demanding execution time. If you suspect that a process or a program is consuming too much CPU time, check the Processes tab. If a process is consuming 90 percent or more of the CPU use for an extended period of time, you may have a rogue process. It's still recommended that you watch the status for at least 5 to 10 minutes before taking further action. It is not uncommon for intense activities by a single process to consume a significant amount of CPU attention. This does not indicate a problem with the process, but rather shows that either your system is underpowered or that some activities require a bit more time on the CPU to complete than most. If you determine that a process really has gone bad, you can select it from the list and click the End Process button. You'll be prompted to confirm the termination. The process is then removed from memory and the process queue, and its system resources are returned to the available pool. If other processes were dependent on the terminated process, those processes may terminate as well or stop functioning until the process is launched again.

This ability to terminate individual processes is an important one to remember, especially if you work with in-house or custom applications, DOS applications, or Win16 applications (that is, 16-bit applications written for Windows 3.x or Windows for Workgroups). Terminating a process is often the only solution to a poorly behaving application, short of rebooting. Most Win32 applications that go bad typically attempt to consume CPU or memory; terminating them restores the system to normal operation. All DOS applications are launched within a separate Windows NT Virtual DOS Machine (NTVDM). When you are unable to exit a DOS application gracefully, you can terminate the NTVDM hosting the application. All Win16 applications are launched within an environment created by WOWEXEC that is similar to the NTVDM, yet itself runs within an NTVDM. Terminating the WOWEXEC, NTVDM, or application process tears down the entire environment. Keep in mind that, by default, all Win16 applications are launched into the same WOWEXEC environment. When one application fails and is terminated, all the other applications are often terminated as well.

Another useful feature of the Processes tab is the ability to alter the execution priority of processes. Even though Windows 2000 has 32 levels of execution priority, you are only granted the ability to access the following 6 levels:

- *Realtime*—Sets the process to an execution priority level of 24. This setting is restricted to administrators.

- *High*—Sets the process to an execution priority level of 13.

- *AboveNormal*—Sets the process to an execution priority level of 10.

- *Normal*—Sets the process to an execution priority level of 8.

- *BelowNormal*—Sets the process to an execution priority level of 6.

- *Low*—Sets the process to an execution priority level of 4.

Changing a process's priority is accomplished by right-clicking a process, selecting the Set Priority submenu from the pop-up menu, and then clicking an execution priority level. You'll be prompted to confirm the priority change. The Realtime priority level is restricted to administrators. Even as an administrator, you can only change the execution priorities of User mode processes. However, it is possible to launch Task Manager (and any other tool) with a system-level privilege context using the **At** command. AT is the command-line tool used to define automated or scheduled tasks. The command **At <time> /interactive taskman.exe** launches the Task Manager at the specified time with system-level privileges. After Task Manager is launched in this manner, you can alter the execution priority of any active process. Be extremely cautious about altering the execution priority of system or kernel processes. The alteration of process priorities is not retained across reboots or even the termination and relaunch of the process during the same boot session.

Defining the execution priority of an application or process upon launching can be performed using the **Start** command. The syntax of the command string is **Start /<priority> <program>**. Any of the execution priority levels—Realtime, AboveNormal, Normal, BelowNormal, and Low—can be used. For more details on the **Start** command, enter **Start /?** at a command prompt. This technique can be used at a command prompt, through the **Run** command, or as the target command string of a shortcut.

The Performance tab, shown in Figure 9.17, offers you a brief glimpse into the performance levels of the system. This tab presents performance data focused on CPU, memory, and processes statistics. It contains a thermometer bar graph and a history graph for both CPU usage and memory usage. The thermometer bar graph displays the most recent level of activity, and the history graph shows the last 20 measurements. Below these graphs are 12 performance metrics:

- *Totals: Handles*—Indicates how many system objects are in use, such as files, registry keys, and virtual machines
- *Totals: Threads*—Indicates how many execution threads are present from all active processes
- *Totals: Processes*—Indicates the number of active processes
- *Physical Memory (K): Total*—Indicates the size of physical random access memory (RAM)
- *Physical Memory (K): Available*—Indicates the amount of unused physical RAM
- *Physical Memory (K): File Cache*—Indicates the amount of physical RAM being used for caching files
- *Commit Charge (K): Total*—Indicates the total amount of virtual memory allocated to processes or the system
- *Commit Charge (K): Limit*—Indicates the maximum amount of virtual memory on this computer
- *Commit Charge (K): Peak*—Indicates the maximum amount of virtual memory used during this boot session

- *Kernel Memory (K): Total*—Indicates the amount of memory used by the kernel

- *Kernel Memory (K): Paged*—Indicates the amount of total kernel memory that can be saved to a swap file

- *Kernel Memory (K): Nonpaged*—Indicates the amount of kernel memory that always remains in physical RAM

The graphs on this tab can be altered using the CPU History submenu and View|Show Kernel Times command. The CPU History submenu can be used to display a single graph for all CPUs or multiple graphs (one for each CPU). The Show Kernel Times command causes the graphs to display the amount of Kernel mode process CPU and memory consumption in red, and the remainder used by User mode processes is in green.

This tab can be used to determine in general if your system is overloaded. A consistent level of 90 percent or greater CPU use may indicate a rogue process or an underpowered system. Likewise, too little remaining available memory can indicate problems as well—from needing more RAM to a leaky application (one that consumes too many resources). You'll find Task Manager is the first tool you'll use to diagnose a problem before proceeding to more specialized tools, such as System Monitor or Network Monitor (both native to Windows 2000 Server), or even to a third-party tool.

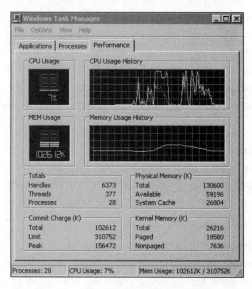

Figure 9.17   The Task Manager's Performance tab.

Managing Virtual Memory

Working with virtual memory is managing your paging file. That's the only real control of how Windows 2000 uses memory. Windows 2000 uses a flat linear, 32-bit addressing scheme to manage a contiguous block of memory. Within Windows 2000, memory is called *virtual memory* because it's created through combining physical RAM and storage space on a hard drive within one or more paging files. Windows 2000 Professional and Server can both manage 4 gigabytes (GB) of memory. Windows 2000 Advanced Server boasts support for 8GB of memory, and Windows 2000 Datacenter Server promises support for 64GB of memory. The amount of memory supported by any version of Windows 2000 is the total maximum amount of memory created through the combination of physical RAM and paging file space.

The Virtual Memory Manager (VMM) component of the Windows 2000 Executive is responsible for managing virtual memory. It is responsible for numerous complex activities, including moving pages to and from physical RAM and paging files, maintaining the distinct address spaces for each virtual machine present on the system, managing the correlation between Virtual Machine (VM) address space and virtual memory, and managing the state of memory pages located in both physical RAM and paging files.

By default, a paging file is created in the root directory of the boot partition by Windows 2000 upon installation. This paging file will be the same size as the physical RAM on Windows 2000 Professional systems or 64 megabytes (MB) larger than the amount of physical RAM on Windows 2000 Server systems. The paging file can be moved, enlarged, and altered in any manner with only one exception. If the Startup and Recovery options for the system are configured to create a dump file in the event of a STOP error, you must have a 2MB or greater paging file on the boot partition that must be one megabyte greater than the amount of physical RAM on the system.

Alterations to the paging file are performed through the Virtual Memory dialog box (see Figure 9.18). This dialog box is opened from the System applet by selecting the Advanced tab, clicking the Performance Options button, and then clicking the Change button on the Performance Options dialog box under the Virtual Memory heading.

To alter the size of a paging file, select the drive where the paging file is located in the top list window, alter the initial size and maximum size values, and then click Set. The initial size value determines how much drive space is allocated to the paging file. The maximum size value sets the upper limit for how large the paging file can grow. The value in the initial size is guaranteed, whereas the amount of

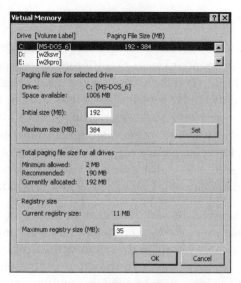

Figure 9.18   The Virtual Memory dialog box.

drive space required to meet the maximum size is not guaranteed and may not be present when requested by the VMM. Notice the middle section labeled Total Paging File Size For All Drives. This area lists some very important numbers. The minimum allowed number indicates the smallest paging file that must exist, and, in most cases, this minimal paging file must reside on the boot partition. The recommended size is the size of the paging file that the system thinks is adequate to perform currently active tasks. The currently allocated value is the total amount of allocated drive space for the paging file across all volumes.

Spreading the paging file across multiple drives simply means adding another paging file to a different volume. This is accomplished by selecting a volume that does not already have a paging file, providing initial and maximum values, and then clicking Set. Removing a paging file is accomplished by setting the initial and maximum values to zero.

It's a good idea to move the paging file (or all but the minimal required) from the boot partition to some other volume not on the same physical hard drive. When multiple paging files are created, the greatest performance benefit is reaped only when each paging file segment is on a unique physical hard drive. Placing a paging file on two or more partitions or volumes on the same hard drive causes performance degradation.

User Profiles

User profiles are employed by Windows 2000 to retain custom user environments across logon sessions even when those sessions occur on different systems on the network. User profiles can also enforce a common or restricted desktop environment when customization is not allowed. Every user has a user profile. By default, these are local, customizable user profiles. A user profile is really little more than the contents of a few user-specific directories, history lists, favorites, and a subsection of the registry stored in a file named ntuser.dat. A user profile can store Start menu layout, sound schemes, color schemes, desktop icons, mapped network shares, last accessed documents, Web site favorites, and more.

User profiles can be local only or roaming. In addition, user profiles can be customizable or mandatory. A local-only user profile exists on a single computer. A roaming user profile is available no matter where on the network the user logs on. A customizable user profile records the changes to the environment each time that the user logs off; this allows the last saved state of the environment to be returned to him or her at the next logon. A mandatory user profile does not save changes made during a logon session; this means the original mandatory environment will be returned to the user at the next logon. A mandatory profile can be shared by multiple users because no customization is possible.

User profiles from Windows 2000 and Windows NT are compatible, but user profiles from Windows 98 or Windows 95 are not. Therefore, users can move from Windows 2000 clients to Windows NT clients and back while maintaining the same environment throughout. However, after a user moves to a Windows 98 or Windows 95 system, he or she will not be presented with the normal profile, but rather the default local profile for that system. Both Windows 98 and Window 95 and Windows 2000 and Windows NT user profiles can exist on the same network, and both types support roaming and mandatory configuration. However, to keep confusion to a minimum, users should stick with one system type or the other.

The first time that a user logs in to a computer, the system looks for a roaming profile on a network share for that user. The path to the storage location of a user's roaming profile is defined in his or her domain user account's properties. If no roaming user profile is found, a local user profile is created by duplicating the local default user profile. When a local user profile is created on a Windows 2000 system (whether from a copy of the local default user profile or a copy of the roaming user profile from its network storage location), it is placed in a subfolder of the \Documents and Settings directory, which has the same name as the user account. If a roaming user profile path is defined for a user, but no profile is stored there when the system checks, the newly created user profile will be copied to the network share location. The next time that the user logs on anywhere, his or her roaming user profile will be found and loaded. If a roaming user profile path is not defined for the user, the newly created user profile will remain a local profile, which will only be available on the one system where it is created. To transform a local user profile into a roaming user profile, just add a user profile path to the user account's properties. The next time that the user logs on and then logs off, the user's profile will become a roaming user profile stored on the provided network share path.

NOTE: *By default, all user profiles can be customized by the user. This means that all changes made to the environment during a logon session will be saved when the user logs out. This is true both for local and roaming user profiles.*

The only user account that does not have or cannot have its own unique user profile is the Guest account. Each time the Guest account is used to log on, the default user profile is given to that user. No changes made by the guest user are saved, and no user profile directory is created.

Each time that a user logs on to a system, his or her roaming user profile will be cached locally. The next time that the user logs on to the same system, only the changed items will be transferred across the network. This also allows users to log on even if the domain controller cannot be contacted to authenticate them. However, if the user profile is a mandatory profile and the domain controller cannot be contacted, the user will not be allowed to log on.

Roaming user profiles are created or defined by providing a Universal Naming Convention (UNC) path statement for the storage location for the profile. This is done on the Profile tab, shown in Figure 9.19, of a user account's Properties

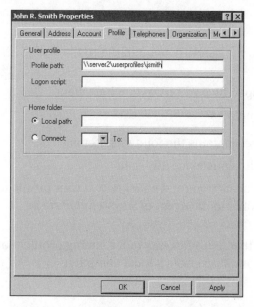

Figure 9.19   The Profile tab of a user account's Properties dialog box, accessed through the Active Directory Users And Computers console.

dialog box, accessed through the Active Directory Users And Computers console. A UNC path statement takes the form of \\<**servername**>\<**sharename**>\ <**directoryname**>, where **directoryname** is often the user account's name.

NOTE: *The directory name can be a folder tree path as well, such as* \users\profiles\admins\department1\jsmith.

If you examine the contents of a user profile's storage folder, you'll see the following subfolders:

- *Application Data*—Contains application-specific data, such as configuration files, custom dictionaries, and file cache for Internet Explorer or Outlook Express

- *Cookies*—Contains the cookies accepted by the user

- *Desktop*—Contains the icons, files, shortcuts, and folders found on the desktop

- *Favorites*—Contains the list of bookmarked uniform resource locators (URLs) from Internet Explorer

- *Local Settings*—Contains user-specific application data, history data, and temporary files

- *My Documents*—Contains a user's saved files

- *NetHood*—Contains network mappings and items in Network Places

- *PrintHood*—Contains printer mappings and items in the printer folder

- *Recent*—Contains links to the most recently used resources (documents and folders)

- *SendTo*—Contains items found in the Send To menu of the right-click pop-up menu

- *Start Menu*—Contains the user-specific portions of the Start menu

- *Templates*—Contains a user's templates

The user profile's storage folder also contains the following items:

- *Ntuser.dat*—A registry file containing user-specific data

- *Ntuser.dat.log*—A file that logs transactions and changes to a user profile for the purpose of re-creating the profile in the event of a system failure or element corruption

- *Ntuser.ini*—A configuration file that lists elements of a roaming profile that are not to be uploaded to a network share from a local computer

The System applet's User Profiles tab, shown in Figure 9.20, offers a few management functions. This tab lists all profiles stored or cached locally. Therefore, only the profiles for users who have logged on to the system locally will appear here. This interface can be used to delete local copies of local user profiles or roaming user profiles from the local hard drive. It can also be used to prevent changes made on the local machine to a roaming user profile from being uploaded back to its network share storage location. This is known as converting a roaming user profile to a local user profile. The Copy To button is used to duplicate an existing profile to a new location. This can be used to create a backup of a profile or to jump-start a new user's profile with something other than the default user profile.

Any profile can be converted to a mandatory profile by renaming the registry file from ntuser.dat to ntuser.man. This name change must be made in the main storage location of the profile (that is, the network share instead of a local cache in the case of a roaming user profile). After a profile is set to mandatory, no changes made by the user during a logon session will be saved. To return a profile to a customizable state, just change the name of the registry file back to ntuser.dat.

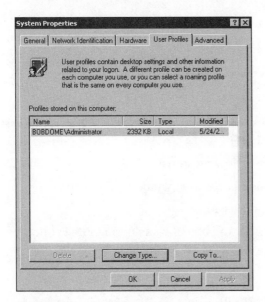

Figure 9.20   The User Profiles tab of the System applet.

Immediate Solutions

Disabling or Enabling Autorun

Autorun is the ability of the operating system (OS) to automatically launch a program or to play music from an inserted CD. This feature doesn't have a GUI configuration setting to manage it. It must be altered using the registry. To manage Autorun using REGEDIT, perform the following steps:

1. Click Start, select Run, type "REGEDIT", and click OK.

2. Locate the HKEY_LOCAL_MACHINE\System\CurrentControlSet\ Services\CDRom key.

3. Select the Autorun value entry.

4. Change the value to 0 to disable Autorun or change the value to 1 to enable Autorun.

5. Close the registry editor.

Setting Permissions on a File

To set file permissions, perform the following steps:

1. Click Start, and select Programs|Accessories|Windows Explorer.

2. Locate and select a file to set permissions.

3. Open the Properties dialog box for the object by selecting File|Properties.

4. Select the Security tab (refer to Figure 9.1).

5. Click Add.

6. Select the Authenticated Users group.

7. Click Add.

8. Click OK. Authenticated Users is added to the Name field of the Security tab.

9. While Authenticated Users is selected, mark or unmark the checkboxes under Allow or Deny of each of the listed permissions to set the level of access to grant this group (or user).

10. Repeat Steps 5 through 9 for each user or group desired.

11. Select the Everyone group.

12. Click the Remove button.

13. Click OK to close the Properties dialog box.

Configuring Advanced Permissions

To configure advanced permissions, perform the following steps:

1. Click Start, and select Programs|Accessories|Windows Explorer.

2. Locate and select a file on which to set permissions.

3. Open the Properties dialog box for the object by selecting File|Properties.

4. Select the Security tab.

5. Click Advanced.

6. On the Permissions tab, click Add.

7. Select the Server Operators group.

8. Click OK.

9. Mark or unmark the checkboxes under Allow or Deny of each of the listed detail permissions to set the level of access to grant this group (or user).

10. Click OK.

11. The Server Operators group now appears in the list of permission entries.

12. Repeat Steps 6 through 10 for each user or group desired.

13. Click OK to return to the Security tab.

14. Click OK to close the Properties dialog box.

Configuring Auditing

To configure auditing, perform the following steps:

1. Click Start, and select Programs|Accessories|Windows Explorer.

2. Locate a resource object (file or folder) on which to configure auditing.

3. Select File|Properties.

4. Select the Security tab.

5. Click Advanced.

6. Select the Auditing tab.

9. Windows 2000 Configuration

7. Click Add.

8. Select the user or group to audit.

9. Click OK.

10. Select the access functions to be audited on a success or failure basis by selecting checkboxes.

11. Click OK.

12. The added user or group will appear in the Auditing Entries list.

13. Repeat Steps 7 through 11 for each user and group desired.

14. Click OK to return to the Security tab.

15. Click OK to close the Properties dialog box.

Managing Ownership

If you own an object, you have Full Control of that object. Users with the Take Ownership user right or the specific object permission can recapture ownership of an object. To establish ownership, perform the following steps:

1. Click Start, and select Programs|Accessories|Windows Explorer.

2. Locate a resource object (file or folder) on which to configure ownership.

3. Open the Properties dialog box for the object by selecting File|Properties.

4. Select the Security tab.

5. Click Advanced.

6. Select the Owner tab (refer to Figure 9.5).

7. A list of valid possible owners is displayed.

8. Select the user or group to become the new owner of the object, and then click OK.

9. Click OK to close the Properties dialog box.

Enabling Fax Receiving

By default, the Windows 2000 fax system is set to send faxes, but not to receive faxes. To configure fax receiving, perform the following steps:

1. Open the Fax Service Management tool by clicking Start and selecting Programs|Accessories|Communications|Fax|Fax Service Management.

2. Select the Devices node in the left pane (refer to Figure 9.8).

3. Select the fax device in the right pane.

4. Select Action|Properties.

5. Select the Enable Receive checkbox.

6. Set the field for Rings Before Answer to 1.

7. Click OK to close the Properties dialog box.

8. Close the Fax Service Management tool by clicking the close button on the title bar.

Configuring the Recycle Bin

The Recycle Bin stores recently deleted files. To manage Recycle Bin settings, perform the following steps:

1. Select the Recycle Bin icon on the desktop.

2. Right-click the Recycle Bin, and select Properties from the pop-up menu. The Recycle Bin Properties dialog box opens (refer to Figure 9.9).

3. Make sure the Use One Setting For All Drives radio button is selected.

4. Make sure the Do Not Move Files To The Recycle Bin. Remove Files Immediately When Deleted checkbox is not marked.

5. Move the slider that determines the amount of drive space to be used by the Recycle Bin to 5 pecent.

6. Make sure the Display Delete Confirmation Dialog checkbox is marked.

7. Click OK.

Restoring a File from the Recycle Bin

If a deleted file is still stored in the Recycle Bin, it can be recovered. Here are the steps to follow:

NOTE: *This solution requires that one or more files be deleted and present in the Recycle Bin.*

1. View the desktop.

2. Select the Recycle Bin icon on the desktop.

3. Right-click the Recycle Bin, and then select Open from the pop-up menu.

9. Windows 2000 Configuration

4. Select the file (or files) to recover.

5. Take note of the path listed in the Original Location column.

6. Select File|Restore.

7. Click Yes in the Confirm File Replace window.

8. Close the Recycle Bin view window by selecting File|Close.

9. Use Windows Explorer or another tool to view the path of the file's original location to access the restored file (or files).

Selecting Files for Storage Offline

To be able to access network files when you're not connected to the network requires that those files be cached locally in offline files. Work through the following steps to configure file resources for storage of offline files:

NOTE: *This solution requires Windows 2000 Professional.*

1. Access My Network Places through its desktop icon or through Windows Explorer.

2. Locate and select a file or folder from a network share to make available when not connected to the network.

3. Right-click the selected item, and select Make Available Offline from the pop-up menu.

4. If a folder was selected, you'll be prompted whether to make just this folder and its nonsubfolder contents available or the folder and all file and subfolder contents available. Select Yes, Make This Folder And All Its Subfolders Available Offline.

5. Click OK.

6. A synchronization dialog box will display the progress of the transfer.

Configuring Offline Files

To alter the default configuration and operation of offline files, perform the following steps:

NOTE: *This solution requires Windows 2000 Professional.*

1. Click Start, and select Programs|Accessories|Windows Explorer.

2. Select Tools|Folder Options.

3. Select the Offline Files tab.

4. Make sure the checkboxes for Enable Offline Files and Synchronize All Offline Files Before Logging Off are marked.

5. If you want to be reminded when you are using resources cached by offline files, mark the Enable Reminders checkbox, and set the Repeat Reminder interval.

6. If you want an offline files shortcut on the desktop, mark that checkbox.

7. Set the maximum amount of drive space that can be used to host offline files to 3 percent of the drive.

8. Click Delete to delete cached files by shared folder.

9. Click View to see a list of cached files.

10. Click OK to save settings and return to Windows Explorer.

Compressing a File or Folder to Save Drive Space

To compress files and folders, perform the following steps:

NOTE: *Only files and folders on NTFS volumes can be compressed. An encrypted file cannot be compressed and vice versa.*

1. Click Start, and select Programs|Accessories|Windows Explorer.

2. Select a file or folder to compress.

3. Open the Properties dialog box for the selected object.

4. Click the Advanced button.

5. Mark the Compress Contents To Save Disk Space checkbox.

6. Click OK twice.

7. If the object is a folder, you'll be prompted whether to compress just the folder and its contents or the folder, its contents, and any subfolders.

9. Windows 2000 Configuration

Decompressing a File or Folder

To decompress files and folders, perform the following steps:

NOTE: *Only files and folders on NTFS volumes can be compressed. Make sure enough free drive space is available to accommodate the uncompressed files.*

---

1. Click Start, and select Programs|Accessories|Windows Explorer.
2. Select a compressed file or folder to decompress.
3. Open the Properties dialog box for the selected object.
4. Click the Advanced button.
5. Unmark the Compress Contents To Save Disk Space checkbox.
6. Click OK twice.
7. If the object is a folder, you'll be prompted whether to decompress just the folder and its contents or the folder, its contents, and any subfolders.

Encrypting a File or Folder

To encrypt a file or folder, perform the following steps:

NOTE: *Only files and folders on NTFS volumes can be encrypted. Only the person who encrypts an object can access it or decrypt it. An encrypted file cannot be compressed and vice versa.*

---

1. Click Start, and select Programs|Accessories|Windows Explorer.
2. Select a file or folder to encrypt.
3. Open the Properties dialog box for the selected object.
4. Click the Advanced button.
5. Mark the Encrypt Contents To Secure Data checkbox.
6. Click OK twice.
7. If the object is a folder, you'll be prompted whether to encrypt just the folder and its contents or the folder, its contents, and any subfolders.

Decrypting a File or Folder

Decrypting a file or folder removes the security protection from the file and makes it accessible to other users. To decrypt a file or folder, follow these steps:

NOTE: *Only files and folders on NTFS volumes can be encrypted. Only the person who encrypts an object can access it or decrypt it.*

1. Click Start, and select Programs|Accessories|Windows Explorer.
2. Select an encrypted file or folder to decrypt.
3. Open the Properties dialog box for the selected object.
4. Click the Advanced button.
5. Unmark the Encrypt Contents To Secure Data checkbox.
6. Click OK twice.
7. If the object is a folder, you'll be prompted whether to decrypt just the folder and its contents or the folder, its contents, and any subfolders.

Creating a Mount Point

To grant easy access to a volume that does not have an assigned drive letter, create a mount point by performing the following steps:

1. Click Start, and select Programs|Accessories|Windows Explorer.
2. Create a new directory to be used as the mount point.
3. Click Start, and select Programs|Computer Management|Disk Management.
4. Select the volume to be mounted.
5. Select Action|All Tasks|Change Drive Letter And Path.
6. Click Add.
7. Select the Mount In This NTFS Folder radio button.
8. Use the Browse button to locate and select the directory created in Step 2.
9. Click OK.
10. Close the Disk Management/Computer Management interface.
11. The mounted volume is now accessible through the mount point directory.

9. Windows 2000 Configuration

Cleaning Up a Drive

The Disk Cleanup tool can be used to recover drive space by removing files and compressing others. Here are the steps to follow:

1. Click Start, and select Programs|Accessories|Windows Explorer.
2. Right-click a drive to clean up, and select Properties from the pop-up menu.
3. Click the Disk Cleanup button on the General tab.
4. Wait while the Disk Cleanup tool performs an inspection of your drive.
5. When prompted, mark or unmark the checkboxes beside each of the available means to recover space on your hard drive. When files are to be deleted, a list of those files can be viewed.
6. Click OK to perform the selected space-recovery activities.
7. When completed, close the drive's Properties dialog box.

Testing for Errors on a Drive

To use ScanDisk to test a drive for errors, perform the following steps:

1. Click Start, and select Programs|Accessories|Windows Explorer.
2. Right-click a drive to test for errors, and select Properties from the pop-up menu.
3. Select the Tools tab.
4. Click the Check Now button.
5. Select the Automatically Fix File System Errors checkbox.
6. Select the Scan For And Attempt Recovery Of Bad Sectors checkbox.
7. If ScanDisk is unable to perform its operations while Windows 2000 is booted, you'll be prompted whether to schedule ScanDisk to launch at the next bootup.
8. After ScanDisk completes, a report of its findings will be displayed.
9. Close ScanDisk.
10. Close the drive's Properties dialog box.

Defragmenting a Drive

The Disk Defragmenter tool is used to improve the organization of files on volumes. If you suspect your drives are highly fragmented, use the following steps to defragment your hard drive:

1. Click Start, and select Programs|Accessories|Windows Explorer.

2. Right-click a drive to test for errors, and select Properties from the pop-up menu.

3. Select the Tools tab.

4. Click the Defragment Now button.

5. Select a volume from the list.

6. Click the Defragment button.

7. Wait while the process is performed.

8. Repeat Steps 5 through 7 until all volumes are defragmented.

9. Close the Disk Defragmenter tool.

10. Close the drive's Properties dialog box.

Configuring Quotas

To use quotas to control user consumption of network shared drives, perform the following steps:

1. Click Start, and select Programs|Accessories|Windows Explorer.

2. Right-click the drive on which to enable quotas, and select Properties from the pop-up menu.

3. Select the Quota tab.

4. Select the Enable Quota Management checkbox.

5. Select the Deny Disk Space To Users Exceeding Quota Limit checkbox.

6. Set Limit Disk Space to 100MB (or other value consistent with your needs).

7. Set the warning level to 90MB (or a similar value for your own limit setting).

8. Mark both Log Event checkboxes.

9. Click Quota Entries.

10. Select Quota|New Quota Entry to add a custom quota setting for the administrator.

11. Select the administrator.

12. Click Add.

13. Click OK.

14. Select the Do Not Limit Disk Usage radio button.

15. Click OK.

16. Select Quota|New Quota Entry to add a custom quota setting for the Guest account.

17. Select the Guest account.

18. Click Add.

19. Click OK.

20. Select the Limit Disk Space To radio button.

21. Set the limit to 25MB and the warning level to 20MB.

22. Click OK.

23. Select Quota|Close.

24. Click OK to close the drive's Properties dialog box.

Chapter 10

Windows 2000 File Systems, Fault Tolerance, and Recovery

In Depth

It is important that you understand the file systems supported by Windows 2000 to use some of its most powerful and helpful features. This chapter deals not only with these file systems, but with some of the management tasks that go with them. These include old features, such as security, compression, and auditing, as well as new, long-awaited features, such as disk quotas and encryption.

This chapter also deals with disk management in Windows 2000. This discussion includes working with disks, partitions, and volumes. In addition, some of the recovery tools that ship with Windows 2000 are discussed.

The File Systems

Although many different file systems exist, only the four that Windows 2000 supports are covered in this chapter. These include file allocation table (FAT), FAT32, and Windows NT File System (NTFS) 4 and 5. The benefits and drawbacks of each of these file systems are listed in the sections that follow.

FAT

The FAT file system is the most widely supported file system. Almost all major operating systems support this particular file system, including disk operating system (DOS), Windows 3.x, Windows 9x, Windows NT, Windows 2000, Macintosh Operating System (OS), and many flavors of Unix. Table 10.1 compares the pros and cons of the FAT file system.

TIP: *There's another version of FAT known as FAT16. FAT and FAT16 are the same file system. The new name is to differentiate it from FAT32, which is described in the next section. Another file system known as Virtual FAT (VFAT) is an enhanced version of FAT that allows long file names to be used. These three terms (FAT, FAT16, and VFAT) are used interchangeably in most Windows documentation.*

FAT32

Windows 95 OSR2 (OEM Service Release 2) introduced FAT32. This 32-bit file system is backward compatible with FAT and has better long file name support, larger partition support, and the ability to change the sector block size. Table 10.2 compares the pros and cons of the FAT32 file system.

Table 10.1   The good and bad of the FAT file system.

Pros	Cons
Most widely used file system	No support for local security
Can be supported on small partitions and diskettes	No automatic file recovery
	Uses standard 8.3 file names
	2 gigabyte (GB) drive size limit
	512-entry limit in root directory
	No quotas
	No compression
	No encryption

Table 10.2   The good and bad of FAT32.

Pros	Cons
Support for long file names	No support for local security
Can be supported on small partitions	No automatic file recovery
4GB file size limit	No compression
Larger than 4GB partition size limit	No quotas
Supports up to 2 terabyte disks	No encryption

TIP: *If you're planning on multibooting between different operating systems, it's recommended that you use FAT32 when using Windows 95 OSR2, Windows 98, or Windows 2000. Regular Windows 95 and Windows NT will require FAT formatted drives. If you're strictly using Windows 2000, format NTFS.*

NTFS 4

NTFS 4 is the file system used by Windows NT 4. It operates much like a relational database rather than a flat file system (which is used in FAT and FAT32). It introduced file-level security, auditing, and compression to Windows.

NTFS also introduced a technology known as *cluster remapping*. With this technology, when the operating system finds a bad cluster, it automatically moves the data to a new stable cluster and marks the original cluster as bad. This technology is also known as *self-healing*.

NTFS supports compressions, file- and folder-level security, and auditing. NTFS also supports an extremely large file system: 16 exabytes (EB), which is 16 billion GB. Although this is a theoretical limit (no hardware system currently exists that can support this), the file system will be able to scale to the hardware when it is available.

NOTE: *As an example of the size of this limit, if every man, woman, and child on the planet had a 3,000-page document, and each of those pages was 3 kilobytes (KB) in size, and these documents were all placed into a single file system, this would only account for one-sixteenth of 1EB. NTFS supports 16EB.*

Table 10.3 compares the pros and cons of NTFS 4.

NTFS 5

NTFS 5 is the new file system introduced with Windows 2000. This file system has all the features of NTFS 4, but adds the long-awaited quotas and encryption features.

One of the major downfalls of NTFS 5 is that the only system that supports it out of the box is Windows 2000. Windows NT 4 supports NTFS 5 only if it is running Service Pack 4 (SP4) or higher. Table 10.4 compares the pros and cons of NTFS 5.

TIP: *The only reason to use a file system other than NTFS 5 with Windows 2000 is for dual-boot purposes. If a system is not dual-booted, it is a good idea to convert all partitions to NTFS 5. Microsoft does not recommend configuring a server for dual boot.*

Table 10.3   The good and bad of NTFS 4.

Pros	Cons
Support for long file names	No quotas
Local security	No encryption
Very large partition and file size support	Cannot be supported on small partitions or diskettes
Self-healing	No automatic file recovery
Compression support	Only works with Windows NT and Windows 2000

Table 10.4   The good and bad of NTFS 5.

Pros	Cons
Support for long file names	Not supported by non-Windows NT or Windows 2000 systems
Local security	Cannot be supported on small partitions or diskettes
Self-healing	No automatic file recovery
Compression support	
Quota support	
Very large partition and file size support	
Encryption support	

Choosing and Implementing Windows 2000 File Systems

The simplest way to choose the correct file system is by operating system. Although some would think that the features of the file system are more important, if the operating system installed cannot support the file system, it also cannot support the features. Refer to Table 10.5 to decide which file system to use with which operating system.

File System Management

Some very important features have been added to Windows 2000 to assist in managing file systems. These features are covered in the following sections.

Compressing Folders and Files

Much like Windows NT, NTFS provides the ability to compress partitions, folders, and individual files. Although compression should not be used on all files all the time, it can be used on files that are not accessed often or if extra disk space is temporally required (for example, while awaiting a hardware maintenance window). This is because the overhead needed to compress and then uncompress the files will slow the system down. Note that compression does not work with encryption.

Table 10.5   File system support by operating system.

Operating System(s)	File System
DOS	FAT
Windows 3.x	FAT
Windows 3.x or DOS dual-booted with Windows 9x/NT/2000	FAT
Windows 95 First Edition	FAT
Windows 95 First Edition dual-booted with Windows NT	FAT
Windows 95 Second Edition dual-booted with Windows NT	FAT
Windows 95 Second Edition dual-booted with Windows 2000	FAT32
Windows 98 dual-booted with Windows NT	FAT
Windows 98 dual-booted with Windows 2000	FAT32
Windows NT	NTFS 4
Windows NT with pre-SP5 dual-booted with Windows 2000	NTFS 4
Windows NT with SP5 dual-booted with Windows 2000	NTFS 5
Windows 2000	NTFS 5

Defragmenting Drives

Although NTFS is better than FAT, all drives get fragmented. When a file is saved on the hard drive, the operating system will attempt to fill any empty gaps on the disk to use as much of the drive as possible. This, however, slows file access.

NOTE: *Imagine if the first five pages of this chapter started on page 200, the next five on page 250, the next five on page 124, and so on. It would take you longer to read through the chapter than if all the pages were in order.*

Defragmentation of disks moves files around so that all the components of an individual file are all placed in the same location. Windows 2000 ships with a basic defragmentation tool. "Immediate Solutions" shows you how to defragment a drive using Windows 2000's built-in defragmenter.

Disk Cleanup

Windows 2000 includes a feature for scanning disks for files that can be removed. These include downloaded files, temporary Internet files, Recycle Bin files, and temporary files. The disk cleanup utility also scans hard drives for files that have not been accessed in a long period of time and will automatically compress those files if you select the appropriate option.

Finally, the disk cleanup utility can also be configured to scan for rarely used Windows 2000 components and rarely used installed applications. These can be automatically uninstalled as well.

Working with Quotas

One of the features that has been missing in the Windows operating system is support for disk quotas. Until now, a user with access to a server could singlehandedly bring the server to its knees by filling the server's hard drives with data. Windows 2000 with NTFS 5 can now be configured to support quotas for individual users or global quotas. It is also possible to create different quotas for individual partitions and volumes.

After disk quotas are enabled for a specific volume and drive letter, these rules are applicable to all users on that drive. For some unknown reason, members of the Administrators group are not subject to these blanket quotas unless specifically defined in user-based quota entries. You can also specifically set quotas on a user-by-user basis. This is done on the same drive properties page under the Quotas tab that is used to enable quotas to begin with. By using the Quota Entries button, you can see a list of all users that have ever stored data on the drive. From here, you can set quota limits and warning levels for each user listed. This is where you would set quota limits for members of the Administrators group.

Because individual quota entries are linked only to a single drive or volume, you may want to copy specific user entries from one drive to another. You can export the entries from within the Quota Entries window. You can also drag and drop quota entries from one drive or volume into another drive or volume.

A Word about Distributed File System

Because of the nature of the real world, it's not unusual to have a hard drive on a server run out of space. Usually, what you'd do is either upgrade or replace the drive; restore from tape (if appropriate); and try to find a way to reconfigure shares, scripts, and drive mappings so that the users wouldn't notice. The Windows 2000 Distributed File System (DFS) is designed to help alleviate this caliber of user disruption (because it's rare that you could actually get away with shuffling data without affecting the user population). DFS allows you to tack on additional hard disk space just like you'd build an additional wing to a castle. From the outside, you can usually tell when the original building ends and the new wing begins. From the inside (where the users are), you can't really tell the difference as you walk from one hallway to another. DFS works in the same way by adding linking data from a separate drive to a preexisting share and then having it all appear as one drive to the user.

DFS also has other features, such as a centralized data store for users, which cuts down on confusion. Having your data distributed across multiple drives and servers can be a great fault-tolerant feature in the event that a single server dies. Theoretically, improved performance should also be a benefit of using DFS. Because of its distributed nature, DFS allows multiple servers to work on what could be a single data request from the network.

On the other hand, if your user data is scattered across many different network servers, this can quickly become an administrative—and documenting—nightmare. DFS is not specifically related to the hard drive or disk format. Instead, DFS is more of a networking creature, and as such, I will discuss DFS benefits, drawbacks, and configuration in Chapter 11.

A Word about Encrypting File System

Windows 2000 and NTFS 5 have finally provided the ability to use encryption to protect files. With Encrypting File System (EFS), files can be protected so that no one except the owner of the files or the designated recovery agent can read and modify them. This takes security beyond NTFS permissions. With EFS, only the person who encrypted the files can decrypt them. Now, if someone steals a laptop or other network hardware, the files are secure, even if the administrator password is known. Because Windows 2000 EFS is less of a file system topic and more of a security topic, I will discuss the details of EFS and EFS recovery in Chapter 20.

Disk Management

Similar to Windows NT, disk management in Windows 2000 is performed using the Disk Manager program. True to the Windows 2000 form, however, Disk Manager is available through the DISKMGMT.MSC Microsoft Management Console (MMC) snap-in. You can also get to it by right-clicking the My Computer icon from the desktop and selecting Manage from the pop-up menu.

Basic Disks vs. Dynamic Disks

Windows 2000 has introduced a new way of dealing with disks. These new disks can be modified and moved from one system to another without partition loss and can eliminate most disk configuration reboots. These new disks are known as *dynamic disks*.

Windows 2000 still fully supports disks that were formatted under Windows 95, Windows 98, and Windows NT. In the Windows 2000 world, these legacy disks are known as *basic disks*. Windows 2000 can still manage, format, and modify these disks, but some of the more advanced disk-manipulation methods now require dynamic disks.

It is important to realize that dynamic disks are no different than basic disks in a physical sense. Only the way in which the disk is formatted and written to is changed. To differentiate between partitions created on a basic disk, Windows 2000 has new naming conventions for the different types of disks it can support. Instead of dealing with partitions, Windows 2000 deals with *volumes*. Table 10.6 shows the differences between the Windows NT basic disk naming conventions and Windows 2000 dynamic disks.

Basic disks are also limited in the number of partitions that can be created on them. With Windows 95, Windows 98, and Windows NT, a disk can have up to four partitions: either four primary partitions or three primary partitions and one extended partition. This limitation no longer exists with dynamic disks in Windows 2000.

Table 10.6   Basic vs. dynamic disks.

Windows NT/Basic	Windows 2000/Dynamic
Partition	Simple volume
Volume set	Spanned volume
Mirror set	Mirrored volume
Stripe set	Striped volume
Stripe set with parity	Redundant Array of Inexpensive Disks (RAID) 5 volume

RAID

RAID was a concept that was originally created as a hardware solution to increase fault tolerance and performance on minicomputers. The concept eventually bled into the personal computer (PC) server market in the form of multiple hard disk drives and specialized RAID controllers that handled advanced disk functions. It wasn't long until some software vendors and operating systems figured out how to emulate certain RAID features in a software solution to provide some of the same basic RAID features available with a hardware solution.

RAID: Software vs. Hardware

One of the most common methods of designing fault-tolerant disk systems is by using RAID. Each RAID configuration is given a level (most commonly from Level 0 to Level 5). Windows 2000 supports three of the levels: Levels 0, 1, and 5.

NOTE: *RAID also stands for Redundant Array of Independent Disks. Although workstation-grade hard drives have dropped in price, high-speed, high-throughput Small Computer System Interface (SCSI) drives are still very expensive. This is why "independent" has replaced the word "inexpensive."*

RAID Level 0 is known in the Windows 2000 world as a *striped volume*. Although Level 0 does not give the disks any fault tolerance, it does increase performance on the disks by reading from multiple disks at the same time, thus accomplishing the same tasks in a fraction of the time. RAID Level 1 is disk mirroring/disk duplexing, where data on a single drive is dynamically cloned to a second drive at all times. These methods protect the data from a single disk failure. RAID Level 5 is the most commonly used RAID configuration on the market today. With Windows 2000, it is simply referred to as a *RAID 5 volume*. With RAID 5, parity information is stored separate from the data in such a manner that the system can completely recover the data should any single disk fail.

There are two different ways of dealing with RAID. The first is *software RAID*, which is done with Windows 2000, and the second is *hardware RAID*. Although hardware RAID is much more expensive than software RAID (no special hardware is required with the software implementation of RAID), it is far superior in its performance.

As you may imagine, calculating the parity information and writing to multiple disks by the operating system uses valuable central processing unit (CPU) cycles. With a high-end server, these cycles are needed to support the users and applications. With hardware RAID, a dedicated interface card does all the calculations. The controller then presents the operating system with a single logical disk. Although the RAID array may consist of 3 or more (up to 32) disks, Windows 2000 "sees" the disk as a single disk.

By and large, if you have the opportunity to truly do RAID, use a hardware solution. If you have the money, choosing hardware RAID is just plain better than software RAID for several reasons:

- Hardware RAID can use hot-swapping technology that will allow you to remove and replace failed hard disk drives without taking down the server.
- Hardware RAID can also use hot-plugging technology that will allow a spare hard disk drive to be used automatically when a disk drive fails.
- Hardware RAID supports striped boot volumes.
- Hardware RAID eliminates the huge performance hit you'll see when using software RAID.

Don't get me wrong. I've used software RAID before because of the fault-tolerant features and its cost. Zero is a really good price, and it's a great relief to be able to know that if a single drive fails, I won't be pulling an all-nighter restoring data from tape. I've also used hardware RAID and can testify that hardware RAID runs faster. With hardware RAID, the CPU and memory that would normally be used to maintain data algorithms on a software RAID server are now run on the RAID controller.

Disk Mirroring and Disk Duplexing

It is important to understand the differences between disk mirroring and disk duplexing. Both fault-tolerant methods maintain identical copies of the data on two physically separate disks. Where they differ is in the disk controller hardware.

Disk mirroring saves all data to two different disks that are connected to a single controller. Should one of the disks fail, the second disk has an identical copy. However, should the controller fail, neither disk will be available to the system (although the data on them might be intact).

With disk duplexing, on the other hand, each of the two mirrored disks are connected to a different controller. Should a single disk fail, the second disk will have an exact copy of the data. However, should one of the controllers fail, the second controller will continue to maintain the disk—and therefore its data—online.

Opportunities for Optimization

RAID does provide certain advantages in the performance department when it is implemented properly. Outside of the fact that software RAID will run slower than hardware RAID on any system, disk striping with parity (RAID 5) reads faster than disk mirroring and duplexing (RAID 1), but writes slower than striping without parity (RAID 0).

> **TIP:** *RAID 0, striping without parity, should only be used in high-performance networked environments where speed is of the essence. This particularly applies for networked drives where temporary files are large, frequent, and often changing. Examples would be drives where print-spooling files are stored for large print jobs or drives where temporary files are stored for drafting or graphics-rendering applications. Outside of these particular applications, you need to remember that RAID is not redundant or fault tolerant and, if you lose a drive in a RAID 0 array, the entire array is lost.*

There are ways to add additional optimization and fault tolerance to a RAID array, but these methods are restricted to hardware RAID and are out of the scope of this book.

Disaster Recovery

Windows 2000 includes several disaster recovery tools that are far superior to the ones found in Windows NT. In this section, I will look at the Windows 2000 backup program, the emergency repair disk (ERD), and a new feature called Recovery Console.

Windows 2000 Backup

Windows NT has always included a backup program. Many would argue that the backup program that ships with Windows NT is not very functional. The most common complaint about that iteration of the program is that data can only be backed up to tape. If data needs to be backed up to removable media (such as a CD-ROM, Zip, or Jaz drive), third-party programs, which are too expensive for some smaller organizations, are needed.

The Windows 2000 backup program fixes some of these complaints. It now has the ability to back up to tape or to a file. This file can reside on the floppy drive, on any local hard drive, on a network share, or on a removable device. It can also be transferred to a CD-ROM (for this method, a backup file, which is then burned onto the CD-ROM, must be created).

> **NOTE:** *This built-in backup application is written by VERITAS, one of the largest vendors of backup solutions for Windows NT and Windows 2000. If, during your journeys through the Windows 2000 backup program, you find yourself wanting additional features, such as building catalogs on the fly, you can purchase the full-blown backup application, and it will read your existing backup tapes.*

One additional feature that goes with the backup program is the removable storage folders within computer management. Many backup applications work on the concept of building media pools to manage groups of backup tapes. This type of management is necessary when the computer needs to deal with situations where multiple backups may span multiple tapes or media. Most of these backup applications handle this media management within the application itself. Windows 2000 allows this type of media management within the operating system (OS). This also comes in handy because Windows 2000 can recognize many different types of removable media, including CD recordable (CD-R), Zip, and Object Request Broker (ORB) drives. Although this is a great improvement that allows you to create media pools for these types of media, the Windows 2000 backup application often will not back up directly to these media types as they exist within media pools. Instead, it will back up to drive letters, but without compression.

If you are running NTBACKUP with a tape drive, you will need to deal with removable storage to create and mount media pools and tapes for use within the application. Again, this is because NTBACKUP will not run a scheduled backup without first ensuring that the appropriate tape is in the drive.

I have one word of warning with regard to NTBACKUP. It's still not ready for primetime. Let's say that you have flagged your mission-critical files for backup using NTBACKUP and have scheduled the backup to occur every evening. During this configuration process, you must define a specific tape for use for this backup. Because you've scheduled this job to occur on a daily basis, the backup will request the same tape every evening when the schedule kicks off. This is bad because most of us usually have a tape rotation scheme in place where we use different tapes every evening. If the scheduled backup does not receive the requested tape, the backup will not run, and, because logging is virtually nonexistent, it could be days or weeks before you'd notice, and that can become a serious problem. You can customize the process two different ways to get it to work. The first way is to save the backup job as a file, use NTBACKUP to open the file, and make a new scheduled job for every time that a given tape is rotated. An example would be to create a job to use the "Monday" tape every Monday and to create another job to use the "Tuesday" tape every Tuesday. The second way involves the scheduling application itself. When configuring a job for scheduling, NTBACKUP passes a command line to the scheduler that defines everything that needs to be backed up, including the name of the backup job and the backup tape. Create the first scheduled backup to occur every Monday, for example. Then, go into the scheduler, copy the command line, and create a new scheduled event for every other day where a different tape should be used. When you're creating a scheduled task, copy the original command line in place, and change the tape names that appear after the **/n** and **/d** switches. Don't worry. Tape names will be there from the original instance where you used NTBACKUP to create and schedule the job. All you have to do is replace the original tape names with the new tape names, such as "Tuesday" and "Wednesday."

When using removable media, be sure to change the media names to something that makes sense (such as days, weeks, or numbers that are meaningful) so that you can better modify any scheduled backup command lines and also be able to restore from tape without going through your entire library.

If all of this effort seems a bit much to perform backups, you may be right. My personal preference is to purchase a full-blown backup application that isn't quite so restricted when it comes to tape names.

Restoring Active Directory

In the event that the Active Directory database becomes corrupt, or even when an OU or other important objects is accidentally deleted, Microsoft has provided us with a means for restoring the Active Directory relatively easily. Actually, in order to make sure that everything's on the up and up, we begin in the same manner as we would for performing a full tape restore, and that's by booting into the Directory Services Restore Mode. The Directory Services Restore Mode (DSRM) is similar to Safe mode in that it is a clipped version of Windows 2000 that is not running the Active Directory, but is capable of running NTBACKUP and other repair utilities. If you can get into the DSRM, you can restore from tape, and also restore all or part of the Active Directory. In order to enter DSRM, press F8 during system boot when the boot options appear. From there, the boot menu will appear, and you'll have the option to enter the Directory Services Restore Mode. From there, the system will boot and you will be able to access applications. Be aware that Windows 2000 may complain about AD services failing; this is normal, as the AD ins't running in DSRM.

There are two different ways to restore the Active Directory. The first method is simply by restoring the system state from backup. The AD will be restored, and other DCs in the domain will replicate back to the restored AD to fill in any gaps that occurred between the time of backup and the time of restore. If, on the other hand, the problem ends up being replicated to the other DCs in the domain, this type of restore won't do any good because the problem will just end up being replicated back to the restored "good" database. In this situation, you'll need to perform what's known as an Authoritative Restore. This type of restoration method basically flags there stored data as authoritative and allows outbound replication only. Basically, the other "damaged" DCs that are running the AD databases will not replicate to the authoritatively restored DC. This type of authoritative restore is done after you actually restore the system state from tape backup. Through a command-line utility called NTDSUTIL.EXE, you can type in the words "authoritative restore" and press enter. After that, type "help" to display your options. From there you can choose to restore the entire AD database, or only a specific subtree.

ERD

Much like Windows NT, Windows 2000 supports an ERD. The ERD contains information about the specific system that enables an administrator to recover some of the system settings in case of a failure. The information stored on the ERD includes the boot sector and the startup configuration.

Although Windows NT's ERD maintained copies of some of the main registry keys, this is no longer done in Windows 2000. Instead, the DOS subsystem files (autoexec.nt and config.nt) and the setup.log file are copied to the disk. The setup.log file points the recovery process to the location on your disk for the recovery files.

WARNING! Many administrators believe that all ERDs are the same. This is not the case. Each ERD is unique to the server on which it was created. Using an ERD from one server on another server can have disastrous consequences. If an organization has 1,000 servers, it should maintain an ERD for each server.

Every time that a major change is made to the system, such as disk, security, or hardware changes, the ERD should be updated. In the past, the ERD was created using the RDISK utility. In Windows 2000, the backup program performs this task.

NOTE: The ERD is not bootable; you must use it in conjunction with a boot disk.

Recovery Console

One of the coolest tools for recovery introduced with Windows 2000 is the Recovery Console. The Recovery Console allows administrators to boot Windows 2000 into a DOS-like interface, which allows them to reset parts of the registry, repair corrupted files, and modify files (such as the boot.ini file).

The Recovery Console is not installed by default, but it ships on the Windows 2000 installation CD-ROM. The process of installing and using the Recovery Console is described in "Immediate Solutions" in this chapter.

Immediate Solutions

Converting to NTFS 5

To convert to NTFS 5 using Method 1, perform the following steps:

1. Click Start, and select Programs|Accessories|Command Prompt.

2. Type the following:

```
convert volume /FS:NTFS
```

3. Press Enter. A successful conversion is shown in Figure 10.1.

To convert to NTFS 5 using Method 2, perform the following steps:

NOTE: *Method 2 is used if the convert application cannot gain exclusive access to the drive being converted.*

1. Click Start, and select Programs|Accessories|Command Prompt.

2. Type the following:

```
convert volume /FS:NTFS
```

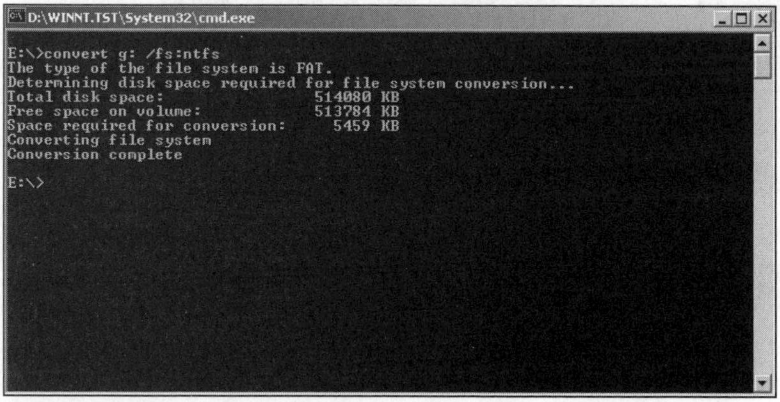

Figure 10.1   A successful conversion.

3. Type "Y", and press Enter (see Figure 10.2).

4. Reboot the server. When the server restarts, it converts the file system (see Figure 10.3).

Figure 10.2   Scheduling a volume conversion upon reboot.

Figure 10.3   Disk conversion after a reboot.

Converting to NTFS 5 Using Verbose Mode

To convert a volume to NTFS 5 in Verbose mode, perform the following steps:

1. Click Start, and select Programs|Accessories|Command Prompt.

2. Type the following:

```
convert volume /FS:NTFS /v
```

3. Press Enter. A successful verbose conversion is shown in Figure 10.4.

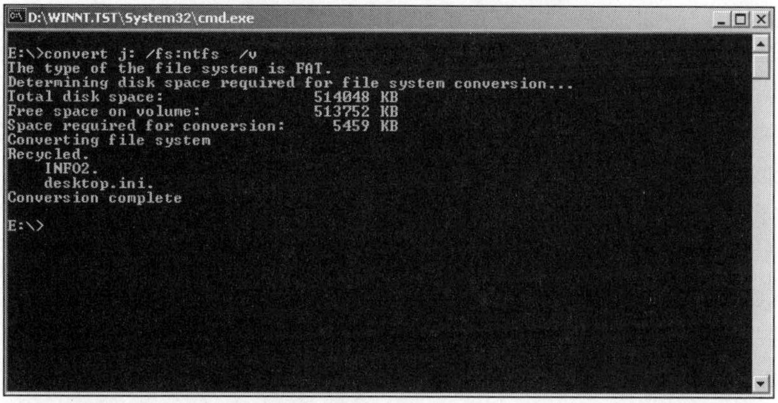

```
D:\WINNT.TST\System32\cmd.exe

E:\>convert j: /fs:ntfs /v
The type of the file system is FAT.
Determining disk space required for file system conversion...
Total disk space:            514048 KB
Free space on volume:        513752 KB
Space required for conversion:   5459 KB
Converting file system
Recycled.
    INFO2.
    desktop.ini.
Conversion complete

E:\>
```

Figure 10.4   A successful verbose conversion.

Working with Compression

A number of management tasks are involved with compressed data. The following sections explore these tasks.

Configuring How Compressed Information Is Displayed

To configure the display of compression information, perform the following steps:

1. Click Start, and select Programs|Accessories|Windows Explorer.

2. Select Tools|Folder Options, and select the View tab.

3. Select the Display Compressed Files And Folders With Alternate Color option.

4. Click OK. All compressed files and folders will now be shown in blue.

Compressing a File

To compress a file, perform the following steps:

1. Click Start, and select Programs|Accessories|Windows Explorer.

2. Right-click the file that you would like compressed, and choose Properties from the pop-up menu.

3. On the General tab, click the Advanced button.

4. In the Compress Or Encrypt Attributes section of the Advanced Attributes window, check the Compress Contents To Save Disk Space checkbox, and click OK.

5. Click OK.

Uncompressing a File

To uncompress a file, perform the following steps:

1. Click Start, and select Programs|Accessories|Windows Explorer.

2. Right-click the file that you would like uncompressed, and choose Properties from the pop-up menu.

3. On the General tab, click the Advanced button.

4. In the Compress Or Encrypt Attributes section of the Advanced Attributes window, clear the Compress Contents To Save Disk Space checkbox, and click OK.

5. Click OK.

Compressing a Folder

To compress a folder, perform the following steps:

1. Click Start, and select Programs|Accessories|Windows Explorer.

2. Right-click the folder that you would like compressed, and choose Properties from the pop-up menu.

3. On the General tab, click the Advanced button.

4. In the Compress Or Encrypt Attributes section of the Advanced Attributes window, check the Compress Contents To Save Disk Space checkbox, and click OK.

5. If you would like to compress only the folder, choose the Apply Changes To This Folder Only option, and click OK.

6. If you would like to compress the folder and its contents, choose the Apply Changes To This Folder, Subfolders, And Files option, and click OK.

Uncompressing a Folder

To uncompress a folder, perform the following steps:

1. Click Start, and select Programs|Accessories|Windows Explorer.

2. Right-click the folder that you would like uncompressed, and choose Properties from the pop-up menu.

3. On the General tab, click the Advanced button.

4. In the Compress Or Encrypt Attributes section of the Advanced Attributes window, clear the Compress Contents To Save Disk Space checkbox, and click OK.

5. If you would like to uncompress only the folder, choose the Apply Changes To This Folder Only option, and click OK.

6. If you would like to uncompress the folder and its contents, choose the Apply Changes To This Folder, Subfolders, And Files option, and click OK.

Compressing a Volume

To compress a volume, perform the following steps:

1. Click Start, and select Programs|Accessories|Windows Explorer.

2. Right-click the disk that you would like compressed, and choose Properties from the pop-up menu.

3. Check the Compress Drive To Save Disk Space checkbox, and click OK.

4. If you would like to compress only the drive, but not the files and folders within the drive, choose the Apply Changes To *Drive*:\ Only option, and click OK.

5. If you would like to compress the entire drive, including all files and folders, choose the Apply Changes To *Drive*:\, Subfolders, And Files option, and click OK.

Uncompressing a Volume

To uncompress a volume, perform the following steps:

1. Click Start, and select Programs|Accessories|Windows Explorer.

2. Right-click the disk that you would like uncompressed, and choose Properties from the pop-up menu.

3. Clear the Compress Drive To Save Disk Space checkbox, and click OK.

4. If you would like to uncompress only the drive, but not the files and folders within the drive, choose the Apply Changes To *Drive*:\ Only option, and click OK.

5. If you would like to uncompress the entire drive, including all files and folders, choose the Apply Changes To *Drive*:\, Subfolders, And Files option, and click OK.

Managing Files and Folders

A number of tasks are involved in managing files and folders. The following sections explore these tasks.

Viewing File and Folder Permissions

To view file and folder permissions, perform the following steps:

1. Click Start, and select Programs|Accessories|Windows Explorer.
2. Select the file or folder for which you would like to view permissions.
3. Right-click the item, and choose Properties from the pop-up menu.
4. Select the Security tab.
5. If you would like to see more advanced properties, click Advanced. Click OK when done.
6. Click OK.

Setting File and Folder Permissions

To set file and folder permissions, perform the following steps:

1. Click Start, and select Programs|Accessories|Windows Explorer.
2. Select the file or folder for which you would like to view permissions.
3. Right-click the item, and choose Properties from the pop-up menu.
4. Select the Security tab, and click Add.
5. Select a group or user, and click Add.
6. Assign any desired permissions to the group or user, and click OK.

Copying Files and Folders

The four methods for copying files and folders are covered next.

To copy a file or folder using Method 1, perform the following steps:

1. Click Start, and select Programs|Accessories|Windows Explorer.
2. Select the files or folders that you would like to copy.
3. Select Edit|Copy.

4. Navigate to where you would like the files copied.

5. Select Edit|Paste.

To copy a file or folder using Method 2, perform the following steps:

1. Click Start, and select Programs|Accessories|Windows Explorer.

2. Select the files or folders that you would like to copy.

3. Press Ctrl+C.

4. Navigate to where you would like the files copied.

5. Press Ctrl+V.

To copy a file or folder using Method 3, perform the following steps:

1. Click Start, and select Programs|Accessories|Windows Explorer.

2. Select the files or folders that you would like to copy.

3. Right-click, drag the files or folders to the destination folder, and release the mouse button.

4. Choose the Copy Here option from the pop-up menu.

To copy a file or folder using Method 4, perform the following steps:

1. Click Start, and select Programs|Accessories|Windows Explorer.

2. Select the files or folders that you would like to copy.

3. Select Edit|Copy To.

4. Navigate to where you would like the files copied, and click OK.

Moving Files and Folders

The two methods for moving files and folders are covered next.

To move a file or folder using Method 1, perform the following steps:

1. Click Start, and select Programs|Accessories|Windows Explorer.

2. Select the files or folders that you would like to move.

3. Select Edit|Move To.

4. Navigate to where you would like the files moved, and click OK.

To move a file or folder using Method 2, perform the following steps:

1. Click Start, and select Programs|Accessories|Windows Explorer.

2. Select the files or folders that you would like to move.

3. Right-click, drag the files or folders to the destination folder, and release the mouse button.

4. Choose Move Here from the pop-up menu.

Creating Folders

The two methods for creating files and folders are covered next.

To create a file or folder using Method 1, perform the following steps:

1. Click Start, and select Programs|Accessories|Windows Explorer.
2. Navigate to the location where you would like the new folder created.
3. Right-click, and select New|Folder.
4. Enter a name for the new folder, and press Enter.

To create a file or folder using Method 2, perform the following steps:

1. Click Start, and select Programs|Accessories|Windows Explorer.
2. Navigate to the location where you would like the new folder created.
3. Select File|New|Folder.
4. Enter a name for the new folder, and press Enter.

Enabling Auditing

To enable auditing, perform the following steps:

1. Click Start, and select Programs|Administrative Tools|Local Security Policy.
2. Navigate to the Audit Policy container in the Local Policies container.
3. Right-click the Audit Object Access policy in the right pane, and choose Security from the pop-up menu.
4. To enable auditing of successful object access, check the Success checkbox.
5. To enable auditing of failed object access, check the Failure checkbox.
6. Click OK.

Setting Up Auditing of Files and Folders

To establish file and folder auditing, perform the following steps:

1. Click Start, and select Programs|Accessories|Windows Explorer.
2. Select the file or folder that you would like to audit.
3. Right-click the file, and choose Properties from the pop-up menu.
4. Select the Security tab, and click Advanced.
5. Select the Auditing tab.
6. Click Add.

7. Select the group or user to audit, and click OK.

8. Choose which components to audit and how to apply them, and click OK.

9. Click OK.

Taking Ownership of Files and Folders

To take ownership of files and folders, perform the following steps:

1. Click Start, and select Programs|Accessories|Windows Explorer.

2. Select the file or folder for which you would like to take ownership.

3. Right-click it, and choose Properties from the pop-up menu.

4. Select the Security tab, and click Advanced.

5. Select the Owner tab.

6. Select a new owner, and click OK.

7. Click OK.

Restoring Deleted Files from the Recycle Bin

To restore files or folders that have been deleted, perform the following steps:

1. Double-click the Recycle Bin icon on the desktop.

2. Select the item that you would like to recover.

3. Right-click the item, and choose Restore from the pop-up menu.

NOTE: You can recover items from other Recycle Bins (assuming that you have the correct permissions) by navigating to the Recycler folder in Windows Explorer and choosing the appropriate Recycle Bin. This folder is hidden by default, and you must change the folder view to show hidden files. Refer to Figure 10.5 for an example.

Customizing the Recycle Bin

To customize Recycle Bin settings, perform the following steps:

1. Right-click the Recycle Bin icon on the desktop, and choose Properties from the pop-up menu.

2. Select whether to configure all the drives together by choosing the Use One Setting For All Drives radio button or to configure the drives individually by choosing the Configure Drives Independently radio button (see Figure 10.6).

3. Make any necessary configuration changes, and click OK when done.

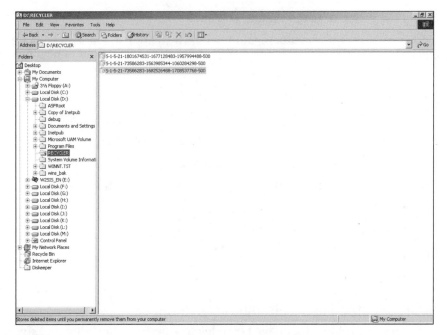

Figure 10.5   The Recycler folder showing multiple recycle bins.

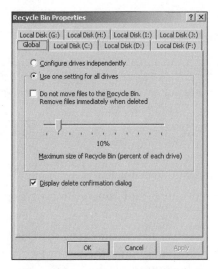

Figure 10.6   The Recycle Bin Properties dialog box.

Working with Quotas

A number of tasks are involved with managing disk quotas; these are discussed next.

Enabling Disk Quotas

To enable disk quotas, perform the following steps:

1. Click Start, and select Programs|Accessories|Windows Explorer.

2. Right-click the disk for which you would like to establish a quota, and choose Properties from the pop-up menu.

3. Select the Quota tab.

4. Check the Enable Quota Management checkbox, as shown in Figure 10.7.

5. Configure any other quota management properties, and click OK when done.

Setting Quotas

To set disk quotas, perform the following steps:

1. Click Start, and select Programs|Accessories|Windows Explorer.

2. Right-click the disk for which you would like to set a quota, and choose Properties from the pop-up menu.

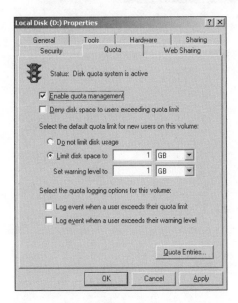

Figure 10.7   Enabling quota management.

3. Select the Quota tab.

4. Click Quota Entries. The Quota Entries console appears (see Figure 10.8).

5. Select Quota|New Quota Entry.

6. Select the user or users, and click Add. Click OK.

7. Select the Limit Disk Space To radio button, and enter a quota limit amount and an amount for when a warning should be sent to the user.

8. Click OK.

Disabling Quotas

To disable disk quotas, perform the following steps:

1. Click Start, and select Programs|Accessories|Windows Explorer.

2. Right-click the disk for which you would like to disable a quota, and choose Properties from the pop-up menu.

3. Select the Quota tab.

4. Clear the Enable Quota Management checkbox.

5. Click OK when done.

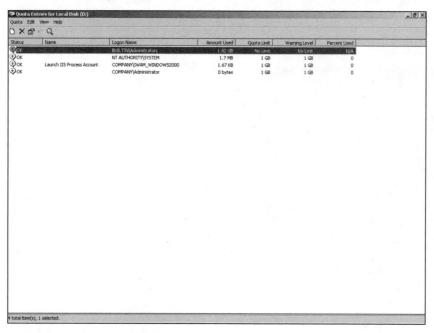

Figure 10.8   The Quota Entries console.

Working with Encryption

A number of tasks are involved in managing encryption. These tasks are discussed in the following sections.

Encrypting a File

To encrypt a file, perform the following steps:

1. Click Start, and select Programs|Accessories|Windows Explorer.
2. Right-click the file that you would like to encrypt, and choose Properties from the pop-up menu.
3. Click Advanced.
4. Check the Encrypt Contents To Secure Data checkbox, and click OK.
5. Click OK.
6. If you want to encrypt the file and its parent folder, choose the Encrypt The File And Parent Folder option, and click OK.
7. If you want to encrypt only the file, choose the Encrypt The File Only option, and click OK.

Decrypting a File

To decrypt a file, perform the following steps:

1. Click Start, and select Programs|Accessories|Windows Explorer.
2. Right-click the file that you would like to decrypt, and choose Properties from the pop-up menu.
3. Click Advanced.
4. Check the Decrypt Contents To Secure Data checkbox, and click OK.
5. Click OK.

Encrypting a Folder

To encrypt a folder, perform the following steps:

1. Click Start, and select Programs|Accessories|Windows Explorer.
2. Right-click the folder that you would like to encrypt, and choose Properties from the pop-up menu.
3. Click Advanced.
4. Check the Encrypt Contents To Secure Data checkbox, and click OK.
5. Click OK.

Decrypting a Folder

To decrypt a folder, perform the following steps:

1. Click Start, and select Programs|Accessories|Windows Explorer.

2. Right-click the folder that you would like to decrypt, and choose Properties from the pop-up menu.

3. Click Advanced.

4. Check the Decrypt Contents To Secure Data checkbox, and click OK.

5. Click OK.

Managing Disks

The following sections explore the tasks involved with disk management.

Analyzing a Disk

To analyze disk fragmentation, perform the following steps:

1. Click Start, and select Programs|Accessories|System Tools|Disk Defragmenter.

2. Select the disk that you would like to analyze, and click Analyze (see Figure 10.9).

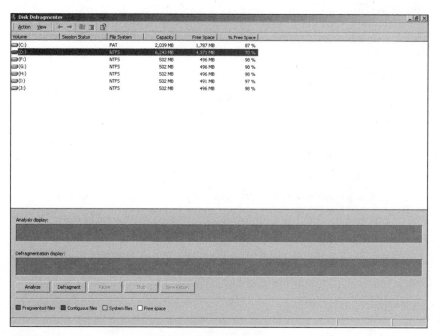

Figure 10.9   The built-in Disk Defragmenter utility.

3. When the analysis is complete, click View Report to view what the analysis turned up.

4. Click Defragment to defragment the drive.

Defragmenting a Disk

To defragment a disk, perform the following steps:

1. Click Start, and select Programs|Accessories|System Tools|Disk Defragmenter.

2. Select the disk that you would like to defragment, and click Defragment.

3. Click Close.

Running Cleanup on a Disk

To run disk cleanup, perform the following steps:

1. Click Start, and select Programs|Accessories|Windows Explorer.

2. Right-click the disk that you would like to clean up, and choose Properties from the pop-up menu.

3. Click Disk Cleanup. The Disk Cleanup Wizard scans the disk.

4. The Disk Cleanup Wizard, shown in Figure 10.10, lists all files that can be deleted to clean up the system. Select any desired files, and click OK.

5. You can view the files that are to be deleted by selecting the files to be deleted and clicking View Files.

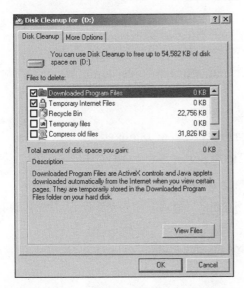

Figure 10.10   The Disk Cleanup Wizard.

6. You can also have the wizard check for unused or rarely used Windows components and installed applications by clicking the More Options tab.

7. Click Yes to confirm the file cleanup.

Formatting a Disk

To format a disk, follow these steps:

1. Click Start, and select Programs|Administrative Tools|Computer Management.

2. In the left pane, select Disk Management.

3. Select the disk that is to be formatted.

4. Select Action|All Tasks|Format.

5. Select the desired formatting parameters, and click OK.

6. Click Yes to confirm the format.

Marking a Disk Active

To mark a disk active, follow these steps:

1. Click Start, and select Programs|Administrative Tools|Computer Management.

2. In the left pane, select Disk Management.

3. Select the disk that is to be marked as active.

4. Select Action|All Tasks|Mark Partition Active.

Assigning Drive Letters

To assign a drive letter to a disk, follow these steps:

1. Click Start, and select Programs|Administrative Tools|Computer Management.

2. In the left pane, select Disk Management.

3. Select the disk for which the drive letter is to be changed.

4. Choose Action|All Tasks|Change Drive Letter And Path.

5. Click Edit.

6. From the Assign A Drive Letter list, select the letter to assign to this disk.

7. Click OK.

8. Click Yes to confirm the drive letter change.

Upgrading from a Basic Disk to a Dynamic Disk

To upgrade from a basic disk to a dynamic disk, follow these steps:

1. Click Start, and select Programs|Administrative Tools|Computer Management.

2. In the left pane, select Disk Management.

3. Select the basic disk that is to be upgraded to a dynamic disk.

4. Select Action|All Tasks|Upgrade To Dynamic Disk.

5. Select the desired disk, and click OK.

Converting from a Dynamic Disk to a Basic Disk

To convert from a dynamic disk to a basic disk, follow these steps:

1. Click Start, and select Programs|Administrative Tools|Computer Management.

2. In the left pane, select Disk Management.

3. Select the dynamic disk that is to be converted to a basic disk.

4. Choose Action|All Tasks|Revert To Basic Disk.

NOTE: You need to be sure that you want to perform this task because converting a dynamic disk back to a basic disk may result in the loss of other features. Plus, you'll need to back up or remove all data and volumes from the drive before performing this conversion because if the drive had any dynamic disk functions applied to it, all data on those drives will be lost during the downgrade. For example, after completing this process, you can only create partitions and logical drives on the basic disk; you can't create volumes, which is a dynamic disk function.

Managing Partitions

A number of issues are involved with partition management in Windows 2000. The following sections explore these tasks.

Creating a Primary Partition

To create a primary partition, follow these steps:

1. Click Start, and select Programs|Administrative Tools|Computer Management.

2. In the left pane, select Disk Management.

3. Select the disk where a primary partition is to be created.

Figure 10.11   The Create Partition Wizard.

4. Select Action|All Tasks|Create Partition. The Create Partition Wizard will appear, as shown in Figure 10.11.

5. Click Next.

6. Ensure that the Primary Partition radio button is selected, and click Next.

7. Enter the amount of disk space that is to be allocated to this partition, and click Next.

8. Decide whether to assign the partition a drive letter, mount it as a folder, or not assign it a drive letter on this window. Click Next.

9. If this partition is to be formatted, select Format This Partition With The Following Settings, choose the desired settings, and click Next. If not, select Do Not Format This Partition, and click Next.

10. Click Finish.

Deleting a Primary Partition

To delete a primary partition, follow these steps:

1. Click Start, and select Programs|Administrative Tools|Computer Management.

2. In the left pane, select Disk Management.

3. Select the primary partition that is to be deleted.

4. Select All Tasks|Delete Partition.

5. Click Yes to confirm the deletion.

Creating an Extended Partition

To create an extended partition, follow these steps:

1. Click Start, and select Programs|Administrative Tools|Computer Management.

2. In the left pane, select Disk Management.

3. Select the disk where a primary partition is to be created.

4. Select Action|All Tasks|Create Partition.

5. Click Next.

6. Ensure that the Extended Partition radio button is selected, and click Next.

7. Enter the amount of disk space that is to be allocated to this partition, and click Next.

8. Click Finish.

Creating a Logical Partition

To create a logical partition, follow these steps:

1. Click Start, and select Programs|Administrative Tools|Computer Management.

2. In the left pane, select Disk Management.

3. Select the extended partition where a logical partition is to be created.

4. Select Action|All Tasks|Create Partition.

5. Click Next.

6. Click Next.

7. Enter the amount of disk space that is to be allocated to this partition, and click Next.

8. Decide whether to assign the partition a drive letter, mount it as a folder, or not assign it a drive letter on this window. Click Next.

9. If this partition is to be formatted, select Format This Partition With The Following Settings, choose the desired settings, and click Next. If not, select Do Not Format This Partition, and click Next.

10. Click Finish.

Deleting a Logical Partition

To delete a logical partition, follow these steps:

1. Click Start, and select Programs|Administrative Tools|Computer Management.

2. In the left pane, select Disk Management.

3. Select the logical partition that is to be deleted.

4. Select Action|All Tasks|Delete Logical Partition.

5. Click Yes to confirm the deletion.

Deleting an Extended Partition

To delete an extended partition, follow these steps:

1. Click Start, and select Programs|Administrative Tools|Computer Management.

2. In the left pane, select Disk Management.

3. Select the extended partition that is to be deleted.

NOTE: *If the extended partition contains any logical partitions, they must be deleted before the Disk Management application will allow you to delete the extended partition.*

---

4. Select Action|All Tasks|Delete Partition.

5. Click Yes to confirm the deletion.

Managing Volumes

A number of issues are involved with volume management in Windows 2000. The following sections explore these tasks.

Creating a Simple Volume

To create a simple volume, follow these steps:

1. Click Start, and select Programs|Administrative Tools|Computer Management.

2. In the left pane, select Disk Management.

3. Select the dynamic disk on which the simple volume is to be created.

4. Select Action|All Tasks|Create Volume. The Create Volume Wizard will appear, as shown in Figure 10.12.

5. Click Next.

6. In the Select Volume Type window, shown in Figure 10.13, ensure that the Simple Volume radio button is selected, and click Next.

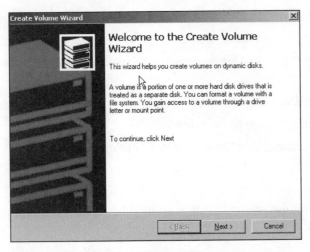

Figure 10.12   The Create Volume Wizard.

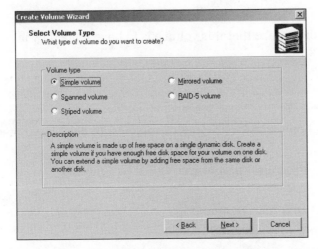

Figure 10.13   The Select Volume Type window.

7. Enter the amount of disk space that is to be allocated to this volume in the
    Size section, and click Next.

8. Decide whether to assign the partition a drive letter, mount it as a folder, or
    not assign it a drive letter on this window. Click Next.

9. If this partition is to be formatted, select Format This Partition With The
    Following Settings, choose the desired settings, and click Next. If not,
    select Do Not Format This Partition, and click Next.

10. Click Finish.

Extending a Simple Volume

To extend a simple volume, follow these steps:

1. Click Start, and select Programs|Administrative Tools|Computer Management.

2. In the left pane, select Disk Management.

3. Select the simple volume that is to be extended.

4. Select Action|All Tasks|Extend Volume. The Extend Volume Wizard will appear.

5. Click Next.

6. To add a disk to the volume, select the disk in the All Available Dynamic Disks section, and click Add.

TIP: *If the disk that the volume is created on has free space, you can use that disk to extend the partition. In this situation, an extra disk is not needed.*

---

7. Enter the amount of disk space that this volume is to be extended by in the Size section, and click Next.

8. Click Finish.

Deleting a Volume

The method outlined here holds true for all types of volumes. To delete a volume, follow these steps:

1. Click Start, and select Programs|Administrative Tools|Computer Management.

2. In the left pane, select Disk Management.

3. Select the volume that is to be deleted.

4. Select Action|All Tasks|Delete Volume.

5. Click Yes to confirm the deletion.

Creating a Spanned Volume

To create a spanned volume, follow these steps:

1. Click Start, and select Programs|Administrative Tools|Computer Management.

2. In the left pane, select Disk Management.

3. Select the dynamic disk on which the spanned volume is to be created.

4. Select Action|All Tasks|Create Volume.

5. Click Next.

6. In the Select Volume Type window (refer to Figure 10.13), ensure that the Spanned Volume radio button is selected, and click Next.

7. Select one or more dynamic disks from the All Available Dynamic Disks section, and click Add.

8. Enter the amount of disk space that is to be allocated to this volume in the Size section, and click Next. This can be configured independently on each dynamic disk.

9. Decide whether to assign the partition a drive letter, mount it as a folder, or not assign it a drive letter on this window. Click Next.

10. If this partition is to be formatted, select Format This Partition With The Following Settings, choose the desired settings, and click Next. If not, select Do Not Format This Partition, and click Next.

11. Click Finish.

Extending a Spanned Volume

To extend a spanned volume, follow these steps:

1. Click Start, and select Programs|Administrative Tools|Computer Management.

2. In the left pane, select Disk Management.

3. Select the spanned volume that is to be extended.

4. Select Action|All Tasks|Extend Volume. The Extend Volume Wizard will appear.

5. Click Next.

6. To add a disk to the volume, select the disk in the All Available Dynamic Disks section, and click Add.

7. Enter the amount of disk space that this volume is to be extended by in the Size section, and click Next.

8. Click Finish.

Creating a Striped Volume

To create a striped volume, follow these steps:

1. Click Start, and select Programs|Administrative Tools|Computer Management.

2. In the left pane, select Disk Management.

3. Select the dynamic disk on which the striped volume is to be created.

4. Select Action|All Tasks|Create Volume.

5. Click Next.

6. In the Select Volume Type window (refer to Figure 10.13), ensure that the Striped Volume radio button is selected, and click Next.

7. Select one or more dynamic disks from the All Available Dynamic Disks section, and click Add.

8. Enter the amount of disk space that is to be allocated to this volume in the Size section, and click Next. This size is for the entire volume with equal amounts on each disk.

9. Decide whether to assign the partition a drive letter, mount it as a folder, or not assign it a drive letter on this window. Click Next.

10. If this partition is to be formatted, select Format This Partition With The Following Settings, choose the desired settings, and click Next. Otherwise, select Do Not Format This Partition, and click Next.

11. Click Finish.

Creating a Mirrored Volume

To create a mirrored volume, follow these steps:

1. Click Start, and select Programs|Administrative Tools|Computer Management.

2. In the left pane, select Disk Management.

3. Select the dynamic disk that is to be used to create the mirrored volume.

4. Select Action|All Tasks|Create Volume.

5. Click Next.

6. In the Select Volume Type window (refer to Figure 10.13), ensure that the Mirrored Volume radio button is selected, and click Next.

7. Select one dynamic disk from the All Available Dynamic Disks section, and click Add.

8. Enter the amount of disk space that is to be allocated to this volume in the Size section, and click Next.

9. Decide whether to assign the partition a drive letter, mount it as a folder, or not assign it a drive letter on this window. Click Next.

10. If this partition is to be formatted, select Format This Partition With The Following Settings, choose the desired settings, and click Next. If not, select Do Not Format This Partition, and click Next.

11. Click Finish.

Adding a Mirror to an Existing Simple Volume

To add a mirror to an existing simple volume, follow these steps:

1. Click Start, and select Programs|Administrative Tools|Computer Management.

2. In the left pane, select Disk Management.

3. Select the simple volume that is to be mirrored.

4. Select Action|All Tasks|Add Mirror.

5. Select the dynamic disk that this volume is to be mirrored with, and click Add Mirror.

Breaking a Mirrored Volume

To break a mirrored volume, follow these steps:

1. Click Start, and select Programs|Administrative Tools|Computer Management.

2. In the left pane, select Disk Management.

3. Select the mirrored volume that is to be broken.

4. Select Action|All Tasks|Break Mirror.

5. Click Yes to confirm the breaking of the mirror.

Recovering from a Failed Mirror Volume

Should one of the volumes in the mirrored volume fail, the notification shown in Figure 10.14 will be displayed. To recover the mirror, follow these steps:

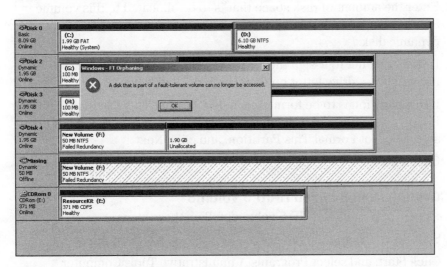

Figure 10.14   The Failed Disk Notification window.

1. Shut down the system, replace the faulty disk, and boot up the system.

2. Click Start, and select Programs|Administrative Tools|Computer Management.

3. In the left pane, select Disk Management.

4. Select one of the disks in the mirrored volume.

5. Right-click the disk, and select Reactivate Disk from the pop-up menu.

Creating a RAID 5 Volume

To create a RAID 5 volume, follow these steps:

1. Click Start, and select Programs|Administrative Tools|Computer Management.

2. In the left pane, select Disk Management.

3. Select the dynamic disk on which the simple volume is to be created.

4. Select Action|All Tasks|Create Volume.

5. Click Next.

6. In the Select Volume Type window (refer to Figure 10.13), ensure that the RAID 5 Volume radio button is selected, and click Next.

7. Select two or more dynamic disks from the All Available Dynamic Disks section, and click Add.

NOTE: *At least three disks must be selected for a RAID 5 volume.*

---

8. Enter the amount of disk space that is to be allocated to this volume in the Size section, and click Next. This can be configured independently on each dynamic disk.

9. Decide whether to assign the partition a drive letter, mount it as a folder, or not assign it a drive letter on this window. Click Next.

10. If this partition is to be formatted, select Format This Partition With The Following Settings, choose the desired settings, and click Next. If not, select Do Not Format This Partition, and click Next.

11. Click Finish.

Recovering from a Failed RAID 5 Volume

To recover from a failed RAID 5 volume, follow these steps:

1. Shut down the system, replace the faulty disk, and boot the system.

2. Click Start, and select Programs|Administrative Tools|Computer Management.

3. In the left pane, select Disk Management.

4. Select one of the disks in the RAID 5 volume.

5. Right-click the disk, and select Reactivate Disk from the pop-up menu.

Importing Disks from Another System

In some instances, you will need to remove a hard drive from one system and place it on another. With Windows 2000 and dynamic disks, the partition information is stored on the drives. For this reason, the drives will need to be imported. Figure 10.15 shows how foreign disks appear in the Disk Management applet. To import disks from another system, perform the following steps:

1. Click Start, and select Programs|Administrative Tools|Computer Management.

2. In the left pane, select Disk Management.

3. Select the disk that is to be imported, and select Action|All Tasks|Import Foreign Disks.

4. Select the disk(s) to import, and click OK.

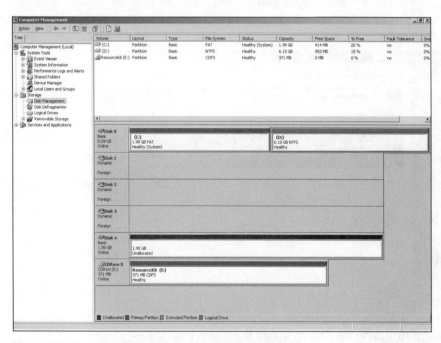

Figure 10.15   Importing disks in Disk Management.

Managing Backup and Recovery

A number of issues are involved with backing up and recovering a Windows 2000 system. The following sections explore these tasks.

Backing Up the System

To back up the system, follow these steps:

1. Click Start, and select Programs|Accessories|System Tools|Backup.

2. Click Backup Wizard. The Backup Wizard will appear.

3. Click Next.

4. Choose one of the three options: Backup Everything, Selected Files, or System State.

5. Click Next.

6. Select the backup media type and the corresponding media or file name, and click Next.

7. As shown in Figure 10.16, click Finish to start the backup, or click Advanced to select the backup type, verify the backup, use hardware compression (if available), append or replace existing data, create a label for the backup set and media, and choose whether to schedule the backup.

8. When the backup is complete, click Close.

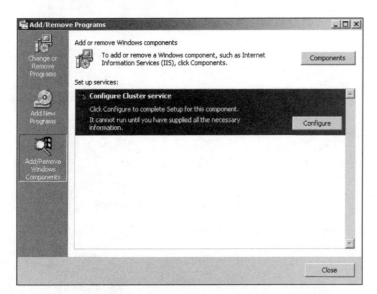

Figure 10.16   Using the Backup wizard to perform a backup.

Recovering the System

To recover the system, follow these steps:

1. Click Start, and select Programs|Accessories|System Tools|Backup.

2. Click Restore Wizard. The Restore Wizard will appear.

3. Click Next.

4. Select the backup set to restore, and click Next.

5. Click Finish to start the restoration, or click Advanced to select the restoration location and choose whether to replace files.

6. Click Close.

Creating an ERD

To create an ERD, follow these steps:

1. Click Start, and select Programs|Accessories|System Tools|Backup.

2. Click ERD.

3. Make sure that you have a formatted, blank disk in your floppy drive.

4. If you would also like to back up the registry information to the Repair folder on the hard drive, check the appropriate checkbox.

5. Click OK.

6. Click OK again to begin creating the disks.

Using an ERD

To use an ERD, follow these steps:

1. Start the Windows 2000 installation process.

2. On the Welcome to Setup window, press R to repair the current Windows 2000 installation.

3. Press R to recover using the ERD.

4. Press M for manual selection of recovery options or F for fast recovery (fast recovery selects all the options).

5. If you have the ERD, press Enter.

6. Insert the disk, and press Enter.

Installing the Recovery Console

To install the Recovery Console, follow these steps:

1. Insert the Windows 2000 CD-ROM.

2. Click Start, and select Run.

3. Type "*CD-ROMDrive*:\i386\winnt32\cmdcons", where *CD-ROMDrive* is the drive letter assigned to the CD-ROM drive, and click OK.

4. Click Yes to install the Recovery Console.

Using the Recovery Console

To use the Recovery Console, follow these steps:

1. Start the Windows 2000 installation process.

2. On the Welcome to Setup window, press R to repair the current Windows 2000 installation.

3. Press C to recover using the Recovery Console.

4. Click OK.

5. Click OK.

6. Close the Control Panel.

7. Click Start, and select Programs|Administrative Tools|Cluster Administrator.

8. In the left pane, select the node where diagnostic logging is to be enabled, and select File|Stop Cluster Service.

9. In the left pane, select the node where diagnostic logging is to be enabled, and select File|Start Cluster Service.

Chapter 11

Local and Small Business Networking

In Depth

Entire books have been devoted to the subject of connecting servers to a network and the different protocols that can be used to make these connections. For this reason, this chapter will be more of an overview than a complete description.

Meet the Protocols

Although Windows 2000 supports many third-party protocols, four main protocols are supported out of the box. These include the following:

- Transmission Control Protocol/Internet Protocol (TCP/IP)
- NWLink Internet Packet Exchange/Sequenced Packet Exchange/Network Basic Input/Output System (IPX/SPX/NetBIOS) Compatible Transport Protocol
- NetBIOS Enhanced User Interface (NetBEUI)
- AppleTalk

Each of these protocols is discussed in the following sections.

TCP/IP

The most popular protocol currently used in networks today is TCP/IP. The Internet is the main reason that this is the most used protocol in the world. The Internet would not be what it is today without TCP/IP.

TCP/IP is the most complex, and therefore the slowest, protocol covered in this chapter. It is also the most complex to configure. As you'll see, some of the services that are available to you with Windows 2000 make configuring TCP/IP simpler and more manageable.

Although each network operating system originally had its own protocol, all now rely on TCP/IP (including NetWare and Apple Computer and Macintosh). With the popularization of the Internet, TCP/IP has even been adopted as a default protocol in the Novell NetWare world, which relied on IPX/SPX for many years.

NWLink (IPX/SPX)

Until a few years ago, Novell NetWare was the market leader in network operating systems. The protocol used by NetWare is known as IPX/SPX. This protocol, for the most part, is self-addressing and can still be used in large routed networks. It's also extremely fast.

When Microsoft decided to go against NetWare in the network operating system market, it knew that it had to support the IPX/SPX protocol. Companies are much more likely to convert from one network operating system to another if both can operate together for a time. Not surprisingly, NetWare did not give Microsoft access to the IPX/SPX protocol. Microsoft, therefore, had to come up with its own version of the protocol. This version of the protocol is known as *NWLink* or *NWLink IPX/SPX/NetBIOS Compatible Transport Protocol.*

NetBEUI

Microsoft adapted an IBM-designed protocol to work with its operating systems in small network environments. That protocol is NetBEUI. Although this protocol is extremely fast and configures itself automatically, it does have limitations. For one, it is chatty. Because it is self-configuring, it has to communicate continuously with all other systems on the network. Also, this self-configuration is partially done using broadcasts. Because of these broadcasts, NetBEUI cannot be used on a wide area network (by default, routers do not route broadcasts from one network to another). If you need to install a network between a small number of computers, all you need to do is connect the computers to the network and install NetBEUI.

NOTE: *Once upon a time, it was necessary to run NetBIOS in order to accomplish peer-to-peer networking in the Microsoft world. This was because each computer was known by a NetBIOS name, and it was necessary to run the NetBIOS name in order to find and communicate across the network. This is no longer necessary in a pure Windows 2000 network. Windows 2000 networking will automatically load TCP/IP. TCP/IP communicates through unique TCP/IP addresses that are aliased fully qualified domain names (FQDNs). Unlike previous versions of Windows, Windows 2000 masks these FQDNs in such a manner that they look and act the same as NetBIOS names while still having all of the qualities of an FQDN. This effectively allows you to communicate in a peer-to-peer network without loading NetBIOS. In larger environments, NetBIOS is far from gone, especially in situations where different versions of Windows are running or when an application server uses NetBIOS as its protocol for communications. In many peer-to-peer and smaller networks, however, you'll only need to run TCP/IP on your Windows 2000 computers.*

Additional Protocols

Several additional protocols ship with Windows 2000. The one covered in this chapter, however, is AppleTalk. AppleTalk is the protocol invented by Apple Computer to work with its Macintosh line of computers.

When Microsoft originally designed File and Print Services for Macintosh, it approached Apple Computer and got Apple's permission to design Windows NT to operate like a Macintosh server. In fact, a Windows NT (or 2000) Server running services for the Macintosh is 100 percent compatible with a Macintosh server.

TCP/IP for the Small Business

Before a system can use TCP/IP to communicate with another system on the local network, two pieces of information are required: the IP address and the subnet mask. If the same system needs to communicate outside the local network, it must do so through a default gateway, which can be a router or computer that acts as the door through which all communications must go. The IP address and the subnet mask are used to pinpoint the computer on the network in much the same way that a street address and ZIP code are used to pinpoint a building in a city. Originally, the IP address, in combination with the subnet mask, had to be unique in the world. This is to say that no two IP addresses could ever be the same, or there was no way to ensure that the connections were being made to the correct computer. With more modern technology and engineering practices, this is now much less of a concern or problem.

Subnets

TCP/IP operates within what are known as subnets. Each subnet makes its own LAN, and can also be compared to a room in a house. Each computer on the network has its own TCP/IP address and subnet mask, so these rooms are boundaries where outbound communications and data are funneled through a single device acting as a gateway to other subnets and the Internet. In order to accomplish this, each computer on the subnet must be configured with the IP address of the gateway device. Essentially, it must know where the door to the room is. This gateway is usually a router or some other device, such as a computer or modem, that is configured to act as a router.

TCP/IP communications contain IP address information about the source and destination computers, and many routers and routing devices can be configured to replace the source computer IP address with the router IP address. In the Microsoft world, this is called Network Address Translation, and it's used not only for security purposes, but also to ensure that systems behind that router don't need a globally unique TCP/IP address. It's almost like posting guards at the door to ensure that everything going through that door looks presentable. This allows the computers in the room to be assigned any IP address as long as they do not duplicate within the subnet. This is because all outbound communications at the door (also known as a gateway or router) can be configured to change the source IP address to the IP address of the router.

Gateways and Routers

With NAT in place, routers, in turn, can also have addresses that may be duplicated somewhere in the world. Just like your home where you can have rooms within rooms, each room can have its own door, represented by a router. These doors within the house may be identical to other doors in other homes, but there cannot be duplicates within the home itself. Ultimately, you reach the front door to the home, where the street address is unique in the world. If each door in the house were represented by a router, only the IP address assigned to the router that's at the front door needs to be unique in the entire world. It works in just the same way as the address to your home that is represented by a number, street, city, state, and ZIP code. These doors can be identical to other doors in other houses, and there is some duplication allowed within the house, as shown in Figure 11.1, but duplicates must always be safely represented behind a nonduplicate door within the house. Again, if you look at Figure 11.1, you'll see a house where the bathroom addresses and the closet addresses are the same. This is allowable only because the addresses assigned to each bedroom door are different, and

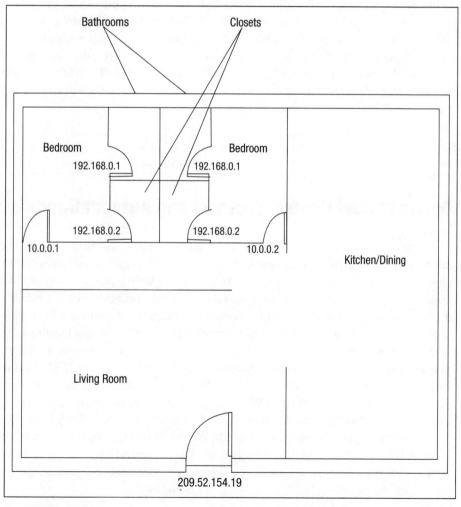

Figure 11.1 TCP/IP configuration. Each room is a subnet; each door is a router or gateway.

those doors will safely change these duplicate addresses to their own. In the computer world, the front door—the one with the unique street address—is the same as a router and must have a unique IP address in all the world. Each room that has a door is a subnet or network, and each door is a gateway or router, and NAT must be configured in each router in order to allow these types of duplications to occur. Without NAT, we would be required to purchase and register a globally unique TCP/IP address for every computer and router that needs to access the Internet.

You'll also notice in Figure 11.1 that the addresses for the bathrooms and closets start with 192.168. This is for a specific purpose. The people who created and designed TCP/IP designated several reserved IP addresses to handle very specific uses. One of these reserved address blocks is the 192.168.xxx.xxx range. Other address blocks are 10.0.0.0 and 172.16.0.0. These addresses, by definition, are not routable. What this means is that TCP/IP data that contains the source information from a computer with an address in this range will not go beyond the router. If your router is not configured to replace outbound communications addresses (this is called Network Address Translation, or NAT), you've effectively isolated all computers on this subnet because data will not go in or out of that particular door.

NOTE: *Incidentally, another reserved address is 127.0.0.1. This address is reserved for internal loopback. You can use the **PING** command on this address to determine if your TCP/IP is functioning properly.*

Dynamic Host Control Protocol and Autoconfiguration

Look again at Figure 11.1, and consider that several hundred computers could reside within each room or subnet. In order to ensure and maintain unique IP addresses, you will need to assign addresses to each computer manually and make sure that, when the computer is moved to a different subnet, the IP address changes appropriately. As you can imagine, this can become something of a nightmare in documentation and maintenance. Wouldn't it be great if you could configure a program to hand out IP addresses to computers on the network automatically and then configure the network with reservations for computers and systems that need specific IP addresses? Dynamic Host Control Protocol (DHCP) is a service that can be run on Windows NT or Windows 2000 server that will do this. Many small companies that run Windows 2000 don't require DHCP because of a new feature called Automatic Private IP Addressing (APIPA), which I will discuss in a moment. If you are running multiple Windows platforms, purchasing a Windows NT or Windows 2000 Server system that will run DHCP is an investment well worth the effort to avoid IP configuration conflicts and problems. DHCP basics are discussed in "DHCP in the Small Business."

When you configure the TCP/IP protocol on Windows clients, you need to enter either IP address information (usually a TCP/IP address, subnet mask, and a connection. You also have the ability to share network connections, even when the connection does not go to the Internet. The process is done by configuring the local network card to forward or route information to other network connections on the computer. A few details are associated with ICS that you should be aware of prior to configuring it. The ICS computer must be using the IP address 192.168.0.1, and all network computers must be referring to this same address as their default gateway. If these computers are using DHCP for IP address configuration, you'll need to add a gateway entry on the DHCP server showing 192.168.0.1 as the gateway server. If the networked computers are using the APIPA feature of Windows 2000, you'll need to add a gateway address in the advanced TCP/IP settings for each computer on the network. This does require some footwork, but not nearly as much as if IP configuration were manual.

TCP/IP Tools

You can use several tools to troubleshoot and find information about TCP/IP. All of these tools are command-line utilities and are accessed through a command prompt. The following shows the syntax of the utility, followed by a description of when and how to use it:

- *PING 127.0.0.1*—Tests to see if TCP/IP on the local computer is functioning properly. This does not mean that there might not be problems, but, for the most part (and especially in a small business network), if you receive a response, TCP/IP is working on the local computer.

- *PING NNN.NNN.NNN.NNN*—Tests to see if the TCP/IP protocol is working on another computer. You'll need to replace *NNN.NNN.NNN.NNN* with the IP address of the computer that you want to test. For the most part, if you're running an IP network, and you receive positive results from this test, it's safe to say that the tested computer is up and running.

- *TRACERT NNN.NNN.NNN.NNN*—Tests to see if the IP protocol is working on another computer, which is similar to **PING**. It will also display every gateway and router that is between the local computer and the computer indicated by *NNN.NNN.NNN.NNN*.

- *IPCONFIG*—Displays the current IP address configuration. Several different options (called switches) are available with this utility to display or perform certain tasks. The **/all** switch displays detailed IP configuration information. The **/release** switch removes IP address information, and the **/renew** switch will allow reconfiguration. You can also release and renew IP configuration for specific network adapter cards. More information on IPCONFIG is covered in Chapter 16. **IPCONFIG /?** displays all available options.

- *NETSTAT*—Displays active TCP/IP connections. With the **–r** switch, it shows the current routing table. A routing table is a list of routes that can

default gateway) or select an option that allows the computer to re
information from a DHCP server. With Windows 2000 Server and P
computers, if no DHCP server is available, the system will automatic
ure a nonroutable IP address within the 169.254.0.0-169.254.255.255 add
This feature is called Automatic Private IP Addressing.

NOTE: *Every network card made has a unique MAC address that is similar to a serial number. TCP/IP v6*
address as the local computer TCP/IP address, and the router provides subnet and network pieces of the
address. This eliminates the need for DHCP and manually or computer-generated unique IP addresses. B
Windows 2000 uses standard TCP/IP, but IP v6 is supported and must be configured.

Getting Out to the Internet

Many individual users have had no problems connecting to the Intern
phone dial-up, Integrated Services Digital Network (ISDN), digital sub
(DSL), digital satellite, or cable. These methods usually involve a l
nected modem or device of some sort and a process that opens the c
or, in the case of DSL, satellite, and cable, the connection is always
need only begin to surf the Web. The overriding problem has been s
single-user connectivity into the multiuser needs of a business. For
frustration has been centered around the fact that you could share fil
drives, data, printers, and even fax capabilities on the network, but yo
share the device that connected you to the Internet. The result was
need to equip individual computers with connectivity devices or to pu
pensive routing equipment and dedicated lines to enable the netwo
use a single device as a gateway to the Internet. As home users, home of
telecommuters have increased the demand for affordable Internet co
the methods and technologies for business connectivity have become
more available with greater access and affordability.

One of these technologies is a result of evolving methods and greater a
An example is the ability to purchase a DSL connection with a certain
at a fraction of the cost of a dedicated line. This same technology exist
users, but the difference is in the device. Instead of using a DSL mode
necting a single computer to the Internet, a DSL router can be instal
lows networked computers to refer to the DSL router as a default gat
allowing network access to the Internet.

Another technology is exclusive to Windows 2000, and that is called Int
nection Sharing (ICS). ICS allows any computer that has access to the
share its Internet connection with other computers on the network. C
puters on the network refer to the ICS computer as their default gat
voila! Everything works. ICS will work for any computer running any i

be used by the system to communicate with particular computers on the network. In this case, the routing table should consist of routes for 127.0.0.1, the local default gateway, and several other addresses and aliases that your computer will respond to. Again, more information is covered in Chapter 16, and **NETSTAT /?** displays all available options.

DHCP in a Small Business

As I discussed before, manually assigning and maintaining TCP/IP addresses can be a time-consuming chore. If two systems on the same network or subnet use the same IP address, either one of them will fail, or both will cause errors. Also, if the subnet mask is wrong on a single computer on the network, it will not be able to communicate properly with other systems in its network. Finally, if the default gateway address is wrong, the workstation will not be able to communicate with systems on remote networks. IP address configuration also has many additional options to define different types of servers that the computer might require access to in certain situations. Problems can also occur if the IP addresses for these specialized servers are incorrect.

When you're configuring a few machines, making such an error is not likely, but, in time, it can still grow to be painful. When you're configuring several hundred or thousand computers, the likelihood of an error becomes increasingly more probable. Fixing errors on such a large network can also be extremely difficult (imagine trying to find the two computers that share the same IP address on your network of several thousand computers).

To allow administrators to automate this task, *DHCP* was created. As the name says, this protocol dynamically assigns IP addresses to any system that asks, assuming that the system is authorized and is asking correctly. Not only will DHCP assign the requesting workstation an IP address, but it will also specify the subnet mask, default gateway, DNS servers, and any other servers and services that the administrator configures it to. As shown in "Immediate Solutions," the configuration of DHCP requires an understanding of scopes and leases. A *scope* is the range (or ranges) of IP addresses that the DHCP server is allowed to assign to computers. A *lease* is also normally assigned when the server assigns the IP address information. This lease is much like that on a car. The address is assigned to the client for the duration of the lease. When the lease expires, the client must either renew the lease or return it. At that point, the computer loses its TCP/IP address and will no longer be able to communicate on the network using TCP/IP.

DHCP deals with three types of scopes: regular scopes, superscopes, and multicast scopes. As mentioned, a scope is a boundary that is set on the IP addresses that can be assigned by the DHCP server. A *superscope* is a "scope of scopes." It is a scope that is made up of two or more scopes that are in the same network space.

Finally, a *multicast scope* is used for multicasting information to systems. Multicasting is the process of sending a single stream of data to multiple machines. Examples of this include streaming audio and video from the Internet and cloning multiple machines on the network simultaneously. You are unlikely to use superscopes and multicast scopes in a small business environment, so they will be covered in Chapter 12.

Network Resources with Security and Style

You should be aware of additional features available with Windows 2000 Professional and Server if you are in a small to midsize business. These deal primarily with user requests that happen in any type of company of any size, so we will discuss them in some detail here.

Distributed File System

Distributed File System (DFS) is a feature that is available only with Windows 2000 Server. It does not require Active Directory. DFS allows users to view data residing on multiple computers as a single share on their computer. This makes it easier for the user to access data and information, and it also allows for some loose fault tolerance. As an administrator, you'll be tempted to use DFS when you run out of disk space on a server and cannot upgrade or add another drive to the same system. Instead, you can purchase a new drive or simply configure DFS and add a shared folder from another server to the overall mix, thus increasing available drive space. Theoretically, you can develop a DFS scheme that will optimize performance by manually splitting frequently accessed data across multiple servers in such a manner that the resource loads are balanced across these servers. DFS has many other uses in larger enterprise environments, which we will discuss in Chapter 12. In the meantime, let's discuss some applicable details here.

As you can imagine, you need to know some details about DFS prior to implementing it. First, in order for the network computers to view DFS shares as a single entity, they'll need to be either Windows 2000, Windows NT 4 Service Pack 3 (SP3), or Windows 9x. For Windows 95, you'll need to download the DFS client, and you'll need to do the same for Windows 98 or NT if you're running DFS in an Active Directory domain. Second, you do have the capability of integrating Windows NT 4 shares into Windows 2000 DFS, but only when you're not dealing with a domain environment.

DFS structurally may seem similar in nature to Active Directory structure. This is because shares can be grafted into what appears to be a single DFS tree. Each branch can be a share residing on a Windows 2000, Windows NT, Windows 9x, or NetWare computer. The only hitch is that the data must be available using a universal naming convention (UNC) path. You might better recognize a UNC path by example, such as \\servername\sharename. Each branch is grafted onto the DFS root folder, which resides on a host server that is either standalone or a member of a domain. Again, we'll talk about domain DFS in Chapter 12.

Encrypting File System

Encryption has been used in wars for many years so that the armies could communicate in a manner that was secure from prying eyes and ears. With the use of computers, encryption algorithms have become more and more complex and difficult to break or decode. For any environment, Encrypting File System (EFS) can be either completely overkill or ideal for the situation.

Basically, take a document, and encrypt it. At this point, anybody who can figure out the encryption code can decrypt it. Instead, take the document and encrypt it with your own specific encryption algorithm. This is more secure, but anyone who knows your algorithm can still decrypt the document. The most secure means of encrypting is to encrypt a document with your specific encryption algorithm and also to encrypt it with the algorithm assigned to the person who is going to decrypt it. This way, the document is encrypted once specifically for you and then again specifically for the person who ultimately will read it. Each encryption algorithm is known as a key. Your personal encryption algorithm is your private key, and the target person's algorithm is known as a public key. Your private key is yours and cannot be shared, and a person's public key is given to others for them to encrypt to that person. This is how applications such as Pretty Good Privacy (PGP) work.

EFS works similarly, but instead of having the option of encrypting data to someone else, the system automatically encrypts data with your own public key. This can be good, and it can be bad. This is good because users can be assured that they will be the only person who can decrypt the data. This is bad because if the user leaves the company, changes accounts (such as during a domain restructure or migration), or has a fit, you may never see that data again. It's also safe to assume that if it's important enough to encrypt, it's pretty important to the company. In the event that something like this happens, EFS does have one safety fallback, which is known as the recovery agent. I'll discuss how EFS is used to decrypt data in "Immediate Solutions."

As with everything else in life, EFS does have a couple other gotchas. The first is that it is machine specific and local. EFS files cannot be stored on the network, but must be stored on the local computer. What's more, if users need to decrypt an EFS file from a different computer, their public and private keys must be copied to the other computer. Keep this in mind if file security is paramount.

Immediate Solutions

Configuring TCP/IP

The following sections detail the various tasks involved with configuring the TCP/IP protocol suite.

Configuring Static Addresses

To configure static IP addresses, perform the following steps:

1. Click Start, and select Settings|Control Panel.
2. Double-click the Network And Dial-Up Connections applet.
3. Double-click the network connection for which you would like to configure a static address.
4. Click Properties.
5. On the General tab, select the Internet Protocol (TCP/IP) option, and click Properties.
6. Select the Use The Following IP Address radio button.
7. Enter an IP address, a subnet mask, and a default gateway.
8. Enter a preferred DNS server and an alternate DNS server.
9. Click OK.

Configuring Additional TCP/IP Addresses

Sometimes you may need the same computer or server to respond to more than one TCP/IP address. To configure additional IP addresses, perform the following steps:

1. Click Start, and select Settings|Control Panel.
2. Double-click the Network And Dial-Up Connections applet.
3. Double-click the network connection for which you would like to configure additional IP addresses.
4. Click Properties.
5. On the General tab, select the Internet Protocol (TCP/IP) option, and click Properties.

6. Click Advanced.

7. On the IP Settings tab, click Add in the IP Addresses section of the window.

8. Enter an additional IP address and subnet mask, and then click Add.

9. Repeat if desired. Click OK.

10. Click OK.

Configuring DHCP Client or APIPA

In the event that a DHCP server is unavailable, or you wish to take advantage of automatic IP addressing without a DHCP server on the network (APIPA), you only need to perform the following steps:

1. Click Start, and select Settings|Control Panel.

2. Double-click the Network And Dial-Up Connections applet.

3. Double-click the network connection for which you would like to configure a dynamic address.

4. Click Properties.

5. On the General tab, select the Internet Protocol (TCP/IP) option, and click Properties.

6. Select the Obtain An IP Address Automatically radio button.

7. Click OK.

Using Static DNS with TCP/IP

To use static DNS with TCP/IP, perform the following steps:

1. Click Start, and select Settings|Control Panel.

2. Double-click the Network And Dial-Up Connections applet.

3. Double-click the network connection for which you would like to configure a static DNS entry.

4. Click Properties.

5. On the General tab, select the Internet Protocol (TCP/IP) option, and click Properties.

6. Select the Use The Following DNS Server Addresses radio button. Then, enter the preferred DNS server and alternate DNS server addresses.

7. Click OK.

Using Windows Internet Naming System with TCP/IP

To use Windows Internet Naming System (WINS) with TCP/IP, perform the following steps:

1. Click Start, and select Settings|Control Panel.

2. Double-click the Network And Dial-Up Connections applet.

3. Double-click the network connection for which you would like to configure a WINS address.

4. Click Properties.

5. On the General tab, select the Internet Protocol (TCP/IP) option, and click Properties.

6. Click Advanced.

7. Select the WINS tab.

8. Click Add.

9. Enter the IP address of the WINS server in the TCP/IP WINS Server section, and click Add.

10. Repeat this process for any other WINS servers you want to include. When you're done, click OK.

Enabling the LMHOSTS File to Resolve NetBIOS Names

To configure clients to use an LMHOSTS file for NetBIOS name resolution, perform the following steps:

1. Click Start, and select Settings|Control Panel.

2. Double-click the Network And Dial-Up Connections applet.

3. Double-click the network connection for which you would like to enable LMHOSTS resolution.

4. Click Properties.

5. On the General tab, select the Internet Protocol (TCP/IP) option, and click Properties.

6. Click Advanced.

7. Select the WINS tab.

8. Select the Enable LMHOSTS Lookup checkbox.

9. Click Import LMHOSTS, and navigate to its location.

10. Click OK.

Using TCP/IP Filtering

To enable TCP/IP filtering, perform the following steps:

1. Click Start, and select Settings|Control Panel.

2. Double-click the Network And Dial-Up Connections applet.

3. Double-click the network connection for which you would like to configure TCP/IP filtering.

4. Click Properties.

5. On the General tab, select the Internet Protocol (TCP/IP) option, and click Properties.

6. Click Advanced.

7. Select the Options tab.

8. Select the TCP/IP Filtering option, and click Properties.

9. Select the desired configuration, and click OK.

Using IPSec Security

To enable IPSec security, perform the following steps:

1. Click Start, and select Settings|Control Panel.

2. Double-click the Network And Dial-Up Connections applet.

3. Double-click the network connection for which you would like to configure IPSec.

4. Click Properties.

5. On the General tab, select the Internet Protocol (TCP/IP) option, and click Properties.

6. Click Advanced.

7. Select the Options tab.

8. Select the IP Security option, and click Properties.

9. Select the Use This IP Security Policy radio button.

10. Choose the desired security policy from the drop-down list.

11. Click OK.

Installing Simple TCP/IP Services

To install TCP/IP services, perform the following steps:

1. Click Start, and select Settings|Control Panel.
2. Double-click the Add/Remove Programs applet.
3. Click Add/Remove Windows Components.
4. When the Windows Component Wizard appears, click Next.
5. Select Networking Services, and click Details.
6. Select Simple TCP/IP Services in the Subcomponents Of Networking Services window, and click OK.
7. Click Next.
8. Click Finish.

Working with Servers and DHCP

The following sections detail the various tasks involved in working with DHCP.

Installing DHCP

To install DHCP, perform the following steps:

1. Select Start|Settings|Control Panel.
2. Double-click the Add/Remove Programs applet.
3. Click Add/Remove Windows Components.
4. When the Windows Component Wizard appears, click Next.
5. Select Networking Services, and click Details.
6. Select the Dynamic Host Configuration Protocol (DHCP) option, and click OK.
7. Click Next.
8. Click Finish.

Starting a DHCP Server

To start a DHCP server, perform the following steps:

1. Click Start, and select Programs|Administrative Tools|DHCP. The DHCP console will appear, as shown in Figure 11.2.
2. Right-click the server to start, and choose All Tasks|Start from the pop-up menu.

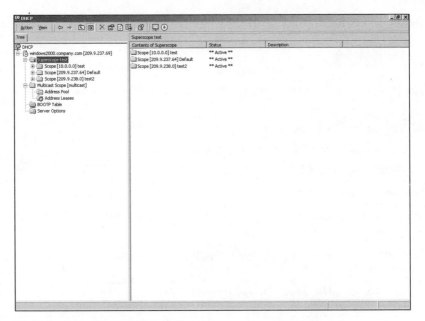

Figure 11.2   The DHCP console.

Starting a DHCP Server Using the Command Prompt

To start a DHCP server from the command prompt, perform the following steps:

1. Click Start, and select Programs|Accessories|Command Prompt.

2. Type the following command:

```
net start dhcpserver
```

3. Press Enter.

Stopping a DHCP Server

To stop a DHCP server, perform the following steps:

1. Click Start, and select Programs|Administrative Tools|DHCP.

2. Right-click the server to stop, and choose All Tasks|Stop from the pop-up menu.

Stopping a DHCP Server Using the Command Prompt

To stop a DHCP server from the command prompt, perform the following steps:

1. Click Start, and select Programs|Accessories|Command Prompt.

11. Local and Small
Business Networking

2. Type the following command:

```
net stop dhcpserver
```

3. Press Enter.

Connecting to a DHCP Server

To connect to a DHCP server, perform the following steps:

1. Click Start, and select Programs|Administrative Tools|DHCP.
2. Navigate to the DHCP container.
3. Right-click the container, and choose Add Server from the pop-up menu. The Add Server window appears.
4. Select either this server or another DHCP server that has been authorized.

TIP: *DHCP within Windows 2000 must be 'authorized' in order to function properly.*

---

5. Click OK.

Deleting a DHCP Server

To delete a DHCP server, perform the following steps:

1. Click Start, and select Programs|Administrative Tools|DHCP.
2. Select the server from which to disconnect.
3. Right-click the server, and choose Delete from the pop-up menu.
4. Click Yes to confirm the server's deletion.

Repairing the DHCP Database

To repair the DHCP database, perform the following steps:

1. Click Start, and select Programs|Administrative Tools|DHCP.
2. Navigate to the server whose database you would like to repair.
3. Right-click the server, and choose Reconcile All Scopes from the pop-up menu.
4. Click Verify.
5. If the database checks out properly, click OK.
6. Click Cancel.

Repairing the DHCP Database Manually

To repair the DHCP database manually, perform the following steps:

1. Click Start, and select Programs|Accessories|Command Prompt.

2. Stop the DHCP server by typing "net stop dhcpserver" and pressing Enter.

3. Type "cd %systemroot%\system32\dhcp", and press Enter.

4. Type "jetpack dhcp.mdb tmp.mdb", and press Enter.

5. Start the DHCP server by typing "net start dhcpserver" and pressing Enter.

Managing DHCP Servers

The following sections detail the various tasks involved in working with DHCP servers.

Authorizing a DHCP Server in Active Directory

To authorize a DHCP server in Active Directory, perform the following steps:

1. Click Start, and select Programs|Administrative Tools|DHCP.

2. Navigate to the server to authorize in Active Directory.

3. Right-click the server object, and choose Authorize from the pop-up menu.

Unauthorizing a DHCP Server in Active Directory

To unauthorize a DHCP server in Active Directory, perform the following steps:

1. Click Start, and select Programs|Administrative Tools|DHCP.

2. Right-click the DHCP container, and choose Manage Authorized Servers from the pop-up menu.

3. Select the server to unauthorize, and click Unauthorize.

4. Click Close.

Working with DHCP Scopes

The following sections detail the tasks involved in managing DHCP scopes.

Creating a New Scope

To create a DHCP scope, perform the following steps:

1. Click Start, and select Programs|Administrative Tools|DHCP.

2. Navigate to the server where you would like the new scope created.

3. Right-click the server, and choose the New Scope option. The New Scope Wizard appears.

4. Click Next.

5. Enter a name and an optional description for the scope.

6. Enter the start and end TCP/IP addresses.

7. Enter either the subnet mask or the subnet length, and click Next.

8. If you want to exclude any addresses, enter the start and end IP addresses, and click Add.

TIP: *If you want to enter a single IP address, enter the same address in both the Start and End fields.*

---

9. Click Next.

10. Set the duration for the DHCP lease, and click Next.

11. If you would like to configure any DHCP options, select the Yes, I Want To Configure These Options Now radio button, and click Next. Otherwise, select the No, I Will Configure These Options Later radio button, and click Next.

12. Click Finish.

Deleting a Scope

To delete a DHCP scope, perform the following steps:

1. Click Start, and select Programs|Administrative Tools|DHCP.

2. Navigate to the server where you would like the new scope deleted.

3. Right-click the scope, and choose Delete from the pop-up menu.

4. Click Yes to confirm the scope deletion.

Activating a Scope

To activate a DHCP scope, perform the following steps:

1. Click Start, and select Programs|Administrative Tools|DHCP.

2. Navigate to the scope to activate.

3. Right-click the scope, and choose Activate from the pop-up menu.

Deactivating a Scope

To deactivate a DHCP scope, perform the following steps:

1. Click Start, and select Programs|Administrative Tools|DHCP.

2. Navigate to the scope to deactivate.

3. Right-click the scope, and choose Deactivate from the pop-up menu.

4. Click Yes to confirm the deactivation.

Modifying a Scope's Properties

To modify a DHCP scope's properties, perform the following steps:

1. Click Start, and select Programs|Administrative Tools|DHCP.

2. Navigate to the scope with the properties that you would like to modify.

3. Right-click the scope, and choose Properties from the pop-up menu.

4. Modify any desired properties, and click OK when done.

Excluding TCP/IP Addresses from a Scope

To exclude IP addresses from a scope, perform the following steps:

1. Click Start, and select Programs|Administrative Tools|DHCP.

2. Navigate to the Address Pool container in the scope from which you would like to exclude IP addresses.

3. Right-click Address Pool, and choose New Exclusion Range from the pop-up menu.

4. Click Add.

5. Repeat this process for any other addresses that need to be excluded, and click Close when done.

Modifying a Scope's Duration

To modify a DHCP scope's duration, perform the following steps:

1. Click Start, and select Programs|Administrative Tools|DHCP.

2. Navigate to the scope for which you would like to modify the duration properties.

3. Right-click the scope, and choose Properties from the pop-up menu.

4. Modify the Lease Duration For DHCP Clients section of the General tab.

5. Click OK.

Reconciling a Scope

To reconcile a scope, perform the following steps:

1. Click Start, and select Programs|Administrative Tools|DHCP.

2. Navigate to the scope to reconcile.

3. Right-click the scope, and choose Reconcile from the pop-up menu.

  4. Click Verify.

  5. Click OK.

  6. Click Cancel.

Working with Leases

The following sections detail the various tasks involved in working with DHCP leases.

Viewing a Client Lease

To view a client lease, perform the following steps:

  1. Click Start, and select Programs|Administrative Tools|DHCP.

  2. Navigate to the Address Lease container under the desired server and zone.

  3. Double-click the desired client lease in the view pane (the right pane) of the DHCP console.

Verifying a Client Lease

To verify a client lease, perform the following steps:

  1. On the client computer, click Start, and select Programs|Accessories|Command Prompt.

  2. Type "ipconfig /all", and press Enter.

  3. The lease information will be listed.

Terminating a Client Lease

To terminate a client lease, perform the following steps:

  1. On the client computer, click Start, and select Programs|Accessories|Command Prompt.

  2. Type "ipconfig /release", and press Enter.

  3. The client lease is now released.

Renewing a Client Lease

To renew a client lease, perform the following steps:

  1. On the client computer, click Start, and select Programs|Accessories|Command Prompt.

  2. Type "ipconfig /renew", and press Enter.

  3. The client will now terminate the lease and then immediately renew it.

Configuring DHCP Reservations

The following sections detail the various tasks involved in working with DHCP reservations.

Adding a Reservation

To add a reservation, perform the following steps:

1. Click Start, and select Programs|Administrative Tools|DHCP.

2. Navigate to the Reservations container under the server and zone where you would like to add a reservation.

3. Right-click, and choose New Reservation from the pop-up menu.

4. Enter a name for the reservation, the IP address that's to be reserved, the MAC address for the reserved system, and a description.

5. Select the reservation type: Both, DHCP Only, or BOOTP Only.

6. Click Add.

7. Repeat this process for any other reservations that you want. Click Close when done.

Modifying a Reservation

To modify a reservation, perform the following steps:

1. Click Start, and select Programs|Administrative Tools|DHCP.

2. Navigate to the Reservations container under the server and zone where you would like to modify the reservation.

3. Select the desired reservation.

4. Right-click the reservation, and choose Properties from the pop-up menu.

5. Make any desired changes, and click OK when done.

Configuring Options for a Reservation

To configure options for a reservation, perform the following steps:

1. Click Start, and select Programs|Administrative Tools|DHCP.

2. Navigate to the Reservations container under the server and zone where you would like to configure options for the reservation.

3. Select the desired reservation.

4. Right-click the reservation, and choose Configure Options from the pop-up menu.

5. Configure any desired options, and click OK when done.

Monitoring DHCP

The following sections detail the various tasks involved in monitoring DHCP.

Enabling Logging

To enable logging, perform the following steps:

1. Click Start, and select Programs|Administrative Tools|DHCP.
2. Navigate to the server where you would like to enable logging.
3. Right-click the server, and select Properties from the pop-up menu.
4. Select the Enable DHCP Audit Logging checkbox on the General tab, and click OK.

Viewing Server Statistics

To view server statistics, perform the following steps:

1. Click Start, and select Programs|Administrative Tools|DHCP.
2. Navigate to the server for which you would like to view statistics.
3. Right-click the server, and choose Display Statistics from the pop-up menu.
4. Click Close when done.

Viewing Server Properties

To view server properties, perform the following steps:

1. Click Start, and select Programs|Administrative Tools|DHCP.
2. Navigate to the server whose properties you would like to view.
3. Right-click the server, and choose Properties from the pop-up menu.
4. The server properties will be displayed. Click OK when done.

Enabling Address Conflict Detection

To enable address conflict detection, perform the following steps:

1. Click Start, and select Programs|Administrative Tools|DHCP.
2. Navigate to the server where you would like to enable address conflict detection.
3. Right-click the server, and choose Properties from the pop-up menu.
4. Select the Advanced tab.
5. Increase the Conflict Detection Attempts by setting to a number higher than zero, and click OK.

Refreshing Server Statistics

To refresh server statistics, perform the following steps:

1. Click Start, and select Programs|Administrative Tools|DHCP.

2. Navigate to the server where you would like to refresh the server statistics.

3. Right-click the server, and choose Display Statistics from the pop-up menu.

4. Click Refresh.

5. Click Close when done.

Testing TCP/IP

The following sections detail the various tasks involved with testing TCP/IP.

Using the **PING** Command to Test a Connection

To use **PING**, perform the following steps:

1. Click Start, and select Programs|Accessories|Command Prompt.

2. Type the following command:

```
PING destination
```

3. Press Enter. If the **PING** command is successful, you'll see a response saying so.

Using the **NET VIEW** Command to Test Connection

To use **NET VIEW**, perform the following steps:

1. Click Start, and select Programs|Accessories|Command Prompt.

2. Type the following command:

```
net view \\destination
```

3. Press Enter. If the **NET VIEW** command is successful, you'll see a response that says so.

Using the **TRACERT** Command to Trace a TCP/IP Path

To use **TRACERT**, perform the following steps:

1. Click Start, and select Programs|Accessories|Command Prompt.

2. Type the following command:

```
tracert destination
```

3. Press Enter.

Viewing the NetBIOS Name Table

Viewing the NetBIOS name table allows you to see which NetBIOS names assigned to computers have been detected on the network. To view the NetBIOS name table, perform the following steps:

1. Click Start, and select Programs|Accessories|Command Prompt.

2. Type the following command:

```
nbtstat -n
```

3. Press Enter.

Refreshing the NetBIOS Name Table

To refresh the NetBIOS name table, perform the following steps:

1. Click Start, and select Programs|Accessories|Command Prompt.

2. Type the following command:

```
nbtstat -R
```

3. Press Enter.

Viewing the Address Resolution Protocol Table

The Address Resolution Protocol (ARP) table is filled with information that essentially equates the TCP/IP address to the MAC address that's assigned to the compter. To view the ARP table, perform the following steps:

1. Click Start, and select Programs|Accessories|Command Prompt.

2. Type the following command:

```
arp -a
```

3. Press Enter.

Adding a Static ARP Entry

To add a static ARP entry, perform the following steps:

1. Click Start, and select Programs|Accessories|Command Prompt.

2. Type the following command:

```
arp -s inet_address eth_address
```

3. Press Enter.

NOTE: *For example, to create a static ARP entry for a system with a MAC address of 12-34-56-78-90-AB and an IP address of 192.168.1.2, you would enter the following:*

```
Arp -s 192.168.1.2 12-34-56-78-90-AB
```

Working with EFS

When you choose to encrypt a file, you will be given the option to encrypt the parent folder that it belongs to. Any folders that are encrypted act as encryption agents for any items within those folders. What this means is that any file or folder that you add to an encrypted folder will in turn become encrypted using the keys belonging to the owner of the file. Any file or folder that is removed from an encrypted folder will maintain its encryption properties until the file or folder's properties cease to include encryption.

Encrypting a File or Folder

To encrypt a file or folder, perform the following steps:

1. Right-click the file or folder, and choose Properties from the pop-up menu.

2. Click the Advanced button, and select the Encrypt Contents To Secure Data checkbox.

3. Click OK, and click OK again to close the window.

Decrypting a File or Folder

To decrypt a file or folder, perform the following steps:

1. Right-click the file or folder within Explorer, and choose Properties from the pop-up menu.

2. Click Advanced, and ensure that the Encrypt Contents To Secure Data checkbox is not selected.

3. Click OK, and click OK again to close the window.

Exporting Public and Private Keys

You will want to export your public and private keys for two reasons. The first reason is when you may want to view encrypted data from another computer. The second is when you lose or corrupt your keys. Certificates also exist for the recovery agent and are required in order to decrypt or access encrypted files where the original keys have been lost or are unrecoverable. You'll need to export the recovery agent certificates and import them back when this situation occurs. To export public and private keys, perform the following steps:

1. Open the Certificate Manager Microsoft Management Console (MMC) by clicking Start, selecting Run, typing "CERTMGR.MSC", and pressing Enter.

2. Right-click an EFS key. Move the mouse arrow to the All Tasks from the popup menu, and click on the |Export option from the flyout menu that appears.

3. The Certificate Export Wizard will start. PKCS #12 formats are password protected and will hold private keys. PKCS #7 will hold any keys.

4. When prompted, enter a target path for the exported certificate.

Importing Public and Private Keys

To import public and private keys, perform the following steps:

1. Open the Certificate Manager MMC console by clicking Start, selecting Run, typing "CERTMGR.MSC", and pressing Enter.

2. Right-click the certificate category that you want to import into. Select All Tasks|Import from the pop-up menu.

3. When prompted, browse to the location of the exported keys. Double-click the file.

4. If the importing certificate is in PKCS #12 format, you'll be prompted for a password.

Working with DFS

In many small to midsized businesses, you'll want to use DFS to make additional disk space available on the network for usage without creating additional shares and drive mappings for users.

Configuring DFS

To configure DFS, perform the following steps:

1. Launch the DFS MMC by clicking Start, selecting Run, typing "DFS", and pressing Enter.

2. Select Action|New DFS Root, and click Next.

3. The New DFS Root Wizard appears. You'll have the option to choose a standalone or domain DFS system. If the current computer is a member of a Windows 2000 domain, choose to create a domain DFS root. Otherwise, choose to create a standalone DFS root.

4. Click Next, and choose the domain name, if applicable.

5. Click Next, and click Browse. Browse the network until you find the appropriate server that will hold the DFS root share. Click Next.

6. You will be prompted to choose an existing share on that server or to create a new one. Fill out the information appropriately, and click Next.

7. Enter a name for the DFS root. It's recommended that the DFS root name be unique and different from any other share names on the network. Click Next, and click Finish.

Adding Shares to the DFS Tree

When you need to add a share from a server into the overall DFS tree, perform the following steps:

1. Launch the DFS MMC by clicking Start, selecting Run, typing "DFS", and pressing Enter.

2. Highlight the DFS root that will be changed, and select Action| NewDFS Link.

3. A DFS link dialog box appears. Enter a link name, and browse to the server and folder that will be linked to the DFS tree. Be sure to enter a comment to help document where the data resides.

4. Click OK.

Working with ICS

ICS is probably the greatest single improvement for small and home offices alike. Using ICS, you can now use a single computer on a LAN to dial up or otherwise connect to the internet, and share that connection with other systems on the network.

Configuring the ICS Server

In order to properly configure ICS, you'll need to configure the ICS server to share the LAN connection.

1. Right-click on the My Network Places on the desktop, and click on Properties from the popup menu.

2. Right-click on the network connection that is associated with the network card that will be receiving internet requests, and click on Properties from the popup menu.

3. Click on the Sharing tab, and click on the Enable Internet Connection Sharing for this Connection checkbox.

4. Click on the OK button. A message will appear as shown in Figure 11.3. Click on OK.

TIP: *The system will automatically reconfigure your TCP/IP address as 192.168.0.1. If you need to have specific DNS, WINS, or default gateway addresses, you'll need to manually alter the TCP/IP properties to add that information. If this particular system resides in a DHCP environment, you may consider altering the DHCP scopes to use the 192.168.xxx.xxx subnet so that client computers will be able to maintain communications with the ICS server. If DHCP does not exist in the environment, you really should just configure TCP/IP to Obtain an IP Address Automatically and manually configure any DNS, WINS, or default gateway addresses.*

---

5. Click on the OK button to close the network interface properties.

Configuring ICS Clients

Once the ICS server is configured appropriately, you'll need to basically set the computers on the network to look at the ICS server as a default gateway. Any Windows client (Windows 3.11, Win95/98, Windows NT, Windows 2000) can use ICS in this manner. The following instructions are for a Windows 2000 system.

1. Right-click on the My Network Places icon on the desktop, and choose Properties from the popup menu.

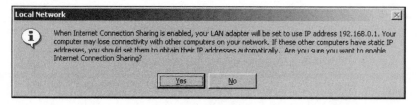

Figure 11.3   ICS configuration message indicating that 192.168.0.1 must be assigned to the network adapter.

2. Right-click on the Network Adapter card that is attached to the network and click Properties from the popup menu.

3. Click on the Internet Protocol (TCP/IP) button and click on the Properties button.

4. Click on the Obtain an IP Address Automatically radio button, and click on the Advanced button at the bottom of the window.

5. Under Default Gateways, click on the Add button, and enter 192.168.0.1 and click on the OK button.

6. Click on the OK button to close the Advanced TCP/IP Settings window.

7. Click on the OK button to close the Internet Protocol (TCP/IP) Properties window.

11. Local and Small
Business Networking

Chapter 12

Large Business and Enterprise Networking

In Depth

Domain Name Service (DNS)

When computers communicate, they use a unique number that's assigned to every networking device made today. This number is known as the *Media Access Control (MAC) address*. It is a unique 48-bit number. The MAC address is usually written in hexadecimal bytes with either colons (:) or dashes (-) separating the bytes. For example, a MAC address might be 1A-34-DC-37-91-AB. The first three bytes are assigned to the company that created the networking device, and the last three bytes are a unique serial number for the device. All the major network protocols use this address to communicate, including Transmission Control Protocol/Internet Protocol (TCP/IP) and NWLink.

With TCP/IP, however, each network host is given a four-byte IP address separated by periods, for example, 192.168.54.145. As you can imagine, most people would have difficulty remembering what the MAC address or IP address of Microsoft's Web site is. Therefore, fully qualified domain names (FQDNs) are used to communicate on the Internet, for example, **www.microsoft.com**.

Therefore, we have a bit of a problem. We humans use FQDNs, and computers use IP addresses. We need a method to translate between the two in order to ensure that communications from Point A always reach the correct recipients at Point B. The most common method used for this type of translation today is known as the *Domain Name Service (DNS)*. Simply put, DNS automatically converts from one format to another. You give a computer the FQDN, and it finds the IP address; you give the computer an IP address, and it returns the FQDN.

DNS is made up of objects called zones. Each zone is basically a container that contains one or more DNS domains or subdomains. In turn, these domains contain the records listing what IP addresses are associated with which FQDNs. There are five types of zones within Windows 2000 DNS:

1. *Forward Lookup* zones handle the name resolution that DNS is known for. The forward lookup zone will tell the system that **www.microsoft.com** is 207.46.230.218.

2. *Reverse Lookup* zones are opposite from forward lookup zones. Instead of presenting the system with an IP address upon receipt of a FQDN, they deliver an FQDN upon receipt of an IP address.

3. *Primary* zones are "standard" zones that may be Active Directory–integrated, but not necessarily. A Primary zone basically contains the DNS zone information (FQDNs and the resolved IP addresses) that can be updated.

4. *Secondary* zones are essentially backup zones for non-AD-integrated DNS systems. Secondary zones contain read-only copies of the DNS zone information that cannot be updated. Secondary zones are used for fault tolerance and also for balancing DNS traffic across multiple servers.

5. *Active Directory-integrated* zones are exactly that: DNS zones that are integrated into AD. Windows 2000 Active Directory requires DNS, but not necessarily Windows 2000 DNS. Remember that it can work with versions of Unix DNS running BIND 4.9.7 or higher (preferably higher . . . 8.1.2+) The primary reason for using AD-integrated zones is to take advantage of the built-in replication that AD gives us. Additionally, AD-integrated DNS zones replicate only where necessary. For instance, let's say you configured DNS with two AD-integrated zones, one at the corporate office and another at the remote office, and you have a DC in the remote office that runs DNS. The entire DNS database shouldn't replicate to the remote office because the remote office's DNS server is configured with only the appropriate zone.

NOTE: *Active Directory-integrated zones are new to the DNS world because they essentially place DNS within Active Directory itself. Instead of maintaining a separate database, DNS records become separate objects within Active Directory. This can be a huge benefit because you won't need to deal with DNS replication between DNS servers. Instead, DNS information will replicate appropriately along with AD replication. A possible downside may deal with security because any DC in the domain then has the capability of updating the DNS database (via the Dynamic Update feature).*

Within a small company or peer-to-peer network that doesn't have the support of a domain controller, you can still accomplish DNS-type name resolution through the HOSTS file located on each client computer. The HOSTS file exists for all Windows clients. If a DNS server does not exist, or if it is unavailable, the client computer will automatically refer to the HOSTS file for resolution. The format of the file is simple: it lists FQDNs, followed by their associated IP addresses. The HOSTS file is a decentralized method of name resolution, and it requires manual intervention to update or change the listed computers. Considering that a single change would have to be manually updated on every computer on the network, it might be a good idea to take this into consideration when planning your network. Also keep in mind that if your network is small, you probably won't be needing DNS name resolution anyway, and you may even be able to refer to your ISP's DNS server address for what little Internet-related name resolution you require.

NOTE: *DNS does not perform any IP address-to-MAC address translation. The protocol that accomplishes this is known as Address Resolution Protocol (ARP). This is done automatically in the background. Under normal circumstances, you will not be required to modify any ARP information. The conversion from MAC addresses to IP addresses is performed by Reverse ARP (RARP).*

There is a new feature available with Windows 2000 DNS that is known as dynamic DNS. Traditionally, a DNS database required manual intervention. Basically, if you need name resolution for a computer on the network, you must manually add it into the DNS database in order to enable that resolution through DNS. This is particularly annoying when DHCP clients change IP addresses every so often. In order to ease this administrative headache, you can enable Windows 2000 DNS for dynamic updates. Dynamic DNS allows for the following to occur:

- DHCP client addresses will be automatically inserted into the DNS database.

- WINS client addresses will be automatically inserted into the DNS database.

- Address scavenging will automatically remove old, dead entries in the DNS database.

- Windows 2000 clients will automatically update themselves into the DNS database.

These new features are an incredible time savings in your standard DNS administration. Indeed, if you are considering or planning a migration to Windows 2000, these particular features of dynamic DNS may come in handy if you're considering whether to lay out additional money to upgrade or maintain Unix DNS or use Windows 2000 DNS for the enterprise.

In addition to standard name resolution services (A-Records or Hosts), DNS can resolve specific types of addresses such as Email servers (MX records) or Routers.

Dynamic Host Configuration Protocol (DHCP)

If you've ever managed a large network, you'll be one of the first to agree that assigning an IP address to each workstation can be a tedious task. With IP, every workstation must have a unique IP address assigned to it. If two systems use the same IP address, either one of them will fail, or both will cause errors. Also, if the subnet mask is wrong on a single computer on the network, it will not be able to communicate properly with other systems in its network. Finally, if the default gateway address is wrong, the workstation will not be able to communicate with systems on remote networks. Problems can also occur with incorrectly defined domain names, DNS servers, WINS servers, and so on.

When you're configuring a few machines, making such an error is not likely. When you're configuring several hundred or thousand computers, the likelihood of an error becomes increasingly more probable. Fixing errors on such a large network can also be extremely difficult. Imagine trying to find the two computers that share the same IP address on your network of several thousand computers.

To allow administrators to automate this task, *Dynamic Host Configuration Protocol (DHCP)* was created. As the name says, this protocol dynamically assigns IP addresses to any system that asks, assuming that the system is authorized and is asking correctly. Not only will DHCP assign the requesting workstation an IP address, it will also specify the subnet mask, default gateway, DNS servers, and any other servers and services that the administrator configures it to. As shown in the "Immediate Solutions" section, the configuration of DHCP requires an understanding of scopes and leases. A *scope* is the range (or ranges) of IP addresses that the DHCP server is allowed to assign to computers. A *lease* is also normally assigned when the server assigns the IP address information. This lease is much like that on a car. The address is assigned to the client for the duration of the lease. When the lease expires, the client must either renew the lease or return it. At that point, the computer loses its TCP/IP address and will no longer be able to communicate on the network using TCP/IP.

DHCP deals with three types of scopes: regular scopes, superscopes, and multicast scopes. As mentioned, a scope is simply a boundary that is set on the IP addresses that can be assigned by the DHCP server. A *superscope* is a "scope of scopes." It is a scope that is made up of two or more groups of addresses that are in the same network space. An example of a superscope would be where DHCP assigns addresses from both the 120.100.100.1-120.100.100.255 and the 130.100.100.1-100.130.100.-255 groups. Finally, a *multicast scope* is used for multicasting information to systems. Multicasting is the process of sending a single stream of data to multiple machines. Examples of this include streaming audio and video from the Internet and cloning multiple machines on the network simultaneously.

A DHCP scope is created to use a specific range of IP addresses. If a specific address within that range needs to always be assigned to a particular system or server, you can configure what's known as an *exclusion* within the scope. An exclusion is a specific address that lies within the range of IP addresses defined within a scope that will not be assigned by DHCP. Exclusions are also often used to document statically assigned servers and systems in order to better track IP address utilization, and also dynamic DNS functionality.

A couple of notes about DHCP. First, if you're running DHCP in Windows 2000, you must register it before it will work properly. This basically registers DHCP as a resource within Active Directory, and opens the door for dynamic update for DNS. Second, if you're running DHCP in a network containing multiple subnets, you may want to install a DHCP relay agent in each subnet that doesn't contain a DHCP server. Remember that subnets basically isolate communications (among other things) and that if there's no DHCP server in the subnet, the clients won't be able to get IP addresses. It is possible to install a DHCP server in each subnet, but this is overkill in time, effort, and administration. Instead, installing a DHCP relay agent in each subnet will enable DHCP clients to receive IP addresses from the DHCP server even when it's not in their subnet.

Windows Internet Naming Service (WINS)

Most Windows computers on the network use a Network Basic Input/Output System (NetBIOS) name rather than the FQDN. For example, your system might be known as both johnw2k (the NetBIOS name) and johnw2k.company.com (the FQDN). With Windows 2000, NetBIOS is not used as long as you follow this simple rule: There cannot be any non-Windows 2000 systems on the network. Quite a catch!

You see, in the past, peer-to-peer networking relied upon the NetBIOS protocol along with assigned NetBIOS computer names in order to communicate on the network without maintaining a centralized repository such as a server or domain controller. In fact, many network applications manufacturers relied upon NetBIOS in order to appeal to a broader audience that didn't necessarily require an additional server or domain controller. Unfortunately, NetBIOS isn't the best protocol in the world to work with. For one thing, it's not routable without essentially disguising it to look like a different protocol. Another reason NetBIOS isn't so hot is because computers running NetBIOS need to constantly maintain a "who's who" list of what systems are on the network in order to ensure that communications run smoothly. This list doesn't just come out of nowhere. Basically, it's built on the fly by a regular barrage of interviews (called broadcasts) from each NetBIOS system on the network to every other NetBIOS system on the network. As you may imagine, this constant chatter on the network takes up bandwidth and can become cumbersome. As time went by, the NetBIOS protocol wasn't really required for peer-to-peer or workgroup networking, but the NetBIOS computer names still existed, along with the same types of network traffic that go with them. To fix this problem, Microsoft created *WINS*. Simply put, this service converts between NetBIOS names and IP addresses (and the reverse) in much the same way that DNS converts between FQDNs and IP addresses. Instead of broadcasting their presence on the network, systems configured with WINS send their information directly to the WINS server. When a computer needs to find another computer on the network, it asks the WINS server for the other computer's IP address.

Unfortunately, WINS isn't really very much quieter on the network than all of the NetBIOS clients regularly broadcasting messages either. It just provides us with centralized and controllable services that we can take care of.

Remember that there are two basic reasons for using the NetBIOS protocol to begin with: one was peer-to-peer communications using NetBIOS computer names, and the other was for applications that use NetBIOS. WINS still exists with Windows 2000, but if Microsoft has anything to do with it, it won't exist for much longer. This is because Microsoft, with Windows 2000, seamlessly converts what appear to be NetBIOS computer names to FQDNs without the user knowing what's going on. This, in effect, eliminates the need for WINS in many situations where a network application doesn't require it. Basically, if you aren't running a NetBIOS-reliant network application, you're running a pure Windows 2000 client environment, and humans still need to know computers by their names; you don't need WINS to do NetBIOS name to IP translation for you because Windows 2000 automatically translates computer names to FQDNs on the fly. Indeed, Active Directory registers these computers by their FQDNs, but displays them as regular old computer names.

Keep in mind that WINS is dynamically updated, which makes it somewhat indiscriminate as far as what's included in the WINS resolution database. This can lead to problems that are sometimes difficult to resolve, such as multiple entries for the same IP address or multiple IP addresses using the same NetBIOS name. WINS has a built-in utility called scavenging to help with these problems and remove "dead" entries.

In much the same way that the local HOSTS file has a means of handling FQDN-to-IP address name resolution instead of DNS, WINS has one, too. It is known as the LMHOSTS file. The *LMHOSTS* file is used to convert between TCP/IP addresses and NetBIOS names and back.

Distributed File System

As I discussed in Chapter 11, basic DFS can be implemented to upgrade available network disk space seamlessly in such a manner that a user won't know the difference. In an enterprise or single-domain network, this particular functionality is standard. However, Microsoft DFS offers additional features that are more often used within an enterprise environment. DFS has the ability to be fault tolerant by essentially replicating selected DFS volumes to different DFS servers. The ideal result is that if a particular DFS server were to go down, files and resources can still be accessed at a different server containing replicated information.

Accessing and managing standard DFS occurs through the DFS Microsoft Management Console (MMC) snap-in (also know as dfsgui.msc). From there, you can configure fault-tolerant DFS, which can also be referred to as replicated or domain-based DFS. After DFS has been replicated, you can maintain and document replicated DFS branches from within the Active Directory Users And Computers console under System|File Replication.

Network Load Balancing and Cluster Services

Other tools that you may find handy within an enterprise environment are *Network Load Balancing (NLB)* and *clustering*. There is definitely some confusion in the industry as to the definitions of these two types of servers. As discussed here, please remember that I am speaking in Microsoftish. Any time that you are seriously considering load balancing and clustering packages for your server(s), be sure to gauge all products by their feature sets rather than the fuzzy moniker of NLB or cluster service.

A load balancing cluster is a group of two or more servers that are used to balance high volumes of network requests. If three different Web servers were members of the same load balancing cluster, all incoming requests would be balanced across all three of the servers. Although all servers within a load-balanced cluster are balancing against the same application, they share no data among themselves. If one member of the load-balanced cluster fails, the cluster is automagically reconfigured for balancing among the remaining servers, and life goes on with a near-zero service failure from a client point of view.

Server clustering is load balancing with the additional feature of shared data. Instead of each cluster member relying on its own data for functionality, they all rely on a single point of data—preferably an external shared drive or Network Access Server (NAS) system—for both load balancing and complete service redundancy. If one member of the cluster fails, the cluster is automatically configured, one of the other cluster members restarts any applicable services, and life goes on.

In the real world, you'd see load balancing being used for application servers or any server that sees high use. Load balancing of this nature is particularly great in situations where you don't need to share data, but you do have more traffic than one server can deal with. Relatively static Web servers are a great example, especially because multiple Internet Information Servers (IISs) can be used to point to the same external data source outside of the load-balancing function.

You are likely to see clustered servers in conjunction with major enterprise applications, such as Citrix MetaFrame, Citrix XP, or Oracle. In order to fully integrate an enterprise application into a clustered environment so that various application services can be fully supported and redundant, you are more likely to see a true clustered system as a complete package from an original equipment manufacturer (OEM) or value-added reseller (VAR).

IIS

The Internet has become part of everyone's life. All you have to do is turn on the television or radio, and you will hear a reference to the Internet. Most people understand that the Internet is there, but do not know what happens in the background when you enter an address in your Internet browser. You simply enter an address into your favorite Internet browser, and content (text, images, and multimedia) returns to you. The hidden, or server side, of this equation is IIS. This is the component that replies to the request from your browser and sends it the desired information back.

IIS is more complex than that, but, when simplified, that's all it really does. IIS also gives you the ability to host multiple Web sites on a single Web server, control how each site is accessed, and specify the security for each.

File Transfer Protocol

Although the Hypertext Transfer Protocol (HTTP) used by the Web servers and browsers has taken the wind out of the File Transfer Protocol's (FTP's) sails, FTP is still a widely used protocol. This protocol is designed for one thing, and one thing only: to transfer files from one location to another across a TCP/IP network.

In the same way that the Internet browser has a server side to it in IIS, the FTP service is the server side of the equation, and FTP clients act as the client side. The Microsoft implementation of FTP allows you to configure both private and public FTP sites as well as multiple FTP sites on a single server.

Integrating with NetWare

Microsoft designed the Windows operating systems to work with Novell NetWare. Many people are unaware of this, but Novell does not have a desktop operating system. It only builds the server side of the equation. The Novell NetWare operating system runs on top of a secondary operating system—disk operating system (DOS), for example. Novell NetWare has used the Microsoft suite of desktop operating systems for almost the entire span of its lifecycle. Microsoft would like you to use its client software to connect to Novell's servers using Novell's version of the client software.

Many arguments can be started by asking this question: Which client is better, the Microsoft one or the Novell one? This question is best answered by your specific needs.

Novell NetWare can be configured to run in one of two modes: bindery and Novell Directory Service (NDS). Windows 2000 allows you to connect to Novell NetWare networks running in one of these two modes. With NetWare versions 3.x and earlier, Novell used a flat directory system called the bindery (not unlike that of Windows NT). When Novell introduced NetWare 4.x, it unveiled a new directory service known as *NDS (Netware Directory Services)*. This directory service is a relational database-type system similar to Active Directory. With the Microsoft Client For NetWare, your system can connect to both NDS NetWare servers and the older bindery-based systems.

When connecting a Windows 2000 Professional system to a NetWare network, you can use the Client Services For NetWare (CSNW). This client allows you to log on to a Novell NetWare network and access files and printers on that network. Each version of NetWare also provides client software for Windows 2000 systems to access the NetWare server. Again, which one you choose is dependent upon the environment and what you want to accomplish. Using the Gateway Services For NetWare (GSNW), you can also configure a Windows 2000 server to act as a gateway between Windows 2000 (and NT & 9x) clients and the Netware Server without loading CSNW on each client computer. GSNW gives you the ability to connect to the Novell NetWare network in the same way as with Windows 2000 Professional, but it also allows your server to act as a gateway into the Novell network, sharing its file and printer resources with non-Novell clients.

Integrating with Macintosh Networks

Windows 2000 Server includes support for Macintosh systems. When you install the File And Print Services for Macintosh on your Windows 2000 Server, your server effectively becomes a Macintosh server. The Macintosh clients cannot distinguish the Windows 2000 Server from a true Macintosh server.

There are no requirements for sharing Windows 2000 printers with Macintosh systems, other than installing the Print Services for Macintosh. For file sharing, however, at least one partition must be formatted with the Window NT File System (NTFS).

Immediate Solutions

Working with Servers and DNS

The following sections detail configuring DNS.

Installing DNS

To install DNS, perform the following steps:

1. Click Start, and select Settings|Control Panel.

2. Double-click the Add/Remove Programs applet.

3. Click Add/Remove Windows Components.

4. When the Windows Component Wizard appears, click Next.

5. Select Networking Services, and click Details.

6. Select the Domain Name System (DNS) option, and click OK.

7. Click Next.

8. Click Finish.

Configuring a DNS Server

To configure a DNS server, perform the following steps:

1. Click Start, and select Programs|Administrative Tools|DNS. The DNS console appears, as shown in Figure 12.1.

2. Navigate to the server where you would like the DNS server configured, right-click the server, and choose the Configure The Server option from the pop-up menu.

3. When the Configure DNS Server Wizard appears, click Next.

4. Select the zone type (Active Directory-Integrated, Standard Primary, or Standard Secondary), and click Next.

5. Enter the name for the new zone, and click Next.

6. Select the Create A New File With This Name Or Use This Existing File option. Enter the name of the file, and click Next.

7. Click Finish.

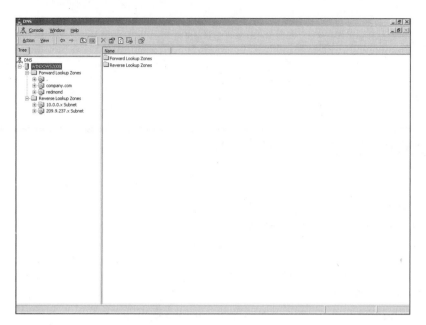

Figure 12.1   The DNS console.

Configuring a Secondary DNS Server

To configure a secondary DNS server, perform the following steps:

1. Click Start, and select Programs|Administrative Tools|DNS.

2. Navigate to the server where you would like the secondary DNS server configured, right-click the server, and choose the New Zone option from the pop-up menu.

3. When the Configure DNS Server Wizard appears, click Next.

4. Select the zone type (Active Directory-Integrated, Standard Primary, or Standard Secondary), and click Next.

5. Enter the name of the new zone, and click Next

6. If you selected to make the zone Active Directory-integrated, you only need to click Next, and Finish.

7. If you selected Standard Secondary, then you need to enter the IP addresses of the Master DNS server from which the zone will be copied.

8. If you selected Standard Primary, then you need to select the Create A New File With This Name or Use This Existing File option. Click on the Next button.

9. Click Finish.

Configuring a Caching-Only DNS Server

To configure a caching-only DNS server, perform the following steps:

1. Install DNS as described in "Installing DNS."

2. Do not configure any zones.

3. Ensure that the root servers are configured.

Configuring DNS Forwarders

To configure DNS forwarders, perform the following steps:

1. Click Start, and select Programs|Administrative Tools|DNS.

2. Navigate to the desired DNS server, right-click it, and choose the Properties option from the pop-up menu.

3. Select the Forwarders tab.

4. Select the Enable Forwarders option.

5. Enter the TCP/IP address of any servers that will act as forwarders for this DNS server.

6. Click OK.

TIP: *If you want the DNS server to use only the configured forwarders, select the Do Not Use Recursion checkbox. This will basically configure the server as a slave—which means that it will forward all queries to the forwarding server.*

Managing DNS Servers

The following projects detail the various tasks involved in managing a DNS server.

Starting a DNS Server

To start a DNS server, perform the following steps:

1. Click Start, and select Programs|Administrative Tools|DNS.

2. Navigate to the desired DNS server.

3. Right-click the server, navigate to All Tasks, and choose the Start option.

Starting a DNS Server from the Command Prompt

To start DNS from a command prompt, perform the following steps:

1. Click Start, and select Programs|Accessories|Command Prompt.

2. Type the following command:

```
net start dns
```

3. Press Enter.

Stopping a DNS Server

To stop a DNS server, perform the following steps:

1. Click Start, and select Programs|Administrative Tools|DNS.

2. Navigate to the desired DNS server.

3. Right-click the server, navigate to All Tasks, and choose the Stop option.

Stopping a DNS Server from the Command Prompt

To stop DNS from the command prompt, perform the following steps:

1. Click Start, and select Programs|Accessories|Command Prompt.

2. Type the following command:

```
net stop dns
```

3. Press Enter.

Restarting a DNS Server

To restart a DNS server, perform the following steps:

1. Click Start, and select Programs|Administrative Tools|DNS.

2. Navigate to the desired DNS server.

3. Right-click the server, navigate to All Tasks, and choose the Restart option.

Modifying the DNS Boot Sequence

You may wish to change the DNS boot sequence when moving DNS from one server to another. To modify the DNS boot sequence, perform the following steps:

1. Click Start, and select Programs|Administrative Tools|DNS.

2. Navigate to the server you would like to modify the boot sequence for.

3. Right-click the selected server, and choose Properties from the pop-up menu.

4. Select the Advanced tab.

5. From the Load Zone Data On Startup drop-down list, choose one of the following:

   • From Registry

- From File
- From Active Directory And Registry

6. Click OK.

TIP: *If you select the From File option, the text file must be named "boot" and must be located in the \winnt\system32\dns folder.*

Working with DNS Zones

The following sections detail managing DNS zones.

Adding a Forward Lookup Zone

To add a forward lookup zone, perform the following steps:

1. Click Start, and select Programs|Administrative Tools|DNS.

2. Navigate to the Forward Lookup Zones container under the desired server.

3. Right-click the container, and select the New Zone option.

4. When the New Zone Wizard appears, click Next.

5. Select the zone type (Active Directory-Integrated, Standard Primary, or Standard Secondary), and click Next.

6. Select the Forward Lookup Zone option, and click Next.

7. Enter the name for the new zone, and click Next.

8. Select the Create A New File With This Name Or Use This Existing File option. Enter the name of the file, and click Next.

9. Click Finish.

Adding a Reverse Lookup Zone

To add a reverse lookup zone, perform the following steps:

1. Click Start, and select Programs|Administrative Tools|DNS.

2. Navigate to the Reverse Lookup Zones container under the desired server.

3. Right-click the container, and select the New Zone option.

4. When the New Zone Wizard appears, click Next.

5. Select the zone type (Active Directory-Integrated, Standard Primary, or Standard Secondary), and click Next.

6. Select the Reverse Lookup Zone option, and click Next.

7. Enter the network ID or the name for the new zone, and click Next.

8. Select the Create A New File With This Name Or Use This Existing File option. Enter the name of the file, and click Next.

9. Click Finish.

Modifying the Zone Type

To modify the zone type, perform the following steps:

1. Click Start, and select Programs|Administrative Tools|DNS.

2. Navigate to the zone to modify.

3. Right-click the container, and select the Properties option.

4. Click Change on the General tab.

5. Select the new zone type and click OK.

Configuring Authoritative Servers for a Zone

To configure an authoritative server for a zone, perform the following steps:

1. Click Start, select Programs|Administrative Tools|DNS.

2. Navigate to the zone for which you would like to configure authoritative servers.

3. Right-click the container, and select the Properties option.

4. Select the Name Server tab.

5. Click Add.

6. Enter the IP addresses of the DNS servers.

7. Click OK.

Configuring DNS to Work with WINS

To configure DNS to work with WINS, perform the following steps:

1. Click Start, and select Programs|Administrative Tools|DNS.

2. Navigate to the zone for which you would like to configure WINS.

3. Right-click the container, and select the Properties option.

4. Select the WINS tab.

NOTE: *For a reverse lookup zone, select the WINS-R tab.*

---

5. Select the Use WINS Forward Lookup option.

NOTE: *For a reverse lookup zone, select the Use WINS-R Lookup option.*

---

6. Enter the IP address of the WINS server.

7. Click Add.

8. Click OK.

Starting a Zone Transfer at a Secondary DNS Site

To start a zone transfer at a secondary DNS site, perform the following steps:

1. Click Start, and select Programs|Administrative Tools|DNS.

2. Navigate to the zone to transfer.

3. Right-click the zone object, and choose the Transfer From Master option from the pop-up menu.

Permitting Dynamic Updates

To enable dynamic updates, perform the following steps:

1. Click Start, and select Programs|Administrative Tools|DNS.

2. Navigate to the zone for which you would like to configure dynamic updates.

3. Right-click the container, and select the Properties option.

4. Ensure that the zone type is set either to Active Directory-Integrated or Primary. Select Allow Dynamic Updates|Yes.

5. Click OK.

Using Secure Dynamic Updates

To configure secured dynamic updates, perform the following steps:

1. Click Start, and select Programs|Administrative Tools|DNS.

2. Navigate to the zone for which you would like to configure secure dynamic updates.

3. Right-click the container, and select the Properties option.

4. Ensure that the zone type is set either to Active Directory-Integrated or Primary. If the zone type is Active Directory-Integrated, select Allow Dynamic Updates|Only Secure Updates.

5. Click OK.

Changing the Refresh Interval

To change the refresh interval, perform the following steps:

1. Click Start, and select Programs|Administrative Tools|DNS.

2. Navigate to the zone for which you would like to change the refresh interval.

3. Right-click the container, and select the Properties option.

4. Ensure that the zone type is set to either Active Directory-Integrated or Primary. Click the Start Of Authority (SOA) tab.

5. Modify the Refresh Interval setting as needed, and click OK.

Changing the Expire Interval

To change the expire interval, perform the following steps:

1. Click Start, and select Programs|Administrative Tools|DNS.

2. Navigate to the zone for which you would like to change the expire interval.

3. Right-click the container, and select the Properties option.

4. Ensure that the zone type is set either to Active Directory-Integrated or Primary. Click the Start Of Authority (SOA) tab.

5. Modify the Expires After Interval setting as needed, and click OK.

Changing the Default Time-to-Live Settings

To modify the default time-to-live (TTL) settings, perform the following steps:

1. Click Start, and select Programs|Administrative Tools|DNS.

2. Navigate to the zone for which you would like to change the default TTL.

3. Right-click the container, and select the Properties option.

4. Ensure that the zone type is set either to Active Directory-Integrated or Primary. Click the Start Of Authority (SOA) tab.

5. Modify the Minimum (Default) TTL Interval setting as needed, and click OK.

Changing the TTL for a Record

To change the TTL for a record, perform the following steps:

1. Click Start, and select Programs|Administrative Tools|DNS.

2. Navigate to the record for which you would like to change the TTL.

3. Right-click the container, and select the Properties option.

4. Ensure that the zone type is set either to Active Directory-Integrated or Primary. Click the Start Of Authority (SOA) tab.

5. Modify the TTL for This Record Interval setting as needed, and click OK.

Adding a Host (A) Record

To add a host (A) record, perform the following steps:

1. Click Start, and select Programs|Administrative Tools|DNS.

2. Navigate to the zone where you would like to add the host record.

3. Right-click the container, and choose New Host from the pop-up menu.

4. Enter a name for the new host.

5. Enter the IP address for the new host.

6. If desired, enter the pointer (PTR) record for this host by checking the Create Associated Pointer (PTR) Record checkbox.

7. Click Add Host.

WARNING! *The pointer record will only be created if the corresponding reverse lookup zone was created.*

Adding an Alias (CNAME) Record

To add an alias (CNAME) record, perform the following steps:

1. Click Start, and select Programs|Administrative Tools|DNS.

2. Navigate to the zone where you would like to add the alias record.

3. Right-click the container, and choose New Alias from the pop-up menu.

4. Enter a name for the alias.

5. Enter the fully qualified name for the target host (or browse to it).

6. Click OK.

Adding a Mail Exchanger (MX) Record

To add a mail exchanger (MX) record, perform the following steps:

1. Click Start, and select Programs|Administrative Tools|DNS.

2. Navigate to the zone where you would like to add the MX record.

3. Right-click the container, and choose New Mail Exchanger from the pop-up menu.

4. Enter a host or domain name.

5. Enter the name of the mail server (or browse to it).

6. Enter the Mail Server Priority setting.

7. Click OK.

Adding a Domain Record

To add a domain record, perform the following steps:

1. Click Start, and select Programs|Administrative Tools|DNS.

2. Navigate to the zone where you would like to add the domain record.

3. Right-click the container, and choose New Domain from the pop-up menu.

4. Enter the domain name.

5. Click OK.

Adding Other Records

To add other records, perform the following steps:

1. Click Start, and select Programs|Administrative Tools|DNS.

2. Navigate to the zone where you would like to add the other record.

3. Right-click the container, and choose Other New Records from the pop-up menu.

4. Select the desired record type from the Select A Resource Record Type list box, and click Create Record.

5. When you're done creating the record, click OK.

Modifying a Record

To modify a record, perform the following steps:

1. Click Start, and select Programs|Administrative Tools|DNS.

2. Navigate to the record to modify.

3. Right-click the container, and choose Properties from the pop-up menu.

4. Make any desired changes, and click OK when done.

Deleting a Record

To delete a record, perform the following steps:

1. Click Start, and select Programs|Administrative Tools|DNS.

2. Navigate to the record to delete.

3. Right-click the container, and choose Delete from the pop-up menu.

4. Click OK to confirm the deletion.

Setting the Aging and Scavenging Properties on a DNS Server

To set the aging and scavenging DNS properties, perform the following steps:

1. Click Start, and select Programs|Administrative Tools|DNS.

2. Navigate to the server to configure aging and scavenging.

3. Right-click the container, and choose Set Aging/Scavenging For All Zones from the pop-up menu.

4. Select the Scavenge Stale Resource Records checkbox.

5. Click OK.

6. Click OK.

Scavenging for Stale Resource Records

To find stale resource records, perform the following steps:

1. Click Start, and select Programs|Administrative Tools|DNS.

2. Navigate to the server where you would like to scavenge for stale resource records.

3. Right-click the container, and choose Scavenge Stale Resource Records from the pop-up menu.

4. Click OK to start the scavenging process.

Working with DHCP Servers

The following sections detail the various tasks involved in working with DHCP.

Installing DHCP

To install DHCP, perform the following steps:

1. Click Start, and select Settings|Control Panel.

2. Double-click the Add/Remove Programs applet.

3. Click Add/Remove Windows Components.

4. When the Windows Component Wizard appears, click Next.

5. Select Networking Services, and click Details.

6. Select the Dynamic Host Configuration Protocol (DHCP) option, and click OK.

7. Click Next.

8. Click Finish.

Starting a DHCP Server

To start a DHCP server, perform the following steps:

1. Click Start, and select Programs|Administrative Tools|DHCP. The DHCP console will appear, as shown in Figure 12.2.

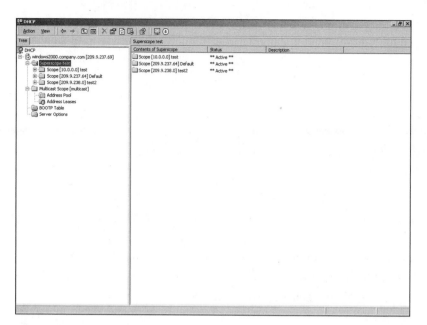

Figure 12.2   The DHCP console.

2. Right-click the server to start, and choose All Tasks|Start from the pop-up menu.

Starting a DHCP Server Using the Command Prompt

To start a DHCP server from the command prompt, perform the following steps:

1. Click Start, and select Programs|Accessories|Command Prompt.

2. Type the following command:

```
net start dhcpserver
```

3. Press Enter.

Stopping a DHCP Server

To stop a DHCP server, perform the following steps:

1. Click Start, and select Programs|Administrative Tools|DHCP.

2. Right-click the server to stop, and choose All Tasks|Stop from the pop-up menu.

Stopping a DHCP Server Using the Command Prompt

To stop a DHCP server from the command line, perform the following steps:

1. Click Start, and select Programs|Accessories|Command Prompt.

2. Type the following command:

```
net stop dhcpserver
```

3. Press Enter.

DHCP Database Diagnostics

To check the DHCP database, perform the following steps:

1. Click Start, and select Programs|Administrative Tools|DHCP.
2. Navigate to the server for the database that you would like to repair.
3. Right-click the server, and choose Reconcile All Scopes from the pop-up menu.
4. Click Verify.
5. If the database checks out properly, click OK.
6. Click Cancel.

Repairing the DHCP Database Manually

To repair the DHCP database manually, perform the following steps:

1. Click Start, and select Programs|Accessories|Command Prompt.
2. Stop the DHCP server by typing "net stop dhcpserver" and pressing Enter.
3. Type "cd %systemroot%\system32\dhcp", and press Enter.
4. Type "jetpack dhcp.mdb tmp.mdb", and press Enter.
5. Start the DHCP server by typing "net start dhcpserver", and pressing Enter.

Managing DHCP Servers

The following sections detail the various tasks involved in working with DHCP servers.

Authorizing a DHCP Server in Active Directory

Remember that DHCP must be authorized in order to work properly. To authorize a DHCP server in Active Directory, perform the following steps:

1. Log in as an enterprise admin.
2. Click Start, and select Programs|Administrative Tools|DHCP.
3. Navigate to the server to authorize in Active Directory.
4. Right-click the server object, and choose Authorize from the pop-up menu.

Unauthorizing a DHCP Server in Active Directory

To authorize a DHCP server in Active Directory, perform the following steps:

1. Click Start, and select Programs|Administrative Tools|DHCP.

2. Right-click the DHCP container, and choose Manage Authorized Servers from the pop-up list.

3. Select the server to unauthorize, and click Unauthorize.

4. Click Close.

Working with DHCP Scopes

The following sections detail the tasks involved in managing DHCP scopes.

Creating a New Scope

To create a DHCP scope, perform the following steps:

1. Click Start, and select Programs|Administrative Tools|DHCP.

2. Navigate to the server where you would like the new scope created.

3. Right-click the server, and choose the New Scope option. The New Scope Wizard appears.

4. Click Next.

5. Enter a name and an optional description for the scope.

6. Enter the start and end TCP/IP addresses.

7. Enter either the subnet mask or the subnet length, and click Next.

8. If you want to exclude any addresses, enter the start and end IP addresses, and click Add.

TIP: If you want to enter a single IP address, enter the same address in both the Start and End fields.

---

9. Click Next.

10. Set the duration for the DHCP lease, and click Next.

11. If you would like to configure any DHCP options, select the Yes, I Want To Configure These Options Now radio button, and click Next. Otherwise, select the No, I Will Configure These Options Later radio button, and click Next.

12. Click Finish.

Deleting a Scope

To delete a DHCP scope, perform the following steps:

1. Click Start, and select Programs|Administrative Tools|DHCP.

2. Navigate to the server where you would like the new scope deleted.

3. Right-click the scope, and choose Delete from the pop-up menu.

4. Click Yes to confirm the scope deletion.

Activating a Scope

To activate a DHCP scope, perform the following steps:

1. Click Start, and select Programs|Administrative Tools|DHCP.

2. Navigate to the scope to activate.

3. Right-click the scope, and choose the Activate option from the pop-up menu.

Modifying a Scope's Properties

To modify DHCP scope properties, perform the following steps:

1. Click Start, and select Programs|Administrative Tools|DHCP.

2. Navigate to the scope with the properties that you would like to modify.

3. Right-click the scope, and choose Properties from the pop-up menu.

4. Modify any desired properties, and click OK when done.

Excluding IP Addresses from a Scope

To exclude IP addresses from a scope, perform the following steps:

1. Click Start, and select Programs|Administrative Tools|DHCP.

2. Navigate to the Address Pool container in the scope from which you would like to exclude IP addresses.

3. Right-click Address Pool, and choose New Exclusion Range from the pop-up menu.

4. Click Add.

5. Repeat this process for any other addresses that need to be excluded, and click Close when done.

Modifying a Scope's Lease Duration

To modify a DHCP scope's lease duration, perform the following steps:

1. Click Start, and select Programs|Administrative Tools|DHCP.

2. Navigate to the scope for which you would like to modify the duration properties.

3. Right-click the scope, and choose Properties from the pop-up menu.

4. Modify the Lease Duration For DHCP Clients section of the General tab.

5. Click OK.

Reconciling a Scope

To reconcile a scope, perform the following steps:

1. Click Start, and select Programs|Administrative Tools|DHCP.

2. Navigate to the scope to reconcile.

3. Right-click the scope, and choose Reconcile from the pop-up menu.

4. Click Verify.

5. When the process is complete, click OK.

6. Click Cancel to close the window.

Working with DHCP Multicast Scopes

The following sections detail the various tasks involved in working with DHCP multicast scopes.

Creating a Multicast Scope

To create a muticast scope, perform the following steps:

1. Click Start, and select Programs|Administrative Tools|DHCP.

2. Select the server where you would like the multicast scope to be created.

3. Right-click the server, and choose New Multicast from the pop-up menu.

4. When the New Multicast Scope Wizard window appears, click Next.

5. Enter a name for the new multicast scope and an optional description, and click Next.

6. Enter starting and ending IP addresses for the multicast scope and a TTL, and click Next.

NOTE: *A multicast address ranges from 224.0.0.0 to 239.255.255.255.*

---

7. If you want to exclude any addresses, enter the start and end IP addresses, and click Add.

8. Click Next.

9. Set the duration for the multicast scope lease, and click Next.

10. If you would like to activate the multicast now, select the Yes radio button, and click Next. Otherwise, select the No radio button, and click Next.

11. Click Finish.

Deleting a Multicast Scope

To delete a muticast scope, perform the following steps:

1. Click Start, and select Programs|Administrative Tools|DHCP.

2. Select the multicast scope to delete.

3. Right-click the multicast scope, and choose Delete from the pop-up menu.

4. Click Yes to confirm the deletion.

Setting a Multicast Scope TTL

To set a muticast scope TTL, perform the following steps:

1. Click Start, and select Programs|Administrative Tools|DHCP.

2. Select the multicast scope for which you would like to modify the TTL.

3. Right-click the multicast scope, and choose Properties from the pop-up menu.

4. Select the Lifetime tab.

5. Modify the TTL for the multicast scope, and click OK.

Configuring DHCP Options

The following sections detail the various tasks involved with configuring DHCP.

Configuring a Server-Based Option

To configure a server-based option, perform the following steps:

1. Click Start, and select Programs|Administrative Tools|DHCP.

2. Navigate to the Server Options container under the server where you would like to configure a new option.

3. Right-click the container, and choose the Configure Options option.

4. Select any desired options in the Available Options list.

5. Enter any desired information about the selected options in the Data Entry field.

6. Repeat these steps for any additional server options that you want.

7. Click OK.

Configuring a Scope-Based Option

To configure a scope-based option, perform the following steps:

1. Click Start, and select Programs|Administrative Tools|DHCP.

2. Navigate to the Scope Options container under the scope for which you would like to configure a new option.

3. Right-click the container, and choose the Configure Options option.

4. Select any desired options in the Available Options list.

5. Enter any desired information about the selected options in the Data Entry field.

6. Repeat these steps for any additional scope options that you want.

7. Click OK.

Creating a New Option

To create a new option, perform the following steps:

1. Click Start, and select Programs|Administrative Tools|DHCP.

2. Navigate to the server where you would like to create the new option.

3. Right-click the server, and choose Set Predefined Options from the pop-up menu.

4. When the Predefined Options And Values window appears, click Add.

5. Enter all the appropriate information in the Option Type window, and click OK.

6. Click OK.

Deleting an Option

To delete an option, perform the following steps:

1. Click Start, and select Programs|Administrative Tools|DHCP.

2. Navigate to the server where you would like to delete an option.

3. Right-click the server, and choose Set Predefined Options from the pop-up menu.

4. When the Predefined Options And Values window appears, select the option to delete, and click Delete.

5. Click OK.

Modifying an Option

To modify an option, perform the following steps:

1. Click Start, and select Programs|Administrative Tools|DHCP.

2. Navigate to the server where you would like to modify an option.

3. Right-click the server, and choose Set Predefined Options from the pop-up menu.

4. When the Predefined Options And Values window appears, select the option to modify, and click Edit.

5. Enter all the appropriate information in the Option Type window, and click OK.

6. Click OK.

Working with WINS Servers

The following sections detail the various tasks involved in working with WINS.

Installing a WINS Server

To install a WINS server, perform the following steps:

1. Click Start, and select Settings|Control Panel.

2. Double-click the Add/Remove Programs applet.

3. Click Add/Remove Windows Components.

4. When the Windows Component Wizard appears, click Next.

5. Select Networking Services, and click Details.

6. Select the Windows Internet Naming System (WINS) option, and click OK.

7. Click Next.

8. Click Finish.

Starting a WINS Server

To start a WINS server, perform the following steps:

1. Click Start, and select Programs|Administrative Tools|WINS. The WINS console will appear, as shown in Figure 12.3.

2. Navigate to the desired WINS server.

3. Right-click the server, navigate to All Tasks, and choose the Start option.

Starting a WINS Server Using the Command Prompt

To start a WINS server from the command prompt, perform the following steps:

1. Click Start, and select Programs|Accessories|Command Prompt.

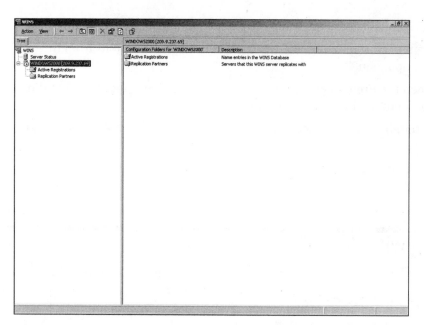

Figure 12.3   The WINS console.

2. Type the following command:

```
net start wins
```

3. Press Enter.

Stopping a WINS Server

To stop a WINS server, perform the following steps:

1. Click Start, and select Programs|Administrative Tools|WINS.

2. Navigate to the desired WINS server.

3. Right-click the server, navigate to All Tasks, and choose the Stop option.

Stopping a WINS Server Using the Command Prompt

To stop a WINS server from the command prompt, perform the following steps:

1. Click Start, and select Programs|Accessories|Command Prompt.

2. Type the following command:

```
net stop wins
```

3. Press Enter.

Adding a WINS Server

To add a WINS server, perform the following steps:

1. Click Start, and select Programs|Administrative Tools|WINS.

2. Right-click the WINS container, and choose Add Server from the pop-up menu.

3. Enter the name of the WINS server to add to the console, or browse to it, and click OK.

Deleting a WINS Server

To delete a WINS server, perform the following steps:

1. Click Start, and select Programs|Administrative Tools|WINS.

2. Navigate to the server to be deleted.

3. Right-click the server, and choose Delete from the pop-up menu.

4. Click Yes to confirm the deletion.

Changing Backup Settings

To change backup settings, perform the following steps:

1. Click Start, and select Programs|Administrative Tools|WINS.

2. Navigate to the server for which you would like to modify the backup settings.

3. Right-click the server, and choose Properties from the pop-up menu.

4. In the Database Backup section, make any necessary changes to the backup configuration, and click OK when done.

Changing the Renew Interval

To change the renew interval, perform the following steps:

1. Click Start, and select Programs|Administrative Tools|WINS.

2. Navigate to the server for which you would like to change the renew interval.

3. Right-click the server, and choose Properties from the pop-up menu.

4. Select the Intervals tab.

5. Modify the renew interval as desired.

6. Click OK.

Changing the Extinction Interval

To change the extinction interval, perform the following steps:

1. Click Start, and select Programs|Administrative Tools|WINS.

2. Navigate to the server for which you would like to change the extinction interval.

3. Right-click the server, and choose Properties from the pop-up menu.

4. Select the Intervals tab.

5. Modify the extinction interval as desired.

6. Click OK.

Changing the Extinction Timeout

To change the extinction timeout, perform the following steps:

1. Click Start, and select Programs|Administrative Tools|WINS.

2. Navigate to the server for which you would like to change the extinction timeout interval.

3. Right-click the server, and choose Properties from the pop-up menu.

4. Select the Intervals tab.

5. Modify the extinction timeout as desired.

6. Click OK.

Changing the Verification Interval

To change the verification interval, perform the following steps:

1. Click Start, and select Programs|Administrative Tools|WINS.

2. Navigate to the server for which you would like to change the verification interval.

3. Right-click the server, and choose Properties from the pop-up menu.

4. Select the Intervals tab.

5. Modify the verification interval as desired.

6. Click OK.

Configuring the Logging Properties

To configure logging properties, perform the following steps:

1. Click Start, and select Programs|Administrative Tools|WINS.

2. Navigate to the server for which you would like to configure logging.

3. Right-click the server, and choose Properties from the pop-up menu.

4. Select the Advanced tab.

5. Check the Log Detailed Events To Windows Event Log checkbox.

6. Click OK.

Specifying the WINS Database Path

To specify the WINS database path, perform the following steps:

1. Click Start, and select Programs|Administrative Tools|WINS.

2. Navigate to the server for which you would like to configure the WINS database.

3. Right-click the server, and choose Properties from the pop-up menu.

4. Select the Advanced tab.

5. Enter the desired path in the Database Path field.

TIP: *Instead of entering the drive letter and system directory (for example, C:\WINNT) you can use %windir%. This is a variable that maps to whichever system directory is created.*

---

6. Click OK.

Viewing the WINS Server Statistics

To view WINS server statistics, perform the following steps:

1. Click Start, and select Programs|Administrative Tools|WINS.

2. Navigate to the server for which you would like to view the server statistics.

3. Right-click the server, and choose Display Server Statistics from the pop-up menu.

4. Click Close when done.

Refreshing the WINS Server Statistics

To refresh WINS server statistics, perform the following steps:

1. Click Start, and select Programs|Administrative Tools|WINS.

2. Navigate to the server for which you would like to refresh the server statistics.

3. Right-click the server, and choose Display Server Statistics from the pop-up menu.

4. Click Refresh.

5. Click Close when done.

Resetting the WINS Server Statistics

To reset WINS server statistics, perform the following steps:

1. Click Start, and select Programs|Administrative Tools|WINS.

2. Navigate to the server for which you would like to view the server statistics.

3. Right-click the server, and choose Display Server Statistics from the pop-up menu.

4. Click Refresh.

5. Click Close when done.

Viewing WINS Information

The following sections detail the various tasks involved in viewing WINS information.

Viewing a WINS Record's Properties

To view a WINS record's properties, perform the following steps:

1. Click Start, and select Programs|Administrative Tools|WINS.

2. Navigate to the Active Registrations container under the server for which you would like to view a record.

3. In the right pane, right-click the desired record, and choose Properties from the pop-up menu.

4. Click OK.

Filtering the WINS Database

To filter the WINS database, perform the following steps:

1. Click Start, and select Programs|Administrative Tools|WINS.

2. Navigate to the server for which you would like to filter records.

3. Right-click the server, and choose Find By Owner from the pop-up menu.

4. Select the Record Types tab.

5. Clear the checkbox for any record type that you would like to exclude from the view.

6. Click Find Now.

Adding a Filter

To add a filter, perform the following steps:

1. Click Start, and select Programs|Administrative Tools|WINS.

2. Navigate to the server to add a filter to.

3. Right-click the server, and choose Find By Owner from the pop-up menu.

4. Select the Record Types tab.

5. Click Add.

6. Enter the ID and description for the new filter.

7. Click OK.

8. Repeat steps 4 through 7 if necessary, and click Find Now when done.

Deleting a Filter

To delete a filter, perform the following steps:

1. Click Start, and select Programs|Administrative Tools|WINS.

2. Navigate to the server from which you would like to delete a filter.

3. Right-click the server, and choose Find By Owner from the pop-up menu.

4. Select the Record Types tab.

5. Select the record to delete.

WARNING! You can only delete records that you have created.

6. Click Delete.

7. Click Yes to confirm the record deletion.

8. Click Find Now.

Modifying a Filter

To modify a filter, perform the following steps:

1. Click Start, and select Programs|Administrative Tools|WINS.

2. Navigate to the server for which you would like to modify a filter.

3. Right-click the server, and choose Find By Owner from the pop-up menu.

4. Select the Record Types tab.

5. Select the record to modify.

WARNING! You can only modify records that you have created.

6. Click Edit.

12. Large Business and
Enterprise Networking

7. Modify the description of the record.

8. Click OK.

9. Click Find Now.

Clearing the Filters

To clear a filter, perform the following steps:

1. Click Start, and select Programs|Administrative Tools|WINS.

2. Navigate to the server to which you would like to add a filter.

3. Right-click the server, and choose Find By Owner from the pop-up menu.

4. Select the Record Types tab.

5. Click Clear All.

6. Click OK.

Setting Up and Managing WINS Replication

The following sections detail the various tasks involved with setting up and managing WINS replication.

Adding a Replication Partner

To add a replication partner, perform the following steps:

1. Click Start, and select Programs|Administrative Tools|WINS.

2. Navigate to the Replication Partners container of the server.

3. Right-click the container, and choose New Replication Partner from the pop-up menu.

4. Enter the name or IP address of the replication partner computer, or browse to it.

5. Click OK.

Deleting a Replication Partner

To delete a replication partner, perform the following steps:

1. Click Start, and select Programs|Administrative Tools|WINS.

2. Navigate to the Replication Partners container of the server.

3. Select the replication partner to delete from the right pane, right-click it, and choose Delete from the pop-up menu.

4. Click Yes to confirm the deletion.

Configuring a Push Partner

To configure a push partner, perform the following steps:

1. Click Start, and select Programs|Administrative Tools|WINS.
2. Navigate to the Replication Partners container of the server.
3. Right-click the container, and choose Properties from the pop-up menu.
4. Select the Push Replication tab.
5. Make any desired modifications, and click OK.

Configuring a Pull Partner

To configure a pull partner, perform the following steps:

1. Click Start, and select Programs|Administrative Tools|WINS.
2. Navigate to the Replication Partners container of the server.
3. Right-click the container, and choose Properties from the pop-up menu.
4. Select the Pull Replication tab.
5. Make any desired modifications, and click OK.

Starting Replication

To start replication, perform the following steps:

1. Click Start, and select Programs|Administrative Tools|WINS.
2. Navigate to the Replication Partners container of the server.
3. Right-click the container, and choose Replicate Now from the pop-up menu.
4. Click Yes to confirm the replication.

Adding Static Mapping

To add static mapping, perform the following steps:

1. Click Start, and select Programs|Administrative Tools|WINS.
2. Navigate to the Active Registrations container of the server.
3. Right-click the container, and select New Static Mapping from the pop-up menu.
4. Enter the computer name, an optional NetBIOS scope, a mapping type (choose from Unique, Group, Domain Name, Internet, or Multihomed), and an IP address.
5. Click OK.

Modifying Static Mapping

To modify static mapping, perform the following steps:

1. Click Start, and select Programs|Administrative Tools|WINS.

2. Navigate to the Replication Partners container of the server.

3. Select the static mapping to modify.

4. Right-click it, and choose Properties from the pop-up menu.

5. Modify the IP address of the mapping, and click OK.

Importing Static Mappings

To import static mappings, perform the following steps:

1. Click Start, and select Programs|Administrative Tools|WINS.

2. Navigate to the Replication Partners container of the server.

3. Right-click the container, and choose Import LMHOSTS File from the pop-up menu.

4. Navigate to the location of the LMHOSTS file, and click Open.

5. Click OK when done.

Backing Up the WINS Database

To back up the WINS database, perform the following steps:

1. Click Start, and select Programs|Administrative Tools|WINS.

2. Navigate to the server with the database to back up.

3. Right-click the server, and choose Backup Database from the pop-up menu.

4. Navigate to the desired backup location, and click OK.

5. Click OK.

Restoring the WINS Database

To restore the WINS database, perform the following steps:

1. Click Start, and select Programs|Administrative Tools|WINS.

2. Navigate to the server with the database to restore.

3. Right-click the server, and choose All Tasks|Stop. This will stop the WINS service.

4. Right-click the server, and choose Restore Database from the pop-up menu.

5. Navigate to the location of the backup, and click OK.

6. The database will be restored, and WINS will automatically be started. Click OK when done.

Scavenging the WINS Database

To scavenge the WINS database, perform the following steps:

1. Click Start, and select Programs|Administrative Tools|WINS.

2. Navigate to the server to scavenge.

3. Right-click the server, and choose Scavenge Database from the pop-up menu.

4. Click OK.

5. Any errors will be logged in the Event Viewer.

Working with DFS

The following sections detail how to configure and administer DFS. Configuring DFS in a domain.

DFS configuration in a domain environment is different from the process used for peer-to-peer or non-Windows 2000 environments. To configure DFS in a domain environment, perform the following steps:

1. Launch the DFS MMC by clicking Start, selecting Run, typing "DFS", and pressing Enter.

2. Select Action|New DFS, and click Next.

3. The New DFS Root Wizard appears. You'll have the option to choose a standalone or domain DFS system. If the current computer is a member of a Windows 2000 domain, choose to create a domain DFS root. If not, choose to create a standalone DFS root.

4. Click Next, and choose the domain name, if applicable.

5. Click Next, and click Browse. Browse the network until you find the appropriate server that will hold the DFS root share. Click Next.

6. You will be prompted to choose an existing share on that server or to create a new one. Fill out the information appropriately, and click Next.

7. Enter a name for the DFS root. It's recommended that the DFS root name be unique and different from any other share names on the network. Click Next, and click Finish.

Adding Shares to the DFS Tree

When you need to add a share from a server into the overall DFS tree, follow this process:

1. Launch the DFS MMC by clicking Start, Programs, Admin Tools, DFS.

2. Highlight the DFS root that will be changed, and select Action|New DFS Link.

3. A DFS Link dialog box appears. Enter a link name, and browse to the server and folder that will be linked to the DFS tree. Be sure to enter a comment to help document where the data resides.

4. Click OK.

Configuring Fault-Tolerant DFS

After initially configuring DFS as shown in Chapter 11, you may want to make DFS fault tolerant by configuring multiple locations to hold the same data. To do this, perform the following steps:

1. In order to save time and network bandwidth, create a replica of the DFS folder data on a different server by copying it from the source to the target folder. Share the new folder.

2. Click Start, and select Program Files|Administrative Tools|Distributed File System.

3. Right-click on the source folder that you copied in Step 1, and select New Replica from the pop-up menu.

4. Click Browse to locate the duplicate target folder that you created in Step 1. Double-click this folder.

5. Select Automatic Replication, and click on OK.

6. When the Replication Policy dialog box appears, highlight the original source folder, and click Set Master.

7. Highlight the folder shares, and click Enable to activate replication.

8. Click OK.

Checking DFS Fault-Tolerance Configuration

After you've configured DFS replication (fault tolerance), you'll need to document and monitor the status of these fault-tolerant folders. To do this, perform the following steps:

1. Click Start, and select Program Files|Administrative Tools|Active Directory Users And Computers.

2. Expand the domain, and click the System Folder.

3. Expand the File Replication Service folder by clicking the plus sign to the left of the folder.

4. Expand the DFS Volume folder, and locate the share that has been replicated.

5. Two entries should be under the share. Each entry corresponds with one of the servers that replication has been configured for.

Working with IIS

The following sections detail the various tasks involved with managing IIS.

Installing the IIS Service

To install IIS, perform the following steps:

1. Click Start, and select Settings|Control Panel.

2. Double-click the Add/Remove Programs applet.

3. Click Add/Remove Windows Components.

4. When the Windows Component Wizard appears, click Next.

5. Select Internet Information Services (IIS), and click Next.

6. Click Finish.

Starting the IIS Service

To start IIS, perform the following steps:

1. Click Start, and select Programs|Administrative Tools|Internet Services Manager.

2. The IIS console will appear, as shown in Figure 12.4. Right-click the server where you would like to start the IIS Service, and choose the Restart IIS option from the pop-up menu.

3. Select the Start Internet Services on *Servername* option from the drop-down list, and click OK.

Starting the IIS Service Using the Command Prompt

To start IIS from the command prompt, perform the following steps:

1. Click Start, and select Programs|Accessories|Command Prompt.

2. Type the following command:

```
net start w3svc
```

3. Press Enter.

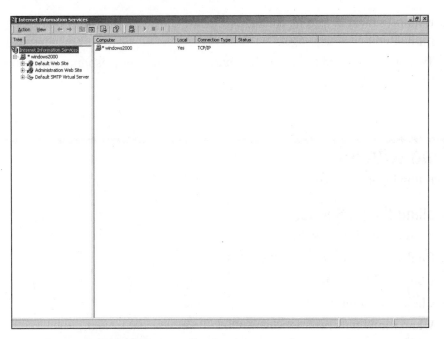

Figure 12.4   The Internet Information Services console.

Stopping the IIS Service

To stop IIS, perform the following steps:

1. Click Start, and select Programs|Administrative Tools|Internet Services Manager.

2. The IIS console will appear. Right-click the server where you would like to stop the IIS service, and choose Restart IIS from the pop-up menu.

3. Select the Start Internet Services on *Servername* option from the drop-down list, and click OK.

4. The console will wait 30 seconds before shutting the service down. If you would like the service shut down immediately, click End Now.

Stopping the IIS Service Using the Command Prompt

To stop IIS from the command prompt, perform the following steps:

1. Click Start, and select Programs|Accessories|Command Prompt.

2. Type the following command:

```
net stop w3svc
```

3. Press Enter.

Creating a New Web Site

To create a new Web site, perform the following steps:

1. Click Start, and select Programs|Administrative Tools|Internet Services Manager.

2. Navigate to the server where you would like a new Web site created.

3. Right-click the server, and choose New|Web Site from the pop-up menu.

4. When the Web Site Creation Wizard appears, click Next.

5. Enter a description for the new Web site, and click Next.

6. Enter the IP address, the port, and the host header for this site, and click Next.

7. Select a path for the new Web site.

8. If you would like anonymous access to be allowed for this site, check the Allow Anonymous Access To This Web Site checkbox, and click Next.

9. Specify the allowed permissions for this Web site, and click Next.

10. Click Finish.

Modifying a Web Site

To modify a new Web site, perform the following steps:

1. Click Start, and select Programs|Administrative Tools|Internet Services Manager.

2. Navigate to the Web site to modify.

3. Right-click the Web site, and choose Properties from the pop-up menu.

4. Make any necessary modifications to the site, and click OK when done.

Deleting a Web Site

To delete a Web site, perform the following steps:

1. Click Start, and select Programs|Administrative Tools|Internet Services Manager.

2. Navigate to the Web site to delete.

3. Right-click the Web site, and choose Delete from the pop-up menu.

4. Click Yes to confirm the deletion.

Starting a Web Site

To start a Web site, perform the following steps:

1. Click Start, and select Programs|Administrative Tools|Internet Services Manager.

2. Navigate to the Web site to start.

3. Right-click the Web site, and choose Start from the pop-up menu.

Stopping a Web Site

To stop a Web site, perform the following steps:

1. Click Start, and select Programs|Administrative Tools|Internet Services Manager.

2. Navigate to the Web site to stop.

3. Right-click the Web site, and choose Stop from the pop-up menu.

Changing the Web Port

To change a Web port, perform the following steps:

1. Click Start, and select Programs|Administrative Tools|Internet Services Manager.

2. Navigate to the Web site for which you would like to change the port.

3. Right-click the Web site, and choose Properties from the pop-up menu.

4. On the Web Site tab, modify the TCP Port value (the default is 80).

5. Click OK.

Using the Administration Web Site

To use the administration Web site, perform the following steps:

1. Click Start, and select Programs|Administrative Tools|Internet Services Manager.

2. Navigate to the Administration Web Site container.

3. Right-click the container, and choose Properties from the pop-up menu.

4. Note the value of the TCP port.

5. Close the IIS console.

6. Start Internet Explorer.

7. In the Address field, enter "http://localhost:*portnumber/*", and press Enter.

8. The IIS administration site will appear, as shown in Figure 12.5.

Changing the Administration Web Site Port

To change the administration Web site port, perform the following steps:

1. Click Start, and select Programs|Administrative Tools|Internet Services Manager.

2. Navigate to the Administration Web Site container.

Figure 12.5   The IIS administration Web site.

3. Right-click the container, and choose Properties from the pop-up menu.

4. Modify the TCP Port setting, and click OK.

Working with the FTP Service

The following sections detail the various tasks involved with managing FTP.

Installing the FTP Service

To install FTP, perform the following steps:

1. Click Start, and select Settings|Control Panel.

2. Double-click the Add/Remove Programs applet.

3. Click Add/Remove Windows Components.

4. When the Windows Component Wizard appears, click Next.

5. Select Internet Information Server, and click Details.

6. Select the File Transfer Protocol (FTP) Server option, and click OK.

7. Click Next.

8. Click Finish.

Starting the FTP Service

To start the FTP service, perform the following steps:

1. Click Start, and select Programs|Administrative Tools|Services.

2. Select the FTP Publishing Service item, right-click it, and choose the Start option.

Starting the FTP Service Using the Command Prompt

To start the FTP service from the command prompt, perform the following steps:

1. Click Start, and select Programs|Accessories|Command Prompt.

2. Type the following command:

```
net start msftpsvc
```

3. Press Enter.

Stopping the FTP Service

To stop the FTP service, perform the following steps:

1. Click Start, and select Programs|Administrative Tools|Services.

2. Select the FTP Publishing Service item, right-click it, and choose the Stop option.

Stopping the FTP Service Using the Command Prompt

To stop the FTP service from the command prompt, perform the following steps:

1. Click Start, and select Programs|Accessories|Command Prompt.

2. Type the following command:

```
net stop msftpsvc
```

3. Press Enter.

Creating a New FTP Site

To create a new FTP site, perform the following steps:

1. Click Start, and select Programs|Administrative Tools|Internet Services Manager.

2. Navigate to the server where you would like a new FTP site created.

3. Right-click the server, and choose the New|FTP Site option from the pop-up menu.

4. When the New FTP Site Creation Wizard appears, click Next.

5. Enter a description for the new FTP site, and click Next.

6. Enter the IP address and the TCP port for this site, and click Next.

7. Select a path for the new FTP site.

8. Specify the allowed permissions for this FTP site, and click Next.

9. Click Finish.

Modifying an FTP Site

To modify an FTP site, perform the following steps:

1. Click Start, and select Programs|Administrative Tools|Internet Services Manager.

2. Navigate to the FTP site that you would like to modify.

3. Right-click the FTP site, and choose Properties from the pop-up menu.

4. Make any necessary modifications to the site, and click OK when done.

Deleting an FTP Site

To delete an FTP site, perform the following steps:

1. Click Start, and select Programs|Administrative Tools|Internet Services Manager.

2. Navigate to the FTP site to delete.

3. Right-click the FTP site, and choose Delete from the pop-up menu.

4. Click Yes to confirm the deletion.

Starting an FTP Site

To start an FTP site, perform the following steps:

1. Click Start, and select Programs|Administrative Tools|Internet Services Manager.

2. Navigate to the FTP site to start.

3. Right-click the FTP site, and choose Start from the pop-up menu.

Stopping an FTP Site

To stop an FTP site, perform the following steps:

1. Click Start, and select Programs|Administrative Tools|Internet Services Manager.

2. Navigate to the FTP site to stop.

3. Right-click the FTP site, and choose Stop from the pop-up menu.

Changing the FTP Port

To change the FTP port, perform the following steps:

1. Click Start, and select Programs|Administrative Tools|Internet Services Manager.

2. Navigate to the FTP site for which you would like to change the port.

3. Right-click the FTP site, and choose Properties from the pop-up menu.

4. On the FTP Site tab, modify the TCP Port value (the default is 21).

5. Click OK.

Working with Routers

The following sections detail the various tasks involved with routes.

Viewing the Routing Table

To view the routing table, perform the following steps:

1. Click Start, and select Programs|Accessories|Command Prompt.

2. Type the following command:

```
route print
```

3. Press Enter. A screen similar to the one shown in Figure 12.6 appears.

Figure 12.6   The routing table.

Adding a Static Route from the Command Line

To add a static route, perform the following steps:

1. Click Start, and select Programs|Accessories|Command Prompt.

2. Type the following command:

```
route add destination mask netmask gateway metric metric IF interface
```

3. Press Enter.

NOTE: *For example, if you wanted to create a static route to the 192.168.0.0 network with a subnet mask of 255.255.0.0, a gateway of 192.168.1.1, and a metric of 1, you can type the following:*

```
Route add 192.168.0.0 mask 255.255.0.0 192.168.1.1 metric 1
```

Deleting a Static Route from the Command Line

To delete a static route, perform the following steps:

1. Click Start, and select Programs|Accessories|Command Prompt.

2. Type the following command:

```
route add destination mask netmask gateway metric metric IF interface
```

3. Press Enter.

NOTE: *If you were to delete the route created in the previous example, you would type in the following command:*

```
Route delete 192.168.0.0
```

Working with Routing Protocols

The following sections detail the various tasks involved with managing routing protocols.

Installing RRAS

To install RRAS, perform the following steps:

1. Click Start, and select Programs|Administrative Tools|Routing And Remote Access.

2. In the Routing And Remote Access console, shown in Figure 12.7, right-click the Routing And Remote Access container, and choose the Add Server option from the pop-up menu.

3. Right-click the newly added server, and choose the Configure And Enable Routing And Remote Access option.

4. When the Routing And Remote Access Server Setup Wizard appears, click Next.

5. Select the desired configuration for the server. (This example uses the Manually Configured Server option.) Click Next.

6. Click Finish.

7. Click Yes to start RRAS.

Adding an IP Routing Protocol

To add an IP routing protocol, perform the following steps:

1. Click Start, and select Programs|Administrative Tools|Routing And Remote Access.

2. Navigate to the General container of the IP routing protocol in the desired server container.

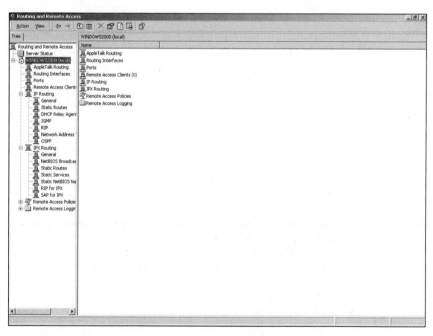

Figure 12.7   The Routing And Remote Access console.

3. Right-click the General Container, and choose the New Routing Protocol option from the pop-up menu.

4. Select the desired routing protocol, and click OK.

Deleting an IP Routing Protocol

To delete an IP routing protocol, perform the following steps:

1. Click Start, and select Programs|Administrative Tools|Routing And Remote Access.

2. Navigate to the General container of the IP routing protocol in the desired server container.

3. Right-click the routing protocol to delete, and choose Delete from the pop-up menu.

4. Click Yes to confirm the deletion.

Adding a Static Route

To add a static route, perform the following steps:

1. Click Start, and select Programs|Administrative Tools|Routing And Remote Access.

2. Navigate to the General container of the IP routing protocol in the desired server container.

3. Right-click the Static Routes container, and choose New Static Route from the pop-up menu.

4. Enter the static route information, and click OK.

Deleting a Static Route

To delete a static route, perform the following steps:

1. Click Start, and select Programs|Administrative Tools|Routing And Remote Access.

2. Navigate to the General container of the IP routing protocol in the desired server container.

3. Right-click the static route to delete, and choose Delete from the pop-up menu.

Configuring Routing Information Protocol

To configure Routing Information Protocol (RIP), perform the following steps:

1. Click Start, and select Programs|Administrative Tools|Routing And Remote Access.

2. Navigate to the General container of the IP routing protocol in the desired server container.

3. Right-click the General container, and choose New Routing Protocol from the pop-up menu.

4. Select Routing Internet Protocol (RIP), and click OK.

Configuring Open Shortest Path First

To configure Open Shortest Path First (OSPF), perform the following steps:

1. Click Start, and select Programs|Administrative Tools|Routing And Remote Access.

2. Navigate to the General container of the IP routing protocol in the desired server container.

3. Right-click the General container, and choose New Routing Protocol from the pop-up menu.

4. Select Open Shortest Path First (OSPF), and click OK.

Configuring Network Address Translation

To configure Network Address Translation (NAT), perform the following steps:

1. Click Start, and select Programs|Administrative Tools|Routing And Remote Access.

2. Navigate to the General container of the IP routing protocol in the desired server container.

3. Right-click the General container, and choose New Routing Protocol from the pop-up menu.

4. Select Network Address Translation (NAT), and click OK.

Working with NWLink

The following sections detail the various tasks involved with managing NWLink.

Installing NWLink

To install NWLink, perform the following steps:

1. Click Start, and select Settings|Control Panel.

2. Double-click the Network And Dial-Up Connections applet.

3. Double-click the network connection for which you would like to install NWLink.

4. Click Properties.

5. On the General tab, click Install.

6. Select the Protocol option, and click Add.

7. In the Select Network Protocol window, select NWLink IPX/SPX/NetBIOS Compatible Transport Protocol, and click OK.

8. Click Yes to reboot the server.

Removing NWLink

To remove NWLink, perform the following steps:

1. Click Start, and select Settings|Control Panel.

2. Double-click the Network And Dial-Up Connections applet.

3. Double-click the network connection for which you would like to uninstall NWLink.

4. Click Properties.

5. On the General tab, select the NWLink IPX/SPX/NetBIOS Compatible Transport Protocol option.

6. Click Uninstall.

7. Click Yes to confirm the deletion.

8. Click Close.

Changing the Internal Network Number

To change the internal network number, perform the following steps:

1. Click Start, and select Settings|Control Panel.

2. Double-click the Network And Dial-Up Connections applet.

3. Double-click the network connection for which you would like to change the internal network number.

4. Click Properties.

5. On the General tab, select the NWLink IPX/SPX/NetBIOS Compatible Transport Protocol option.

6. Click Properties.

7. Enter a new internal network number.

8. Click OK.

9. Click Close.

Changing the Frame Type

To change frame type settings, perform the following steps:

1. Select Start|Settings|Control Panel.

2. Double-click the Network And Dial-Up Connections applet.

3. Double-click the network connection for which you would like to change the frame type.

4. Click Properties.

5. On the General tab, select the NWLink IPX/SPX/NetBIOS Compatible Transport Protocol option.

6. Click Properties.

7. Select either to detect the frame type automatically (by selecting Auto Frame Type Detection) or manually (by selecting Manual Frame Type Detection).

8. For manual frame type detection, click Add, enter the frame type properties, and click OK.

9. Click Close.

Connecting to a Novell NetWare Server

The following sections detail the various tasks involved with connecting to NetWare computers.

Installing GSNW

To install GSNW, perform the following steps:

1. Click Start, and select Settings|Control Panel.

2. Double-click the Network And Dial-Up Connections applet.

3. Double-click the network connection for which you would like to install GSNW.

4. Click Properties.

5. On the General tab, click Add.

6. Select the Client option, and click Add.

7. Select Gateway (And Client) Services For NetWare, and click OK.

Removing GSNW

To remove GSNW, perform the following steps:

1. Click Start, and select Settings|Control Panel.

2. Double-click the Network And Dial-Up Connections applet.

3. Double-click the network connection for which you would like to install GSNW.

4. Click Properties.

5. Select the Gateway (And Client) Services For NetWare, and click Uninstall.

6. Click Yes to confirm the deletion.

7. Click Yes to reboot the server.

Setting a Preferred Server for Bindery Emulation

To set a preferred server for bindery emulation, perform the following steps:

1. Click Start, and select Settings|Control Panel.

2. Double-click the Network And Dial-Up Connections applet.

3. Double-click the network connection for which you would like to install Gateway Services For NetWare.

4. Click Properties.

5. Select Gateway (And Client) Services For NetWare, and click Properties.

6. Select the Preferred Server radio button, and enter the name of the preferred server.

7. Click OK.

8. Click Close.

Setting a Default Tree and Context for NDS

To set a default tree and context for NDS, perform the following steps:

1. Click Start, and select Settings|Control Panel.

2. Double-click the Network And Dial-Up Connections applet.

3. Double-click the network connection for which you would like to install Gateway Services For NetWare.

4. Click Properties.

5. Select Gateway (And Client) Services For NetWare, and click Properties.

6. Select the Default Tree And Context radio button, and enter the name of the default tree and context.

7. Click OK.

8. Click Close.

Installing Services for the Macintosh

The following sections detail the various tasks involved with configuring Services for Macintosh.

Installing the AppleTalk Protocol

To install AppleTalk, perform the following steps:

1. Click Start, and select Settings|Control Panel.
2. Double-click the Network And Dial-Up Connections applet.
3. Double-click the network connection for which you would like to install AppleTalk.
4. Click Properties.
5. On the General tab, click Install.
6. Select the Protocol option, and click Add.
7. In the Select Network Protocol window, select AppleTalk Protocol, and click OK.
8. Click Yes to reboot the server.

Removing the AppleTalk Protocol

To remove AppleTalk, perform the following steps:

1. Click Start, and select Settings|Control Panel.
2. Double-click the Network And Dial-Up Connections applet.
3. Double-click the network connection for which you would like to uninstall AppleTalk.
4. Click Properties.
5. On the General tab, select the AppleTalk Protocol option.
6. Click Uninstall.
7. Click Yes to confirm the deletion.
8. Click Close.

Modifying the AppleTalk Zone

To modify the AppleTalk zone, perform the following steps:

1. Click Start, and select Settings|Control Panel.
2. Double-click the Network And Dial-Up Connections applet.
3. Double-click the network connection for which you would like to modify the AppleTalk zone.

4. Click Properties.

5. On the General tab, select the AppleTalk Protocol option.

6. Click Properties.

7. Select the zone from the drop-down menu, and click OK.

8. Click Done.

Working with Clusters

Clustering is becoming more and more common. This section assumes that you have dedicated cluster hardware that is on the Windows 2000 Hardware Compatibility List (HCL). When preparing for the installation, install Windows 2000 Advanced Server as outlined in Chapter 5. The only difference is that you need to select Cluster Service from the Windows 2000 Components window.

Adding the First Node of the Cluster

To add the first node of the cluster, follow these steps:

1. Upon the final reboot of the server, the Configure Your Server window will appear. Click Finish.

2. In the Add/Remove Programs applet, click the Configure button to the right of Cluster Service (see Figure 12.8). The Cluster Service Configuration Wizard will appear.

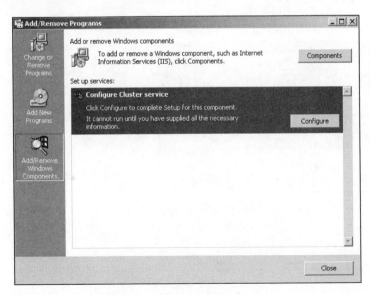

Figure 12.8   Installing the Cluster service.

3. Click Next.

4. Click I Understand, and then click Next.

5. Select the First Node In The Cluster radio button, and click Next, as shown in Figure 12.9.

6. Enter the name for the cluster, and click Next.

7. Enter the username, password, and domain for the cluster administrator. Click Next.

8. Click Next to confirm the user information.

9. Select the cluster file storage volume, and click Next.

10. Select the desired connections, and click Next. Repeat this if more than one network adapter is installed on the system.

11. Click OK.

12. Assign a cluster IP address, and click Next.

13. Click Finish.

Adding Subsequent Cluster Nodes

To add subsequent cluster nodes, follow these steps:

1. Upon final reboot of the server, the Configure Your Server window will appear. Click Finish.

2. In the Add/Remove Programs applet, click the Configure button to the right of Cluster Service. The Cluster Service Configuration Wizard will appear.

3. Click Next to formally launch the wizard.

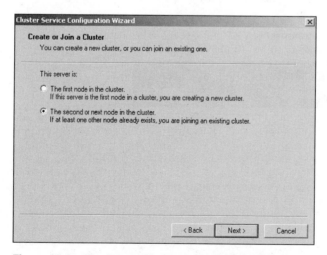

Figure 12.9   The Create Or Join A Cluster window.

4. Click I Understand, and then click Next.

5. Select the Second Or Next Node In The Cluster radio button, and click Next.

6. Enter the existing cluster information, and click Next.

7. Click OK.

8. Select an account and password, and then click Next.

9. Click Finish.

Evicting a Cluster Node Resource

To evict a cluster node, follow these steps:

1. Click Start, and select Programs|Administrative Tools|Cluster Administrator.

2. In the left pane, select the node that is to be evicted, and select File|Stop Cluster Service.

3. Select File|Evict Node.

4. Uninstall the Cluster service.

Adding a New Resource

To add a new resource to a cluster node, follow these steps:

1. Click Start, and select Programs|Administrative Tools|Cluster Administrator.

2. Double-click the Groups folder in the left pane.

3. In the right pane, select the group to which the new resource is to belong.

4. Right-click the group, and choose New|Resource from the pop-up menu.

5. In the New Resource Wizard screen, enter the name and description of the new resource, select the resource type and group, and click Next.

6. Add any desired owner for the resource, and click Next.

7. To add dependencies, select a resource under the Available Resources section, and click Add.

8. Repeat Step 7 to add any other resource dependencies, and click Finish when done.

Deleting a Resource

To delete a resource from a cluster node, follow these steps:

1. Click Start, and select Programs|Administrative Tools|Cluster Administrator.

2. Select the Resources folder in the left pane.

3. Right-click the resource that is to be deleted, and select Delete from the pop-up menu.

Bringing a Resource Online

To bring a resource online, follow these steps:

1. Click Start, and select Programs|Administrative Tools|Cluster Administrator.

2. Select the Resources folder in the left pane.

3. Right-click the resource that is to be brought online, and select File|Bring Online.

Taking a Resource Offline

To take a resource offline, follow these steps:

1. Click Start, and select Programs|Administrative Tools|Cluster Administrator.

2. Select the Resources folder in the left pane.

3. Right-click the resource that is to be taken offline, and select File|Take Offline.

Adding a DHCP Server Resource

To add a DHCP server resource to a cluster node, follow these steps:

1. Click Start, and select Programs|Administrative Tools|Cluster Administrator.

2. Double-click the Groups folder in the left pane.

3. In the right pane, select the group for which the DHCP server resource is to belong.

4. Right-click the group, and choose New|Resource from the pop-up menu.

5. In the New Resource Wizard screen, enter the name and description of the new resource, select the DHCP Service resource type and group, and click Next.

6. Add any desired owner for the resource, and click Next.

7. To add dependencies, select a resource under the Available Resources section, and click Add.

8. Repeat Step 7 to add any other resource dependencies, and click Next.

9. Enter the appropriate database, audit file, and backup paths.

10. Click Finish.

Adding a File Share Resource

To add a file share resource to a cluster node, follow these steps:

1. Click Start, and select Programs|Administrative Tools|Cluster Administrator.

2. Double-click the Groups folder in the left pane.

3. In the right pane, select the group to which the file share resource is to belong.

4. Right-click the group, and choose New|Resource from the pop-up menu.

5. In the New Resource Wizard screen, enter the name and description of the new resource, select the file share resource type and group, and click Next.

6. Add any desired owner for the resource, and click Next.

7. To add dependencies, select a resource under the Available Resources section, and click Add.

8. Repeat Step 7 to add any other resource dependencies, and click Next.

9. Enter a share name, path, and comment.

10. If desired, enter a user limit and permissions.

11. Click Advanced.

12. Select the share type (Normal Share, DFS Root, or Share Subdirectories).

13. Click OK.

14. Click Finish.

Adding an IIS Server Resource

To add an IIS server resource to a cluster node, follow these steps:

1. Click Start, and select Programs|Administrative Tools|Cluster Administrator.

2. Double-click the Groups folder in the left pane.

3. In the right pane, select the group to which the IIS server resource is to belong.

4. Right-click the group, and choose New|Resource from the pop-up menu.

5. In the New Resource Wizard screen, enter the name and description of the new resource, select the IIS server resource type and group, and click Next.

6. Add any desired owner for the resource, and click Next.

7. To add dependencies, select a resource under the Available Resources section, and click Add.

8. Repeat Step 7 to add any other resource dependencies, and click Next.

9. Select whether this resource is for an FTP site or a Web site, choose the desired site from the IIS server drop-down list, and click Finish.

Adding a Print Spooler Resource

To add a print spooler resource to a cluster node, follow these steps:

1. Click Start, and select Programs|Administrative Tools|Cluster Administrator.
2. Double-click the Groups folder in the left pane.
3. In the right pane, select the group to which the print spooler resource is to belong.
4. Right-click the group, and choose New|Resource from the pop-up menu.
5. In the New Resource Wizard screen, enter the name and description of the new resource, select the Print Spooler resource type and group, and click Next.
6. Add any desired owner for the resource, and click Next.
7. To add dependencies, select a resource under the Available Resources section, and click Add.
8. Repeat Step 7 to add any other resource dependencies, and click Next.
9. Enter the path to the spool folder.
10. Select a desired Job Completion Timeout setting.
11. Click Finish.

Adding an IP Address Resource

To add an IP address resource to a cluster node, follow these steps:

1. Click Start, and select Programs|Administrative Tools|Cluster Administrator.
2. Double-click the Groups folder in the left pane.
3. In the right pane, select the group to which the IP address resource is to belong.
4. Right-click the group, and choose New|Resource from the pop-up menu.
5. In the New Resource Wizard screen, enter the name and description of the new resource, select the IP Address resource type and group, and click Next.
6. Add any desired owner for the resource, and click Next.
7. To add dependencies, select a resource under the Available Resources section, and click Add.
8. Repeat Step 7 to add any other resource dependencies, and click Next.
9. Enter an IP address and subnet mask.
10. Select the appropriate network from the drop-down list.

11. If NetBIOS is to be enabled, check the Enable NetBIOS For This Address checkbox.

12. Click Finish.

Adding a WINS Server Resource

To add a WINS server resource to a cluster node, follow these steps:

1. Click Start, and select Programs|Administrative Tools|Cluster Administrator.

2. Double-click the Groups folder in the left pane.

3. In the right pane, select the group to which the WINS server resource is to belong.

4. Right-click the group, and choose New|Resource from the pop-up menu.

5. In the New Resource Wizard screen, enter the name and description of the new resource, select the WINS server resource type and group, and click Next.

6. Add any desired owner for the resource, and click Next.

7. To add dependencies, select a resource under the Available Resources section, and click Add.

8. Repeat Step 7 to add any other resource dependencies, and click Next.

9. Enter the appropriate database and backup paths.

10. Click Finish.

Enabling Diagnostic Logging

To enable diagnostic logging on a cluster, follow these steps:

1. Click Start, and select Settings|Control Panel.

2. Double-click the System applet.

3. Select the Advanced Tab.

4. Click Environmental Variables.

5. Click New under the System Variables section.

6. In the Variable Name field, enter the name of the variable: "clusterlog".

7. In the Variable Value field, enter the variable's value: "c:\cluster\cluster.log".

8. Click OK.

9. Click OK.

10. Close Control Panel.

11. Click Start, and select Programs|Administrative Tools|Cluster Administrator.

12. In the left pane, select the node where diagnostic logging is to be enabled, and select File|Stop Cluster Service.

13. In the left pane, select the node where diagnostic logging is to be enabled, and select File|Start Cluster Service.

Disabling Diagnostic Logging

To disable diagnostic logging on a cluster, follow these steps:

1. Click Start, and select Settings|Control Panel.

2. Double-click the System applet.

3. Select the Advanced Tab.

4. Click Environmental Variables.

5. Select the Clusterlog variable in the System Variable section.

6. Click Delete.

7. Click OK.

8. Click OK to close the window.

9. Close the Control Panel.

10. Click Start, and select Programs|Administrative Tools|Cluster Administrator.

11. In the left pane, select the node where diagnostic logging is to be enabled, and select File|Stop Cluster Service.

12. In the left pane, select the node where diagnostic logging is to be enabled, and select File|Start Cluster Service.

Chapter 13

The Windows 2000 Boot Process

In Depth

The bootup process of a modern personal computer (PC) is fairly standard. Although some systems, such as Compaq and International Business Machines (IBM), go through their own processes, the basic design is the same. Every PC goes through a process known as power-on self-test (POST). The "Windows 2000 Bootup—Step by Step" section covers POST in more detail.

Important Windows 2000 Boot Files

Before Windows 2000 can start properly, several files need to be present. Many of these files are interchangeable between systems, assuming that the same operating system and service pack are installed on both systems. Some, however, such as boot.ini and bootsect.dos, are specific to the system on which they were installed.

Table 13.1 lists most of the files that might exist on your Windows 2000 installation and their location on the system. Any files that exist on all Windows 2000 systems are marked as default and are listed in the order in which they are loaded.

Table 13.1   Windows 2000 startup files.

File	Default?	Location
ntldr	Yes	In the active partition (usually C:\)
boot.ini	Yes	In the active partition (usually C:\)
bootsect.dos	No	In the active partition (usually C:\)
ntdetect.com	Yes	In the active partition (usually C:\)
ntbootdd.sys	No	In the active partition (usually C:\)
ntoskrnl.exe	Yes	%systemroot%\System32
hal.dll	Yes	%systemroot%\System32

Windows 2000 Bootup—Step by Step

As outlined in Microsoft's *Windows 2000 Professional Resource Kit* (Microsoft Press, ISBN 1-57231-808-2), the startup process for Windows 2000 follows these eight steps:

1. POST
2. Initial startup process
3. Bootstrap loader process
4. Operating system selection
5. Hardware detection
6. Hardware configuration selection
7. Kernel loading
8. Operating system logon process

Each of these boot sequences is covered in the following sections.

POST

Almost every computer made today goes through the same boot process. The order, responses, and what it displays on the screen might be different, but the process is the same nonetheless. It's important to know that up until the time when the operating system (Windows 2000) loads, the basic input/output system (BIOS) is in control. The BIOS is a computer chip that resides on the system that issues instructions to the central processing unit (CPU) during the boot process in order to initialize everything and to get all of the BIOS running.

One of the first things that the BIOS does when the power is turned on is that it goes through a POST process where it wakes up and checks to make sure that all of the arms and legs are attached and working.

When you first turn on your computer, the system will begin to do this by initializing the video card and displaying a brief message. At this point, many brand-name servers and systems will mask the goings-on of POST with what's known as a splash screen that usually shows the company logo or something of that sort and gives you the option to enter the setup or configuration windows. While this is going on, the system will check the memory on the system and test it in an attempt to detect any errors. The hard drives will be detected next, along with some of the installed devices. These devices might include communication ports, parallel ports, Universal Serial Bus (USB) ports, and P/S2 ports.

Initial Startup Process

One of the important things that occurs right after POST is the detection of peripherals located on the PCI bus. For plug-and-play (PnP)-compliant computers, most types of BIOS will have a setting to trigger PnP features. If this setting is turned on, the BIOS will take an inventory of all devices on the PCI bus and attempt to detect the nature of these devices. Those devices that are PnP compliant will respond with a set of specific instructions indicating the basic configuration information for those devices. If these PnP devices do not have this basic configuration installed—input/output (I/O) addresses, interrupt requests (IRQs), and so forth—the BIOS will automatically configure those devices appropriate to what's available on the system. This information is stored in a miniature database that is passed on to the PnP-compliant operating system, where the information is stored and referenced for use during I/O processes.

After this hard drive is detected, the BIOS will look for a Master Boot Record (MBR). The MBR contains all the information necessary to boot the operating system. The BIOS loads the MBR into memory, launches it, and passes control to it.

Although there's only one MBR, each operating system's MBR is different. Essentially, it knows how to load the operating system. For example, Windows 9x's MBR will look for the io.sys file and pass control to it, whereas Windows NT and Windows 2000's MBR will look for (and load) the NTLDR file.

Bootstrap Loader Process

The MBR passes control to the NTLDR program. NTLDR is known as the *bootstrap loader* for Windows 2000. Its role is to load the operating system boot files, display the operating system selection menu, and control hardware profiles selection and device detection.

NTLDR will not operate properly unless specific files exist on the system. These files are the boot.ini file and the ntdetect.com file.

NOTE: *If you have a non-Windows NT or non-Windows 2000 operating system installed on your system and you are dual-booting the computer, a bootsect.dos file will exist as well. This file maintains a copy of the MBR for the secondary operating system. If that operating system is selected, the MBR from the bootsect.dos file is loaded, and control is passed to it. At this point, the Windows 2000 startup process is stopped, and the secondary operating system boot process takes over.*

After NTLDR is loaded and launched, it clears the screen and displays a message, such as "OS Loader V5.0." The exact message may vary depending on the version of the operating system or service pack installed.

NTLDR is responsible for performing several tasks. First, it will switch the processor from Real mode (the default startup for the system) to 32-bit Memory mode. If this step does not occur, NTLDR will fail.

Operating System Selection

Next, the file system drivers are loaded. These include the file allocation table (FAT) and Windows NT File System (NTFS) drivers. If these drivers are not loaded, the rest of the boot process will fail because the startup programs will not be able to read any information on the hard drives.

At the next phase of NTLDR's execution, the program will search for a boot.ini file. As stated earlier, the boot.ini file is a simple text file that informs NTLDR what operating systems are installed on the system, where they are located, which one to boot by default, and the timeout on the default selection. After this file is analyzed, NTLDR will display the normal operating system selection screen (see Figure 13.1). Several different switches can be used in the boot.ini files. These switches and their uses are listed in Table 13.2.

From the operating system selection screen, you can either choose the operating system to boot, let NTLDR automatically choose it for you (assuming that a timeout has been set), or use a troubleshooting/advanced setup option (by pressing F8). This troubleshooting/advanced setup menu is shown in Figure 13.2.

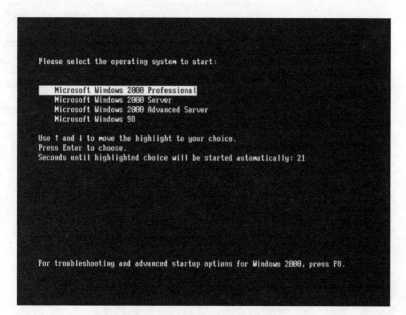

Figure 13.1   The operating system selection menu.

Table 13.2   The boot.ini switches.

Switch	Use
/basevideo	Starts the operating system using industry-standard Video Graphics Array (VGA) drivers. All video cards support this boot method.
/baudrate=xx	Used for debugging. Sets the baud rate that will be used when the server is debugged. The **/debug** option will be automatically run.
/crashdebug	Loads the debugger, but does not launch it until Windows 2000 has a kernel error.
/debug	Loads the debugger so that it can be used when a connection is made to the server through a host PC.
/debugport=comx	Selects the communication port that will be used for the debugging. The **/debug** option will be automatically run.
/fastdetect=comx	Prevents Windows 2000's ntdetect.com from attempting to detect a mouse on the specified communication port. This switch is used when an uninterruptable power supply (UPS) is connected to the serial port.
/maxmem:x	Limits the amount of memory that can be used by Windows 2000. This switch is used if a faulty memory chip is suspected.
/nodebug	Turns off debugging.
/numproc=x	Limits the number of processors that a multiprocessor Windows 2000 system will use.
/pae	Enables the physical address extension.
/sos	Displays all device drivers on the screen as they are loaded. Used to find a specific device driver that may be causing a problem on the network.

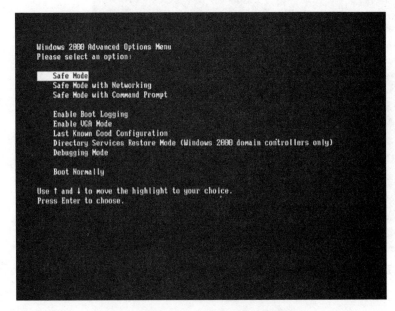

Figure 13.2   The troubleshooting/advanced setup menu.

Hardware Detection

After the operating system—including any special startup instructions—is selected, NTLDR will launch an application called ntdetect.com whose role is to detect the hardware devices installed on the system. One of the things that ntdetect.com will do is pull the PnP inventory information that was gathered earlier during the boot process. It will subsequently verify each of the devices against the BIOS information and will also verify the hardware information that is already configured within the operating system. Necessary updates are made, and the boot process continues. These hardware devices can include the following:

- Video
- Keyboard
- Mouse
- Ports (communication, parallel, and USB)
- Floppy drives
- CD-ROM drives

Hardware Profile Selection

While ntdetect.com is running, you have the option to select a different hardware profile if more than one profile has been defined. Hardware profiles are most commonly used with notebook computers. Many of today's notebook computers have docking bays that can greatly enhance functionality.

Because Windows 2000 PnP features will automatically detect hardware changes when a system's hardware changes, the time involved during this detection process can become lengthy and time-consuming, especially if you're dealing with a notebook computer whose hardware configuration changes at least twice a day. You can configure Windows 2000 either to autodetect hardware changes or to let you select a hardware profile. This selection will automatically load the known changes for you so that the detection process is much faster. The hardware profile screen is shown in Figure 13.3.

Kernel Loading

The last task that NTLDR performs is to load the Windows 2000 kernel (ntoskrnl.exe) and pass control to it. You'll know that this step has occurred when you see the graphical Windows 2000 startup screen.

Ntoskrnl will now load the hardware abstraction layer (HAL) file (hal.dll) and the system configuration from the registry (HKEY_LOCAL_MACHINE/SYSTEM). It then starts loading the system services and low-level device drivers.

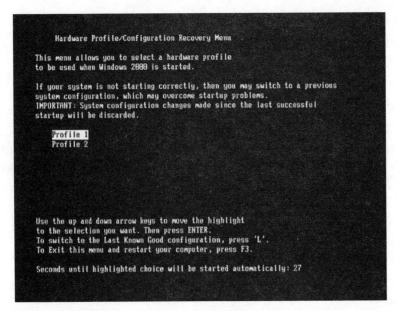

Figure 13.3   The hardware profile selection menu.

NOTE: *If you select a Last Known Good Configuration, the system configuration information will be read from HKEY_ LOCAL_MACHINE/SYSTEM/ControlSetxxx. The value of xxx is read from the LastKnownGood entry in the Select key.*

Final Preparation

After the hardware is loaded and initialized, the system will examine other configuration settings to load local computer and user profiles and also to initialize network settings. After computer and user profiles are loaded, the system will investigate the networking settings associated with the installed network card(s). The system will load any configured protocols, and, if the Transmission Control Protocol/Internet Protocol (TCP/IP) settings call for a dynamically assigned IP address, the system will query the network for a local Dynamic Host Control Protocol (DHCP) server. After the IP address information is received from the DHCP server, the system will again check to determine what kind of networked configuration it has. If it is a member of a domain, the computer will register itself with the domain and DDNS (if applicable), will receive any applicable computer group policies, and will execute appropriate startup scripts. If the system is not a member of a domain, it will immediately move to the logon process.

Logon Process

The final step in the startup process is launching the Windows 2000 Logon subsystem. This subsystem (winlogon.exe) will start the Local Security Administration system (lsass.exe). At this point, the Welcome To Windows logon window appears.

Immediate Solutions

Using the Windows 2000 Boot Menu

To use the Windows 2000 boot menu, perform the following steps:

1. Boot the system.
2. If you would like the countdown stopped, press any key.
3. Select an operating system option by using the up or down arrow key.
4. After you've chosen the operating system to boot, press Enter.

Modifying the Windows 2000 Boot Menu

There are a few ways to customize the Windows 2000 boot menu. These are discussed in the following sections.

Changing the Default Operating System

To change the default operating system using the Control Panel, perform the following steps:

1. Click Start, and select Settings|Control Panel.
2. Double-click the System applet.
3. Click the Advanced tab.
4. Click Startup And Recovery (see Figure 13.4). The Startup And Recovery dialog box appears.
5. Select the operating system that you want booted by default from the Default Operating System drop-down list.
6. Click OK.

Manually Modifying the Default Operating System

To change the default operating system manually, perform the following steps:

1. Double-click My Computer.
2. Navigate to and select the C:\ drive.
3. Right-click the boot.ini file.

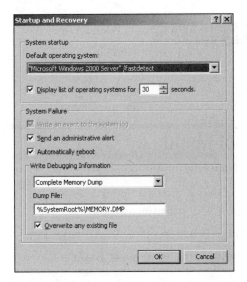

Figure 13.4   The Startup And Recovery dialog box.

TIP: If the boot.ini file is not visible, follow these steps:

1. Click Start, and select Settings|Control Panel.

2. Select Tools|Folder Options.

3. Select the View tab.

4. Select the Show Hidden Files And Folders radio button.

5. Uncheck the Hide Protected Operating System Files checkbox.

6. Uncheck the Hide File Extensions For Known File Types checkbox.

7. Click OK.

The boot.ini file will now appear as a faded icon.

---

4. In the boot.ini Properties window, ensure that the Read-Only checkbox is cleared.

5. Click OK.

6. Double-click the boot.ini file.

7. Find the path to the operating system that you want to become the default from the Operating Systems section of the boot.ini file (to the left of the equal sign).

8. Copy the path to the Default parameter of the Boot Loader section of the boot.ini file.

9. Save the file, and exit Notepad.

10. Reboot the server.

Manually Modifying the Boot Order

To change the boot order manually, perform the following steps:

1. Double-click My Computer.

2. Navigate to and select the C:\ drive.

3. Right-click the boot.ini file.

TIP: *If the boot.ini file is not visible, follow these steps:*

1. Click Start, and select Settings\Control Panel.

2. Select Tools\Folder Options.

3. Select the View tab.

4. Select the Show Hidden Files And Folders radio button.

5. Check the Hide File Extensions For Known File Types checkbox.

6. Click OK.

The boot.ini file will now appear as a faded icon.

---

4. In the boot.ini Properties window, ensure that the Read-Only checkbox is cleared.

5. Click OK.

6. Double-click the boot.ini file.

7. Rearrange the items in the Operating Systems section to your liking.

8. Save the file, and exit Notepad.

9. Reboot the server.

Disabling and Enabling the Boot Menu Countdown

To enable or disable the boot menu countdown, perform the following steps:

1. Click Start, and select Settings\Control Panel.

2. Double-click the System applet, and click the Advanced tab.

3. Click Startup And Recovery.

4. Clear the Display List Of Operating Systems For *X* Seconds checkbox to disable the countdown. You can also click this option, set the number of seconds to count down to enable it, and click OK.

5. Click OK.

Modifying the Boot Menu Timeout

To change the amount of time before the boot menu times out, perform the following steps:

1. Click Start, and select Settings\Control Panel.

2. Double-click the System applet.

3. Click the Advanced tab.

4. Click Startup And Recovery.

5. Check the Display List Of Operating Systems For *X* Seconds checkbox.

6. Enter the amount of time (in seconds) for the boot menu to count down before making a default operating system selection.

7. Click OK two times.

Manually Modifying the Boot Menu Timeout

To change the boot menu timeout manually, perform the following steps:

1. Double-click My Computer.

2. Navigate to, and select the C:\ drive.

3. Right-click the boot.ini file.

TIP: *If the boot.ini file is not visible, follow these steps:*

1. Click Start, and select Settings/Control Panel.

2. Select Tools/Folder Options.

3. Select the View tab.

4. Select the Show Hidden Files And Folders radio button.

5. Check the Hide File Extensions For Known File Types checkbox.

6. Click OK.

The boot.ini file will now appear as a faded icon.

---

4. In the boot.ini Properties window, ensure that the Read-Only checkbox is cleared.

5. Click OK.

6. Double-click the boot.ini file.

7. Modify the Timeout value in the Boot Loader section of the boot.ini file to the desired value.

TIP: *If you do not want the boot menu to wait for a user selection, set the timeout value to 0 (zero).*

---

8. Save the file, and exit Notepad.

9. Reboot the server.

Working with Hardware Profiles

A number of issues are involved in hardware profile management. The following sections explore these tasks.

Adding a Hardware Profile

To add a hardware profile, perform the following steps:

1. Click Start, and select Settings|Control Panel.

2. Double-click the System applet.

TIP: You can also access the System applet by right-clicking My Computer and choosing Properties from the pop-up menu.

3. Select the Hardware tab.

4. Click Hardware Profiles. The Hardware Profiles applet will appear, as shown in Figure 13.5.

5. Select the hardware profile that you would like to base the new profile on, and click Copy.

6. Enter a name for the new hardware profile in the To field, and click OK.

7. Select the newly created profile in the Available Hardware Profiles section, and click Properties.

Figure 13.5   The Hardware Profiles applet.

8. If this system is a portable system, you can select whether it has a docking station by selecting The Docking State Is Unknown, The Computer Is Docked, or The Computer Is Undocked option. This will notify the operating system which hardware components are available in the docked/undocked state.

9. If you would like this hardware profile to always be displayed as an option when Windows 2000 starts, check the Always Include This Profile As An Option When Windows Starts checkbox. This option will display the hardware profile during startup even if Windows 2000 detects that the system is docked or undocked. This allows you to boot into a docked configuration even if the workstation is not docked.

10. Click OK when done.

11. Click OK twice.

Deleting a Hardware Profile

To delete a hardware profile, perform the following steps:

1. Click Start, and select Settings|Control Panel.

2. Double-click the System applet.

3. Select the Hardware tab.

4. Click Hardware Profiles.

5. Select the hardware profile that you would like to delete, and click Delete.

6. Click Yes to confirm the deletion.

7. Click OK twice.

Renaming a Hardware Profile

To rename a hardware profile, perform the following steps:

1. Click Start, and select Settings|Control Panel.

2. Double-click the System applet.

3. Select the Hardware tab.

4. Click Hardware Profiles.

5. Select the hardware profile that you would like to rename, and click Rename.

6. Enter a new name for the hardware profile in the To field, and click OK.

7. Click OK twice.

Copying a Hardware Profile

To copy a hardware profile, perform the following steps:

1. Click Start, and select Settings|Control Panel.

2. Double-click the System applet.

3. Select the Hardware tab.

4. Click Hardware Profiles.

5. Select the hardware profile that you would like to copy, and click Copy.

6. Enter a name for the new hardware profile in the To field, and click OK.

7. Click OK twice.

Booting with a Different Hardware Profile

To boot using a different hardware profile, perform the following steps:

1. Boot the system.

2. Select the operating system that you would like to boot.

3. When the Hardware Profile/Configuration Recovery Menu window appears, select the hardware profile that you would like to boot with, and press Enter.

Selecting the Hardware Profile Timeout

To specify the amount of time before a hardware profile times out, perform the following steps:

1. Click Start, and select Settings|Control Panel.

2. Double-click the System applet.

3. Select the Hardware tab.

4. Click Hardware Profiles.

5. In the Hardware Profiles Selection section of the window, select either the Wait Until I Select A Hardware Profile or the Select The Files Profile Listed If I Don't Select A Profile In X Seconds option.

6. If you choose the countdown option, enter a number (in seconds) for the system to wait before automatically making the hardware profile selection for you.

7. Click OK when done.

Enabling and Disabling a Device for a Specific Hardware Profile

To enable or disable a device for a hardware profile, perform the following steps:

1. Click Start, and select Settings|Control Panel.

2. Double-click the System applet.

3. Select the Hardware tab.

4. Click Device Manager. The Device Manager will launch.

5. Select the device that you would like to enable in the currently loaded hardware profile.

6. To enable the device, right-click the device, and choose Properties from the pop-up menu.

7. In the Device Usage drop-down box, select the Use This Device (Enable) option.

8. Click OK.

9. To disable a device, select the device that you would like to disable from the hardware profiles.

NOTE: *Some devices cannot be disabled because disabling some devices, such as the video display, will render the system inoperative.*

---

10. Right-click the device, and choose Properties from the pop-up menu.

11. In the Device Usage drop-down box, select the Do Not Use This Device In Any Hardware Profile (Disable) option.

12. Click OK.

13. Close the Device Manager.

14. Click OK to close the System applet.

Modifying System Services for Hardware Profiles

There are a few issues regarding the management of system services in hardware profiles. The following sections discuss these tasks.

Changing a Service Startup Type to Automatic

To change a service type to automatic, perform the following steps:

1. Click Start, and select Programs|Administrative Tools|Services.

2. Select the service that you would like modified.

3. Right-click the service, and choose Properties from the pop-up menu.

4. In the Startup Type drop-down list, choose the Automatic option.

5. Click OK.

Changing a Service Startup Type to Manual

To change a service type to manual, perform the following steps:

1. Click Start, and select Programs|Administrative Tools|Services.

2. Select the service that you would like modified.

3. Right-click the service, and choose Properties from the pop-up menu.

4. In the Startup Type drop-down, choose the Manual option.

5. Click OK.

Disabling and Enabling a Service for a Hardware Profile

To enable or disable a service for a hardware profile, perform the following steps:

1. Click Start, and select Programs|Administrative Tools|Services.

2. Select the service that you would like modified.

3. Right-click the service, and choose Properties from the pop-up menu.

4. To disable the service, select the Disable option in the Startup Type drop-down list.

5. Click OK.

6. To enable a service, right-click the service, and select Properties from the pop-up menu.

7. Select the Log On tab.

8. Select the hardware profile for which you would like to enable this service from the Hardware Profile section, and click Enable.

9. Repeat these steps for any other hardware profiles for which a service needs to be enabled or disabled.

10. Click OK.

Managing Services

A number of issues are involved with managing system services. The following sections explore these tasks.

Modifying Service Logon Information

To modify service logon information, perform the following steps:

1. Click Start, and select Programs|Administrative Tools|Services.

2. Select the service that you would like modified.

3. Right-click the service, and choose Properties from the pop-up menu.

4. Select the Log On tab.

5. If you would like the service to use the Local System account, select the Local System Account radio button. If you would like the service to be allowed to interact with the desktop, check the Allow Service To Interact With The Desktop checkbox. Click OK when done.

6. If you would like the service to use a specific user account, select the This Account radio button. Enter the username (or click Browse to list the available users) and password, and then confirm the password. Click OK when done.

Configuring a Service to Autorestart after a Service Failure

To configure a service to autorestart after a service failure, perform the following steps:

1. Click Start, and select Programs|Administrative Tools|Services.

2. Select the service that you would like modified.

3. Right-click the service, and choose Properties from the pop-up menu.

4. Select the Recovery tab (see Figure 13.6).

5. Select the Restart The Service option from the First Failure drop-down list.

6. Enter an amount of time (in minutes) in the Restart Service After dialog box.

7. Enter a time (in days) for the failure count to be reset in the Reset Fail Count After field.

8. Click OK.

Configuring a Program to Run after a Service Failure

To configure a program to run after a service failure, perform the following steps:

1. Click Start, and select Programs|Administrative Tools|Services.

2. Select the service that you would like modified.

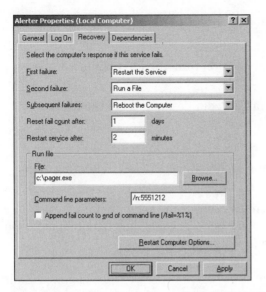

Figure 13.6   The Alerter Properties window's Recovery tab.

3. Right-click the service, and choose Properties from the pop-up menu.

4. Select the Recovery tab.

5. Select the Run A File option from the First Failure drop-down list.

6. Enter the full path to the application, or click Browse to navigate to the application.

7. Enter a time (in days) for the failure count to be reset in the Reset Fail Count After field.

8. Enter the required command-line parameters (if any) in the Command Line Parameters dialog box.

9. If you would like to append a fail count to the command line, check the Append Fail Count To End Of Command Line checkbox.

NOTE: *If you select to append a fail count to the command line, the application that's executed must support this feature.*

---

10. Click OK.

Configuring a Server Reboot after a Service Failure

To configure a server reboot after a service failure, perform the following steps:

1. Click Start, and select Programs|Administrative Tools|Services.

2. Select the service that you would like modified.

3. Right-click the service, and choose Properties from the pop-up menu.

4. Select the Recovery tab.

5. Select the Reboot The Computer option from the First Failure drop-down list.

6. Enter a time (in days) for the failure count to be reset in the Reset Fail Count After field.

7. Click Restart Computer Options.

8. Enter a time (in minutes) for the system to wait before rebooting in the Restart Computer After field.

9. If you would like a message sent to users of the server before the server is rebooted, check the Before Restart, Send This Message To Computers On The Network checkbox, and enter the message.

10. Click OK two times.

Dealing with Multiple Service Startup Failure Attempts

To manage multiple service startup failure attempts, perform the following steps:

1. Click Start, and select Programs|Administrative Tools|Services.

2. Select the service that you would like modified.

3. Right-click the service, and choose Properties from the pop-up menu.

4. Select the Recovery tab.

5. Select the desired actions from the First Failure drop-down list, and configure the parameters (if any).

6. Select the desired actions from the Second Failure drop-down list, and configure the parameters (if any).

7. Select the desired actions from the Subsequent Failures drop-down list, and configure the parameters (if any).

8. Click OK.

Starting a Service

To start a service, perform the following steps:

1. Click Start, and select Programs|Administrative Tools|Services.

2. Select the service that you would like to start.

3. Right-click the service, and choose Start from the pop-up menu.

Starting a Service from the Command Prompt

To start a service from the command prompt, perform the following steps:

1. Click Start, and select Programs|Accessories|Command Prompt.

2. Type "net start *ServiceName*".

TIP: *If you do not know the name of the service, you can find it in the registry key, HKEY_LOCAL_MACHINE/SYSTEM/ CurrentControlSet/Services.*

---

3. Press Enter.

Stopping a Service

To stop a service, perform the following steps:

1. Click Start, and select Programs|Administrative Tools|Services.

2. Select the service that you would like to stop.

3. Right-click the service, and choose Stop from the pop-up menu.

Stopping a Service from the Command Prompt

To stop a service from the command prompt, perform the following steps:

1. Click Start, and select Programs|Accessories|Command Prompt.

2. Type "net stop *ServiceName*".

TIP: *If you do not know the name of the service, you can find it in the registry key, HKEY_LOCAL_MACHINE/SYSTEM/ CurrentControlSet/Services.*

---

3. Press Enter.

Pausing a Service

To pause a service, perform the following steps:

1. Click Start, and select Programs|Administrative Tools|Services.

2. Select the service to pause.

NOTE: *Some services cannot be paused.*

---

3. Right-click the service, and choose Pause from the pop-up menu.

Pausing a Service from the Command Prompt

To pause a service from the command prompt, perform the following steps:

1. Click Start, and select Programs|Accessories|Command Prompt.

2. Type "net pause *ServiceName*".

TIP: *If you do not know the name of the service, you can find it in the registry key, HKEY_LOCAL_MACHINE/SYSTEM/ CurrentControlSet/Services.*

---

3. Press Enter.

Resuming a Paused Service

To resume a paused service, perform the following steps:

1. Click Start, and select Programs|Administrative Tools|Services.

2. Select the service to resume.

3. Right-click the service, and choose Resume from the pop-up menu.

Resuming a Paused Service from the Command Prompt

To resume a paused service from the command prompt, perform the following steps:

1. Click Start, and select Programs|Accessories|Command Prompt.

2. Type "net continue *ServiceName*".

TIP: *If you do not know the name of the service, you can find it in the registry key, HKEY_LOCAL_MACHINE/SYSTEM/ CurrentControlSet/Services.*

---

3. Press Enter.

Restarting a Service

To restart a service, perform the following steps:

1. Click Start, and select Programs|Administrative Tools|Services.

2. Select the service to restart.

3. Right-click the service, and choose Restart from the pop-up menu.

Checking Service Dependencies

To verify service dependencies, perform the following steps:

1. Click Start, and select Programs|Administrative Tools|Services.

2. Select the service to modify.

3. Right-click the service, and choose Properties from the pop-up menu.

4. Select the Dependencies tab.

5. The dependencies for this service (if any) will appear on this tab.

Building a Minimal Boot Disk

To build a boot disk, perform the following steps:

1. Place a blank disk in the floppy drive.

2. Double-click My Computer.

3. Right-click the A:\ drive, and choose Format from the pop-up menu.

4. Click Start.

5. Copy the following files from the i386 directory of the Windows 2000 CD-ROM: NTLDR, ntdetect.com, and boot.ini.

Manually Shutting Down Windows 2000

There are a couple of different methods for shutting down Windows 2000.

The first method for shutting down Windows 2000 is as follows:

1. Click Start, and select Shut Down.

2. Choose the Shutdown option from the What Do You Want The Computer To Do? drop-down list.

3. Click OK.

The second method for shutting down Windows 2000 is as follows:

1. Press Ctrl+Alt+Delete.

2. Click Shut Down.

3. Choose the Shutdown option from the What Do You Want The Computer To Do? drop-down list.

4. Click OK.

Manually Rebooting Windows 2000

There are a couple of different methods for rebooting Windows 2000.

The first method for rebooting Windows 2000 is as follows:

1. Click Start, and select Shut Down.
2. Choose the Restart option from the What Do You Want The Computer To Do? drop-down list.
3. Click OK.

The second method for rebooting Windows 2000 is as follows:

1. Press Ctrl+Alt+Delete.
2. Click Shut Down.
3. Choose the Restart option from the What Do You Want The Computer To Do? drop-down list.
4. Click OK.

Using Remote Shutdown to Shut Down a Local System

To use remote shutdown to shut down a system, perform the following steps:

1. Run the shutdown.exe application (see Figure 13.7).
2. Enter the name of the server or browse to it.
3. Clear the Kill Applications Without Saving Data checkbox.
4. Clear the Reboot After Shutdown checkbox.
5. Enter a message in the Message Text field.

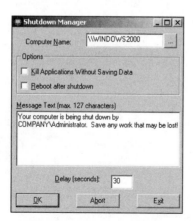

Figure 13.7   The Shutdown Manager.

6. Enter an amount of time (in seconds) that the application should wait before initiating the shutdown.

7. Click OK.

NOTE: *The Remote Shutdown application (shutdown.exe) is found on the Windows 2000 Resource Kit in the drive:\Program Files\Resource Kit\ folder.*

Using Remote Shutdown to Reboot a System

To use remote shutdown to reboot a system, perform the following steps:

1. Run the shutdown.exe application.

2. Enter the name of the server or browse to it.

3. Clear the Kill Applications Without Saving Data checkbox.

4. Check the Reboot After Shutdown checkbox.

5. Enter a message in the Message Text field.

6. Enter an amount of time (in seconds) that the application should wait before initiating the shutdown.

7. Click OK.

WARNING! *This method kills all services and applications without saving the data. Use caution with this method because it can corrupt your system. Only use this as a last resort.*

Chapter 14

Windows 2000
Administration Tools

In Depth

This chapter explores the Windows 2000 administrative tools and the Control Panel. Nearly every administration, control, management, configuration, or monitoring task performed on a Windows 2000 system starts with using the tools found in these two areas. You'll recognize many of the tools in the Control Panel from Windows NT or Windows 98, and a few of the administrative tools may remind you of utilities from Windows NT. In any case, familiarity with these tools is essential to managing a Windows 2000 installation.

Microsoft Management Console

Windows 2000 is the first operating system from Microsoft to employ the Microsoft Management Console (MMC) interface for most of its administration and management functions. The MMC is a standardized graphical interface that hosts management tools called *snap-ins*. The MMC itself is nothing more than a structured architecture environment; it can perform no administration or management on its own. It is through the loading of snap-ins into the MMC that control of a computer system is gained. The MMC was designed to provide a versatile, customizable interface mechanism that allows administrators to create tool sets that match their regular activities.

The MMC is a shell into which consoles (similar to documents) are loaded. Within each console, one or more snap-ins can be loaded. Each snap-in can then be expanded with add-ons called *extensions*. Each snap-in's capabilities focus on a single object type within the Windows 2000 environment, such as storage, networking, users, and so on. The extensions expand the capabilities of a snap-in through the inclusion of additional functions. This multilevel modular design offers you the flexibility to build a tool set that is right for you. In addition, most of the tools based on snap-ins can manage objects locally or remotely.

The MMC was previously introduced to the Windows NT 4 environment through the Windows NT 4 Option Pack. It was required to manage Internet Information Server (IIS) 4.

In addition to the snap-in tools and utilities included with Windows 2000, administrators can write or create their own snap-ins. MMC is a fully Independent Software Vendor (ISV)-extensible control framework, which means that it complies with basic programming standards to allow third parties to create tools that will function within its predefined versatile environment.

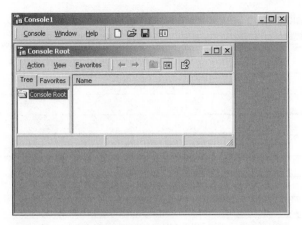

Figure 14.1   The MMC (empty).

The MMC can be launched without loading any snap-ins. This is done by typing "MMC" from a command prompt or from the Run command. The empty MMC window, shown in Figure 14.1, displays the main menu, containing the Console, Window, and Help drop-down menus, and a movable mini-icon bar with New, Open, Save, and New Window buttons. The display area can support multiple console windows that can be cascaded, tiled, or minimized as icons.

Each console window has a console menu bar, a console tree, and a details pane. The console menu bar contains the Action and View pull-down menus and another mini-icon bar containing Back, Forward, Up One Level, Show/Hide Console Tree/Favorites, and Help buttons. The console tree section is the area to the left that has a Tree tab and a Favorites tab. The console tree shows the organization of loaded plug-ins and extensions, along with context selections. A context selection depends on the plug-in's management object, such as domain, computer, organizational unit (OU), user, folder, or service. The details pane is the area to the right; items displayed in the details pane are determined by the selection in the console tree. The contents of the console menu bar change based on the selected element within the console tree or details pane.

Starting from a blank MMC interface and an empty console window, you can load and customize your own administration tools using any or all of the snap-ins included with Windows 2000 Professional and/or Server. The set of snap-ins shown in Table 14.1 can be executed through their standard access points—Start menu, programs, administrative tools, and so forth—or by simply entering the file name from the Run line on the Start menu. If the snap-in is not available, then the particular component needs to be installed appropriately.

NOTE: *Default snap-ins may vary, depending on the various utilities and applications that you have loaded.*

Table 14.1   Windows 2000 Professional and Server MMC snap-ins.

Snap-In Name	File Name
Active Directory Domains And Trusts	DOMAIN.MSC
Active Directory Schema Manager	SCHMMGMT.MSC
Active Directory Sites And Services	DSSITE.MSC
Active Directory Users And Computers	DSA.MSC
ADSI Edit	ADSIEDIT.MSC
Certificate Manager	CERTMGR.MSC
Certificate Services	CERTSRV.MSC
Component Services	COMEXP.MSC
Computer Management	COMPMGT.MSC
Device Manager	DEVMGMT.MSC
DHCP Manager	DHCPMGMT.MSC
Disk Defragmenter	DFRG.MSC
Disk Manager	DISKMGMT.MSC
Distributed File System	DFSGUI.MSC
DNS Manager	DNSMGMT.MSC
Domain Controller Security Policy	DCPOL.MSC
Domain Security Policy	DOMPOL.MSC
Event Viewer	EVENTVWR.MSC
Fax Service Management	FAXSERV.MSC
Group Policy	GPEDIT.MSC
Indexing Service	CIADV.MSC
Internet Authentication Service	IAS.MSC
Internet Information Server	IIS.MSC
IP Security Policy Management	IPSEC.MSC
Local Security Policy	SECPOL.MSC
Local Users And Groups	LUSRMGR.MSC
Performance Monitor	PERFMON.MSC
RRAS Manager	RRASMGMT.MSC
Remote Storage Management	RSADMIN.MSC
Removable Storage Management	NTMSMGR.MSC
Removable Storage Operator Requests	NTMSOPRQ.MSC
Services	SERVICES.MSC

(continued)

Table 14.1   Windows 2000 Professional and Server MMC snap-ins *(continued)*.

Snap-In Name	File Name
Shared Folders	FSMGMT.MSC
SIDWalker Security Manager	SIDWALK.MSC
System Information	MSINFO32.MSC
Telephony Management	TAPIMGMT.MSC
Terminal Services Manager	TSCC.MSC
WINS Manager	WINSMGMT.MSC
WinMgmt Control	WMIMGMS.MSC

These snap-ins are the same elements used to create the utilities found in administrative tools. By using one or more of the snap-ins, you can create a custom console. After your console is configured, you can save the console for later use using one of four formats:

- *Author Mode*—Enables users to add and remove snap-ins, create new windows, view the entire console tree, and save new versions of the console

- *User mode: Full Access*—Allows users to create new windows and view the entire console tree, but prevents adding or removing snap-ins or resaving console files

- *User mode: Delegated Access, Multiple Windows*—Allows users to create new windows, but restricts access to portions of the console tree, adding or removing snap-ins, or resaving console files

- *User mode: Delegated Access, Single Window*—Restricts users from creating new windows, accessing portions of the console tree, adding or removing snap-ins, or resaving console files

To set the mode of the console, select Console|Options. Then, use the Save or Save As command to save the console to a file. MMC console settings are stored in MSC files. After you've created an MSC file, it can be distributed and used on any system with MMC.

Windows 2000 uses the MMC for many of its administration and management utilities. All the MMC snap-in predefined utilities (that is, preconfigured consoles) are found in Administrative Tools (see Figure 14.2). Administrative Tools can be accessed either from the Control Panel or from the Start menu.

NOTE: *The Administrative Tools section of the Start menu | Programs is disabled by default on Windows 2000 Professional systems.*

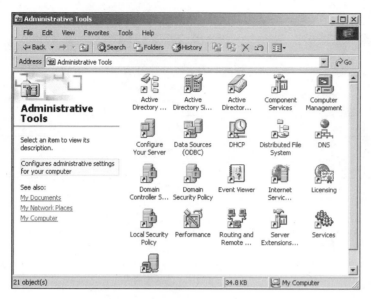

Figure 14.2   The Administrative Tools window.

The utilities found in the Administrative Tools area include the following:

- *Active Directory Domains And Trusts*—Used to create and manage domains and trusts. This includes operations, such as setting the domain names operation manager, changing a domain's mode, creating trusts between domains, and defining a managing user account. This tool is discussed in Chapter 3.

- *Active Directory Sites And Services*—Used to configure server settings, site settings, and replication. This tool is discussed in Chapter 3.

- *Active Directory Users And Computers*—Used to create and manage users, groups, and computers within a domain. As a domain administrator, this is where you will be spending most of your Win2k administration time. This is because all user and group administration occurs here, along with domain OU, Group Policy, and software distribution administration. This tool is discussed in Chapter 4.

- *Component Services*—The renamed Microsoft Transaction Server, Component Services is used to deploy and control Component Object Model (COM)+, automate tasks using scripting or programming languages, manage transactions between processes, and create scalable component-based applications. For more details, see the *Windows 2000 Server Resource Kit* (Microsoft Press, ISBN 1-57231-805-8) or the Windows 2000 and IIS 5.0 Software Development Kits (SDKs).

- *Computer Management*—Offers single-interface access to several commonly used local computer management utilities, such as Event Viewer, Disk Management, and the Services applet (discussed later in the "Computer Management" section).

- *Data Sources (Open Database Connectivity [ODBC])*—Used to define Data Source Names (DSNs) employed by applications and services to access database management systems. See the *Windows 2000 Server Resource Kit* for details.

- *Dynamic Host Configuration Protocol (DHCP)*—Used to configure the dynamic client configuration service. See Chapters 11 and 12 for details.

- *Distributed File System*—Used to create and manage a distributed file system (DFS) for a domain. See Chapters 11 and 12 for details.

- *Domain Name Service (DNS)*—Used to configure the domain name-to-Internet Protocol (IP) address resolution service for a domain. See Chapter 12 for details.

- *Domain Controller Security Policy*—Used to configure and define the security policy for all domain controllers. See Chapter 20 for details.

- *Domain Security Policy*—Used to configure and define the security policy for a domain. See Chapter 20 for details.

- *Event Viewer*—Used to view and manage the logs of Windows 2000.

- *Internet Services Manager*—Used to manage Internet information services, such as the Web and File Transfer Protocol (FTP). See the *Windows 2000 Resource Kit* or the *IIS 5.0 Documentation* (Microsoft Press, ISBN 0-7356-0652-8) for details.

- *Licensing*—Used to configure and manage the licenses of Windows 2000 and installed applications.

- *Local Security Policy*—Used to configure and define the security policy for the local system. See Chapter 20 for details.

- *Performance*—Used to monitor and record the performance levels of the system. See Chapter 20 for details.

- *Routing And Remote Access*—Used to configure and manage routing and remote access for a system. See Chapter 19 for details.

- *Server Extensions Administrator*—Used to manage FrontPage server extensions. See the *Windows 2000 Server Resource Kit, IIS 5.0 Documentation,* or the *Official Microsoft FrontPage 2000 Book* (Microsoft Press, ISBN 0-57231-992-5) for details.

14. Windows 2000 Administration Tools

NOTE: *The Configure Your Server element of Administrative Tools is not an MMC snap-in tool; instead, it's a wizard with multiple menus for configuring a server. See Chapter 3 for details. The Services element is not an MMC snap-in; it's an applet. See the "Control Panel Tools" section later in this chapter. Finally, the Telnet Server element is not an MMC snap-in; it's a text-based menu system used to configure and manage the Telnet server service. See Chapter 20 for details.*

This is not an exhaustive list of the possible tools that can be found in Administrative Tools. Other tools may be added, or some of these tools might not be present, based on the services installed on your Windows 2000 system. Many of these tools are found only on Windows 2000 Server (that is, those used to manage network services for a domain).

Computer Management

The Computer Management tool, shown in Figure 14.3, is an MMC console configured to grant quick access to many commonly used administration tools. This tool is divided into three sections: System Tools, Storage, and Services And Applications.

The System Tools section contains six tools:

- *Event Viewer*—Used to view and manage the event logs of Windows 2000.

- *System Information*—Used to view configuration, status, and setting information about the system. The multileveled information hierarchy, shown in Figure 14.4, displays the current data regarding the system, hardware resources, installed components and devices, software environment, and native

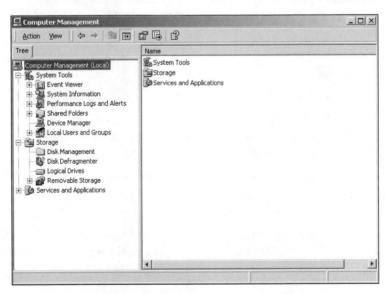

Figure 14.3   The Computer Management administrative tool.

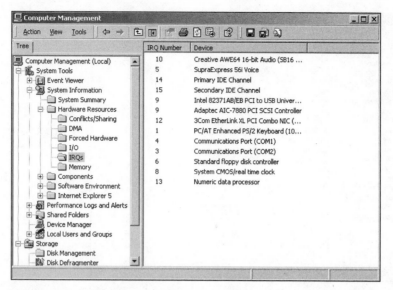

Figure 14.4 The System Information tool accessed from the Computer Management window.

Microsoft applications, such as Internet Explorer 5. This tool is extremely handy in discovering system model numbers, free interrupt requests (IRQs), resource conflicts, and component configurations.

- *Performance Logs And Alerts*—Used to create and manage Performance Monitor counter logs, trace logs, and alerts. See Chapter 16 for details.

- *Shared Folders*—Used to create and manage shared folders on the local system. This tool displays both standard and hidden shares (see Figure 14.5), current sessions, and open files.

- *Device Manager*—Used to display and configure the settings of installed hardware devices. System resources can be altered, new drives can be installed, and device conflicts can be resolved.

- *Local Users And Groups*—Used to configure and manage local users and groups. This tool is disabled when Active Directory is present.

The Storage section of Computer Management has four tools:

- *Disk Management*—Used to manage partitions and volumes on hard drives. Its capabilities include converting from basic to dynamic storage; deleting, formatting, assigning drive letters; and creating Redundant Array of Inexpensive Disks (RAID) drive configurations. See Chapter 13 for details.

- *Disk Defragmenter*—Used to analyze the fragmentation level and to defragment a volume. See Chapter 13 for details.

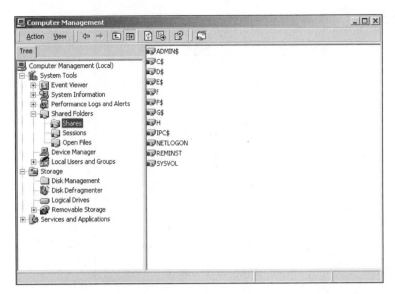

Figure 14.5   The Shared Folders tool accessed from the Computer Management window.

- *Logical Drives*—Used to view data about logical drives (formatted volumes and partitions). This is the same information shown by opening the Properties dialog box on a drive from My Computer or Windows Explorer. See Chapter 13 for details.

- *Removable Storage*—Used to track and manage definable libraries or media pools of removable media, including floppies, tapes, CDs, CD recordables (CD-Rs), CD rewritables (CD-RWs), and more (see Figure 14.6). See Chapter 13 for details.

The Services And Applications section of Computer Management has a variable number tools that depend upon installed services and applications. Possible tools include the following:

- *DHCP*—Used as another access point for the DHCP configuration and management interface. See Chapter 9 for details.

- *Telephony*—Used to configure the installed communication providers (same as the Advanced tab of the Phone And Modem applet) and to define user access for each provider. See Chapter 20 for details.

- *Windows Management Instrumentation (WMI)*—Used to enable system management through a consistent interface.

- *Services*—Used to start and stop services and to define their initialization and security credentials (discussed in the "Services" section of this chapter).

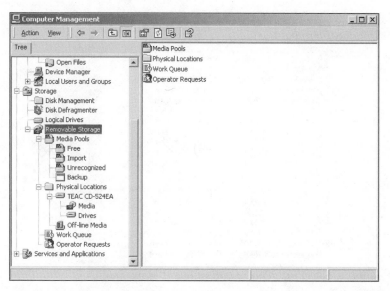

Figure 14.6   The Removable Storage tool accessed from the Computer Management window.

14. Windows 2000
Administration Tools

- *Indexing Service*—Used to define the folders that will be included in the Indexing Service's index, as distinguished between system and Web. See Chapter 6 for details.

- *Internet Information Services*—Used to configure and manage the Web, FTP, and Simple Mail Transport Protocol (SMTP) services of IIS 5. See Chapter 6 for details.

- *DNS*—Used to configure and manage the DNS service. See Chapter 9 for details.

Event Viewer

The Event Viewer is used to view the log files created by Windows 2000. There are three main log files—System, Application, and Security—plus log files specific to installed applications or services, such as Directory Service, DNS Server, and File Replication Service (see Figure 14.7). The Event Viewer can be used to view logs locally or from remote systems. The Event Viewer is accessed through Administrative Tools on the Start menu or Control Panel and through the Computer Management window.

The Windows 2000 log files record event details. An *event detail* is a report containing information specific to a condition, situation, or occurrence (that is, an event). Events can range from access denials, to driver failures, and to service initialization announcements.

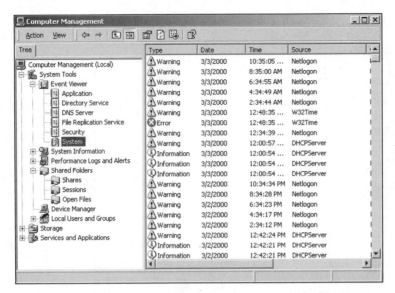

Figure 14.7   The Event Viewer tool accessed from the Computer Management window.

Information, warning, and error event details are recorded in the system and application logs. Audit success and failure event details are recorded in the security log. An event detail includes time and date, source, category, user account, computer account, and more.

NOTE: For audit events to be recorded, auditing must be enabled and configured. See Chapter 19 for details.

Logs can be customized as to their displayed name, the maximum size of the log, and how to manage a full log. Full logs can have the oldest events overwritten by new events or can have only events more than a specific number of days old overwritten by new events, or new events can be discarded until the log is manually cleared. These configuration options are defined through the Properties dialog box for each log.

You can also define a display filter (through the View|Filter) that reduces the number of event details shown. View|Find is used to perform a keyword search in the selected log. Both of these tools will prove invaluable when you have to locate a single event in a log of thousands.

Licensing

The Licensing MMC snap-in is accessed through Administrative Tools. This utility, shown in Figure 14.8, is used to manage the use license for Windows 2000 and for distributed applications hosted on the system as well.

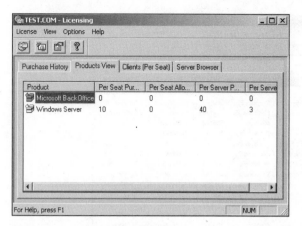

Figure 14.8   The Licensing tool.

Windows 2000 licensing is available in two types: Per Server and Per Seat. Per Server licensing grants client-access licenses to a server. One client computer is able to establish a connection with the server for each installed client license. The client licenses can only be used on the server that holds the licenses. Per Seat licensing grants client access licenses to the client. The client can use that license to connect to any server on the network. Per Server licensing makes the most sense in smaller networks with fewer servers. Per Seat licensing makes the most sense in larger networks with lots of servers. You have the ability to convert your license mode from Per Server to Per Seat once, but the conversion cannot be reversed.

If a product, such as Microsoft BackOffice, is installed, it will automatically be added to the list of products that the Licensing tool can manage. The Purchase History tab is used to add newly purchased licenses to a product. The Products View tab shows the number of Per Seat and Per Server licenses available and used for each product. The Clients (Per Seat) tab lists details about users employing licenses to access products. The Server Browser tab is used to view the license settings on other systems on the network.

Through Options|Advanced, you can create or edit license groups. A *license group* is used to manage the use of licenses properly when the number of users, computers, and licenses are not identical. For example, if you have 100 users and 10 computers, you only need 10 licenses and a single user group with access to those licenses.

Services

The Services utility within Computer Management , shown in Figure 14.9, is used to start and stop services and to define the initialization credentials of services.

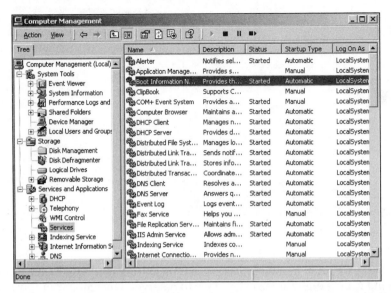

Figure 14.9   The Services utility.

All installed services are listed along with a description, current status, startup type, and "log on as" credential. The status will either be started or paused. A blank here indicates the service is stopped. The startup type indicates how the system will handle the service; the options are Automatic (starts when the operating system [OS] starts), Manual (starts by a user or a dependent service), and Disabled (prevents a service from being launched). The Log On As option lists the user account whose access credentials that the service will use. A value of LocalSystem indicates the service is launched with system-level privileges. Any defined user account can be employed by a service.

Each service has a Properties dialog box consisting of four tabs. The General tab, shown in Figure 14.10, is used to define the displayed name, description, startup type, and start parameters as well as to start, stop, pause, or resume the service. The Log On tab is used to define the privilege level of the service as either system level or a user account. This tab is also used to enable or disable a service within a hardware profile. The Recovery tab is used to define how the system will react to the first, second, and later failures of the service. The options are Take No Action, Restart The Service, Run A File, and Reboot The Computer. The Dependencies tab lists the services on which this service is dependent and the services that are dependent on this service.

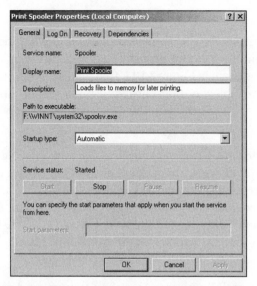

Figure 14.10   The Services Properties dialog box.

Control Panel Tools

The Control Panel is a collection of configuration applets used to manage the installation of new hardware and software. The Control Panel is accessed either through the Start menu (by clicking the Start menu and selecting Settings|Services) or as an element in both My Computer and Windows Explorer. The Control Panel is basically an access window you can use to launch applets by double-clicking them. The set of applets that appears depends on the computer system (for example, if it is a notebook computer, the PC Card applet will be present) and installed applications and services (QuickTime, RealPlayer, Norton AntiVirus, TweakUI, and so on). The common Control Panel applets are described in the following sections.

Accessibility Options

The Accessibility Options applet is used to configure special keyboard, sound, display, mouse, and other features that improve interaction for the seeing-, hearing-, or movement-impaired user. Some of the features accessible through this applet are StickyKeys (pressing Ctrl, Shift, or Alt once instead of holding down the key), SoundSentry (a visual clue, such as a flashing title bar, that's assigned to all sounds), high-contrast color schemes, and the use of the numeric keypad to control mouse movements. If you need more information about the accessibility options, consult the *Windows 2000 Server Resource Kit*.

Add/Remove Hardware

The Add/Remove Hardware applet is used to perform several tasks, such as adding a new device, troubleshooting a device, and uninstalling or removing a device. The applet is actually a wizard, shown in Figure 14.11, that walks you through the selected activity. Adding and troubleshooting hardware tasks are grouped into the first selection, and tasks related to uninstalling and removing a device are grouped as the second selection.

To add a new device, select the Add/Troubleshoot radio button, and click Next. The system will search for new hardware first; then, it will prompt you with a list of located devices. If you want to troubleshoot a listed device, select it. Devices with problems will have a yellow exclamation point or a stop sign over their device icon. If you want to install a new device, select the Add A New Device item. The rest of the wizard walks you through the process of either troubleshooting or installing the device.

To remove a device, select the Uninstall/Remove option. You then must decide whether just to unplug or eject the device (the driver stays installed) or to uninstall the device (remove the driver from the system). The former process will allow you to reattach the device at a later time without reinstalling the driver, and it will retain its original configuration (such as for a modem or network interface card). The latter process should only be used when a device is being permanently removed or when a corrupt driver is present.

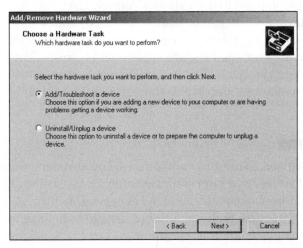

Figure 14.11   The Add/Remove Hardware Wizard.

Add/Remove Programs

The Add/Remove Programs applet is used to perform three types of software management:

- *Change Or Remove Programs*—Change or remove installed third-party applications (that is, applications not natively included with Windows 2000 or on its distribution CD)

- *Add New Programs*—Install new applications from a vendor-supplied disk or CD

- *Add/Remove Windows Components*—Add or remove Windows 2000 components

The applet launches by default in the Change Or Remove Programs mode. This mode lists all installed applications along with details, such as size (total amount of drive space consumed by files), used status (often, seldom, or rarely), and last used date. There's also a Change/Remove button, which will either launch the selected application's own Configure/Remove tool or launch Windows 2000's removal tool.

The Add New Programs mode can pull software from a CD or disk, from the Microsoft Update Web site, or from a network distribution site, or from local files. It's used to initiate the setup procedure and to ensure the process is recorded by the Windows 2000 removal tool for later management through the Change Or Remove Programs mode.

The Add/Remove Windows Components mode displays a list of all available components of Windows 2000 found on the distribution CD that are still available to be installed on the current system. This interface can also be used to remove already installed components. Simply mark the items that you want installed and then clear the checkmarks for the items that you no longer want present on your system. The tool manages adding and removing components based on your checkbox markings.

Administrative Tools

Administrative Tools is a link to another Control Panel-like window that hosts all the MMC snap-in tools used to manage and configure the operating system environment. These tools were discussed in the "Microsoft Management Console" section earlier in this chapter.

Date/Time

The Date/Time applet is used to set the calendar, date, and clock time for the local system. This interface is used to set the day, month, year, and time (to the second) as well as the time zone. After you make a time or date change using this applet, it is immediately recorded onto the system's complementary metal oxide semiconductors (CMOS).

Display

The Display applet is used to control a wide range of desktop interface settings. The settings on each of the tabs of this applet dialog box include the following:

- *Background*—Used to define the desktop wallpaper
- *Screen Saver*—Used to set the screen saver and idle time, enable password protection, and access the power-saving features of the monitor
- *Appearance*—Used to define the color scheme; can be selected from pre-defined sets or can be custom configured
- *Web*—Used to configure the Active Desktop components
- *Effects*—Used to define desktop icons and to enable or disable several visual effects (such as menu transitions, smooth screen fonts, use all colors for icons, and so on)
- *Settings*—Used to set the display area and color depth and to change adapter- or monitor-specific settings

Windows 2000 supports multiple displays. If multiple video adapters are installed (that is, the hardware is installed and configured by also installing their drivers using the Add/Remove Hardware applet), the Settings tab will display a monitor icon for each installed video adapter. You can drag these icons into the arrangement of your choice and then associate an adapter with each of the numbered monitor icons. The color depth and resolution can be set for each adapter/display. Using multiple displays requires compliance with the following rules:

- All video adapters must be Accelerated Graphics Port (AGP) and/or Peripheral Component Interconnect (PCI).
- Windows 2000 should be installed with only a single adapter. Additional adapters can be installed after installation has completed.

Fax

The Fax applet is used to manage faxing. Windows 2000 includes native support for basic fax capabilities, such as sending faxes, receiving faxes, and managing cover pages. Faxing requires a fax-capable modem, which must be installed using the Phone And Modem Options applet). See Chapter 6 for a discussion on using faxing.

Folder Options

The Folder Options applet is the interface accessed when you select Tools|Folder Options in Windows Explorer or My Computer. The following list explains the features of each tab in this applet:

- *General*—Used to enable/disable the Active Desktop, Web, or classic view of folders, open folders in the same or a different window, or select single or double clicks to open an item.

- *View*—Used to configure the advanced settings of displayed information, such as hidden files, known extensions, and so on, as well as to hide protected files.

- *File Types*—Used to configure registered associations between file extensions and applications.

- *Offline Files*—Used to enable and disable caching of network files locally for use offline. This process is described in detail in Chapter 6.

Fonts

The Fonts folder contains a list of all installed fonts. New fonts can be added and existing fonts can be removed through this interface.

Game Controllers

The Game Controllers applet is used to manage gaming controls, such as joysticks and steering wheels. New devices can be installed, and existing devices can be removed or configured.

Internet Options

The Internet Options applet controls how Internet Explorer functions. The tabs in this applet are used to configure the following settings:

- *General*—Used to define the home page, the path for temporary Internet files, site visit history, colors, fonts, languages, and accessibility options, which are all specific to Web surfing.

- *Security*—Used to define the security level of four Web zones. The security controls govern within that zone whether software will be automatically downloaded and installed, whether form data will be submitted, and whether cookies will be used.

- *Content*—Used to configure the Content Advisor (site-blocking control), manage certificates, configure AutoComplete, and define your online identity.

- *Connections*—Used to configure how an Internet connection is established if one is not already present.

- *Programs*—Used to associate applications with types of Internet services encountered on Web sites (email, newsgroups, and so on).

- *Advanced*—Used to configure advanced features, such as Hypertext Transfer Protocol (HTTP) 1.1 Microsoft virtual machine, multimedia, printing, searching, security, and accessibility.

Keyboard and Mouse

The Keyboard applet is used to manage the keyboard and to configure settings, such as repeat delay and cursor blink rate. The Mouse applet is used to manage the mouse and to configure settings, such as double click speed and tracking acceleration.

Licensing

The Licensing applet is used to change licensing options. From within this applet, you can change from Per Server licensing to Per Seat and can add or remove licenses.

Network And Dial-Up Connections

The Network And Dial-Up Connections applet controls all network interfaces, including LAN, RAS, direct cable, and VPN connections. This applet is discussed in Chapters 9 and 20.

Phone And Modem Options

The Phone And Modem Options applet manages dialing locations, modem installation and configuration, as well as Remote Access Service (RAS) and Telephony Application Programming Interface (TAPI) drivers and services. This applet is discussed in Chapter 20.

Power Options

The Power Options applet manages a system's power-saving capabilities. For desktop systems, this includes powering down the monitor and hard drives. For portable systems, this can include hibernation and other device-specific controls. Predefined power schemes can be used, or you can customize your own. Simply select a scheme or create your own by configuring devices to power down after a defined time interval. Keep in mind that the system BIOS may be configured to also deal with power options. In order to avoid problems, be sure to check both the BIOS and the Power Options to ensure that conflicts do not occur.

Printers

The Printers folder manages printers, including installation, sharing, configuration, and queue control. This applet manages both plain paper printers, as well as specialty printers and fax devices. This applet is discussed in Chapter 18.

Regional Settings

The Regional Settings applet manages geographic location-specific conventions for numbers, currency, time, dates, and more. You can select from a predefined scheme for a language and country or can define your own.

Scanners And Cameras

The Scanners And Cameras applet manages the installation and configuration of digital cameras and scanners. Use this applet to install vendor-supplied drivers (if Windows 2000 does not automatically detect the device upon system boot); then, use this applet to access vendor or device-specific property control interfaces.

Scheduled Tasks

The Scheduled Tasks folder manages task scheduling. With this tool, programs or batch files can be configured to launch automatically at a specific time or when an event occurs. Tasks can be launched with specific user credentials and can be allowed to run only when the system is idle or only when the system is not running on batteries. An Add Scheduled Task Wizard is used to create tasks. Then, advanced options can be set by opening the Properties dialog box of a defined task. In spite of all the capabilities offered by this tool, it's amazingly simple to operate.

Sounds And Multimedia

The Sounds And Multimedia applet manages the association between system events and sounds, the creation and use of sound schemes, the setting of preferred playback and recording devices, and the troubleshooting and configuration of multimedia hardware.

System

The System applet manages many system and core functions of Windows 2000. The General tab of this applet displays the system version, registration information, and basic computer platform details. The Network Identification tab is used to change the name of the computer and to join a domain or workgroup. The Hardware tab has links to the Add/Remove Hardware applet, the Driver Signing Options dialog box, the Device Manager, and the Hardware Profiles dialog box.

The User Profiles tab is used to create roaming profiles (see Chapter 6). The Advanced tab has links to performance options, environmental variables, and startup and recovery settings.

NOTE: *The options available on these tabs may vary depending on the software you have installed.*

Driver Signing Options

The Driver Signing Options dialog box defines how the system will handle nonsigned drivers when you're installing new hardware. A signed driver is a device driver digitally signed by Microsoft to validate its authenticity. The system can be configured to ignore signing, warn when nonsigned drivers are being used, or block all but signed drivers from being installed.

Device Manager

The Device Manager is a tool that displays all installed hardware. From this list, you can access the Properties dialog box for each device to change settings, update drivers, or troubleshoot problems. In the list of devices, the device icon may be enhanced with a yellow exclamation point or a red stop sign. These icons indicate problems or conflicts with the device or its driver. The list of devices can be displayed by type or connection. You can also view a list of system resources—direct memory access (DMA), input/output (I/O) address, IRQ, and memory—by type or connection.

Hardware Profiles

A *hardware profile* is used to define a set of device drivers for a specific configuration of hardware. Hardware profiles make the most sense when used on portable computers that have changing hardware components, such as a docking bar, removable storage devices, or a Personal Computer Memory Card Industry Association (PCMCIA)/PC card slot. Every Windows 2000 system has a single default hardware profile. When secondary and additional hardware profiles are defined, the system attempts to match the current state of hardware with a hardware profile upon bootup. If a match cannot be made, you'll be prompted to select a profile to use. One hardware profile is defined as the default. Through the Hardware Profiles interface, you can configure the system to use the default profile automatically. You set a specified length of time to wait for you to select an alternate profile in the event that the system cannot automatically determine the hardware profile to use.

A hardware profile is created by copying an existing hardware profile and then booting using the copy. After it is booted, devices can be enabled and disabled through the Device Manager by changing the Device Usage pull-down list on a device's Properties dialog box to Use This Device (Enable) or Do Not Use This Device In The Current Hardware Profile (Disable).

Performance Options

The Performance Options dialog box is used to configure the system optimization and virtual memory. The system can be optimized for applications or background services. By default, Windows 2000 Professional is optimized for applications. By default, Windows 2000 Server is optimized for background services.

Virtual memory is the memory scheme used by Windows 2000; it combines physical random access memory (RAM) with a paging file on a storage device to increase the amount of available memory to the system and hosted processes. Windows 2000 creates a paging file by default of one and a half times the amount of physical RAM installed. For example, if you have 128 megabytes (MB) of RAM, the paging file will be 192MB. This initial paging file is placed on the boot partition.

To alter the paging file settings, click the Change button on the Performance Options dialog box. The Virtual Memory dialog box, shown in Figure 14.12, displays the current paging file configuration and is used to alter the paging file settings. The system automatically calculates an optimum size for the paging file and displays this value under the Total Paging File Size For All Drives section (labeled as Recommended). You should configure one or more paging files as large or larger than this value.

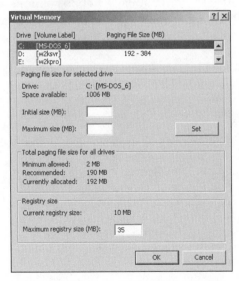

Figure 14.12   The Virtual Memory dialog box.

New paging files are created by selecting a host volume, defining the initial and maximum size values, and then clicking Set. The initial size is the amount of drive space exclusively allocated to the paging file. The maximum size is how large the paging file can grow, but that space is not allocated. In most cases, setting these numbers to the same value is recommended. Existing paging files are altered by selecting them and changing their initial and maximum values. Settings the values to zero removes the paging file from that volume.

Environment Variables

The Environment Variables dialog box, shown in Figure 14.13, displays the variables and definitions or values defined for the currently logged on user and the system. These values can be edited when necessary by someone who is logged into the system with administrative authority. In most cases, the default values are sufficient. Installed applications will often alter or add environmental variables as necessary.

Startup And Recovery

The Startup And Recovery dialog box, shown in Figure 14.14, controls some aspects of the boot menu and how the system manages STOP errors. The System Startup section sets the default OS and the display timeout for the boot menu. The System Failure section configures whether an administrative alert, an automatic reboot, and/or a memory dump file is performed when a STOP error occurs. The Send An Administrative Alert and Automatically Reboot options are useful, but the memory dump can only be interpreted by a Microsoft technical

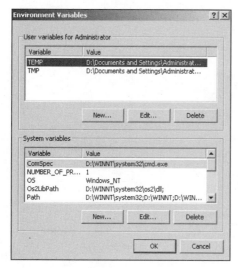

Figure 14.13   The Environment Variables dialog box.

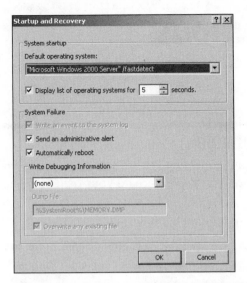

Figure 14.14   The Startup And Recovery dialog box.

specialist with specific debugging tools. Therefore, you can opt out from creating a memory dump file (debugging information file). If you do enable debugging, you must have a paging file on the boot partition as large or larger than the amount of physical RAM present in the system. The default file name and path for the dump file is %systemroot%\memory.dmp.

Users And Passwords

The Users And Passwords applet is used to manage local user accounts and group memberships. This applet also manages certificates and whether Ctrl+Alt+Delete is required for logging on. This applet is not present on Windows 2000 Server systems.

Immediate Solutions

Creating a Custom MMC Console

As an administrator, you want to create your own set of tools to facilitate your common management tasks. Therefore, you should create your own MMC console. Here are the steps to follow:

1. Click Start, and then click Run. The Run dialog box opens.

2. Type "mmc", and then click OK. An empty MMC window opens. Refer to Figure 14.1.

3. Select Console|Add/Remove Snap-In. The Add/Remove Snap-In dialog box opens.

4. Click the Add button. The Add Standalone Snap-In dialog box opens.

5. Locate and select the snap-in of choice. Figure 14.15 shows Device Manager as an example. Click Add.

6. Select the local computer, and then click Finish.

7. Locate and select System Information. Click Add.

8. Select the local computer, and then click Finish.

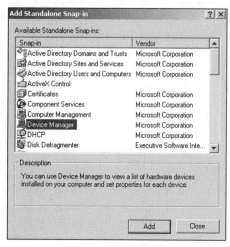

Figure 14.15   The Add Standalone Snap-In dialog box with Device Manager selected.

9. Click Close. You are returned to the Add/Remove Snap-In dialog box.

10. Click OK. You are returned to the MMC window.

11. Select Console|Options. The Options dialog box opens.

12. Change the Console Mode pull-down list to User Mode - Limited Access, Single Window.

13. Click OK.

14. Select Console|Save As.

15. Provide a file name, such as devices. The default storage location should be within the Administrative Tools folder of the currently logged on user's Start menu. Click Save.

16. Select Console|Exit to close the MMC window.

17. Click the Start menu, and select Programs|Administrative Tools|Devices.msc. Your newly created MMC console is launched.

18. Select Console|Exit to close the MMC window.

Viewing System Information

When you need to install a new device, you want to make sure that you have free system resources, such as IRQs and I/O addresses. Checking the resource status before adding new devices is always a good first step. Here's how:

NOTE: *On Windows 2000 Professional systems, the Administrative Tools section of the Start menu is disabled by default. You can also access Administrative Tools through the Control Panel.*

---

1. Click Start, and select Programs|Administrative Tools|Computer Management. The Computer Management window opens.

2. Select the System Information tool under the System Tools section.

3. Expand the System Information tool by clicking the plus sign.

4. Select the System Summary item. Notice the amount of available physical memory. If this is less than 10MB, add more physical RAM.

5. Expand the Hardware Resources item.

6. Select the Conflicts/Sharing item. Take note of whether the resources are shared or in contention.

7. Select the IRQ item (see Figure 14.16). Take note of whether IRQs are still available. (Note that the IRQs are not always shown in numeric order. Click the IRQ Number button to put them in order.)

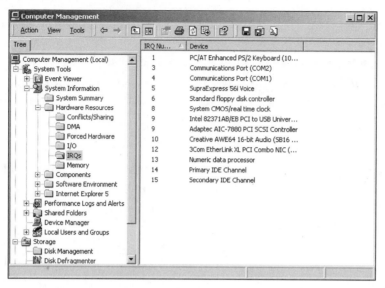

Figure 14.16   The IRQ item selected in the System Information utility in the Computer Management interface.

8. Explore the other areas of this tool for items or issues specific to the device that you want to install.

9. Close the Computer Management window by clicking the close button (the X button) in the title bar.

Viewing and Managing Local Shares

You'll periodically want to verify that the correct drives are shared and whether users are accessing those drives. This is done through the Shared Folders tool of Computer Management. Follow these steps:

NOTE: *On Windows 2000 Professional systems, the Administrative Tools section of the Start menu is disabled by default. You can also access Administrative Tools through the Control Panel.*

1. Click Start, and select Programs|Administrative Tools|Computer Management. The Computer Management window opens.

2. Select the Shared Folders utility.

3. Expand the Shared Folders utility by clicking the plus sign.

4. Select the Shares item. Notice that it lists all normal, hidden, and system shares of the local system.

5. Select Action|New File Share. The Create Shared Folder Wizard appears.

6. Click the Browse button. Locate and select a drive or folder to share. Then click OK.

7. Provide a share name and a share description. Then click Next.

8. Select the permission level for this share. Your options are All Users Have Full Control, Administrators Have Full Control And Other Users Have Read-Only Access, Administrators Have Full Control And Other Users Have No Access, and Custom Settings.

9. Click Finish to create the share.

10. You'll be prompted to indicate whether you want to create another share. Click No.

11. Notice that your new share now appears in the list of shares for this system.

12. Select the Sessions item. A list of all users and computers currently accessing resources from shares off this system are displayed.

13. By selecting an entry in this list and selecting Action|Close Session, you can terminate an active session.

14. Select the Open Files item. A list of all open files and folders is displayed.

15. Close the Computer Management window by clicking the close button (the X button) in the title bar.

Using the Event Viewer

When system problems occur, you'll want to investigate the details as recorded in the Event Viewer. Here are the steps:

NOTE: *On Windows 2000 Professional systems, the Administrative Tools section of the Start menu is disabled by default. You can also access Administrative Tools through the Control Panel.*

1. Click Start, and select Programs|Administrative Tools|Event Viewer. The Event Viewer opens.

2. Select the System log. A list of events should be displayed in the right pane.

3. Double-click any listed Information event (its icon is a blue "i" inside a thought bubble).

4. View the data captured for this event.

5. Click OK to close this event detail.

6. Double-click any listed Warning event (its icon is a yellow triangle with a black exclamation point.)

7. View the data captured for this event.

8. Click OK to close this event detail.

9. Double-click any listed Error event (its icon is a red circle with a white X).

10. View the data captured for this event.

11. Click OK to close this event detail.

12. Select Action|Properties. The System Log Properties dialog box opens.

13. Change the maximum log size from its 512 kilobyte (KB) default to 1,024KB.

14. Select the Overwrite Events As Needed radio button.

15. Click OK.

16. Select View|Filter. The System Log Properties dialog box opens with the Filter tab selected.

17. Deselect all event types but Warning.

18. Change the From and To pull-down lists to Events On; then change the dates to yesterday's and today's dates, respectively. Click OK.

19. The Event Viewer should be displaying only Warning events that occurred yesterday or today.

20. Close the Event Viewer window by clicking the close button (the X button) in the title bar.

Managing Licensing

This solution should only be performed if you are actually purchasing real licenses. Knowing how many licenses are being used on your server can help you determine whether you need to purchase more. Here are the steps:

NOTE: *On Windows 2000 Professional systems, the Administrative Tools section of the Start menu is disabled by default. You can also access Administrative Tools through the Control Panel.*

1. Click Start, and select Programs|Administrative Tools|Licensing. The Licensing window opens.

2. Select the Products View tab.

3. Take note of the values for the Windows Server product.

4. If the Per Seat Allocated value is close to or more than the Per Seat Purchased value, you need to purchase more Per Seat licenses. If the Per Server Reached value is close to or more than the Per Server Purchased value, you need to purchase more Per Server licenses. Contact your license reseller before continuing with this solution.

5. Click the Purchase History tab.

6. Select License|New License. The New Client Access License dialog box appears.

7. In the Product window, select Windows Server.

8. Change the quantity to the number of additional licenses you've purchased.

9. Select the Per Seat or Per Server mode (if applicable).

10. Provide a comment about the set of added licenses. Click OK.

11. Check the I Agree checkbox, and then click OK.

12. Notice that the newly added licenses appear on the Purchase History tab.

13. Select the Products View tab. Notice that the number of Per Seat Purchased or Per Server Purchased license values has incremented.

14. Select License|Exit.

Working with Services

From time to time, you may need to stop, restart, or reconfigure a service. This is done through the Services tool. Here's how:

NOTE: *On Windows 2000 Professional systems, the Administrative Tools section of the Start menu is disabled by default. You can also access Administrative Tools through the Control Panel.*

1. Click Start, and select Programs|Administrative Tools|Services. The Services window opens.

2. Notice that the right pane contains a list of all services installed in Windows 2000, along with description, status, startup type, and log on as information.

3. Select the Alerter service.

4. Select Action|Properties. The Properties dialog box for the selected service opens.

5. Click the Stop button. The service is stopped.

14. Windows 2000 Administration Tools

6. Click the Start button. The service is restarted.

7. Select the Log On tab.

8. Select the This Account radio button.

9. Click Browse. Locate and select the Administrator user account. Click OK.

10. Type in the password and a confirmation for this user account.

11. Select the Recovery tab.

12. Change the Second Failure setting to Restart The Service.

13. Change the Subsequent Failure setting to Reboot The Computer.

14. Set the Reset Fail Count setting to 3 Days.

15. Select the Dependencies tab. Notice the services that this service depends on.

16. Click Cancel to discard all settings and to return the service to its original state.

17. Close the Services window by clicking the close button (the X button) in the title bar.

Enabling Accessibility Options

If a user is seeing, hearing, or movement impaired, several features of Windows 2000 can be turned on or altered to improve interaction and control. Here are the steps to follow:

NOTE: *To return your system to normal activity, simply reopen the Accessibility Options applet, and deselect all enabled functions.*

---

1. Click Start, and select Settings|Control Panel. The Control Panel opens.

2. Double-click the Accessibility Options applet. The Accessibility Options applet opens.

3. Enable StickyKeys by selecting its checkbox.

4. Click Settings under StickyKeys. The Settings For StickyKeys dialog box opens.

5. Make sure that all setting checkboxes are marked. Click OK.

6. Enable ToggleKeys by selecting its checkbox.

7. Click Settings under ToggleKeys. The Settings For ToggleKeys dialog box opens.

8. Make sure the Settings checkbox is marked. Click OK.

9. Select the Sound tab.

10. Enable SoundSentry by selecting its checkbox.

11. Click Settings under SoundSentry. The Settings For SoundSentry dialog box opens.

12. Set the warning to Flash Active Caption Bar.

13. Select the General tab.

14. Select the Turn Off Accessibility Features After Idle For checkbox.

15. Set the minutes to five.

16. Click OK to close the Accessibility Options dialog box.

17. Close the Control Panel by selecting File|Close.

Troubleshooting a Device

When a hardware device does not function, you can use the Add/Remove Hardware applet to perform basic troubleshooting. To do so, follow these steps:

1. Click Start, and select Settings|Control Panel. The Control Panel opens.

2. Double-click the Add/Remove Hardware applet. The Add/Remove Hardware applet opens (see Figure 14.11).

3. Select the Add/Troubleshoot radio button. Click Next.

4. From the list, select the device that's having difficulties that you want to troubleshoot. It will most likely have a yellow triangle or red stop sign added to its device icon. Click Next.

5. The final window of the Add/Remove Hardware Wizard shows the current status of the device and indicates that the Troubleshooter will launch after this wizard is closed. Click Finish. The Troubleshooter opens.

6. The Troubleshooter is a question-and-answer wizard that helps determine the problem and offers you possible solutions. Answer the questions, and follow the instructions.

7. When this is complete, close the Troubleshooter by clicking the close button (the X button) in the title bar.

8. Close the Control Panel by selecting File|Close.

Adding New Hardware

If you've installed a new hardware device, but Windows 2000 did not automatically detect it, you'll need to use the Add/Remove Hardware applet. Here's how:

1. Click Start, and select Settings|Control Panel. The Control Panel opens.

2. Double-click the Add/Remove Hardware applet. The Add/Remove Hardware applet opens.

3. Select the Add/Troubleshoot radio button. Click Next.

4. Select the Add New Device item. Click Next.

5. Select the Yes, Search For New Hardware option, and then click Next. The system will attempt to locate any new hardware.

6. If the hardware is located, a Found New Hardware window will be displayed with the name of the detected hardware. Windows 2000 will attempt to locate the driver(s) for the detected device(s). If necessary, you'll be prompted for the distribution CD or a driver disk. A list of found devices will be displayed. Review this list, and then click Next. A completed message is displayed. Click Finish. The drivers are installed. You may be asked to reboot your system.

7. If the new device is not detected, a message will be displayed stating this. Click Next.

8. Select the type of device from the list provided.

9. Select the manufacturer and model from the list provided, or click the Have Disk button to install nonlisted devices or new drivers for listed devices.

10. A window listing the name of the device to be installed is shown. Click Next to install the driver.

11. After the driver is installed, a completed message is displayed. Click Finish. The drivers are installed. You may be asked to reboot your system.

12. Close the Control Panel by selecting File|Close.

Removing a Device Permanently

If you remove a device from a computer and that device will never be reinstalled, you should remove the driver associated with that device as well. This is done through the Add/Remove Hardware applet. Follow these steps:

1. Click Start, and select Settings|Control Panel. The Control Panel opens.

2. Double-click the Add/Remove Hardware applet. The Add/Remove Hardware applet opens.

3. Select the Uninstall/Unplug radio button. Click Next.

4. Select Uninstall a Device. Click Next.

5. From the list of devices, select the device to install. If the device is not listed, check the Show Hidden Devices checkboxes, and look again. After the device is selected, click Next.

6. Select the Yes, I Want To Uninstall This Device option, and click Next.

7. A Completing message is displayed. Click Finish. The driver (or drivers) is removed. You may be asked to reboot your system.

8. Close the Control Panel by selecting File|Close.

Rejecting or Unplugging a Device Temporarily

If you need to remove or unplug a device temporarily, you don't need to remove the driver. Instead, you can just have the system disable the driver until the device is returned to the system. This is done through the Add/Remove Hardware applet. Here are the steps:

1. Click Start, and select Settings|Control Panel. The Control Panel opens.

2. Double-click the Add/Remove Hardware applet. The Add/Remove Hardware applet opens.

3. Select the Uninstall/Unplug radio button. Click Next.

4. Select Unplug/Eject A Device. Click Next.

5. Select the device that you want to unplug or eject. Click Next.

6. A Completing message is displayed. Click Finish. The driver (or drivers) is removed. You may be asked to reboot your system.

7. Close the Control Panel by selecting File|Close.

Installing New Applications

If you need to install a new software application, use the Add/Remove Programs applet. Follow these steps:

1. Click Start menu, and select Settings|Control Panel. The Control Panel opens.

2. Double-click the Add/Remove Programs applet. The Add/Remove Programs applet opens.

3. Click the Add New Programs button.

4. Place the installation CD or floppy in the drive of the computer.

5. Click the CD or Floppy button, and then click Next.

6. If an installation launch tool is found, its path will be displayed. If not, or if the displayed path and file name are incorrect, use the Browse button to find and select the installation routine for the application. Click Finish.

7. The installation routine for the application is launched. Follow its prompts as necessary. When complete, you may be asked to reboot your system.

8. Close the Add/Remove Programs applet by clicking the Close button.

9. Close the Control Panel by selecting File|Close.

Removing an Installed Application

If you want to remove an installed application, use the Add/Remove Programs applet. Here are the steps:

1. Click Start, and select Settings|Control Panel. The Control Panel opens.

2. Double-click the Add/Remove Programs applet. The Add/Remove Programs applet opens.

3. Click the Change Or Remove Programs button.

4. Select the program that you want to remove.

5. Click the Change/Remove button.

6. Follow the application-specific prompts for removing or changing the product.

7. After this is complete, you may be asked to reboot your system.

8. Close the Add/Remove Programs applet by clicking the Close button.

9. Close the Control Panel by selecting File|Close.

Changing Installed Windows Components

If you want to add or remove Windows 2000 components from the original distribution, use the Add/Remove Programs applet. Here's how:

1. Click Start, and select Settings|Control Panel. The Control Panel opens.

2. Double-click the Add/Remove Programs applet. The Add/Remove Programs applet opens.

3. Click the Add/Remove Windows Components button. The Windows Components Wizard opens.

4. Use this interface to select or deselect Windows components. Selecting a component and clicking Details will display the subcomponents. When all the subcomponents are selected, the checkbox will be marked with a white background. When at least one subcomponent, but not all, are selected, the checkbox will be marked with a gray background. After you have made your selections, click Next.

5. The Windows Components Wizard will install or remove files based on your selections. When the Completing message is displayed, click Finish.

6. Close the Add/Remove Programs applet by clicking the Close button.

7. Close the Control Panel by selecting File|Close.

Changing Display and Desktop Settings

To alter the appearance of your desktop environment, use the Display applet. Here are the steps:

NOTE: *The Display applet can be reached by right-clicking an area of the desktop without an icon and selecting Properties from the pop-up menu.*

1. Click Start, and select Settings|Control Panel. The Control Panel opens.

2. Double-click the Display applet. The Display applet opens.

3. On the Background tab, select a graphics file for your desktop wallpaper. If necessary, select to tile the image. You may be prompted to enable Active Desktop. Click Yes.

4. Select the Screen Saver tab.

5. Select a screen saver from the pull-down list. Set the wait interval to 10 minutes.

6. Select the Appearance tab.

7. Select a scheme from the pull-down list.

8. Select the Web tab.

9. Select the Smooth Edges Of Screen Fonts and Show Window Contents While Dragging checkboxes.

10. Select the Settings tab.

11. Set your screen resolution to 800 x 600 and the color to 16-Bit High Color.

12. Click OK.

13. Close the Control Panel by selecting File|Close.

Configuring Regional Settings

If your computer is based in a country other than the United States, you are using a language other than English, or you want to change the conventions of your computer, you can do so through the Regional Settings applet. Here are the steps to follow:

1. Click Start, and select Settings|Control Panel. The Control Panel opens.

2. Double-click the Regional Settings applet. The Regional Settings applet opens (with a title of Regional Options).

3. On the General tab, select the location of your computer.

4. Check any additional languages that you want to install on this system.

5. Select the Numbers tab.

6. The default conventions for the language/location of your computer are shown. To alter any settings, use the pull-down list.

7. Select the Currency tab.

8. The default conventions for the language/location of your computer are shown. To alter any settings, use the pull-down list.

9. Select the Time tab.

10. The default conventions for the language/location of your computer are shown. To alter any settings, use the pull-down list.

11. Select the Date tab.

12. The default conventions for the language/location of your computer are shown. To alter any settings, use the pull-down list.

13. Select the Input Locales tab. This tab is where the hotkeys to switch to an alternate location are defined. Take note of the defaults or define your own.

14. Click OK to close the Regional Settings applet.

15. Close the Control Panel by selecting File|Close.

Scheduling a Task

If you want to perform a task automatically without user input, use the Task Scheduler. Here's how:

1. Click Start, and select Settings|Control Panel. The Control Panel opens.

2. Double-click the Scheduled Tasks applet. The Scheduled Tasks applet opens into the same window as Control Panel.

3. Double-click the Add Scheduled Task Wizard. The wizard opens.

4. Click Next.

5. Select an application to launch, or click the Browse button to select programs or batch files not listed. Click Next.

6. Set the frequency of this task. Click Next.

7. Set the start time, repeat intervals, start date, or other frequency-specific details, as prompted. Click Next.

8. Provide the user name and password for the user account that this task will be executed under. Click Next.

9. Select the Open Advanced Properties For This Task When I Click Finish checkbox. Click Finish. The Properties dialog box for the scheduled task opens.

10. Select the Settings tab.

11. Select the Delete The Task If It Is Not Scheduled To Run Again checkbox.

12. Set the Stop The Task If It Runs For option to eight hours.

13. Select the Only Start The Task If The Computer Has Been Idle For At Least checkbox, and set the idle time to five minutes.

14. Click OK. Notice that the scheduled task now appears in the Scheduled Task window.

15. Click the Back button to return to the Control Panel.

16. Close the Control Panel by selecting File|Close.

Configuring a Sound Scheme

If you have a multimedia-capable system, you can customize the sounds that your system makes based on application and interface events through the Sounds and Multimedia applet. Follow these steps:

1. Click Start, and select Settings|Control Panel. The Control Panel opens.

2. Double-click the Sounds and Multimedia applet. The Sounds and Multimedia applet opens.

3. Select a scheme from the pull-down list.

4. To customize a sound for an event, select the event from the Sound Events list. Then, use the Name pull-down list, shown in Figure 14.17, or the Browse button to select a sound. Click the play button (the triangle pointing to the right, like a play button on a tape recorder) to hear the selected sound.

5. After you've customized all desired sound events, click the Save As button. Provide a name for your new sound scheme. Click OK.

6. Click OK to close the Sounds and Multimedia applet.

7. Close the Control Panel by selecting File|Close.

Figure 14.17   The Name pull-down list in the Sounds And Multimedia Properties dialog box.

Setting Driver Signing Options

If you're concerned about corrupted drivers being installed on your system, use the driver signing options to protect yourself. Here are the steps:

1. Click Start|, and select Settings|Control Panel. The Control Panel opens.

2. Double-click the System applet. The System applet opens.

3. Select the Hardware tab.

4. Click the Driver Signing button. The Driver Signing Options dialog box opens, as shown in Figure 14.18.

5. Select the Block radio button to prevent nonsigned drivers from being installed.

6. Click OK to close the Driver Signing Options dialog box.

7. Click OK to close the System applet.

8. Close the Control Panel by selecting File|Close.

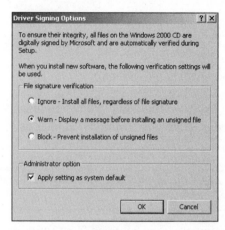

Figure 14.18   The Driver Signing Options dialog box.

Creating Hardware Profiles

If you have a computer with hardware devices that change periodically, you can use hardware profiles to define a set of drivers for each unique hardware configuration. Here are the steps to follow:

1. Click Start, and select Settings|Control Panel. The Control Panel opens.

2. Double-click the System applet. The System applet opens.

3. Select the Hardware tab.

4. Click the Hardware Profiles button. The Hardware Profiles dialog box opens.

5. Select the Profile 1 hardware profile. Click Copy.

6. Type a name for the new profile. Click OK.

7. Click Start, and select Shutdown. Select Reboot, and then click OK.

8. When prompted during the booting process, use the arrow keys to select the new hardware profile that you named in Step 6. After you've made your selection, press Enter.

9. After the computer has booted, log on using Ctrl+Alt+Delete.

10. If the Control Panel is not open, click Start, and select Settings|Control Panel. The Control Panel opens.

11. Double-click the System applet. The System applet opens.

12. Select the Hardware tab.

13. Click the Device Manager button. The Device Manager opens.

14. Expand the list of devices. Select a device that will not be present when this hardware profile is used.

15. Select Action|Properties.

16. Change the Device Usage pull-down list from Use This Device (Enable) to Do Not Use This Device In The Current Hardware Profile (Disable), as shown in Figure 14.19. Click OK.

NOTE: *If you want to add a device back into a hardware profile, change the Device Usage setting from Do Not Use This Device In The Current Hardware Profile (Disable) to Use This Device (Enable).*

---

17. Repeat Steps 14 through 16 for each device to be removed from this hardware profile.

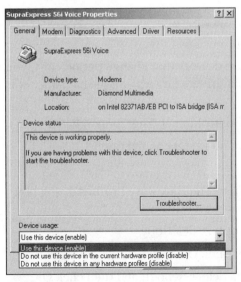

Figure 14.19   A device's Properties dialog box from the Device Manager.

18. When this is complete, shut down the system. Click Start, and then select Shutdown. Select Shutdown, and then click OK.

19. After the power is off, change the hardware configuration of the system to match the newly created hardware profile.

20. Power on the system. The hardware profile should be automatically selected.

21. After the computer has booted, log on using Ctrl+Alt+Delete.

22. Repeat this solution to create other hardware profiles.

Chapter 15

Windows 2000 Registry: Structure, Editing, and Important Keys

In Depth

Although many people think that Windows 95 and Windows NT were the first operating systems to have a registry, that's not the case. In fact, Windows 3.x and Windows NT 3.1 had registries of sorts. They were just stored and modified differently.

Anyone who worked with Windows 3.x will recall having to edit initialization (INI) files. These INI files get their name from the .ini extension that's most commonly assigned to the files. The INI files were simple text files. You could edit them from the disk operating system (DOS) using the **edit** command or through Notepad in Windows. Having these configuration files stored as text files was great because they were very easy to edit. However, because they were easy to edit, they were easily corrupted. Any user or application could go into these files and modify them.

Windows NT 3.1 introduced a new way of storing configuration information: using the registry. The registry introduced in Windows NT 3.1 has not changed much in its format and structure and is very similar to the one you find in Windows 2000.

The registry stores all configuration information about the system. This includes networking components, security, applications, desktop settings, and the actual appearance of the user interface.

Hives, Files, and Structures

The Windows 2000 registry is designed much like a file system. Each component in the file system has a corresponding component in the registry. The registry is stored in binary databases on the local hard drive.

You have a couple of ways to access the information stored in the registry databases. The first is using either built-in or third-party registry tools. The other is through a Win32 application programming interface (API).

As stated, the registry can be compared to a file system. A file system consists of three main components: the disk, the folders, and the files. The root of the file system is the disk. It's most commonly assigned a letter (for example, C:). Underneath the root exists folders and files. Folders are containers that can hold other folders and/or files. Finally, the lowest part of the structure is the files. Files cannot contain other folders or files (archive files, such as Zip files, are a special case).

With the registry, the structure is similar. Only the names have changed. At the root of the registry are the root keys. There are five root keys (also known as *hives*): HKEY_CLASSES_ROOT (HKCR), HKEY_CURRENT_USER (HKCU), HKEY_LOCAL_MACHINE (HKLM), HKEY_USERS (HKU), and HKEY_CURRENT_CONFIG (HKCC). These root keys are listed in Table 15.1 with their descriptions.

Keep in mind that changes to the HKEY_CURRENT_USER and HKEY_CURRENT_CONFIG hives are specific to the current configuration and logged-in user. When the user is logged out, these changes will be integrated into HKLM and HKU appropriately. These same changes will only appear for that specific user. If you need to make changes for all users or all configurations, you need to find the appropriate identical structure within HKLM or HKU.

Below the root keys are the keys. Several of the main keys are referred to as *subkeys*. Table 15.2 deals with some of the most commonly used (and most important) subkeys.

Table 15.1 The root keys.

Root Key	Description
HKEY_CLASSES_ROOT (HKCR)	Creates the links between file extensions and old class system components. These links tell the system which application to launch for a specific extension (for example, launch Microsoft Word when a DOC file is opened).
HKEY_CURRENT_USER (HKCU)	Specifies the configuration properties of the currently logged-on user. When the user logs on, the user's profile is written to this root key. When the user logs off, information from this root key is written into the user's profile.
HKEY_LOCAL_MACHINE (HKLM)	Stores all configuration information about the current system. This includes hardware, software, and operating system information.
HKEY_USERS (HKU)	Stores a copy of the profile of each user who has logged into this system before.
HKEY_CURRENT_CONFIG (HKCC)	Stores information about the current system configuration.

Table 15.2 The main subkeys.

Subkey	Description
HKLM\HARDWARE	Stores all hardware configurations currently known about the system. This subkey is created when the system is first started.
HKLM\SAM	Stores all the information about the user databases. In Windows 2000, this is stored in Active Directory. The Security Account Manager (SAM) is no longer used as it was in Windows NT. The subkey is named SAM for backward compatibility.

(continued)

Table 15.2   The main subkeys (continued).

Subkey	Description
HKLM\SECURITY	This subkey stores the security information for the system, such as the currently logged-on user's credentials and policy information. You cannot modify this subkey.
HKLM\SOFTWARE	This subkey stores information about the different software packages installed on the system. The Windows 2000 operating system is defined as one of these applications, so you'll find many of the configuration properties for Windows 2000 within this subkey.
HKLM\SYSTEM	Stores all information about the currently loaded session (including services). This subkey also stores the configuration for the Last Known Good Configuration boot option.

Manipulating the Windows 2000 Registry

Because of the way the registry is stored on the system, you need specialized tools to control all the changes in the registry. Many of the day-to-day changes to the registry are performed through the Control Panel applets. Sometimes, however, a manual registry edit is required. Some of the tools available to perform these tasks are covered in this section.

WARNING! Incorrectly editing the registry can render your system unusable. Many of the tools discussed here will make the changes immediately and can crash your system if not used properly. Only edit the registry directory as a last resort, if you have a current backup and you are absolutely certain that you know what you're editing.

Registry Access Tools and Editors

Windows 2000 ships with two registry editing tools: regedit.exe, shown in Figure 15.1, and regedt32.exe, shown in Figure 15.2. The differences between the two will become apparent in this section and throughout the chapter. Both perform the same basic tasks, but as you'll see, one is considerably more powerful for editing the registry.

These two editors have different backgrounds. When Microsoft shipped Windows NT 3.1, it included a tool to modify the registry known as *regedt32.exe*. This tool could be used to view and modify the registry, set permissions on the registry, and search keys within the registry. When Windows 95 was developed, Microsoft quickly realized that although Windows 95 needed a registry—and therefore a registry editor—the format of regedt32.exe did not fit. Therefore, the Windows 95 registry editor, *regedit.exe*, was developed. This editor had all the basic capabilities of regedt32.exe, but did not have the option of modifying registry permissions. The reason for this is simple. There is no way in Windows 9x to control

Figure 15.1   The REGEDIT application.

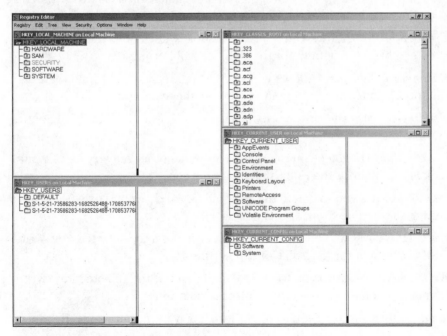

Figure 15.2   The REGEDT32 application.

permissions by users. However, regedit.exe provided a more flexible search component (you could now search for keys, values, and data rather than only keys, as with regedt32.exe), better importing and exporting tools, the ability to rename keys, and the ability to copy key names.

When Windows 2000 shipped, Microsoft decided to include both editors in the operating system. Although this might seem redundant, it is, in fact, not. Although it would be nice to have a single tool that does everything, Microsoft kept the two tools that administrators are used to.

Registry Permissions

From within REGEDT32, it's possible to set security permissions on registry hives, subtrees, and keys in just the same manner as you would assign Windows NT File System (NTFS) permissions to files and folders. All you have to do to set permissions is to select Security|Permissions. The dialog at that point should look very familiar. By default, you have only two permission types: Read and Full Control. Advanced permissions are as follows:

- *Query Value*—Allows you to read data entries within a key. Query Value is a default for the Read permission.

- *Set Value*—Allows you to write, create, and change data entries within a key. Set Value is a default for the Full Control permission.

- *Create Subkey*—Allows you to create a subkey key under the selected key. Create Subkey is a default for the Full Control Permission.

- *Enumerate Subkeys*—Allows you to view and read subkeys and their data. Enumerate Subkeys is a default for the Read permission.

- *Notify*—Enables auditing. Notify is a default for both read and full control permissions.

- *Create Link*—Enables you to create a link to another registry key. Create Link is a default for the Full Control permission.

- *Delete*—Allows you to delete the selected key and any subkeys. Delete is a default for the Full Control permission

- *Write DAC*—Allows you to change permissions on the selected key. Write DAC is a default for the Full Control permission.

- *Write Owner*—Allows you to change the owner of the selected key. Write Owner is a default for the Full Control permission.

- *Read Control*—Allows you to read the security permissions list. Read Control is a default for the Read permission.

15. Windows 2000 Registry: Structure, Editing, and Important Keys

As with all registry functions, be very careful what you do here. Try not to remove the Administrators group from any permissions list unless you have an adequately permissioned replacement planned and ready. Also, avoid making permission changes to any system keys because these are traditionally modified by applications during installation.

Backing Up the Registry

You can perform registry backups in several ways, and many of them have existed since the days of Windows 95. As with a tape backup, it is possible to back up all or part of the registry using several different processes.

The System State

The Windows 2000 registry is part of what's known as the *system state*. The system state can probably best be defined as a group of the most important files on a Windows 2000 system. In a Windows 2000 professional or member server, the system state is the registry, boot files, and Component Object Model (COM)+ extensions. In a domain controller, the SYSVOL volume and the Active Directory database are included. For the most part, the easiest way to back up the registry fully is to flag the system state for backup within the backup program you're using. If the program that you use is not fully Windows 2000-compliant and does not have an entry for the system state, you can back up the registry in other ways, but, before you choose an alternative, you need to be aware of the special features that come with the system state package.

Just like with Active Directory, changes to the registry are stored in log files. Every time that a full backup of the system state occurs, the log files are purged, and a new set begins with every change that occurs. Any restore process that occurs after a partial or complete failure results in missing data, namely all of the information that changed since the last applicable backup process. These log files also allow you to recover from this particular data loss. If the registry becomes partially or fully corrupt, it can be restored from backup, and the log files can be implemented to create a completely restored registry in a process that's known as an authoritative restore. These log files are located in the %systemroot%\system32\config directory.

These log files can be a very valuable addition to an overall disaster recovery plan that may well justify the purchase or upgrade of a Windows 2000-compliant backup program. In any case, remember that NTBACKUP.EXE comes with Windows 2000 and will back up the System State. If, for some reason, you cannot purchase a third-party backup program, schedule NTBACKUP to back up the System State regularly to a location on the network that can be backed up by your standard tape backup program.

Every time that the System State is backed up with NTBACKUP, a copy of the registry is stored in the %systemroot%\repair\regback. You can restore this copy of the registry much faster than using a tape catalog. In addition, if your registry is ruined, it's highly unlikely that you'll be able even to access NTBACKUP, let alone a tape drive.

Remote Backup

It's possible to access and back up other Windows 2000 system registries remotely. The process is really only copying the appropriate files, but appropriate permissions are required.

Most registry files on any Windows 2000 system are located in the %systemroot%\system32\config directory. Be aware that another copy of the registry is located in the %systemroot%\repair directory, but this particular registry is a snapshot of the registry as it was when Windows 2000 was first installed or upgraded. Making a backup of this may be useful to you, but it's far more important to copy the contents of the config folder. You may also consider copying the %systemroot%\repair\regback folder as an additional layer of backup in the event of a failure. The registry located in the config folder will be your first option, followed by the copy located in regback (which should be the equivalent of a tape backup), and then the copy in the repair directory.

TIP: *Although a viable copy of the registry is located in the %systemroot%\repair directory, keep in mind that it's a copy of the registry when you first installed or upgraded Windows 2000. Restoring it as a last-ditch effort may not improve the situation if your mission-critical applications aren't appropriately on that registry. It may cause more problems than you care to deal with.*

User data constitutes another part of the registry that is stored separately in order to maximize efficiency. If you are performing a remote (or manual) backup of the registry, you'll need to find and copy all instances of NTUSER.DAT. In pure Windows 2000 systems, the NTUSER.DAT file is located in the *documents and settings**<username>* folder. For systems that are upgraded from Windows NT 4, NTUSER.DAT will continue to be in the %system root%\profiles.

Piecemeal Backups

It is possible to back up pieces of a registry. Reasons for doing so range from troubleshooting, to cleanup, to distributing changes. From within REGEDT32.EXE, you can back up specific keys by clicking the registry key and using the Registry menu to save the key as a hive file. Both REGEDIT and REGEDT32 can save selected keys as text files by selecting the key and selecting the Registry menu to export (for REGEDIT) or save the subtree (within REGEDT32).

Any time that you manually change the registry, it's recommended that you use REGEDIT to export the keys that you're going to be playing with. The exported text files have an extension of .reg, and, if you double-click them, they will automatically insert themselves back into the registry appropriately, overwriting any blunders. This is another reason why, if you have a simple registry hack or change that needs to be distributed with little or no effort, you should simply make your change (test it first!) and export the changed key. Copy the .reg file to any and all systems that require the change, double-click, and, voilà, your changes are done.

Restoring the Registry

As I discussed in "Piecemeal Backups," restoring an exported key is easy and somewhat convenient. Restoring a larger piece of the registry, or indeed the entire registry, can become a bit more dicey and is certainly more so in an emergency situation. As I'm sure you've heard quite often, the registry can be the only thing standing between you and a fully functioning system. It's important to ensure that you are aware of the appropriate recovery methods in the event of a failure or problem so that you don't end up losing the rest of the data located on the system. Without these recovery methods, a corrupt registry can render your hard drive into not much more than a hockey puck with a lot of valuable—yet inaccessible—data on it.

Simple Restore

Simply restoring a corrupt registry can be one of the most daunting tasks you'll ever have to do simply because it may not be possible to get to the backup application to restore the tape. You may need to install Windows 2000 to a separate directory in order to boot and get to the backup program. For the same reason that it's difficult to change a carpet if you're standing on it, it's also nearly impossible to restore system files if you're using them. The best that you can hope for is a mishmash of new and old restored data, which can be unpredictable at best. It's far better for you to install Windows 2000 in a separate directory and to coordinate the restoration efforts from there rather than from the original location.

If the boot menu offers you another operating system to choose from, by all means, do so and use the alternate reboot to restore your registry. You may be able to restore most of the registry manually by copying the contents of the %systemboot%\repair\regback directory to the %systemboot%\system32\config folder. If you're booting to a separate copy of Windows 2000, this is just the same as installing Windows 2000 to a separate directory. From there, you should be able to use NTBACKUP (or whatever the backup program) to restore the registry or the System State.

Directory Services Restore Mode

If you're dealing with a single domain controller environment, you can use the boot menu to press F8 and boot to Directory Services Restore mode and restore the System State from the %systemroot%\repair\regback location. You'll need to use NTDSUTIL to perform an authoritative restore (see Chapter 10) if you're working in a multiple domain controller environment where Active Directory may have been corrupted and replicated to other domain controllers.

Emergency Repair Disks

You can restore the registry from the emergency repair disks (ERDs). However, be very aware that, although this may seem to be the most comfortable, familiar, and fastest method of restoring a corrupt registry, it's only good as a last-ditch effort. I mentioned before that the contents of the %systemroot%\repair are created from day one of the system's existence. The ERD uses this copy of the registry to restore from, and, indeed, this is the preferred method of restoring the registry back to its original clean working state.

Recovery Console

You have the capability of restoring large pieces of the registry from within the Windows 2000 Recovery Console. You can boot to the Windows 2000 installation CD, select R for repair, and C to enter the recovery console and restore the registry there. However, this will only work if the security hive isn't corrupt. If per chance the security hive is corrupt or this particular method does not work, it's advisable that you restore from within Directory Services Restore mode.

Last Known Good

If the registry blows up on you, you can still use one recovery method before you start thinking about tape backups and copies of the registry. I'm specifically talking about the Last Known Good option that's available when the system boots. Last Known Good is an option where you can press F8 from the boot menu to boot to the last configuration where the system successfully booted.

Here's the perfect scenario where the Last Known Good comes in handy. You install an application or driver that causes your system to get the blue screen of death (BSOD), which is a situation where a blue screen appears with a cryptic message that basically means that something went wrong and the system cannot recover from it. You have no choice but to reboot the system. When you reboot, you choose the Last Known Good option, and the system comes up with the same registry settings that it had before you installed the application, driver, or whatever the offending component was.

The Last Known Good option was available with Windows NT, but it wasn't very effective. Windows NT keeps a single list of configuration changes that changes every time the system initializes. Basically, if you get to the logon prompt, the system assumes that the boot was successful, purges the list of configuration changes, and starts a new list. Basically, if a BSOD occurs, you reboot, log in, and subsequently get another BSOD, the Last Known Good configuration has been overwritten with what actually was the last known bad configuration. For some reason, Microsoft assumed that you would always be aware of the situation and never pass up an opportunity to use the Last Known Good feature.

With Windows 2000, Microsoft fixed this problem by making several copies of configuration changes in such a manner that you can be sure that different versions of the registry still exist. If there's a problem, you should always be able to take advantage of the Last Known Good feature while still maintaining a copy of configuration changes that failed. If you somehow lose track of the Last Known Good configuration, you can manually configure the registry to point to a particular configuration as long as you can boot and get into a registry editor.

The system keeps four copies of registry configuration changes located in HKEY_LOCAL_MACHINE\System. There can be more or less than four, but you can always distinguish a configuration change by its name, which will always include the word "controlset". The control sets labeled "ControlSet001," "ControlSet002," and so on are official backup configurations, and the CurrentControlSet key is what is currently active and being used. It does not contain any backup information. Although it's difficult to tell exactly which control set contains what changes, you can tell which one is currently being used, which one is the default, and which one would be used if the Last Known Good option were triggered. Within the HKEY_LOCAL_MACHINE\System\Select key, you'll notice four different entries: current, default, LastKnownGood, and failed. Each one contains data in the form of a hexadecimal number that equates to the control set that will be referenced. These entries are as follows:

- *Current*—Lists the control set that is currently being used
- *Default*—Lists the control set that will be used if Last Known Good is not triggered
- *LastKnownGood*—Points to the control set that will be used if Last Known Good is triggered
- *Failed*—Points to the control set that contains configuration data from a failed boot

If the Last Known Good option is triggered, the contents of the CurrentControlSet are moved to a backup control set (ControlSetNNN where NNN represents a number) and that control set is entered into the Failed entry under the Select subkey.

If the Last Known Good option is not triggered, the contents of the CurrentControlSet are moved to a backup control set and that control set is entered into the Default entry and Current entry under the Select subkey.

Let's say that you install a driver on your Windows 2000 system. Those changes are reflected in the CurrentControlSet key under HKEY_LOCAL_MACHINE\ System. If the system gives you the BSOD, you reboot it, choose the Last Known Good option, and the contents of the CurrentControlSet are dumped into ControlSet003, for example, the entry for HKEY_LOCAL_MACHINE\ System\Select\Failed (shown in Figure 15.3) reads 0x00000003(3), and the controlset listed in the HKEY_LOCAL_MACHINE\System\Select\LastKnownGood entry is loaded instead. In this example, let's say that LastKnownGood points to ControlSet002. When the system boots, ControlSet002 will be loaded, and the contents of the HKEY_LOCAL_MACHINE\System\Select will read Current=2, Default=1, Failed=3, LastKnownGood=2. If you subsequently reboot the system without invoking Last Known Good, the HKEY_LOCAL_MACHINE\System\ Select key entries will be changed to read Current=2, Default=2, Failed=3, LastKnownGood=1. Subsequent successful changes cycle through over time. At no point should you ever see the current and default entries being equal to the LastKnownGood.

My point in this detail over the Last Known Good is simple. If you choose not to take advantage of the Last Known Good option, yet the system continues to give

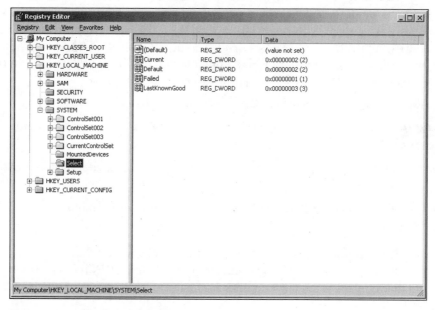

Figure 15.3   The System Subkey.

you a BSOD, you should still be able to choose the Last Known Good option. If, for some reason, that doesn't work, you can still manually change the control set to use one of the other two control set backups located in HKEY_LOCAL_ MACHINE\System. Once you access the registry either via Safe mode or before the BSOD kicks in, all you need to do is look at the contents of the HKEY_ LOCAL_MACHINE\System\Select. You can assume that, because you've rebooted in a bad state more than once, the current and default sets are not going to do you any good. You may have already used the control set that LastKnownGood is pointing to, so you might consider changing the LastKnownGood entry to whatever the last one is.

Again, I cannot emphasize enough how delicate these operations are. It's very easy to cause more problems by invoking a control set that contains a previous disaster's configuration. It's even easier to cycle control sets accidentally to the point where the good control set is shuffled to oblivion in favor of bad control sets that the system believes are good because you didn't choose the LastKnownGood option. My best advice in situations like this is to keep your head, write everything down, export the backup control sets if you can (so you can double-click and bring them back in if you've accidentally replaced the good control set with bad ones), and keep track of what's going on in the HKEY_LOCAL_MACHINE\System\Select key so that you can get an idea of what's happening to those control sets. If you really want to manipulate the LastKnownGood control sets, I'd recommend that you check out the TechNet article Q142033 on the Microsoft Web site.

Registry Size Limits

Windows 2000 loads the registry into memory when the system is booted. The purpose is primarily for efficiency, but also somewhat for security purposes. This is also why the NTUSER.DAT user registry hives are stored separately. Loading all user registry entries is unnecessary and useless. In order to keep control of how much memory is being used by the registry, a size limit is imposed on the amount of memory that the registry is allowed to use. Keep in mind here that you're not imposing a limit on the size of the registry itself, but rather how much memory it consumes when it is loaded into memory. If the size limit is too small, you may see error messages where the printers folder won't open, user profiles won't load, or the system indicates that there's not enough disk space to complete certain operations when there's plenty of space on the system drive. You can change the limit of memory that's taken up by the registry by changing the limit. To do this, select Control Panel|System, click the Advanced Tab, click Performance Options, and change the virtual memory settings for the maximum registry size.

Windows 2000 Server Resource Kit Registry Tools

The *Windows 2000 Server Resource Kit* (Microsoft Press, ISBN: 1-57231-805-8) is a must for all Windows 2000 administrators. Although Windows 2000 has most of the tools that an administrator needs, the *Windows 2000 Server Resource Kit* has more advanced tools (but not always pretty) to help with everyday tasks. These tools are available with the resource kit itself, and also downloadable from Microsoft's Web site. Several registry tools and help files ship with the resource kit, and this chapter looks at the following six:

- Regback.exe
- Regrest.exe
- Regdmp.exe
- Regfind.exe
- Scanreg.exe
- Dureg.exe

Regback.exe

The *Windows 2000 Server Resource Kit* ships with a program that can be used to back up the registry. This file, regback.exe, is found in the %root%\Program Files\Resource Kit folder and is executed using the following format:

```
REGBACK [-m \\servername] directoryPath [-u | -U outputFile]
```

The regback.exe application can be used to back up the registry on the local machine or on a remote machine. It can also be used to back up the user profile. This is useful if you've created a profile that you would like to back up easily and use with other users.

Regrest.exe

The flip side of regback.exe is regrest.exe. It can take the files backed up with regback.exe and restore them to the registry. One nice feature of the regrest.exe application is that it will automatically back up the information in the registry before restoring the new information. The format for running this application is as follows:

```
regrest <newfilename> <savefilename> <hivetype> <hivename>
```

WARNING! The regrest.exe file does not actually overwrite any files. Instead, it moves the current registry file to the location specified in the <savefilename> switch and then moves the new registry file, as specified in the <newfilename> switch. For this reason, all files must reside on the same volume. For example, if the new files are on the D: drive and the current files are on the C: drive, you'll need to move the files from the D: drive to the C: drive.

Regdmp.exe

This application allows you to dump the contents of the registry to the screen, a file, or a printer. The regdmp.exe application uses the following format:

```
REGDMP [-m \\servername | -h hivefile hiveroot |
-w Win95 Directory][-i n][-o outputWidth][-s]
[-o outputWidth] RegistryPath
```

Regfind.exe

Although regedit.exe gives you some fairly good registry search capabilities, its searching capabilities pale in comparison to those of regfind.exe. This tool not only allows you to search the registry for a string, but it also allows you to replace those found strings automatically. Its format is as follows:

```
REGFIND [-m \\machinename | -h hivefile hiveroot | -w Win95 Directory][-i n]
[-o outputWidth][-p RegistryKeyPath][-z | -t DataType][-b | -B][-y]
[-n][searchString [-r ReplacementString]]
```

Scanreg.exe

Scanreg.exe has been called the "grep" of the registry. *Grep* is a Unix command-line tool for performing very complex searches on directories, files, and data. Scanreg.exe allows you to search the registry for a specific string. You can have only keys, values, or data searched, or you can search all three. It also displays the output with different colors assigned to each type that it finds. Scanreg.exe uses the following structure:

```
scanreg <[-s] string> < [-k][-v][-d] > [[-r] key][-c][-e][-n]
```

Dureg.exe

Dureg.exe is a tool that can be used to find the size of the registry, a root key, or any key within the local registry. Its format is as follows:

```
DuReg [/a | /cr | /cu | /u | /lm][/s | /d]
["Registry path"]["string to search"]
```

Immediate Solutions

Working with Registry Keys and Values

The following sections explore the tasks involved with managing registry keys and values.

Making a Shortcut to Regedt32.exe or Regedit.exe

By default, the registry editors do not have a shortcut assigned to them on the Start menu. The following steps create a shortcut for the registry editor of your choice:

1. Click Start, and select Settings|Taskbar and Start Menu.

2. Click the Advanced tab (see Figure 15.4).

3. Click Add.

4. When the Create Shortcut Wizard appears, enter the location of regedt32.exe or regedit.exe (by default, they're located in the %systemroot%\system32\ folder), or use the Browse button to locate it, select the file, and click Next.

5. Navigate to the location in the Start menu where you would like the short-cut created, and click Next.

Figure 15.4   Modifying the Start menu.

6. Enter a display name for the registry editor (for example, "Registry Editor 32" or "Regedit"), and click Finish.

7. Click OK to close the Taskbar and Start Menu applet.

Finding a Registry Key

The two registry editors search for keys somewhat differently. For this reason, both methods are presented.

Finding a Key Using Regedt32.exe

To find a key using regedt32.exe, perform the following steps:

1. Click Start, and select Run.

2. Enter "regedt32.exe" in the Open field, and click OK.

3. Select View|Find Key.

4. The Find window will appear, as shown in Figure 15.5. Enter the name of the key in the Find What field, and click Find Next.

5. To find subsequent keys with the same name, press F3.

Finding a Key Using Regedit.exe

To find a key using regedit.exe, perform the following steps:

1. Click Start, and select Run.

2. Enter "regedit.exe" in the Open field, and click OK.

3. Select Edit|Find.

4. The Find window will appear, as shown in Figure 15.6. Enter the name of the key in the Find What field, ensure that the Keys checkbox is checked, and click Find Next.

5. To find subsequent keys with the same name, press F3.

Finding a Registry Value

Whereas regedt32.exe will only search for keys, regedit.exe will search for keys, values, and data. To do so, perform the following steps:

1. Click Start, and select Run.

2. Enter "regedit.exe" in the Open field, and click OK.

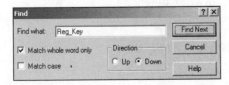

Figure 15.5   Finding a registry key in regedt32.exe.

15. Windows 2000 Registry: Structure, Editing, and Important Keys

Figure 15.6   Finding a registry key in regedit.exe.

3. Select Edit|Find.

4. The Find window will appear. Enter the name of the value in the Find What field, ensure that the Values checkbox is checked, and click Find Next.

5. To find subsequent values with the same name, press F3.

Running the Registry Editor in Read-Only Mode

When you modify the registry using regedt32.exe, changes are made immediately. Because a simple mistake can make your system inoperative, regedt32.exe has the option to set the registry editor to Read Only. To do this, perform the following steps:

1. Click Start, and select Run.

2. Enter "regedt32.exe" in the Open field, and click OK.

3. Select Options|Read Only Mode.

Saving a Registry Key

You can save a registry key as a backup or you can duplicate a configuration from one system to another. To do so, perform the following steps:

1. Click Start, and select Run.

2. Enter "regedt32.exe" in the Open field, and click OK.

3. Select the key that you would like to save.

4. Select Registry|Save Key.

5. Specify a location and a name for the saved key file, and click OK.

Saving a Registry Subtree

To save a registry subtree, perform the following steps:

1. Click Start, and select Run.

2. Enter "regedt32.exe" in the Open field, and click OK.

3. Select the key that you would like to save.

4. Select Registry|Save Subtree As.

5. Specify a location and a name for the saved subtree file, and click OK.

Creating a New Key

The method for creating new keys varies between regedit.exe and regedt32.exe. Therefore, both methods are listed here.

Creating a New Key Using Regedt32.exe

To create a new key using regedt32.exe, perform the following steps:

1. Click Start, and select Run.

2. Enter "regedt32.exe" in the Open field, and click OK.

3. Navigate to where you would like the new key created.

4. Select Edit|Add Key.

5. Enter a name for the new key in the Key Name field, enter a class for the key in the Class field, and click OK.

Creating a New Key Using Regedit.exe

To create a new key using regedit.exe, perform the following steps:

1. Click Start, and select Run.

2. Enter "regedit.exe" in the Open field, and click OK.

3. Navigate to where you would like the new key created.

4. Select Edit|New|Key.

5. A new key will appear with a temporary name of New Key # n. Enter the name for the key, and press Enter.

Creating a New Key on a Remote System

The two registry editors create keys somewhat differently. For this reason, both methods are presented.

Creating a Key on a Remote System Using Regedt32.exe

To create a key on a remote system using regedt32.exe, perform the following steps:

1. Click Start, and select Run.

2. Enter "regedt32.exe" in the Open field, and click OK.

3. Select Registry|Select Computer.

4. Either enter the name of the computer to which you would like to connect or use the Browse button to locate it.

5. Click OK.

6. Select Edit|Add Key.

7. Enter a name for the new key, and click OK.

Creating a Key on a Remote System Using Regedit.exe

To create a key on a remote system using regedit.exe, perform the following steps:

1. Click Start, and select Run.

2. Enter "regedit.exe" in the Open field, and click OK.

3. Select Registry|Connect Network Registry.

4. Enter the name of the computer, or use the Browse button to locate it.

5. Click OK.

6. Navigate to where the value is to be created.

7. Select Edit|New_Key.

8. Enter the name of the new key, and press Enter.

Creating a New Value

The two registry editors create values somewhat differently. For this reason, both methods are presented.

Creating a New Value Using Regedt32.exe

To create a new value using regedt32.exe, perform the following steps:

1. Click Start, and select Run.

2. Enter "regedt32.exe" in the Open field, and click OK.

3. Navigate to where you would like the new value created.

4. Select Edit|Add Value.

5. Enter a name for the new value in the Value Name field, select the data type from the Data Type menu, and click OK.

6. Enter the data for the value, and click OK.

Creating a New Value Using Regedit.exe

To create a new value using regedit.exe, perform the following steps:

1. Click Start, and select Run.

2. Enter "regedit.exe" in the Open field, and click OK.

3. Navigate to where you would like the new value created.

4. Select Edit|New|String Value.

NOTE: *You can also use this method to create a binary or DWORD value by selecting Edit|New|Binary Value or Edit|New|DWORD Value.*

5. A new value will appear with a temporary name of New Value # n. Enter the name for the value, and press Enter.

6. Double-click the newly created value, enter its data, and click OK.

Creating a New Value on a Remote System

The two registry editors create new values on a remote system somewhat differently. For this reason, both methods are presented.

Creating a Value on a Remote System Using Regedt32.exe

To create a value on a remote system using regedt32.exe, perform the following steps:

1. Click Start, and select Run.

2. Enter "regedt32.exe" in the Open field, and click OK.

3. Select Registry|Select Computer.

4. Either enter the name of the computer to which you would like to connect, or use the Browse button to locate it.

5. Click OK.

6. Select Edit|Add Value.

7. A new value will appear with a temporary name of New Value # n. Enter the name for the value, and press Enter.

8. Double-click the newly created value, enter its data, and click OK.

Creating a Value on a Remote System Using Regedit.exe

To create a value on a remote system using regedit.exe, perform the following steps:

1. Click Start, and select Run.

2. Enter "regedit.exe" in the Open field, and click OK.

3. Select the Connect Network Registry option.

4. Enter the name of the computer, or use the Browse button to locate it.

5. Click OK.

6. Navigate to where the value is to be created.

7. Select Edit|New|String.

8. Enter the name of the new value, and press Enter.

9. Select the value, and select Edit|Modify.

10. Enter the data for the value, and click OK.

Copying a Key Name

To copy a key name, perform the following steps:

1. Click Start, and select Run.

2. Enter "regedit.exe" in the Open field, and click OK.

3. Navigate to the location of the key that you would like to copy the name of.

4. Select Edit|Copy Key Name.

NOTE: You can only copy a key using regedit.exe.

Renaming a Key

To rename a key, perform the following steps:

1. Click Start, and select Run.

2. Enter "regedit.exe" in the Open field, and click OK.

3. Navigate to the location of the key that you would like to rename.

4. Select Edit|Rename.

5. Enter the new name for the key, and press Enter.

NOTE: Only regedit.exe can be used to rename a key.

Renaming a Value

To rename a value, perform the following steps:

1. Click Start, and select Run.

2. Enter "regedit.exe" in the Open field, and click OK.

3. Navigate to the location of the value that you would like to rename.

4. Select Edit|Rename.

5. Enter the new name for the value, and press Enter.

NOTE: Only regedit.exe can be used to rename a value.

Editing an Existing Value

The two registry editors edit values somewhat differently. For this reason, both methods are presented.

Editing a Key Using Regedt32.exe

To edit a key using regedt32.exe, perform the following steps:

1. Click Start, and select Run.

2. Enter "regedt32.exe" in the Open field, and click OK.

3. Navigate to the value to be edited.

4. Select the value and select Edit|Binary, String, DWORD, or Multi String, depending on the value data type.

5. Modify the value as desired, and click OK when done.

Editing a Key Using Regedit.exe

To edit a key using regedit.exe, perform the following steps:

1. Click Start, and select Run.

2. Enter "regedit.exe" in the Open field, and click OK.

3. Navigate to the value to be edited.

4. Select the value, and select Edit|Modify.

5. Edit the value as desired, and click OK when done.

Editing an Existing Value on a Remote System

The two registry editors edit values on a remote system somewhat differently. For this reason, both methods are presented.

Editing a Value on a Remote System Using Regedt32.exe

To edit a value on a remote system using regedt32.exe, perform the following steps:

1. Click Start, and select Run.

2. Enter "regedt32.exe" in the Open field, and click OK.

3. Select Registry|Select Computer.

4. Either enter the name of the computer to which you would like to connect or use the Browse button to locate it.

5. Click OK.

6. Navigate to the value to be edited.

7. Select the value, and select Edit|Binary, String, DWORD, or Multi String, depending on the value data type.

8. Modify the value as desired, and click OK when done.

Editing a Value on a Remote System Using Regedit.exe

To edit a value on a remote system using regedit.exe, perform the following steps:

1. Click Start, and select Run.

2. Enter "regedit.exe" in the Open field, and click OK.

3. Select the Connect Network Registry option.

4. Enter the name of the computer, or use the Browse button to locate it.

5. Click OK.

6. Navigate to the value to be edited.

7. Select the value and Select Edit|Binary, String, DWORD, or Multi String, depending on the value data type.

8. Modify the value as desired, and click OK when done.

Deleting a Registry Key

To delete a key, perform the following steps:

1. Click Start, and select Run.

2. Enter "regedt32.exe" or "regedit.exe" in the Open field, and click OK.

3. Navigate to the key to be deleted.

4. Select the key, and select Edit|Delete.

5. Click Yes to confirm the deletion.

Deleting a Registry Key on a Remote System

The two registry editors delete keys on a remote system somewhat differently. For this reason, both methods are presented.

Deleting a Key on a Remote System Using Regedt32.exe

To delete a key on a remote system using regedt32.exe, perform the following steps:

1. Click Start, and select Run.

2. Enter "regedt32.exe" in the Open field, and click OK.

3. Select Registry|Select Computer.

4. Either enter the name of the computer to which you would like to connect or use the Browse button to locate it.

5. Click OK.

6. Navigate to the key to be deleted.

7. Select Edit|Delete.

8. Click Yes to confirm the deletion.

Deleting a Key on a Remote System Using Regedit.exe

To delete a key on a remote system using regedit.exe, perform the following steps:

1. Click Start, and select Run.

2. Enter "regedit.exe" in the Open field, and click OK.

3. Select the Connect Network Registry option.

4. Enter the name of the computer, or use the Browse button to locate it.

5. Click OK.

6. Navigate to the key to be deleted.

7. Select Edit|Delete.

8. Click Yes to confirm the deletion.

Deleting a Registry Value

To delete a value, perform the following steps:

1. Click Start, and select Run.

2. Enter "regedt32.exe" or "regedit.exe" in the Open field, and click OK.

3. Navigate to the value to be deleted.

4. Select the value, and select Edit|Delete.

5. Click Yes to confirm the deletion.

Deleting a Registry Value on a Remote System

The two registry editors delete values on a remote system somewhat differently. For this reason, both methods are presented.

Deleting a Value on a Remote System Using Regedt32.exe

To delete a value on a remote system using regedt32.exe, perform the following steps:

1. Click Start, and select Run.

2. Enter "regedt32.exe" in the Open field, and click OK.

3. Select Registry|Select Computer.

4. Either enter the name of the computer to which you would like to connect, or use the Browse button to locate it.

5. Click OK.

6. Navigate to the value to be deleted.

7. Select Edit|Delete.

8. Click Yes to confirm the deletion.

Deleting a Value on a Remote System Using Regedit.exe

To delete a value on a remote system using regedit.exe, perform the following steps:

1. Click Start, and select Run.

2. Enter "regedit.exe" in the Open field, and click OK.

3. Select the Connect Network Registry option.

4. Enter the name of the computer, or use the Browse button to locate it.

5. Click OK.

6. Navigate to the value to be deleted.

7. Select Edit|Delete.

8. Click Yes to confirm the deletion.

Importing Registry Settings

To import a registry, perform the following steps:

1. Click Start, and select Run.

2. Enter "regedit.exe" in the Open field, and click OK.

3. Select Registry|Import Registry File.

4. Navigate to the registry file that you would like imported, and click OK (see Figure 15.7).

5. You'll be notified when the information has been successfully imported into the registry.

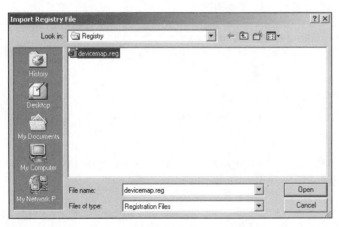

Figure 15.7   Importing the registry.

Manually Importing Registry Information

To import registry information manually, perform the following steps:

1. Find the file you created (either manually or through the export process).

TIP: *The registry file will have a .reg extension.*

---

2. Right-click the file, and select Merge from the pop-up menu.

3. Click Yes to confirm the registry merge.

4. Click OK when you are notified that the merge has completed.

Exporting the Entire Registry

To export a registry, perform the following steps:

1. Click Start, and select Run.

2. Enter "regedit.exe" in the Open field, and click OK.

3. Select Registry|Export Registry File.

4. Select the All radio button in the Export Range section of the Export Registry File window, as shown in Figure 15.8.

5. Navigate to a location to save the file, enter a name for the file, and click OK.

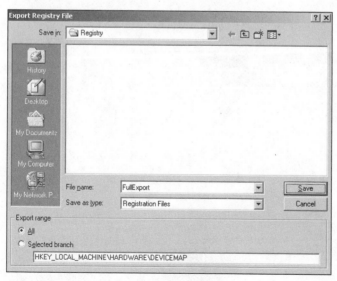

Figure 15.8   Exporting the entire registry.

Exporting a Registry Branch

To export a registry branch, perform the following steps:

1. Click Start, and select Run.

2. Enter "regedit.exe" in the Open field, and click OK.

3. Navigate to the key or subkey from where you would like to export registry information.

4. Select Registry|Export Registry File.

5. Select the Selected Branch radio button in the Export Range section of the Export Registry File window (see Figure 15.9).

6. Navigate to a location to save the file, enter a name for the file, and click OK.

Creating Your Own REG File

You can use a REG file to apply several registry modifications very quickly to multiple computers. You may want to create a REG file with your default configurations. To do so, perform the following steps:

1. Click Start, and select Programs|Accessories|Notepad.

2. Type "Windows Registry Editor Version 5.00".

3. Leave a blank line. This line is required.

4. Enter the full path to the key in square brackets. Here's an example:

```
[HKEY_LOCAL_MACHINE\SOFTWARE\Microsoft\Windows NT\CurrentVersion]
```

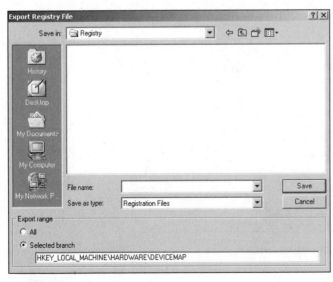

Figure 15.9   Exporting a registry branch.

5. Enter values using the notation "Value"="Data". (The double quotes are required.)

6. For any values that have a DWORD data type, you can use the following notation:

```
"Value"=dword:000001
```

7. Save the file with a .reg extension.

Backing Up the Registry

To back up the registry, perform the following steps:

1. Click Start, and select Programs|Accessories|System Tools|Backup.

2. Select the Backup tab.

3. Select the System State checkbox (see Figure 15.10).

4. Select the Backup Destination option from the drop-down menu.

5. Enter any media-specific information.

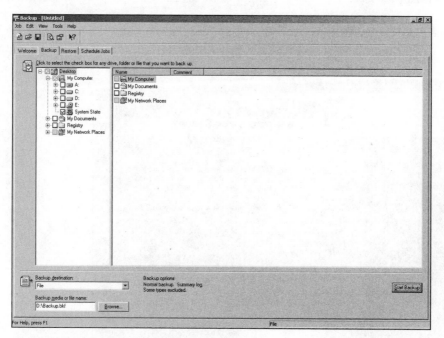

Figure 15.10   Backing up the registry.

6. Click Start Backup.

7. If you would like to verify the files after the backup, click Advanced, check the Verify Data After Backup option, and click OK.

8. If you want to schedule the backup, click Schedule. Otherwise, click Start Backup.

9. When the backup is completed, click Close.

Restoring the Registry

To restore the registry, perform the following steps:

1. Click Start, and select Programs|Accessories|System Tools|Backup.

2. Select the Restore tab.

3. Navigate to the backup set that you would like to recover, and check the System State checkbox (see Figure 15.11).

WARNING! If the system for which you're trying to restore the registry is also running Active Directory, you'll need to reboot the server, and select Troubleshooting|Directory Services Restore Mode. Otherwise, your restore will fail.

4. Click Start Restore.

5. Click Close.

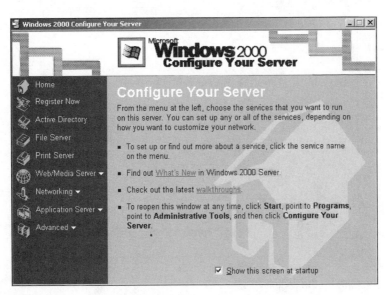

Figure 15.11   Restoring the registry.

Finding Registry Information

The following sections explore how to find information in the registry.

Finding the Installed Basic Input/Output System Date

Basic input/output system (BIOS) updates are common tasks. The BIOS date can be found through the registry rather than through a system reboot. Here's how:

1. Click Start, and select Run.

2. Enter "regedt32.exe" in the Open field, and click OK.

3. Select the HKEY_LOCAL_MACHINE On Local Machine window.

4. Navigate to HARDWARE\DESCRIPTION\System.

5. Find the SystemBiosDate value in the right pane. This is the date associated with your system's BIOS.

Finding the Installed BIOS Version

BIOS updates are common tasks. The BIOS version number can be found through the registry rather than through a system reboot. Here's how:

1. Click Start, and select Run.

2. Enter "regedt32.exe" in the Open field, and click OK.

3. Select the HKEY_LOCAL_MACHINE On Local Machine window.

4. Navigate to HARDWARE\DESCRIPTION\System.

5. Find the SystemBiosVersion value in the right pane. This is the BIOS version.

Finding the Processor Type

To find the processor type, perform the following steps:

1. Click Start, and select Run.

2. Enter "regedt32.exe" in the Open field, and click OK.

3. Select the HKEY_LOCAL_MACHINE On Local Machine window.

4. Navigate to HARDWARE\DESCRIPTION\System\CentralProcessor.

5. Expand this key. You'll notice at least one key below CentralProcessor. Each processor has its own key. For example, on a single-processor system, you'll have a 0 key. With a dual-processor system, you'll have a 0 and a 1 key.

6. In the right pane, find the Identifier value. This is the processor type.

Finding the Processor Speed

To find the processor speed, perform the following steps:

1. Click Start, and select Run.

2. Enter "regedt32.exe" in the Open field, and click OK.

3. Select the HKEY_LOCAL_MACHINE On Local Machine window.

4. Navigate to HARDWARE\DESCRIPTION\System\CentralProcessor.

5. Expand this key. You'll notice at least one key below CentralProcessor. Each processor has its own key. For example, on a single-processor system, you'll have a 0 key. With a dual-processor system, you'll have a 0 and a 1 key.

6. In the right pane, find the ~MHz value. This is the processor speed in hexadecimal.

7. To view the processor speed in decimal notation, double-click the ~MHz value, and select the Decimal radio button.

Finding the Current Windows 2000 Build

To find the current Windows 2000 build, perform the following steps:

1. Click Start, and select Run.

2. Enter "regedt32.exe" in the Open field, and click OK.

3. Select the HKEY_LOCAL_MACHINE On Local Machine window.

4. Navigate to SOFTWARE\Microsoft\Windows NT\CurrentVersion.

5. Find the CurrentBuildNumber value. This is the currently installed Windows 2000 build.

Modifying the Registry

You can make numerous changes to the registry. The remainder of this chapter is dedicated to some of the most common registry changes.

Modifying the Registered Owner

Sometimes, systems move from one person to another. By modifying the registered owner, you can customize the owner settings to fit the person using the system. Here are the steps to follow:

1. Click Start, and select Run.

2. Enter "regedt32.exe" in the Open field, and click OK.

3. Select the HKEY_LOCAL_MACHINE On Local Machine window.

4. Navigate to SOFTWARE\Microsoft\Windows NT\CurrentVersion.

5. Double-click the RegisteredOwner value.

6. In the String field, enter the new name for the owner, and click OK.

Modifying the Registered Organization

If your organization changes its name or merges with another organization, it may be necessary to modify the name used to install the system. Here are the steps to follow:

1. Click Start, and select Run.

2. Enter "regedt32.exe" in the Open field, and click OK.

3. Select the HKEY_LOCAL_MACHINE On Local Machine window.

4. Navigate to SOFTWARE\Microsoft\Windows NT\CurrentVersion.

5. Double-click the RegisteredOrganization value.

6. In the String field, enter a new name for the organization, and click OK.

Changing the Path for the Windows 2000 Source Files

When Windows 2000 is installed, it logs the initial location of the installation files. These locations, however, may change. Unfortunately, Windows 2000 will search for any additional files in this original location. You can use the following method to modify this location:

1. Click Start, and select Run.

2. Enter "regedt32.exe" in the Open field, and click OK.

3. Select the HKEY_LOCAL_MACHINE On Local Machine window.

4. Navigate to SOFTWARE\Microsoft\Windows NT\CurrentVersion.

5. Double-click the SourcePath value.

6. In the String Field, enter the new path where the Windows 2000 source files are stored, including the drive letter, and click OK.

Viewing Installed Hot Fixes in the Registry

To view hot fixes in the registry, perform the following steps:

1. Click Start, and select Run.

2. Enter "regedt32.exe" in the Open field, and click OK.

3. Select the HKEY_LOCAL_MACHINE On Local Machine window.

4. Navigate to SOFTWARE\Microsoft\Windows NT\CurrentVersion\HotFix.

15. Windows 2000 Registry: Structure, Editing, and Important Keys

5. Expand the HotFix key.

6. All installed hot fixes are listed under this key. Their names appear as Q*xxxxxx* (for example, Q147222).

Disabling the Ctrl+Alt+Delete Logon Screen

To disable the Ctrl+Alt+Delete logon screen, perform the following steps:

1. Click Start, and select Run.

2. Enter "regedt32.exe" in the Open field, and click OK.

3. Select the HKEY_LOCAL_MACHINE On Local Machine window.

4. Navigate to SOFTWARE\Microsoft\Windows NT\CurrentVersion\Winlogon.

5. Select Edit|Add Value.

6. In the Value Name field, enter "DisableCAD".

7. Select the REG_DWORD option from the Data Type drop-down menu.

8. Click OK.

9. Enter a value of 0 to enable the Ctrl+Alt+Delete logon screen or a value of 1 to disable the Ctrl+Alt+Delete logon screen.

10. Click OK.

Hiding the Last Logged-On Username

For security reasons, you might want to hide the name of the previously logged-on user. Here are the steps to follow:

1. Click Start, and select Run.

2. Enter "regedt32.exe" in the Open field, and click OK.

3. Select the HKEY_LOCAL_MACHINE On Local Machine window.

4. Navigate to SOFTWARE\Microsoft\Windows\CurrentVersion\Policies\system.

5. Select Edit|Add Value.

6. In the Value Name field, enter "dontdisplaylastusername".

7. Select the REG_DWORD option from the Data Type drop-down menu.

8. Click OK.

9. Enter a value of 0 to display the last logged-on user or a value of 1 to hide the last logged-on user.

10. Click OK.

NOTE: *This particular change is also available via Group Policy.*

Displaying a Warning Window before Logon

Some organizations require a warning window to appear before the user is presented with the logon screen. This information is stored in the registry. Here are the steps to follow:

1. Click Start, and select Run.

2. Enter "regedt32.exe" in the Open field, and click OK.

3. Select the HKEY_LOCAL_MACHINE On Local Machine window.

4. Navigate to SOFTWARE\Microsoft\Windows\CurrentVersion\ Policies\system.

5. Select Edit|Add Value.

6. In the Value Name field, enter "legalnoticecaption".

7. Select the REG_SZ option from the Data Type drop-down menu.

8. Click OK.

9. Enter the text that is to appear on the top of the caption window.

10. Click OK.

11. In the Value Name field, enter "legalnoticetext".

12. Select the REG_SZ option from the Data Type drop-down menu.

13. Click OK.

14. Enter the text that is to appear in the caption window.

15. Click OK.

Controlling the Shutdown Button on the Logon Screen

A shutdown button exists on the logon screen. In Windows 2000 Professional systems, this button is enabled by default. In Windows 2000 Server systems, the button is disabled by default. The shutdown button allows you to shut down or reboot the system without logging on to the system. For security purposes, you may want to modify this button. Here's how:

1. Click Start, and select Run.

2. Enter "regedt32.exe" in the Open field, and click OK.

3. Select the HKEY_LOCAL_MACHINE On Local Machine window.

4. Navigate to SOFTWARE\Microsoft\Windows\CurrentVersion\ Policies\system.

5. Select Edit|Add Value.

6. In the Value Name field, enter "shutdownwithoutlogon".

7. Select the REG_DWORD option from the Data Type drop-down menu.

8. Click OK.

9. Enter a value of 0 to disable the Shutdown button or a value of 1 to enable the Shutdown button.

10. Click OK.

NOTE: *This particular change is also available via Group Policy.*

Modifying the Default Logon Domain Name

To modify the default logon domain name, perform the following steps:

1. Click Start, and select Run.

2. Enter "regedt32.exe" in the Open field, and click OK.

3. Select the HKEY_LOCAL_MACHINE On Local Machine window.

4. Navigate to SOFTWARE\Microsoft\Windows NT\CurrentVersion\Winlogon.

5. In the right pane, select the DefaultDomainName value.

6. Select Edit|String.

7. Enter the new name for the domain.

8. Click OK.

Modifying the Number of Cached Logons

To modify the number of cached logons, perform the following steps:

1. Click Start, and select Run.

2. Enter "regedt32.exe" in the Open field, and click OK.

3. Select the HKEY_LOCAL_MACHINE On Local Machine window.

4. Navigate to SOFTWARE\Microsoft\Windows NT\CurrentVersion\Winlogon.

5. In the right pane, select the cachedlogoncount value.

6. Select Edit|String.

7. Enter the number of logons that should be cached.

8. Click OK.

Forcing Windows 2000 to Perform a Memory Dump with a Keystroke

To enable a keystroke memory dump, perform the following steps:

1. Click Start, and select Run.

2. Enter "regedt32.exe" in the Open field, and click OK.

3. Select the HKEY_LOCAL_MACHINE On Local Machine window.

4. Navigate to \SYSTEM\CurrentControlSet\Services\i8042prt\Parameters.

5. Select Edit|New Value.

6. In the Value Name field, enter "CrashOnCtrlScroll".

7. Choose the REG_DWORD option from the Data Type drop-down menu.

8. Click OK.

9. In the String field, enter a value of 0 to disable the registry value or a value of 1 to enable the registry value.

10. Click OK.

11. Reboot the system. When you press the Ctrl+Scroll Lock key combination, the system performs a memory dump.

Configuring the System to Reboot Automatically on System Failure

To configure the system to reboot automatically on system failure, perform the following steps:

1. Click Start, and select Run.

2. Enter "regedt32.exe" in the Open field, and click OK.

3. Select the HKEY_LOCAL_MACHINE On Local Machine window.

4. Navigate to \SYSTEM\CurrentControlSet\Control\CrashControl.

5. Select the AutoReboot value.

6. Select Edit|DWORD.

7. In the String field, enter a value of 0 to disable the registry value or a value of 1 to enable the registry value.

8. Click OK.

Working with Welcome Tips

When users first log in to the system, they are presented with a "Welcome to Windows" window. This window gives users different tips for getting the most out of their desktop experience. This registry manipulation shows you how to modify these tips:

1. Click Start, and select Run.

2. Enter "regedt32.exe" in the Open field, and click OK.

3. Select the HKEY_LOCAL_MACHINE On Local Machine window.

4. Navigate to \SOFTWARE\Microsoft\Windows\CurrentVersion\Explorer\Tips.

5. To delete a tip, select the value associated with that tip, select Edit|Delete, and click Yes to confirm the deletion.

6. To modify a tip, select the value of the tip that you would like to modify, select Edit|String, enter a new tip, and click OK.

7. To add a tip, find the next subsequent value number (there are 50 by default, starting at 0 and ending with 49), and select Edit|Add Value.

8. Enter the tip number in the Value Name field, choose the REG_SZ option from the Data Type drop-down menu, and click OK.

9. Enter the tip, and click OK.

Displaying/Hiding the Welcome Window

To display or hide the Welcome window, perform the following steps:

1. Click Start, and select Run.

2. Enter "regedt32.exe" in the Open field, and click OK.

3. Select the HKEY_USERS On Local Machine window.

4. Navigate to *SID*\Software\Microsoft\Windows\CurrentVersion\Explorer\tips.

5. Select the Show value.

6. Select Edit|String.

7. In the String field, enter a value of 0 to disable the registry value or a value of 1 to enable the registry value.

8. Click OK.

Controlling the Cascading of the Control Panel Menu

To control the cascading of the Control Panel menu, perform the following steps:

1. Click Start, and select Run.

2. Enter "regedt32.exe" in the Open field, and click OK.

3. Select the HKEY_USERS On Local Machine window.

4. Navigate to *SID*\Software\Microsoft\Windows\CurrentVersion\Explorer\Advanced.

5. Select the CascadeControlPanel value.

6. Select Edit|String.

7. To enable the cascading menu, enter "YES", and click OK.

8. To disable the cascading menu, enter "NO", and click OK.

Controlling the Cascading of the My Documents Menu

To control the cascading of the My Documents menu, perform the following steps:

1. Click Start, and select Run.

2. Enter "regedt32.exe" in the Open field, and click OK.

3. Select the HKEY_USERS On Local Machine window.

4. Navigate to *SID*\Software\Microsoft\Windows\CurrentVersion\
   Explorer\Advanced.

5. Select the CascadeMyDocuments value.

6. Select Edit|String.

7. To enable the cascading menu, enter "YES", and click OK.

8. To disable the cascading menu, enter "NO", and click OK.

Controlling the Cascading of the Network Connections Menu

To control the cascading of the Network Connections menu, perform the following steps:

1. Click Start, and select Run.

2. Enter "regedt32.exe" in the Open field, and click OK.

3. Select the HKEY_USERS On Local Machine window.

4. Navigate to *SID*\Software\Microsoft\Windows\CurrentVersion\
   Explorer\Advanced.

5. Select the CascadeNetworkConnections value.

6. Select Edit|String.

7. To enable the cascading menu, enter "YES", and click OK.

8. To disable the cascading menu, enter "NO", and click OK.

Controlling the Cascading of the Printers Menu

To control the cascading of the Printers menu, perform the following steps:

1. Click Start, and select Run.

2. Enter "regedt32.exe" in the Open field, and click OK.

3. Select the HKEY_USERS On Local Machine window.

4. Navigate to *SID*\Software\Microsoft\Windows\CurrentVersion
   \Explorer\Advanced.

5. Select the CascadePrinters value.

6. Select Edit|String.

7. To enable the cascading menu, enter "YES", and click OK.

8. To disable the cascading menu, enter "NO", and click OK.

Enabling the Administrative Tools Menu

To enable the Administrative Tools menu, perform the following steps:

1. Click Start, and select Run.

2. Enter "regedt32.exe" in the Open field, and click OK.

3. Select the HKEY_USERS On Local Machine window.

4. Navigate to *SID*\Software\Microsoft\Windows\CurrentVersion\ Explorer\Advanced.

5. Select the StartMenuAdminTools value.

6. Select Edit|String.

7. To enable the Administrative Tools menu, enter "YES", and click OK.

8. To disable the Administrative Tools menu, enter "NO", and click OK.

Enabling the Windows 2000 IntelliMenu

You can configure the Start menu to track your most commonly used applications. Any applications that are not used are hidden until you request them. To control this behavior, follow these steps:

1. Click Start, and select Run.

2. Enter "regedt32.exe" in the Open field, and click OK.

3. Select the HKEY_USERS On Local Machine window.

4. Navigate to *SID*\Software\Microsoft\Windows\CurrentVersion\ Explorer\Advanced.

5. Select the IntelliMenus value.

6. Select Edit|String.

7. To enable IntelliMenu, enter "YES", and click OK.

8. To disable IntelliMenu, enter "NO", and click OK.

Controlling How Compressed Files and Folders Are Displayed

To control how compressed files and folders are displayed, perform the following steps:

1. Click Start, and select Run.

2. Enter "regedt32.exe" in the Open field, and click OK.

3. Select the HKEY_USERS On Local Machine window.

4. Navigate to *SID*\Software\Microsoft\Windows\CurrentVersion\
   Explorer\Advanced.

5. Select the ShowCompColor value.

6. Select Edit|String.

7. In the String field, enter a value of 0 to disable the registry value or a value
   of 1 to enable the registry value.

8. Click OK.

Displaying the Full Path in the Address Bar

To display the full path in the address bar, perform the following steps:

1. Click Start, and select Run.

2. Enter "regedt32.exe" in the Open field, and click OK.

3. Select the HKEY_USERS On Local Machine window.

4. Navigate to *SID*\Software\Microsoft\Windows\CurrentVersion\
   Explorer\CabinetState.

5. Select the FullPathAddress value.

6. Select Edit|String.

7. In the String field, enter a value of 0 to disable the registry value or a value
   of 1 to enable the registry value.

8. Click OK.

Chapter 16

Scripting, Automation, and Command-Line Tools

In Depth

No matter where you go or what you read, there never seems to be enough information about scripting and command-line utilities. For the most part, this is because graphical user interfaces (GUIs) handle most of the day-to-day administrative tasks, and it's not necessary to delve deeply into disk operating system (DOS) land. It's only when something needs to be done that takes too long within a GUI, or when you want to automate a procedure that can be scheduled that a script or command-line application comes into play. On the other hand, many command-line applications are left without enhanced GUI equivalents intentionally in order to discourage the fainthearted from tampering with volatile or dangerous ground.

Command-Line Tools

There are many different types of command-line utilities. Most of us with some history usually equate "command-line" with DOS. This is no longer the case. The further away you get from native DOS means the more utilities that are created for use specifically within the Windows 2000 command line that simply won't work or function on any other operating system.

For the purpose of this book, you can assume that command-line tools and utilities need to be run from within a command prompt. The command prompt is a throwback to DOS when the command interpreter—that is to say, the DOS equivalent of a user interface—was called COMMAND.COM. You can get to the command prompt in several different ways, and all of them either use the **CMD** function or the **COMMAND** function. The **COMMAND** function is actually a DOS 16-bit emulator that kicks off the Windows NT Virtual DOS Machine (NTVDM). By default, **COMMAND** is less flexible than the **CMD** function, which is the Windows 2000 32-bit equivalent. Reasons for this are numerous, but all you need to keep in mind is that **COMMAND** won't run 32-bit applications or utilities. Also, it won't support many of the utilities that are described in this entire section.

Windows 2000 is very careful to note the difference between the **CMD** and **COMMAND** environments. For one thing, the COMMAND program is not located in the Start |Programs and is only launched manually by typing "COMMAND" in the Run line of the Start menu or when a 16-bit DOS application is run. The 32-bit CMD environment is similarly launched by typing "CMD" in the Run line of the Start menu, but is also accessed from the Start|Programs|Accessories|Command

Prompt. Note the difference here. Older versions of Windows used DOS prompts to launch the equivalent of the COMMAND program.

Any COMMAND or CMD window can be closed by typing "EXIT" and pressing Enter. It is also possible to close the window in the same manner as you'd close any other window or application. You can double-click the button in the upper left-hand corner or click the X button in the upper right-hand corner. If the window is maximized to a full screen, you can exit again by typing "EXIT" and pressing Enter. If you need to switch windows and get back into the Windows 2000 desktop interface without closing the CMD window, you can hold down Alt and press Tab to rotate between the standard Windows 2000 desktop and any or all other running applications. You can also hold down Ctrl and press Esc to trigger the Start menu.

DOS Commands

With this in mind, let's investigate those DOS commands that are still valid within the Windows 2000 environment. All of these commands exist by default within the Windows 2000 environment and do not require any preloading. It's important to keep in mind that there's a difference between a DOS command and a DOS utility. An example would be the command **COPY**, which is used to copy files, and the utility FDISK, which is used to display and create partitions. This section will focus on the verbs of DOS commands. All other traditional DOS utilities will fall under the "Networking" or "Local Administration" sections.

START

The **START** command is used to launch an application from within a batch file. All of the same options apply here as they do within the regular Windows 2000 interface: **/MIN**, **/MAX**, **/LOW**, **/NORMAL**, and **/HIGH**. Other options are available, but these are the most frequently used. The **START** command can be used to kick off any Component Object Model (COM), executable (EXE), batch (BAT), or CMD file or application.

DIR

The **DIR** command is probably the most frequently used command within DOS, with possible exception of **CD**. The **DIR** command will list all of the contents in the current directory. The **/P** switch will break up the display by pages so that you'll need to press a key to advance from page to page. The **DIR** command can also be used as a search tool by using wildcards or a specific file, followed by the **/S** switch. The **/S** switch will find and display the file if it is within the scope of the files queried. **DIR *.** will display only directories. **DIR *.* /ON** will sort by alphabetic name, and **DIR *.* /OE** will sort by the file extension name. **DIR *.* /OS** will sort the output by size with the smallest first. One of the more valuable switches is **DIR *.* /OD**, which will sort by date and time and which will display the oldest file first. **DIR *.* -OD** will do the same, but will display the newest file first.

ATTRIB

The **ATTRIB** command is similar to the **DIR** command in that it displays files located in the current directory (or folder). The difference is that the **ATTRIB** command will also display the file attributes that are associated with the displayed files. You can run **ATTRIB** using wildcards (*), and it will show you any files that apply to that wildcard. In the first line of the syntax example that follows, **ATTRIB** is used to display all files ending in a .sys extension:

```
ATTRIB *.SYS
ATTRIB *.SYS -S -H -R
ATTRIB *.SYS +S
ATTRIB NETWORK.SYS +R
```

In the previous example, the second line of the syntax example shows the removing of the system, hidden, and read-only attributes associated with all files with the extension of .sys. The third line of the syntax example adds the system attribute to those same files. The last line of the syntax example adds the read-only attribute to the NETWORK.SYS file.

When you run the **DIR** command from the command line, it will not display hidden files. This is one situation where you may want to use the **ATTRIB** command. Another reason is to remove the read-only attribute so that you can modify a read-only file.

NOTE: *One note with regard to hidden and read-only files within Windows 2000 is that you have the ability to configure Explorer to display hidden files and folders from within Tools|Folder Options. If you choose to display hidden files and folders, they will appear as somewhat grayed out and lighter in color from within Explorer. You should also be aware that you can change the read-only and hidden attributes of a file or folder by right-clicking the item, clicking Properties, and selecting or deselecting the read-only or hidden attribute at the bottom of the dialog box.*

FC

The **FC** command will compare two files that are entered by the user. The user is not prompted to enter the two files like the **COMP** command. An example of the **FC** syntax is the following, where the comparison data is being put into a file called COMP.TXT. If you want to display the comparison data on the screen, simply remove the **>COMP.TXT** from the line.

```
FC FILE1.TXT FILE2.TXT>COMP.TXT
```

COMP

The **COMP** command is similar to **FC** in that both utilities compare two files. The **COMP** command will prompt you for the applicable file names. If you want a file output of the comparison data, you'll need to use the **FC** command and redirect the output to a file. If you feel more comfortable with some guidance in this area, use the **COMP** command.

> and >>

These two symbols aren't really commands, but they are immensely valuable in both command-line utilities and in batch programming. Basically, you place these symbols after a command followed by a filename, and the output from that command will be redirected to that file. The > symbol will create a new file. If that file exists, it will be overwritten. The >> will create a new file containing the command output if one doesn't exist, or, if the file already exists, it will append the command output to an existing file. This comes in handy if you're creating log entries that are written after each command. An example is the following:

```
COPY NET.EXE .. > NETLOG.TXT
COPY IPXODI.SYS>>NETLOG.TXT
```

CLS

CLS is a DOS command that clears the screen.

TYPE

The **TYPE** command is similar to the **ECHO** command. The difference is that **TYPE** will display the contents of a listed file. **TYPE AUTOEXEC.BAT** will display the AUTOEXEC.BAT file on the screen.

COPY

The **COPY** command for DOS will copy a file from one location to another. It can also rename the file with the appropriate syntax, as in the following example:

```
COPY AUTOEXEC.BAT AUTOEXEC.BAK
COPY C:\AUTOEXEC.BAT A:\BACKUPS\AUTOEXEC.BAT
COPY *.BAT A:\*.BAK
```

The first line of the example copies the AUTOEXEC.BAT file and renames it in the process. Both files will be located in the same place. The second line of the example copies the AUTOEXEC.BAT located in the C: drive to the A:\BACKUPS directory on the A: drive. The third line of the example copies all batch files (extension .bat) to the A: drive with the extension of .bak.

XCOPY

The **XCOPY** command is similar to the **COPY** command in that it is used to copy files from one location to another. **XCOPY** has the added ability to copy entire directory structures by using the **/S** switch.

MOVE

The **MOVE** command is used to move files from one location to another. Personally, I do not recommend ever using the **MOVE** command because of the risk of failure. If you are moving multiple files and a failure occurs, you have no idea exactly which files were successfully moved and intact. If you use the **COPY** command followed by **DELETE**, you can be sure that the copy was successful before deleting the original files without running the risk of losing data if there is a failure.

DEL

The **DEL** command is used to delete files, as in the following example:

```
DEL *.TXT
DEL C:\PERSONAL\NOTES.TXT
```

The first line of the example deletes all text files in the same directory where the command is executed. The second line of the example deletes the NOTES.TXT located in the PERSONAL directory of the C: drive.

SET

The **SET** command is usually used within batch programs, but it can also be performed on the command line. The **SET** command is used to declare variables. Because that was programmer lingo, let me put it this way. You can use variables (just like algebra) within batch programs. These variables can change. In order to use a new variable, you must initialize, or declare it, before you use it. Many variables come with the system by default: username, homedrive, homepath, logonserver, operating system (OS), userdomain, userprofile, and others. In order to reference a variable within a batch command, you must place percent signs around the variable, for example, %username%.

ECHO

ECHO is a command that will copy whatever text follows to the screen. You'll usually use it in a batch file when you want the user to be notified of a particular event occurring. You can also use it when you want to display a message followed by a pause where the user should press a key to continue.

MD

The **MD** command is used to make a directory.

RD

The **RD** command is used to delete a directory. If you attempt to use **RD** to remove a directory that has files, the system won't allow you to do this. This is because hidden files may exist within a directory, and you won't see them unless you know to run the **ATTRIB** command.

CD

The **CD** command is a standard DOS command that you use to navigate from one directory to another. Figure 16.1 shows a series of **CD** commands that are used first to change to the WINNT directory and then to the system32 directory. The third command backs you up one level to the WINNT directory, and the fourth command takes you back to the root of the drive. The fifth command (cd winnt\system32) drops you into the system32 directory just the same as the second command, but in a single step instead of changing first to WINNT and then system32. The last command backs you up one level and sends you to a different directory from that level.

NOTE: *Remember that DOS was created almost as a child of Unix. DOS was intended to be a cheaper and easier-to-use alternative. As such, most true DOS commands are either similar or identical to commands within UNIX.*

DOSKEY

DOSKEY is a DOS utility that keeps a running list of the last 20 commands executed on the command line. In order to avoid retyping commands again and again, you can press the up arrow several times until the appropriate command appears. You can then change parts of the command by back-spacing and entering in the new text.

EXIT

The **EXIT** command will close the CMD window.

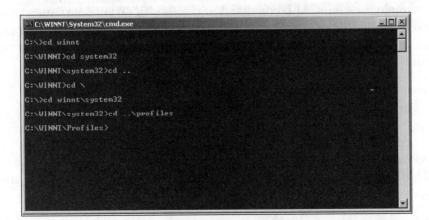

```
C:\WINNT\System32\cmd.exe                              _ □ ×

C:\>cd winnt

C:\WINNT>cd system32

C:\WINNT\system32>cd ..

C:\WINNT>cd \

C:\>cd winnt\system32

C:\WINNT\system32>cd ..\profiles

C:\WINNT\Profiles>
```

Figure 16.1   Using the **CD** command to navigate directories within DOS.

16. Scripting, Automation, and Command-Line Tools

RENAME

The **RENAME** command is used to rename one or many files (with wildcards), as in the following example:

```
RENAME *.BAT *.BAK
```

The previous command renames all batch files to BAK files.

TREE

The **TREE** command will display all directories on the disk drive in an outline, or tree, format.

VOL

The **VOL** command will display the current volume information on the screen.

Batch Language

The original versions of DOS had a built-in scripting language that allowed automation to occur using any DOS command along with some low-level logic. Batch is something of a language of its own. Batch commands in Windows 2000 are gathered together to accomplish simple tasks that you can do using DOS or any other command-line tool or utility available to Windows 2000. Creating a batch script consists of using a text editor, such as notepad or EDIT; typing the script; and naming the file with a .bat extension.

CALL

The **CALL** command is specific to batch files. The **CALL** command is used within a batch script to instruct the program to execute a different batch file. The following example uses the **CALL** command to run the NETWORK.BAT file. After the NETWORK.BAT file runs, control will return to the original batch file. Keep in mind that the parent batch file will pause while the CALLed batch file runs and will continue after the CALLed script is completed.

```
NET TIME
CALL NETWORK.BAT
NET USE M: \\MARKETING\SHARESTUFF
```

The previous example sets the system time, calls the NETWORK.BAT file, and, after the batch file is complete, maps the M: drive to the MARKETING server and SHARESTUFF folder.

FOR

The **FOR** command is a logic tool specifically for use within batch files. The syntax is similar to a FOR loop that you'd see in BASIC programming language. The syntax is as follows:

```
FOR <variable> IN <set> DO <command>
```

Its explanation is that, as long as the **<variable>** (whatever the variable has been defined as) is in the files declared as part of the **<set>**, the system will do whatever the **<command>** is.

GOTO

The **GOTO** command is used within a batch program to skip to a separate line. Be careful when using the **GOTO** command because line numbers are not displayed. It is easy to make changes, add a line, and have your **GOTO** statement fail because the line number that the application is referencing no longer applies.

IF

The **IF** statement is another logic tool used within batch programs. It can be used in one of three ways. The ERRORLEVEL add-on is used to perform the subsequent command only if the returned ERRORLEVEL from the application is the number indicated. Any time that you run a command from within a batch file, it will output an **ERRORLEVEL** variable. Typically, if the **ERRORLEVEL** is 0, everything is okay. You can use the ERRORLEVEL logic with the **IF** statement to ensure that a prior command executed successfully and behaved appropriately. You can also compare strings using the **IF** statement. By this, I mean that you can declare variables or compare two different items and execute the subsequent command if those two items are equal. Last, but not least, you can use the **IF** statement to check to see if a file exists. This is particularly handy if you choose to redirect output or to create log files at different times during the program. An example is the following:

```
COPY A:\DATA1.DAT C:\DATA1.DAT>COPYLOG.TXT
IF ERRORLEVEL=1 ECHO COPY FAILED ELSE ECHO COPY SUCCESSFUL
IF EXIST COPYLOG.TXT TYPE COPYLOG.TXT
```

The previous snippet of code copies a file and redirects the screen output to the COPYLOG.TXT file. If the copy failed, the message "COPY FAILED" appears on the screen. On the other hand, if the ERRORLEVEL is not 1, the copy is successful, and the message "COPY SUCCESSFUL" appears on the screen. The final line checks for the COPYLOG.TXT file and subsequently types the contents of the file on the screen.

PAUSE

The **PAUSE** command is used as part of a batch file to stop processing temporarily. The user is prompted with a "Press Any Key to Continue" message.

16. Scripting, Automation, and Command-Line Tools

TITLE

The **TITLE** command is usually used within batch files to change the name of the window being opened or used. You would use the **TITLE** command as an extra professional touch to a window that is being opened by a batch file.

REM

The **REM** command is used within batch files to indicate a remark. Remarks are automatically ignored by the computer when it processes the code. **REM** statements are a good idea because they enable you to document exactly what you're attempting to do with the code.

CMD

The CMD utility can be accessed in two ways. You can type "CMD" on the Run line to get to the 32-bit command line. From within the command window, you can type "CMD", and the system will display the current version of the command interpreter for you.

Networking

Several command-line utilities are specifically designed to display, diagnose, and/or configure network settings and information. For the most part, the Transmission Control Protocol/Internet Protocol (TCP/IP)-related utilities are useful in day-to-day troubleshooting, but you may need to use several others on occasion.

IPCONFIG

The IPCONFIG utility will display IP configuration information. The **/ALL** switch will display all information for all network adapters. The **/RELEASE** switch will flush the IP configuration. The **/RENEW** switch will query the nearest Dynamic Host Configuration Protocol (DHCP) server for new IP configuration information.

NETSTAT

NETSTAT will display IP connection statistics. Using this, you can determine what active connections (using the IP protocol, of course) exist to the server or workstation. You can also use the **–R** switch to show the routing table. This can help you while troubleshooting connectivity issues.

PING

PING is a utility that is used to determine if the TCP/IP protocol is working on the computer that is being PINGed. An example is the following:

```
PING 127.0.0.1
```

This particular statement will PING the local loopback address to determine if TCP/IP is being properly loaded.

TRACERT

TRACERT is a command that is similar to PING, except that it displays the name and IP address of every router or gateway that your PING command travels across while navigating to its destination, which is the device that is being PINGed.

PATHPING

The **PATHPING** command is similar to **TRACERT**. The difference is that **TRACERT** displays the transmit time between each hop on the list. **PATHPING** will compute and report network statistics.

NOTE: Don't make the mistake of typing PATH PING instead of PATHPING as one word. The PATH command is used to show the current directories that are actively tracked and used by the operating system without requiring a full path. If you run PATH PING, you'll inadvertently blow away all of those directories and replace them with the word PING.

NET

The **NET** command is the most powerful networking command in this list. Table 16.1 shows its different options and features.

Table 16.1   NET commands.

Command	Description
NET ACCOUNTS	Displays and allows modification of standard account features, such as minimum password age, password history, lockout threshold/duration, and computer role.
NET COMPUTER	This utility is used to add and remove computers from the domain. This must be executed on a domain controller.
NET CONFIG	Displays and allows limited administration of either the SERVER or WORKSTATION service.
NET CONTINUE	Allows you to continue a paused service.
NET FILE	Shows the active files that are being used on the system.
NET GROUP	Allows complete command-line domain group administration. You have the ability to create and delete groups and also to add and remove members to groups.
NET LOCALGROUP	Allows complete command-line local group administration. You have the ability to create and delete groups and also to add and remove members to groups.
NET NAME	Creates an alias for use with the **NET SEND** command. If you enter this command, it will show you the existing default aliases.
NET PAUSE	Allows you to pause a service.
NET PRINT	Allows you to administer print jobs in a print queue. You must know the computer name to which the printer is defined.
NET SEND	Sends an immediate console message to anyone on the network.

(continued)

16. Scripting, Automation, and Command-Line Tools

Table 16.1   NET commands *(continued).*

Command	Description
NET SESSION	Displays any active sessions on the system. This is particularly useful when using Terminal Services. You also have the ability to delete a session using this tool.
NET SHARE	Allows you to create, delete, and administer shares on a workstation or server.
NET START	Allows you to start a service manually.
NET STATISTICS	Displays access statistics for either the server or workstation service.
NET STOP	Stops the listed service.
NET TIME	Synchronizes the time with a time server.
NET USE	Maps a network drive.
NET USER	Allows you to complete domain user administration.
NET VIEW	Lists the computers on the network.

FTP COMMANDS

File Transfer Protocol (FTP) is often used to upload and download files from Microsoft and Unix servers. Table 16.2 shows some of the major FTP commands that you may use from the command line. Keep in mind that Windows Explorer will do FTP downloads. You may want to use FTP from this command line if you need to upload files or if you prefer to keep an eye on exactly what's going on during the file transfers. FTP commands also come in handy in scripts. It is possible to launch an FTP session from a batch file and have the FTP session refer to an FTP script for instructions on what to do.

IPXROUTE

This command will display the routing tables for the Internet Packet Exchange (IPX) protocol.

NBTSTAT

This utility will display and release/refresh Network Basic Input/Output System (NetBIOS) protocol information, including the NetBIOS names that have been resolved to IP addresses using Windows Internet Naming System (WINS) and broadcast resolution methods.

ROUTE

This command displays, prints, and allows you to configure the TCP/IP routing table.

NETDIAG

This command displays statistics and runs diagnostics on the network card.

Table 16.2   FTP commands.

Command	Description
FTP	Allows you to enter into the FTP shell.
OPEN	Opens a specific FTP connection. Connections can be initiated in one of two ways. First, run FTP from the command prompt, and then run **OPEN** followed by the FTP server address. The second way is to run FTP followed by the FTP server address all as the same command. After the connection is opened, most FTP servers will request a username and a password.
LCD	Changes the local directory. When you upload or download files, the system will assume that the files are located in the directory that you were in when you entered FTP to begin with. If you need to upload a file from a different directory, you can either enter the pathname along with the filename, or you can change the local directory and continue the upload. When performing downloads, you may need to change the local directory in order to have the system place the downloaded files in the proper place.
CD	Changes the directory.
LS	Lists the contents of the current directory. Wildcards (*) work with this command, for example, **LS *.txt**.
GET/MGET	The **GET** command is used to download a single file. The **MGET** command is used to download multiple files. **MGET** requires wildcards, but GET will not even accept them. For example **GET FILE.TXT** or **MGET *.TXT**.
PUT/MPUT	The **PUT** command is used to upload a single file. The **MPUT** command is used to upload multiple files. **MPUT** requires wildcards, but PUT will not even accept them. For example, **PUT FILE.TXT** or **MPUT *.TXT**.
MDELETE	Deletes multiple files. **MDELETE** requires wildcards. Keep in mind that, if this command does not work, you may not have permissions to delete files on the FTP server.
DELETE	Deletes a single file. Again, keep in mind that, if this command does not work, you may not have permissions to delete files on the FTP server.
BYE/QUIT	Quits the FTP session.

Local Administration

Most of the local administration tools that you'll use on the command line can be interchangeable as DOS utilities. Many of these have been improved since the real DOS days. Many of these utilities are also available within the Windows 9x environment, but don't be surprised if they don't work immediately because many of them are known by different names.

FTYPE

The **FTYPE** command is used in association with the **ASSOC** command to change or add a program to a file type that was defined using the **ASSOC** command. The following example opens NOTEPAD.EXE any time that a file of type TEXT is executed. The **ASSOC** command is used to assign the file type TEXT to files of extension .txt.

```
FTYPE TEXT=NOTEPAD.EXE
```

ASSOC

Have you ever noticed that when you double-click on a file within Windows Explorer, 9 out of 10 times an application will open with the file you double-clicked? This is because most files are named to include an extension (such as .TXT, .DOC, and .BMP), and Windows 2000 associates these extensions with applications. Normally, this is automated, but there are times when you may want to do this association yourself manually. This is particularly useful when an installed application associates a file extension incorrectly. The easiest way of doing associations is by right-clicking the file that has an extension that needs to be associated and then selecting Properties. The General tab will appear, and you can click Change, next to the Opens With line, and the Opens With dialog will appear. Most of the applications installed on the computer will be represented in the list. Just double-click the application, and click OK. If the application is not represented in the list, click Browse to browse out to the appropriate application. If, for some reason, you don't want to use the GUI method of associating files, you can associate files manually using the **ASSOC** command as the first step in a two-part process. The **ASSOC** command will give a file type name to the extension. This is because the extension isn't always indicative of the application to which it belongs. Typing the **ASSOC** command from a command prompt will display all of the file associations, and you can use the **ASSOC** command as follows to perform the file type assignment:

```
ASSOC .TXT=TEXT
```

The previous syntax for the **ASSOC** command assigns the TEXT file type to all files with extensions of .txt.

CACLS

CACLS is similar to the **ATTRIB** command in that it displays specific information about a file or folder. In particular, **CACLS** will show you the Access Control List (ACL) for a file. The **CACLS** command will accept wildcards, thus enabling you to change the basic security permissions for several items at once. The most important options are **/E** (edit, don't replace permissions), **/G** (grant permissions), **/R** (remove permissions), **/P** (replace permissions), and **/D** (deny permissions). The available permissions that you can use are None, Read, Write, Change, and Full Control (NRWCF, respectively).

```
CACLS *.TXT /G JOE:F
CACLS *.TXT /E /R ENGINEERS
```

```
CACLS *.TXT /P ENGINEERS:N
CACLS *.TXT /D JOE
```

The previous syntax examples show different ways that the **CACLS** command can be used to modify user access permissions to local and network resources. The first example grants Full Control permissions to Joe for all TXT files in the current directory. The second example revokes all permissions for all TXT files in the current directory only for the Engineers group. The third example replaces the Engineers group's permissions for all TXT files with the No Access permission. The last example denies access for all TXT files to the members of Joe.

*TIP: Remember that you can type in any command on the command line followed by a **/?**, and syntax and description information will appear for that particular command.*

CONVERT

The CONVERT utility is the only way to change a file allocation table (FAT) or FAT32 disk to Windows NT File System (NTFS) format. Sample syntax is as follows.

```
CONVERT C: /FS:NTFS
```

The first argument, shown by the C:, can be replaced by any drive letter. /FS:NTFS indicates what the file system will be converted to.

RECOVER

The **RECOVER** command is command-exclusive, and does not have a counterpart in the GUI world. Use the **RECOVER** command to recover data from a bad or damaged disk. You'll need to know the file name in question, and there's no guarantee that the system will be able to recover the damaged data intact.

SUBST

The **SUBST** command has been around for a while, and it's very handy. The **SUBST** command allows you to designate a folder or directory on the hard drive and assign a separate drive letter to that folder or directory.

```
SUBST P: C:\APPS\PERSDATA
```

This particular SUBST command creates a drive letter called P: and assigns the contents located in the C:\APPS\PERSDATA to it.

COLOR

You can use the **COLOR** command to change the text and background colors that are displayed within the CMD window. Type the word "color", followed by the number or letter of the text color and the number or letter of the background color. Table 16.3 shows the color codes.

Table 16.3   Color codes for the COLOR utility.

Code	Color
0	Black
1	Blue
2	Green
3	Aqua
4	Red
5	Purple
6	Yellow
7	White
8	Gray
9	Light Blue
A	Light Green
B	Light Aqua
C	Light Red
D	Light Purple
E	Light Yellow
F	Bright White

DATE/TIME

Both the **DATE** and **TIME** commands will display the current date and time (respectively) and offer you the option of changing the date and time. If you do not want to change the date or time, press Enter.

FORMAT

FORMAT A: will format the A: drive. Similarly, **FORMAT C:** will format the C: drive. You can format NTFS by entering "FORMAT /FS:NTFS". Similarly, you can format FAT by entering "FORMAT /FS:FAT".

CHKDSK

The CHKDSK utility is used to check and repair FAT and FAT32 disks.

CHKNTFS

The CHKNTFS utility runs diagnostics and repairs NTFS disks.

Domain Administration

Several new command utilities have been created specifically for domain administration since Windows NT 3.5x came out. Many of these utilities have been updated and improved for Windows 2000, and several others deal with Windows

2000 Active Directory domains as well. Remember that Windows 2000 Active Directory is Lightweight Directory Access Protocol (LDAP) compliant. Because LDAP is an industry standard similar to X.500, you should be able to run any LDAP utility from any manufacturer to view and modify the Active Directory environment. Keep in mind, however, that, in the same manner that Microsoft has created LDAP utilities tuned specifically for Active Directory, Novell and International Business Machines (IBM) have also tuned other LDAP utilities specifically for NetWare and Lotus Notes. Be careful what you do with these third-party utilities, and make sure that you have a thorough understanding of LDAP. You should also understand how the Active Directory structure is LDAP-compliant before you make any changes whatsoever.

NET COMPUTER

The NET COMPUTER utility will add a computer to the domain. It must be executed from a Windows 2000 domain controller.

NTDSUTIL

NTDSUTIL is a complex utility that allows you to display and modify certain aspects of the Active Directory database. NTDSUTIL is also where you perform an authoritative restore of the Active Directory. NTDSUTIL ROLES will allow you to change flexible single master operation (FSMO) role master servers. You can also use NTDSUTIL to locate and clean duplicate security identifiers (SIDs), connect to other servers, and perform an authoritative restore of the Active Directory database. NTDSUTIL is different from all other utilities in that you navigate by entering nested prompts. You'll start out in an NTDSUTIL prompt. If you enter "?", a list of options will be displayed. From there, you choose an option, enter it, and enter another "?" to display a different set of options based upon what you entered. NTDSUTIL has many levels, and it can become quite confusing. Just try to remember that it is most often used to perform an authoritative restore and to change FSMO roles.

NSLOOKUP

NSLOOKUP behaves in a similar manner to NTDSUTIL in the sense that running the application places you in an application-specific prompt. If you enter "?", options will appear. Using NSLOOKUP, you can check Domain Name Service (DNS) to determine aliases and host services.

MOVETREE

The MOVETREE utility is used when restructuring two separate Active Directory databases into a single database.

Miscellaneous Command Utilities

The following are some miscellaneous command utilities that may be important for you to know.

EXPAND

The EXPAND utility is a command-line tool that is used by most Microsoft applications to decompress installation files. Basically, you can use the EXPAND command to decompress any file that has an extension ending with an underscore. EXPAND can also be used to decompress cabinet (*.cab) files:

```
EXPAND COMMAND.SY_ COMMAND.SYS
EXPAND INSTALL.CAB .\INSTALL
EXPAND -D INSTALL.CAB
```

The first of these three commands expands the COMMAND.SY_ file and renames it into COMMAND.SYS. The second command decompresses the contents of the INSTALL.CAB file into a subdirectory called INSTALL. The third command displays the contents of the INSTALL.CAB file.

COMPACT

The COMPACT utility is a command-line tool that compresses files. The compression algorithm is specific to Microsoft and is different from WinZip. There are several switches available with the COMPACT tool, which you can determine in detail by using **COMPACT /?**. The syntax is as follows:

```
COMPACT /C DATA.DAT
COMPACT /U DATA.DAT
COMPACT /C DATADIR
```

The first two lines of the previous example compress and decompress the file named DATA.DAT. The third line of the example compresses the DATADIR directory. After this compression takes place, any file that is added to that directory is compressed automatically.

FIND

The **FIND** command is used to locate a specific string of text within a file. You can use wildcards with the **FIND** command to narrow down the results in the same manner as you would with the Search utility from the Start menu.

FINDSTR

The **FINDSTR** command is more complex than the **FIND** command because it can also include wildcards within the string that you're searching for. Several other options are available, such as searching for string matches at the beginning of a word within a file, the end of a word within the file, and other similar combinations. A simple example follows.

```
FINDSTR "DMI" HPSUPPT.TXT
```

This particular example searches for the string DMI within the HPSUPPT.TXT file. You can use the FINDSTR command to search for multiple strings, literal strings, and combination strings within one or more files. FINDSTR can even search for a series of strings listed in a separate file to determine if any of those strings are found in one or more files indicated within the command.

TIP: Again, remember that you can find more information on any command by running it followed by the /?.

DISKCOMP

DISKCOMP is usually used to compare two floppy disks.

DISKCOPY

DISKCOPY is used to duplicate two floppy disks. This utility does not require two drives because it will copy the contents of the first disk into memory and then prompt for the second disk. Enter "DISKCOPY A: A:" to do this. Use "DISKCOPY A: B:" to copy two disks in separate drives. Note that both disks must be the same size because DISKCOPY will duplicate formatted and bootable disks.

Scripting

Talk to any Unix administrator about why Unix is better than Windows NT, and you'll start a war. When the smoke settles, one of the strengths of Unix is its ability to script administrative tasks easily. Before Windows Scripting Host (WSH), the only way to create administrative scripts in Windows NT was by using DOS batch files. Although batch files are great for simple scripts and are easy to create, they fall apart when you try to accomplish any complex tasks.

All that changed when Microsoft released WSH (Windows Scripting Host). WSH gives administrators the ability to create very complex scripts using common scripting languages to perform complex tasks easily.

WSH is automatically installed with Windows 2000. It also installs two scripting engines: VBScript and JScript. These two scripting languages are Visual Basic Script and JavaScript, respectively. Any scripts written with these languages will be executed properly in Windows 2000.

Another nice feature of WSH is its ability to host most scripting languages, including PerlScript, Python, Tool Command Language (TCL), and Rexx. These third-party scripting languages, however, need to be installed separately.

Two different scripting engines exist with WSH: WScript and CScript.

16. Scripting, Automation, and Command-Line Tools

WScript

WScript is the 32-bit Windows-based scripting engine. This is the engine that's used to execute a script when you double-click the script file. You can, however, use it to run scripts from the command prompt and to configure how scripts are run.

When executing WScript from the command prompt, the following format must be used:

```
WScript scriptname.extension [//B | //I][//D][//E:Engine][//H:scripthost][//
Job:nnn] [//Logo | //Nologo][//S][//T:nn][//X]
```

Table 16.4 lists all the command-line switches that can be used with WScript to configure the script execution.

CScript

CScript.exe is the command-line-based scripting engine. This engine will only be used if the script is configured to use it by default (the default is to run the script using WScript) or when a CScript command is issued, as follows:

```
CScript scriptname.extension [//B | //I][//D][//E:Engine][//H:scripthost][//
Job:nnn][//Logo | //Nologo][//S][//T:nn][//X][//U]
```

Table 16.4   The WScript.exe command-line switches.

Switch	Description
//B	Specifies that the script should run in batch mode. Batch mode stops the script errors and prompts from displaying.
//D	Turns on active debugging.
//E:engine	Uses the specified engine.
//H:CScript	Specifies that Cscript.exe should be used as the default script host.
//H:WScript	Specifies that Wscript.exe should be used as the default script host. This is the default setting.
//I	Specifies that the script should run in Interactive mode. All script errors and prompts are displayed. This is the default setting.
//Job:xxxx	Executes the specified WScript job.
//Logo	Displays the logo. This is the default setting.
//Nologo	Hides the logo.
//S	Saves current command-line options for the user.
//T:nn	Specifies the maximum amount of time that the script is allowed to execute. The timeout is in seconds.
//X	Executes the script in the debugger.

The command-line switches that are used with CScript to configure script execution are the same as the ones listed in Table 16.4 for WScript. There's only one additional one for CScript, **//U,** which is for using Unicode for redirected input/output (I/O) from the console.

Microsoft has supplied many different sample scripts to work with. Some sample scripts are found at **msdn.microsoft.com/scripting**. These scripts are also listed in Table 16.5. These scripts may not work properly without modification on your Windows 2000 system because they were released before Windows 2000. More up-to-date scripts are found in the *Windows 2000 Server Resource Kit* (Microsoft Press, ISBN: 1-57231-805-8) under the "Remote Administration Scripts" section, and they are also listed in Table 16.6. Most of these scripts are also available on the Microsoft Web site.

Table 16.5   Microsoft-supplied sample scripts.

Script File	Description
Addusers.vbs	A VBScript to add users to Active Directory
DelUsers.vbs	A VBScript to delete users from Active Directory
Chart.vbs	A VBScript to create a chart in Microsoft Excel and to rotate it
Chart.js	A JScript to create a chart in Microsoft Excel and to rotate it
Excel.vbs	A VBScript to write application properties into a Microsoft Excel spreadsheet
Excel.js	A JScript to write application properties into a Microsoft Excel spreadsheet
Showvar.vbs	A VBScript to display variables configured on the system
Network.vbs	A VBScript to display network properties
Network.js	A JScript to display network properties
Registry.vbs	A VBScript to display or change registry information
Registry.js	A JScript to display or change registry information
Shortcut.vbs	A VBScript to create a shortcut
Shortcut.js	A JScript to create a shortcut

Table 16.6   *Resource Kit*-supplied sample scripts.

Script File	Description
Bootconfig.vbs	Displays the boot configuration
Bus.vbs	Displays the bus information
Cacheinfo.vbs	Displays the cache information
Cdromdrives.vbs	Displays the CD-ROM configuration
CheckBios.vbs	Displays the BIOS configuration

(continued)

16. Scripting, Automation, and Command-Line Tools

Table 16.6   *Resource Kit*-supplied sample scripts *(continued)*.

Script File	Description
Chkusers.vbs	Checks a domain for users
CodecFile.vbs	Displays codec information
CompSys.vbs	Displays the system properties
CreateUsers.vbs	Creates users in Active Directory
Desktop.vbs	Displays the desktop properties
Device.vbs	Controls a device
Devicemem.vbs	Displays device memory information
DiskPartition.vbs	Displays disk partition information
Dmachan.vbs	Displays the direct memory access (DMA) channel information
Drives.vbs	Displays physical disk information
EnableDhcp.vbs	Enables DHCP on the system
Eventlogmon.vbs	Monitors event log commands
Exec.vbs	Executes a command
Fileman.vbs	Manages a file
Group.vbs	Displays a list of groups in a domain
Groupdescription.vbs	Displays the description for a group
IrqRes.vbs	Displays the interrupt request (IRQ) resources
Keyboard.vbs	Displays the keyboard configuration
Ldordergrp.vbs	Displays service dependency groups
ListAdapters.vbs	Displays network adapters
Listdcs.vbs	Displays all domain controllers
ListDisplayConfig.vbs	Displays the display configuration
Listdomains.vbs	Displays all domains in a specified namespace
ListFreeSpace.vbs	Displays free space on all drives
Listmembers.vbs	Displays the members of a group
ListOs.vbs	Displays the OS properties
ListPrinters.vbs	Displays the installed printers
ListSpace.vbs	Displays the size of the physical drives
Logmeminfo.vbs	Displays logical memory configuration
Llstdpconinfo.vbs	Displays the display controller configuration
Modifyusers.vbs	Modifies user account properties
Motherboard.vbs	Displays motherboard information

(continued)

Table 16.6 *Resource Kit*-**supplied sample scripts** *(continued).*

Script File	Description
NetConnections.vbs	Displays network connections
NetworkProtocol.vbs	Displays network protocols
OsReconfig.vbs	Displays and changes OS Recover mode
PageFile.vbs	Displays the page file information
Parallelport.vbs	Displays parallel port configuration
PointDev.vbs	Displays mouse configuration
Processor.vbs	Displays processor information
ProtocolBinding.vbs	Displays protocol binding configuration
Ps.vbs	Displays all processes running on the system
Regconfig.vbs	Displays registry configuration
Restart.vbs	Restarts a local or remote computer
Schemadiff.vbs	Compares schema from two different forests
ScsiController.vbs	Displays Small Computer System Interface (SCSI) controller information
SerialPort.vbs	Displays serial port configuration
Service.vbs	Controls a service
Share.vbs	Modifies shares on the system
Sounddevice.vbs	Displays sound card configuration
Startup.vbs	Displays the startup programs on the system
SystemAccount.vbs	Displays the system account information
TapeDrive.vbs	Displays tape drive configuration
Thread.vbs	Displays all threads on the system
UserAccount.vbs	Displays user account information
Usergroup.vbs	Adds or deletes multiple users from a group

Automation

There are technically two different ways to perform automated tasks within Windows 2000. The first is AT and WinAT, and the second is the task scheduler.

AT and WinAT

The AT and WinAT applications from Microsoft can be used to schedule tasks. The first, AT.EXE, is built into the operating system and is found in the %windir%\system32 folder. The second utility is available on the *Windows NT Server 4 Resource Kit* using the WINAT.EXE file name. Both of these applications rely on the Microsoft Task Scheduler service to run.

> **WARNING!** *For some reason, WINAT.EXE does not ship with the Windows NT Server Resource Kit. It is, however, included in the Windows NT Server 4 Resource Kit and runs properly under Windows 2000. Considering the current availability of these reskits, you might want to check the Microsoft Web site to see if it's available for download.*

These two applications are the same except for the user interface. AT.EXE is strictly a text-based application, which means that you have to run a command prompt to control it, and WINAT.EXE is a graphical version of AT.EXE.

Because of AT.EXE's command-line execution mode, the following format must be used before AT.EXE will operate properly:

```
AT [\\Systemname][[id][/delete] | /delete [/yes]] time [/interactive][/
every:date][/next:date] "Command"
```

Table 16.7 lists the command-line switches that may be used with the AT.EXE command along with their descriptions. (Note that you can retrieve the information in Table 16.7 by typing "at /?" at the command line.)

Task Scheduler

Windows 2000 also comes with a built-in task scheduler. The Task Scheduler is accessed through the Control Panel. This is a simple graphical wizard that can be run to automate many administrative tasks without scripting.

Table 16.7   The AT command-line switches.

Switch	Description
\\systemname	Specifies a remote computer. Commands are scheduled on the local computer if this parameter is omitted.
Id	An identification number assigned to a scheduled command.
/delete	Cancels a scheduled command. If Id is omitted, all the scheduled commands on the computer are canceled.
/yes	Used with the cancel all jobs command when no further confirmation is desired.
time	Specifies the time when the command is to run.
/interactive	Allows the job to interact with the desktop of the user who is logged on at the time the job runs.
/every:date[,...]	Runs the command on each specified day of the week or month. If date is omitted, the current day of the month is assumed.
/next:date[,...]	Runs the specified command on the next occurrence of the day (for example, next Thursday). If date is omitted, the current day of the month is assumed.
"command"	Specifies the Windows NT command or batch program to be run.

Immediate Solutions

Working with Scripts

Creating the actual VBScript and JScript is beyond the scope of this book. For this reason, you'll look at ready-made scripts that Microsoft has made available as demo scripts. These scripts are found in a couple of places. The sample files can be found at **msdn.microsoft.com/scripting** and in the *Windows 2000 Server Resource Kit*. Each time that one of these scripts is used, the script's name and location will be supplied.

Executing a Script Using CScript

To execute a script using CScript, follow these steps:

1. Click Start, and select Programs|Accessories|Command Prompt.

2. Type "CScript *scriptname*", and press Enter.

3. Add the **//b** switch to run the script in Batch mode or the **//I** switch to run the script in Interactive mode. With Interactive mode, all messages will be sent to the console, and, with Batch mode, these messages are suppressed.

4. Add the **//d** switch to turn active debugging on, or add **//x** to run the script in the debugger.

5. Add the **//e:*engine*** switch to run the script in a specific engine.

6. Add the **//h:CScript** switch to set the default script engine to CScript or the **//h:WScript** switch to set the default script engine to WScript.

7. Add the **//job:*nnn*** switch to run a specific WScript job.

8. Add the **//logo** switch to display a logo during execution or the **//nologo** switch to suppress the logo.

9. Add the **//s** switch to save the configuration for the currently logged-on user. This is used when setting the script execution defaults for the user.

10. Add the **//t:*nn*** switch to control the amount of time the specified script has to execute before it is terminated by the scripting engine.

11. Add the **//u** switch to use Unicode for all redirected I/O for non-English operating systems.

Executing a Script Using WScript

Because WScript is the default scripting engine, there are two ways to execute a script using WScript.

To use Method 1, perform the following steps:

1. Navigate to the script that you would like to execute.

2. Double-click the script.

NOTE: *When using this method, the script will be executed using any default settings defined for the scripting engine. For example, if you have not modified the scripting engine, the script will execute in Interactive mode with the logo being displayed and in the WScript engine.*

To use Method 2, perform the following steps:

1. Click Start, and select Programs|Accessories|Command Prompt.

2. Type "WScript *scriptname*", and press Enter.

3. Add the **//b** switch to run the script in Batch mode or the **//I** switch to run the script in Interactive mode. With Interactive mode, all messages will be sent to the console, and, with Batch mode, these messages are suppressed.

4. Add the **//d** switch to turn active debugging on or **//x** to run the script in the debugger.

5. Add the **//e:*engine*** switch to run the script in a specific engine.

6. Add the **//h:CScript** switch to set the default script engine to CScript or the **//h:WScript** to set the default script engine to WScript.

7. Add the **//job:*nnn*** switch to run a specific WScript job.

8. Add the **//logo** switch to display a logo during execution or the **//nologo** switch to suppress the logo.

9. Add the **//s** switch to save the configuration for the currently logged-on user. This is used when setting the script execution defaults for the user.

10. Add the **//t:*nn*** switch to control the amount of time that the specified script has to execute before it is terminated by the scripting engine.

Setting Script Properties

To set script properties, follow these steps:

1. Navigate to the script for which you would like to modify the properties.

2. Right-click the script, and choose Properties from the pop-up menu.

3. Select the Script tab.

4. To set the timeout on the script, check the Stop Script After A Specified Number Of Seconds checkbox, and enter an amount of time in the Seconds field.

5. To keep the logo from being displayed, clear the Display Logo When Script Executed In Command Console checkbox.

6. Click OK.

Setting Script Properties Using WSH Files

To set script properties using WSH files, follow these steps:

1. Create a text file with the same name as the desired script, but with the .wsh extension.

2. Use the following format in the file:

```
[ScriptFile]
Path=%Systemroot%\folder\script.vbs
[Options]
Timeout=0
DisplayLogo=1
BatchMode=0
```

3. The Path field is the location of the script file to be executed. This can be a VBScript file, a JScript file, or any other supported scripting language file.

4. Specify a timeout (if any) in the Timeout field.

5. To display a logo, set the DisplayLogo field to 1. To suppress the logo, set the property to 0.

6. To run the script in Interactive mode, set the BatchMode Property to 0. To run the script in Batch mode, set it to 1.

Running a Simple VBScript

To run a simple VBScript, follow these steps:

NOTE: *Externally, the only difference between a VBScript file and a JScript file is the extension. VBScript files use the .vbs extension, and JScript files use the .js extension.*

---

1. Navigate to the script that you would like to execute.

2. Double-click the script to run it.

3. To set properties on the script, follow the instructions on running the script using CScript/WScript. Also see the "Setting Script Properties" or "Setting Script Properties Using WSH Files" solution.

Running a Simple JScript

To run a simple JScript, follow these steps:

NOTE: *Externally, the only difference between a VBScript file and a JScript file is the extension. VBScript files use the .vbs extension, and JScript files use the .js extension.*

---

1. Navigate to the script that you would like to execute.

2. Double-click the script to run it.

3. To set properties on the script, follow the instructions on running the script using CScript/WScript. Also see the "Setting Script Properties" or "Setting Script Properties Using WSH Files" solution.

Adding a Scripting Language

To add a scripting language to the system, follow these steps:

1. Click Start, and select Run.

2. Enter "regedt32.exe" in the Open field, and click OK.

3. Select the HKEY_LOCAL_MACHINE on the Local Machine window.

4. Navigate to SOFTWARE\Microsoft\Windows Scripting Host\Script Extensions.

5. Select Edit|New Key.

6. In the Key Name field, enter the name of the scripting engine extension beginning with a period (for example, .scr).

7. Click OK.

8. Select the newly created key.

9. Select Edit|New Value.

10. Leave the Value Name field blank, select REG_SZ from the Data Type drop-down menu, and click OK.

11. In the String field, enter a description for the extension (for example, SCRScript Script File), and click OK.

12. Select Edit|New Value.

13. In the Value Name field, enter "DefaultIcon", select REG_SZ from the Data Type drop-down menu, and click OK.

14. In the String field, enter "%SystemRoot%\System32\wscript.exe,n", where n is the nth icon in the wscript.exe file. There are only four icons in the wscript.exe files; therefore, only a value from one to four may be used.

15. Click OK.

16. Select Edit|New Value.

17. In the Value Name field, enter "EngineID", select REG_SZ from the Data Type drop-down menu, and click OK.

18. In the String field, enter the engine ID (for example, SCRScript).

19. Click OK.

20. Select Edit|New Value.

21. In the Value Name field, enter "ScriptID", select REG_SZ from the Data Type drop-down menu, and click OK.

22. In the String field, enter the script ID (for example, SCRFile).

23. Click OK.

Working with the Task Scheduler Service

The Windows 2000 **AT** and **WinAT** commands rely on a service called the Task Scheduler service. If this service is not running, no AT and WinAT events can be scheduled. This section deals with controlling this service:

TIP: This service is the same as the Windows NT Scheduler Service. Only the name has changed.

Starting the Task Scheduler Service

To start the Task Scheduler service, follow these steps:

1. Click Start, and select Programs|Administrative Tools|Services.

2. Select Task Scheduler.

3. Right-click the service, and choose Start from the pop-up menu.

Stopping the Task Scheduler Service

To stop the Task Scheduler service, follow these steps:

1. Click Start, and select Programs|Administrative Tools|Services.

2. Select Task Scheduler.

3. Right-click the service, and choose Stop from the pop-up menu.

16. Scripting, Automation, and Command-Line Tools

Using the **AT** Command

The text-based task-scheduling application is AT.EXE. This section illustrates some of the most common tasks for this application.

Adding an **AT** Command

To add an **AT** command, follow these steps:

1. Click Start, and select Programs|Accessories|Command Prompt.

2. Type "AT *hh:mm Command*", and press Enter. The time is entered in 24-hour notation, and the command can be a batch file, a script, or any executable.

3. The **AT** command will return an ID for the command using a format similar to what's shown in Figure 16.2.

Adding an Interactive **AT** Command

To add an interactive **AT** command, follow these steps:

1. Click Start, and select Programs|Accessories|Command Prompt.

2. Type "AT *hh:mm Command* /Interactive", and press Enter. The time is entered in 24-hour notation, and the command can be a batch file, a script, or any executable.

3. The **AT** command will assign the next available ID.

Viewing the Configured **AT** Commands

To view the configured **AT** commands, follow these steps:

1. Click Start, and select Programs|Accessories|Command Prompt.

Figure 16.2   Creating a new AT command.

2. Type "AT", and press Enter.

3. All currently scheduled tasks will be listed.

Deleting an **AT** Command

To delete an **AT** command, follow these steps:

1. Click Start, and select Programs|Accessories|Command Prompt.

2. To delete a single command, type "AT *id* /delete", and press Enter. Note that *id* is the ID for the task to be deleted.

3. To delete all scheduled tasks, type "AT /delete", press Enter, and press Y to confirm the deletion.

Creating a Recurring **AT** Command

To create a recurring **AT** command, follow these steps:

1. Click Start, and select Programs|Accessories|Command Prompt.

2. Type "AT *hh:mm /every:{Su,m,t,w,th,f,sa} Command*", and press Enter. You can pick and choose the days of the week to run the task.

3. Alternatively, type "AT *hh:mm /next:{Su,m,t,w,th,f,sa} Command*", and press Enter. You can pick and choose the days of the week to run the task.

Using the **WinAT** Command

The graphical version of the **AT** command is the WinAT application. The *Windows 2000 Server Resource Kit* does not include WINAT.EXE; the *Windows NT Server Resource Kit*, however, does. After you copy the WinAT files to your system, you can execute the WinAT application, as shown in Figure 16.3. Notice that any tasks scheduled with the **AT** command appear here because they share the same database.

Adding a **WinAT** Command

To add a **WinAT** command, follow these steps:

1. Run the WINAT.EXE application.

2. Select Edit|Add. The window shown in Figure 16.4 appears.

3. Type the command to be executed in the Command field.

4. Select a day (or days) from the Days section.

5. Select the execution time.

6. Click OK.

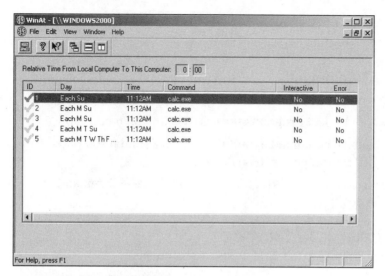

Figure 16.3   The WinAT application.

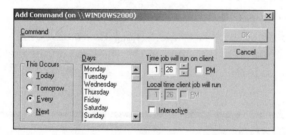

Figure 16.4   The WinAT Add Command window.

Adding an Interactive **WinAT** Command

To add an interactive **WinAT** command, follow these steps:

1. Run the WINAT.EXE application.

2. Select Edit|Add.

3. Type the command to be executed in the Command field.

4. Select a day (or days) from the Days section.

5. Select the execution time.

6. Check the Interactive checkbox.

7. Click OK.

Deleting a **WinAT** Command

To delete a **WinAT** command, follow these steps:

1. Run the WINAT.EXE application.

2. Select the command that you would like to delete.

3. Select Edit|Remove.

4. Click Yes to confirm the deletion.

Creating a Recurring **WinAT** Command

To create a recurring **WinAT** command, follow these steps:

1. Run the winat.exe application.

2. Select Edit|Add.

3. Type the command to be executed in the Command field.

4. Select the Recurrence property from the This Occurs section of the window.

5. Select a day (or days) from the Days section.

6. Select the execution time.

7. If desired, check the Interactive checkbox.

8. Click OK.

Using the Windows 2000 Task Scheduler

To use the built-in Task Scheduler, perform the following steps:

1. Click Start, and select Settings|Control Panel.

2. Double-click the Scheduled Tasks icon.

3. Double-click Add Scheduled Task.

4. The Scheduled Task Wizard appears. Click Next.

5. Select a task to be automated. For this example, I'll select Disk Cleanup.

NOTE: *The steps that follow may vary depending on the task selected. Follow the on-screen prompts to complete automation settings for particular tasks.*

6. Enter a name for the task in the field provided, and select how often the task is to be performed (see Figure 16.5). Click Next.

7. Enter the start time for the task and the day on which the task is to be performed (see Figure 16.6). Click Next.

TIP: *Depending on the task, it's best to select a time and day when server activity and usage are at a minimum.*

16. Scripting, Automation, and Command-Line Tools

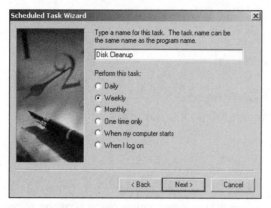

Figure 16.5   Entering a name and setting the frequency for a scheduled task.

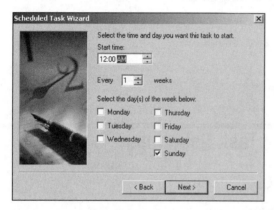

Figure 16.6   Setting the time and day for a scheduled task.

8. Enter the username and password (and confirm the password) under which the scheduled task will be run. Click Next.

9. If desired, check the Open Advanced Properties For This Task When I Click Finish checkbox if advanced settings are needed.

10. Click Finish.

11. Close the Scheduled Tasks applet.

Chapter 17
Tuning and Optimization

In Depth

One of the most difficult tasks that a Windows 2000 administrator (or any systems administrator, for that matter) encounters is answering client complaints on system slowness. One question that you should ask yourself when a user notifies you of a slow system is: "What is slow?" What is slow on one system might not be slow on another. To truly know when a system is slowing down, a baseline should be created and used. The next section deals with just that.

For NT administrators, there is some confusion between Performance Monitor, the Performance Tool, and System Monitor. This is understandable, because Microsoft basically shuffled things around on us. With Windows NT, there was only Performance Monitor, and its application was PERFMON.EXE. With Windows 2000, the Performance Tool, whose application name is PERFMON.EXE, doesn't really do anything. Instead, it contains an entry called System Monitor, which is what we know as Performance Monitor. As we continue to discuss System Monitor and the Performance Tool, just keep in mind that Performance Monitor is now System Monitor despite the fact that the PERFMON.EXE application changed hands.

Building and Using Baselines

A *baseline* is simply an average of how a system performs during normal operation over the course of at least a day, and usually a week or so. Normal operation, to a system, means that users should be logged in and operating normally during the baseline calculation. Ultimately, your baselines should tell you when your server is receiving the most usage, when it is experiencing errors, and when it's hardly used at all. Creating a baseline on a production system during regular operations involves taking a snapshot of the system's performance. Down the road (say, a few weeks or months), a second measurement can be taken and compared to the first. This comparison shows the growth of the system, thus allowing an administrator to predict when a system upgrade should be scheduled, at what time of day, and how long the system should be down.

When creating a baseline, you should log the information about your system (memory, processor, disks, and network) for a prolonged time period with an interval that is longer than the default (say, every 30 seconds or 1 minute). This will decrease the log file size while giving you a good snapshot. Also, make sure that the baseline runs for at least 24 hours. Extra baselines should be created for especially heavy days, such as the first or fifteenth of the month.

TIP: Using any monitoring tools will have an impact on the performance of a server. If you are seeking a good baseline on a troubled or slow server, keep in mind that while you're running the monitoring tools, the system will run slower.

When creating a baseline, you should use applications such as System Monitor (within the Performance tool, see the following section) and Network Monitor to gather activity information about hard disks, memory, paging, and network use every minute, 5 minutes, or 10 minutes for a period lasting at least a full day. Ideally, you should gather this baseline information over the course of at least a week so that you can get a good idea of what days of the week or month are more critical than others. This will also give you a better idea of what the expansion rate is on your server's memory, hard disk, and central processing unit (CPU), and what the network usage is.

Performance Tool and System Monitor

The System Monitor will be your primary means of creating baselines for trouble-shooting and maintenance purposes. System Monitor works by configuring what's known as a counter and using it to monitor specific events occurring on the server. For those of you familiar with Simple Network Management Protocol (SNMP), counters are very similar to traps.

As you might imagine, the different types of counters available with the Performance tool are wide and varied. As you navigate through System Monitor in an attempt to add or modify counters (right-click on the right windowpane, and click on Add Counters from the pop-up window), it's easy to get confused. An Explain button is on the right of the window that will display a description for the high-lighted counter. There are about 34 different categories of counters, which are called performance objects within the application. By and large, almost every conceivable performance object category is included by default, even if you aren't running that particular service, such as Internet Authentication Service (IAS) or Remote Access Server (RAS). Additional performance objects may be added to this list depending upon what services and applications you install on your Windows 2000 system.

Of all of the performance object categories available, a few should be included in any baseline process. These are Memory, PhysicalDisk, and Processor. These three elements interreact heavily, are the core of the operation of the system, and are your best link to the hardware side of the overall picture.

The Memory object is primarily used to baseline and determine if the random access memory (RAM) is being used fully and if the RAM has any problems. The Pages/Sec counter will serve two purposes in telling you how much RAM is being used and whether or not you need to get more. Paging is a process whereby less-critical active memory is shoveled temporarily to the hard disk in a configuration that is designed to trick the system into thinking that this particular hard disk space is RAM. Windows 2000 will not function without paging. However, excessive paging can occur when there's not enough RAM on the system and the operating system (OS) is forced to page memory nearly constantly. Cache Faults and Page Faults/Sec can also give you an idea of whether or not your RAM is going bad. Under normal circumstances, it's safe to say that if the RAM is bad, the system will beep during the power-on self test (POST) to notify you of this. Once in a great while, however, single chips on the *single inline memory module (SIMM) board* will become faulty, and you'll see strange behavior as a result. You can use Cache Faults and Page Faults/Sec counters to help you in that area.

The Processor object has several counters, but you'll primarily need to look at the % Processor Time. This particular counter will tell you if the processor is overloaded and if you need an upgrade. If the processor is always pegged at near 100 percent levels, you may need to consider either upgrading the current processor or adding a second processor to the system.

The PhysicalDisk object also has several counters that are all related to the hard disk drive. The % Disk Time counter will give you an idea of how much and how often the hard disk is being used. As a rule of thumb, anything more than 60 percent on a regular basis may warrant additional hard disk space or could be indicative of impending drive failures. If you're worried about drive failure, run Scandisk and Defrag at your earliest opportunity. These two utilities may resolve the problem, and, if not, they can determine if a physical disk problem is occurring. Also, when you see these higher performance numbers, remember that it may not be due to a need for hard disk, but it may be due to a need for RAM. If this is the case, you'll need to pay particular attention to the Memory object's Pages/Sec counter in order to determine what the specific problem is.

Network Monitor

Much like their predecessor Windows NT, Windows 2000 Server and Advanced Server ship with a Network Monitor utility that monitors network data as it crosses the server. By default, the network card installed on a system will only accept packets of information addressed to it. Any packets addressed to another system are ignored. The Network Monitor utility places the network card in what is known as *promiscuous mode* (the card must support this). In this mode, the network card accepts all packets of information. The Network Monitor utility can then be used to view—and therefore troubleshoot—these packets.

Two different versions of Network Monitor exist. One ships with Windows 2000, and the other ships with Microsoft System Management Server (SMS). The difference between the two is simple. The SMS version is more advanced in that it allows for packet captures to occur between any two systems on the network.

The Windows 2000 version will only capture information between the local system and another system.

Many different types of packets exist on the network. Network Monitor uses what are known as *protocol parsers* to define what these packets are. This is done with the use of a separate dynamic link library (DLL) file for each of the protocols.

Network Monitor is able to monitor a variety of protocols:

- AARP
- ADSP
- AFP
- AH
- ARP_RARP
- ASP
- ATMARP
- ATP
- BONE
- BOOKMARK
- BPDU
- BROWSER
- CBCP
- CCP
- COMMENT
- DDP
- DHCP
- DNS
- EAP
- ESP
- ETHERNET
- FDDI
- FINGER
- FRAME
- FTP
- GENERIC
- GRE
- ICMP

- IGMP
- IP
- IPCP
- IPX
- IPXCP
- IPXWAN
- ISAKMP
- L2TP
- LAP
- LCP
- LLC
- LPR
- MESSAGE
- MSRPC
- NBFCP
- NBIPX
- NBP
- NBT
- NCP
- NDR
- NetBIOS
- NETLOGON
- NFS
- NMPI
- NSP
- NWDP
- ODBC
- OSPF
- PAP
- PPP
- PPPCHAP
- PPPML
- PPPPAP

- PPTP
- R_LOGON
- R_LSARPC
- R_WINSPOOL
- RADIUS
- RIP
- RIPX
- RPC
- RPL
- RSVP
- RTMP
- SAP
- SMB
- SMT
- SNAP
- SNMP
- SPX
- SSP
- STATS
- TCP
- TMAC
- TOKENRING
- TPCTL
- TRAIL
- UDP
- VINES_FRAG
- VINES_IP
- VINES_TL
- XNS
- ZIP

Although nobody expects you to be familiar with all of these protocols and messaging methods, it might come in handy to realize that Network Monitor can be used to monitor network traffic of all types, including Apple/Macintosh, Unix, NetWare, token ring, fiber, and even some wide area network (WAN) protocols.

Immediate Solutions

Working with Network Monitor

All the tasks covered in this section are available in the second version of Network Monitor. Any features not available in the Network Monitor application that ships with Windows 2000 Server are marked as such.

Installing Network Monitor

To install Network Monitor, follow these steps:

1. Click Start, and select Settings|Control Panel.

2. Double-click the Add/Remove Programs applet.

3. Click Add/Remove Windows Components. If the Add/Remove Windows Components Wizard appears, go to Step 4. Otherwise, click Components to start the Add/Remove Windows Components Wizard.

4. Select Management And Monitoring Tools, and click Details.

5. Check the Network Monitor Tools checkbox, and click OK.

6. Click Next.

7. Click Finish. Then click Close.

Installing the Network Monitor Driver

To install Network Monitor driver, follow these steps:

1. Right-click My Network Places, and choose Properties from the pop-up menu.

2. Select Local Area Connection.

3. Select File|Properties.

4. Click Install.

5. Select Protocol, and click Add.

6. Select the Network Monitor driver, and click OK.

7. Click OK.

Starting Network Monitor

To start Network Monitor, follow these steps:

1. Click Start, and select Programs|Administrative Tools|Network Monitor.

2. If prompted for the network selection, click OK.

3. From the window in Figure 17.1, select the network to capture data on, and click OK.

Starting a Network Capture

To start a network capture, follow these steps:

1. Click Start, and select Programs|Administrative Tools|Network Monitor.

2. Select Capture|Start. Network Monitor will begin the network capture, as shown in Figure 17.2.

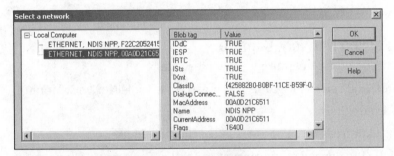

Figure 17.1   Making the network selection.

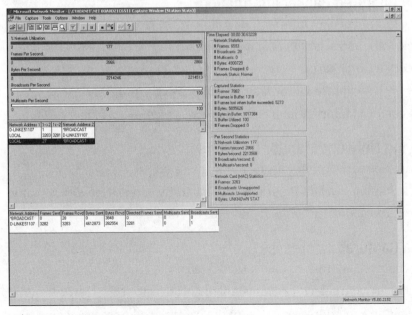

Figure 17.2   A network capture.

Stopping a Network Capture

To stop a network capture, follow these steps:

1. Click Start, and select Programs|Administrative Tools|Network Monitor.
2. Select Capture|Stop.

Pausing a Network Capture

To pause a network capture, follow these steps:

1. Click Start, and select Programs|Administrative Tools|Network Monitor.
2. Select Capture|Start.
3. When the capture is to be paused, select Capture|Pause.

Starting a Paused Network Capture

To start a paused network capture, follow these steps:

1. Click Start, and select Programs|Administrative Tools|Network Monitor.
2. Select Capture|Start.
3. When the capture is to be paused, select Capture|Pause.
4. To continue the paused network capture, select Capture|Continue.

Viewing Captured Packet Information

To view captured packet information, follow these steps:

1. Click Start, and select Programs|Administrative Tools|Network Monitor.
2. Select Capture|Start.
3. To view the captured information, select Capture|Stop And View.
4. The captured information will be displayed as shown in Figure 17.3.

Identifying Network Monitor Users

To identify Network Monitor users, follow these steps:

1. Click Start, and select Programs|Administrative Tools|Network Monitor.
2. Select Tools|Identify Network Monitor Users.

Viewing Captured Addresses

To view captured addresses, follow these steps:

1. Click Start, and select Programs|Administrative Tools|Network Monitor.
2. Select Capture|Addresses. A list of the captured addresses appears, as shown in Figure 17.4.

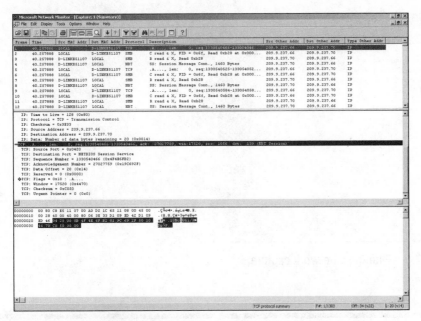

Figure 17.3   Network capture data.

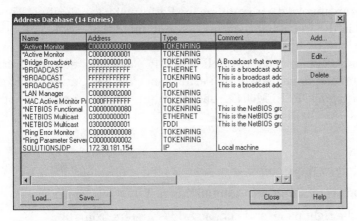

Figure 17.4   Viewing captured addresses.

Applying a Capture Filter

To apply a capture filter, follow these steps:

1. Click Start, and select Programs|Administrative Tools|Network Monitor.

2. Select Capture|Filter.

3. If the built-in version of Network Monitor is the one running, a warning message will be displayed specifying that this version only captures packets to or from the local system. Click OK.

4. Define your filter as desired (see Figure 17.5), and click OK.

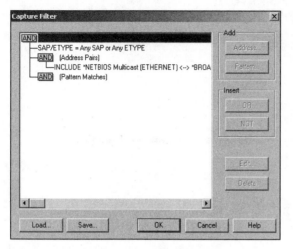

Figure 17.5   Filtering a network capture.

Working with System Monitor

A number of issues are involved with running the Performance application. These tasks are covered in the following sections. Keep in mind that System Monitor can be opened in one of three ways: clicking Start and selecting Programs| Administrative Tools|Performance; right-clicking My Computer, selecting Manage from the pop-up menu, and selecting Performance from the available icons on the left page; or typing "PERFMON" from Start|Run. The Performance application appears as shown in Figure 17.6.

Adding Counters

To add a counter, follow these steps:

1. Click Start, and select Programs|Administrative Tools|Performance.

2. Right-click in the right pane, and choose Add Counters from the pop-up menu.

3. From the Add Counters window, shown in Figure 17.7, select to monitor either the current system by choosing Use Local Computer Counters or a remote system by entering a computer name in Select Counters From Computer.

NOTE: When entering a name for a remote computer, use the Universal Naming Convention (UNC), for example, \\server.

4. Choose a performance object from the Performance Object drop-down list.

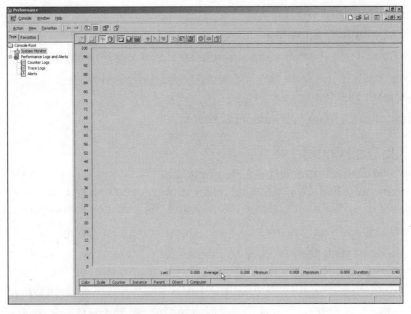

Figure 17.6   The Performance application.

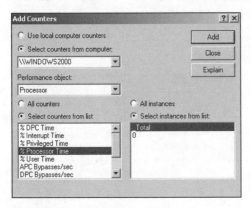

Figure 17.7   Adding a counter.

5. Select the counters to monitor. Shift+click (to select a range) and Ctrl+click (to select individual counters) can be used for the selection.

6. If multiple instances exist, choose the desired instance.

7. For extra information on a specific counter, select the counter, and click Explain.

8. Click Add to add the counter.

9. Repeat Steps 3 through 8 for any other desired performance objects and counters.

10. Click Close.

Removing Counters

To remove a counter, follow these steps:

1. Click Start, and select Programs|Administrative Tools|Performance.

2. Choose the counter to be deleted in the bottom right counter pane, and either click Delete or press Delete.

3. Repeat Step 2 for any additional counters.

Controlling Disk Counters

Windows 2000 allows for much more flexibility than Windows NT did in how disk counters are controlled. By default, all disk counters are off during the boot process. This solution deals with all the different options available for disk counters:

1. Click Start, and select Programs|Accessories|Command Prompt.

2. To turn on all disk performance counters at boot time, type "diskperf -y", and press Enter. Restart the system for the setting to take effect.

3. To turn on disk performance counters for physical disks, type "diskperf -yd", and press Enter. Restart the system for the setting to take effect.

4. To turn on disk performance counters for logical disks, type "diskperf -yv", and press Enter. Restart the system for the setting to take effect.

5. To disable disk performance counters, type "diskperf -n", and press Enter. Restart the system for the setting to take effect.

6. To disable disk performance counters for physical disks, type "diskperf -nd", and press Enter.

7. To disable disk performance counters for logical disks, type "diskperf -nv", and press Enter.

TIP: A \\system switch can be added to the options in Steps 2 through 7 to control disk performance counters on a remote system.

Creating a Counter Log

To create a counter log, follow these steps:

1. Click Start, and select Programs|Administrative Tools|Performance.

2. In the left pane, select the Performance Logs And Alerts|Counter Logs container.

3. Right-click Counter Logs, and choose New Log Settings from the pop-up menu.

4. Enter a name for the new counter log, and click OK.

5. To add a counter, click Add, and choose the counter or counters to be added to the log.

6. To remove a counter, select the counter, and click Remove.

7. Specify the logging interval by entering in the number in the Interval field and the units for the interval (seconds, minutes, hours, or days) in the Units field.

8. Click the Log Files tab. Enter the log file information, including name, location, size, and type.

9. Click Schedule, and enter the start and/or stop information for the counter log.

10. Click OK.

Starting a Counter Log

To start a counter log, follow these steps:

1. Click Start, and select Programs|Administrative Tools|Performance.

2. In the left pane, select the Performance Logs And Alerts|Counter Logs container.

3. Right-click the counter log in the right pane, and choose Start from the pop-up menu.

Stopping a Counter Log

To stop a counter log, follow these steps:

1. Click Start, and select Programs|Administrative Tools|Performance.

2. In the left pane, select the Performance Logs And Alerts|Counter Logs container.

3. Right-click the counter log in the right pane, and choose Stop from the pop-up menu.

Scheduling a Counter Log

To schedule a counter log, follow these steps:

1. Click Start, and select Programs|Administrative Tools|Performance.

2. In the left pane, select the Performance Logs And Alerts|Counter Logs container.

3. Right-click the counter log in the right pane, and choose Properties from the pop-up menu.

4. Click the Schedule tab.

5. In the Start Log section, select the At radio button.

6. Enter a time and date on which this counter is to be started.

7. To specify a counter log with no scheduled end time, choose Manually (using the shortcut menu).

8. To stop the counter log after a set number of seconds, minutes, hours, or days, choose the After radio button, and enter the number of units that the system is to wait before stopping the counter log.

9. To stop the counter log on a specific date and time, choose At, and enter the desired date and time.

10. If a command is to be executed after the log file closes, check the Run This Command checkbox, and enter the command path, name, and desired switches.

11. Click OK.

Modifying the Counter Log Logging Rate

To modify the counter log logging rate, follow these steps:

1. Click Start, and select Programs|Administrative Tools|Performance.

2. In the left pane, select the Performance Logs And Alerts|Counter Logs container.

3. Right-click the counter log in the right pane, and choose Properties from the pop-up menu.

4. In the General tab, modify the interval and interval unit, and click OK.

Creating a Trace Log

To create a trace log, follow these steps:

1. Click Start, and select Programs|Administrative Tools|Performance.

2. In the left pane, select the Performance Logs And Alerts|Trace Logs container.

3. Right-click Trace Logs, and choose New Log Settings from the pop-up menu.

4. Enter a name for the new trace log, and click OK.

5. To log system provider events, (events that are related to the base system functionality) select the Events Logged By System Provider radio button, and select the desired providers from which to create the trace log.

6. To log nonsystem providers, select the Nonsystem Providers radio button.

7. Click Add (assuming that Step 5 was not performed).

8. Select the nonsystem providers to log, and click OK.

9. Click the Log Files tab. Enter the log file information, including name, location, size, and type.

10. Click Schedule, and enter the start and/or stop information for the counter log.

11. Click OK.

Starting a Trace Log

To start a trace log, follow these steps:

1. Click Start, and select Programs|Administrative Tools|Performance.

2. In the left pane, select the Performance Logs And Alerts|Trace Logs container.

3. Right-click the trace log in the right pane, and choose Start from the pop-up menu.

Stopping a Trace Log

To stop a trace log, follow these steps:

1. Click Start, and select Programs|Administrative Tools|Performance.

2. In the left pane, select the Performance Logs And Alerts|Trace Logs container.

3. Right-click the trace log in the right pane, and choose Stop from the pop-up menu.

Scheduling a Trace Log

To schedule a trace log, follow these steps:

1. Click Start, and select Programs|Administrative Tools|Performance.

2. In the left pane, select the Performance Logs And Alerts|Trace Logs container.

3. Right-click the trace log in the right pane, and choose Properties from the pop-up menu.

4. Click the Schedule tab.

5. In the Start Log section, select the At radio button.

6. Enter a time and date on which this trace log is to be started.

7. To specify a trace log with no scheduled end time, choose Manually (using the shortcut menu).

8. To stop the trace log after a set number of seconds, minutes, hours, or days, choose the After radio button, and enter the number of units that the system is to wait before stopping the trace log.

9. To stop the trace log on a specific date and time, choose At, and enter the desired date and time.

10. If a command is to be executed after the log file closes, check the Run This Command checkbox, and enter the command path, name, and desired switches.

11. Click OK.

Creating an Alert

To create an alert, follow these steps:

1. Click Start, and select Programs|Administrative Tools|Performance.

2. In the left pane, select the Performance Logs and Alerts|Alerts container.

3. Right-click in the right pane, and choose New Alert Settings from the pop-up menu.

4. Enter a name and an optional description for the alert.

5. To add a counter, click Add, select the desired counter, click Add, and click Close.

6. Ensure that the counter is selected. Choose to cause an alert when the counter is either over or under the limit by selecting Over/Under from the Value drop-down list and selecting the limit in the Limit field.

7. To remove a counter, highlight the counter, and click Remove.

8. Specify the logging interval by entering the number in the Interval field and the units for the interval (seconds, minutes, hours, or days) in the Units field.

9. Select the Action tab.

10. To log an entry, check the Log An Entry In The Application Event Log checkbox.

11. To send an alert, check the Send A Network Message To checkbox, and enter the username(s) or group name(s) in the field.

12. To start a performance log, check the Start Performance Data Log checkbox, and choose the appropriate log type from the drop-down list.

13. To run an external program, check the Run This Program checkbox, and enter the path and name of the program. To assign it command-line switches, click Command Line Arguments, choose the desired switches, and click OK.

14. To start the alert automatically, choose the At radio button, and enter a date and time.

15. To specify an alert with no scheduled end time, choose Manually (using the shortcut menu).

16. To stop the alert after a set number of seconds, minutes, hours, or days, choose the After radio button and enter the number of units that the system is to wait before stopping the counter log.

17. To stop the alert on a specific date and time, choose At, and enter the desired date and time.

18. Click OK.

Configuring Alert Thresholds

To configure the alert thresholds, follow these steps:

1. Click Start, and select Programs|Administrative Tools|Performance.

2. In the left pane, select the Performance Logs And Alerts|Trace Logs container.

3. Double-click the desired alert.

4. Select the counter for which the threshold is to be set.

5. Choose either the Over or Under option from the drop-down list.

6. Enter a value for the threshold.

7. Click OK.

Configuring Alert Actions

To configure the alert actions, follow these steps:

1. Click Start, and select Programs|Administrative Tools|Performance.

2. In the left pane, select the Performance Logs And Alerts|Trace Logs container.

3. Double-click the desired alert.

4. Click the Action tab in the Alert dialog box (see Figure 17.8).

5. To log an entry, check the Log An Entry In The Application Event Log checkbox.

6. To send an alert, check the Send A Network Message To checkbox, and enter the username(s) or group name(s) in the field.

7. To start a performance log, check the Start Performance Data Log checkbox, and choose the appropriate log type from the drop-down list.

8. To run an external program, check the Run This Program checkbox, and enter the path and name of the program. To assign it command-line switches, click Command Line Arguments, choose the desired switches (see Figure 17.9), and click OK.

9. Click OK.

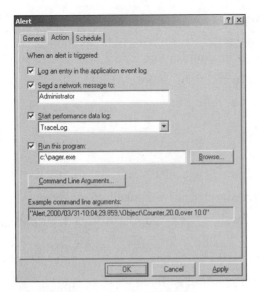

Figure 17.8   Configuring alert actions.

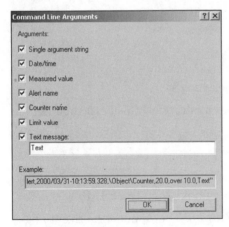

Figure 17.9   Configuring command-line switches.

Starting an Alert

To start a configured alert, follow these steps:

1. Click Start, and select Programs|Administrative Tools|Performance.

2. In the left pane, select the Performance Logs And Alerts|Alerts container.

3. Right-click the alert in the right pane, and choose Start from the pop-up menu.

Stopping an Alert

To stop an alert, follow these steps:

1. Click Start, and select Programs|Administrative Tools|Performance.

2. In the left pane, select the Performance Logs And Alerts|Alerts container.

3. Right-click the alert in the right pane, and choose Stop from the pop-up menu.

Highlighting a Desired Counter

To highlight a desired counter, follow these steps:

1. Click Start, and select Programs|Administrative Tools|Performance.

2. Right-click the right pane, and choose Add Counters from the pop-up menu.

3. From the Add Counters window, select to monitor either the current system by choosing Use Local Computer Counters or a remote system by entering a computer name in Select Counters From Computer.

4. Choose a performance object from the Performance Object drop-down list.

5. Select the counters to monitor. Shift+click and Ctrl+click can be used for multiple selections.

6. If multiple instances exist, choose the desired instance.

7. For extra information on a specific counter, select the counter, and click Explain.

8. Click Add to add the counter.

9. Repeat Steps 3 through 8 for any other desired performance objects and counters.

10. Select the counter to be highlighted in the bottom right counter pane.

11. Press Ctrl+H. The counter is now highlighted (see Figure 17.10).

12. To change the highlighted counter, select a different counter.

Exporting Data to a Hypertext Markup Language File

To export data to a Hypertext Markup Language (HMTL) file, follow these steps:

1. Click Start, and select Programs|Administrative Tools|Performance.

2. Right-click the right pane, and choose Add Counters from the pop-up menu.

3. From the Add Counters window, select to monitor either the current system by choosing Use Local Computer Counters or a remote system by entering a computer name in Select Counters From Computer.

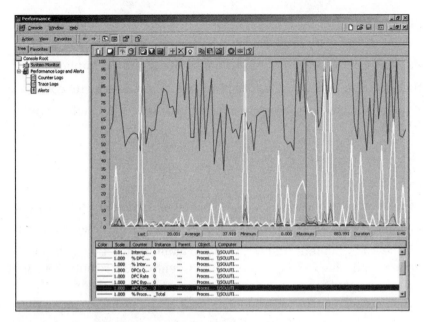

Figure 17.10   Highlighting a counter.

4. Choose a performance object from the Performance Object drop-down list.

5. Select the counters to monitor. Shift+click (to select a range of counters) and Ctrl+click (to select individual counters) can be used for the selection.

6. If multiple instances exist, choose the desired instance.

7. For extra information on a specific counter, select the counter, and click Explain.

8. Click Add to add the counter.

9. Repeat for any other desired performance objects and counters.

10. Right-click the counter graph, and choose Save As from the pop-up menu.

11. Enter a name for the HTML page, and click Save.

Working with Events

A number of issues exist when working with Event Viewer. The following sections deal with these issues.

Viewing Event Details

To view event details, follow these steps:

1. Click Start, and select Programs|Administrative Tools|Event Viewer.

2. Choose the desired log in the console tree (the left pane).

3. Right-click the event to be viewed, and choose Properties from the pop-up menu.

4. To skip to the next event, click the down arrow button.

5. To move to the previous event, click the up arrow button.

6. Click OK when finished.

Creating a New Log View

To create a new log view, follow these steps:

1. Click Start, and select Programs|Administrative Tools|Event Viewer.

2. Choose the log for which you would like a new view created in the left pane.

3. Right-click the log, and choose New Log View from the pop-up menu.

4. Right-click the newly created log, and choose Rename from the pop-up menu.

5. Enter a new name for the log, and press Enter.

6. Right-click the log, and choose Properties from the pop-up menu.

7. Choose the Filter tab.

8. Check the checkboxes for the event types that are to be displayed in this log view.

9. Choose more advanced filters if required.

10. Click OK when finished.

Saving the Log to a File

To save the logs to a file, follow these steps:

1. Click Start, and select Programs|Administrative Tools|Event Viewer.

2. In the right pane, right-click the event log that is to be saved, and choose Save Log File As from the pop-up menu.

3. Enter a name for the log file in the File Name field.

4. Ensure that Event Log (*.evt) is selected in the Save As Type list.

5. Click Save.

Saving the Log to a Tab-Delimited File

To save the log to a tab-delimited file, follow these steps:

1. Click Start, and select Programs|Administrative Tools|Event Viewer.

2. In the right pane, right-click the event log that is to be saved, and choose Save Log File As from the pop-up menu.

3. Enter a name for the log file in the File Name field.

4. Ensure that Text (Tab Delimited) (*.txt) is selected in the Save As Type pop-up list.

5. Click Save.

Saving the Log to a Comma-Delimited File

To save the log to a comma-delimited file, follow these steps:

1. Click Start, and select Programs|Administrative Tools|Event Viewer.

2. In the right pane, right-click the event log that is to be saved, and choose Save Log File As from the pop-up menu.

3. Enter a name for the log file in the File Name field.

4. Ensure that CSV (Comma Separated Variable) (*.csv) is selected in the Save As Type list.

5. Click Save.

Viewing a Log File

To view a saved log file, follow these steps:

1. Click Start, and select Programs|Administrative Tools|Event Viewer.

2. Right-click the Event Viewer container, and click Open Log File in the pop-up menu.

3. Enter the name of the saved log file in the File Name field.

4. Specify the log type in the Log Type list.

5. Enter a display name in the Display Name field.

6. Click OK.

Connecting to a Remote System

To connect to a remote system, follow these steps:

1. Click Start, and select Programs|Administrative Tools|Event Viewer.

2. Right-click the Event Viewer container, and choose Connect To Another Computer from the pop-up menu.

3. Enter the name of the remote computer in the Another Computer field (or click Browse to search for it).

4. Click OK.

Displaying Event Logs from Multiple Computers

To display the event logs of multiple computers, follow these steps:

1. Click Start, and select Run.

2. Type "MMC", and click OK.

3. Choose the Add/Remove snap-in from the Console menu.

4. Click Add.

5. Select Event Viewer, and click Add.

6. Select the Another Computer radio button.

7. Enter the path to the remote computer, and click Finish.

8. Repeat Steps 5 through 7 for any additional computers to be connected to.

9. Click Close.

10. Click OK.

Searching for Events

To search for events, follow these steps:

1. Click Start, and select Programs|Administrative Tools|Event Viewer.

2. Right-click the log to be searched, and choose View|Find from the pop-up menu.

3. Select the types of events to search for.

4. Specify additional information about the events to be searched for in the Event Source, Category, Event ID, User, Computer, and Description sections.

5. Click Find Next.

Configuring the Log

To configure the event log, follow these steps:

1. Click Start, and select Programs|Administrative Tools|Event Viewer.

2. Right-click the log to be configured, and choose Properties from the pop-up menu.

3. In the Log Size section, specify the maximum size for the log.

4. Choose the task to be performed should the maximum log size be reached.

5. Click OK.

Clearing the Log

To clear the event log, follow these steps:

1. Click Start, and select Programs|Administrative Tools|Event Viewer.

2. Right-click the log to be cleared, and choose Clear All Events from the pop-up menu.

3. If you would like the log saved before it is cleared, click Yes, enter a file name, and click Save. Otherwise, click No.

Chapter 18

Remote Access, Remote Control, and Windows 2000

In Depth

Windows 2000 offers a wide range of remote access options, including dial-up, dial-out, Virtual Private Networks (VPNs), and Terminal Services. These options and abilities expand the type of clients that can be used in a Windows 2000 environment as well as the physical range of clients that can connect to a Windows 2000 network.

Remote Control vs. Remote Access

Remote control and remote access are two technologies that are often confused. *Remote control* is the function of taking control of a remote system using a keyboard, monitor, and mouse. *Remote access* is the function of establishing a network connection between two systems so that normal network activities can take place.

Using remote control, the local system's functions are all sent to the remote system, where they actually control the system. The local system is often called a *dumb terminal* because it does no actual processing, but instead just relays the input/output (I/O) from keyboard, mouse, and monitor to and from the remote system. Remote control applications such as Symantec's PCAnywhere can be used with Windows 2000, however the Terminal Server that comes with Windows 2000 Server is used in the same manner.

Using remote access, the local system's functions control the local system, and network resources can be requested across the remote access link. The local system retains all of its normal capabilities and still performs all local processing. Remote access grants a true network connection with distant clients. Remote control gives distant clients control of a system. Remote access clients can establish network connections across wide area network (WAN) links, such as phone, Integrated Services Digital Network (ISDN), cable modem, Asymmetric Digital Subscriber Line (ADSL), and so on. Remote control clients must use an existing network connection (either a direct cable connection or preestablished remote access connection).

Terminal Services

Terminal Services is a Windows 2000 service that's more like remote control than it is remote access. Additional Terminal Services licenses can be purchased and configured for remote access purposes; however, the base product that comes with Windows 2000 Server is more like remote control than remote access. Terminal Services enables thin clients (or computers with low capabilities) to make a remote control-like connection with a server. The terminal clients don't actually take control of the server, but are logged in to the server and presented with their own desktop environment. Terminal Services allows thin clients to take advantage of the powerful features and applications of Windows 2000 without having Windows 2000 installed locally. Terminal clients can employ either a direct cable connection to the network or a preestablished remote access connection to the network to gain communication with the Terminal Services server.

Terminal Services is an add-on component for Windows 2000 Server that's used to support terminal clients. Terminal clients are network devices that perform little or no processing locally, but exchange I/O from the keyboard, mouse, and monitor with the Terminal Services server. This allows the power of Windows 2000 and applications to be accessed from devices without having Windows 2000 installed locally. Terminal Services supports all the Microsoft Windows operating systems as clients, plus many non-Windows platforms—such as the Apple Computer, disk operating system (DOS), and Unix—when running a third-party client product. Therefore, as a Terminal Services client, even a Macintosh system can exploit the power of Windows 2000.

The types of systems that can be used as Terminal Services clients include the following:

- Windows CE-based terminals and handheld professional devices (H/PC Pro)
- All 32-bit Windows-based computers supporting Windows 95, Windows 98, Windows NT 3.51 Server, Windows NT 3.51 Workstation, Windows NT 4 Server, Windows NT 4 Workstation, or Windows 2000 Professional
- All 16-bit Windows-based computers supporting Windows for Workgroups 3.11 with Microsoft Transmission Control Protocol/Internet Protocol (TCP/IP)-32
- Many non-Windows platforms, including Apple Computer, DOS, Linux, and Unix, supporting a third-party terminal client product, such as that available from Citrix (**www.citrix.com**)

Terminal Services can be deployed for numerous specific purposes, including remote administration, remote access, line-of-business applications, and centralized desktop management. Each of these purposes requires different features or capabilities from Windows 2000 Server and the licensing manager (see Table 18.1).

Table 18.1   Terminal Services functions and feature requirements.

Feature	Remote Administration	Remote Access	Line of Business Application	Centralized Desktop Deployment
Domain structure	Yes	No	Yes	Yes
License server	No	Yes	Yes	Yes
Licensing	No	Yes	Yes	Yes
Load balancing	No	Yes	Yes	Yes
Local printing	Yes	Yes	Yes	Yes
Roaming profiles	No	Yes	No	No
Security	Yes	Yes	Yes	Yes

This table is extracted from the Windows 2000 Server Resource Kit.

Terminal Services can be used in one of two ways: in Remote Administration mode or Application Server mode. System management and administration tasks can be performed from any terminal client when Remote Administration mode is employed. This is the only mode currently supported by Cluster service. Central access to applications and resources from any terminal client is supported by the Application Server mode. Unfortunately, these modes are mutually exclusive. Terminal Services is managed through four tools added to Administrative Tools: Terminal Services Client Creator, Terminal Services Configuration, Terminal Services Licensing, and Terminal Services Manager.

The basic process of deploying Terminal Services is as follows:

1. Install Terminal Services on a Windows 2000 Server. This can be performed at the same time that the main operating system (OS) is being installed or at any point after the main OS has been installed.

2. To configure Terminal Services clients, you must install the client software on those systems. This can be performed in at least two ways. You can use the Terminal Services Client Creator to create client software installation disks, or you can create a network distribution point where the client installation software is stored and accessible from all network clients.

3. Create client-based connection profiles.

4. Configure the Terminal Services server.

5. Establish a terminal session.

The Terminal Services Client Creator utility is very straightforward. Select whether to build client installation disks for 16-bit Windows or for 32-bit Windows, indicate the destination floppy drive, select whether to format the disks, and click OK to initiate the creation. Keep in mind that 16-bit Windows client installation software requires four floppies, but 32-bit Windows client installation software requires only two floppies.

Installing the client software from either floppies or a network distribution point requires that the setup.exe file be launched. You'll need to agree to the license agreement and then answer a few system-specific prompts. After these tasks are completed, the computer will be able to connect to Terminal Services.

Terminal Services server configuration is performed using the Terminal Services Configuration utility. There is only a single native connection type, namely Microsoft Remote Desktop Protocol (RDP) 5. This tool is used to configure each connection type's settings and server-related properties. Connection-type settings include control of encryption level, session timeouts, program launch on session initialization, remote control options, client drive and printer mappings, network adapter controls, session permissions, and logon credential management. Server-related property controls include deleting temporary folders on session termination, allowing Internet access from sessions, supporting Active Desktop within sessions, and determining whether permissions are compatible with just Windows 2000 or all possible terminal clients.

Connection-specific configuration settings are accessed through the Connections node of the Terminal Services Configuration tool. Select the connection, and select Action|Properties to view the Properties dialog box for that connection. This eight-tabbed configuration dialog box offers the following configuration controls:

- *Encryption Level*—Used to configure the level of encryption used by the client and server. Settings are Low, Medium, and High.

- *Logon Credentials*—Used to configure how client sessions are authenticated. Options include unique credentials for each user or to authenticate all sessions through a single user account. You can also configure if a password is required to grant access even when a shared user account is employed for authentication.

- *Session Timeouts*—Used to configure the length of time that a session can continue. Timeout values for inactive and active sessions can be determined from either the client or the server side of the connection.

- *Launch Program*—Used to configure whether a program or batch file is launched at the start of each session and whether to allow desktop wallpaper.

- *Remote Control*—Used to configure the ability to control or observe a connected session.

- *Client Settings*—Used to configure whether to retain and use a client's settings for network drive mappings and printers. This is also used to configure whether to disable network drive, printer, LPT port, communication (COM) port, clipboard, and audio mappings.

18. Remote Access, Remote Control, and Windows 2000

- *Network Adapter*—Used to configure which network interfaces can be used by Terminal Services and the number of sessions that can occur across that network interface card (NIC).

- *Permissions*—Used to configure which users and groups can establish Terminal Services sessions and what level of access these sessions will be assigned: Full Control, User Access, or Guest Access.

Server-specific configuration settings are listed under the Server Settings node. These elements include the following:

- *Terminal Server Mode*—Used to display the mode of the Terminal Services server; it will display either Remote Administration or Application Server. This cannot be changed without removing and reinstalling Terminal Services.

- *Delete Temporary Folders On Exit*—Used to configure whether to remove temporary files and folders on Terminal Services shutdown. The default is Yes.

- *Use Temporary Folders Per Session*—Used to configure whether to remove temporary files and folders each time that a session is terminated. The default is Yes.

- *Internet Connector Licensing*—Used to configure the sharing of Windows-based software with up to 200 Internet-connected users. This feature requires specific-use licenses and is set to Disable by default.

- *Active Desktop*—Used to configure whether to allow Active Desktop during Terminal Services sessions. This is set to Enable by default. To conserve server resources, set it to Disable.

- *Permission Compatibility*—Used to configure whether to use permissions that are specific to Windows 2000 only or that are compatible with any possible Terminal Services client. This is configured to the latter option by default.

User licensing and license management is required to deploy Terminal Services in Application Server mode. The Terminal Services Licensing utility, shown in Figure 18.1, is used to perform this function. You'll need to contact a Microsoft license distributor with this tool to activate your user licenses. Windows 2000 includes the Terminal Services software, but it does not include any actual use licenses. You are granted a 90-day grace period to obtain your licenses before you'll be operating in violation of the purchase and license agreement from Microsoft. If you'll be using Terminal Services in Remote Administration mode, there is a limit of two users, but licenses are not required. However, if you'll be using Terminal Services in Application Server mode, you'll need to purchase additional licenses.

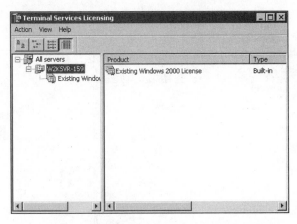

Figure 18.1   The Terminal Services License utility.

The Terminal Services Manager, shown in Figure 18.2, is used to manage active terminal client sessions. This tool is also used to initiate remote control of other terminal sessions when it is launched by an administrator from a terminal session. You can quickly view details about sessions, users, servers, and session processes, and you can send messages to sessions, terminate active sessions, terminate processes within sessions, and reset connection protocols.

When Terminal Services is installed, several of the native Windows 2000 management utilities are enhanced to control Terminal Services-specific capabilities and features:

- *Active Directory Users And Computers (Windows 2000 Server) and Local Users And Groups (Windows 2000 Professional)*—These tools are enhanced to offer user account controls specific to Terminal Services sessions. These new controls include Terminal Services user profiles, logon enablement, session timeouts, reconnection procedures, remote control capability, application launch at session startup, and retaining of mapped drives and printers.

- *System Monitor*—The User object and Session object are added to this performance-monitoring tool so that Terminal Services session-specific activities can be monitored. Also, the Process and System objects are enhanced with several Terminal Services-specific counters.

- *Task Manager*—Two new process information optional columns are added to the Processes tab, namely Session ID and User Name. Plus, the ability is added to terminate all processes associated with all Terminal Services sessions.

- *Add/Remove Programs*—This application installation tool has been enhanced to support the installation of software used on multisession environments.

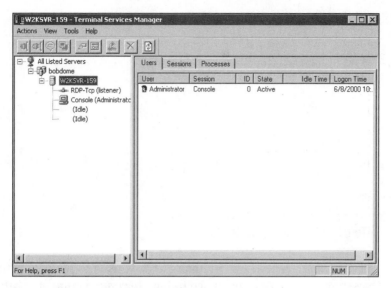

Figure 18.2   The Terminal Services Manager utility.

Most of the functions of Terminal Services can be performed using command-line tools.

Terminal Services can share applications specifically designed for multiuser environments as well as those that are not. However, if Terminal Services is ever disabled and then re-enabled, some programs will need to be reinstalled to function properly. Also, keep the use of 16-bit applications within Terminal Services sessions to a minimum. The overhead required to support 16-bit applications reduces the capabilities of a server to support multiple sessions by 40 percent, and the amount of memory used by each session increases by 50 percent.

Troubleshooting Terminal Services involves employing one or more of the following tactics:

- Double-check configuration settings on the Terminal Services server and all terminal clients.

- Reboot the Terminal Services server system.

- Check the Properties dialog boxes of user accounts that use Terminal Services. The last four tabs configure session details.

- Check that users have proper permissions to establish terminal sessions and to access resources.

- Automatic logon will not function for Windows NT clients. Therefore, manual logon is required.

- If an application fails to operate correctly, after rebooting the Terminal Server, remove and then reinstall the application.

- You cannot use both Offline Files and Terminal Services at the same time; these services are mutually exclusive.

More information on Terminal Services and its use in a Windows 2000 network are discussed in the *Windows 2000 Server Resource Kit* and the original manuals.

Remote Access as a Client

Remote access allows Windows 2000 to serve as a network router, Internet connection proxy, a VPN sever, or a dial-in/dial-out server. Some of the features of the Remote Access Service (RAS) are the following:

- Supports a wide range of clients, including Windows 2000, Windows NT, Windows 95, Windows 98, Windows for Workgroups, DOS (with Microsoft network client software installed), LAN Manager, plus any client that supports Point-to-Point Protocol (PPP).

- Supports PPP for inbound connections and can employ PPP or Serial Line Internet Protocol (SLIP) for outbound connections. PPP can tunnel TCP/IP, NWLink, and Network Basic Input/Output System Enhanced User Interface (NetBEUI). AppleTalk Remote Access Protocol (ARAP) is also supported for inbound connections from Macintosh clients.

- Supports VPN through Point-to-Point Tunneling Protocol (PPTP) or Layer Two Tunneling Protocol (L2TP).

- Supports most WAN connectivity technologies, including phone line, ISDN, T-carrier lines, ADSL, and more. It also supports X.25, Asynchronous Transfer Mode (ATM), and RS-232C null modem connections.

- Supports channel aggregation through multilink PPP.

- Provides integration with Windows 2000 logon, domain, and file-level security.

- Protects dial-up connections with callback security.

- Supports restartable file copy for failed transfers caused by disconnection.

- Supports idle disconnect.

- Supports autodial, logon dial, and dial on demand.

Remote access is a default component of Windows 2000 that's integrated into the networking capabilities and is therefore a required component even if you do not employ its special remote access capabilities. Remote access connections are managed through the Network And Dial-Up Connections utility (see Figure 18.3). See Chapter 8 for general (non-RAS-specific) interface information on this tool.

All RAS connection objects must be created manually. This is done by double-clicking the Make New Connection icon in the Network And Dial-Up Connections applet (see Figure 18.4).

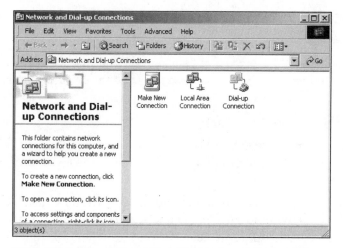

Figure 18.3   The Network And Dial-Up Connections utility.

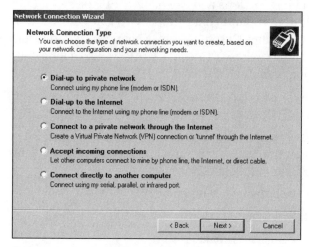

Figure 18.4   The Network Connection Wizard.

This tool is used to create the following types of remote connections:

- *Dial-Up To Private Network*—Creates a connection object to link with a Windows 2000 or Windows NT RAS server

- *Dial-Up To The Internet*—Creates a connection object to link with an Internet service provider (ISP) for Internet access

- *Connect To A Private Network Through The Internet*—Creates a connection object to establish a VPN link using PPTP or L2TP

- *Accept Incoming Connections*—Creates a connection object to configure the system to accept inbound connections

- *Connect Directly To Another Computer*—Creates a connection object to establish a communications link across a serial cable, parallel cable, or infrared port

The Network Connection Wizard is very easy to use. However, it only prompts for minimal unique information. To alter the defaults and to customize a connection object, you'll need to open that object's Properties dialog box. The properties for each object type are discussed in the following sections.

Dial-Up To Private Network

The Dial-Up To Private Network connection object is used to dial up to a Windows 2000 or Windows NT RAS server to establish a network connection. After you are connected, you can participate in any normal network activity (access files and printers, gain proxied Internet access, and so on) with only the speed of your connection as a concern. Also, when this connection object is in use, an icon of two overlapping monitors will appear in the icon tray. Double-clicking this icon opens the connection's status page where you can see information about the link.

The Properties dialog box for a Dial-Up To Private Network connection object has five tabs: General, Options, Security, Networking, and Sharing. The General tab, shown in Figure 18.5, is used to configure the following:

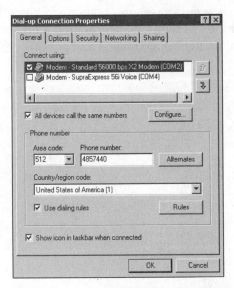

Figure 18.5   A Dial-Up To Private Network connection object's General tab.

You can connect using one or more select devices. What this means is that you can use more than one modem to connect to more than one modem at the remote site. The result ends up being speedier communications.

NOTE: Multilink is enabled simply by selecting two or more devices and providing the necessary phone numbers.

A checkbox sets all devices to dial the same phone number. Choose this option if there is a "lead" phone number associated with a hunt group attached to a modem bank. Each modem has its own phone number, but all inbound communications are associated with the lead phone number. The lead phone number is attached to a single modem, but if that modem/phone line is busy, the call will roll over to the next modem/phone line in the group, and so on. Administratively, this is no more difficult to configure and set up than separate phone numbers for each modem anyway. The advantage is that your users only need to know one phone number.

The Security tab, shown in Figure 18.6, is used to configure several security settings. You can select whether to use typical (recommended) settings or advanced (customized) settings for security. This is where you would enable smart card usage. (See Chapter 19 for more information on Windows 2000 security.) During your dial-up session, you have the ability to define whether secured passwords will be enabled as opposed to unsecured passwords. Basically, it's recommended that you use secured passwords for basic security reasons, however you may be unable to do so if you're using non-Windows clients. When secured passwords are required, automatic use of the local/network logon name and password can

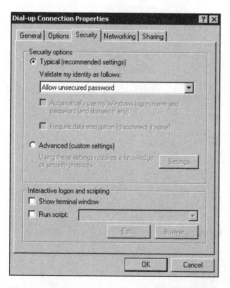

Figure 18.6   A Dial-Up To Private Network connection object's Security tab.

be enabled. This particular feature can become annoying if the local logon name and password are different from the logon name and password of the dial-up server to whom you are connecting.

TIP: *You can automatically encrypt communications by enabling data encryption, but this option is available only when secured passwords or smart cards are enabled. Figure 18.7 shows advanced encryption settings.*

As shown in Figure 18.6, you can configure an automated logon script. Sample scripts are included with Windows 2000 in the %systemroot%\System32\RAS\ folder. These sample scripts can be customized for your own needs using any text editor.

The Networking tab, shown in Figure 18.8, is used to configure network settings. Basically, all you really need to be concerned with here is how the remote server deals with TCP/IP.

If you need to share this particular connection with other systems on your local area network, use the Sharing tab, shown in Figure 18.9. If you enable Internet Connection Sharing, you'll be notified that the computer's IP address will be changed to 192.168.0.1.

TIP: *When using Internet Connection Sharing (ICS), you can enable on-demand dialing for the connection. This means that anytime another computer on the network requires the connection, the connecting machine will automatically dial the connection. Personally, I've found this handy, but not 100% reliable. If the connection dumps for some reason, the system will redial automatically, but I've never seen it actually demand dial.*

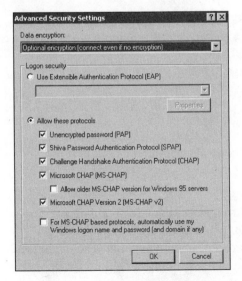

Figure 18.7   The Advanced Security Settings dialog box.

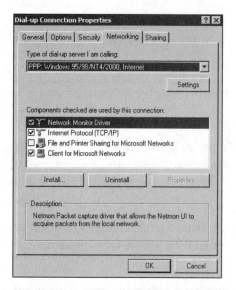

Figure 18.8   A Dial-Up To Private Network connection object's Networking tab.

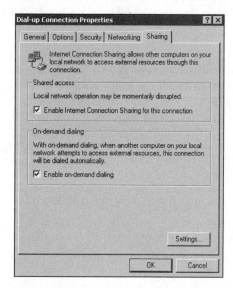

Figure 18.9   A Dial-Up To Private Network connection object's Sharing tab.

Dial-Up To The Internet

The Dial-Up To The Internet connection object is used to establish a link with an ISP to obtain Internet access. This object can be configured to create a new Microsoft Network (MSN) account, transfer an existing MSN account to this system, connect to the Internet using a modem, or connect to the Internet across a local area network (LAN). The Properties dialog box for this type of connection object is the same as a Dial-Up To Private Network connection object.

See Chapter 6 for more information about Internet access, utilities, and services related to Windows 2000.

Connect To A Private Network Through The Internet

The Connect To A Private Network Through The Internet connection object is used to establish a VPN connection across the Internet using PPTP or L2TP. VPN connections encrypt all data transferred between the client and server and enable long-distance connections without the associated long-distance charges. The RAS server that you are connecting to must have an Accept Incoming Connections connection object properly defined to accept your connection.

The Properties dialog box for this connection object type is similar to the previous two objects. The General tab sets the domain name or IP address of the VPN server and whether to connect to the Internet using an alternate connection object first. The Options tab sets dialing options and redial (reattempt) parameters. The Security tab sets the security requirements for the connection. The Networking tab sets the VPN server type to automatic, PPTP, or L2TP, and it binds available network components to this object. The Sharing tab enables Internet Connection Sharing and on-demand dialing for this connection.

Accept Incoming Connections

The Accept Incoming Connections connection object is used to transform a system into a RAS server that accepts inbound connections from VPN, ISDN, X.25, telephone lines, or direct cable mediums.

The Properties dialog box for this type of connection has three tabs: General, Users, and Networking. The General tab sets the devices or connection types that can accept inbound calls and whether to allow VPN connections. The Users tab sets which users have permission to connect to this RAS server and configures user-specific security settings, such as callback. The Networking tab sets the binding for networking components to this object.

Connect Directly To Another Computer

The Connect Directly To Another Computer connection object is used to create a link between two systems without using NICs. This type of connection can take place across a serial cable, a parallel cable, or infrared (IR) ports. Before creating this link, go ahead and attach the cable or orient the IR ports. You'll need to create one of these objects on each system, selecting one to be the host (server) and the other to be the guest (client).

18. Remote Access, Remote Control, and Windows 2000

The Properties dialog box for the host connection object is the same as an Accept Incoming Connections connection object. The Properties dialog box for the guest connection object is the same as a Dial-Up To Private Network connection object.

Remote Access as a Server

With the help of wizards, configuring Remote Access, from a Windows 2000 Server perspective, is actually quite easy. If you want to provide remote users access to your network, several options are available, all of which use the same basic components that are automatically flavored (by those handy-dandy wizards) to suit the method of remote access. The largest of these basic components is routing. In order to configure remote access, you'll need to set up your server with both security and authentication protocols. However, you also need to set up routing in order to allow outside communications to wander around the internal network as if the remote user were on site. Windows 2000 server supports, out of the box, remote access through dial-up modems, VPN, and as a router between two subnets or networks. Routing And Remote Access Server (RRAS) is the means by which it accomplishes these things.

For most environments, you'll be implementing remote access through VPN rather than dial-up for several reasons. It's usually cheaper for the company, especially if you have traveling personnel. With a dial-up remote access connection, a person who is accessing the system remotely will either pay high long distance bills from the hotel room by dialing into the local phone number attached to your modem, or you will pay higher long-distance bills for maintaining an 800 number for the remote user's convenience. Instead, all you'll need to do is configure VPN on your server and set up your traveling personnel with nationwide ISP accounts that have local access numbers. This will eliminate the long distance fees while still providing remote access for your users and speedier Web access, too. By far, if the corporate security policy does not require dedicated-line or callback features, use VPN.

Remote Authentication Dial-In User Service and Internet Authentication Service

I've had people ask me about Remote Authentication Dial-In User Service (RADIUS) just because the word sounds nifty and is synonymous with remote access. The truth of the matter is that, unless you're (a) using dial-up as your remote access method of choice along with several servers acting in that capacity or (b) you want to maintain security logs for access and authentication, you don't need a RADIUS server. RADIUS, put simply, is a centralized server that handles all authentication and logging for remote access. It's only necessary when you're dealing with multiple RRAS servers, or when you specifically want to track who is remotely accessing the network. Remember that you can track general system logons through auditing, so, if you're seriously looking at logging, you may consider the built-in tools as an effective alternative to RADIUS.

As I briefly mentioned before, RADIUS is something of a mystery unless you've specifically looked into it. It's not a brand name of server, but rather a type of server in the same way as Domain Name Service (DNS) is a type of server. Microsoft's answer to RADIUS is Internet Authentication Service (IAS). IAS can be installed from the Add/Remove Programs applet within Control Panel. Keep in mind that RADIUS will use valuable system resources, so you'll only want to use it if you require centralized authentication (for when you have multiple dial-up servers) or remote access logging for both dial-up and VPN connections.

Installing and Configuring RRAS

Before you even consider configuring RRAS on your server, you must have two communications devices installed on the server. By this, I mean that you must have either one NIC and at least one modem or two NICs. The purpose of this is to enable the server to isolate and appropriately route network traffic effectively from one connection to the other. The second NIC or modem in this case is being used to connect to the remote network (be it the Internet, another subnet, or dial-up), and RRAS binds it all together by generating a routing table and only allowing configured traffic through specific ports to travel between the two connections.

Configuring remote access for Windows 2000 server is simply done by getting into Administrative tools and then starting the Routing and Remote Access snap-in. From there, you right-click the server, and choose the Configuration option from the pop-up menu. You'll be presented with options to configure this server as a gateway for Internet Connection Sharing, remote access using dial-up, remote access using VPN, or as a network router between two networks or subnets.

Phone And Modem Options

The Phone And Modem Options applet in the Control Panel is used to manage location-based dialing rules; configure modems; and add, remove, or configure the Telephone Application Programming Interface (TAPI) service providers. Location-based dialing rules are profiles used by dial-out connection objects to define how to establish a communication link across standard telephone lines. These profiles include settings such as area code, open line prefix, disable call waiting, and make credit card calls. The ability to manage modem configurations is the same as that found in the Device Manager. Managing TAPI services is usually unnecessary because they offer few user settings and are installed automatically based on connection types.

Immediate Solutions

Installing Terminal Services

To support terminal clients, Terminal Services must be installed on a Windows 2000 Server system. This can be performed during initial installation of the OS, through the Configure Your Server Wizard, or using the Control Panel (as described here):

NOTE: *Windows 2000 Server is required for this solution.*

1. Log into the system as administrator.
2. Open the Control Panel, and double-click the Add/Remove Programs applet.
3. Click Add/Remove Windows Components.
4. Click Next.
5. Locate and select Terminal Services from the list of components.
6. If you will be using Terminal Services in Applications Server mode, you should also select Terminal Services Licensing (see Figure 18.10).
7. Click Next.

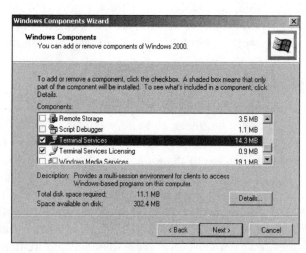

Figure 18.10   Installing Terminal Services and Terminal Services Licensing.

8. Select whether to use Terminal Services in Remote Administration mode or Application Server mode (see Figure 18.11).

9. Click Next.

10. Select whether Terminal Services will use permissions exclusive to Windows 2000 or will employ permissions compatible with any Terminal Services-compatible client (see Figure 18.12).

11. Click Next.

12. The wizard displays a list of possible problematic applications (see Figure 18.13). Review this list.

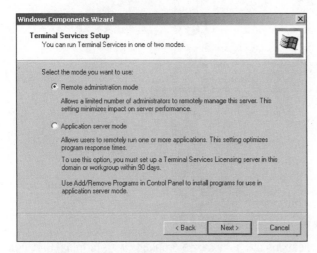

Figure 18.11   Selecting the Terminal Services mode.

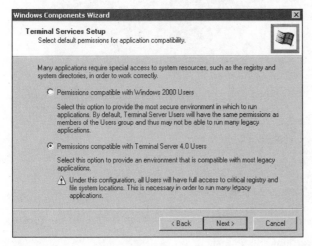

Figure 18.12   Selecting the Terminal Services user permissions.

13. Click Next.

14. Select whether to make the license server available only to this domain or workgroup or to the entire enterprise (see Figure 18.14). (This item only appears if Terminal Services Licensing was selected.)

15. Click Next.

16. Provide the Windows 2000 Server CD-ROM when or if prompted.

17. When prompted, click Finish.

18. When prompted, reboot the system.

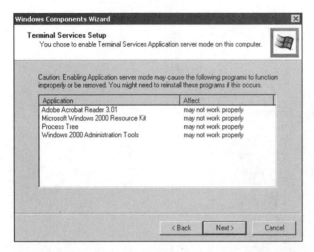

Figure 18.13   Identifying applications that may cause problems with Terminal Services.

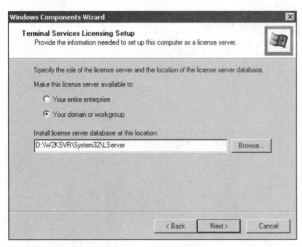

Figure 18.14   Selecting the Terminal Services licensing setup.

Creating a Network Distribution Point for Terminal Services

A *network distribution* point is a shared folder where the client software installation files reside. To create a network distribution point, perform the following steps:

1. Launch Windows Explorer or My Computer.

2. Locate and select the %systemroot%\system32\clients\tsclient\net folder. The Terminal Services installation automatically created it.

3. Select File|Sharing.

4. Select the Share This Folder radio button, and define a share name, such as TSClients.

5. Click Permissions. Change the Everyone group's permissions to Read Only (that is, deselect the Full Control and Modify permissions). Click OK.

6. Click OK.

Creating Terminal Services Installation Disk Sets

If a terminal client-to-be device is not already connected to the network or is unable to access the network distribution point, you can create a set of installation floppies. To create Terminal Services installation disks, perform the following steps:

1. Gather floppies. Four disks are required for the 16-bit client. Two disks are required for the 32-bit client.

2. Launch the Terminal Services Client Creator tool from Administrative Tools.

3. Select either the 16-bit client or the 32-bit client.

4. Select the correct letter for the floppy drive.

5. Select whether to format the disks.

6. Click OK.

7. Follow the prompts to insert the disks.

8. As you remove the disks, be sure to label them properly (for example, Terminal Services client 16-bit disk 1/4).

Installing the Terminal Services Client Software

To install the client software for Terminal Services, perform the following steps:

NOTE: *This solution can only be performed for Windows 95, Windows 98, Windows NT, and Windows 2000 clients. Special instructions are included in the Windows 2000 Resource Kit and the Windows 2000 manuals for installing the client software on Windows CE clients.*

1. If you want to install from a floppy set, place the first disk in the floppy drive.
2. Select Start|Run.
3. Click Browse.
4. Locate the setup.exe file from either the local floppy or the network distribution point. (This is the share named TSClients from an earlier solution.)
5. Agree to the license agreement.
6. Select to install the software for all users.

Connecting to a Terminal Services Server from a Terminal Services Client

The whole purpose of the Terminal Services client software is to establish communication sessions with the Terminal Services server. This can be accomplished in two ways. Either use the Terminal Services client from Administrative Tools to connect immediately, or create a connection profile with unique settings and then employ that profile to connect. Here are the steps to follow:

1. Launch the Client Connection Manager.
2. Select File|New Connection.
3. Click Next.
4. Define a name for the connection profile, and then provide the server name or IP address of the terminal server.
5. Click Next.
6. Select whether to enable automatic logon for this connection profile. If this is enabled, provide the user account logon credentials.
7. Click Next.

8. Select a screen resolution and whether to display the connection full screen. Click Next.

9. Select whether to enable data compression and/or caching of bitmaps. Click Next.

10. Select if a program or batch file should be launched upon logging in. If this option is selected, provide the path to the executable or batch file and the startup directory. Click Next.

11. Select an icon to associate with this connection profile and then select a program group in the Start menu where this connection profile will be placed. Click Next.

12. Click Finish.

13. Double-click the connection profile object from within the Client Connection Manager, or select it from its location in the Start menu to connect to the terminal server.

There is another Terminal Services client called the Terminal Services Advanced Client (TSAC) that serves Terminal sessions over an Internet connection. This is actually rather fast and definitely easier to handle on the client side. The TSAC is freely downloadable from the Microsoft Web site.

Creating a Dial-Up To Private Network Connection Object

To establish a network link with a remote network (a Dial-Up To Private Network connection object is required), perform the following steps:

1. Double-click the Make New Connection icon in the Network And Dial-Up Connections utility. The Network Connection Wizard launches. Click Next.

2. Select the Dial-Up To Private Network radio button. Click Next.

3. Select one or more communication devices for this object by marking their checkboxes.

4. Provide the dial-up phone number to the remote network's RAS server.

5. If this system is a portable computer, select the Use Dialing Rules checkbox, and provide the area code and select the country/region code. Click Next.

6. Select whether to allow all users of this computer to use this connection object or restrict access to just your user account. Click Next.

7. Provide a name for this connection object.

8. Select whether to add a shortcut for this connection object to the desktop by marking the appropriate checkbox.

9. Click Finish.

Creating a Dial-Up To The Internet Connection Object

To establish a link to the Internet (a Dial-Up To The Internet connection object is required), perform the following steps:

1. Double-click the Make New Connection icon in the Network And Dial-Up Connections utility. The Network Connection Wizard launches. Click Next.

2. Select the Dial-Up To The Internet radio button. Click Next.

3. Select one of the following options. For this solution, select to Configure The Internet Connection Manually.

   • Create A New Internet Account (creates a new MSN account)

   • Transfer An Existing Internet Account To This Computer (transfers an existing MSN account)

   • Configure Internet Connection Manually Or Connect Through A LAN (allows you to dial any ISP or use LAN Internet access)

4. Click Next.

5. Select whether to create a connection object that uses a modem or the LAN to obtain Internet access.

6. Click Next. If you selected LAN, skip to Step 14.

7. Select the communication device. Click Next.

8. Provide the telephone number for the ISP. Verify the settings for area code and country/region. Click Next.

9. Enter the username and password used to log in to the ISP. Click Next.

10. Type in a name for the connection object. Click Next.

11. If you need to configure Outlook Express for Internet email, select Yes. Otherwise, select No. Click Next.

12. If you selected Yes to configure Outlook Express, provide the requested information for profile name, email address, email server addresses, and email server logon credentials. Click Next.

13. Deselect the To Connect To The Internet Immediately, Select This Box Then Click Finish checkbox. Click Finish.

14. By selecting a LAN connection, you must provide the details to obtain Internet access on the LAN. This may be using automatic detection, a configuration script at a uniform resource locator (URL), a manually configured proxy server, or direct routing (clear all checkboxes). Click Next.

15. If your LAN uses a proxy server, you may be presented with further proxy-specific configuration settings. Usually the defaults are correct. Click Next to continue.

16. If your LAN uses a proxy server, you may be presented with the option to provide addresses that will bypass the proxy when accessed. Configure as necessary, and then click Next.

17. If you need to configure Outlook Express for Internet email, select Yes. Otherwise, select No. Click Next.

18. If you selected Yes to configure Outlook Express, provide the requested information for profile name, email address, email server addresses, and email server logon credentials.

19. Click Next.

20. Deselect the To Connect To The Internet Immediately, Select This Box Then Click Finish checkbox.

Creating a Connect To A Private Network Through The Internet Connection Object

To establish a VPN link across the Internet (a Connect To A Private Network Through The Internet connection object is required), perform the following steps:

1. Double-click the Make New Connection icon in the Network And Dial-Up Connections utility. The Network Connection Wizard launches. Click Next.

2. Select the Connect To A Private Network Through The Internet radio button. Click Next.

3. Select whether to dial an Internet connection object. If this option is selected, also select which defined connection object should be used to establish an Internet connection before the VPN link is attempted. Click Next.

4. Supply the domain name or IP address of the Windows 2000 or Windows NT RAS server that you will establish a VPN connection with across the Internet. Click Next.

5. Select whether this link will be used by all users or just your user account. Click Next.

6. Type in a name for the connection object. Click Finish.

Creating an Accept Incoming Connections Connection Object

To answer inbound calls to your system (an Accept Incoming Connections connection object is required), perform the following steps:

1. Double-click the Make New Connection icon in the Network And Dial-Up Connections utility. The Network Connection Wizard launches. Click Next.

2. Select the Accept Incoming Connections radio button. Click Next.

3. Select one or more devices across which inbound connections will be answered. Click Next.

4. Select whether to allow VPN connections across inbound links. Click Next.

5. Select which users will be granted permission to connect to this system using this connection object. Click Next.

6. Alter any bindings and change any network component configurations for this connection object. Click Next.

7. Type in a name for the connection object. Click Finish.

Creating a Connect Directly To Another Computer Connection Object

To establish a direct link to another computer across a serial, parallel, or IR port (a Connect Directly To Another Computer connection object is required), perform the following steps:

NOTE: *Two Connect Directly To Another Computer connection objects must be created, one on each computer (that is, one configured as the host and the other configured as the guest).*

1. On the system to serve as the host (server), double-click the Make New Connection icon in the Network And Dial-Up Connections utility. The Network Connection Wizard launches. Click Next.

2. Select the Connect Directly To Another Computer radio button. Click Next.

3. Select the Host radio button. Click Next.

4. Select the device type for the link. Click Next.

5. Select the users to grant permission to use this connection object. Click Next.

6. Type in a name for this connection object. Click Finish.

7. On the system to serve as the guest (client), double-click the Make New Connection icon in the Network And Dial-Up Connections utility. The Network Connection Wizard launches.

8. Click Next.

9. Select the Connect Directly To Another Computer radio button. Click Next.

10. Select the Guest radio button. Click Next.

11. Select the device type for the link (it must be the same as the host's). Click Next.

12. Select the users to grant permission to use this connection object. Click Next.

13. Type in a name for this connection object. Click Finish.

14. In the Connect Direct Connection dialog box, provide your username and password.

15. Click Connect to establish the connection.

Working with RRAS

RRAS is the Windows 2000 answer to remote access. Windows 2000 will support remote access through a modem or dial-up connection and VPN. RRAS will also allow you to configure the server as an Internet gateway or to connect to another network or subnet.

Configuring Remote Access Using Dial-up

1. Click Start, and select Programs|Administrative Tools|Routing And Remote Access.

2. In the left pane of the Microsoft Management Console (MMC) snap-in, right-click the server object labeled with the server name.

3. Select Configure|Enable Routing And Remote Access from the pop-up menu.

4. The Routing and Remote Access Server Setup Wizard will appear. Click Next.

5. Select the Remote Access Server radio button, and click Next.

6. Ensure that the radio button labeled Yes, All Of The Required Protocols Are On This List is selected, and click Next.

NOTE: *You have the option here to add protocols, but keep in mind that the more protocols you use across these links, the less secure your network becomes.*

---

7. RRAS will automatically assign TCP/IP address information to the dial-up clients. If you're running Dynamic Host Configuration Protocol (DHCP), choose the radio button labeled Automatically. If you're not running DHCP, choose the radio button labeled From a Specified Range of Addresses, and fill in the appropriate range of IP addresses from which RRAS can draw from.

8. Click Next.

9. If you are configuring more than one dial-up server, you may consider installing and configuring IAS as a RADIUS server. If you have already installed IAS, you will want to choose to configure RRAS to use a RADIUS server. If this is the case, select the radio button labeled Yes, I Want To Use A RADIUS Server. Otherwise, select No, I Don't Want To Set Up This Server To Use RADIUS Now.

10. Click Next, and click Finish to complete the configuration process.

Configuring Remote Access Through a VPN

To configure remote access through a VPN, perform the following steps:

1. Click Start, and select Programs|Administrative Tools|Routing And Remote Access.

2. In the left pane of the MMC snap-in, right-click the server object labeled with the server name.

3. Select Configure|Enable Routing and Remote Access from the pop-up menu.

4. The Routing and Remote Access Server Setup Wizard will appear. Click Next.

5. Select the Virtual Private Network Server radio button, and click Next.

6. Ensure that the radio button labeled Yes, All Of The Required Protocols Are On This List is selected, and click Next.

NOTE: *You have the option here to add protocols, but keep in mind that the more protocols you use across these links, the less secure that your network becomes.*

7. The Internet Connection dialog box will appear. Choose the NIC that leads to the Internet, and click Next.

8. RRAS will automatically assign TCP/IP address information to the dial-up clients. If you're running DHCP, choose the radio button labeled Automatically. If you're not running DHCP, choose the radio button labeled From A Specified Range Of Addresses, and fill in the appropriate range of IP addresses from which RRAS can draw from.

9. Click Next.

10. If you are configuring more than one dial-up server, you may consider installing and configuring IAS as a RADIUS server. If you have already installed IAS, you will want to choose to configure RRAS to use a RADIUS server. If this is the case, select the radio button labeled Yes, I Want To Use A RADIUS server. Otherwise, select No, I Don't Want To Set Up This Server To Use RADIUS Now.

11. Click Next, and click Finish to complete the configuration process.

Stopping RRAS

To stop RRAS, perform the following steps:

1. Click Start, and select Programs|Administrative Tools|Routing and Remote Access.

2. In the left pane of the MMC snap-in, right-click the server object labeled with the server name.

3. Select Disable Routing And Remote Access from the pop-up menu.

NOTE: *Be aware that if you stop RRAS in this method, you will be required to reconfigure it again in order to get it back up and running.*

Enabling Domain Users for Remote Access

RRAS has its own Remote Access Policy that denies access to everyone on the system at all times. With this particular policy in place, the only way that someone can remotely access the system is by performing the following steps:

1. Click Start, and select Programs|Administrative Tools|Active Directory Users And Computers.

2. Right-click the user that requires remote access, and select Properties from the pop-up menu.

3. Select the Dial-In tab, and select the Allow Access radio button.

4. Click OK, and close the Active Directory Users And Computers console.

NOTE: *Microsoft officially recommends that you set RRAS options via a group policy, or configure RADIUS to use a centralized RRAS policy. Personally, configuring a template account to grant or deny remote access is easier than either of these options if all I want is simple dial-up.*

Configuring Callback Options for Remote Access Users

RRAS has an option to call back remote access users on demand. What happens is that, when the remote access user calls the RRAS server, the user's computer identifies itself and then hangs up. The RRAS server then calls the user's computer back. When the user's computer answers the line, the remaining authentication steps take place, and the connection is established. There are basically two options. You can have the server call back a phone number that is entered by the user during the first half of the transaction or always call back to a specified number. This is a valuable feature for higher security situations where you want to ensure that the remote user is accessing network data in a fully authorized manner. To configure callback options, perform the following steps:

1. Click Start, and select Programs|Administrative Tools|Active Directory Users And Computers.

2. Right-click the user that requires dial-up options, and select Properties from the pop-up menu.

3. Select the Dial-In tab, and select Set by Caller or Always Callback To.

4. Click OK, and close the Active Directory Users And Computers console.

Chapter 19

Security

In Depth

It is the administrator's job to make sure that a network and all its data are secure. Windows 2000 provides a number of features to assist in this quest. An administrator must prevent unauthorized access to information and damage (either unintentional or malicious) to data and systems. However, security restrictions should not prevent authorized users from getting access to the data that they require. The following Windows 2000 features help secure various components of a server:

- Extensible Authentication Protocol (EAP)
- Kerberos 5
- Microsoft Challenge Handshake Authentication Protocol 2 (MS-CHAP 2)
- Password Authentication Protocol (PAP)
- Secure Sockets Layer/Transport Layer Security (SSL/TLS)
- Windows NT Local Area Network (LAN) Manager (NTLM)

Kerberos 5

Windows 2000 implements a standardized domain authentication method known as Kerberos. The purpose of using Kerberos is primarily additional security. However, because Kerberos is an industry standard, it does mean that Windows 2000 can finally boast secure interoperability with other applications and operating systems, such as Unix.

Kerberos authentication is used in Windows 2000 domains containing Windows 2000 clients. Windows 3.x, Windows 9x, and Windows NT systems all function within a Windows 2000 domain, but they do not use Kerberos authentication. Instead, they use NTLM authentication for domain authentication and also for local logons and workgroup networking.

Kerberos operates by adding an additional security gate between a Windows 2000 system and the resource that it is attempting to access. This security gate is known as the Key Distribution Center (KDC). When a client system requests access to another system (the Products server in Figure 19.1), the KDC sends the client an encrypted message (Figure 19.2). If the client can decrypt the message correctly, the KDC then gives it a ticket known as a session key, which is a pass indicating that the client has passed through the gate. From there, the KDC creates another ticket for the client and sends a copy to the Products server. Once the client goes

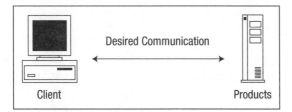

Figure 19.1   A Kerberos example.

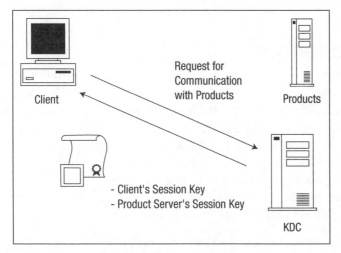

Figure 19.2   Key-encrypted communication.

to the Products server for final authentication, the Products server ensures that the client is carrying the same ticket as it is holding, and grants appropriate resource access (see Figure 19.3).

After the server receives this information, it decrypts the client's ticket using the session key that it shares with the KDC. This is how the server ensures that the client is not carrying a forged ticket. If all of this is successful, the Product server now trusts the client and can communicate with it.

TIP: *The session key, or ticket, has a limited lifespan and may only be used for a single logon session. After it expires, a new session key must be generated.*

This process is a bit complicated, but it also creates a very secure method of authentication, which makes Windows 2000 the most secure Microsoft operating system ever.

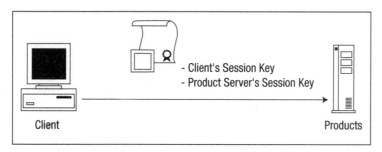

- Client's Session Key
- Product Server's Session Key

Client   Products

Figure 19.3   Session communication.

Keys and Certificates

One of the ways that encryption occurs is through a public and private keying system called public key infrastructure (PKI). Although it may be difficult to understand, the process has been in use for quite a while now. Rather than attempt to explain the specifics on how PKI works, it's easier to give you an example. Let's say that you need to send an encrypted message to me. In order to send it, you must encrypt it specifically to me so that nobody but me can decrypt it. In order to make that happen, I generate a public and a private key and give you the public key. You use that public key to encrypt the message specifically to me and send it. When I get the message, I decrypt it using my private key.

I've personally used applications, such as Pretty Good Privacy (PGP), to encrypt emails and documents on my system. The process is simple. I encrypt the data and then choose a public key from a list of public keys to encrypt the data with. This effectively ensures that only one person (whoever has the private key that goes with that public key) can decrypt the data. When I installed PGP, the program generated a public and private key. I subsequently trade public keys with other people using the same program. When I receive a key, I install it into PGP, and, after that, I'm able to send messages and encrypt to the person whose public key I just installed.

PGP relies heavily on user intervention to encrypt and decrypt data. Windows 2000, on the other hand, uses certificates and the certification authority (CA) to do almost everything for you seamlessly. Instead of manually trading public keys, systems called CAs issue certificates that contain their public key along with several other pieces of information, such as an expiration, that add value and security to the overall system. After a system has received a certificate for a target recipient, it can automatically encrypt information for that system.

Additionally, Windows 2000 certificates are issued by a centralized server called a *certificate authority (CA)*. The CA handles and distributes certificates on behalf of the client computers on the network. Similar to a power of attorney, the CA has the authority to manage my certificates and to distribute my certificates to others on the network.

Certificate administration comes in two flavors: client and server. The client side of certificate management comes from the Certificates Microsoft Management Console (MMC) snap-in that can be launched by typing "CERTMGR.MSC" in the Run line from the Start menu. Certificates will show you the current valid (as opposed to expired) certificates that are active on your system. Server certificate management comes after installing Certificate Services on the server. After installation, certificates are distributed by the newly installed CA using Group Policies (Computer Configuration|Security Settings|Public Key Policies).

Smart Cards

Smart cards seem to be the latest of black box buzzwords. By this, I mean that they sound really nifty. Smart cards are additional pieces of authentication equipment, usually a credit card-sized piece of plastic that requires a cardreader at each computer, but sometimes a Smart Card is a small key that plugs into a Universal Serial Bus (USB), parallel, or serial port on a client system. These smart cards must be present in order for login and authentication to occur.

Smart cards require Certificate Services to be present on the network because the cards themselves act as repositories for a user's certificates. Although Windows 2000 supports smart card implementation, it does not do so natively. If you're interested in this additional level of security, you'll need to investigate third-party software packages to determine the feature set and implementation that's best for your company. When you check out these third-party packages, be sure to inquire as to whether the hardware (the card writers and readers for each client machine) is both Windows 2000-compliant and included in the package or if it needs to be purchased separately.

Internet Protocol Security Policies

Internet Protocol Security (IPSec) is a means of encrypting network traffic. By default, domain communications are initialized using Kerberos authentication, which is in itself encrypted. These types of Kerberos communications are encrypted, but only for the authentication and authorization processes. Simple data transfers are performed with no encryption enabled. IPSec is a method of data encryption that allows a fuller and more robustly secure system. IPSec allows various shades of implementation through IPSec policies within Group Policy. Using IPSec Policies (available within Group Policy Computer Configuration| Windows Settings|Security Settings|IP Security Policies in Active Directory), you have the ability to require secure communications (this would be the Secure Server option); request, but not require, secure communications (this is the Server option); or respond with secure communications when requested to do so (this is the Client option).

When you create an IPSec policy, you do have the option to use certificates, but, if you do not have Certificate Services enabled, you'll need to use the Windows 2000 default authentication method, which uses Kerberos 5.

Working with Hot Fixes and Service Packs

One of the inevitable tasks of administering an operating system as large and complex as Windows 2000 is installing updates. Microsoft provides two different types of updates: hot fixes and service packs. As you would expect with an operating system as complex as Windows 2000 (or any other operating system for that matter), flaws, security holes, and bugs will exist. These are fixed using hot fixes and service packs.

Hot fixes are usually used to fix any major bugs or security holes. These are applied individually, but they usually must be applied in a specific order. A list of the currently available hot fixes can be found on the Microsoft Web site.

Service packs are a collection of hot fixes and add-ons. Any time that a hot fix is released, it is automatically added to the service pack that will be released next. Service packs also include product enhancements that are associated with fixing other issues. Some of the utilities and applications that Microsoft was working on for Windows 2000 were either not finished or not stable enough to release with the operating system in February 2000. These utilities and applications are therefore included in the service packs. Many administrators install the service packs to keep ahead of hackers and to protect their operating system from intrusion. What many do not realize is that the service packs are much more than that; they enhance the operating system as well. Service packs can be downloaded from the Microsoft Web site.

The normal steps involved in applying hot fixes and service packs are to install the most recent service pack and then install the hot fixes released after that service pack (known as the *post-service pack hot fixes*).

One of the major drawbacks with service packs in the past (with Windows NT) was that a service pack had to be reapplied every time that a new application was installed on the system. The reason for this is simple. Suppose that the required.dll file that ships on the Windows 2000 CD has a security hole in it. The administrator therefore applies a service pack (or hot fix) that replaces required.dll with a fixed version. Next, an application that relies on required.dll is installed. As with many applications, the required.dll file that was used in the creation of the application is also copied to the system. If this required.dll file is the one with the security hole, the fix applied by the service pack or hot fix has been reversed. The service pack or hot fix must therefore be reapplied.

With Windows 2000, Microsoft has come up with a new method of installing service packs to prevent this problem. This method is known as *slipstreaming*. Slipstreaming assumes that the Windows 2000 installation files (the i386 directory) exist either on the system or on a network share. An administrator can then apply the service pack to this directory. The service pack will then fix any issues with the original files. Any time files (such as required.dll) are needed, the updated ones will be used from this folder. This means that service packs need only be applied once.

Several command-line switches are available to the administrator when installing service packs. These switches, along with their descriptions, are shown in Table 19.1.

Auditing for Security

Much like in Windows NT, Windows 2000 enables the administrator to control what access is audited by the system. Windows 2000, however, does provide some extra auditing features not found in Windows NT.

Here's a list of the available audit policies:

- Audit Account Logon Events
- Audit Account Management
- Audit Directory Service Access
- Audit Logon Events
- Audit Object Access
- Audit Policy Change

Table 19.1   The service pack command-line switches.

Switch	Description
/f	Forces all running applications to shut down before the system is restarted.
/n	Does not back up the current information before installing the service pack. This does not allow the administrator to uninstall the service pack.
/o	Overwrites all original equipment manufacturer (OEM) files without asking the operator for permission.
/q	Runs the service pack installation in Quiet mode. No user intervention is required.
/s	Slipstreams the installation.
/u	Runs an unattended service pack installation.
/z	Does not restart the system when the installation of the service pack is completed.

- Audit Privilege Use
- Audit Process Tracking
- Audit System Events

It is important to note that enabling some of these policies starts auditing immediately, whereas others are just an intermediary step (as with object access). For example, when an administrator enables the audit policy, an event will be logged immediately in the Security section of the Event Viewer and will specify that the audit policy has been modified. On the other hand, no events will be logged when the administrator enables the audit object Access Audit Policy (unless, of course, the Audit Policy Change policy is enabled). After the audit object Access Audit Policy is enabled, the administrator must selectively specify which users (and/or groups) that the policy is to be applied to and which objects should be audited for access.

Auditing is logged as one of two events: a success or a failure. These audit log entries are viewed in the Security Log section of the Event Viewer (see Figure 19.4). Successful audits are displayed with a key icon, and failed audits use a lock icon.

It is important to control what is audited rather than turning all success and failure events on for all audit policies. Even on a rarely used server, turning everything on will overload both the system logs and the administrator who's attempting

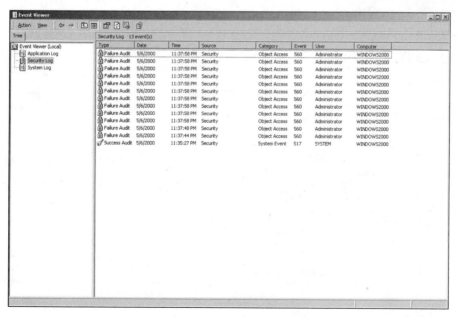

Figure 19.4   Viewing audited events in the Event Viewer.

to go through the log files. Only turn on the audit policies that make sense for your organization. For example, failed logon attempts are much more useful than successful logon events unless you're tracking usage for accounts that should see little or no usage. (Many of us assign Administrative privileges to all of our IT admins and subsequently 'lockup' the Administrator password. It may be wise to audit successful logons for the Administrator in order to track unauthorized usage.) Also, unauthorized access to your company's confidential information (such as payroll) is more important than unauthorized access to nonsensitive information (such as what is being served for lunch on Thursday). In situations such as this, both the successful and failed attempts should be logged on the sensitive information, and no auditing should be logged on the nonsensitive information. This is another reason why object access is audited on a per-object basis rather than an all-or-none basis.

About Organizational Security Policies

Two tools allow an administrator to control security policies: Local Security Policy and Domain Security Policy. The one used depends on the configuration. Their names are self-explanatory. The first is used to apply security to the local machine, and the latter is used to apply security policies to the domain.

Local Security Policy is divided into four sections: account policies (which include password and account lockout policies), local policies (which include audit policies, user rights assignment, and security options), public key policies (which include encrypted data recovery agents), and IPSec policies. Table 19.2 lists all the local policies and their containers.

Table 19.2   Local security policies.

Policy	Location
Enforce Password History	Account Policies|Password Policy
Maximum Password Age	Account Policies|Password Policy
Minimum Password Age	Account Policies|Password Policy
Minimum Password Length	Account Policies|Password Policy
Passwords Must Meet Complexity Requirements	Account Policies|Password Policy
Store Passwords Using Reversible Encryption For All Users	Account Policies|Password Policy
Account Lockout Duration	Account Policies|Account Lockout Policy
Account Lockout Threshold	Account Policies|Account Lockout Policy
Reset Account Lockout Counter After	Account Policies|Account Lockout Policy
Audit Account Logon Events	Local Policies|Audit Policy

(continued)

Table 19.2   Local security policies *(continued)*.

Policy	Location
Audit Account Management	Local Policies|Audit Policy
Audit Directory Service Access	Local Policies|Audit Policy
Audit Logon Events	Local Policies|Audit Policy
Audit Object Access	Local Policies|Audit Policy
Audit Policy Change	Local Policies|Audit Policy
Audit Privileged Use	Local Policies|Audit Policy
Audit Process Tracking	Local Policies|Audit Policy
Audit System Events	Local Policies|Audit Policy
Access This Computer From The Network	Local Policies|User Rights Assignment
Act As Part Of The Operating System	Local Policies|User Rights Assignment
Add Workstations To Domain	Local Policies|User Rights Assignment
Back Up Files And Directories	Local Policies|User Rights Assignment
Bypass Traverse Checking	Local Policies|User Rights Assignment
Change The System Time	Local Policies|User Rights Assignment
Create A Pagefile	Local Policies|User Rights Assignment
Create A Token Object	Local Policies|User Rights Assignment
Create Permanent Shared Objects	Local Policies|User Rights Assignment
Debug Programs	Local Policies|User Rights Assignment
Deny Access To This Computer From The Network	Local Policies|User Rights Assignment
Deny Logon As A Batch Job	Local Policies|User Rights Assignment
Deny Logon As A Service	Local Policies|User Rights Assignment
Deny Logon Locally	Local Policies|User Rights Assignment
Enable Computer And User Accounts To Be Trusted	Local Policies|User Rights Assignment
Force Shutdown From A Remote System	Local Policies|User Rights Assignment
Generate Security Audits	Local Policies|User Rights Assignment
Increase Quotas	Local Policies|User Rights Assignment
Increase Scheduling Priority	Local Policies|User Rights Assignment
Load And Unload Device Drivers	Local Policies|User Rights Assignment
Lock Pages In Memory	Local Policies|User Rights Assignment
Log On As A Batch Job	Local Policies|User Rights Assignment
Log On As A Service	Local Policies|User Rights Assignment
Log On Locally	Local Policies|User Rights Assignment

(continued)

Table 19.2   Local security policies *(continued).*

Policy	Location
Manage Auditing And Security Log	Local Policies|User Rights Assignment
Modify Firmware Environment Values	Local Policies|User Rights Assignment
Profile Single Process	Local Policies|User Rights Assignment
Profile System Performance	Local Policies|User Rights Assignment
Remove Computer From Docking Station	Local Policies|User Rights Assignment
Replace A Process Level Token	Local Policies|User Rights Assignment
Restore Files And Directories	Local Policies|User Rights Assignment
Shut Down The System	Local Policies|User Rights Assignment
Synchronize Directory Service Data	Local Policies|User Rights Assignment
Take Ownership Of Files Or Other Objects	Local Policies|User Rights Assignment
Additional Restrictions For Anonymous Connections	Local Policies|Security Options
Allow Server Operators To Schedule Tasks	Local Policies|Security Options
Allow System To Be Shut Down Without Having To Log On	Local Policies|Security Options
Allowed To Eject Removable NTFS Media	Local Policies|Security Options
Amount Of Idle Time Required Before Disconnecting Session	Local Policies|Security Options
Audit The Access Of Global System Objects	Local Policies|Security Options
Audit Use Of Backup And Restore Privilege	Local Policies|Security Options
Automatically Log Off Users When Logon Time Expires	Local Policies|Security Options
Clear Virtual Memory Pagefile When System Shuts Down	Local Policies|Security Options
Digitally Sign Client Communication (Always)	Local Policies|Security Options
Digitally Sign Client Communication (When Possible)	Local Policies|Security Options
Digitally Sign Server Communication (Always)	Local Policies|Security Options
Digitally Sign Server Communication (When Possible)	Local Policies|Security Options
Disable Ctrl+Alt+Delete Requirement For Logon	Local Policies|Security Options
Do Not Display Last Username In Logon Screen	Local Policies|Security Options
LAN Manager Authentication Level	Local Policies|Security Options
Message Text For Users Attempting To Log On	Local Policies|Security Options
Message Title For Users Attempting To Log On	Local Policies|Security Options
Number Of Previous Logons To Cache	Local Policies|Security Options
Prevent System Maintenance Of Computer Account Pwd	Local Policies|Security Options
Prevent Users From Installing Printer Drivers	Local Policies|Security Options
Prompt User To Change Password Before Expiration	Local Policies|Security Options

(continued)

Table 19.2   Local security policies *(continued)*.

Policy	Location
Recovery Console: Allow Automatic Administrative Logon	Local Policies|Security Options
Recovery Console: Allow Floppy Copy	Local Policies|Security Options
Rename Administrator Account	Local Policies|Security Options
Rename Guest Account	Local Policies|Security Options
Restrict CD-ROM Access To Locally Logged-On User Only	Local Policies|Security Options
Restrict Floppy Access To Locally Logged-On User Only	Local Policies|Security Options
Send Unencrypted Password To Connect To 3rd Part SMB	Local Policies|Security Options
Shut Down System Immediately If Unable To Log Security	Local Policies|Security Options
Smart Card Removal Behavior	Local Policies|Security Options
Strengthen Default Permissions	Local Policies|Security Options
Unsigned Driver Installation Behavior	Local Policies|Security Options
Unsigned Non-Driver Installation Behavior	Local Policies|Security Options

The second tool, Domain Security Policy, is used to configure the system policies for the entire domain. With exception to Domain Controllers, these policies override the ones set at the local level. Table 19.3 lists all the domain Group Policies and the containers in which they are located.

Table 19.3   Domain security policies.

Policy	Location
Enforce Password History	Account Policies|Password Policy
Maximum Password Age	Account Policies|Password Policy
Minimum Password Age	Account Policies|Password Policy
Minimum Password Length	Account Policies|Password Policy
Passwords Must Meet Complexity Requirements	Account Policies|Password Policy
Store Passwords Using Reversible Encryption For All Users	Account Policies|Password Policy
Account Lockout Duration	Account Policies|Account Lockout Policy
Account Lockout Threshold	Account Policies|Account Lockout Policy
Reset Account Lockout Counter After	Account Policies|Account Lockout Policy
Enforce User Logon Restrictions	Account Policies|Kerberos Policy
Maximum Lifetime For Service Ticket	Account Policies|Kerberos Policy
Maximum Lifetime For User Ticket	Account Policies|Kerberos Policy
Maximum Lifetime For User Ticket Renewal	Account Policies|Kerberos Policy

(continued)

Table 19.3   Domain security policies *(continued).*

Policy	Location
Maximum Tolerance For Computer Clock Synchronization	Account Policies|Kerberos Policy
Audit Account Logon Events	Local Policies|Audit Policy
Audit Account Management	Local Policies|Audit Policy
Audit Directory Service Access	Local Policies|Audit Policy
Audit Logon Events	Local Policies|Audit Policy
Audit Object Access	Local Policies|Audit Policy
Audit Policy Change	Local Policies|Audit Policy
Audit Privileged Use	Local Policies|Audit Policy
Audit Process Tracking	Local Policies|Audit Policy
Audit System Events	Local Policies|Audit Policy
Access This Computer From The Network	Local Policies|User Rights Assignment
Act As Part Of The Operating System	Local Policies|User Rights Assignment
Add Workstations To Domain	Local Policies|User Rights Assignment
Back Up Files And Directories	Local Policies|User Rights Assignment
Bypass Traverse Checking	Local Policies|User Rights Assignment
Change The System Time	Local Policies|User Rights Assignment
Create A Pagefile	Local Policies|User Rights Assignment
Create A Token Object	Local Policies|User Rights Assignment
Create Permanent Shared Objects	Local Policies|User Rights Assignment
Debug Programs	Local Policies|User Rights Assignment
Deny Access To This Computer From The Network	Local Policies|User Rights Assignment
Deny Logon As A Batch Job	Local Policies|User Rights Assignment
Deny Logon As A Service	Local Policies|User Rights Assignment
Deny Logon Locally	Local Policies|User Rights Assignment
Enable Computer And User Accounts To Be Trusted	Local Policies|User Rights Assignment
Force Shutdown From A Remote System	Local Policies|User Rights Assignment
Generate Security Audits	Local Policies|User Rights Assignment
Increase Quotas	Local Policies|User Rights Assignment
Increase Scheduling Priority	Local Policies|User Rights Assignment
Load And Unload Device Drivers	Local Policies|User Rights Assignment
Lock Pages In Memory	Local Policies|User Rights Assignment
Log On As A Batch Job	Local Policies|User Rights Assignment

(continued)

19. Security

Table 19.3   Domain security policies *(continued)*.

Policy	Location
Log On As A Service	Local Policies|User Rights Assignment
Log On Locally	Local Policies|User Rights Assignment
Manage Auditing And Security Log	Local Policies|User Rights Assignment
Modify Firmware Environment Values	Local Policies|User Rights Assignment
Profile Single Process	Local Policies|User Rights Assignment
Profile System Performance	Local Policies|User Rights Assignment
Remove Computer From Docking Station	Local Policies|User Rights Assignment
Replace A Process-Level Token	Local Policies|User Rights Assignment
Restore Files And Directories	Local Policies|User Rights Assignment
Shut Down The System	Local Policies|User Rights Assignment
Synchronize Directory Service Data	Local Policies|User Rights Assignment
Take Ownership Of Files Or Other Objects	Local Policies|User Rights Assignment
Additional Restrictions For Anonymous Connections	Local Policies|Security Options
Allow Server Operators To Schedule Tasks	Local Policies|Security Options
Allow System To Be Shut Down Without Having To Log On	Local Policies|Security Options
Allowed To Eject Removable NTFS Media	Local Policies|Security Options
Amount Of Idle Time Required Before Disconnecting Session	Local Policies|Security Options
Audit The Access Of Global System Objects	Local Policies|Security Options
Audit Use Of Backup And Restore Privilege	Local Policies|Security Options
Automatically Log Off Users When Logon Time Expires	Local Policies|Security Options
Clear Virtual Memory Pagefile When System Shuts Down	Local Policies|Security Options
Digitally Sign Client Communication (Always)	Local Policies|Security Options
Digitally Sign Client Communication (When Possible)	Local Policies|Security Options
Digitally Sign Server Communication (Always)	Local Policies|Security Options
Digitally Sign Server Communication (When Possible)	Local Policies|Security Options
Disable Ctrl+Alt+Delete Requirement For Logon	Local Policies|Security Options
Do Not Display Last Username In Logon Screen	Local Policies|Security Options
LAN Manager Authentication Level	Local Policies|Security Options
Message Text For Users Attempting To Log On	Local Policies|Security Options
Message Title For Users Attempting To Log On	Local Policies|Security Options
Number Of Previous Logons To Cache	Local Policies|Security Options
Prevent System Maintenance Of Computer Account Pwd	Local Policies|Security Options

(continued)

Table 19.3   Domain security policies *(continued)*.

Policy	Location
Prevent Users From Installing Printer Drivers	Local Policies|Security Options
Prompt User To Change Password Before Expiration	Local Policies|Security Options
Recovery Console: Allow Automatic Administrative Logon	Local Policies|Security Options
Recovery Console: Allow Floppy Copy	Local Policies|Security Options
Rename Administrator Account	Local Policies|Security Options
Rename Guest Account	Local Policies|Security Options
Restrict CD-ROM Access To Locally Logged-On User Only	Local Policies|Security Options
Restrict Floppy Access To Locally Logged-On User Only	Local Policies|Security Options
Send Unencrypted Password To Connect To 3rd Part SMB	Local Policies|Security Options
Shut Down System Immediately If Unable To Log Security	Local Policies|Security Options
Smart Card Removal Behavior	Local Policies|Security Options
Strengthen Default Permissions	Local Policies|Security Options
Unsigned Driver Installation Behavior	Local Policies|Security Options
Unsigned Non-Driver Installation Behavior	Local Policies|Security Options
Maximum Application Log Size	Event Log|Settings For Event Logs
Maximum Security Log Size	Event Log|Settings For Event Logs
Maximum System Log Size	Event Log|Settings For Event Logs
Restrict Guest Access To Log	Event Log|Settings For Event Logs
Retain Application Log	Event Log|Settings For Event Logs
Retain Security Log	Event Log|Settings For Event Logs
Retain System Log	Event Log|Settings For Event Logs
Retention Method For Application Log	Event Log|Settings For Event Logs
Retention Method For Security Log	Event Log|Settings For Event Logs
Retention Method For System Log	Event Log|Settings For Event Logs
Shut Down The Computer When The Security Audit Log Is Full	Event Log|Settings For Event Logs

Encrypting File System

Encrypting File System (EFS) is a new feature in Windows 2000 that allows users to encrypt their files and directories. EFS allows users to protect their data without worrying about unauthorized users accessing the data. EFS can only be used on disks formatted as Windows NT File System (NTFS). This gives Windows 2000 an added level of protection on shared systems.

NOTE: *With Windows NT, administrators could usually view all files even if they did not have permissions. With EFS, however, these documents are secure from all prying eyes. If you're not the person who encrypted the file, the only way to decrypt it is through the Recovery Agent. By default, the initial administrator in the domain is the Recovery Agent.*

Encrypting and decrypting files is a simple task. In Windows Explorer, right-click the object, choose Properties, click Advanced, and check the Encrypt Contents To Secure Data checkbox. Windows 2000 also ships with a command-line utility (cipher.exe) that performs the same task. This tool, however, gives the user more control of what is encrypted and decrypted. The format for the **cipher** command (as shown in the Windows 2000 Help) is as follows:

```
Cipher [/E|/D][/S:dir][/A][/I][/F][/Q][H][/K][path]
```

Table 19.4 lists the command-line switches and their tasks.

Table 19.4   The cipher command-line switches.

Switch	Description
/A	Encrypts or decrypts files and directories.
/D	Decrypts the specified directory. All files added to the directory will not be encrypted.
/E	Encrypts the specified directory. All files added to the directory will be encrypted.
/F	Forces encryption of all objects, regardless of whether they have been encrypted before.
/H	Displays all files (including hidden and system files).
/I	Ignores any errors encountered.
/K	Creates a new encryption key for the user.
/Q	Reports only essential information.
/S	Encrypts or decrypts all subdirectories.

Immediate Solutions

Controlling Objects

One of the most common lapses in security involves locking down objects (files, folders, and printers). This section deals with how this is done.

Managing Drive Permissions

To manage drive permissions, perform the following steps:

1. Right-click the desired disk, and choose Properties from the pop-up menu.

2. Select the Security tab.

WARNING! The Security tab will only appear on the drive's Properties dialog box if the disk is formatted with NTFS.

3. To add a user or group, click Add, choose the user or group, and assign the desired Allow or Deny permissions (see Figure 19.5).

4. To remove a user or group, select the object to be removed, and click Remove.

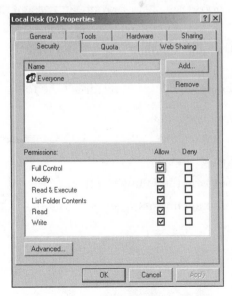

Figure 19.5   Setting disk permissions.

5. To view all the permissions individually, enable auditing, or set the disk owner, click Advanced.

6. Click OK to set the permissions.

Managing File Permissions

To manage file permissions, perform the following steps:

1. Right-click the desired file, and choose Properties from the pop-up menu.

2. Select the Security tab.

3. To add a user or group, click Add, choose the user/group, and assign the desired Allow or Deny permissions.

4. To remove a user or group, select the object to be removed, and click Remove.

5. To view all the permissions individually, enable auditing, or set the file owner, click Advanced.

6. Click OK to set the permissions.

Managing Folder Permissions

To manage folder permissions, perform the following steps:

1. Right-click the desired folder, and choose Properties from the pop-up menu.

2. Select the Security tab.

3. To add a user or group, click Add, choose the user or group, and assign the desired Allow or Deny permissions.

4. To remove a user or group, select the object to be removed, and click Remove.

5. To view all the permissions individually, enable auditing, or set the folder owner, click Advanced.

6. Click OK to set the permissions.

Managing Shared Folder Permissions

To manage shared folder permissions, perform the following steps:

1. Right-click the desired shared folder, and choose Properties from the pop-up menu.

2. Select the Sharing tab.

3. Click Permissions.

4. To add a user or group, click Add, choose the user or group, and assign the desired Allow or Deny permissions.

5. To remove a user or group, select the object to be removed, and click Remove.

6. Click OK to set the permissions.

7. Click OK to close the folder's Properties dialog box.

NOTE: *If the shared folder resides on an NTFS drive, both share permissions and NTFS permissions apply with the effective permissions being the most restrictive between the two.*

Managing Printer Permissions

To manage printer permissions, perform the following steps:

1. Right-click the desired printer, and choose Properties from the pop-up menu.

2. Select the Security tab.

3. To add a user or group, click Add, choose the users or groups, and assign the desired Allow or Deny permissions.

4. To remove a user or group, select the object to be removed, and click Remove.

5. To view all the permissions individually, enable auditing, or set the printer owner, click Advanced.

6. Click OK to set the permissions.

Taking Ownership

To take ownership of an object, perform the following steps:

1. Right-click the desired object, and choose Properties from the pop-up menu.

2. Select the Security tab.

3. Click on the Advanced button and select the user account that will become the owner of the object.

4. Click on the View/Edit button and click on the checkbox labeled Take Ownership in the Permissions window.

5. Click on OK.

6. From this point on, the future owner of the object will need to log in to the system.

7. From within Explorer, Right-click the desired object, and choose Properties from the pop-up menu.

8. Select the Security tab, and click on the Advanced button.

9. Select the Owner tab.

10. Select the user or group that is to become the new owner, and click OK.

11. Click OK twice.

Granting Domain Controller Logon Permission

By default, all users are not allowed to log on to the domain controller locally (that is, by physically sitting in front of the domain controller). To grant a user the right to log on to a domain controller, perform the following steps:

1. Click Start, and select Programs|Administrative Tools|Domain Security Policy.

2. Double-click Security Settings in the left pane, expand Local Policies, and select User Rights Assignment.

3. Double-click the Log On Locally policy in the right pane; the Log On Locally Policy window will appear (see Figure 19.6).

4. Mark the Define These Policy Settings checkbox, and click Add to add a user or a group.

5. Assign the right to the desired users or groups.

6. Click OK.

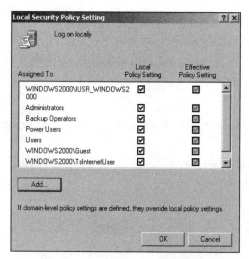

Figure 19.6   The Log On Locally policy window.

Using Audit Policies

A few issues are involved with audit policies. These tasks are discussed in the following sections.

Setting an Audit Policy

To establish an audit policy, perform the following steps:

1. Click Start, and select Programs|Administrative Tools|Domain Security Policy (or Local Security Policy).

2. Double-click the audit policy to be enforced.

3. Select whether to audit successes, failures, or both (see Figure 19.7). Click OK.

Enabling Auditing on Objects

To enable object auditing, perform the following steps:

1. Right-click the object that is to be audited, and choose Properties from the pop-up menu.

2. Select the Security tab.

3. Click Advanced (see Figure 19.8).

4. Select the Auditing tab.

5. To add a user or group, click Add, select the user or group, and select the access to audit. Click OK.

6. To remove a user or group, highlight the user or group, and click Remove.

7. Click OK twice.

Figure 19.7   Enabling an auditing policy.

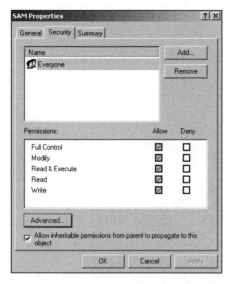

Figure 19.8   Setting permissions to audit an object.

Viewing the Security Log

To view the security log, perform the following steps:

1. Click Start, and select Programs|Administrative Tools|Event Viewer.

2. Select the security log to view.

Working with Encryption

A new feature of Windows 2000's NTFS allows users to encrypt their files and folders. The following sections illustrate how this is done.

Encrypting Files and Folders

To encrypt files and folders, perform the following steps:

1. Right-click the file or folder to be encrypted, and choose Properties from the pop-up menu.

2. Click Advanced.

3. Check the Encrypt Contents To Secure Data checkbox.

4. Click OK twice.

Encrypting Files from the Command Prompt

To encrypt files from the command prompt, perform the following steps:

1. Click Start, and select Programs|Accessories|Command Prompt.
2. Navigate to the folder where the files to be encrypted are located.
3. Type "cipher /e *filename*", and press Enter.

Encrypting Folders from the Command Prompt

To encrypt folders from the command prompt, perform the following steps:

1. Click Start, and select Programs|Accessories|Command Prompt.
2. Navigate to the folder where the files to be encrypted are located.
3. Type "cipher /e *folder*", and press Enter.

Decrypting Files and Folders

To decrypt files and folders, perform the following steps:

1. Right-click the file or folder to be decrypted, and choose Properties from the pop-up menu.
2. Click Advanced.
3. Clear the Encrypt Contents To Secure Data checkbox.
4. Click OK twice.

Encrypting Remote Files and Folders

To encrypt remote files and folders, perform the following steps:

1. Map a drive to the location of a remote file or folder.
2. Right-click the file or folder to be encrypted, and choose Properties from the pop-up menu.
3. Click Advanced.
4. Check the Encrypt Contents To Secure Data checkbox.
5. Click OK twice.

Decrypting Files from the Command Prompt

To decrypt files from the command prompt, perform the following steps:

1. Click Start, and select Programs|Accessories|Command Prompt.
2. Navigate to the folder where the files to be decrypted are located.
3. Type "cipher /d *filename*", and press Enter.

Decrypting Folders from the Command Prompt

To decrypt folders from the command prompt, perform the following steps:

1. Click Start, and select Programs|Accessories|Command Prompt.

2. Navigate to the folder where the folders to be decrypted are located.

3. Type "cipher /d *folder*", and press Enter.

Displaying Encryption and Decryption Information from the Command Prompt

To display encryption and decryption information from the command prompt, perform the following steps:

1. Click Start, and select Programs|Accessories|Command Prompt.

2. Navigate to the folder where the folders to be decrypted are located.

3. Type "cipher", and press Enter.

NOTE: *Any encrypted object will show the letter "E" in the left column, and unencrypted files will show the letter "U".*

Decrypting Remote Files and Folders

To decrypt remote files and folders, perform the following steps:

1. Map a drive to the location of a remote file or folder.

2. Right-click the file or folder to be decrypted, and choose Properties from the pop-up menu.

3. Click Advanced.

4. Clear the Encrypt Contents to Secure Data checkbox.

5. Click OK twice.

Using Group Policy to Delegate Recovery

To use Group Policy to delegate recovery, perform the following steps:

1. Click Start, and select Programs|Administrative Tools|Group Policy.

2. Navigate to Computer Configuration|Windows Settings|Security Settings|Public Key Policies.

3. Right-click Encrypted Data Recovery Agents, and choose Add from the pop-up menu.

4. When the Add Recovery Agent Wizard window appears, click Next.

5. If the recovery certificates are located on the file system, click Browse Folders, navigate to the location, and click OK.

6. If the recovery certificates are located in Active Directory, click Browse Directory, navigate to the container, and click OK.

7. Repeat Steps 5 or 6 for any additional recovery agents.

8. Click Next.

9. Click Finish.

Adding a Recovery Agent for the Local Computer

To add a recovery agent for the local computer, perform the following steps:

1. Click Start, and select Run.

2. Type "MMC", and click OK.

3. Select Console|Add/Remove Snap-In.

4. Click Add.

5. Select Group Policy.

6. Click Add.

7. Click Browse.

8. Ensure that the This Computer radio button is selected, and click OK.

9. Click Finish.

10. Click Close.

11. Click OK.

12. Expand Local Computer Policy.

13. Expand Computer Configuration.

14. Expand Windows Settings.

15. Expand Security Settings.

16. Expand Public Key Policies.

17. Right-click Encrypted Data Recovery Agents, and select Add from the pop-up menu.

18. Click Add.

19. When the Add Recovery Agent Wizard appears, click Next.

20. Click Browse Folders.

21. Navigate to the CER file, and click OK.

22. Click Next.

23. Click Finish.

Changing the Recovery Policy for the Local Computer

To change the recovery policy for the local computer, perform the following steps:

1. Click Start, and select Run.
2. Type "MMC", and click OK.
3. Select Console|Add/Remove Snap-In.
4. Click Add.
5. Select Group Policy.
6. Click Add.
7. Click Browse.
8. Ensure that the This Computer radio button is selected, and click OK.
9. Click Finish.
10. Click Close.
11. Click OK.
12. Expand Local Computer Policy.
13. Expand Computer Configuration.
14. Expand Windows Settings.
15. Expand Security Settings.
16. Expand Public Key Policies.
17. Right-click Encrypted Data Recovery Agents, and select Delete Policy from the pop-up menu.
18. Click Yes.

Adding an Encrypted Data Recovery Agent for a Group Policy Object

To add an encrypted data recovery agent for a Group Policy Object, perform the following steps:

1. Click Start, and select Programs|Administrative Tools|Group Policy.
2. Expand Local Computer Policy.
3. Expand Computer Configuration.
4. Expand Windows Settings.
5. Expand Security Settings.
6. Expand Public Key Policies.

7. Right-click Encrypted Data Recovery Agents, and select Add from the pop-up menu.

8. Click Add.

9. When the Add Recovery Agent Wizard appears, click Next.

10. Click Browse Folders.

11. Navigate to the CER file, and click OK.

12. Click Next.

13. Click Finish.

Working with Security Templates

Windows 2000 has some MMC snap-ins available to the administrator for setting security policies. These tools must be configured the first time (as shown in the first solution). The following solutions all assume that this MMC snap-in is created.

Starting the Security Templates Snap-In

To enable the Security Templates snap-in, perform the following steps:

1. Click Start, and select Run.

2. Type "MMC" in the Open field, and click OK.

3. Select Console|Add/Remove Snap-In.

4. Click Add.

5. Select Security Templates, and click Add.

6. Select Security Configuration And Analysis.

7. Click Close.

8. Click OK.

9. Select Console|Save.

10. Enter a desired name, and click Save.

Modifying an Existing Security Template

To modify a security template, perform the following steps:

1. Select the Security Templates snap-in configured previously.

2. Double-click the default path folder.

3. Right-click the security template to be modified, and choose Save As from the pop-up menu.

4. Enter a name for the template, and click Save.

5. Double-click the newly created template.

6. Make the desired modifications.

Creating a New Security Template

To create a security template, perform the following steps:

1. Select the Security Templates snap-in configured previously.

2. Right-click the default path folder, and choose New Template from the pop-up menu.

3. Enter a name and description for the new security template, and click OK.

4. Double-click the newly created security template.

5. Make any desired modifications.

Deleting a Security Template

To delete a security template, perform the following steps:

1. Select the Security Templates snap-in configured previously.

2. Right-click the security template to be deleted, and choose Delete.

3. Click Yes to confirm the deletion.

Applying a Security Template

To apply a security template, perform the following steps:

1. Select the Security Templates snap-in configured previously.

2. Right-click Security Configuration And Analysis, and choose Open Database from the pop-up menu.

3. Enter a name for the database, and click Open.

4. Select Import Template.

5. Right-click Security Configuration And Analysis, and choose Configure System Now.

Working with Service Packs

A few issues are involved in the management of service packs. The following sections discuss these tasks.

Installing a Service Pack

To install a service pack, perform the following steps:

1. Click Start, and select Run.

2. Enter the path to the service pack (either a CD or the network), and click OK.

3. The Windows 2000 Service Pack Setup window will appear (see Figure 19.9). Accept the license agreement by checking the Accept The License Agreement checkbox, and then click Install.

4. If the Uninstall feature of the service pack is required, check the Backup Files Necessary To Uninstall This Service Pack At A Later Time checkbox, and click Install.

NOTE: *If enough space exists on your hard drive, the setup program will automatically back up the required information.*

---

5. Click Restart to restart the system.

Installing a Service Pack Using Slipstreaming

To install a service pack using slipstreaming, perform the following steps:

1. Click Start, and select Run.

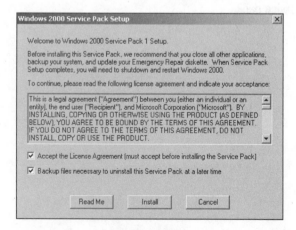

Figure 19.9   The Windows 2000 Service Pack Setup window.

2. Enter "*drive:\i386\update\update.exe /s:installfolder*" (where *drive* is the CD drive where the service pack exists and *installfolder* is the location of the Windows 2000 installation files).

3. Click OK. Figure 19.10 illustrates the slipstream process.

Uninstalling a Service Pack

To uninstall a service pack, perform the following steps:

1. Click Start, and select Settings|Control Panel.

2. Double-click Add/Remove Programs.

3. Select the service pack to be removed, and click Change/Remove.

4. Click Yes to uninstall the service pack.

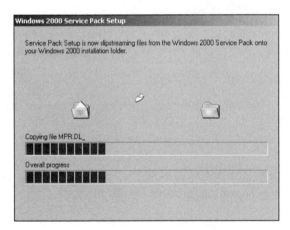

Figure 19.10   Slipstreaming a service pack.

Chapter 20

Providing Print Services

(continued)

In Depth

The terms used by Windows 2000 for printing must be defined for printers to be understood fully. The whole subject of printers with Windows operating systems has been extremely confusing in the past.

With Windows NT, the actual physical printer was referred to as the *print device*, and the software was known as the *printer*. This has been extremely confusing, especially for those of us who also dealt with NetWare printing, where the physical printer was the printer and the software was the print server. To make matters worse, these terms have changed yet again with Windows 2000. The physical printer is now known as the *print device*, the software component is the *logical printer*, and the print queue is called the printer.

This chapter will use this new Windows 2000 naming convention. However, in the interest of your own sanity and the understanding of those around you, you should choose names that work for you and stick with them.

If you understand the process Windows 2000 follows when printing, troubleshooting printer problems will become easier. This section describes the process that Windows 2000 follows when sending a print job through the server, finally arriving at the printer.

When the print option is selected in a Windows application, the application sends the data to the graphics device interface (GDI). The GDI is a Windows internal memory stack that makes the applications independent of the printers. It handles anything dealing with graphics as well.

In the old disk operating system (DOS) world, it was the application's job to talk to the printer and print the actual print job. If a word processor was running on a system and a printer of type X was installed, the application required specific support for that printer. If the application didn't support the printer, you couldn't print from that application. You could, however, have any number of other applications that would print to the printer because they would support printer X. This was true for each application installed on the system. Each one of these applications required a dedicated driver.

GDI changed all that. Instead of requiring each application to maintain its own graphics memory and functions, GDI allowed for all applications to share the same memory and graphics functions to display and print. Now, the application needs to know only how to communicate with GDI, and GDI needs to know how to communicate with the printer. The application now sends the print job to the GDI, which formats it using the printer driver, using the minidriver/unidriver model, and sends it to the spooler.

The spooler passes the print job to the remote print provider (RPP), which then sends it across the network to the print router on the server. The print router is part of the print spooler service on the server. It is this service that's responsible for passing the print job to the print monitor.

The print monitor manages all the printers and print jobs on the server. It is the print monitor that controls scheduling and priority. When the printer is ready, the print monitor will send the print job to the printer.

Printers and Networks

There are two main methods for connecting printers to the physical network: by using print servers and by using network printers. Each of these technologies is presented and explained in the following sections.

Working with Print Servers

Print servers come in two different flavors: either a network device or a computer. The network device—known as a *print server*, or computer with the appropriate software installed—acts as the communication link between the clients attempting to print to the printer and the physical printer.

Generally speaking, the print server device is separate from the printer itself and has a network connection and a printer connection. The print server device essentially plugs into the network on one side of the box, and into the printer on the other side of the box. Quite often, print server devices can be installed within the printer. The print server can also be a computer, which essentially acts as the controller for the print queue. In these cases, either the printer device is connected directly to the computer or a network card is installed on the printer and an IP address assigned to that NIC. The computer, in turn, configures the printer using the IP address. The print server device is very similar to a network printer in its operation, but it's normally used on older printers that do not have network capabilities.

WARNING! All versions of Windows 2000 will operate as print servers. However, be aware that a limitation has been set on Windows 2000 Professional. Although Windows 2000 Server and Advanced Server have no limitations on the number of users supported on a single printer, Windows 2000 Professional only allows 10 concurrent users to connect.

There are really two approaches to how computer-based print servers operate. Microsoft has taken the "intelligent" approach, whereas most Unix systems have taken the "dumb" approach. It is important that these two approaches not be taken as good and bad, respectively. Instead, just remember that they are different, but perform the same task. With the intelligent approach, the print server performs all the tasks necessary for printing to occur. This includes providing the necessary printer drivers to the clients when they connect to the printer and handling the actual communication between the client and the printer. All spooling tasks occur at the print server, not at the client. That is to say, it is the print server that controls all the print jobs when multiple jobs are sent to the printer at the same time.

With the dumb approach, the print server is just an interface between the network and the printer. It is up to each client to maintain the printer driver and the printer queue when multiple print jobs are sent to the printer at the same time. This task is sometimes performed by the printer as well. The most popular implementation of this method is known as the *Line Printer Daemon* (LPD). The clients must then connect to the print server using the line printer remote (LPR) service to send the print jobs to the printer.

NOTE: *Windows 2000 can operate as both an LPD server and an LPR client. Both these services are optional and are not installed by default.*

TIP: *A third service exists, known as line printer queue (LPQ). This service is used to control print jobs already at the print server. LPQ can be used to display information about the currently queued print jobs as well as to modify or delete jobs.*

Working with Network Printers

Network printers are simply regular printers that have additional networking hardware installed. These printers can usually support multiple protocols, such as Transmission Control Protocol/Internet Protocol (TCP/IP), Internet Packet Exchange (IPX), and AppleTalk. After they are connected to the network and are configured, they simply become another device on the network. Basically, for a TCP/IP printer, you assign the printer a valid TCP/IP address and then use Windows 2000 to attach to that IP address.

These network printers are normally used in conjunction with print servers, such as a Windows 2000 Server. Although most printers have client software available to allow the clients to connect directly to the printer, this method is not always the desired approach for a couple of reasons. The first is security. If clients have the appropriate software installed to connect to the network printer, it becomes extremely difficult to control who has rights to print to the printer. The second is scalability. If, for example, a network printer supports 100 clients and breaks down or cannot handle the volume, it needs to be either repaired or replaced. If each client is connected directly to the printer, each of those clients will have to be reconfigured. However, if all the clients connect through a Windows 2000 print server, only the server needs to be modified. The clients will automatically get the new printer drivers installed the next time they connect to the print server.

Fixing Printer Problems

For the most part, printing problems are one of the biggest problems that an administrator has to live with. Luckily, these are fairly easy to fix. The two troubleshooting fixes listed in this section should fix about 90 percent of printer problems, excluding physical problems.

The first problem deals with print jobs coming out garbled with foreign characters on the printer. The problem is most commonly caused by corrupted printer memory or drivers (either on the server or on the client). When this occurs, turn off the printer and turn it on again. If this doesn't work, simply reinstall the printer driver. If the problem is occurring on a single system, reinstall the client's driver. If, however, the problem is occurring from all the systems, the driver must be reinstalled on the server.

The second problem is caused when the spooler service gets corrupted and ceases to respond to requests. Fixing this problem is easy. Simply stop and restart the service on the system controlling the printer or printers. At times, the spooler is using so much of the system's central processing unit (CPU) cycles that it's easier to restart the service from a remote system.

TIP: Keep in mind that often when corruption occurs, it's for a reason. You may consider moving the Print Spooler from the %systemroot%\system32 folder to another drive or partition. This will help reduce the possibility of the spooler growing so large that it leaves no room for the operating system to function.

Immediate Solutions

Creating a Parallel Port Printer

To create a parallel port printer, perform the following steps:

1. Click Start, and select Settings|Printers.

2. Double-click Add Printer. The Add Printer Wizard appears.

3. Click Next.

4. Ensure that the Local Printer radio button is selected, as shown in Figure 20.1, and click Next.

5. Select a parallel (LPT) port, and click Next, as shown in Figure 20.2.

6. Select the printer manufacturer and the model, as shown in Figure 20.3, and click Next.

7. Enter a printer name, and click Next.

8. To share the printer, choose the Share As radio button, enter a share name, and click Next. To not share the printer, choose the Do Not Share This Printer radio button, and click Next.

9. If the printer is to be shared, enter a location and a printer description, and click Next.

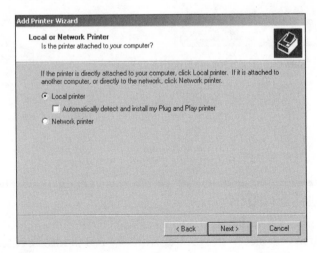

Figure 20.1   Adding a printer.

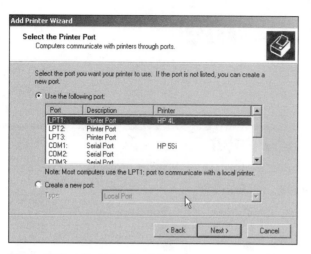

Figure 20.2   Choosing a printer port.

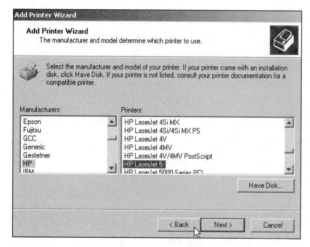

Figure 20.3   Selecting the printer manufacturer and model.

10. If desired, select to print a test page, and click Next.

11. Click Finish.

Creating a TCP/IP Port Printer

After a network printer has been installed and given a valid TCP/IP address, you'll need to use Windows 2000 to connect to the printer by its TCP/IP address. Afterward, you can then share the printer as a network resource to other computers. To connect to the printer by its TCP/IP address, perform the following steps:

1. Click Start, and select Settings|Printers.

2. Double-click Add Printer. The Add Printer Wizard appears.

3. Click Next.

4. Ensure that the Local Printer radio button is selected, and click Next.

5. Select the Create New Port radio button, and click Next.

6. Choose the standard TCP/IP port from the Type drop-down list, and click Next. The Add Standard TCP/IP Printer Port Wizard appears.

7. Click Next.

8. Enter the TCP/IP address for the printer, and click Next.

9. Select the device type, and click Next.

10. Click Finish.

11. Select the printer manufacturer and the model, and click Next.

12. Enter a printer name, and click Next.

13. To share the printer, choose the Share As radio button, enter a share name, and click Next. To not share the printer, choose the Do Not Share This Printer radio button, and click Next.

14. If the printer is to be shared, enter a location and a printer description, and click Next.

15. If desired, select to print a test page, and click Next.

16. Click Finish.

Publishing a Printer in Active Directory

To publish a printer in Active Directory, perform the following steps:

1. Click Start, and select Settings|Printers.

2. Right-click the printer that is to be published in Active Directory, and choose Sharing from the pop-up menu.

3. If the printer is not shared, select the Shared As radio button, and enter a share name for the printer.

4. Check the List In The Directory checkbox.

NOTE: *Active Directory must be installed on the system for this checkbox to be visible.*

---

5. Click OK.

Sharing a Printer

To share a printer, perform the following steps:

1. Click Start, and select Settings|Printers.

2. Highlight the printer to be shared.

3. Right-click the printer, and choose Sharing from the pop-up menu.

4. Select the Shared As radio button.

5. Enter a share name for the printer, and click OK.

Setting Printing Security

To modify printer security, perform the following steps:

1. Click Start, and select Settings|Printers.

2. Highlight the printer for which security is to be set.

3. Right-click the printer, and choose Properties from the pop-up menu.

4. Select the Security tab.

5. To add a user or group, click the Add button, select the user or group, and click OK.

6. Assign any desired permissions to the selected user or group.

7. For more advanced features, click the Advanced button.

8. Click OK when done.

Auditing Printers

To audit printer use, perform the following steps:

1. Click Start, and select Settings|Printers.

2. Highlight the printer to be audited.

3. Right-click the printer, and choose Properties from the pop-up menu.

4. Select the Security tab.

5. Click Advanced.

6. Select the Auditing tab.

7. Click Add.

8. Choose the user or group for which auditing on the printer is to be enabled, and click OK.

9. Select the access types to audit (Print, Manage Printers, Manage Documents, Read Permissions, Change Permissions, and Take Ownership) and whether to audit success and failure. Click OK.

10. Click OK.

11. Click OK.

Restarting a Stalled Print Job

To restart a stalled print job, perform the following steps:

1. Click Start, and select Settings|Printers.

2. Highlight the printer where the stalled print job exists.

3. Right-click the printer, and choose Open from the pop-up menu.

4. Highlight the stalled print job.

5. Select Document|Resume.

Pausing a Print Job

To pause a print job, perform the following steps:

1. Click Start, and select Settings|Printers.

2. Highlight the printer where the print job to be paused exists.

3. Right-click the printer, and choose Open from the pop-up menu.

4. Highlight the print job.

5. Select Document|Pause.

Removing a Print Job

To remove a print job, perform the following steps:

1. Click Start, and select Settings|Printers.

2. Highlight the printer where the print job is to be removed.

3. Right-click the printer, and choose Open from the pop-up menu.

4. Highlight the print job to be removed.

5. Select Document|Cancel.

Deleting All Print Jobs

To delete pending print jobs, perform the following steps:

1. Click Start, and select Settings|Printers.

2. Highlight the printer where the print jobs to be deleted reside.

3. Right-click the printer, and choose Open from the pop-up menu.

4. Select Printer|Cancel All Documents.

Taking Ownership of a Printer

To take ownership of a printer, perform the following steps:

1. Click Start, and select Settings|Printers.

2. Highlight the printer of which you want to take ownership.

3. Right-click the printer, and choose Properties from the pop-up menu.

4. Select the Security tab.

5. Click Advanced.

6. Select the Ownership tab.

7. Choose the user or group that is to take ownership, and click OK.

8. Click OK.

9. Click OK.

Creating a Printing Pool

To create a printing pool, perform the following steps:

1. Create all the printers that will participate in the pool.

TIP: Microsoft recommends that only printers of the same make and model be used when creating a printing pool. In practice, however, as long as all the printers can use the same driver, they may be pooled.

---

2. Click Start, and select Settings|Printers.

3. Highlight the first printer in the printing pool.

4. Right-click the printer, and choose Properties from the pop-up menu.

5. Choose the Ports tab.

6. Check the Enable Printer Pooling checkbox.

7. Select one or more extra ports, and click OK (see Figure 20.4).

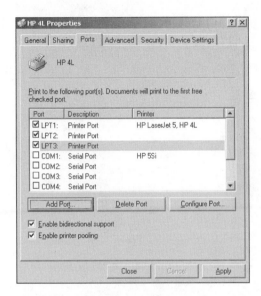

Figure 20.4   Creating a printer pool.

Configuring Multiple Printers for a Single Device

Sometimes, you need to create printers with different configuration properties assigned to them. For example, if only a single printer exists, the administrator might want to schedule the printer differently for managers and users. For this, the administrator can create multiple printers for a single device. Here's how:

1. Click Start, and select Settings|Printers.

2. Create the first printer as outlined in the procedures for Creating a Parallel Port Printer or a TCP/IP Port Printer.

3. Create the second printer, and assign it to the same port.

4. Repeat if desired.

Scheduling Printing

To set up scheduled printing, perform the following steps:

1. Click Start, and select Settings|Printers.
2. Highlight the printer to be scheduled.
3. Right-click the printer, and choose Properties from the pop-up menu.
4. Select the Advanced tab.
5. Choose the Available From radio button (see Figure 20.5).
6. Enter the start and end times that this printer is to be available.
7. Click OK.

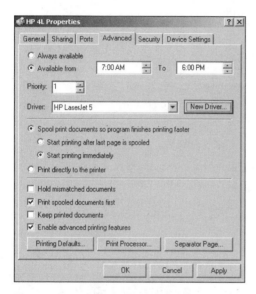

Figure 20.5   Scheduling a printer.

Configuring Printer Priorities

To configure printer priorities, perform the following steps:

1. Click Start, and select Settings|Printers.
2. Highlight the printer for which the priority is to be set.
3. Right-click the printer, and choose Properties from the pop-up menu.
4. Select the Advanced tab.
5. Choose the priority from the Priority section.
6. Click OK.

Using Separator Pages

To set up the use of separator pages between print jobs, perform the following steps:

1. Click Start, and select Settings|Printers.

2. Highlight the printer on which to use separator pages.

3. Right-click the printer, and choose Properties from the pop-up menu.

4. Select the Advanced tab.

5. Click Separator Page.

6. Enter the name of the separator page (or browse to it).

NOTE: *Separator pages are used to separate print jobs when the printer switches modes, for example, changing from postscript to Printer Control Language (PCL). Several separator pages ship with Windows 2000 that end with the .sep extension.*

7. Click OK.

8. Click OK.

Installing Multiple Operating System-Specific Drivers

To install multiple operating system print drivers, perform the following steps:

1. Click Start, and select Settings|Printers.

2. Highlight the printer for which multiple operating system drivers need to be added.

3. Right-click the printer, and choose Properties from the pop-up menu.

4. Select the Sharing tab.

5. Click Additional Drivers. The Additional Drivers page is displayed, see Figure 20.6.

6. Select the operating system or systems for which drivers need to be installed.

7. Click OK.

8. Insert the requested CD-ROM.

9. Click Close.

Figure 20.6   The Additional Drivers window.

Updating the Printer Driver

To update a printer driver, perform the following steps:

1. Click Start, and select Settings|Printers.

2. Highlight the printer that needs the updated driver.

3. Right-click the printer, and choose Properties from the pop-up menu.

4. Select the Advanced tab.

5. Click New Driver. The New Driver Wizard appears.

6. Click Next.

7. Select the manufacturer and printer, or click Have Disk to install a new driver.

8. Click Next.

9. Click Finish.

10. Click OK.

Managing Printers

A few issues are involved in managing existing printers. These are discussed in the following sections.

Managing Printers from Windows 2000

To manage an existing printer, perform the following steps:

1. Click Start, and select Settings|Printers.

2. Highlight the printer to manage.

3. Right-click the printer, and choose Open from the pop-up menu.

4. Make any management changes needed, and click OK.

Managing Printers Through a Browser

To manage a printer through Internet Explorer, perform the following steps:

1. Click Start, and select Programs|Internet Explorer.

NOTE: *Internet Information Services (IIS) must be installed for this feature to be functional.*

2. In the Address field, enter "http://*Servername*/Printers", and click OK.

3. The printer list appears, as shown in Figure 20.7.

4. Select the printer that is to be managed. The printer's properties window appears, as shown in Figure 20.8.

5. To pause the printer, click the Pause option under the Printer Actions section.

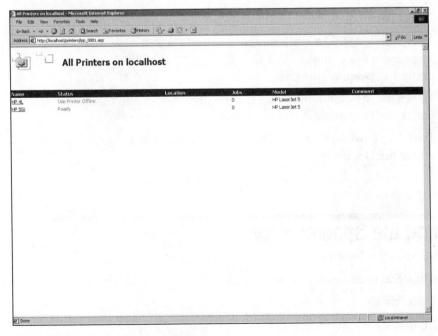

Figure 20.7   The Internet printer list.

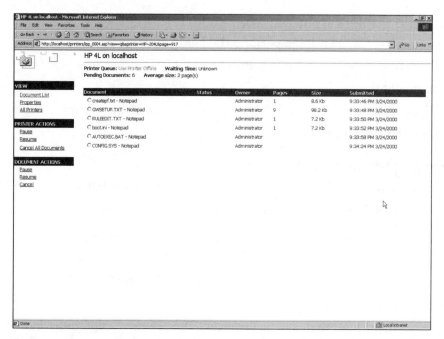

Figure 20.8   The printer's Properties window.

6. To resume the printer, click the Resume option under the Printer Actions section.

7. To cancel all documents, click the Cancel All Documents option under the Printer Actions section.

8. To pause a document, select the document, and click the Pause option under the Document Actions section.

9. To resume a document, select the document, and click the Resume option under the Document Actions section.

10. To delete a print job, select the document, and click the Cancel option under the Document Actions section.

Stopping the Spooler Service

To stop the spooler service, perform the following steps:

1. Click Start, and select Programs|Administrative Tools|Services.

2. Highlight the spooler service.

3. Right-click the service, and choose Stop from the pop-up menu.

Starting the Spooler Service

To start the spooler service, perform the following steps:

1. Click Start, and select Programs|Administrative Tools|Services.

2. Highlight the spooler service.

3. Right-click the service, and choose Start from the pop-up menu.

Modifying the Print Spool Folder Location

To modify the print spool folder location, perform the following steps:

1. Click Start, and select Settings|Printers.

2. Select File|Server Properties.

3. Choose the Advanced tab.

4. Enter a new path for the spool folder in the Spool Folder field.

5. Stop and restart the Spooler service.

6. Click OK.

Setting Printing Preferences

Many different printing options can be set in Windows 2000. The available options depend on the type of printer installed and on the printer driver. The following solutions deal with some of the common preferences set on printers.

Setting Paper Size

To set the paper size, perform the following steps:

1. Click Start, and select Settings|Printers.

2. Right-click the printer that is to be configured, and choose Printing Preferences from the pop-up menu.

3. Click Advanced.

4. Under the Paper/Output section, click Paper Size.

5. Select the desired paper size.

6. Click OK.

7. Click OK.

Modifying Page Orientation

To modify the page orientation, perform the following steps:

1. Click Start, and select Settings|Printers.

2. Right-click the printer for which the page orientation is to be configured, and choose Printing Preferences from the pop-up menu.

3. Choose the Layout tab.

4. Select the desired orientation from the Orientation section.

NOTE: *Three different page orientations are available: portrait, landscape, and rotated landscape. Portrait prints the print job vertically on the page, landscape prints the print job horizontally on the page, and rotated landscape prints the print job rotated 90 degrees counterclockwise on the page.*

---

5. Click OK.

Setting Print Resolution

To set the print resolution, perform the following steps:

1. Click Start, and select Settings|Printers.

2. Right-click the printer for which the print resolution is to be set, and choose Printing Preferences from the pop-up menu.

3. Click Advanced.

4. Select Graphic|Print Quality.

5. Choose the desired resolution from the pop-up menu.

6. Click OK.

7. Click OK.

Monitoring Printer Queue Performance

To monitor printer queue performance, perform the following steps:

1. Click Start, and select Programs|Administrative Tools|Performance.

2. Click the + button.

3. Choose the print server computer to be monitored from the Select Counters From Computer list box.

4. Select Print Queue from the Performance Object list box.

5. Choose the counter to be monitored, and click Add.

6. Repeat Step 5 for each additional counter.

7. Click Close when finished.

Tracking Printer Usage

To track printer usage, perform the following steps:

1. Click Start, and select Settings|Printers.

2. Right-click the printer for which usage is to be tracked, and choose Properties from the pop-up menu.

3. Choose the Security tab.

4. Click Advanced.

5. Choose the Auditing tab.

6. Click Add.

7. Select the user or group for which to track usage, and click OK.

8. Choose the successful and failed printing events to be audited, and click OK.

9. Click OK to confirm the audit configuration.

10. Click OK to close the window.

Keeping a Copy of Print Jobs

To keep a copy of all print jobs, perform the following steps:

1. Click Start, and select Settings|Printers.

2. Right-click the printer for which this feature is to be enabled, and choose Properties from the pop-up menu.

3. Choose the Advanced tab.

4. Check the Keep Printed Documents checkbox.

TIP: To delete all kept printed documents from the spool, clear the Keep Printed Documents checkbox, click Apply, check the Keep Printed Documents checkbox, and click OK.

---

5. Click OK.

Disabling Completed Print Job Notification

To enable completed print job notification, perform the following steps:

1. Select Start|Settings|Printers.

2. Select File|Server Properties.

3. Choose the Advanced tab.

4. Clear the Notify When Remote Documents Are Printed checkbox.

5. Click OK.

Setting Printer Priorities

To set printer priority, perform the following steps:

1. Click Start, and select Settings|Printers.

2. Highlight the printer for which the priority is to be set.

3. Right-click the printer and choose Properties from the pop-up menu.

4. Choose the Advanced tab.

5. Set the desired priority by entering a value in the Priority field or by clicking the up or down arrow.

NOTE: With printer priorities, 1 is the lowest priority level, and 99 is the highest.

---

6. Choose the Security tab.

7. Ensure that only the users or groups that are to be given this priority have permission to connect and print to this printer.

8. Click OK.

9. Double-click Add Printer to add another logical printer for the same physical printer. See "Creating a Parallel Port Printer" in this chapter for a step-by-step description.

10. Right-click the newly created printer, and choose Properties from the pop-up menu.

11. Choose the Advanced tab.

12. Set the desired priority by entering a value in the Priority field or by clicking the up or down arrow.

13. Choose the Security tab.

14. Ensure that only the users or groups that are to be given this priority have permission to connect and print to this printer.

15. Click OK.

Chapter 21

Troubleshooting Windows 2000

In Depth

Even though Windows 2000 is a very robust operating system, problems can and do occur. This chapter takes a look at some of the troubleshooting tools and techniques that you can use to restore a system to full working order.

Troubleshooting 101

Before diving into any troubleshooting endeavor, take a moment, step back, breathe, and then analyze the problem with a calm mind. Attempting to force a solution or performing operations and alterations hurriedly or with an angry and frustrated disposition will often just cause you more stress without resolving the issue. In many cases, problems occur at the most inopportune times, such as when you are against a deadline, all your users are online, or you are on vacation. If you can take the time to relax and examine the situation, you'll often find that your troubleshooting efforts will consume less time than when they are attempted in a less positive mood.

To help you overcome the stress of the situation and to obtain satisfactory results, keep the following commonsense rules and procedures about troubleshooting in mind:

- *Try to be patient*—Being rushed, hostile, angry, or frantic will often exacerbate the problem rather than help you to remedy it.

- *Know your system's hardware and software*—Nothing can substitute for thorough and intimate knowledge of your system and network. If you don't know what is normal or how a system is configured, you'll have more difficulty resolving problems. Before something goes wrong, check system documentation, gather baseline operating data, and also be sure to look up manufacturer and model information on the Internet. If all else fails, and if you have the ability to do so, crack the case and look inside the server itself.

- *Use a process of elimination to isolate the problem*—Systematically testing and removing from suspicion segments of a system or a network will help locate and isolate the problem.

- *Undo any recent alterations*—In many cases, the most recent change to a system is the cause of the current problem. A common first step is to repeal the last changes. Keep in mind that this may include configuration changes, software upgrades, or adding or removing hardware devices.

NOTE: *Be sure to run a tape backup of the system any time major configuration changes are made. Doing so could save your job in the event of a failure.*

- *Review previous points of failure*—If you have experienced repeated problems on the same system or network, always double-check those areas where problems occurred before. In many cases, the weak link in your system is acting up again.

- *Attempt the quick fixes first*—Although they're not always the most obvious, in the long run, attempting to resolve the problem with the simplest solutions first will save time. Trying system reboots, replacing cables, and using different user accounts may result in a cheaper, faster, and easier resolution than the more involved and tedious solutions, such as registry hacking, software reinstallation, and hardware replacement.

- *Make one change at a time*—Only make a single significant alteration to a system at a time. Then, reboot (if applicable), and test the alteration. This process may reveal that your resolution is incorrect or that changes are not working properly. If the change didn't have the desired effect, change it back to the way it was. This process will also reveal the exact alteration that resolves the issue, which is an important data item in the event of a future reoccurrence.

- *Cause the failure to reoccur*—In some cases, only repeating the failure and monitoring various aspects of your system with human eyes as well as automated monitoring tools is the only way to locate the exact problem. If you are unable to repeat a failure on demand, you'll need to implement an automated monitoring system to watch for the next occurrence.

- *Maintain a problem and solution log for each server*—Documenting the process of troubleshooting can provide invaluable information for resolving future issues. Keep track of what the problem was, its symptoms, the attempted solutions that failed, and the solution that succeeded.

Although there's probably very little new to you in this list of basic troubleshooting procedures, it never hurts to review the obvious, especially because you may forget the important basics in a crisis.

Troubleshooting

The following sections explore troubleshooting specific problems that can occur with Windows 2000 Server.

Installation

Windows 2000 is a very robust operating system. This robustness extends even into the installation process. In most cases, with hardware that is Hardware Compatibility List (HCL) compatible, Windows 2000 will install without a hitch. However, even in the perfect world according to Microsoft, problems can and do occur. Generally, installation problems are related to one of the following four issues:

- *Media errors*—These occur either with a damaged distribution CD or when a corrupted or missing file is present in the copied version of the files from the distribution CD. Media errors can also occur between the storage location of the files and the system reading the files due to network link interruptions or damaged hardware. When a media error occurs, you must change CDs, recopy the material to the distribution point, or use a different pathway to get to the distribution files.

- *Domain controller communications*—When attempting to join a domain or installing a second domain controller, you must be able to communicate with an existing domain controller on the network. What's more, you must be able to successfully query the DNS server for the domain controller's name. Human errors in typing in the name, password, and domain name on the client computer can cause problems, and improperly configured DNS on the server can also prevent communications. Also, network communication interruptions can cause problems. Make sure that both the domain controller and DNS are online and that other systems can communicate with it.

- *Hardware/driver problems*—Using the wrong driver or a device not listed on the HCL (**www.microsoft.com/windows2000/upgrade/compat/search/devices.asp** or **www.microsoft.com/hcl**) can prevent the installation from completing successfully. Both of these can cause STOP errors. The only solution is to use the correct driver and replace all non-HCL-compliant devices. Another effective way to determine if the driver is compliant or fully compatible is to install it as a test and see if it is 'signed' by Microsoft. Drivers that have been signed in such a manner have been tested by Microsoft for compliance and support. During driver installation (and this is by default), the system will display a message if the driver is not signed.

- *Dependency issues*—When one service or driver fails, other services or drivers that depend upon that service or driver can also fail. This is known as a *dependency failure*. If your network interface card (NIC) driver fails, the networking components of Windows 2000 will fail, which will prevent you from communicating with the domain controller. If Windows 2000 boots, check the Event Viewer's System log for details on what element of the system failed. In most cases, the issue will be a bad or corrupted driver or a non-HCL-compliant device. If Windows 2000 will not boot, try to view the %systemroot%\ntbtlog.txt file created using Advanced Boot Options|Enable

Boot Logging. In fact, during the actual installation, Windows 2000 creates six log files at various stages along the way. All six logs are created within the %systemroot% or %systemroot%\Debug folders (C:\WINNT and C:\WINNT\DEBUG, by default). You can use these six logs to troubleshoot installations.

No matter which of these situations is the actual cause of an installation failure, you must always restart the installation from the beginning after the issue has been resolved. Don't assume that a partially completed installation will function properly.

Booting

When problems occur that cause Windows 2000 not to boot properly anymore, you need to use special boot troubleshooting techniques and tools. In many cases, you'll be able to restore a system with minimum effort, but having a full system backup is always an important insurance policy against total catastrophe. Restoring a system to bootable capability can require additional elements or components, such as the following:

- The four setup boot disks for your version of Windows 2000. These disks can be created by running the MAKEBT32.exe application on the Windows 2000 installation CD, or manually built using the files from the \bootdisk folder.

- The original Windows 2000 distribution CD and any applied service packs.

- An emergency repair disk (ERD) built using the Backup utility.

- A recent full backup of your entire system (including the system state).

With these tools, you can attempt to repair the boot problem.

Advanced Startup Options

Your first course of action should be to employ one or more of the advanced startup options. In some cases, just booting into Safe mode and then rebooting normally will restore a system. To access these alternate boot settings, you must press F8 when the boot menu is displayed before the timer expires (the default setting for the timer is 30 seconds). Fortunately, a message prompts you to press F8 when this menu is displayed so that you'll know exactly when to press the key. The Advanced Options menu that appears due to this keystroke looks like this:

```
OS Loader v5.0
Windows 2000 Advanced Options Menu
Please select an option:
Safe Mode
Safe Mode with Networking
```

```
Safe Mode with Command Prompt

Enable Boot logging
Enable VGA Mode
Last Known Good Configuration
Directory Services Restore Mode (Windows 2000 domain controllers only)
Debugging Mode

Use [up] and [down] to move the highlight to your choice.
Press Enter to choose.
```

The selections in this menu offer the following controls for booting and system activities:

- *Safe Mode*—Boots Windows 2000 using only the required minimal drivers and system files. The components required for networking are not loaded.

- *Safe Mode With Networking*—Boots Windows 2000 using only the required minimal drivers and system files plus the components required for networking. However, the drivers for personal computer (PC) card services are not loaded, so PC card network connections are not enabled.

- *Safe Mode With Command Prompt*—Boots Windows 2000 using only the required minimal drivers and system files. Boots to a text-only command prompt instead of the graphical user interface (GUI) desktop.

- *Enable Boot Logging*—Turns on the logging process to record the names of loaded drivers and services in the %systemroot%\ntbtlog.txt file.

- *Enable VGA Mode*—Boots Windows 2000 with only standard Video Graphics Array (VGA) video drivers and a desktop resolution of 640 by 480 at 256 or 16 colors.

- *Last Known Good Configuration*—Boots Windows 2000 using the registry configuration stored at the point of the last successful logon.

- *Directory Service Restore Mode*—Boots Windows 2000 and rebuilds or restores Active Directory. This option is only used on Windows 2000 domain controllers.

- *Debugging Mode*—Boots Windows 2000 and transmits debugging data across the serial port to be captured by a second system. See the *Windows 2000 Server Resource Kit* for more information.

See Chapter 9 for detailed information on the Windows 2000 boot process.

Startup File Repair

If the advanced startup options don't enable your system to boot, you may have problems with the boot files or some of the basic system files. Windows 2000 includes a repair process that can often rebuild or restore these essential files. The process involves the four setup boot floppies.

If neither the advanced startup options or the startup file repair process returns your system to a functioning state, your only remaining options are to restore the system (and system state) from backup and to perform an upgrade or fresh installation.

Printers

Resolving printer problems typically involves one or more of the following actions:

- Verify that all physical aspects of the printer are addressed. This includes parallel cable, power, network connection (if applicable), paper, toner, and so on. Also be sure that the printer is online.
- Verify that a logical printer has been created on the system that acts as the print server.
- Verify that the printer is shared with the network (if applicable).
- Verify that a logical printer has been created on the client that connects to the correct network printer share.
- See whether any stalled print jobs are present in the print queue. Delete and resend any stalled jobs.
- Reinstall the printer drivers.
- Test the printer by printing from a different application and a different client.
- Verify that the user has proper permissions to print.
- Stop and restart the spooler service.
- Verify that there is enough free space. Usually, 100 megabytes (MB) is sufficient, but heavier printer loads (for example, more printing users, larger print jobs, and types of data being printed) will require more. If necessary, change the spooler destination folder (see Figure 21.1).

See Chapter 20 for detailed information on printing in Windows 2000.

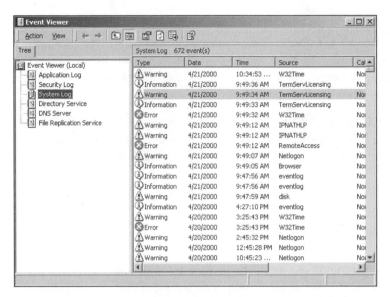

Figure 21.1   The Printer Server Properties dialog box, where the spooler folder is defined.

Remote Access

Remote access is an area that can experience several problems. Here are some recommended resolution actions that may help eliminate problems:

• Verify that all physical connections are tightly seated and that all cables and connections are undamaged.

• Verify that the communication medium itself—phone line, cable, Integrated Services Digital Network (ISDN), and so on—is working properly. This can involve calling your service company.

• Verify that the communication device (that is, modem) is installed properly and that the correct drivers are present. Update the drivers if necessary.

• Verify the settings of the communication device. The settings should match that of the answering system.

• Verify that both the client and the server systems are attempting to use the same protocol, connection medium, security settings, and other configurations related to your remote access connection.

• Verify that the user account has dial-out privileges.

• View the contents of the device.log and modemlog.txt file for information on where problems are occurring.

• Verify that you are not attempting to use multilink and callback on the same connection. They are mutually exclusive.

- Verify that a common authentication protocol and encryption level is present on both the server and the client. Mismatched authentication protocols will prevent user logon and system communication.

One thing that you can do with remote access and networking is to PING the remote server that you're attempting to communicate with. PING it by its name. If the name resolves to an Internet Protocol (IP) address, you've passed one important gateway because that means that Domain Name Service (DNS) is working. Remember that DNS allows your system to know what the IP address is for the domain name that you're trying to talk to.

See Chapter 18 for detailed information on remote access in Windows 2000.

Networking

Network problems are most often related to misconfiguration or damage to the physical connections. Therefore, here are some actions that you can take to help eliminate problems:

- Verify that all physical connections are secure.
- Verify that all media cables and connectors are undamaged.
- Ensure that all standalone network devices are powered and online (when applicable).
- Verify the protocol settings on each system. When working with Transmission Control Protocol/Internet Protocol (TCP/IP), make sure no IP addresses are repeated, that all subnet masks are appropriate, and that the correct gateway is defined.
- Verify that a common authentication protocol and encryption level is present on both the server and the client. Mismatched authentication protocols will prevent user logon and system communication.
- Verify that the NIC is functioning. Update the driver if necessary. Resolve all hardware conflicts.
- Verify that the user account has proper access to connect to the system and/ or network.
- Verify that all Windows NT and Windows 2000 systems have a computer account in the domain.

When you're troubleshooting networking, it's a good idea to use TCP/IP utilities to troubleshoot connectivity. IPCONFIG can be used to determine what the current IP address is. If you're using Dynamic Host Control Protocol (DHCP) on your network, you can quickly use IPCONFIG /RELEASE and IPCONFIG /RENEW both to test network connectivity and to confirm IP configuration. You can also use tools like PING to test IP connections and both TRACERT and PATHPING to check Internet connectivity.

See Chapters 11 and 12 for detailed information on networking Windows 2000.

Permissions

When a user is unable to access a resource, you may have permission problems. These can often be resolved through the following tasks:

- Check for multigroup memberships with conflicting permissions.
- Using the same client, access the same resource using an administrator account.
- Using the same client, access a different resource.
- Using a different client, access the same resource.
- Verify that network connectivity is functioning.
- Verify that the user is authenticated to the domain with the correct account.
- Check for Deny settings for this user and any group memberships.
- Verify that the resource has permissions granted to the user either directly or through groups.
- After changing group memberships, force the user to log on again so that a new access token is generated.

Any time that you're checking permissions, try not to become confused between share and Windows NT File System (NTFS) permissions. Remember that NTFS permissions are attached to the files themselves, and share permissions are associated with sharing files and folders across the network. Keep in mind that a user, when attempting to access a network share, will come across the share permissions first. Only then, if the share permissions allow, will the user's credentials will be presented to the NTFS permissions associated with the files and/or folders. Therefore, the overriding rule of thumb when combining NTFS and share permissions is that the most restrictive permission wins. If the share permissions indicate No Access, the user will never even see the NTFS permissions. If, on the other hand, the Share permissions indicate Full Control, the user will then be passed to the NTFS permissions. If the NTFS permissions indicate No Access, the user won't see the data.

The Registry

The registry is the central storage location for all configuration information about the Windows 2000 environment. This hierarchical database should be protected. Unfortunately, it's fairly easy to damage or overwrite portions of the registry. Nearly every installed application, driver, and service makes a change to the registry. When you discover the need to edit the registry, first attempt to locate a Control Panel applet, administrative tool, or Microsoft Management Console (MMC) snap-in that will provide you with a GUI interface to make setting changes. If you must edit the registry directly, use extreme caution.

The registry is not an exhaustive collection of the settings that control how Windows 2000 operates. Instead, it is only a collection of exceptions to the defaults. This means that many components of Windows 2000, including drivers, services, and applications, will operate based on their own internally defined default values when an alternate value is not found in the registry. This makes locating and altering the operation of Windows 2000 very difficult. If you do not know the exact syntax, spelling, location, and valid values required to alter a default behavior, your alterations may result in a dead system. The *Windows 2000 Server Resource Kit* includes a help file that contains all the native registry entries and valid values, namely regentry.chm. I highly encourage you to employ this tool when working with the registry.

The registry is divided into five keys, as shown in Figure 21.2. Each key has several subdivisions of subkeys, each of which can contain further subkeys and/or value entries. A *value entry* is a named parameter placeholder that contains a value. The value is the setting change that modifies the default behavior of a component. A value entry can contain a single binary digit, a decimal value, a string of American Standard Code for Information Interchange (ASCII) characters, or a hexadecimal number.

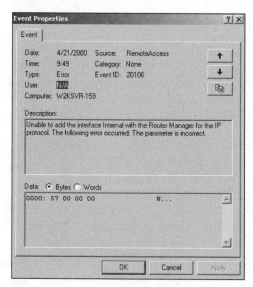

Figure 21.2   REGEDIT showing the five registry keys.

The five registry keys are as follows:

- *HKEY_LOCAL_MACHINE*—Contains the value entries specific to the local computer hardware. The contents of this key are not dependent on a user account or any applications, services, or processes in use.

- *HKEY_CLASSES_ROOT*—Contains the value entries that define the relationships between file extensions (that is, file formats) and applications. This key is actually just a redirector to the HKEY_LOCAL_MACHINE\Software\Classes subkey.

- *HKEY_CURRENT_CONFIG*—Contains the value entries used to control the currently active hardware profile. This key is built each time that the system boots by duplicating the contents of the HKEY_LOCAL_MACHINE\System\CurrentControlSet\HardwareProfiles\### subkey relative to the active hardware profile.

- *HKEY_CURRENT_USER*—Contains the value entries specific to the currently logged-on user. This key is built each time that a user logs on by duplicating the user-specific subkey from the HKEY_USERS key and the ntuser.dat or ntuser.man file from the user's profile.

- *HKEY_USERS*—Contains the value entries for all users who have ever logged onto this system, plus a default user profile for new users who do not already have a user profile.

NOTE: *A sixth key may appear when Windows 95 applications are installed onto a Windows 2000 system. The HKEY_DYN_DATA key acts as a redirector to HKEY_CLASSES_ROOT key, where the data required by the application actually resides under Windows 2000.*

The registry is stored in files on the hard drive. Each time that Windows 2000 boots these files are loaded into memory. While active, Windows 2000 interacts with only the in-memory version of the registry. The registry is saved back to disk when a flush occurs. A flush occurs only when the system is shut down, when an application forces one (such as Backup), or immediately after an alteration.

Chapter 15 provides detailed information about the Windows 2000 registry.

Value Entries

A value entry is defined by three elements: its name, its data type, and the value or data that it contains. The name of a value entry is usually a multiword phrase without spaces and often with intercap or title capitalization, for example, WinLogon and LastLoggedOnUserAccount. The data type specifies how the value is stored. The value or data stored within a value is limited (in length and content) by its value type. The supported value types under Windows 2000 are as follows:

- *REG_BINARY*—Binary format

- *REG_DWORD*—Binary, hex, or decimal format
- *REG_SZ*—Text-string format
- *REG_MULTI_SZ*—Text-string format that contains multiple human-readable values separated by null characters
- *REG_EXPAND_SZ*—Expandable text-string format that contains a variable that's replaced by an application when it is used (for example, %Systemroot%\file.exe)

After a value entry is created, its data type cannot be changed without deleting and re-creating the value entry.

Registry Storage Files

The files used to store the registry are located in the %systemroot%\system32\config folder on the boot partition. Only the HKEY_LOCAL_MACHINE and HKEY_USERS keys are actually stored in files because all the others are either copies or redirectors or are rebuilt each time they are needed. The files used to store and protect the integrity of the registry are shown in Table 21.1.

Troubleshooting Toolbelt

In this section, we will discuss different tools and utilities that you can use during the troubleshooting process.

Event Viewer

The Event Viewer, shown in Figure 21.3, is used to access the Windows 2000 system logs. There are three default or common logs as well as numerous service- and application-specific logs that may be present in the Event Viewer.

Table 21.1   Files used to store the registry.

Registry Hive	File names
HKEY_LOCAL_MACHINE\SAM	Sam, Sam.log, and Sam.sav
HKEY_LOCAL_MACHINE\Security	Security, Security.log, and Security.sav
HKEY_LOCAL_MACHINE\Software	Software, Software.log, and Software.sav
HKEY_LOCAL_MACHINE\System	System, System.alt, System.log, and System.sav
HKEY_USERS\.DEFAULT	Default, Default.log, and Default.sav
HKEY_USERS\<user_SID>	\Documents and Settings\<username>\NTUSER.DAT or NTUSER.MAN
HKEY_CURRENT_USER	Ntuser.dat and Ntuser.dat.log
(Not associated with a hive)	Userdiff and Userdiff.log

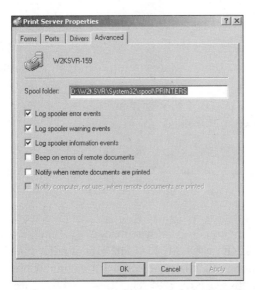

Figure 21.3   The Event Viewer with the System log selected.

The common Event Viewer logs are the following:

- *System log*—Records details about hardware and software issues related to Windows 2000 itself and installed drivers

- *Security log*—Records details about security occurrences and audit events

- *Application log*—Records various application-specific details

The logs record event details. An event detail contains information relevant to the event that caused the log record to be created (see Figure 21.4). These details include date, time, source, category, event, user identification (ID), computer name, and some level of detail about the error, such as an error code number or a detailed description with a memory hexadecimal buffer capture. Through the details captured in a log, you can discover where problems have occurred and, often, what steps are necessary to resolve them.

NOTE: *Microsoft TechNet should be at the top of the list on your troubleshooting toolbelt. Searching the TechNet online at **www.microsoft.com/technet** with the exact error message quite often will give you detailed answers—even when the problem lies with a non-Microsoft product.*

Performance Tool

You can also use the Performance tool (PERFMON.MSC from the run line) to take a look at the current system activity. Hopefully you'll have a baseline to compare with so that you can accurately determine if memory, disk, or swapfile usage is inappropriate. If you don't, that doesn't mean that using the Performance tool does you no good. It can still give you an idea of where to go next. Important

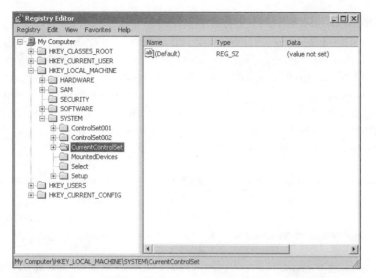

Figure 21.4   An event detail from the Event Viewer's System log.

counters to monitor include % Processor Time under the Processor object, Pages/ Sec under the Memory object, % Usage under the Paging File object, and % Disk Time under the PhysicalDisk object. For the most part, these counters should be able to point you in the direction of determining whether you have a CPU, memory, or disk problem. Be careful, though, because excessive usage anywhere could be the sign of a rogue process or application. Be sure to examine all counters and objects within the Performance tool so that you can get a good idea of exactly what it can monitor for you.

Task Manager/Performance

If you're really in a crunch, and you need to look at what's going on with the memory and CPU on the system realtime, you can access the Task Manager (Ctrl+Alt+Delete, Task Manager button) and select the Performance tab. From there, you will receive an ongoing and immediate graph of CPU and memory utilization. Use this in conjunction with the Performance Tool to track usage over time and attempt to plot a pattern of incidence. (For example, does it happen at certain times of day?) Don't be surprised if the CPU seems to be at 100%. Remember that one of the reasons the CPU is so fast is that nearly all of its effort is put into the task at hand, so it's not surprising to see 100% utilization followed by nearly 0% when it is idle. The Memory utilization, however, can be key to several different issues, including server slowdown, lockup, and a plethora of client-related issues. Take a look at the Processes tab of the Task Manager and try to track which process may be causing the problem(s). This may take some time, as quite often it requires a reboot or two to effectively isolate a memory leak or rogue process, but you'll be better informed and able to resolve the issue in the long run.

Registry Editors: REGEDIT and REGEDT32

Two registry editors are included with Windows 2000. REGEDIT, shown in Figure 21.5, is a 16-bit application that can be used to search the entire registry at once and to edit or add those portions that the current user has access rights to. REGEDT32 is a 32-bit application that can be used to edit the security of keys and subkeys, search on a key-by-key basis, configure auditing, and enable a Read-Only mode to prevent accidental changes. Both tools must be manually launched from the **Run** command or a command prompt.

WARNING! When using either of these tools to modify the registry, be sure to perform the following tasks:

- *Back up the system.*
- *Use these tools to create a backup of the registry.*
- *Reboot the system.*
- *Alter only a single value entry at a time. Test each change before proceeding to the next alteration.*
- *Reboot after all modifications are complete, even if not prompted by the system.*
- *Always test registry alterations on a nonessential system first.*

Registry Tools from the Windows 2000 Resource Kits

The Windows 2000 Server and Professional Resource Kits include many tools that offer functionality in addition to those offered by REGEDIT and REGEDT32 or those that can be used in command-line or batch format. Many of these tools are available free for download from the Microsoft Web site. Using these tools

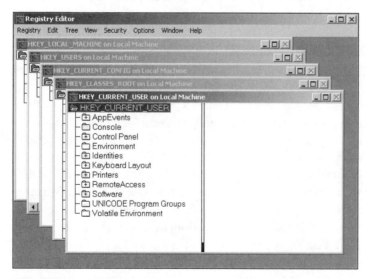

Figure 21.5   REGEDIT.

effectively will require thorough familiarity with a scripting or batch file system. The Resource Kit itself discusses scripting and batching and includes numerous other tools not specific to the registry that you may want to employ as troubleshooting or administrative shortcuts.

Some of the tools from the Resource Kit that are used on the registry are as follows:

- *REG.EXE*—A command-line tool used to perform manipulations and alterations within the registry. It can perform numerous operations, such as adding value entries, changing the value of existing value entries, searching for keywords, copying keys, backing up and restoring keys, and more.

- *REGDUMP.EXE*—A command-line tool used to dump all or part of the registry to the STDOUT. The resultant output from this tool can be used by the REGINI.EXE tool.

- *REGFIND.EXE*—A command-line tool used to search for items in the registry using a keyword or a text string.

- *COMPREG.EXE*—A graphical interface tool used to compare two registry keys. The comparison can occur between local and remote systems. All differences will be highlighted in the display.

- *REGINI.EXE*—A command-line tool used to add keys to the registry.

- *REGBACK.EXE*—A command-line tool used to back up all or part of the registry.

- *REGREST.EXE*—A command-line tool used to restore all or part of the registry from saved key files.

- *SCANREG.EXE*—A graphical interface tool used to search for items in the registry using a keyword or a text string.

The Recovery Console

The Recovery Console is a tool that grants administrators command-line access to system files when the graphical interface will not boot. This tool often affords a method to restore key driver and system files, replace registry items, change service startup settings, repair the Master Boot Record (MBR), format drives, copy files, and more. The Recovery Console is documented thoroughly in the Resource Kit, so, before delving into this complex tool, be sure to review the documentation. Don't forget to check the Microsoft Web site for Resource Kit information.

The Recovery Console can either be launched from the Windows 2000 setup floppies or installed onto the system. To launch the Recovery Console from the setup floppies, select the Recovery Console option when the menu appears. To install the Recovery Console onto your system, execute \i386\winnt32.exe /cmdcons from the Windows 2000 distribution CD. After rebooting, the Recovery Console will now appear as an additional option on the boot menu.

When the Recovery Console is started, you must log on as the administrator for that system. After you are logged on, you are presented with a command prompt from which all your troubleshooting and repair activities will occur. For a complete list of the commands supported by the Recovery Console and details on their use, issue the **help** command.

Troubleshooting Documentation

Microsoft has several publications that include invaluable troubleshooting documentation. When you are in a crunch, nothing can substitute for knowledge, whether it is already in your head or available at your fingertips. Here are four resources you need:

- *Microsoft's Web site*—An overall useful resource on Microsoft's products with numerous technical documents, how-tos, and white papers (**www.microsoft. com/windows/**).

- *The Knowledge Base*—The online and CD collection of technical documents created by Microsoft's support team. It is available online at **support.micro-soft.com/** or offline on the TechNet CD. These documents are based upon the calls, complaints, and feedback coming in to Microsoft technical support. Use the Knowledge Base when you're specifically looking for answers to error messages, behavioral problems, or potential bugs.

- *TechNet*—A monthly subscription service that includes complete documentation and technical resources for all of Microsoft's documentation. It includes all the Resource Kits, numerous utilities and tools unavailable elsewhere, plus CD versions of patches, upgrades, and service packs. For subscription information and online content, visit **www.microsoft.com/technet**. You can also access up-to-the-minute TechNet articles online simply by searching a particular topic or article at the Microsoft Web site.

- *Resource Kits*—The *Windows 2000 Server Resource Kit* and *Windows 2000 Professional Resource Kit* include wonderful information on subjects, such as advanced configuration, administration, and troubleshooting. These kits also include additional documentation not included in the manuals and other tools and utilities that you'll find extremely useful. The Resource Kits are available both as a separate product and as part of TechNet. Most of the resource kit documentation and download information is available on the Microsoft Web site. Searching on the keywords "Resource Kit" will get you there.

Immediate Solutions

Creating the Four Setup Boot Floppies

To create a new set of setup boot floppies, perform the following steps:

NOTE: *You must obtain four floppies for this solution. These floppies should be preformatted.*

1. Insert the Windows 2000 distribution CD into the CD-ROM drive.

2. From the **run** command or a command prompt, execute the **makeboot** (for 16-bit operating systems) or **makebt32** (for 32-bit operating systems) command from the \bootdisk folder on the distribution CD.

3. Type the letter of the floppy driver (most likely this will be "a").

4. Insert the first floppy, and then press any key.

5. Repeat Step 4 for all remaining floppies as prompted.

6. When completed, the disk-building tool will exit. Label each disk clearly as to its number (1/4, 2/4, and so on) and which operating system (OS) it is used for (for example, Windows 2000 Professional or Windows 2000 Server).

Creating an ERD

The ERD is used by the Windows 2000 repair process to restore a system to a functioning state.

NOTE: *This solution requires a blank floppy.*

To build an ERD for a system, perform the following steps:

1. Launch the Backup utility for Windows 2000 by clicking Start and selecting |Programs|Accessories|System Tools|Backup.

2. Click Emergency Repair Disk.

3. Select the Also Back Up The Registry To The Repair Directory checkbox.

4. Insert a floppy into the drive.

5. Click OK.

6. When prompted, remove the floppy, label it as the ERD, and click OK.

7. Close the Backup utility.

Using Startup File Repair

If the essential files on the system partition or key files on the boot partition are damaged or missing, the startup file repair process may return your system to working order. Here are the steps to follow:

NOTE: *This solution requires a set of setup boot floppies for the respective version of Windows 2000. It also requires an ERD for this system.*

1. Place the first boot floppy in the drive of the damaged system.

2. Boot the system from the floppy.

3. Insert each subsequent floppy when prompted.

4. When prompted for a startup option after the fourth disk, press R for Repair to begin the repair process.

5. You'll be prompted whether to repair using the Recovery Console or the Emergency Repair Disk. Press R to select the Emergency Repair Process.

6. Select whether to perform a manual or fast repair. A manual repair requires user response to prompts between repairs; a fast repair suppresses these prompts. Select Fast.

7. When the repair process prompts you, provide the Windows 2000 distribution CD and/or the ERD.

8. Other prompts may appear, depending on the repairs performed and the problems encountered. Respond as necessary to further prompts.

9. After the repair is complete, your system will be rebooted. Be sure to remove any floppies before the reboot occurs.

Searching the Registry Using REGEDIT

To use the 16-bit registry editor for searching through the registry, perform the following steps:

WARNING! This solution should be used with caution to prevent accidental changes to the registry. Always make sure that you have a current, reliable backup of the registry before launching a registry editor.

1. Launch the editor by executing REGEDIT from the **Run** command.
2. Select Edit|Find.
3. Type "DefaultUserName".
4. Click Find Next.
5. The first element that matches this string will be highlighted. The first occurrence found will typically be AltDefaultUserName, which appears in HKLM\…\Winlogon.
6. Select Edit|Find Next.
7. The next element that matches this string is highlighted.
8. Repeat Step 6 until no more matches are discovered.
9. Close the editor by selecting Registry|Exit.

Saving a Registry Key

To store keys into files, perform the following steps:

1. Launch the editor by executing REGEDIT from the **Run** command.
2. Select the HKEY_LOCAL_MACHINE key.
3. Select Registry|Export Registry File.
4. Select a destination folder, and provide a name for the file.
5. Select the Selected Branch radio button to save only the contents of the selected key.
6. Click Save.
7. Close the editor by selecting Registry|Exit.

Restoring a Registry Key

To restore a damaged portion of the registry by importing a saved version of a key, perform the following steps:

WARNING! This solution should be used with caution because the existing registry will be overwritten with the contents of the saved file.

1. Launch the editor by executing REGEDIT from the **Run** command.

2. Select Registry|Import Registry File.

3. Locate and select the registry file containing the portion of the registry that you want to restore.

4. Click Open.

5. Wait for the "Import Completed" message, and then click OK.

6. Close the editor by selecting Registry|Exit.

Viewing the Security Settings on Registry Keys

To use REGEDT32 to work with registry key security, perform the following steps:

1. Launch the editor by executing REGEDT32 from the **Run** command.

2. Select the HKEY_USERS key.

3. Select Security|Permissions.

4. A message may appear that states that you only have View permissions for this key. If so, click OK.

5. The familiar security dialog box appears. View the settings.

6. Click Cancel.

7. Close the editor by selecting Registry|Exit.

Using the Event Viewer

To use the Event Viewer to view the contents of the log files, perform the following steps:

1. Launch the Event Viewer. It is located on the Start menu under Programs|Administrative Tools|Event Viewer.

2. Select the System log.

3. Double-click an event in the right pane.

4. View the contents of this event detail.

5. Click OK.

6. Select a different log.

7. Open an event detail.

21. Troubleshooting Windows 2000

8. Close the event detail by clicking OK.

9. Close the Event Viewer by clicking the X button in the upper-right corner of the title bar.

Booting Windows 2000 into Safe Mode

When a driver or a configuration setting renders your system unusable, booting into Safe mode may resolve the issue. To boot into Safe mode, perform the following steps:

1. Power on the system.

2. When the boot menu is displayed, press F8.

3. On the Advanced Options menu, use the up- and down-arrow keys to select Safe mode.

4. Press Enter.

5. The system will boot into Windows 2000 Safe mode.

6. After the system has booted, click Start, and select Shut Down to restart the system. This will cause the system to reboot back into Normal mode.

Booting Using the Last Known Good Configuration

If you've installed a driver or changed a configuration that causes the system to malfunction or prevent logon, use the Last Known Good Configuration (LKGC) to restore the state of the registry stored by the system at the last successful logon.

NOTE: *Any changes made to the registry since the LKGC was saved will be lost with this procedure.*

To boot a system using the LKGC, perform the following steps:

1. Power on the system.

2. When the boot menu is displayed, press F8.

3. On the Advanced Options menu, use the up- and down-arrow keys to select Last Known Good Configuration.

4. Press Enter.

5. The system will boot into Windows 2000 using the LKGC.

Installing the Recovery Console

The Recovery Console can be used to repair damaged systems. Here's how:

NOTE: *The Recovery Console is an advanced tool. Consult the Windows 2000 Server Resource Kit for instructions on using this tool.*

1. Using the **Run** command, launch WINNT32 /CMDCONS from the Windows 2000 distribution CD.

2. When prompted, click Yes to install the Recovery Console.

3. When the "Finished" message appears, click OK.

4. Restart the system by clicking Start and selecting Shut Down.

5. When the boot menu appears, select Windows 2000 Recovery Console, and press Enter.

6. Type in the number of the operating system from the provided list, and then press Enter.

7. Provide the administrative account password, and press Enter.

8. Type "help", and press Enter to see a list of commands.

9. Type "exit" to reboot the system into Normal mode.

Appendix A
Group Policy Index

The following is a comprehensive index of all Group Policies included with Windows 2000, sorted by category. Use this list to help you troubleshoot Group Policy problems, such as when a Group Policy doesn't work, is duplicated elsewhere, or is overridden by an existing policy.

Accounts

Computer Configuration|Windows Settings|Security Settings|Account Policies|
Account Lockout Policy|Account Lockout Duration
Computer Configuration|Windows Settings|Security Settings|Account Policies|
Account Lockout Policy|Account Lockout Threshold
Computer Configuration|Windows Settings|Security Settings|Account Policies|
Account Lockout Policy|Reset Account Lockout Counter After
Computer Configuration|Windows Settings|Security Settings|Local Policies|
Security Options|Prevent System Maintenance Of Computer Account Password
Computer Configuration|Windows Settings|Security Settings|Local Policies|
Security Options|Rename Administrator Account
Computer Configuration|Windows Settings|Security Settings|Local Policies|
Security Options|Rename Guest Account

Active Directory

User Configuration|Administrative Templates|Desktop|Active Directory|Maximum
Size Of Active Directory Searches
User Configuration|Administrative Templates|Desktop|Active Directory|Enable
Filter In Find Dialog Box
User Configuration|Administrative Templates|Desktop|Active Directory|Hide
Active Directory Folder

Auditing

Computer Configuration|Windows Settings|Security Settings|Local Policies|
Audit Policy|Audit Account Logon Events
Computer Configuration|Windows Settings|Security Settings|Local Policies|
Audit Policy|Audit Account Management
Computer Configuration|Windows Settings|Security Settings|Local Policies|
Audit Policy|Audit Directory Service Access
Computer Configuration|Windows Settings|Security Settings|Local Policies|
Audit Policy|Audit Logon Events
Computer Configuration|Windows Settings|Security Settings|Local Policies|
Audit Policy|Audit Object Access
Computer Configuration|Windows Settings|Security Settings|Local Policies|
Audit Policy|Audit Policy Change
Computer Configuration|Windows Settings|Security Settings|Local Policies|
Audit Policy|Audit Privilege Use
Computer Configuration|Windows Settings|Security Settings|Local Policies|
Audit Policy|Audit Process Tracking
Computer Configuration|Windows Settings|Security Settings|Local Policies|
Audit Policy|Audit System Events
Computer Configuration|Windows Settings|Security Settings|Local Policies|
User Rights Assignment|Generate Security Audits
Computer Configuration|Windows Settings|Security Settings|Local Policies|
User Rights Assignment|Manage Auditing And Security Log
Computer Configuration|Windows Settings|Security Settings|Local Policies|
Security Options|Audit The Access Of Global System Objects
Computer Configuration|Windows Settings|Security Settings|Local Policies|
Security Options|Audit Use Of Backup And Restore Privilege
Computer Configuration|Windows Settings|Security Settings|Local Policies|
Security Options|Shut Down System Immediately If Unable To Log Security
Audits
Computer Configuration|Windows Settings|Security Settings|Event Log|Settings
For Event Log|Shut Down The Computer When The Security Audit Log Is Full

Auto Update

Computer Configuration|Administrative Templates|System|Download Missing COM
Components
User Configuration|Administrative Templates|System|Download Missing Com
Components

Certificates

Computer Configuration|Windows Settings|Security Settings|Local
Policies|Security Options|Digitally Sign Client Communication (Always)
Computer Configuration|Windows Settings|Security Settings|Local Policies|
Security Options|Digitally Sign Client Communication (When Possible)

Computer Configuration|Windows Settings|Security Settings|Local
Policies|Security Options|Digitally Sign Server Communication (Always)
Computer Configuration|Windows Settings|Security Settings|Local Policies|
Security Options|Digitally Sign Server Communication (When Possible)
Computer Configuration|Windows Settings|Security Settings|Local
Policies|Security Options|Unsigned Driver Installation Behavior
Computer Configuration|Windows Settings|Security Settings|Local
Policies|Security Options|Unsigned Non-Driver Installation Behavior
User Configuration|Administrative Templates|Windows Components|Microsoft
Management Console|Restricted/Permitted Snap-Ins|Certificates
User Configuration|Administrative Templates|Windows Components|Microsoft
Management Console|Restricted/Permitted Snap-Ins|Extension Snap-Ins|
Certification Authority
Computer Configuration|Windows Settings|Security Settings|Local
Policies|Security Options|Smart Card Removal Behavior

Control Panel

User Configuration|Administrative Templates|Control Panel|Regional
Options|Restrict Selection Of Windows 2000 Menus And Dialogs Language
User Configuration|Administrative Templates|Network|Offline Files|Disable
User Configuraiton Of Offline Files
User Configuration|Administrative Templates|Control Panel|Disable Control
Panel
User Configuration|Administrative Templates|Control Panel|Hide Specified
Control Panel Applets
User Configuration|Administrative Templates|Control Panel|Show Only
Specified Control Panel Applets
User Configuration|Administrative Templates|Control Panel|Add/Remove
Programs|Disable Add/Remove Programs
User Configuration|Administrative Templates|Control Panel|Add/Remove
Programs|Hide Change Or Remove Programs Page
User Configuration|Administrative Templates|Control Panel|Add/Remove
Programs|Hide Add New Programs Page
User Configuration|Administrative Templates|Control Panel|Add/Remove
Programs|Hide Add/Remove Windows Components Page
User Configuration|Administrative Templates|Control Panel|Add/Remove
Programs|Hide The "Add A Program From Cd-Rom Or Floppy Disk" Option
User Configuration|Administrative Templates|Control Panel|Add/Remove
Programs|Hide The "Add Programs From Microsoft" Option
User Configuration|Administrative Templates|Control Panel|Add/Remove
Programs|Hide The "Add Programs From Your Network" Option
User Configuration|Administrative Templates|Control Panel|Add/Remove
Programs|Go Directly To Components Wizard
User Configuration|Administrative Templates|Control Panel|Add/Remove
Programs|Disable Support Information

User Configuration|Administrative Templates|Control Panel|Add/Remove
Programs|Specify Default Category For Add New Programs

User Configuration|Administrative Templates|Control Panel|Display|Disable
Display In Control Panel

User Configuration|Administrative Templates|Control Panel|Display|Hide
Background Tab

User Configuration|Administrative Templates|Control Panel|Display|Disable
Changing Wallpaper

User Configuration|Administrative Templates|Control Panel|Display|Hide
Appearance Tab

User Configuration|Administrative Templates|Control Panel|Display|Hide
Settings Tab

User Configuration|Administrative Templates|Control Panel|Display|Hide
Screen Saver Tab

User Configuration|Administrative Templates|Control Panel|Display|No Screen
Saver

User Configuration|Administrative Templates|Control Panel|Display|Screen
Saver Executable Name

User Configuration|Administrative Templates|Control Panel|Display|Password
Protect The Screen Saver

User Configuration|Administrative Templates|Control Panel|Printers|Disable
Deletion Of Printers

User Configuration|Administrative Templates|Control Panel|Printers|Disable
Addition Of Printers

User Configuration|Administrative Templates|Control Panel|Printers|Browse
The Network To Find Printers

User Configuration|Administrative Templates|Control Panel|Printers|Default
Active Directory Path When Searching For Printers

User Configuration|Administrative Templates|Control Panel|Printers|Browse A
Common Web Site To Find Printers

Desktop

User Configuration|Administrative Templates|Desktop|Remove My Documents Icon
From Desktop

User Configuration|Administrative Templates|Desktop|Remove My Documents Icon
From Start Menu

User Configuration|Administrative Templates|Desktop|Hide My Network Places
Icon On Desktop

User Configuration|Administrative Templates|Desktop|Hide Internet Explorer
Icon On Desktop

User Configuration|Administrative Templates|Desktop|Do Not Add Shares Of
Recently Opened Documents To My Network Places

User Configuration|Administrative Templates|Desktop|Prohibit User From
Changing My Documents Path

User Configuration|Administrative Templates|Desktop|Disable Adding,
Dragging, Dropping And Closing The Taskbar's Toolbars
User Configuration|Administrative Templates|Desktop|Disable Adjusting
Desktop Toolbars
User Configuration|Administrative Templates|Desktop|Don't Save Settings On
Exit
User Configuration|Administrative Templates|Desktop|Active Desktop|Enable
Active Desktop
User Configuration|Administrative Templates|Desktop|Active Desktop|Disable
Active Desktop
User Configuration|Administrative Templates|Desktop|Active Desktop|Disable
All Items
User Configuration|Administrative Templates|Desktop|Active Desktop|Prohibit
Changes
User Configuration|Administrative Templates|Desktop|Active Desktop|Prohibit
Adding Items
User Configuration|Administrative Templates|Desktop|Active Desktop|Prohibit
Deleting Items
User Configuration|Administrative Templates|Desktop|Active Desktop|Prohibit
Editing Items
User Configuration|Administrative Templates|Desktop|Active Desktop|Prohibit
Closing Items
User Configuration|Administrative Templates|Desktop|Active Desktop|
Add/Delete Items
User Configuration|Administrative Templates|Desktop|Active Desktop|Active
Desktop Wallpaper
User Configuration|Administrative Templates|Desktop|Active Desktop|Allow
Only Bitmapped Wallpaper
User Configuration|Administrative Templates|Desktop|Active Desktop

Domain Administration

Computer Configuration|Windows Settings|Security Settings|Local
Policies|User Rights Assignment|Add Workstations To The Domain
Computer Configuration|Windows Settings|Security Settings|Local
Policies|User Rights Assignment|Synchronize Directory Service Data
Computer Configuration|Windows Settings|Security Settings|Local
Policies|Security Options|Allow Server Operators To Schedule Tasks (Domain
Controllers Only)
Computer Configuration|Administrative Templates|Printers|Automatically
Publish New Printers In Active Directory
Computer Configuration|Administrative Templates|Printers|Allow Pruning Of
Published Printers
Computer Configuration|Administrative Templates|Printers|Printer Browsing
Computer Configuration|Administrative Templates|Printers|Prune Printers That
Are Not Automatically Republished

Computer Configuration|Administrative Templates|Printers|Directory Pruning Interval

Computer Configuration|Administrative Templates|Printers|Directory Pruning Retry

Computer Configuration|Administrative Templates|Printers|Directory Pruning Priority

Computer Configuration|Administrative Templates|Printers|Check Published State

User Configuration|Administrative Templates|Windows Components|Microsoft Management Console|Restricted/Permitted Snap-Ins|Active Directory Users And Computers

User Configuration|Administrative Templates|Windows Components|Microsoft Management Console|Restricted/Permitted Snap-Ins|Active Directory Domains And Trusts

User Configuration|Administrative Templates|Windows Components|Microsoft Management Console|Restricted/Permitted Snap-Ins|Active Directory Sites And Services

User Configuration|Administrative Templates|Windows Components|Microsoft Management Console|Restricted/Permitted Snap-Ins|Group Policy|Group Policy Tab For Active Directory Tools

Computer Configuration|Windows Settings|Security Settings|Local Policies| Security Options|Automatically Log Off Users When Logon Time Expires

Encryption

Computer Configuration|Windows Settings|Security Settings|Local Policies| Security Options|Secure Channel: Digitally Encrypt Or Sign Secure Channel Data (Always)

Computer Configuration|Windows Settings|Security Settings|Local Policies| Security Options|Secure Channel: Digitally Encrypt Secure Channel Data (When Possible)

Computer Configuration|Windows Settings|Security Settings|Local Policies| Security Options|Secure Channel: Digitally Sign Secure Channel Data (When Possible)

Computer Configuration|Windows Settings|Security Settings|Local Policies| Security Options|Secure Channel: Require Strong (Windows 2000 Or Later) Session Key

Computer Configuration|Windows Settings|Security Settings|Local Policies| Security Options|Send Unencrypted Password To Connect To Third-Party Smb Servers

Computer Configuration|Administrative Templates|System|Do Not Automatically Encrypt Files Moved To Encrypted Folders

Computer Configuration|Administrative Templates|System|Group Policy|Efs Recovery Policy Processing

User Configuration|Windows Settings|Security Settings|Public Key Policies| Enterprise Trust

User Configuration|Windows Settings|Security Settings|Ip Security Policies
On Active Directory|Client (Respond Only)
User Configuration|Windows Settings|Security Settings|Ip Security Policies
On Active Directory|Secure Server (Require Security)
User Configuration|Windows Settings|Security Settings|Ip Security Policies
On Active Directory|Server (Request Security)
User Configuration|Administrative Templates|Windows Components|Microsoft
Management Console|Restricted/Permitted Snap-Ins|Extension Snap-Ins|Public
Key Policies

Folder Redirection

User Configuration|Windows Settings|Folder Redirection|Application Data
User Configuration|Windows Settings|Folder Redirection|Desktop
User Configuration|Windows Settings|Folder Redirection|My Documents
User Configuration|Windows Settings|Folder Redirection|My Documents|My
Pictures
User Configuration|Windows Settings|Folder Redirection|Start Menu
User Configuration|Administrative Templates|Windows Components|Microsoft
Management Console|Restricted/Permitted Snap-Ins|Group Policy|Folder
Redirection

Group Policy

Computer Configuration|Administrative Templates|System|Group Policy|Disable
Background Refresh Of Group Policy
Computer Configuration|Administrative Templates|System|Group Policy|Apply
Group Policy For Computers Asynchronously During Startup
Computer Configuration|Administrative Templates|System|Group Policy|Apply
Group Policy For Users Asynchronously During Logon
Computer Configuration|Administrative Templates|System|Group Policy|Group
Policy Refresh Interval For Computers
Computer Configuration|Administrative Templates|System|Group Policy|Group
Policy Refresh Interval For Domain Controllers
Computer Configuration|Administrative Templates|System|Group Policy|User
Group Policy Loopback Processing Mode
Computer Configuration|Administrative Templates|System|Group Policy|Group
Policy Slow Link Detection
Computer Configuration|Administrative Templates|System|Group Policy|Registry
Policy Processing
Computer Configuration|Administrative Templates|System|Group Policy|Internet
Explorer Maintenance Policy Processing
Computer Configuration|Administrative Templates|System|Group Policy|Software
Installation Policy Processing
Computer Configuration|Administrative Templates|System|Group Policy|Folder
Redirection Policy Processing

Computer Configuration|Administrative Templates|System|Group Policy|Scripts Policy Processing

Computer Configuration|Administrative Templates|System|Group Policy|Security Policy Processing

Computer Configuration|Administrative Templates|System|Group Policy|Ip Security Policy Processing

Computer Configuration|Administrative Templates|System|Group Policy|Efs Recovery Policy Processing

Computer Configuration|Administrative Templates|System|Group Policy|Disk Quota Policy Processing

User Configuration|Administrative Templates|System|Group Policy|Group Policy Refresh Interval For Users

User Configuration|Administrative Templates|System|Group Policy|Group Policy Slow Link Detection

User Configuration|Administrative Templates|System|Group Policy|Group Policy Domain Controller Selection

User Configuration|Administrative Templates|System|Group Policy|Create New Group Policy Object Links Disabled By Default

User Configuration|Administrative Templates|System|Group Policy|Enforce Show Policies Only

User Configuration|Administrative Templates|System|Group Policy|Disable Automatic Update Of Adm Files

User Configuration|Administrative Templates|Windows Components|Microsoft Management Console|Restricted/Permitted Snap-Ins|Group Policy|Group Policy Snap-In

User Configuration|Administrative Templates|Windows Components|Microsoft Management Console|Restricted/Permitted Snap-Ins|Group Policy|Administrative Templates (Computers)

User Configuration|Administrative Templates|Windows Components|Microsoft Management Console|Restricted/Permitted Snap-Ins|Group Policy|Administrative Templates (Users)

User Configuration|Administrative Templates|Windows Components|Microsoft Management Console|Restricted/Permitted Snap-Ins|Group Policy|Folder Redirection

User Configuration|Administrative Templates|Windows Components|Microsoft Management Console|Restricted/Permitted Snap-Ins|Group Policy|Internet Explorer Maintenance

User Configuration|Administrative Templates|Windows Components|Microsoft Management Console|Restricted/Permitted Snap-Ins|Group Policy|Remote Installation Services

User Configuration|Administrative Templates|Windows Components|Microsoft Management Console|Restricted/Permitted Snap-Ins|Group Policy|Scripts (Logon/Logoff)

User Configuration|Administrative Templates|Windows Components|Microsoft Management Console|Restricted/Permitted Snap-Ins|Group Policy|Scripts (Startup/Shutdown)

User Configuration|Administrative Templates|Windows Components|Microsoft Management Console|Restricted/Permitted Snap-Ins|Group Policy|Security Settings

User Configuration|Administrative Templates|Windows Components|Microsoft Management Console|Restricted/Permitted Snap-Ins|Group Policy|Software Installation (Computers)

User Configuration|Administrative Templates|Windows Components|Microsoft Management Console|Restricted/Permitted Snap-Ins|Group Policy|Software Installation (Users)

User Configuration|Administrative Templates|Windows Components|Microsoft Management Console|Restricted/Permitted Snap-Ins|Group Policy|Group Policy Tab For Active Directory Tools

Hardware

Computer Configuration|Windows Settings|Security Settings|Local Policies|Security Options|Prevent Users From Installing Printer Drivers

Computer Configuration|Administrative Templates|System|Disable Autoplay

Computer Configuration|Administrative Templates|Printers|Allow Printers To Be Published

User Configuration|Administrative Templates|System|Disable Autoplay

Computer Configuration|Windows Settings|Security Settings|Local Policies|User Rights Assignment|Modify Firmware Environment Values

Computer Configuration|Windows Settings|Security Settings|Local Policies|Security Options|Allowed To Eject Removable Ntfs Media

Computer Configuration|Windows Settings|Security Settings|Local Policies|Security Options|Clear Virtual Memory Pagefile When System Shuts Down

Computer Configuration|Windows Settings|Security Settings|Local Policies|Security Options|Secure System Partition (For Risc Platforms Only)

User Configuration|Administrative Templates|Windows Components|Microsoft Management Console|Restricted/Permitted Snap-Ins|Device Manager

User Configuration|Administrative Templates|Windows Components|Microsoft Management Console|Restricted/Permitted Snap-Ins|Disk Management

User Configuration|Administrative Templates|Windows Components|Microsoft Management Console|Restricted/Permitted Snap-Ins|Removable Storage Management

User Configuration|Administrative Templates|Windows Components|Microsoft Management Console|Restricted/Permitted Snap-Ins|System Information

User Configuration|Administrative Templates|Windows Components|Microsoft Management Console|Restricted/Permitted Snap-Ins|Extension Snap-Ins|Device Manager

User Configuration|Administrative Templates|System|Code Signing For Device Drivers

User Configuration|Administrative Templates|Windows Components|Microsoft Management Console|Restricted/Permitted Snap-Ins|Extension Snap-Ins|Removable Storage

Installation

Computer Configuration|Software Settings|Software Installation

User Configuration|Administrative Templates|Windows Components|Microsoft Management Console|Restricted/Permitted Snap-Ins|Group Policy|Software Installation (Computers)

User Configuration|Administrative Templates|Windows Components|Microsoft Management Console|Restricted/Permitted Snap-Ins|Group Policy|Software Installation (Users)

Interface

User Configuration|Administrative Templates|Start Menu & Taskbar|Remove User's Folders From The Start Menu

User Configuration|Administrative Templates|Start Menu & Taskbar|Disable And Remove Links To Windows Update

User Configuration|Administrative Templates|Start Menu & Taskbar|Remove Common Program Groups From Start Menu

User Configuration|Administrative Templates|Start Menu & Taskbar|Remove Documents Menu From Start Menu

User Configuration|Administrative Templates|Start Menu & Taskbar|Disable Programs On Settings Menu

User Configuration|Administrative Templates|Start Menu & Taskbar|Remove Network & Dial-Up Connections From Start Menu

User Configuration|Administrative Templates|Start Menu & Taskbar|Remove Favorites Menu From Start Menu

User Configuration|Administrative Templates|Start Menu & Taskbar|Remove Search Menu From Start Menu

User Configuration|Administrative Templates|Start Menu & Taskbar|Remove Help Menu From Start Menu

User Configuration|Administrative Templates|Start Menu & Taskbar|Remove Run Menu From Start Menu

User Configuration|Administrative Templates|Start Menu & Taskbar|Add Logoff To The Start Menu

User Configuration|Administrative Templates|Start Menu & Taskbar|Disable Logoff On The Start Menu

User Configuration|Administrative Templates|Start Menu & Taskbar|Disable And Remove The Shut Down Command

User Configuration|Administrative Templates|Start Menu & Taskbar|Disable Drag-And-Drop Context Menus On The Start Menu

User Configuration|Administrative Templates|Start Menu & Taskbar|Disable Changes To Taskbar And Start Menu Settings

User Configuration|Administrative Templates|Start Menu & Taskbar|Disable Context Menus For The Taskbar|

User Configuration|Administrative Templates|Start Menu & Taskbar|Do Not Keep History Of Recently Opened Documents

User Configuration|Administrative Templates|Start Menu & Taskbar|Clear History Of Recently Opened Documents On Exist

User Configuration|Administrative Templates|Start Menu & Taskbar|Disable Personalized Menus

User Configuration|Administrative Templates|Start Menu & Taskbar|Disable User Tracking

User Configuration|Administrative Templates|Start Menu & Taskbar|Add "Run In Separate Memory Space" Check Box To Run Dialog Box

User Configuration|Administrative Templates|Start Menu & Taskbar|Do Not Use The Search-Based Method When Resolving Shell Shortcuts

User Configuration|Administrative Templates|Start Menu & Taskbar|Do Not Use The Tracking-Based Method When Resolving Shell Shortcuts

User Configuration|Administrative Templates|Start Menu & Taskbar|Gray Unavailable Windows Installer Programs Start Menu Shortcuts

User Configuration|Administrative Templates|Desktop|Hide All Icons On Desktop

User Configuration|Administrative Templates|Desktop|Remove My Documents Icon From Desktop

User Configuration|Administrative Templates|Desktop|Remove My Documents Icon From Start Menu

User Configuration|Administrative Templates|Desktop|Hide My Network Places Icon On Desktop

User Configuration|Administrative Templates|Desktop|Hide Internet Explorer Icon On Desktop

User Configuration|Administrative Templates|Desktop|Do Not Add Shares Of Recently Opened Documents To My Network Places

User Configuration|Administrative Templates|Desktop|Prohibit User From Changing My Documents Path

User Configuration|Administrative Templates|Desktop|Disable Adding, Dragging, Dropping And Closing The Taskbar's Toolbars

User Configuration|Administrative Templates|Desktop|Disable Adjusting Desktop Toolbars

User Configuration|Administrative Templates|Desktop|Don't Save Settings On Exit

User Configuration|Administrative Templates|Desktop|Active Desktop|Enable Active Desktop

User Configuration|Administrative Templates|Desktop|Active Desktop|Disable Active Desktop

User Configuration|Administrative Templates|Desktop|Active Desktop|Disable All Items

User Configuration|Administrative Templates|Desktop|Active Desktop|Prohibit Changes

User Configuration|Administrative Templates|Desktop|Active Desktop|Prohibit Adding Items

User Configuration|Administrative Templates|Desktop|Active Desktop|Prohibit Deleting Items

User Configuration|Administrative Templates|Control Panel|Display|Disable Changing Wallpaper

User Configuration|Administrative Templates|Control Panel|Display|Hide Appearance Tab

User Configuration|Administrative Templates|Control Panel|Display|Hide Settings Tab

User Configuration|Administrative Templates|Control Panel|Display|Hide Screen Saver Tab

User Configuration|Administrative Templates|Control Panel|Display|No Screen Saver

User Configuration|Administrative Templates|Control Panel|Display|Screen Saver Executable Name

User Configuration|Administrative Templates|Control Panel|Display|Password Protect The Screen Saver

User Configuration|Administrative Templates|System|Don't Display Welcome Screen At Logon

User Configuration|Administrative Templates|System|Custom User Interface

User Configuration|Administrative Templates|System|Disable The Command Prompt

User Configuration|Administrative Templates|System|Disable Registry Editing Tools

User Configuration|Administrative Templates|System|Run Only Allowed Windows Applications

User Configuration|Administrative Templates|System|Don't Run Specified Windows Applications

User Configuration|Administrative Templates|System|Logon/Logoff|Disable Task Manager

User Configuration|Administrative Templates|System|Logon/Logoff|Disable Lock Computer

User Configuration|Administrative Templates|System|Logon/Logoff|Disable Change Password

User Configuration|Administrative Templates|System|Logon/Logoff|Disable Logoff

Computer Configuration|Windows Settings|Security Settings|Local Policies|User Rights Assignment|Shut Down The System

Computer Configuration|Windows Settings|Security Settings|Local Policies|Security Options|Allow System To Be Shut Down Without Having To Log On

User Configuration|Administrative Templates|Network|Network And Dial-Up Connections|Display And Enable The Network Connection Wizard

Computer Configuration|Windows Settings|Security Settings|Local Policies|Security Options|Do Not Display Last User Name In Logon Screen

Computer Configuration|Windows Settings|Security Settings|Local Policies|Security Options|Message Text For Users Attempting To Log On

Computer Configuration|Windows Settings|Security Settings|Local Policies|Security Options|Message Title For Users Attempting To Log On

Internet Explorer

Computer Configuration|Administrative Templates|Windows Components|Internet Explorer|Security Zones: Use Only Machine Settings

Computer Configuration|Administrative Templates|Windows Components|Internet Explorer|Security Zones: Do Not Allow Users To Change Policies

Computer Configuration|Administrative Templates|Windows Components|Internet Explorer|Security Zones: Do Not Allow Users To Add/Delete Sites

Computer Configuration|Administrative Templates|Windows Components|Internet Explorer|Make Proxy Settings Per-Machine (Rather Than Per-User)

Computer Configuration|Administrative Templates|Windows Components|Internet Explorer|Disable Automatic Install Of Internet Explorer Components

Computer Configuration|Administrative Templates|Windows Components|Internet Explorer|Disable Periodic Check For Internet Explorer Software Updates

Computer Configuration|Administrative Templates|Windows Components|Internet Explorer|Disable Software Update Shell Notifications On Program Launch

Computer Configuration|Administrative Templates|Windows Components|Internet Explorer|Disable Showing The Splash Screen

User Configuration|Windows Settings|Internet Explorer Maintenance|Browser User Interface|Browser Title

User Configuration|Windows Settings|Internet Explorer Maintenance|Browser User Interface|Animated Bitmaps

User Configuration|Windows Settings|Internet Explorer Maintenance|Browser User Interface|Custom Logo

User Configuration|Windows Settings|Internet Explorer Maintenance|Browser User Interface|Browser Toolbar Buttons

User Configuration|Windows Settings|Internet Explorer Maintenance|Connection|Connection Settings

User Configuration|Windows Settings|Internet Explorer Maintenance|Connection|Automatic Browser Configuration

User Configuration|Windows Settings|Internet Explorer Maintenance|Connection|Proxy Settings

User Configuration|Windows Settings|Internet Explorer Maintenance|Connection|User Agent String

User Configuration|Windows Settings|Internet Explorer Maintenance|Urls|Favorites And Links

User Configuration|Windows Settings|Internet Explorer Maintenance|Urls|Important Urls

User Configuration|Windows Settings|Internet Explorer Maintenance|Urls|Channels

User Configuration|Windows Settings|Internet Explorer Maintenance|Security|Security Zones And Content Ratings

User Configuration|Windows Settings|Internet Explorer Maintenance|Security|Authenticode Settings

User Configuration|Windows Settings|Internet Explorer Maintenance|Programs

User Configuration|Administrative Templates|Windows Components|Internet Explorer|Search: Disable Search Customization

User Configuration|Administrative Templates|Windows Components|Internet Explorer|Search: Disable Find Files Via F3 Within The Browser

User Configuration|Administrative Templates|Windows Components|Internet Explorer|Disable External Branding Of Internet Explorer

User Configuration|Administrative Templates|Windows Components|Internet Explorer|Disable Importing And Exporting Of Favorites

User Configuration|Administrative Templates|Windows Components|Internet Explorer|Disable Changing Advanced Page Settings

User Configuration|Administrative Templates|Windows Components|Internet Explorer|Disable Changing Home Page Settings

User Configuration|Administrative Templates|Windows Components|Internet Explorer|Use Automatic Detection For Dial-Up Connections

User Configuration|Administrative Templates|Windows Components|Internet Explorer|Disable Caching Of Auto-Proxy Scripts

User Configuration|Administrative Templates|Windows Components|Internet Explorer|Display Error Message On Proxy Script Download Failure

User Configuration|Administrative Templates|Windows Components|Internet Explorer|Disable Changing Temporary Internet Files Settings

User Configuration|Administrative Templates|Windows Components|Internet Explorer|Disable Changing History Settings

User Configuration|Administrative Templates|Windows Components|Internet Explorer|Disable Changing Color Settings

User Configuration|Administrative Templates|Windows Components|Internet Explorer|Disable Changing Link Color Settings

User Configuration|Administrative Templates|Windows Components|Internet Explorer|Disable Changing Font Settings

User Configuration|Administrative Templates|Windows Components|Internet Explorer|Disable Changing Language Settings

User Configuration|Administrative Templates|Windows Components|Internet Explorer|Disable Changing Accessibility Settings

User Configuration|Administrative Templates|Windows Components|Internet Explorer|Disable Internet Connection Wizard

User Configuration|Administrative Templates|Windows Components|Internet Explorer|Disable Changing Connection Settings

User Configuration|Administrative Templates|Windows Components|Internet Explorer|Disable Changing Proxy Settings

User Configuration|Administrative Templates|Windows Components|Internet Explorer|Disable Changing Automatic Configuration Settings

User Configuration|Administrative Templates|Windows Components|Internet Explorer|Disable Changing Ratings Settings

User Configuration|Administrative Templates|Windows Components|Internet Explorer|Disable Changing Certificate Settings

User Configuration|Administrative Templates|Windows Components|Internet Explorer|Disable Changing Profile Assistant Settings

User Configuration|Administrative Templates|Windows Components|Internet Explorer|Disable Autocomplete For Forms

User Configuration|Administrative Templates|Windows Components|Internet Explorer|Do Not Allow Autocomplete To Save Passwords

User Configuration|Administrative Templates|Windows Components|Internet Explorer|Disable Changing Messaging Settings

User Configuration|Administrative Templates|Windows Components|Internet Explorer|Disable Changing Calendar And Contact Settings

User Configuration|Administrative Templates|Windows Components|Internet Explorer|Disable The Reset Web Settings Feature

User Configuration|Administrative Templates|Windows Components|Internet Explorer|Disable Changing Default Browser Check

User Configuration|Administrative Templates|Windows Components|Internet Explorer|Identity Manager: Prevent Users From Using Identities

User Configuration|Administrative Templates|Windows Components|Internet Explorer|Internet Control Panel|Disable The General Page

User Configuration|Administrative Templates|Windows Components|Internet Explorer|Internet Control Panel|Disable The Security Page

User Configuration|Administrative Templates|Windows Components|Internet Explorer|Internet Control Panel|Disable The Content Page

User Configuration|Administrative Templates|Windows Components|Internet Explorer|Internet Control Panel|Disable The Connections Page

User Configuration|Administrative Templates|Windows Components|Internet Explorer|Internet Control Panel|Disable The Programs Page

User Configuration|Administrative Templates|Windows Components|Internet Explorer|Internet Control Panel|Disable The Advanced Page

User Configuration|Administrative Templates|Windows Components|Internet Explorer|Offline Pages|Disable Adding Channels

User Configuration|Administrative Templates|Windows Components|Internet Explorer|Offline Pages|Disable Removing Channels

User Configuration|Administrative Templates|Windows Components|Internet Explorer|Offline Pages|Disable Adding Schedules For Offline Pages

User Configuration|Administrative Templates|Windows Components|Internet Explorer|Offline Pages|Disable Editing Schedules For Offline Pages

User Configuration|Administrative Templates|Windows Components|Internet Explorer|Offline Pages|Disable Removing Schedules For Offline Pages

User Configuration|Administrative Templates|Windows Components|Internet Explorer|Offline Pages|Disable Offline Page Hit Logging

User Configuration|Administrative Templates|Windows Components|Internet Explorer|Offline Pages|Disable All Scheduled Offline Pages

User Configuration|Administrative Templates|Windows Components|Internet Explorer|Offline Pages|Disable Channel User Interface Completely

User Configuration|Administrative Templates|Windows Components|Internet Explorer|Offline Pages|Disable Downloading Of Site Subscription Content

User Configuration|Administrative Templates|Windows Components|Internet Explorer|Offline Pages|Disable Editing And Creating Of Schedule Groups

User Configuration|Administrative Templates|Windows Components|Internet Explorer|Offline Pages|Subscription Limits

User Configuration|Administrative Templates|Windows Components|Internet Explorer|Browser Menus|File Menu: Disable Save As... Menu Option

User Configuration|Administrative Templates|Windows Components|Internet Explorer|Browser Menus|File Menu: Disable New Menu Option

User Configuration|Administrative Templates|Windows Components|Internet Explorer|Browser Menus|File Menu: Disable Open Menu Option

User Configuration|Administrative Templates|Windows Components|Internet Explorer|Browser Menus|File Menu: Disable Save As Web Page Complete

User Configuration|Administrative Templates|Windows Components|Internet Explorer|Browser Menus|File Menu: Disable Closing The Browser And Explorer Windows

User Configuration|Administrative Templates|Windows Components|Internet Explorer|Browser Menus|View Menu: Disable Source Menu Option

User Configuration|Administrative Templates|Windows Components|Internet Explorer|Browser Menus|View Menu: Disable Full Screen Menu Option

User Configuration|Administrative Templates|Windows Components|Internet Explorer|Browser Menus|Hide Favorites Menu

User Configuration|Administrative Templates|Windows Components|Internet Explorer|Browser Menus|Tools Menu: Disable Internet Options... Menu Option

User Configuration|Administrative Templates|Windows Components|Internet Explorer|Browser Menus|Help Menu: Remove 'Tip Of The Day' Menu Option

User Configuration|Administrative Templates|Windows Components|Internet Explorer|Browser Menus|Help Menu: Remove 'For Netscape Users' Menu Option

User Configuration|Administrative Templates|Windows Components|Internet Explorer|Browser Menus|Help Menu: Remove 'Tour' Menu Option

User Configuration|Administrative Templates|Windows Components|Internet Explorer|Browser Menus|Help Menu: Remove 'Send Feedback' Menu Option

User Configuration|Administrative Templates|Windows Components|Internet Explorer|Browser Menus|Disable Context Menu

User Configuration|Administrative Templates|Windows Components|Internet Explorer|Browser Menus|Disable Open In New Window Menu Option

User Configuration|Administrative Templates|Windows Components|Internet Explorer|Browser Menus|Disable Save This Program To Disk Option

User Configuration|Administrative Templates|Windows Components|Internet Explorer|Toolbars|Disable Customizing Browser Toolbar Buttons

User Configuration|Administrative Templates|Windows Components|Internet Explorer|Toolbars|Disable Customizing Browser Toolbars

User Configuration|Administrative Templates|Windows Components|Internet Explorer|Toolbars|Configure Toolbar Buttons

User Configuration|Administrative Templates|Windows Components|Internet Explorer|Persistence Behavior|File Size Limits For Local Machine Zone

User Configuration|Administrative Templates|Windows Components|Internet Explorer|Persistence Behavior|File Size Limits For Intranet Zone

User Configuration|Administrative Templates|Windows Components|Internet Explorer|Persistence Behavior|File Size Limits For Trusted Sites Zone

User Configuration|Administrative Templates|Windows Components|Internet Explorer|Persistence Behavior|File Size Limits For Internet Zone

User Configuration|Administrative Templates|Windows Components|Internet Explorer|Persistence Behavior|File Size Limits For Restricted Sites Zone

User Configuration|Administrative Templates|Windows Components|Internet Explorer|Administrator Approved Controls|Media Player

User Configuration|Administrative Templates|Windows Components|Internet Explorer|Administrator Approved Controls|Menu Controls

User Configuration|Administrative Templates|Windows Components|Internet Explorer|Administrator Approved Controls|Microsoft Agent

User Configuration|Administrative Templates|Windows Components|Internet Explorer|Administrator Approved Controls|Microsoft Chat

User Configuration|Administrative Templates|Windows Components|Internet Explorer|Administrator Approved Controls|Microsoft Survey Control

User Configuration|Administrative Templates|Windows Components|Internet Explorer|Administrator Approved Controls|Shockwave Flash

User Configuration|Administrative Templates|Windows Components|Internet Explorer|Administrator Approved Controls|Netshow File Transfer Control

User Configuration|Administrative Templates|Windows Components|Internet Explorer|Administrator Approved Controls|DHTML Edit Control

User Configuration|Administrative Templates|Windows Components|Internet Explorer|Administrator Approved Controls|Microsoft Scriptlet Component

User Configuration|Administrative Templates|Windows Components|Internet Explorer|Administrator Approved Controls|Carpoint

User Configuration|Administrative Templates|Windows Components|Internet Explorer|Administrator Approved Controls|Investor

User Configuration|Administrative Templates|Windows Components|Internet Explorer|Administrator Approved Controls|MSNBC

User Configuration|Administrative Templates|Windows Components|Microsoft Management Console|Restricted/Permitted Snap-Ins|Group Policy|Internet Explorer Maintenance

TCP/IP Security

Computer Configuration|Windows Settings|Security Settings|IP Security Policies On Active Directory|Client (Respond Only)

Computer Configuration|Windows Settings|Security Settings|IP Security Policies On Active Directory|Secure Server (Require Security)

Computer Configuration|Windows Settings|Security Settings|IP Security Policies On Active Directory|Server (Request Security)

Computer Configuration|Administrative Templates|System|Group Policy|IP Security Policy Processing

User Configuration|Administrative Templates|Windows Components|Microsoft Management Console|Restricted/Permitted Snap-Ins|IP Security

Local Administration

Computer Configuration|Windows Settings|Security Settings|Local
Policies|User Rights Assignment|Back Up Files And Directories

Computer Configuration|Windows Settings|Security Settings|Local Policies|
User Rights Assignment|Change The System Time

Computer Configuration|Windows Settings|Security Settings|Local Policies|
User Rights Assignment|Create A Pagefile

Computer Configuration|Windows Settings|Security Settings|Local Policies|
User Rights Assignment|Create A Token Object

Computer Configuration|Windows Settings|Security Settings|Local Policies|
User Rights Assignment|Increase Quotas

Computer Configuration|Windows Settings|Security Settings|Local Policies|
User Rights Assignment|Increase Scheduling Priority

Computer Configuration|Windows Settings|Security Settings|Local Policies|
User Rights Assignment|Modify Firmware Environment Values

Computer Configuration|Windows Settings|Security Settings|Local Policies|
Security Options|Recovery Console: Allow Floppy Copy And Access To All
Drives And All Folders

Computer Configuration|Windows Settings|Security Settings|Local Policies|
Security Options|Rename Administrator Account

Computer Configuration|Windows Settings|Security Settings|Local Policies|
Security Options|Rename Guest Account

Computer Configuration|Windows Settings|Security Settings|Local Policies|
Security Options|Restrict CD-ROM Access To Locally Logged-On User Only

Computer Configuration|Windows Settings|Security Settings|System Services|
{All Services}

User Configuration|Administrative Templates|System|Century Interpretation
For Year 2000

User Configuration|Administrative Templates|System|Code Signing For Device
Drivers

Computer Configuration|Windows Settings|Security Settings|Local Policies|
User Rights Assignment|Load And Unload Device Drivers

Computer Configuration|Windows Settings|Security Settings|Local Policies|
User Rights Assignment|Profile Single Process

Computer Configuration|Windows Settings|Security Settings|Local Policies|
User Rights Assignment|Profile System Performance

Computer Configuration|Windows Settings|Security Settings|Local Policies|
User Rights Assignment|Remove Computer From Docking Station

Computer Configuration|Windows Settings|Security Settings|Local Policies|
User Rights Assignment|Restore Files And Directories

Computer Configuration|Windows Settings|Security Settings|Local Policies|
User Rights Assignment|Take Ownership Of Files Or Other Objects

Computer Configuration|Windows Settings|Security Settings|Local Policies|
Security Options|Recovery Console: Allow Automatic Administrative Logon

Computer Configuration|Administrative Templates|Printers|Pre-Populate Printer Search Location Text

User Configuration|Administrative Templates|Windows Components|Microsoft Management Console|Restricted/Permitted Snap-Ins|Computer Management

User Configuration|Administrative Templates|Windows Components|Microsoft Management Console|Restricted/Permitted Snap-Ins|Disk Defragmenter

User Configuration|Administrative Templates|Windows Components|Microsoft Management Console|Restricted/Permitted Snap-Ins|Local Users And Groups

User Configuration|Administrative Templates|Windows Components|Microsoft Management Console|Restricted/Permitted Snap-Ins|Device Manager

User Configuration|Administrative Templates|Windows Components|Microsoft Management Console|Restricted/Permitted Snap-Ins|Disk Management

User Configuration|Administrative Templates|Windows Components|Microsoft Management Console|Restricted/Permitted Snap-Ins|Removable Storage Management

Logging

Computer Configuration|Windows Settings|Security Settings|Event Log|Settings For Event Log|Maximum Application Log Size

Computer Configuration|Windows Settings|Security Settings|Event Log|Settings For Event Log|Maximum Security Log Size

Computer Configuration|Windows Settings|Security Settings|Event Log|Settings For Event Log|Maximum System Log Size

Computer Configuration|Windows Settings|Security Settings|Event Log|Settings For Event Log|Restrict Guest Access To Application Log

Computer Configuration|Windows Settings|Security Settings|Event Log|Settings For Event Log|Restrict Guest Access To Security Log

Computer Configuration|Windows Settings|Security Settings|Event Log|Settings For Event Log|Restrict Guest Access To System Log

Computer Configuration|Windows Settings|Security Settings|Event Log|Settings For Event Log|Retain Application Log

Computer Configuration|Windows Settings|Security Settings|Event Log|Settings For Event Log|Retain Security Log

Computer Configuration|Windows Settings|Security Settings|Event Log|Settings For Event Log|Retain System Log

Computer Configuration|Windows Settings|Security Settings|Event Log|Settings For Event Log|Retention Method For Application Log

Computer Configuration|Windows Settings|Security Settings|Event Log|Settings For Event Log|Retention Method For Security Log

Computer Configuration|Windows Settings|Security Settings|Event Log|Settings For Event Log|Retention Method For System Log

Computer Configuration|Windows Settings|Security Settings|Event Log|Settings For Event Log|Shut Down The Computer When The Security Audit Log Is Full

Logon/Logoff

Computer Configuration|Administrative Templates|System|Disable Boot/Shutdown/Logon/Logoff Status Messages

Computer Configuration|Administrative Templates|System|Verbose Vs Normal Status Messages

Computer Configuration|Administrative Templates|System|Don't Display Welcome Screen At Logon

Computer Configuration|Administrative Templates|System|Logon|Timeout For Dialog Boxes

Computer Configuration|Windows Settings|Security Settings|Local Policies|User Rights Assignment|Deny Logon As A Batch Job

Computer Configuration|Windows Settings|Security Settings|Local Policies|User Rights Assignment|Deny Logon As A Service

Computer Configuration|Windows Settings|Security Settings|Local Policies|User Rights Assignment|Deny Logon Locally

Computer Configuration|Windows Settings|Security Settings|Local Policies|User Rights Assignment|Logon As A Batch Job

Computer Configuration|Windows Settings|Security Settings|Local Policies|User Rights Assignment|Log On As A Service

Computer Configuration|Windows Settings|Security Settings|Local Policies|User Rights Assignment|Log On Locally

Computer Configuration|Windows Settings|Security Settings|Local Policies|Security Options|Automatically Log Off Users When Logon Time Expires

Computer Configuration|Windows Settings|Security Settings|Local Policies|Security Options|Augomatically Log Off Users When The Logon Time Expires (Local)

Computer Configuration|Windows Settings|Security Settings|Local Policies|Security Options|Disable CTRL+ALT+DEL Requirement For Logon

Computer Configuration|Windows Settings|Security Settings|Local Policies|Security Options|Do Not Display Last User Name In Logon Screen

Computer Configuration|Windows Settings|Security Settings|Local Policies|Security Options|LAN Manager Authentication Level

Computer Configuration|Windows Settings|Security Settings|Local Policies|Security Options|Message Text For Users Attempting To Log On

Computer Configuration|Windows Settings|Security Settings|Local Policies|Security Options|Message Title For Users Attempting To Log On

Computer Configuration|Windows Settings|Security Settings|Local Policies|Security Options|Number Of Previous Logons To Cache (In Case Domain Controller Is Not Available)

User Configuration|Administrative Templates|System|Don't Display Welcome Screen At Logon

User Configuration|Administrative Templates|System|Logon/Logoff|Disable Logoff

Maintenance

Computer Configuration|Administrative Templates|System|Windows File
Protection|Set Windows File Protection Scanning

Computer Configuration|Administrative Templates|System|Windows File
Protection|Hide The File Scan Progress Window

Computer Configuration|Administrative Templates|System|Windows File
Protection|Limit Windows File Protection Cache Size

Computer Configuration|Administrative Templates|System|Windows File
Protection|Specify Windows File Protection Cache Location

Microsoft Management Console

User Configuration|Administrative Templates|Windows Components|Microsoft
Management Console|Restrict The User From Entering Author Mode

User Configuration|Administrative Templates|Windows Components|Microsoft
Management Console|Restrict Users To The Explicitly Permitted List Of
Snap-Ins

User Configuration|Administrative Templates|Windows Components|Microsoft
Management Console|Restricted/Permitted Snap-Ins|Active Directory Users And
Computers

User Configuration|Administrative Templates|Windows Components|Microsoft
Management Console|Restricted/Permitted Snap-Ins|Active Directory Domains
And Trusts

User Configuration|Administrative Templates|Windows Components|Microsoft
Management Console|Restricted/Permitted Snap-Ins|Active Directory Sites And
Services

User Configuration|Administrative Templates|Windows Components|Microsoft
Management Console|Restricted/Permitted Snap-Ins|Certificates

User Configuration|Administrative Templates|Windows Components|Microsoft
Management Console|Restricted/Permitted Snap-Ins|Component Services

User Configuration|Administrative Templates|Windows Components|Microsoft
Management Console|Restricted/Permitted Snap-Ins|Computer Management

User Configuration|Administrative Templates|Windows Components|Microsoft
Management Console|Restricted/Permitted Snap-Ins|Device Manager

User Configuration|Administrative Templates|Windows Components|Microsoft
Management Console|Restricted/Permitted Snap-Ins|Disk Management

User Configuration|Administrative Templates|Windows Components|Microsoft
Management Console|Restricted/Permitted Snap-Ins|Disk Defragmenter

User Configuration|Administrative Templates|Windows Components|Microsoft
Management Console|Restricted/Permitted Snap-Ins|Distributed File System

User Configuration|Administrative Templates|Windows Components|Microsoft
Management Console|Restricted/Permitted Snap-Ins|Event Viewer

User Configuration|Administrative Templates|Windows Components|Microsoft
Management Console|Restricted/Permitted Snap-Ins|FAX Service

User Configuration|Administrative Templates|Windows Components|Microsoft
Management Console|Restricted/Permitted Snap-Ins|Indexing Service

User Configuration|Administrative Templates|Windows Components|Microsoft
Management Console|Restricted/Permitted Snap-Ins|Internet Authentication
Service (IAS)

User Configuration|Administrative Templates|Windows Components|Microsoft
Management Console|Restricted/Permitted Snap-Ins|Internet Information
Services

User Configuration|Administrative Templates|Windows Components|Microsoft
Management Console|Restricted/Permitted Snap-Ins|IP Security

User Configuration|Administrative Templates|Windows Components|Microsoft
Management Console|Restricted/Permitted Snap-Ins|Local Users And Groups

User Configuration|Administrative Templates|Windows Components|Microsoft
Management Console|Restricted/Permitted Snap-Ins|Performance Logs And Alerts

User Configuration|Administrative Templates|Windows Components|Microsoft
Management Console|Restricted/Permitted Snap-Ins|Qos Admission Control

User Configuration|Administrative Templates|Windows Components|Microsoft
Management Console|Restricted/Permitted Snap-Ins|Removable Storage
Management

User Configuration|Administrative Templates|Windows Components|Microsoft
Management Console|Restricted/Permitted Snap-Ins|Routing And Remote Access

User Configuration|Administrative Templates|Windows Components|Microsoft
Management Console|Restricted/Permitted Snap-Ins|Security Configuration And
Analysis

User Configuration|Administrative Templates|Windows Components|Microsoft
Management Console|Restricted/Permitted Snap-Ins|Security Templates

User Configuration|Administrative Templates|Windows Components|Microsoft
Management Console|Restricted/Permitted Snap-Ins|Services

User Configuration|Administrative Templates|Windows Components|Microsoft
Management Console|Restricted/Permitted Snap-Ins|Shared Folders

User Configuration|Administrative Templates|Windows Components|Microsoft
Management Console|Restricted/Permitted Snap-Ins|System Information

User Configuration|Administrative Templates|Windows Components|Microsoft
Management Console|Restricted/Permitted Snap-Ins|Telephony

User Configuration|Administrative Templates|Windows Components|Microsoft
Management Console|Restricted/Permitted Snap-Ins|Terminal Services
Configuration

User Configuration|Administrative Templates|Windows Components|Microsoft
Management Console|Restricted/Permitted Snap-Ins|WMI Control

User Configuration|Administrative Templates|Windows Components|Microsoft
Management Console|Restricted/Permitted Snap-Ins|Extension Snap-Ins|Apple
Talk Routing

User Configuration|Administrative Templates|Windows Components|Microsoft
Management Console|Restricted/Permitted Snap-Ins|Extension
Snap-Ins|Certification Authority

User Configuration|Administrative Templates|Windows Components|Microsoft
Management Console|Restricted/Permitted Snap-Ins|Extension
Snap-Ins|Connection Sharing (NAT)

User Configuration|Administrative Templates|Windows Components|Microsoft
Management Console|Restricted/Permitted Snap-Ins|Extension Snap-Ins|DCOM
Configuration Extension

User Configuration|Administrative Templates|Windows Components|Microsoft
Management Console|Restricted/Permitted Snap-Ins|Extension Snap-Ins|Device
Manager

User Configuration|Administrative Templates|Windows Components|Microsoft
Management Console|Restricted/Permitted Snap-Ins|Extension Snap-Ins|DHCP
Relay Management

User Configuration|Administrative Templates|Windows Components|Microsoft
Management Console|Restricted/Permitted Snap-Ins|Extension Snap-Ins|Event
Viewer

User Configuration|Administrative Templates|Windows Components|Microsoft
Management Console|Restricted/Permitted Snap-Ins|Extension Snap-Ins|IAS
Logging

User Configuration|Administrative Templates|Windows Components|Microsoft
Management Console|Restricted/Permitted Snap-Ins|Extension Snap-Ins|IGMP
Routing

User Configuration|Administrative Templates|Windows Components|Microsoft
Management Console|Restricted/Permitted Snap-Ins|Extension Snap-Ins|IP
Routing

User Configuration|Administrative Templates|Windows Components|Microsoft
Management Console|Restricted/Permitted Snap-Ins|Extension Snap-Ins|IPX RIP
Routing

User Configuration|Administrative Templates|Windows Components|Microsoft
Management Console|Restricted/Permitted Snap-Ins|Extension Snap-Ins|IPX
Routing

User Configuration|Administrative Templates|Windows Components|Microsoft
Management Console|Restricted/Permitted Snap-Ins|Extension Snap-Ins|IPX SAP
Routing

User Configuration|Administrative Templates|Windows Components|Microsoft
Management Console|Restricted/Permitted Snap-Ins|Extension Snap-Ins|Logical
And Mapped Drives

User Configuration|Administrative Templates|Windows Components|Microsoft
Management Console|Restricted/Permitted Snap-Ins|Extension Snap-Ins|OSPF
Routing

User Configuration|Administrative Templates|Windows Components|Microsoft
Management Console|Restricted/Permitted Snap-Ins|Extension Snap-Ins|Public
Key Policies

User Configuration|Administrative Templates|Windows Components|Microsoft
Management Console|Restricted/Permitted Snap-Ins|Extension Snap-Ins|RAS
Dialin - User Node

User Configuration|Administrative Templates|Windows Components|Microsoft
Management Console|Restricted/Permitted Snap-Ins|Extension Snap-Ins|Remote
Access

User Configuration|Administrative Templates|Windows Components|Microsoft Management Console|Restricted/Permitted Snap-Ins|Extension Snap-Ins|Removable Storage

User Configuration|Administrative Templates|Windows Components|Microsoft Management Console|Restricted/Permitted Snap-Ins|Extension Snap-Ins|RIP Routing

User Configuration|Administrative Templates|Windows Components|Microsoft Management Console|Restricted/Permitted Snap-Ins|Extension Snap-Ins|Routing

User Configuration|Administrative Templates|Windows Components|Microsoft Management Console|Restricted/Permitted Snap-Ins|Extension Snap-Ins|Send Console Message

User Configuration|Administrative Templates|Windows Components|Microsoft Management Console|Restricted/Permitted Snap-Ins|Extension Snap-Ins|Service Dependencies

User Configuration|Administrative Templates|Windows Components|Microsoft Management Console|Restricted/Permitted Snap-Ins|Extension Snap-Ins|SMTP Protocol

User Configuration|Administrative Templates|Windows Components|Microsoft Management Console|Restricted/Permitted Snap-Ins|Extension Snap-Ins|SNMP

User Configuration|Administrative Templates|Windows Components|Microsoft Management Console|Restricted/Permitted Snap-Ins|Extension Snap-Ins|System Properties

User Configuration|Administrative Templates|Windows Components|Microsoft Management Console|Restricted/Permitted Snap-Ins|Group Policy|Group Policy Snap-In

User Configuration|Administrative Templates|Windows Components|Microsoft Management Console|Restricted/Permitted Snap-Ins|Group Policy|Group Policy Tab For Active Directory Tools

User Configuration|Administrative Templates|Windows Components|Microsoft Management Console|Restricted/Permitted Snap-Ins|Group Policy|Administrative Templates (Computers)

User Configuration|Administrative Templates|Windows Components|Microsoft Management Console|Restricted/Permitted Snap-Ins|Group Policy|Administrative Templates (Users)

User Configuration|Administrative Templates|Windows Components|Microsoft Management Console|Restricted/Permitted Snap-Ins|Group Policy|Folder Redirection

User Configuration|Administrative Templates|Windows Components|Microsoft Management Console|Restricted/Permitted Snap-Ins|Group Policy|Internet Explorer Maintenance

User Configuration|Administrative Templates|Windows Components|Microsoft Management Console|Restricted/Permitted Snap-Ins|Group Policy|Remote Installation Services

User Configuration|Administrative Templates|Windows Components|Microsoft Management Console|Restricted/Permitted Snap-Ins|Group Policy|Scripts (Logon/Logoff)

User Configuration|Administrative Templates|Windows Components|Microsoft
Management Console|Restricted/Permitted Snap-Ins|Group Policy|Scripts
(Startup/Shutdown)

User Configuration|Administrative Templates|Windows Components|Microsoft
Management Console|Restricted/Permitted Snap-Ins|Group Policy|Security
Settings

User Configuration|Administrative Templates|Windows Components|Microsoft
Management Console|Restricted/Permitted Snap-Ins|Group Policy|Software
Installation (Computers)

User Configuration|Administrative Templates|Windows Components|Microsoft
Management Console|Restricted/Permitted Snap-Ins|Group Policy|Software
Installation (Users)

Netmeeting

Computer Configuration|Administrative Templates|Windows Components|
Netmeeting|Disable Remote Desktop Sharing

User Configuration|Administrative Templates|Windows Components|Netmeeting|
Enable Automatic Configuration

User Configuration|Administrative Templates|Windows Components|Netmeeting|
Disable Directory Services

User Configuration|Administrative Templates|Windows Components|Netmeeting|
Prevent Addin Directory Servers

User Configuration|Administrative Templates|Windows Components|Netmeeting|
Prevent Viewing Web Directory

User Configuration|Administrative Templates|Windows Components|Netmeeting|
Set The Intranet Support Web Page

User Configuration|Administrative Templates|Windows Components|Netmeeting|
Set Call Security Options

User Configuration|Administrative Templates|Windows Components|Netmeeting|
Prevent Changing Call Placement Method

User Configuration|Administrative Templates|Windows Components|Netmeeting|
Prevent Automatic Acceptance Of Calls

User Configuration|Administrative Templates|Windows Components|Netmeeting|
Prevent Sending Files

User Configuration|Administrative Templates|Windows Components|Netmeeting|
Prevent Receiving Files

User Configuration|Administrative Templates|Windows Components|Netmeeting|
Limit The Size Of Sent Files

User Configuration|Administrative Templates|Windows Components|Netmeeting|
Disable Chat

User Configuration|Administrative Templates|Windows Components|Netmeeting|
Disable Netmeeting 2.X Whiteboard

User Configuration|Administrative Templates|Windows Components|Netmeeting|
Disable Whiteboard

User Configuration|Administrative Templates|Windows Components|Netmeeting|
Application Sharing|Disable Application Sharing
User Configuration|Administrative Templates|Windows Components|Netmeeting|
Application Sharing|Prevent Sharing
User Configuration|Administrative Templates|Windows Components|Netmeeting|
Application Sharing|Prevent Desktop Sharing
User Configuration|Administrative Templates|Windows Components|Netmeeting|
Application Sharing|Prevent Sharing Command Prompts
User Configuration|Administrative Templates|Windows Components|Netmeeting|
Application Sharing|Prevent Sharing Explorer Windows
User Configuration|Administrative Templates|Windows Components|Netmeeting|
Application Sharing|Prevent Control
User Configuration|Administrative Templates|Windows Components|Netmeeting|
Application Sharing|Prevent Application Sharing In True Color
User Configuration|Administrative Templates|Windows Components|Netmeeting|
Audio & Video|Limit The Bandwidth Of Audio And Video
User Configuration|Administrative Templates|Windows Components|Netmeeting|
Audio & Video|Disable Audio
User Configuration|Administrative Templates|Windows Components|Netmeeting|
Audio & Video|Disable Full Duplex Audio
User Configuration|Administrative Templates|Windows Components|Netmeeting|
Audio & Video|Prevent Changing Directsound Audio Setting
User Configuration|Administrative Templates|Windows Components|Netmeeting|
Audio & Video|Prevent Sending Video
User Configuration|Administrative Templates|Windows Components|Netmeeting|
Audio & Video|Prevent Receiving Video
User Configuration|Administrative Templates|Windows Components|Netmeeting|
Options Page|Hide The General Page
User Configuration|Administrative Templates|Windows Components|Netmeeting|
Options Page|Disable The Advanced Calling Button
User Configuration|Administrative Templates|Windows Components|Netmeeting|
Options Page|Hide The Security Page
User Configuration|Administrative Templates|Windows Components|Netmeeting|
Options Page|Hide The Audio Page
User Configuration|Administrative Templates|Windows Components|Netmeeting|
Options Page|Hide The Video Page

Network

User Configuration|Administrative Templates|Network|Network And Dial-Up
Connections|Enable Access To Properties Of Components Of A LAN Connection
User Configuration|Administrative Templates|Network|Network And Dial-Up
Connections|Enable Adding And Removing Components For A RAS Or LAN
Connection
Computer Configuration|Administrative Templates|System|Logon|Do Not Detect
Slow Network Connections

Computer Configuration|Administrative Templates|System|Logon|Prompt User When Slow Link Is Detected

Computer Configuration|Administrative Templates|System|DNS Client|Primary DNS Suffix

Computer Configuration|Administrative Templates|Network|Network And Dial-Up Connections|Allow Configuration Of Connection Sharing

User Configuration|Administrative Templates|Network|Network And Dial-Up Connections|Enable Connecting And Disconnecting A LAN Connection

User Configuration|Administrative Templates|Network|Network And Dial-Up Connections|Enable Access To Properties Of A LAN Connection

User Configuration|Administrative Templates|Network|Network And Dial-Up Connections|Enable Renaming Of Connections, If Supported

User Configuration|Administrative Templates|Network|Network And Dial-Up Connections|Allow Connection Components To Be Enabled Or Disabled

User Configuration|Administrative Templates|Network|Network And Dial-Up Connections|Display And Enable The Network Connection Wizard

User Configuration|Administrative Templates|Network|Network And Dial-Up Connections|Enable Status Statistics For An Active Connection

User Configuration|Administrative Templates|Network|Network And Dial-Up Connections|Enable The Dial-Up Preferences Item On The Advanced Menu

User Configuration|Administrative Templates|Network|Network And Dial-Up Connections|Enable The Advanced Settings Item On The Advanced Menu

User Configuration|Administrative Templates|Network|Network And Dial-Up Connections|Allow Configuration Of Connection Sharing

User Configuration|Administrative Templates|Network|Network And Dial-Up Connections|Allow TCP/IP Advanced Configuration

User Configuration|Administrative Templates|System|Logon/Logoff|Connect Home Directory To Root Of The Share

Computer Configuration|Windows Settings|Security Settings|Local Policies|User Rights Assignment|Access This Computer From The Network

Computer Configuration|Windows Settings|Security Settings|Local Policies|User Rights Assignment|Deny Access To This Computer From The Network

Computer Configuration|Windows Settings|Security Settings|Local Policies|Security Options|Additional Restrictions For Anonymous Connections

Computer Configuration|Windows Settings|Security Settings|Local Policies|Security Options|Amount Of Idle Time Required Before Disconnecting Session

Computer Configuration|Administrative Templates|System|Logon|Slow Network Connection Timeout For User Profiles

Computer Configuration|Administrative Templates|System|Group Policy|Group Policy Slow Link Detection

User Configuration|Administrative Templates|Windows Components|Microsoft Management Console|Restricted/Permitted Snap-Ins|Distributed File System

User Configuration|Administrative Templates|Windows Components|Microsoft Management Console|Restricted/Permitted Snap-Ins|Routing And Remote Access

User Configuration|Administrative Templates|Windows Components|Microsoft Management Console|Restricted/Permitted Snap-Ins|Shared Folders

User Configuration|Administrative Templates|Windows Components|Microsoft Management Console|Restricted/Permitted Snap-Ins|Extension Snap-Ins|Apple Talk Routing

User Configuration|Administrative Templates|Windows Components|Microsoft Management Console|Restricted/Permitted Snap-Ins|Extension Snap-Ins| Connection Sharing (NAT)

User Configuration|Administrative Templates|Windows Components|Microsoft Management Console|Restricted/Permitted Snap-Ins|Extension Snap-Ins|DHCP Relay Management

User Configuration|Administrative Templates|Windows Components|Microsoft Management Console|Restricted/Permitted Snap-Ins|Extension Snap-Ins|IGMP Routing

User Configuration|Administrative Templates|Windows Components|Microsoft Management Console|Restricted/Permitted Snap-Ins|Extension Snap-Ins|IP Routing

User Configuration|Administrative Templates|Windows Components|Microsoft Management Console|Restricted/Permitted Snap-Ins|Extension Snap-Ins|IPX RIP Routing

User Configuration|Administrative Templates|Windows Components|Microsoft Management Console|Restricted/Permitted Snap-Ins|Extension Snap-Ins|IPX Routing

User Configuration|Administrative Templates|Windows Components|Microsoft Management Console|Restricted/Permitted Snap-Ins|Extension Snap-Ins|IPX SAP Routing

User Configuration|Administrative Templates|Windows Components|Microsoft Management Console|Restricted/Permitted Snap-Ins|Extension Snap-Ins|Logical And Mapped Drives

User Configuration|Administrative Templates|Windows Components|Microsoft Management Console|Restricted/Permitted Snap-Ins|Extension Snap-Ins|OSPF Routing

User Configuration|Administrative Templates|Windows Components|Microsoft Management Console|Restricted/Permitted Snap-Ins|Extension Snap-Ins|RAS Dialin - User Node

User Configuration|Administrative Templates|Windows Components|Microsoft Management Console|Restricted/Permitted Snap-Ins|Extension Snap-Ins|Remote Access

User Configuration|Administrative Templates|Windows Components|Microsoft Management Console|Restricted/Permitted Snap-Ins|Extension Snap-Ins|RIP Routing

User Configuration|Administrative Templates|Windows Components|Microsoft Management Console|Restricted/Permitted Snap-Ins|Extension Snap-Ins|Routing

User Configuration|Administrative Templates|Windows Components|Microsoft Management Console|Restricted/Permitted Snap-Ins|Extension Snap-Ins|Send Console Message

User Configuration|Administrative Templates|Windows Components|Microsoft Management Console|Restricted/Permitted Snap-Ins|Extension Snap-Ins|SNMP

Computer Configuration|Windows Settings|Security Settings|Local Policies|
User Rights Assignment|Force Shutdown From A Remote System

Computer Configuration|Windows Settings|Security Settings|Local
Policies|User Rights Assignment|Create Permanent Shared Objects

Offline Files

Computer Configuration|Administrative Templates|Network|Offline
Files|Enabled

Computer Configuration|Administrative Templates|Network|Offline Files|
Disable User Configuration Of Offline Files

Computer Configuration|Administrative Templates|Network|Offline Files|
Synchronize All Offline Files Before Logging Off

Computer Configuration|Administrative Templates|Network|Offline Files|
Default Cache Size

Computer Configuration|Administrative Templates|Network|Offline Files|Action
On Server Disconnect

Computer Configuration|Administrative Templates|Network|Offline Files|
Non-Default Server Disconnect Actions

Computer Configuration|Administrative Templates|Network|Offline Files|
Disable 'Make Available Offline'

Computer Configuration|Administrative Templates|Network|Offline Files|
Prevent Use Of Offline Files Folder

Computer Configuration|Administrative Templates|Network|Offline Files|Files
Not Cached

Computer Configuration|Administrative Templates|Network|Offline Files|
Administratively Assigned Offline Files

Computer Configuration|Administrative Templates|Network|Offline Files|
Disable Reminder Balloons

Computer Configuration|Administrative Templates|Network|Offline Files|
Reminder Balloon Frequency

Computer Configuration|Administrative Templates|Network|Offline Files|
Initial Reminder Balloon Lifetime

Computer Configuration|Administrative Templates|Network|Offline Files|
Reminder Balloon Lifetime

Computer Configuration|Administrative Templates|Network|Offline Files|At
Logoff, Delete Local Copy Of User's Offline Files

Computer Configuration|Administrative Templates|Network|Offline Files|Event
Logging Level

Computer Configuration|Administrative Templates|Network|Offline Files|
Subfolders Always Available Offline

User Configuration|Administrative Templates|Network|Offline Files|
Synchronize All Offline Files Before Logging Off

User Configuration|Administrative Templates|Network|Offline Files|Action On
Server Disconnect

User Configuration|Administrative Templates|Network|Offline Files|
Non-Default Server Disconnect Actions

User Configuration|Administrative Templates|Network|Offline Files|Disable
'Make Available Offline'

User Configuration|Administrative Templates|Network|Offline Files|Prevent
Use Of Offline Files Folder

User Configuration|Administrative Templates|Network|Offline Files|
Administratively Assigned Offline Files

User Configuration|Administrative Templates|Network|Offline Files|Disable
Reminder Balloons

User Configuration|Administrative Templates|Network|Offline Files|Reminder
Balloon Frequency

User Configuration|Administrative Templates|Network|Offline Files|Initial
Reminder Balloon Lifetime

User Configuration|Administrative Templates|Network|Offline Files|Reminder
Balloon Lifetime

User Configuration|Administrative Templates|Network|Offline Files|Event
Logging Level

Password

Computer Configuration|Windows Settings|Security Settings|Account Policies|
Password Policy|Enforce Password History

Computer Configuration|Windows Settings|Security Settings|Account Policies|
Password Policy|Maximum Password Age

Computer Configuration|Windows Settings|Security Settings|Account Policies|
Password Policy|Minimum Password Age

Computer Configuration|Windows Settings|Security Settings|Account Policies|
Password Policy|Minimum Password Length

Computer Configuration|Windows Settings|Security Settings|Account Policies|
Password Policy|Passwords Must Meet Complexity Requirements

Computer Configuration|Windows Settings|Security Settings|Account Policies|
Password Policy|Store Password Using Reversible Encyption Format

Computer Configuration|Windows Settings|Security Settings|Local Policies|
Security Options|Prompt User To Change Password Before Expiration

User Configuration|Administrative Templates|System|Logon/Logoff|Disable
Change Password

Printers

Computer Configuration|Administrative Templates|Printers|Automatically
Publish New Printers In Active Directory

Computer Configuration|Administrative Templates|Printers|Allow Pruning Of
Published Printers

Computer Configuration|Administrative Templates|Printers|Printer Browsing

Computer Configuration|Administrative Templates|Printers|Prune Printers That Are Not Automatically Republished

Computer Configuration|Administrative Templates|Printers|Directory Pruning Interval

Computer Configuration|Administrative Templates|Printers|Directory Pruning Retry

Computer Configuration|Administrative Templates|Printers|Directory Pruning Priority

Computer Configuration|Administrative Templates|Printers|Check Published State

Computer Configuration|Administrative Templates|Printers|Web-Based Printing

Computer Configuration|Administrative Templates|Printers|Custom Support URL In The Printers Folder's Left Pane

Computer Configuration|Administrative Templates|Printers|Computer Location

Computer Configuration|Administrative Templates|Printers|Pre-Populate Printer Search Location Text

User Configuration|Administrative Templates|Control Panel|Printers|Disable Deletion Of Printers

User Configuration|Administrative Templates|Control Panel|Printers|Disable Addition Of Printers

User Configuration|Administrative Templates|Control Panel|Printers|Browse The Network To Find Printers

User Configuration|Administrative Templates|Control Panel|Printers|Default Active Directory Path When Searching For Printers

User Configuration|Administrative Templates|Control Panel|Printers|Browse A Common Web Site To Find Printers

Computer Configuration|Administrative Templates|Printers|Allow Printers To Be Published

Profiles

Computer Configuration|Administrative Templates|System|Logon|Delete Cached Copies Of Roaming Profiles

Computer Configuration|Administrative Templates|System|Logon|Slow Network Connection Timeout For User Profiles

Computer Configuration|Administrative Templates|System|Logon|Wait For Remote User Profile

Computer Configuration|Administrative Templates|System|Logon|Log Users Off When Roaming Profile Fails

Computer Configuration|Administrative Templates|System|Logon|Maximum Retries To Unload And Update User Profile

User Configuration|Administrative Templates|System|Logon/Logoff|Limit Profile Size

User Configuration|Administrative Templates|System|Logon/Logoff|Exclude Directories In Roaming Profile

Programming

Computer Configuration|Windows Settings|Security Settings|Local Policies|
User Rights Assignment|Replace A Process Level Token

Computer Configuration|Windows Settings|Security Settings|Local Policies|
User Rights Assignment|Debug Programs

Computer Configuration|Windows Settings|Security Settings|Local Policies|
User Rights Assignment|Lock Pages In Memory

Computer Configuration|Windows Settings|Security Settings|Local Policies|
User Rights Assignment|Profile Single Process

Computer Configuration|Windows Settings|Security Settings|Local Policies|
User Rights Assignment|Profile System Performance

Quotas

Computer Configuration|Administrative Templates|System|Disk Quotas|Enable
Disk Quotas

Computer Configuration|Administrative Templates|System|Disk Quotas|Enforce
Disk Quota Limit

Computer Configuration|Administrative Templates|System|Disk Quotas|Default
Quota Limit And Warning Level

Computer Configuration|Administrative Templates|System|Disk Quotas|Log Event
When Quota Limit Exceeded

Computer Configuration|Administrative Templates|System|Disk Quotas|Log Event
When Quota Warning Level Exceeded

Computer Configuration|Administrative Templates|System|Disk Quotas|Apply
Policy To Removable Media

Computer Configuration|Administrative Templates|System|Group Policy|Disk
Quota Policy Processing

RAS

User Configuration|Administrative Templates|Windows Components|Microsoft
Management Console|Restricted/Permitted Snap-Ins|Routing And Remote Access

User Configuration|Administrative Templates|Windows Components|Microsoft
Management Console|Restricted/Permitted Snap-Ins|Extension Snap-Ins|
Connection Sharing (NAT)

User Configuration|Administrative Templates|Windows Components|Microsoft
Management Console|Restricted/Permitted Snap-Ins|Extension Snap-Ins|IGMP
Routing

User Configuration|Administrative Templates|Windows Components|Microsoft
Management Console|Restricted/Permitted Snap-Ins|Extension Snap-Ins|IP
Routing

User Configuration|Administrative Templates|Windows Components|Microsoft
Management Console|Restricted/Permitted Snap-Ins|Extension Snap-Ins|IPX RIP
Routing

User Configuration|Administrative Templates|Windows Components|Microsoft
Management Console|Restricted/Permitted Snap-Ins|Extension Snap-Ins|IPX
Routing

User Configuration|Administrative Templates|Windows Components|Microsoft
Management Console|Restricted/Permitted Snap-Ins|Extension Snap-Ins|IPX SAP
Routing

User Configuration|Administrative Templates|Windows Components|Microsoft
Management Console|Restricted/Permitted Snap-Ins|Extension Snap-Ins|OSPF
Routing

User Configuration|Administrative Templates|Windows Components|Microsoft
Management Console|Restricted/Permitted Snap-Ins|Extension Snap-Ins|RAS
Dialin - User Node

User Configuration|Administrative Templates|Windows Components|Microsoft
Management Console|Restricted/Permitted Snap-Ins|Extension Snap-Ins|Remote
Access

User Configuration|Administrative Templates|Windows Components|Microsoft
Management Console|Restricted/Permitted Snap-Ins|Extension Snap-Ins|RIP
Routing

User Configuration|Administrative Templates|Windows Components|Microsoft
Management Console|Restricted/Permitted Snap-Ins|Extension Snap-Ins|Routing

Computer Configuration|Administrative Templates|Network|Network And Dial-Up
Connections|Allow Configuration Of Connection Sharing

User Configuration|Administrative Templates|Network|Network And Dial-Up
Connections|Enable Deletion Of RAS Connections

User Configuration|Administrative Templates|Network|Network And Dial-Up
Connections|Enable Deletion Of RAS Connections Available To All Users

User Configuration|Administrative Templates|Network|Network And Dial-Up
Connections|Enable Connecting And Disconnecting A RAS Connection

User Configuration|Administrative Templates|Network|Network And Dial-Up
Connections|Allow Access To Current User's RAS Connection Properties

User Configuration|Administrative Templates|Network|Network And Dial-Up
Connections|Enable Access To Properties Of RAS Connections Available To All
Users

User Configuration|Administrative Templates|Network|Network And Dial-Up
Connections|Enable Renaming Of RAS Connections Belonging To The Current User

User Configuration|Administrative Templates|Network|Network And Dial-Up
Connections|Enable Adding And Removing Components For A RAS Or LAN
Connection

User Configuration|Administrative Templates|Network|Network And Dial-Up
Connections|Enable Access To Properties Of Components Of A RAS Connection

RIS

User Configuration|Administrative Templates|Windows Components|Microsoft
Management Console|Restricted/Permitted Snap-Ins|Group Policy|Remote
Installation Services

Run

Computer Configuration|Administrative Templates|System|Run These Programs At User Logon

Computer Configuration|Administrative Templates|System|Disable The Run Once List

Computer Configuration|Administrative Templates|System|Disable Legacy Run List

User Configuration|Administrative Templates|System|Logon/Logoff|Run These Programs At User Logon

User Configuration|Administrative Templates|System|Logon/Logoff|Disable The Run Once List

User Configuration|Administrative Templates|System|Logon/Logoff|Disable Legacy Run List

Scripts

Computer Configuration|Windows Settings|Scripts (Startup/Shutdown)

Computer Configuration|Administrative Templates|System|Logon|Run Logon Scripts Synchronously

Computer Configuration|Administrative Templates|System|Logon|Run Startup Scripts Asynchronously

Computer Configuration|Administrative Templates|System|Logon|Run Startup Scripts Visible

Computer Configuration|Administrative Templates|System|Logon|Run Shutdown Scripts Visible

Computer Configuration|Administrative Templates|System|Logon|Maximum Wait Time For Group Policy Scripts

User Configuration|Windows Settings|Scripts (Logon/Logoff)

User Configuration|Administrative Templates|System|Logon/Logoff|Run Logon Scripts Synchronously

User Configuration|Administrative Templates|System|Logon/Logoff|Run Legacy Logon Scripts Hidden

User Configuration|Administrative Templates|System|Logon/Logoff|Run Logon Scripts Visible

User Configuration|Administrative Templates|System|Logon/Logoff|Run Logoff Scripts Visible

Computer Configuration|Administrative Templates|System|Group Policy|Scripts Policy Processing

User Configuration|Administrative Templates|Windows Components|Microsoft Management Console|Restricted/Permitted Snap-Ins|Group Policy|Scripts (Logon/Logoff)

User Configuration|Administrative Templates|Windows Components|Microsoft Management Console|Restricted/Permitted Snap-Ins|Group Policy|Scripts (Startup/Shutdown)

Security

Computer Configuration|Windows Settings|Security Settings|Local Policies|
Security Options|Strengthen Default Permissions Of Global System Objects
(E.G. Symbolic Links)

Computer Configuration|Windows Settings|Security Settings|Local Policies|
Security Options|Recovery Console: Allow Floppy Copy And Access To All
Drives And All Folders

Computer Configuration|Windows Settings|Security Settings|Account
Policies|Password Policy|Enforce Password History

Computer Configuration|Windows Settings|Security Settings|Account
Policies|Password Policy|Maximum Password Age

Computer Configuration|Windows Settings|Security Settings|Account
Policies|Password Policy|Minimum Password Age

Computer Configuration|Windows Settings|Security Settings|Account
Policies|Password Policy|Minimum Password Length

Computer Configuration|Windows Settings|Security Settings|Account
Policies|Password Policy|Passwords Must Meet Complexity Requirements

Computer Configuration|Windows Settings|Security Settings|Account
Policies|Password Policy|Store Password Using Reversible Encyption Format

Computer Configuration|Windows Settings|Security Settings|Account
Policies|Account Lockout Policy|Account Lockout Duration

Computer Configuration|Windows Settings|Security Settings|Account
Policies|Account Lockout Policy|Account Lockout Threshold

Computer Configuration|Windows Settings|Security Settings|Account
Policies|Account Lockout Policy|Reset Account Lockout Counter After

Computer Configuration|Windows Settings|Security Settings|Local Policies|
Audit Policy|Audit Account Logon Events

Computer Configuration|Windows Settings|Security Settings|Local Policies|
Audit Policy|Audit Account Management

Computer Configuration|Windows Settings|Security Settings|Local Policies|
Audit Policy|Audit Directory Service Access

Computer Configuration|Windows Settings|Security Settings|Local Policies|
Audit Policy|Audit Logon Events

Computer Configuration|Windows Settings|Security Settings|Local Policies|
Audit Policy|Audit Object Access

Computer Configuration|Windows Settings|Security Settings|Local Policies|
Audit Policy|Audit Policy Change

Computer Configuration|Windows Settings|Security Settings|Local Policies|
Audit Policy|Audit Privilege Use

Computer Configuration|Windows Settings|Security Settings|Local Policies|
Audit Policy|Audit Process Tracking

Computer Configuration|Windows Settings|Security Settings|Local Policies|
Audit Policy|Audit System Events

Computer Configuration|Windows Settings|Security Settings|Local Policies|
User Rights Assignment|Access This Computer From The Network

Computer Configuration|Windows Settings|Security Settings|Local Policies|
User Rights Assignment|Act As Part Of The Operating System

Computer Configuration|Windows Settings|Security Settings|Local Policies|
User Rights Assignment|Bypass Traverse Checking

Computer Configuration|Windows Settings|Security Settings|Local Policies|
User Rights Assignment|Deny Access To This Computer From The Network

Computer Configuration|Windows Settings|Security Settings|Local Policies|
User Rights Assignment|Deny Logon As A Batch Job

Computer Configuration|Windows Settings|Security Settings|Local Policies|
User Rights Assignment|Deny Logon As A Service

Computer Configuration|Windows Settings|Security Settings|Local Policies|
User Rights Assignment|Deny Logon Locally

Computer Configuration|Windows Settings|Security Settings|Local Policies|
User Rights Assignment|Enable Computer And User Accounts To Be Trusted For
Delegation

Computer Configuration|Windows Settings|Security Settings|Local Policies|
User Rights Assignment|Generate Security Audits

Computer Configuration|Windows Settings|Security Settings|Local Policies|
User Rights Assignment|Load And Unload Device Drivers

Computer Configuration|Windows Settings|Security Settings|Local Policies|
User Rights Assignment|Logon As A Batch Job

Computer Configuration|Windows Settings|Security Settings|Local Policies|
User Rights Assignment|Log On As A Service

Computer Configuration|Windows Settings|Security Settings|Local Policies|
User Rights Assignment|Log On Locally

Computer Configuration|Windows Settings|Security Settings|Local Policies|
User Rights Assignment|Manage Auditing And Security Log

Computer Configuration|Windows Settings|Security Settings|Local Policies|
User Rights Assignment|Remove Computer From Docking Station

Computer Configuration|Windows Settings|Security Settings|Local Policies|
User Rights Assignment|Replace A Process Level Token

Computer Configuration|Windows Settings|Security Settings|Local Policies|
User Rights Assignment|Restore Files And Directories

Computer Configuration|Windows Settings|Security Settings|Local Policies|
User Rights Assignment|Shut Down The System

Computer Configuration|Windows Settings|Security Settings|Local Policies|
User Rights Assignment|Synchronize Directory Service Data

Computer Configuration|Windows Settings|Security Settings|Local Policies|
User Rights Assignment|Take Ownership Of Files Or Other Objects

Computer Configuration|Windows Settings|Security Settings|Local Policies|
Security Options|Additional Restrictions For Anonymous Connections

Computer Configuration|Windows Settings|Security Settings|Local Policies|
Security Options|Allow Server Operators To Schedule Tasks (Domain
Controllers Only)

Appendix A
Group Policy Index

Computer Configuration|Windows Settings|Security Settings|Local Policies|
Security Options|Secure Channel: Digitally Encrypt Secure Channel Data (When
Possible)

Computer Configuration|Windows Settings|Security Settings|Local Policies|
Security Options|Secure Channel: Digitally Sign Secure Channel Data (When
Possible)

Computer Configuration|Windows Settings|Security Settings|Local Policies|
Security Options|Secure Channel: Require Strong (Windows 2000 Or Later)
Session Key

Computer Configuration|Windows Settings|Security Settings|Local Policies|
Security Options|Secure System Partition (For RISC Platforms Only)

Computer Configuration|Windows Settings|Security Settings|Local Policies|
Security Options|Send Unencrypted Password To Connect To Third-Party SMB
Servers

Computer Configuration|Windows Settings|Security Settings|Local Policies|
Security Options|Shut Down System Immediately If Unable To Log Security
Audits

Computer Configuration|Windows Settings|Security Settings|Local Policies|
Security Options|Smart Card Removal Behavior

Computer Configuration|Windows Settings|Security Settings|Local Policies|
Security Options|Strengthen Default Permissions Of Global System Objects
(E.G. Symbolic Links)

Computer Configuration|Windows Settings|Security Settings|Local Policies|
Security Options|Unsigned Driver Installation Behavior

Computer Configuration|Windows Settings|Security Settings|Local Policies|
Security Options|Unsigned Non-Driver Installation Behavior

Computer Configuration|Windows Settings|Security Settings|Event Log|Settings
For Event Log|Maximum Application Log Size

Computer Configuration|Windows Settings|Security Settings|Event Log|Settings
For Event Log|Maximum Security Log Size

Computer Configuration|Windows Settings|Security Settings|Event Log|Settings
For Event Log|Maximum System Log Size

Computer Configuration|Windows Settings|Security Settings|Event Log|Settings
For Event Log|Restrict Guest Access To Application Log

Computer Configuration|Windows Settings|Security Settings|Event Log|Settings
For Event Log|Restrict Guest Access To Security Log

Computer Configuration|Windows Settings|Security Settings|Event Log|Settings
For Event Log|Restrict Guest Access To System Log

Computer Configuration|Windows Settings|Security Settings|Event Log|Settings
For Event Log|Retain Application Log

Computer Configuration|Windows Settings|Security Settings|Event Log|Settings
For Event Log|Retain Security Log

Computer Configuration|Windows Settings|Security Settings|Event Log|Settings
For Event Log|Retain System Log

Computer Configuration|Windows Settings|Security Settings|Event Log|Settings
For Event Log|Retention Method For Application Log

Computer Configuration|Windows Settings|Security Settings|Event Log|Settings For Event Log|Retention Method For Security Log

Computer Configuration|Windows Settings|Security Settings|Event Log|Settings For Event Log|Retention Method For System Log

Computer Configuration|Windows Settings|Security Settings|Event Log|Settings For Event Log|Shut Down The Computer When The Security Audit Log Is Full

Computer Configuration|Windows Settings|Security Settings|IP Security Policies On Active Directory|Client (Respond Only)

Computer Configuration|Windows Settings|Security Settings|IP Security Policies On Active Directory|Secure Server (Require Security)

Computer Configuration|Windows Settings|Security Settings|IP Security Policies On Active Directory|Server (Request Security)

Computer Configuration|Administrative Templates|System|Do Not Automatically Encrypt Files Moved To Encrypted Folders

User Configuration|Windows Settings|Security Settings|Public Key Policies| Enterprise Trust

User Configuration|Windows Settings|Security Settings|IP Security Policies On Active Directory|Client (Respond Only)

User Configuration|Windows Settings|Security Settings|IP Security Policies On Active Directory|Secure Server (Require Security)

User Configuration|Windows Settings|Security Settings|IP Security Policies On Active Directory|Server (Request Security)

Computer Configuration|Administrative Templates|System|Group Policy|Security Policy Processing

Computer Configuration|Administrative Templates|System|Group Policy|IP Security Policy Processing

User Configuration|Administrative Templates|Windows Components|Microsoft Management Console|Restricted/Permitted Snap-Ins|IP Security

User Configuration|Administrative Templates|Windows Components|Microsoft Management Console|Restricted/Permitted Snap-Ins|Security Configuration And Analysis

User Configuration|Administrative Templates|Windows Components|Microsoft Management Console|Restricted/Permitted Snap-Ins|Security Templates

Computer Configuration|Administrative Templates|System|Group Policy|EFS Recovery Policy Processing

User Configuration|Administrative Templates|Windows Components|Microsoft Management Console|Restricted/Permitted Snap-Ins|Group Policy|Security Settings

Services

Computer Configuration|Windows Settings|Security Settings|System Services|{All Services}

Start Menu

User Configuration|Administrative Templates|Start Menu & Taskbar|Remove User's Folders From The Start Menu

User Configuration|Administrative Templates|Start Menu & Taskbar|Disable And Remove Links To Windows Update

User Configuration|Administrative Templates|Start Menu & Taskbar|Remove Common Program Groups From Start Menu

User Configuration|Administrative Templates|Start Menu & Taskbar|Remove Documents Menu From Start Menu

User Configuration|Administrative Templates|Start Menu & Taskbar|Disable Programs On Settings Menu

User Configuration|Administrative Templates|Start Menu & Taskbar|Remove Network & Dial-Up Connections From Start Menu

User Configuration|Administrative Templates|Start Menu & Taskbar|Remove Favorites Menu From Start Menu

User Configuration|Administrative Templates|Start Menu & Taskbar|Remove Search Menu From Start Menu

User Configuration|Administrative Templates|Start Menu & Taskbar|Remove Help Menu From Start Menu

User Configuration|Administrative Templates|Start Menu & Taskbar|Remove Run Menu From Start Menu

User Configuration|Administrative Templates|Start Menu & Taskbar|Add Logoff To The Start Menu

User Configuration|Administrative Templates|Start Menu & Taskbar|Disable Logoff On The Start Menu

User Configuration|Administrative Templates|Start Menu & Taskbar|Disable And Remove The Shut Down Command

User Configuration|Administrative Templates|Start Menu & Taskbar|Disable Drag-And-Drop Context Menus On The Start Menu

User Configuration|Administrative Templates|Start Menu & Taskbar|Disable Changes To Taskbar And Start Menu Settings

User Configuration|Administrative Templates|Start Menu & Taskbar|Gray Unavailable Windows Installer Programs Start Menu Shortcuts

Task Scheduler

Computer Configuration|Administrative Templates|Windows Components|Task Scheduler|Hide Property Pages

Computer Configuration|Administrative Templates|Windows Components|Task Scheduler|Prevent Task Run Or End

Computer Configuration|Administrative Templates|Windows Components|Task Scheduler|Disable Drag-And-Drop

Computer Configuration|Administrative Templates|Windows Components|Task Scheduler|Disable New Task Creation

Computer Configuration|Administrative Templates|Windows Components|Task Scheduler|Disable Task Deletion

Computer Configuration|Administrative Templates|Windows Components|Task Scheduler|Disable Advanced Menu

Computer Configuration|Administrative Templates|Windows Components|Task Scheduler|Prohibit Browse

User Configuration|Administrative Templates|Windows Components|Task Scheduler|Hide Property Pages

User Configuration|Administrative Templates|Windows Components|Task Scheduler|Prevent Task Run Or End

User Configuration|Administrative Templates|Windows Components|Task Scheduler|Disable Drag And Drop

User Configuration|Administrative Templates|Windows Components|Task Scheduler|Disable New Task Creation

User Configuration|Administrative Templates|Windows Components|Task Scheduler|Disable Task Deletion

User Configuration|Administrative Templates|Windows Components|Task Scheduler|Disable Advanced Menu

User Configuration|Administrative Templates|Windows Components|Task Scheduler|Prohibit Browse

Terminal Services

Computer Configuration|Administrative Templates|System|Remove Security Option From Start Menu (Terminal Services Only)

Computer Configuration|Administrative Templates|System|Remove Disconnect Item From Start Menu (Terminal Services Only)

User Configuration|Administrative Templates|Windows Components|Microsoft Management Console|Restricted/Permitted Snap-Ins|Terminal Services Configuration

Windows Installer

Computer Configuration|Administrative Templates|Windows Components|Windows Installer|Disable Windows Installer

Computer Configuration|Administrative Templates|Windows Components|Windows Installer|Always Install With Elevated Privileges

Computer Configuration|Administrative Templates|Windows Components|Windows Installer|Disable Rollback

Computer Configuration|Administrative Templates|Windows Components|Windows Installer|Disable Browse Dialog Box For New Source

Computer Configuration|Administrative Templates|Windows Components|Windows Installer|Disable Patching

Computer Configuration|Administrative Templates|Windows Components|Windows Installer|Disable IE Security Prompt For Windows Installer Scripts

Computer Configuration|Administrative Templates|Windows Components|Windows Installer|Enable User Control Over Installs

Computer Configuration|Administrative Templates|Windows Components|Windows Installer|Enable User To Browse For Source While Elevated

Computer Configuration|Administrative Templates|Windows Components|Windows Installer|Enable User To Use Media Source While Elevated

Computer Configuration|Administrative Templates|Windows Components|Windows Installer|Enable User To Patch Elevated Products

Computer Configuration|Administrative Templates|Windows Components|Windows Installer|Allow Admin To Install From Terminal Services Session

Computer Configuration|Administrative Templates|Windows Components|Windows Installer|Cache Transforms In Secure Location On Workstation

Computer Configuration|Administrative Templates|Windows Components|Windows Installer|Logging

User Configuration|Administrative Templates|Windows Components|Windows Installer|Always Install With Elevated Privileges

User Configuration|Administrative Templates|Windows Components|Windows Installer|Search Order

User Configuration|Administrative Templates|Windows Components|Windows Installer|Disable Rollback

User Configuration|Administrative Templates|Windows Components|Windows Installer|Disable Media Source For Any Install

Appendix B
Windows 2000 Service Pack 2

Released in May 2001, Windows 2000 Service Pack 2 (SP2) updates Windows 2000 Professional, Windows 2000 Server, Windows 2000 Advanced Server, and Windows 2000 with Server Appliance Kit. This update builds upon Service Pack 1 (SP1) and fixes many of the issues that have arisen with the increased use of Windows 2000 as an operating system in today's enterprises. In this appendix, I discuss the major fixes in Windows 2000 SP2 and how to install SP2, and I'll run through any known issues as of the writing of this book.

SP2 addresses four issues:

• Security

• Windows 2000 setup

• Internet Information Server (IIS)

• Operating system stability

In addition to covering these areas, this appendix discusses where you can get SP2, what the requirements for installation are, and what options are available to you for installation of the service pack. One of the nice things about Microsoft's service packs is the ease of installation because the service packs have progressed from the Windows NT 3.51 days to present day. If you do your homework, test the solution, and use the tools given to you, you will find installing the service packs to be an easy process. First on your list will be installing SP2 and carefully planning the rollout to your network.

Installation

Before you can install Windows 2000 SP2, you will need to get a copy of the SP2 installation package. This can be done in two different ways:

• Download SP2 from any number of Web sites. The Windows 2000 Web site is located at **www.microsoft.com/windows2000**.

- Order the Windows 2000 SP2 CD for $14.95 in the United States or $19.95 in Canada, not including shipping and handling. You can order this from the Windows 2000 Web site as well.

When you download SP2, you will be given an option to do the Express Installation or the Network Installation. The Express Installation is good for single users looking to update their system with a minimal amount of work. Express takes a look at your system and decides which updates are necessary. Some might think of this as a spousal install. (Click Yes dear, Click Yes dear, Click OK dear, and so forth.) The Express Installation ensures that all of the latest updates are downloaded to your system quickly and efficiently.

If you are looking to do more of an enterprise rollout, you will want to download the Network Installation. This downloads all available Windows 2000 SP2 files to your machine. The Network Installation is an excellent choice for the administrator who wants to set up an internal share on the network. As you'll see in the Network Installation section, use this download if you are using Group Policy to mandate an SP2 upgrade on all of your Windows 2000 machines.

NOTE: *This brings up an interesting point. When reading the SP2 frequently asked questions (FAQs), I noticed that someone had asked if Windows 2000 SP2 works on Windows NT 4 workstation. If you have these machines on your network, you will want to install Windows NT 4 service packs on the Windows NT 4 workstations. The last service pack for Windows NT 4 was SP6, and it is also available on Microsoft's Web site.*

Preinstallation

Before you install SP2, you must take several things into consideration. Take some time to read the latest readme documents that accompany the files. They will help identify any new compatibility issues or warnings from Microsoft. You will also want to set up a test group or test lab to make sure that your network doesn't have any adverse reactions. As the saying goes, adverse reactions in a lab versus adverse reactions in the production environment reduce the likelihood of adverse reaction to your career.

The following are additional considerations when installing SP2:

- Close all antivirus programs.
- To maximize recovery of the computer in the event of installation failure, take the following precautionary steps:
  1. Update the system emergency repair disk (ERD) by performing the following steps:
     - Click Start, and select Programs|Accessories|System Tools|Backup.
     - On the Welcome tab, click Emergency Repair Disk.

2. Perform a full backup of the computer, including the registry files and system state (if applicable).

- Check your computer's available disk space.

- The service pack might prompt you to restart if you have made recent changes to your system and have not yet restarted. The error message states that "The system must be restarted before installing the Service Pack, to allow some prior file update operations to complete. (These operations were previously scheduled by some other install or uninstall operation.)"

Space Requirements

When discussing the amount of space required for the installation of SP2, you need to define working space and backup space. *Working space* is the amount of hard disk space necessary to load the temporary files that will install the service pack. If you are planning to give the system the capability of uninstalling SP2, you will need to have additional space on the drive to allow for file backup. Table B.1 shows space requirements for Windows 2000 Professional.

When you install SP2 for Windows 2000 Server, Advanced Server, and Server Appliance Kit, you need a bit more space as shown in Table B.2.

Table B.1 SP2 requirements for Windows 2000 Professional.

Space Use	Space Required for Network Installation	Space Required for CD Installation
Service pack only	20 megabytes (MB) (for the service pack)	20MB (for the service pack)+170MB (for the service pack files contained in the %windir%\servicepackfiles folder)
Working space	70MB	270MB
Uninstallation files*	250MB*	250MB*
Total	270MB(340MB peak during installation)	440MB(770MB peak during installation)

This number could be closer to 380MB if you have installed SP1 before SP2.

Table B.2 SP2 Requirements for Windows 2000 Server.

Space Use	Space Required for Network Installation	Space Required for CD Installation
Service pack only	20MB (for the service pack)	20MB (for the service pack)+215MB (for the service pack files contained in the %windir%\servicepackfiles folder)
Working space	80MB	280MB
Uninstallation files*	315MB*	315MB*
Total	335MB(415MB peak during installation)	550MB(830MB peak during installation)

This number could be closer to 460MB if you have installed SP1 before SP2.

After reviewing the requirements and acquiring SP2, you are ready to install the service pack. I run through two methods of installing the service pack, starting with the easiest, which is the Express Installation.

Remember that this is the recommended installation method for end users looking to update their system with a minimal amount of work. The Express Installation automatically detects which files need to be updated and then copies the appropriate files to a temporary folder on your computer. It then installs those files and updates your computer.

Methods of Installation

The Windows 2000 Service Pack supports three different forms of installation:

- *Update Installation*—This is the standard method used to install Windows NT service packs. If you've done any installations of Windows NT 4 service packs, you will be familiar with this standard type of installation. This is where the Express and Network Installations mentioned in the following sections take place.

- *Integrated Installation*—This is a new installation method that many people were introduced to in SP1 for Windows 2000. It allows you to install Windows 2000 and SP2 at the same time, thus preventing administrators from doing double duty.

- *Combination Installation*—This allows you to install SP2 along with any other components using a combination of update and slipstream installation processes (for example, IIS, Terminal Services, message queuing, and so forth).

One of the great things about the new service packs in the Microsoft world is their ease of installation and the granularity afforded to a network administrator. By combining the installation of SP2 with other options, your valuable time is not eaten up with updates and patches.

Express Installation

To use the Express Installation, perform the following steps:

1. Using a browser, go to **www.microsoft.com/windows2000**.
2. To install SP2, click Download Windows 2000 SP2.
3. Choose a language from the drop-down list, and click Next.
4. Click Express Installation.

Microsoft warns that, if you use a browser other than Internet Explorer 5 or higher, you will more than likely not be able to use Express Installation. If this is the case, you will want to use the Network Installation to download the files to your local hard drive and run the setup from there.

To use the Network Installation, you would use the previous steps, but you would click Network Installation instead of Express Installation. This loads the compressed file, W2ksp2.exe, onto your local drive. From there, you can choose to uncompress the file without installing SP2, or you can double-click W2ksp2.exe and install the service pack on the local machine.

NOTE: *From the command prompt, type "W2ksp2.exe –x" and press Enter to have the files uncompressed to the installation folder, including the Update.exe installation file.*

Network Installation

You can install Windows 2000 SP2 across a network in several ways. I look at two ways in detail: Installation Share and Group Policy.

Performing a network installation with Installation Share should be very familiar to those of you who have used this method back in the Windows NT 4 days. Administrators can extract the files to a network drive and use this share to install SP2 on any machine on that network.

Installing from a Shared Network Folder

To install SP2 from a shared network folder, perform the following steps:

1. Expand W2ksp2.exe to the installation share on your network. At the command prompt, type "W2ksp2.exe /x:*server**share*".

2. On the client computer, connect to the installation distribution share folder. At the command prompt, type "net use *n*: *server**share*", where *n* is the network drive.

3. At the command prompt, type "*n*:" to switch to the network drive.

4. At the command prompt, type "cd i386\update" to switch to the i386\update directory.

5. At the command prompt, type "Update.exe" to begin installing SP2.

6. Follow the directions on the screen to complete the SP2 installation.

You can also use several switches when running Update.exe on your system. For example, you might want to run the installation in Quiet mode (no user intervention). To do this, you would type "Update.exe –q" at the command prompt. Table B.3 lists the available command-line switches that you can use.

Table B.3   SP2 Installation Switches.

Command-Line Switch	Description
-u	Use unattended Setup mode.
-f	Force other applications to close at shutdown.
-n	Do not back up files for uninstall.
-o	Overwrite original equipment manufacturer (OEM) files without prompting.
-z	Do not restart the computer when the installation completes.
-q	Use Quiet mode (no user interaction required).
-s:folder name	Use Integrated Installation mode (to a distribution server location).

Several of these switches can be advantageous for the administrator who is trying to make the installation run as smoothly as possible.

If you are running a Windows 2000 domain and are using the powerful Group Policies, your installation can be even smoother. Windows 2000 SP2 includes the Windows Installer package (Update.msi) for use with a Group Policy that would assign or publish SP2 to specific computers or users. This is a powerful way to test the deployment of SP2. You can set up an organizational unit (OU) for a test group and apply the policy to it. This will help you find any adverse reactions before they occur in the rest of your network. The Windows Installer package contains all the information required to install or uninstall SP2 using the IntelliMirror management technologies of Windows 2000 (for example, Group Policies).

Uninstalling SP2

Believe it or not, you can actually choose to make installing Windows 2000 SP2 a one-way ticket with no chance of uninstalling. This can be a good idea if you have people who tend to play around with Add/Remove Programs in the Control Panel.

During the installation process, the W2ksp2.exe program installs the service pack files on your computer. This program automatically creates a backup of the files and settings that the service pack installer changes, and also saves them in a $NTServicepackUninstall$ folder in your systemroot folder.

Preventing Automatically Created Backups

To prevent W2ksp2.exe from automatically creating backups, use the following methods:

- For an attended installation, clear the Backup Files Necessary To Uninstall This Service Pack At A Later Time checkbox.

- For an unattended installation, add the **-n** switch to the command line when you run W2ksp2.exe.

NOTE: *If you turn off the automatic backup option for W2ksp2.exe, you cannot use the uninstall SP2 mechanism and, therefore, cannot uninstall the service pack.*

As you can see, you need to take several considerations to ensure that you plan an effective installation of SP2. Also, remember that, if you have certain applications or services that rely on SP2, they will have serious issues when you uninstall the service pack. If you use the integrated installation method (installing SP2 as part of the Windows 2000 operating system installation), you will be unable to uninstall SP2 because the two are intertwined.

There are two methods of uninstalling SP2. You can use the Control Panel|Add/Remove Programs, or you can use the command-line prompt Uninstall program.

Add/Remove Programs

To use the Control Panel|Add/Remove Programs to uninstall SP2, perform the following steps:

1. Click Start, and select Settings|Control Panel.

2. Double-click Add/Remove Programs.

3. Click Windows 2000 SP2 in the selections available, and then click Change/Remove.

4. The Uninstall Program wizard will walk you through the steps necessary to remove SP2 from your system.

Command-Line Uninstall

To uninstall SP2 using the command-line Uninstall program, perform the following steps:

1. Click Start, and select Run.

2. At the Open prompt, type "cmd", and then click OK or press Enter.

3. Type "cd %systemroot%\$NtServicePackUninstall$\spuninst\", and then press Enter.

4. Type "spunist.exe", and then press Enter.

What's New and Improved?

As I told you in the beginning of this appendix, SP2 updates and applies fixes to four main areas. I'll cover the majority of fixes in these areas, but the complete list of fixes is quite long. You can see them at **support.microsoft.com/support/kb/articles/Q282/5/22.asp**.

Service packs are cumulative. In other words, the bugs that are fixed in a service pack are also fixed in subsequent service packs. Therefore, Windows 2000 SP2 contains all of the fixes included in Windows 2000 SP1. If you haven't installed SP1, you do not have to install it to install SP2.

Security

One of the biggest updates in Windows 2000 SP2 is the upgrade from 56-bit encryption to 128-bit encryption. When you install SP2, your system security will be upgraded. Any system at a standard encryption level (56 bit) will be moved to a high encryption level (128 bit) in order to offer better online and local security. There is a gotcha. After this upgrade is made, you will not be able to return to 56-bit encryption on your system even if you uninstall SP2.

Because you are upgrading your system security, many areas will be affected. Kerberos, Encrypting File System (EFS), Remote Access Service (RAS), Remote Procedure Call (RPC), Secure Sockets Layer/Transport Layer Security (SSL/TLS), Cryto application programming interface (CryptoAPI), Terminal Services Remote Desktop Protocol (RDP), and Internet Protocol Security (IPSec) will be upgraded and will supply higher levels of security on your system. This also increases encryption levels for your online transactions. Your banking and other transactions will be highly secure.

If your company is global, remember to keep an eye on local laws that prohibit high encryption. All United States (U.S.)-embargoed countries are not allowed to have 128-bit encryption, and several countries ban encryption. France was notorious for its restrictions on encryption, but during the past year or so has relaxed some of those laws. Again, be careful before rolling out SP2 in countries outside the United States if you haven't learned the countries' rules and regulations concerning high encryption.

Table B.4 contains some of the major issues that SP2 fixes in the area of security. For a complete list, go to the Windows 2000 SP2 deployment Web site. Each of these articles can be accessed by going to **www.microsoft.com** and entering the article identification (ID) number (for example, Q263743) in the search line.

Windows 2000 Setup

Microsoft did some incredible work on improving the ease of installation of Windows 2000. It did have its hiccups, but Windows 2000 is one of Microsoft's most stable and robust operating systems. The Windows 2000 SP2 CD includes a Deployment Tools folder that will make your life as an administrator even easier.

Table B.4   Security issues covered by SP2.

TechNet Article	Article title/Issue Fixed with SP2
Q263743	RASDisable and RASForce Winlogon Policies can be bypassed.
Q262539	Memory Leak in Lsass.exe with large built-in groups.
Q262979	Cannot renew Verisign Certificates in IIS 5.0.
Q266684	"Access Denied" after unlocking workstations when the network is disconnected.
Q267556	Auditing doesn't report a security event for resetting passwords on domain controllers.
Q267560	When changing URLs in IIS, you may expose the contents of the file.
Q267868	Renaming the CD-ROM drive creates an Admin$ share to which everyone has full permission.
Q269406	With NTLMv1 on Server, the data is not encrypted when you set or add passwords in User Manager or Server Manager.
Q269731	Domain controllers contain invalid tickets in the Ticket Cache.
Q271641	The "Configure Your Computer" wizard sets a blank Recovery Mode Passcode.
Q272743	HTML e-mail link will transmit a user name and password to an Unauthorized Server.
Q275248	Kerberos doesn't work after connecting to a Windows NT 4.0 share when using Smart Card Logons.

One of the biggest improvements is the updated Windows 2000 System Preparation tool (Sysprep.exe) that is located in the Tools folder.

Sysprep 1.1 is updated to support multiple mass-storage controllers. What this means to you is that you will not need as many images because Sysprep 1.1 can successfully blast images to two machines whose drive controllers are different. Sysprep 1.1 enables administrators to prepare Windows 2000 system images as part of an automated deployment. One of the issues of duplicating Windows 2000 from one computer to another is the unique security identifiers (SIDs). Sysprep allows you to change the SIDs so that each new computer will have a unique identifier. Not only can you duplicate the operating system, but it can also let you allow the end user to set the user-specific information during the first boot. Sysprep 1.1 also allows you to automate the setup and to audit the installation.

If you want to build a Sysprep.inf file (an answer file for Sysprep), you can run the Setup Manager Wizard and use the Install Sysprep option. Answer files assist you in unattended installations by providing you the answers to the installation input screens.

SP2 fixes several things about setup. Table B.5 is a partial list of problems that are fixed in SP2.

Table B.5   Setup issues covered by SP2.

TechNet Article	Article Title/Issue Fixed with SP2
Q255952	Unable to contact DHCP server with RIS boot disk.
Q259144	Computer may hang after using Sysprep on ACPI-enabled computer.
Q260319	Sysprep "-pnp" switch may not install non-native signed drivers.
Q270070	Error message: Windows 2000 is installed on a drive formatted with the OS/2 file system (HPFS).
Q272308	WINNT32/CHECKUPGRADEONLY/UNATTEND is not fully automated.
Q272378	Error message when you use a multiple-processor image on a single processor computer with Sysprep.
Q275206	User must click "Finish" to reboot the computer when the Unattended Installation is complete.
Q282755	Signed drivers may appear as unsigned during setup.
Q285782	Do not uninstall 56-bit hotfixes after installing High Encryption Pack.
Q289192	System Information identifies computers as running Windows 2000 Advanced Server when they are not.
Q289228	When you uninstall IIS, some files are not updated by SP1.
Q296721	Terminal Services Client is not updated when Service Pack 1 is installed.

IIS

With the introduction of IIS as a part of Windows 2000 Server, administrators were given a powerful tool that also served as a back door for many undesirables to gain access to a network. Much has been made of the buffer overflows, port openings, and other miscellaneous holes in the system. SP2 definitely solves many issues, but it must be pointed out that you need to monitor the Windows 2000 Web site for security patches and updates to help in the ongoing war against hackers. However, SP2 will go a long way to help plug up the holes.

IIS also faces other issues, which are fixed with SP2 as well. Many of these issues deal with Component Object Model (COM)+ and Java. Microsoft's Windows 2000 SP2 Web site (go to **www.microsoft.com** and search for Windows 2000 SP2) lists 50 fixes, but I stick with the more recognizable ones.

Remember that IIS 5 is included in Windows 2000 Server, Advanced Server, and Datacenter Server and is installed by default. You can choose to remove these services in Control Panel|Add/Remove Programs. If you don't want to do this, especially if you are using IIS for an intranet Web site, you will want to install all the latest patches. Many of them are included in SP2. I've listed the major issues in Table B.6, but, as always, make sure you check the Web site on a weekly, if not daily, basis for security patches.

Table B.6 IIS issues covered in SP2.

TechNet Article	Article Title/Issue Fixed in SP2
Q262739	Can't administer IIS by using ADSI on Window NT 4.0 IIS 4.0 from Windows 2000 IIS 5.0 and vice versa.
Q251063	Password change notification incorrectly notifies accounts with no password expiration.
Q259076	Cannot Add Users or Groups as operators in default FTP and default Web sites.
Q260353	FIX: use of Java/COM components in COM+ enabled systems can cause delays.
Q263607	New activations of Remote COM Server may not work if Remote Server has been rebooted.
Q264908	Error Message: HTTP 403.15 – Forbidden: Client Access Licenses exceeded.
Q259760	Compression is not enabled on POST request.
Q265379	FIX: Memory leak when calling between configured components.
Q269242	DCOM Bindings not updated when dialing ISP.
Q269285	FTP Server fails to open data connection.
Q265386	FIX: COM+ application Proxy export includes system Dynamic-Link Library (DLL).
Q269476	FIX: COM+ Dispenser Manager doesn't close pooled resources.
Q271456	IIS 4.0 causes heap corruption in CGI application.
Q274294	FrontPage 2000: "Confirm Save. A more recent version of the file has been saved" error message when you try to Save File in WEB.
Q275157	FIX: Access Violation when you activate a pooled COM+ component.
Q276489	Patch for Web Server Folder Traversal vulnerability.
Q277632	Memory leak in Inetinfo.exe when using the Active Directory's IIS provider.
Q277774	Post Windows 2000 SP1 COM+ Hotfix 5.
Q277873	Patch for "Web Server File Request Parsing" vulnerability.
Q278511	Patch for ActiveX parameter validation vulnerability.
Q279207	Access violation in Inetinfo.exe when quitting IIS during heavy usage.
Q280322	FrontPage: Patch for malformed Web form submission security vulnerability.
Q275482	FIX: COM+ 1.0 catalog requires NTLM-based authentication.

Operating System Stability

When you have a computer with an operating system, you want to have it up and running. When you have end users complaining of blue screens and error messages, you spend a lot of time tracking down these issues. You lose valuable time and functionality if your operating system is acting up. This is why you want a stable operating system.

Windows 2000 is one of the most stable operating systems in existence today, but it is far from perfect. SP1 dealt with many of the initial issues that arose with Windows 2000, but, because more and more people are installing Windows 2000 on their systems, they are finding more and more issues. SP2 goes a long way to help solve these issues.

Table B.7 contains some of the fixes and updates that help Windows 2000 become even more stable. This is obviously the biggest portion of the updates and fixes, and, once again, I try to provide you with the most relevant ones.

Table B.7   OS issues covered by SP2.

TechNet Article	Article Title/Issue Fixed by SP2
Q262694	Malicious user can shut down computer browser service.
Q262137	Client Connection Manager for Terminal Service causes Access Violation.
Q257357	Performance degradation when heap is fragmented.
Q259281	Folders are created once an hour if FRS is enabled in DFS root.
Q260241	Registry Quota leak in Windows 2000.
Q261601	Video does not work after resuming from Hibernation on Laptops.
Q261606	Video hangs when you run a 3D graphics program.
Q261643	USB devices are missing in Device Manager after the computer resumes from Hibernation.
Q265003	Windows 2000 overwrites or damages an OS/2 Boot Manager Partition.
Q265365	FRS creates unneeded folders in DFS root alternates.
Q266647	Drive letters automatically assigned to unrecognizable partitions.
Q268094	Windows 2000 cannot read CD-R discs created with DirectCD.
Q271644	Cannot convert FAT32 to NTFS with an IDE hard drive larger than 20GB.
Q272295	Windows 2000 SP1 computer hangs when you use IEEE 1394 digital camera with NetMeeting.
Q272567	FRS improvements made in SP2.
Q272655	Certain PC Cards may not work when system resumes from Suspend mode.
Q273988	Disk Manager prompts you to continue every 5 minutes.
Q276516	Group Policy isn't applied with too many Domain Controllers in a Domain.
Q289195	Computer hangs after attempts to use CD-ROM drive on a computer with Low Memory.
Q289162	Print jobs that are larger than 4MB do not print completely.

Post-SP2 Issues

As of the writing of this book, Windows 2000 SP2 had several know issues. Please understand that this is not an exhaustive list, and you are well advised to go to the Microsoft Windows 2000 SP2 Web site (go to **www.microsoft.com** and search for "Windows 2000 SP2") to find the latest release notes and known issues with SP2.

Having said that, let's take a look at several things you need to be aware of with SP2. Administrators using SP2 have discovered four areas to watch:.

- Networking
- Management/administration
- Setup
- Program compatibility

Because Windows 2000 is a network operating system (NOS), I take a quick look at that area first. I've included the TechNet article and the problem, so make sure you write them down, go to **www.technet.com**, and enter the article number in the Knowledge Base search engine.

Networking issues

With the scalability of Active Directory, Windows 2000 was bound to tie itself into a knot occasionally. As you add more and more servers running services, you'll notice that issues can arise. Some of the more prevalent issues deal with Dynamic Host Configuration Protocol (DHCP). Table B.8 includes some of the highlights.

Table B.8   Networking issues covered by SP2.

TechNet Article	Problem
Q297847	DHCP issues 1. No more than approximately 850 DHCP servers can be authorized in Active Directory. 2. The Active Directory query interval is not configurable. 3. The DHCP authorization process occurs frequently or, in some cases, occurs too often, which causes server performance problems.
Q275286	ISA Server issues 1. Windows 2000 Quality of Service (Qos) Packet Scheduler Service Does Not Filter and Flow Forwarded Traffic. 2. Windows 2000 QoS Packet Scheduler Sends Packets with Wrong Checksum on Network Adapters That Enable Hardware Checksum. 3. Client Computer with High Connect Rate Opens Many Sockets.
Q292640	DHCP Server Management Console issues. If you use the Microsoft Management Console (MMC) to delete or unauthorize a computer that is running Microsoft Windows 2000 as a DHCP server, you may not be able to view all of the DHCP servers in your enterprise network. The Authorized Server MMC snap-in does not display more than 1,000 DHCP servers.

Management/Administration

As an administrator, you need to have tools to help you control your networking environment, and nothing is worse than when those tools don't work. The primary issue in SP1 and SP2 is the inability to install the SP2 Adminpak on any Windows 2000 computer that is running Windows 2000 SP1. That can be a real problem. The answer to this problem is found in Knowledge Base article Q292640, which might look familiar because it deals with several other MMC issues as well as this one.

Follow the directions in the Knowledge Base article, and you'll be running your MMCs in no time.

Setup

A wise network administrator once told me that the only things that mess up perfectly good operating systems are fixes and updates. As you know, you constantly update your networks and machines with the latest patch or service pack, and it is no surprise when the vaccine for the illness causes a little sickness itself.

What happens when you install SP2 on your network? Well, first off, you will find an occasional hiccup in the install process itself, and the first is an antivirus error message if you haven't completely shut down Norton or McAfee. You may also find a few gotchas when the installation runs into other applications that are latently active such as tape backup or apps that track system changes for you. As with other updates, the farther ahead you run from your legacy devices and programs means the more chances that they will give you error messages or refuse to run. Small Computer System Interface (SCSI) is just one of those implementations. Table B.9 contains the most current issues known as of the writing of this book. Again, make sure you check your latest readme files and monitor Microsoft's Windows 2000 Web site at **www.microsoft.com/windows2000**.

Program Compatibility

According to Microsoft's Web site, the only compatibility issue that Microsoft recognizes has to do with BlackIce Defender. Although I'm sure this isn't the only issue, it is the primary one that Microsoft has discovered.

Knowledge Base article Q292642 helps fix the problem that arises when you are installing BlackIce Defender, which is a personal firewall product that helps protect your home network from the hackers on the Internet. Unfortunately, the firewall filter doesn't install if you are running SP2 on your machine. Check out the article to take care of this issue.

Table B.9   Setup issues covered by SP2.

TechNet Article	Article Title/Problem
Q289923	Windows 2000 SP1 or SP2 may need to be reapplied after running a repair.
Q297794	SP2 install doesn't remove SP1 from Control Panel\Add/Remove.
Q298583	Adaptec Easy CD Creator 5.0 can cause a Blue Screen.
Q265824	Norton Antivirus error message when you install Service Pack.
Q296822	ServiceWare: No Add/Remove program entries for SP or IE after reinstalling Windows 2000 Service Pack 2.
Q263125	SP1 upgrade doesn't update Recovery Console files.
Q265813	Running Update.exe for more than one share produces one .log file.
Q265816	Installation path is not updated by Windows 2000 Service Pack Update.exe.
Q268180	Svcpack.log incorrectly records files copied to Winnt\Java\Classes after installation of SP1.
Q268257	Problems with Windows 2000 SP1 Integrated installation updates.
Q268989	Considerations before you uninstall Windows 2000 SP1.
Q297961	SP2 causes SCSI bus resets during startup on an LSI logic controller.

As with any service pack, you occasionally run into issues of programs not liking the new changes to the operating system. Don't be afraid to check the Microsoft Knowledgebase for updates and problems with any and all issues dealing with Windows 2000, including the service packs. A specific search of the Knowledgebase can be performed at **www.microsoft.com/kb**. You can also check out the software vendors' Web sites for their patches and fixes for Windows 2000 and the service packs.

Conclusion

Windows 2000 SP2 is a great update for your Windows 2000 network and provides more flexibility, stability, and overall performance. As Microsoft has progressed through the years of updates and service packs, the ease of installation and the integration of the installation with the operating system itself has provided administrators more opportunity for planning and growth.

Appendix C
Windows 2000 Resources

Many excellent resources for Windows 2000 are available on the Internet. This appendix lists some of the most popular ones. The following list, however, is nowhere near complete:

- *Ask the Experts,* **www.allexperts.com**—AllExperts allows for the exchange of questions and answers. This is a great place to post those hard-to-find-an-answer-for questions.

- *BHS Software,* **www.bhs.com**—This is a good Windows NT and Windows 2000 resource center. It lists many frequently asked questions (FAQs) and also has downloads and tech support.

- *C\Net's Download.com,* **www.download.com**—This is one of the best places on the Internet to find and download demonstration versions of different software packages. Ratings and prices are usually included.

- *C\Net's Shareware.com,* **www.shareware.com**—This is a good place to search for and download shareware programs for Windows 2000.

- *Computerworld,* **www.computerworld.com**—*Computerworld* is one of the most popular magazines available today. The site starts where the magazine ends with resource centers and job postings.

- *Jim Buyen's Web Resources,* **www.interlacken.com**—This site has a great Windows NT and Windows 2000 resource site.

- *@Stake,* **www.atstake.com/research**—This is a site that lists many of the Windows NT and Windows 2000 security holes and how to fix them. It also has tools available to test the security of your network and passwords.

- *DLL Help Database,* **support.microsoft.com/servicedesks/fileversion/dllinfo.asp?fr=0&sd=tech**—Use this Microsoft site to troubleshoot application interoperability issues with dynamic link libraries (DLLs).

- *Microsoft Certified Professional Magazine,* **www.mcpmag.com**—This is the online version of the popular *Microsoft Certified Professional Magazine.*

- *Microsoft Events,* **msevents.Microsoft.com**—Refer to this site every month or so to check for valuable road shows and online seminars.

- *Microsoft MSDN,* **msdn.microsoft.com**—This site is the Microsoft Developer Network online. It has full search capability on the Web and links to demonstration code and applications.

- *Microsoft TechNet,* **www.microsoft.com/technet**—This is the online version of TechNet and is usually more up-to-date than the TechNet CD-ROMs.

- *Microsoft's Windows 2000 Portal,* **www.microsoft.com/windows2000**—This is the main Microsoft Windows 2000 site. It contains all released security fixes, hot fixes, and service packs.

- *NetAdminTools,* **www.netadmintools.com**—This site contains a very comprehensive list of Windows NT and Windows 2000 administration tools. It also has a "Tricks of the Trade" section.

- *NTSecrets.com,* **www.ntsecrets.com**—This site provides a good list of Windows NT and Windows 2000 secrets that an administrator should use on a daily basis.

- *Webopedia,* **www.webopedia.com**—This is an online dictionary for computer terms. Not only are most terms defined, links to more complete definitions are usually included.

- *PCWatch,* **www.pcwatch.com**—This is another online news magazine. This one focuses on the entire PC market, not just Windows NT.

- *The PC Guide,* **www.pcguide.com**—An excellent companion source to **www.webopedia.com**. This site is full of hardware and software information in a clear, concise, and to-the-point format.

- *Microsoft security bulletins,* **www.microsoft.com/technet/security**—Microsoft offers email bulletins on security issues. From this site, you can subscribe and also check for security issues on any Microsoft product.

- *Sunbelt Software,* **www.sunbelt-software.com**—This is a leading software reseller of some of the most powerful software packages for Windows NT and Windows 2000.

- *Sysinternals,* **www.sysinternals.com**—This is the freeware version of **www.winternals.com**. It contains Windows NT and Windows 2000 utilities that should be in every administrator's tool kit.

- *TechWeb,* **www.techweb.com**—Check out the Information Technology (IT) Tech Centers for information on anything from security to careers and training to system management. This is a multiplatform site, so those of you who are living in the real world might benefit from some of the interoperability articles here.

- *Tek-Tips, **www.tek-tips.com**—*This site contains a long list of discussion forums. It is a great place to find information on the latest hardware and software and what experiences other administrators have had with them.

- *Tucows Download, **www.tucows.com**—*This is one of the largest download sites on the Internet with hundreds of mirror sites located all over the world.

- *W2K News, **www.w2knews.com**—*This is a Web news-style site with news, information, history, and downloads on Windows 2000.

- *Windows 2000 hot fixes, downloads, and service packs,* **www.microsoft.com/downloads**—The centralized site for all Microsoft downloads. This includes consumer software (like IE), patches, hot fixes, and demos.

- *Windows 2000 Magazine, **www.win2000mag.com**—*This is the online version of the popular *Windows 2000 Magazine* (formerly *Windows NT Magazine*). Many of the articles are available online in a searchable format.

- *Windows 2000 Professional Documentation on the Web,* **www.microsoft.com/windows2000/en/professional/help/default.asp**—This is the complete Microsoft reference for Windows 2000 Professional.

- *Windows 2000 Server Documentation on the Web, **www.microsoft.com/windows2000/en/server/help/default.asp**—*Microsoft has recognized that a broader offering of documentation on the Web is helpful in the support arena. This site contains comprehensive documentation, support, and instructional articles for Windows 2000 server.

- *The Windows 2000 Resource Kits, **www.microsoft.com/windows2000/techinfo/reskit/en/default.asp**—*Yes, you heard me right. Every single Windows 2000 Resource Kit is on the Web at this site: Server, Professional, Registry, Performance Counters, Group Policy, and Error Messages references.

- *Windows 2000 Secrets, **www.win2ksecrets.com**—*This is the sister site to **www.ntsecrets.com** and is exclusively about Windows 2000.

- *Windows Internals, **www.winternals.com**—*This is the retail side of **www.sysinternals.com**.

- *Windows 2000 FAQ, **www.Windows2000faq.com**—*This is the place to find answers to your Windows 2000 questions.

- *WinPlanet, **www.winplanet.com**—*This is a Windows NT and Windows 2000 site that offers discussions, opinions, reviews, tutorials, and downloads.

Glossary

Active Directory—A centralized resource and security management, administration, and control mechanism in Windows 2000 that is used to support and maintain a Windows 2000 domain. Active Directory is hosted by domain controllers.

Active Directory Domains And Trusts—A Windows 2000 utility used to create and manage domains and trusts. This includes operations, such as setting the domain name's operation manager, changing a domain's mode, creating trusts between domains, and defining a managing user account.

Active Directory Migration Tool (ADMT)—An add-on utility that consists of several wizards used to restructure specific Active Directory objects (user accounts, computer accounts, trusts, and so forth) from one domain to another. ADMT can be used to migrate objects from Windows NT domains to Windows 2000 domains. It can also be used to migrate objects from two Windows 2000 domains.

Active Directory Sites And Services—A Windows 2000 utility used to configure server settings, site settings, and replication.

Active Directory Users And Computers—A Windows 2000 utility used to create and manage users, groups, and computers within a domain.

answer file—A file that contains a complete set of instructions for installing Windows 2000 without sitting at the keyboard to answer queries from the setup program.

application log—Records various application-specific details.

auditing—The process of recording the occurrence of a defined event or action.

authoritative restore—The process of designating a specific domain controller as being the authority. An authoritative restore is performed when all or part of the Active Directory database has been restored and the old or bad database has been replicated to other domain controllers within the domain. Designating the Active Directory authority prevents the bad data located on the other domain controllers from replicating to the authority server and thus causing the problem again. Instead, the authority server replicates to all other domain controllers.

automated task (AT)—A utility that provides a way of programming an operating system to perform management functions automatically.

baseline—A measurement of normal system operation.

basic disks—Standard hard disks that are divided into standard, extended, and logical partitions that are readable by Windows 2000 and other operating systems.

basic input/output system (BIOS)—A set of instructions and data located on a chip on the motherboard. The BIOS contains information about the hardware on the system and also executes boot-up instructions.

boot.ini—The text file that tells a computer how to load an operating system and creates the Windows 2000 boot loader's menu. It is one of the seven files required for booting Windows 2000.

Bootsect.dos—This is one of the seven files required for booting Windows 2000. This file is required only when another operating system is being used on the system.

certificate—A visa of sorts that can be attached to a public key (see encryption) that verifies source, creation, and authenticity of the public key.

ClonePrincipal—A suite of Visual Basic Scripts (VBScripts) that can be run using the Windows 2000 scripting host. These scripts are similar in nature to ADMT in that each one copies components of a Windows 2000 Active Directory to another Windows 2000 Active Directory. Unlike ADMT, ClonePrincipal requires that both domains be Windows 2000.

clustering—A group of Windows 2000 computers that act as a single server by sharing resources and processes.

Component Services—The renamed Microsoft Transaction Server. Component Services are used to deploy and control Component Object Model (COM)+, automate tasks using scripting or programming languages, manage transactions between processes, and create scalable component-based applications.

compression—The process of compacting data to save disk space.

Computer Management—A Windows 2000 utility that offers single-interface access to several commonly used local computer-management utilities, such as Event Viewer, Disk Management, and the Services applet.

console—A Microsoft Management Console (MMC) instance that contains one or more snap-ins.

contact—An Active Directory object that is similar in nature to a user account, but does not have any logon or authentication privileges.

container—An object within Active Directory that can hold other objects.

Control Panel—A collection of tools, called *applets*, within Windows 2000, where most system and hardware configuration takes place.

Counter List—A Resource Kit utility that outputs a list of all the counters installed on a system to a file. This data can be very useful in ensuring that specified logs run on all systems in the network by comparing the counters installed on those systems.

CryptoAPI 2—An application programming interface (API) that enables applications to encrypt or digitally sign data.

CScript—A command-line scripting engine that comes with Windows 2000.

Data Link Control (DLC)—A low-level network protocol designed for International Business Machines (IBM) connectivity, remote booting, and network printing.

data sources (ODBC)—A Windows 2000 utility used to define Data Source Names (DSNs) employed by applications and services to access database management systems in the domain.

defragmentation—The process of reorganizing files so that they are stored contiguously on the hard drive.

delegation—A new feature in Windows 2000 that enables an administrator to assign certain administrative tasks specifically to another user or group.

Device Manager—A Windows 2000 administrative tool used to install, configure, and manage hardware devices.

directory services—A service whereby all network resources within a logical boundary, such as a tree, forest, or domain, are centrally organized. The directory service for Windows 2000 is Active Directory. The directory service for NetWare is Novell Directory Services (NDS).

Glossary

Disk Cleanup—A tool used to regain access to hard drive space through deleting temporary, orphaned, or downloaded files; emptying the Recycle Bin; compressing little-used files; and condensing index catalog files.

distinguished name (DN)—A unique name that identifies an object and its location on a network.

distribution group—A group of accounts or contacts grouped together for the purpose of an application. Exchange 2000 taps into Active Directory distribution groups in order to centralize user authentication and administration.

domain—A logical grouping of network resources, such as computers, users, printers, and so forth.

domain controller—A computer that maintains a Windows 2000 domain's Active Directory, which stores all information and relationships about users, groups, policies, computers, and resources.

Domain Local groups—A group of accounts and other groups that are visible to resources within a domain.

Domain Name Service (DNS)—A naming system used to locate resources on a Transmission Control Protocol/Internet Protocol (TCP/IP)-based network. DNS resolves fully qualified domain names (FQDNs) to TCP/IP addresses.

domain restructure—A process of restructuring a domain or migrating from Windows NT to Windows 2000. A restructure involves moving resources from one domain into another. In the case of a migration scenario, a domain restructure requires that a Windows 2000 domain either be existing or created in order to receive the resources from the Windows NT domain.

domain security policy—A Windows 2000 utility used to configure and define the security policy for a domain.

domain upgrade—A process of migrating a domain from Windows NT to Windows 2000 by upgrading the component domain controllers within the Windows NT domain.

domains—The main structure of Active Directory. By placing objects within one or more domains in an organization, you can duplicate the organization's physical structure.

disk operating system (DOS) subsystem—An environmental subsystem provided to support DOS applications.

driver signing—All drivers from Microsoft and approved vendors are signed. You can configure Windows 2000 to refuse to install any drivers that aren't signed.

duplexing—A RAID configuration identical to mirroring, with two hard drive controllers for added redundancy.

dynamic disks—Hard disks that can only house dynamic volumes created through the Disk Management administrative tool. These disks do not include partitions or logical drives, and they cannot be accessed by any other operating system.

Dynamic DNS—Automates the addition and removal of systems in DNS.

Dynamic Host Control Protocol (DHCP)—A protocol that automates the dynamic assignment of Internet Protocol (IP) addresses to clients.

dynamic trust—A transitive trust.

emergency repair disk (ERD)—A machine-specific disk that can be used to repair a failed system. It's created through the NTBACKUP utility.

Encrypting File System (EFS)—A file system supported by Windows 2000 that provides encryption of data stored on NTFS volumes.

encryption—A method of scrambling data to protect it from anyone who doesn't have a decryption key. Encryption usually occurs using two separate keys, a public and a private key. The public key is used to encrypt data for a specific target user. The private key is used by the target users to decrypt the data that was keyed specifically to them (using the public key).

Event Viewer—A utility used to view and manage the logs of Windows 2000.

Executive Services—The collection of Kernel mode components for operating system management.

explicit trust—A trust that is generated manually. Explicit trusts are also created when upgrading from Windows NT to Windows 2000.

Extensible Authentication Protocol (EAP)—A protocol that provides remote user authentication.

fault tolerance—An operating system's capability to guarantee data integrity after a hardware failure.

file allocation table (FAT)—The file system originally introduced with DOS. FAT does not provide file system security features.

folder redirection—A type of Group Policy that seamlessly redirects local folders to a network location.

forest—A collection of one or more Active Directory trees.

Glossary

fragmentation—The division of data into two or more parts, where each part is stored in a different location on the hard drive. As the level of fragmentation on a drive increases, disk performance decreases.

fully qualified domain name (FQDN)—A friendly name, such as microsoft.com, that's linked to an IP address, such as 207.46.130.45.

Global Catalog—A database that contains a copy of all objects in the current domain and a partial copy of all objects in all other domains in the forest. The Global Catalog is queried against when performing interdomain requests.

Global group—A group of accounts that is visible between domains within a forest.

graphics device drivers—These components manage the graphical rendering of the desktop environment.

graphics device interface (GDI)—The software component and memory stack that interact with the Windows 2000 printing and video systems on behalf of applications.

Group Policy—A means of applying computer- or user-specific restrictions and features to a system.

hardware abstraction layer (HAL)—A loadable kernel-level dynamic link library (DLL) (called Hal.dll and stored in the %*systemroot*%\system32 folder on a Windows 2000 computer) that provides the low-level interface to the hardware of the computer on which Windows 2000 is installed. This is one of the seven required files for booting Windows 2000.

Hardware Compatibility List (HCL)—A list of hardware devices supported by Windows 2000. A version of the HCL appears on the Windows 2000 Server distribution CD, but the version at **www.microsoft.com/hcl/** is updated regularly.

HKEY_CLASSES_ROOT—A registry key that contains the value entries that define the relationships between file extensions (that is, file formats) and applications. This key is actually just a redirector to the HKEY_LOCAL_MACHINE\Software\Classes subkey.

HKEY_CURRENT_CONFIG—A registry key that contains the value entries used to control the currently active hardware profile. This key is built each time the system boots by duplicating the contents of the HKEY_LOCAL_MACHINE\System\CurrentControlSet\HardwareProfiles\### subkey relative to the active hardware profile.

HKEY_CURRENT_USER—A registry key that contains the value entries specific to the currently logged-on user. This key is built each time a user logs on by duplicating the user-specific subkey from the HKEY_USERS key and the ntuser.dat or ntuser.man file from the user's profile.

HKEY_LOCAL_MACHINE—A registry key that contains the value entries specific to the local computer hardware. The contents of this key are not dependent on a user account or any applications, services, or processes in use.

HKEY_USERS—A registry key that contains the value entries for all users who have ever logged onto this system plus a default user profile for new users that do not already have a user profile.

hot fixes—Software releases that are used to fix any major bugs or security holes in an operating system.

input/output (I/O) Manager—A Windows 2000 software component that manages all I/O channels, including file systems and devices.

IntelliMirror—A network desktop-management system that allows administrators to retain control of systems not permanently connected to the network. Each time a portable computer logs back on to the network, the domain's Group Policies are reinforced, software is added or removed, and user data files are updated.

interforest restructure—The process of restructuring two Windows 2000 forests or one Windows NT domain into an existing Windows 2000 forest.

Internet connection sharing (ICS)—Built into Windows 2000's routing support is a basic proxy server. This tool can be used to grant Internet access to a small network without requiring additional hardware or applications, plus the network clients are automatically configured to use the shared connection.

Internet Information Server (IIS) 5—The latest generation of Microsoft IIS is included with Windows 2000. IIS offers a solid platform for building personal Web pages through true distributed, dynamic e-commerce Web sites. IIS integrates with the Windows 2000 system, seamlessly granting Web administrators access to networked resources, security, and management controls.

Internet Protocol Security (IPSec)—A secure, industry-standard implementation of the popular TCP/IP protocol.

Internet Services Manager—A Windows 2000 utility used to manage Internet information services, such as the Web and File Transfer Protocol (FTP).

Internetwork Packet Exchange/Sequenced Packet Exchange (IPX/SPX)—The protocol used on older Novell NetWare networks.

Glossary

intersite replication—Replication that takes place on Global Catalog servers between sites.

intraforest restructure—The process of restructuring two domains within the same Windows 2000 forest into the same domain. This is also called collapsing the forest.

intrasite replication—Replication that takes place between all domain controllers and domains within a site.

IP—An abbreviated reference to TCP/IP.

IPC (Interprocess Communication) Manager—A Windows 2000 software component that manages all transactions between server and client processes, both within the local computer and with remote computers.

Kerberos 5—An encryption-authentication protocol employed by Windows 2000 to verify the identity of a server and a client before data is transferred.

Kernel mode—The level of Windows 2000 where objects can only be manipulated by a thread directly from an application subsystem.

Key Distribution Center (KDC)—A Kerberos service that issues ticket-granting tickets and service tickets for domain authentication.

Layer Two Tunneling Protocol (L2TP)—A protocol that creates a secure connection, relying on other encryption methods (such as IPSec) for communication.

lease—A measurement of time that an IP address assigned by DHCP is assigned to a client.

licensing—A Windows 2000 utility used to configure and manage the license settings for Windows 2000 and installed applications.

Lightweight Directory Access Protocol (LDAP)—An access protocol for Active Directory.

local security policy—The Windows 2000 control mechanism used to configure and define the security policy for a local system, including password restrictions, account lockout, auditing, user rights, security options, public keys, and IP security.

logical printer—The software component that provides print services in Windows 2000.

Master Boot Record (MBR)—The first sector on a disk that contains executable code and a partition table, which stores information about the disk's primary and extended partitions.

Media Access Control (MAC) address—A unique address assigned to a network interface card.

Memory Manager—A Windows 2000 software component that manages virtual memory.

Microsoft Challenge Handshake Authentication Protocol 2 (MS-CHAP 2)—An authentication protocol developed by Microsoft for remote user authentication through remote access or dial-up connections.

Microsoft Installer (MSI)—The process used by both Microsoft applications and Group Policy to install and/or update applications. Microsoft applications, such as Office 2000, are installed using MSI packages. It is possible to create MSI packages for non-Microsoft products using various third-party tools. It is also possible to create customized packages by creating an MST file. A unique feature of Microsoft Installer is that the installed applications are self-aware and repair themselves upon corruption and also automatically install missing components on demand. An example of this feature would be an MSI package that initially installs only Word and Outlook from the Office 2000 suite, but also places icons for Excel and PowerPoint on the desktop. If the user clicks Excel, Microsoft Installer automatically installs Excel at that time.

Microsoft Management Console (MMC)—A new standardized Web-capable management interface. Most of the Windows 2000 administration tasks are accessible through an MMC snap-in.

migration—The process of upgrading or restructuring from Windows NT to Windows 2000 domains. The term migration usually refers to domains, but can be applied to desktop operating systems as well.

mirroring—A RAID configuration requiring at least two hard drives where all data is synchronized between the two hard drives.

mixed mode—A domain setting that enables communication between Active Directory and Windows NT domain controllers.

mount point—A directory on an NTFS volume that's used as an access point to a volume that does not have an assigned drive letter.

MSI—A Microsoft Installer package that is used to install applications. MSI packages always end with a *.msi extension. These installer packages are specifically applied using the Software Installation portion of a Group Policy.

MST—A transformed Microsoft Installer package that contains add-ons, upgrades, or modifications to an existing MSI file. Transformed packages always end with a *.mst extension. For example, an MST file can be created to include specific templates and settings for Microsoft Office 2000.

Glossary

multicast scopes— Used to assign group IP addresses to clients that are subscribing to a multicast media stream, like a video stream. It eliminates the need to unicast to each client

Native mode—A domain setting signifying that all domain controllers on a network are using Active Directory.

Network Address Translation (NAT)—An Internet standard that enables a local area network (LAN) to use one set of IP addresses for internal traffic and a second set of addresses for external traffic.

Network Basic Input/Output System (NetBIOS) Enhanced User Interface (NetBEUI)—A native Microsoft networking protocol that's being phased out with Windows 2000.

Network Load Balancing (NLB)—A service supported by Windows 2000 that distributes network traffic among multiple servers. NLB clusters do not share data.

Network Monitor—A Windows 2000 utility used to view and troubleshoot data packets.

New Technology File System (NTFS)—The preferred file system of Windows 2000. It supports file-level security, encryption, compression, auditing, and more.

Novell Directory Services (NDS)—A distributed database on NetWare servers that maintains network resource information.

NTBOOTDD.SYS—A required file for Windows 2000 when the SCSI controller doesn't have its own ROM.

NTDETECT.COM—One of the seven required files for booting Windows 2000.

NTDSUTIL.EXE—A utility that performs several administrative functions in Active Directory, such as transferring or seizing flexible single master operation (FSMO) roles and performing an authoritative restore.

NTLDR—One of the files required to boot both Windows NT and Windows 2000 successfully. It is one of the seven files required for booting Windows 2000.

NTOSKRNL.EXE—One of the seven required files for booting Windows 2000.

NWLink—The Microsoft implementation of IPX/SPX.

object—An item within Active Directory. Objects can be containers, domains, forests, accounts, OUs, groups, and so forth.

Object Manager—This component manages all resource objects within the system.

Glossary

offline files—A Windows 2000 feature that allows mobile Windows 2000 users to access copies of shared files and folders even when they are not connected to the network.

Open Shortest Path First (OSPF)—A routing protocol that propagates routing information.

Operating System 2, second generation (OS/2) subsystem—An environmental subsystem provided to support OS/2 character-mode applications.

organizational unit (OU)—A container that's used to organize objects into logical administration groups. OUs can contain objects, such as users, groups, printers, computers, applications, file shares, and even other OUs.

paging file—A file, called pagefile.sys, used by the Virtual Memory Manager as a temporary storage container for inactive memory pages.

Password Authentication Protocol (PAP)—A connection-negotiation protocol that passes authentication information in clear text, which is not very secure.

peer-to-peer networking—A network that consists of several systems linked together without a centralized authority. Each system acts as both a server and a client on the network and handles its own security and authentication.

plug and play—A technology that allows an operating system to recognize a device, install the correct driver, and enable the device automatically.

Plug-and-Play Manager—This component manages all plug-and-play-compliant devices and their associated drivers.

Point-to-Point Tunneling Protocol (PPTP)—A protocol used in virtual private networking that allows remote users to access a network across the Internet securely.

POSIX.1 subsystem—An environmental subsystem provided to support POSIX.1 text-only applications.

Power Manager—This component manages the power-conservation capabilities of Windows 2000.

power-on self-test—An internal self-diagnostic that is performed by the central processing unit (CPU) at the request of the BIOS when the system boots.

Pre-Boot Execution Environment (PXE)—A standard process that allows PXE-compliant network cards to boot themselves to the network.

Glossary

primary domain controller (PDC) emulator—A Windows 2000 domain controller that acts as though it were a Windows NT Server to systems that do not support Active Directory.

Print Monitor—The printing component that manages printers and print jobs on the server, as well as print job scheduling and priority.

Process Manager—This component manages the creation, disassembling, and maintenance of processes.

public key infrastructure (PKI)—The settings involved in the management of digital certificates and public and private cryptography keys.

quotas—An assignment in Windows 2000 that limits the amount of disk space available to individual users.

Recovery Console—A command-line control system used in system recovery in the event of a failure of a core system component or driver. Through the Recovery Console, simple commands can be used to restore the operating system to a functional state.

Redundant Array of Inexpensive Disks (RAID)—A type of drive and data storage that is generally synonymous with fault tolerance. This is untrue, however, since RAID 0 is not fault tolerant. RAID 1 is mirroring/duplexing, and RAID 5 is striping with parity. Both RAID 1 and RAID 5 allow for recovery from a single drive failure.

REGEDIT—The registry-editing program intended for use on 16-bit operating systems.

REGEDT32—The 32-bit registry-editing program that only works with Windows NT and Windows 2000. It also shows five variable types versus the three in Regedit.

registry—The hierarchical database that stores the majority of Windows 2000 system information.

Remote Access Service (RAS)—The Windows NT service that allowed remote access to a local network.

Remote Installation Services (RIS)—A service that allows for clients to be installed easily across the network by booting from a PXE read-only memory (ROM) network interface card (NIC) or a boot floppy. The installation routine can be fully automated after the destination computer is turned on, or a full or partial user interaction-required installation can be customized.

reverse lookup zone—A query process in which the IP address of a computer is translated to its DNS name.

RIPrep—A type of installation used with remote operating system installation where an administrator can take an entire image of one Windows 2000 Professional machine and install that image onto other workstations.

roaming profile—Desktop, Start menu, and user settings that are replicated to a network location every time a user logs off or shuts down the system. Roaming profile data is then sent to the system when the user logs back in. This allows users to move from system to system while maintaining the same desktop and Start menu settings.

Routing And Remote Access Service (RRAS)—A Windows 2000 service that provides network routing and remote access to a local network.

ScanDisk—A native tool used to discover and correct problems on hard drives. Both physical and logical errors can be detected by ScanDisk.

schema—The objects and classes and their attributes in Active Directory.

scopes—The range of IP addresses that can be leased to clients by DHCP.

scripts—Flat-text files containing program instructions that are run by the Windows Scripting Host.

Security Account Manager (SAM)—A Windows 2000 service that maintains user account information.

security group—A type of user group within Active Directory that groups user accounts together. All members of a security group have the ability to inherit permissions that are assigned to the security group.

security identifier (SID)—The unique identification number assigned to Windows 2000 objects.

security log—Records details about security occurrences and audit events.

Security Reference Monitor—A Windows component that manages the security services, including authentication, resource access, and group memberships.

service packs (SPs)—A collection of hot fixes and add-ons to fix bugs in an operating system.

site—An Active Directory object that logically groups subnets and domains into a single high-speed network.

slipstreaming—A new way of applying service packs. Slipstreaming ensures that updated files will be used so that service packs need only be applied once.

Glossary

snap-ins—The consoles that can be added to the Microsoft Management Console to manage Windows 2000 features.

Spooler Service—The service responsible for passing a print job to the print monitor.

superscopes—A feature that allows DHCP to use separate scopes of IP addresses for client assignment.

SYSDIFF—The Windows 2000 utility used to take a snapshot of a basic installation and, after changes have been made, record the changes and then apply them to another installation.

SYSPREP—A tool used to duplicate an entire hard drive. This tool is useful when installing Windows 2000 onto multiple identical systems that require identical configurations.

system log—Records details about hardware and software issues related to Windows 2000 itself and installed drivers.

System Management Server (SMS)—A Microsoft package that is used to take inventory and distribute applications. RIS is a scaled-down version of SMS.

SYSVOL volume—A shared folder that is present on every Windows 2000 server in a domain. Everything located in the SYSVOL volume is replicated to every other domain controller in the domain.

Task Scheduler—A Windows 2000 component that automates the execution or launch of programs and batch files based on time and system conditions.

Terminal Services—Windows 2000 includes native Terminal Services (previously available to Windows NT only as an add-on), which allows thin clients to be employed as network clients. Terminal Services grants remote access to applications and offers limitation controls of application access.

time-to-live—The amount of time that a packet is held before being discarded.

Trace Dump—A Resource Kit utility that gathers information in a trace log file (or a realtime trace) and outputs it into a CSV file. A CSV file then allows for the data to be imported into an Excel spreadsheet and manipulated.

Trace Log—A Resource Kit utility that allows an administrator to start, stop, or enable trace logs from the command prompt. This allows for trace logs to be included in startup or login scripts.

transitive trust—A trust that is dynamic in nature and automatically generated by Windows 2000 domains within the same forest.

Glossary

Transmission Control Protocol/Internet Protocol (TCP/IP)—The most popular protocol suite in use today. TCP/IP was originally based on the network protocols developed by the Department of Defense. TCP/IP is the protocol used on the Internet.

tree—A group of Windows 2000 domains arranged hierarchically within the same forest.

Trust—An established relationship between two domains that allows authenticated users in one domain to forego authentication in the second domain when attempting to access resources in the second domain.

unattended installation—A Windows 2000 installation that uses a previously made script to install the operating system without user interaction.

Uniqueness Database File (UDF)—A text file that contains a partial set of instructions for installing Windows 2000 to specify settings for individual users. Used to supplement an answer file when only minor changes are needed that don't require a new answer file.

Universal group—A group of accounts and/or groups that is visible to any system within a forest. Universal groups are unique in that they (a) exist only within Native mode domains and (b) can contain accounts and other groups from any domain and can be used to assign permissions to resources in any domain.

virtual memory—A Windows 2000 service that stores memory pages not currently in use by the system. This frees up memory for other uses. Virtual memory also hides the swapping of memory from applications and higher-level services.

virtual private network (VPN)—An extension of a network that can be accessed securely through a public network, such as the Internet.

Web-Based Enterprise Management (WBEM)—This Distributed Management Force (DMTF) initiative, included in Windows 2000 through Windows Management Instrumentation (WMI), grants you the ability to manage, configure, and control nearly every aspect of your systems and networks remotely—from software to hardware.

Win16 subsystem—An environmental subsystem designed to support Windows 3.x, Windows for Workgroups 3.11, and Win16 Windows 95 applications in a simulated Windows 3.x environment.

Win32 subsystem—An environmental subsystem required by Windows 2000. Win32 supports many essential functions, including maintaining the user's desktop environment and providing a standard interface for graphical and user device I/O.

Glossary

Window Manager—This component manages the input (mouse and keyboard) and display of windowing and dialog boxes.

Windows 2000 Backup—The built-in backup program in Windows 2000.

Windows 2000 Executive—The collection of high-level system services in Windows 2000.

Windows file protection—An automated protection measure that prevents in-use system files, such as SYS, DDL, OCX, TTF, and EXE files, from being over-written by other programs or installation routines.

Windows Internet Naming Service (WINS)—A service that resolves IP addresses to NetBIOS computer names.

Windows Scripting Host (WSH)—Native scripting capabilities of Windows 2000 grant administrators a wider set of automation options. Most tasks can be accomplished through command-line utilities. Using WSH, an administrator can automate many redundant tasks.

workgroup—A specialized peer-to-peer network that usually refers to older Microsoft networks that do not have a centralized server or do not belong to a domain.

Wscript—The 32-bit, Windows-based scripting engine included with Windows 2000.

ZAP—An alternative to MSI packages for use when implementing the Software Installation portion of a group policy. ZAP files are basically scripts that point the installation routine toward the executable that installs the program. ZAP-installed applications are not self-aware and will not automatically repair or install additional components.

zone—A subtree of a DNS database.

Index

O

R

X

Z

What's On The CD-ROM

The *Windows 2000 System Administrator Black Book 2nd Edition*'s companion CD-ROM contains elements specifically selected to enhance the usefulness of this book, including:

- *AutoProf.com's Profile Maker 4*—Profile Maker is a network administration utility for automating the configuration of Windows applications and includes support for messaging applications.

- *Executive Software's Diskeeper 5 Server*—Diskeeper is a disk defragmenter utility that defragments files on file allocation table (FAT), FAT32, and Windows NT File System (NTFS) volumes. Diskeeper Server allows the user to connect to remote computers (that already have Diskeeper installed) and to perform online defragmentation and configuration.

- *Executive Software's Undelete Server 2*—Undelete allows you to recover files that have been deleted.

- *Sunbelt Software's Ultra*　　　 – UltraAdmin is a centralized, domain administration tool that remai　　　 nteroperable as you manage both Windows NT 4 and Windows 2000 con　　　 s, us rs, and groups.

- *Sunbelt Software's UltraBac 5.5*—UltraBac is able to perform live backups of open databases with optional agents for Structured Query Language (SQL) and Exchange.

- *Sunbelt Software's DirectoryAnalyzer 1.04*—This tool manages Active Directory.

- *TIDAL Software's Sys*Admiral 2.3*—This tool is an enterprise job-scheduling and workload-management solution designed to manage complex, dynamic, and geographically dispersed organizations.

- *Trend Micro's PC-cillin 2000*—PC-cillin 2000 provides antivirus features for Windows 2000. For more information, visit **www.trend.com**.

- *VERITAS Software Corp.'s Backup Exec 8 (SL)*—Backup Exec 8.0 provides 100 percent compatibility for the total Windows NT and Windows 2000 environments while offering reliable backup and recovery.

System Requirements

Software

- Your operating system must be Windows 95, 98, or higher.

Hardware

- An Intel (or equivalent) Pentium 100MHz processor is the minimum platform required; an Intel (or quivalent) Pentium 133MHz processor is recommended.
- 32MB of RAM is the minimum requirement.
- A color monitor (256 colors) is recommended.